THE MENTALLY ILL IN AMERICA

From the painting by Robert Fleury

DR. PHILIPPE PINEL AT THE SALPÊTRIÈRE, 1795

The great pioneer of humanitarian reform orders the chains removed from patients at the Paris asylum for insane women.

THE MENTALLY ILL IN AMERICA

A HISTORY OF THEIR CARE AND TREATMENT
FROM COLONIAL TIMES

Albert Deutsch

SECOND EDITION, REVISED AND ENLARGED

Andrew S. Thomas Memorial Library
MORRIS HARVEY COLLEGE, CHARLESTON, W. VA.

COLUMBIA UNIVERSITY PRESS
NEW YORK AND LONDON

COPYRIGHT 1937, 1949, BY THE AMERICAN FOUNDATION
FOR MENTAL HYGIENE, INC.

FIRST EDITION: *First and second printings, 1937, 1938*
Doubleday, Doran & Company, Inc.
FIRST EDITION: *Third printing, 1945, Columbia University Press*
SECOND EDITION: *1949, Columbia University Press*
Sixth printing, 1967

362.2
D489m2

PRINTED IN THE UNITED STATES OF AMERICA

INTRODUCTION

IT IS with deep satisfaction that I introduce this important book to the reading public. If the lessons it teaches are understood and taken to heart by its readers, society will be the author's debtor.

Mr. Deutsch's book, the preparation of which has been made possible by the American Foundation for Mental Hygiene, might be described in a very few words by saying that it traces the evolution of a cultural pattern as represented by the way in which people through the years have thought and felt about the so-called insane. It is an exceedingly illuminating presentation and because of the dramatic material with which it deals, it may well prove to be a spearhead for the penetration of important social facts and the understanding of social processes which, presented with less appealing or less startling illustration, might fail to attract attention.

It is altogether fitting that in the presentation of this extraordinary and important story of man's struggles with himself, the illustrations should be taken more particularly from their American setting. In this way the whole matter is brought home to us who live in this country and we see what has actually been taking place, more especially since early colonial days, and we can feel that we ourselves are a part of the whole story and that the victories that have been won and the ground that has been gained are assets of which we can avail ourselves. It is always an illuminating procedure to trace the path along which we have come, to become acquainted with the historical forces that are driving us, and their directions, because after all we have to conquer, not by opposing these forces, but by conforming to them. Mr. Deutsch's story, therefore, while it may make us ashamed of some aspects of our past and proud of others, offers hope for the future through the realization that the goals toward which we have directed our vision can be attained, but only at the price of unremitting and indefatigable effort. If we are willing to undertake the task, we can feel assured of the future. It is but another instance of the necessity for eternal vigilance if past gains are not to be lost. It is and has been the function of the National Committee for Mental Hygiene, through all the years since its beginning, to symbolize and to exercise this very function of vigilance, sustained by the unflagging faith of its prescient creator, Clifford W. Beers. Though very different in content and approach, this book resembles in a significant way Mr. Beers's classic autobiography, *A Mind That Found Itself*, since it is intended not merely to entertain or inform, but to stimulate to constructive action.

A great amount of research has gone into the making of this book. Hundreds of treatises, reports, articles, and pamphlets have been consulted by Mr. Deutsch in its preparation. His approach to the subject as a social historian rather than as a psychiatrist makes possible an objective view free from the temptations of professional partisanship. His data have been gathered with scrupulous care. Interpretations, where they occur—and they are more often implicit in the text than explicit—flow naturally from the facts.

"Man's inhumanity to man" is an old theme, so old, in fact, that people repeat the phrase with little appreciation of what lies behind the words in terms of actual human suffering. The inhumanity, however, has its foundations in a background of ignorance and misconceptions. Thus in this book we see that inhumanity, with all the ugly facts of ignorance from which it takes root, expressing itself in the end results, not only of neglect, but of actual abuse directed against the helpless and those unable to defend themselves or to retaliate. The average reader, as he follows the presentation from chapter to chapter, will find that the whole ugly story is only too easy to understand. Personal ambition, cupidity, cowardice, all the selfish and hateful passions of man, are seen unleashed here in all their fury; we have only to read the daily press today to see instances

INTRODUCTION vii

of the same kind staring at us from its pages. But, as Mr. Deutsch is at pains to point out, the conditions described in this book are primarily attributable, not to the emotional and mental make-ups of particular individuals, but to broad-based public attitudes corresponding closely to the general manners and mores and to society's phase of development at each stage of its evolution. In the final analysis, too, the effects of such conditions are rather social than individual in their implications.

In the somewhat vague terms of oriental mysticism, this might very well be expressed in the words of Buddha, who said: "Not in the sky, nor in the midst of the sea, nor in the clefts of the mountains, is there known a spot where a man can be freed from an evil act." To put this concept in somewhat more concrete and understandable terms, I will point an analogy. The public health movement came originally into existence by no means as a pure, altruistic effort to save the lives and health of the factory workers who were laboring fourteen, sixteen, and more hours a day under atrocious conditions of light, ventilation, food, poverty and filth. The real impelling force that started movements in this direction was the fact that these *degraded* human beings were the easy prey of disease. Contagions and infections spread rapidly among them, and when they lived, as they often did, in close proximity to the rich man's home, disease, being proverbially no respecter of persons, often found its mark there. The factory owner and the man of wealth, therefore, found in this roundabout way that in order to protect themselves it was necessary to produce different conditions among their employees. This was simply self-preservation.

Here in this book, therefore, the reader may see unfold before him with reference to a particular cultural pattern, a form, model or paradigm into which probably all social movements might reasonably fit. He will see how great personalities stand out as nuclear points about which latent tendencies accumulate and become active by way of their leadership. He will see that progress does not take place in two or even three, but in four dimensions, that the historical unfoldment of a story such as this can not be understood solely from its linear presentation page after page, but must be thought of in all these dimensions, reforms in certain places having progressed further than in others, reforms at certain times having advanced more rapidly and accomplished more than similar efforts at other times. And so he will be prepared to understand the whole complex picture as it is distributed in time and space as the author presents it, and he will realize that the classification of what has happened through the years by chapter headings is but a convenient method of presenting the material which the author, from his point of view, with his vision and background, feels to be most desirable and most practicable. In integrating, wherever possible, the historical process in one particular field of human endeavor with the general cultural pattern, Mr. Deutsch makes an impressive contribution to this kind of historical literature. He has, with much success, resisted the temptation to treat his subject as an entity isolated from the social stream.

Perhaps no single impression will be stronger than the realization one gets from reading these pages of the terrific effort that man must make in order to go ahead. Though it may be temporarily checked here and there, this progressive effort can not be subdued or destroyed by any obstacles, no matter how great. It carries man along the path of what we are pleased to call civilization, sometimes even against his will, perhaps, and accomplishes over and over again results which at the inception of the enterprise, may have seemed impossible of achievement.

Thus as the reader peruses these pages, he will get two pictures of man, diametrically opposed to one another. He will see man in all his weaknesses, the minutest of specks in a gigantic universe, struggling against cosmic forces so great that it seems impossible that he should even survive. He will see him stumbling and blundering along, being eliminated and eliminating himself in vast numbers as the result of his mistakes, but nevertheless somehow continuing to exist. On the other hand, he will see him as exemplifying, incarnating those very cosmic forces which are of such stupendous power, expressing them in his acts and in his thoughts, and surviving in spite of all, a really gigantic character because of what he represents, no longer minute, but cosmic in proportions. And that which survives survives in the thin line that lives on from generation to generation, and that which perishes by the million perishes, at least to some extent, in order that the others may live. It is a marvelous picture that the author paints, a significant part of the great story of man as illustrated in the particular set of circumstances so vividly set forth in these pages.

It is fitting, perhaps, that a final word be said about the future. While man and his affairs present problems infinitely too complex to warrant prophecy in detail, still it is fair to assume that the results in the future, quantitatively at least, will be comparable to results that have been reached elsewhere when science has been brought to bear upon the particular problem involved. Those who can look back in their experience over a period of time will realize that, as a matter of fact, enormous progress has been made and that perhaps the most significant of all results has been attained, namely, the widespread recognition of the existence, the importance and the significance of the problems of mental health. With this recognition and the added fact that science is turning its effort in the direction of their solution, the future may reasonably be considered assured. And so this book of Mr. Deutsch's is not only a record of past atrocities and of great accomplishments, but a presentation of developing cultural patterns and trends of thought which presage wondrous accomplishments for the future.

It is hoped that the readers of this book will not only be intrigued by its contents as dramatic appeal, but will also be able to read the implications between the lines. Such a stage of civilization as we have thus far reached has not been attained by a process of drifting, but only by the hardest kind of sustained effort over long periods of time. The primitive instincts with which man originally battled his way among the crude forces of nature have not perished. They still exist, but man must no longer be at their mercy. He must be able to recapture for socially constructive ends the energies that they represent. That is the lesson of mental hygiene and that is the lesson which this book teaches. It should be widely read, for its message is of the utmost significance.

WILLIAM A. WHITE

January 7, 1937
St. Elizabeths Hospital
Washington, D. C.

INTRODUCTION TO THE SECOND EDITION

ALBERT DEUTSCH has chosen a most opportune time to issue this new edition of his significant history of the treatment of the mentally ill. The decade that has elapsed since the first edition was published has been one of rapid advancements, many of which are described in new chapters of the book. It also has been a period when the need for better understanding of mental and emotional problems has been sharply focused by the brutalities of war and by the unrest and confusion which have characterized the subsequent peace.

In tracing the historical origins of public attitudes toward mental illness, Mr. Deutsch helps us to brush away prejudices and misconceptions inherited from an earlier day. This is an important first step toward the more extensive measures which must be taken if we are to attain the high degree of mental health which modern life demands. Only an eminently sane civilization can survive its potential power for world destruction.

Those who have read the first edition will note with interest that the author has added a review of recent trends which militate toward prevention as well as toward better treatment of mental diseases.

The importance of developing facilities for prevention is underscored by a new chapter describing the conditions which prevail in many mental hospitals today. He translates here into human terms what government statistics have long been revealing. For example, Federal reports show that between 1937 and 1946, overcrowding in State mental hospitals increased from 10.9 per cent to 16.3 per cent. During the same period, the number of patients admitted to these hospitals for the first time increased from 78,000 to 89,000. On the other hand, the ratio of employees decreased, from one employee to 5.8 patients in 1937 to one for 6.2 patients in 1946. In other words, conditions in mental hospitals have grown worse instead of better in the ten years since this book first appeared. And this deterioration has occurred in spite of the fact that we are spending almost twice as much for the care of mental patients—$284 per patient, on the average, in 1937 and $436 in 1946.

To the health officer, one answer to this situation is immediately apparent because it has proved effective in solving other health problems: reduce the influx of patients by better techniques and facilities for case-finding, prevention, and early, energetic treatment by skilled persons.

Basic to public acceptance of this suggestion, however, is the realization that the acute forms of mental illness differ more in degree than in kind from the disturbances which, at one time or another, afflict almost all of us. This fact is apparent to Mr. Deutsch and perhaps explains his splendid perseverance in continuing with the pioneer efforts he began a decade ago to trace the ups and downs of this complex subject. Beckoning him and all of us on, in the search for mental health, is the bright hope that it may lead to the discovery of better ways of managing our own affairs and of planning a more peaceful and ordered world.

From this viewpoint, we follow the author's account of progress with more than academic interest, realizing that each gain against mental illness brings closer the ultimate goal of more complete mental health for us all.

The unique historical contribution of the book is its tracing of the evolution of psychological medicine and its application against the socio-cultural setting down the ages. It portrays the mentally ill in the times in which they lived. In the days when superstition was a dominant factor in society, when health, happiness and prosperity appeared to depend upon appeasement of evil spirits, this social concept determined the treatment accorded to the mentally ill. Learned men, as the author points out, put forth much thought and effort to devise effective means of exorcising the "devils" which were believed to inhabit the souls of the mentally deranged. Mr. Deutsch's carefully recorded data makes this understandable and logical to the reader.

After he has traveled with Mr. Deutsch through the dark days of superstition, the reader is ready to examine the present era of science with a fresh perspective, seeing its limitations as well as its strengths.

Man's absorption, during this later period, with the physical and materialistic aspects of life is reflected in his treatment of the mentally ill. Buildings were constructed to house them; mechanical devices were invented to treat them. Recent years have seen a constructive refinement of this approach. Our mental hospitals, although still a national disgrace, are in general more pleasant and comfortable than those of a century ago. Concentrated search for the physical causes of mental illness has borne significant fruit. We have learned how to prevent many of the mental illnesses that are by-products of physical illness such as syphilis and pellagra. Advances have also been made in treatment, although, regrettably, improvements in care have not in all instances kept pace.

However, just as we have barely begun a scientific approach to solving non-materialistic problems in other fields—such as the economic problem of distributing the wealth of goods which result from mass production, and the political problem of how to get along with the multitudinous nations and peoples who, by virtue of radio and airplane, have become our close neighbors—so this aspect of mental illness is likewise largely unexplored territory, forested with question marks.

The new chapters on developments during and since the war evaluate recent progress, particularly toward better recognition and treatment of neuroses and the psychosomatic aspects of physical disease. This section includes a description of the National Mental Health Act under which the Federal government has been authorized to give substantial support to research, to the training of more psychiatric personnel, and to the expansion of preventive and treatment services for those whose conflicts have not reached such handicapping proportions as to require hospitalization.

The success of this final phase of the national mental health program—treatment of early symptoms—depends in large measure upon the cooperation of a well-informed public. Mr. Deutsch, in the best tradition of his profession, presents this essential public information in a highly readable and dramatic style.

If one has a vague feeling that a person who contracts a mental illness is somehow inferior to one who suffers appendicitis or some other physical illness; if one clings to the theory of punishment rather than treatment for sexual deviates, delinquents, and other social misfits; if one thinks of mental illness as a mysterious affliction for which there is no hope of cure—this book will trace the origin of those misconceptions and dispel them. As one sees how many ideas about mental illness which persist into the present are actually distortions of outmoded superstitions relating to evil spirits, the awe and fears which may have colored our own attitudes about mental illness will disappear.

The common sense approach which Mr. Deutsch takes toward this subject, and which gleams through even in his descriptions of the brutalities inflicted upon the mentally ill through the ages, must inevitably come to be shared by his readers.

This book should be read by all citizens. Only with better public understanding of the problem of mental illness can we hope to attain expanded research, to recruit candidates for training in psychiatric specialties, and to organize improved treatment facilities which are so sorely needed. These are basic requirements if we are to speed the recovery of our half million fellow Americans who are in mental hospitals today, and bring more buoyant mental health to us all.

ROBERT H. FELIX
Chief, Mental Hygiene Division
U.S. Public Health Service

Washington, D.C.
August, 1948

Foreword

THROUGHOUT the greater part of human history the role of the medical man in the care and treatment of the mentally ill has been a minor one. Only in recent decades has the medical approach assumed a dominant position in this field. For many centuries the insane were regarded as demoniacs and were consequently often handed over to the exorcist or even to the executioner, when they were not completely abandoned. In later times they were frequently treated as criminals and paupers and as such came under the supervision of penal and poor law authorities. The story of the mentally ill falls largely within the penumbra of social welfare development; this relationship has served as a major frame of reference in my approach to the subject. I have tried to bring into sharper relief the important though often obscure social factors that have conditioned attitudes toward, and treatment of, mental disease through the centuries.

Since the care and treatment of the mentally ill in America have been profoundly influenced by men and movements abroad, I have traced foreign developments wherever necessary for the clarification of trends in this country. I have also included an introductory chapter outlining the history of the insane from early times to the founding of the American colonies.

In dealing with the medical aspects of the history of the mentally ill, I have been fortunate in receiving the generous aid and advice of a number of specialists in the field. Many technical details in psychiatric development were clarified for me, and many errors avoided, through their valuable suggestions. I am indebted to the following psychiatrists for reading parts of my manuscript submitted to them for criticism: Drs. Earl D. Bond, C. Macfie Campbell, Clarence O.

Cheney, Clarence B. Farrar, Samuel W. Hamilton, Clarence M. Hincks, Nolan D. C. Lewis, Winfred Overholser, Howard W. Potter, Mortimer M. Raynor, Arthur H. Ruggles, William L. Russell, George S. Stevenson, and Edward A. Strecker. Dr. William A. White, whose lamented death occurred shortly before publication of this book, was of great assistance to me during the preparation of my manuscript.

Professor Clarence G. Dittmer of New York University read my manuscript with an eye to sociological content. Professor Sheldon Glueck read the chapters on insanity and the law. Dr. Stanley P. Davies and Mr. Harry L. Lurie also read parts of the manuscript. Dr. Horatio M. Pollock of the New York State Department of Mental Hygiene read the entire work in galley proof. Of course, none of the aforementioned individuals is responsible for errors that may appear in this book, or for interpretations and conclusions.

I am obligated to the staff of the National Committee for Mental Hygiene, particularly Miss Margaret H. Wagenhals and Mr. Paul O. Komora, for their splendid cooperation. Dr. George L. Banay, medical librarian of the Worcester State Hospital, compiled the index. For their many courtesies in affording research facilities I am indebted to the staff members of several libraries, particularly to Mr. Charles F. McCombs of the New York Public Library, Mrs. Bertha C. Hulseman of the Russell Sage Foundation Library, Dr. Jacob Shatzky of the Library of the New York State Psychiatric Institute and Hospital, and Dr. Walter R. Bett, Librarian of the College of Physicians and Surgeons, Columbia University.

I gratefully acknowledge the grant awarded to me by the American Foundation for Mental Hygiene, which made possible the preparation of this work.

Above all, I am deeply indebted to Mr. Clifford W. Beers for his innumerable services during the planning and preparation of the book. He has given unstintingly of his time and energy, facilitating my work at many points, opening up valuable channels of assistance that otherwise would have been difficult of access. His infectious enthusiasm and helpful counsel were constant sources of stimulation to me. Any return that I could make for his splendid cooperation could best be measured in terms of the success this book attains in attracting attention to the cause of the mentally ill—a cause which he has made his life-work.

ALBERT DEUTSCH

CONTENTS

	INTRODUCTION, BY WILLIAM A. WHITE, M.D.	v
	INTRODUCTION TO THE SECOND EDITION, BY ROBERT H. FELIX, M.D.	xi
	AUTHOR'S FOREWORD	xv
I.	PROPHETS, DEMONS AND WITCHES	1
II.	COLONIAL AMERICA: THE OLD WORLD HERITAGE	24
III.	COLONIAL PROVISION FOR THE MENTALLY ILL: PUNISHMENT, REPRESSION AND INDIFFERENCE	39
IV.	RATIONAL HUMANITARIANISM: THE BEGINNINGS OF REFORM	55
V.	BENJAMIN RUSH: THE FATHER OF AMERICAN PSYCHIATRY	72
VI.	THE RISE OF MORAL TREATMENT	88
VII.	RETROGRESSION: OVER THE HILL TO THE POORHOUSE	114
VIII.	THE CULT OF CURABILITY AND THE RISE OF STATE INSTITUTIONS	132
IX.	DOROTHEA LYNDE DIX: MILITANT CRUSADER	158
X.	MID-CENTURY PSYCHIATRISTS	186
XI.	CONFLICT OF THEORIES: RESTRAINT OR NON-RESTRAINT?	213

CONTENTS

XII.	THE TREND TOWARD STATE CARE	229
XIII.	STATE CARE: EXODUS FROM THE POORHOUSE	246
XIV.	PSYCHIATRY EMERGES FROM ISOLATION	272
XV.	THE MENTAL HYGIENE MOVEMENT AND ITS FOUNDER	300
XVI.	HISTORICAL BACKGROUNDS OF MENTAL DEFECT	332
XVII.	CHANGING CONCEPTS IN MENTAL DEFECT	354
XVIII.	INSANITY AND THE CRIMINAL LAW	387
XIX.	OUR COMMITMENT LAWS	418
XX.	MODERN TRENDS IN INSTITUTIONAL CARE AND TREATMENT	442
XXI.	PSYCHIATRY IN WORLD WAR II	458
XXII.	TOWARDS MENTAL HYGIENE	483
	BIBLIOGRAPHY	520
	INDEX	539

ILLUSTRATIONS

PINEL AT THE SALPÊTRIÈRE	*Frontispiece*
BENJAMIN RUSH	72
EIGHTEENTH-CENTURY HOSPITALS FOR THE MENTALLY ILL IN AMERICA	104
DOROTHEA LYNDE DIX	168
THE ORIGINAL THIRTEEN	200
CLIFFORD W. BEERS	328
OLD METHODS OF RESTRAINT AND A MODERN SUBSTITUTE	456
HYDROTHERAPY, OLD AND NEW	488

THE MENTALLY ILL IN AMERICA

CHAPTER I
Prophets, Demons and Witches

BEFORE medicine, there was magic.
Primitive man peoples the world about him with gods and demons. He sees spirits in the trees, in the winds and the moving clouds, in storms and lightning, in the running rivers, in sun and moon, in the very stones he treads upon. These spirits, benevolent and malevolent, control his destiny for good or ill. They are particularly responsible for his misfortunes. The primitive mind does not regard sickness, disease, or even death as the consequence of natural phenomena. Rather are they looked upon as the results of supernatural intervention on the part of the spirits which fill his world. In his naïveté primitive man feels confident that by learning certain secrets and mysteries, certain rituals and incantations, he can in turn gain control of the supernatural spirits and manipulate them to his own purposes and desires, or at least to neutralize them—to ward off illness, for instance. His efforts to manipulate external forces through supernatural means or knowledge constitute the kernel of magic.

The explanation of disease is simple and all-inclusive; it may be brought on by a "good" deity or spirit as a punishment for some sin or slight; more often it is ascribed to an evil demon acting out of sheer malevolence. Sometimes it operates at a distance; at other times it actually enters the body of the intended victim and carries on its nefarious work from within. Disease thus becomes identified with a personal demon. If this theory could serve to explain physical diseases, how much more reasonable must it appear to the untutored mind when applied to mental disorders, which manifest themselves in such awesome and mysterious forms?

Obviously, the ascribed causes of disease in any age determine the methods adopted for prevention and cure. Since mental diseases, along with other forms of illness, are supernaturally induced, prophylaxis and cure are sought in magic. To ward off disease, talismans and amulets are worn, and other magic protective devices are utilized. Sickness is cured by exorcising the demon from the person possessed, through incantation and prayer, through propitiation, cajoling, and even threats. On occasion, when the possessing demon is regarded as a corporal being, physical torture, such as squeezing or scourging the body, may be resorted to in driving him out. In time, the study and practice of magic for healing and other purposes becomes the specialty of a few in the community, and thus is evolved the sorcerer, wizard, medicine man, priest, and priest-physician—all forerunners of the modern doctor.

It is safe to assume that mental disease has always existed among mankind. Of course, we have no means of ascertaining its prevalence in early times. In all probability, however, it was less prevalent in ancient days than it is now. The mental and nervous strains arising from participation in a progressively complex civilization were absent, life was more stratified, competition between individuals less fierce, and breakdowns attributable to social causes of this kind were probably much less frequent. Dr. D. Hack Tuke, in a treatise on this subject, concluded that present-day civilization, with its increasing demands on the individual, and the extreme complexity and divergences of its socio-economic relationships, inevitably carries in its wake an increase in the rate of mental disorders.[1]

From time immemorial, the confounding of mental illness with demoniacal possession has existed. It survives today over great areas of the earth, not only among primitive tribes in Africa, the East Indies and Australia (where the belief is found in its most pristine forms), but even among highly civilized people, either openly espoused or concealed under the cloak of religion. It is interesting to note that not

NOTE: Bibliographical references indicated in the text may be found on pages 497 to 514.

many years ago a brochure by a respectable London physician was published which vigorously defended the belief in demoniacal possession as the cause of mental illness, and advocated exorcism as its cure.[2]

Many instances of possession are mentioned in the Bible. Most familiar, perhaps, is the story of Jesus casting out the devils from two possessed men, and causing the evil spirits to enter into a herd of swine, which forthwith plunge headlong over a cliff to their destruction. (Matthew, viii, 28.) In the Old Testament, the melancholia of King Saul is ascribed to an "evil spirit" sent down by God to trouble him, and is cured by the harp-playing of David—the first record of music used as a therapeutic agent in mental illness. (I Samuel, xvi.) Another famous Biblical instance of insanity is the case of the Babylonian King, Nebuchadnezzar, who seems to have been stricken with madness for a period of seven years. Some authorities interpret his disorder as lycanthropy (a condition in which a person imagines himself to be, and imitates, a wolf or some other animal), since it is stated that he roamed the fields as a beast, and "did eat grass as oxen, and his body was wet with the dew of heaven, till his hairs were grown like eagles' feathers, and his nails like birds' claws." (Daniel, iv, 33.) Popular belief among the ancient Hebrews also attributed mental derangement to the "seizure" of a person's body by the soul of a wicked or murdered man which could find no rest elsewhere.

Among the ancient Egyptians, who attained a remarkably high degree of civilization long before the great age of Greek culture burst upon the world, the care and treatment of the mentally ill was naturally conditioned by the prevailing notion of demoniacal possession. They seem to have regarded all diseases as literally personal demons or spirits. It is interesting to note, in this respect, that the words "cure" and "relieve" seldom occur in the papyrus prescriptions that have been preserved to us. Rather do we find such significant terms as "banishing," "driving out," "terrifying," "destroying" and "shattering" the disease, expressions in which the implication of possession by personal beings is obvious.

In Egypt the art of healing was exclusively practiced by the priesthood, who jealously guarded the secrets of their craft as sacred mysteries. To the temples came those suffering from mental and physical ailments, to be exorcised by the priest-physicians. Elaborate, stylized invocations were used in the resulting ceremonies, the potency of which was greatly heightened if the name of the indwelling demon were known to the exorcist. A common invocation used for head ailments began: "O, enemy, male or female! O dead, male or female! Descend not on the head of M, the son of N," and went on to name the protecting gods of the sufferer in order to strike terror into the possessing spirit.[3] At times, the exorcist would don the disguise of a powerful god to deceive the disease-demon, and to drive him out with dire threats in the name of the deity represented.

With the passing of centuries, incantations came to be accompanied more and more by physical remedies such as herbs, vegetables, and ointments. Precious stones were also prescribed; lapis-lazuli seems to have been a favorite remedy for hysteria.[4] These concoctions, it was believed, had no therapeutic values *per se,* but were imbued by supernatural agencies with magical properties. Through an age-long process of elimination and selection, however, remedies which experience proved to be most efficacious naturally survived the others, and thus there were preserved some really beneficial medicaments, some of which, like hyoscyamus, are still used in the treatment of certain mental diseases. Thus did the pharmaceutical aspects of healing gradually grow in importance, though the mystical and ritualistic trappings continued to dominate the healing art.

Nineteenth century commentators on the history of insanity were prone to regard the practices of ancient Egypt as a "golden age" in the care and treatment of the mentally ill, a tendency which still persists. This idealization of Egyptian practices has resulted in some amusing exaggerations. Thus, one commentator writes:

> In remote times enlightened views of insanity were entertained; intelligent and humane treatment was taught and practiced, first by the

learned priests of Egypt . . . (where) . . . melancholics were brought in considerable numbers to the temples. Whatever gifts of nature or productions of art were calculated to impress the imagination were there united to the solemnities of an imposing superstition. Games and recreations were instituted. The most voluptuous productions of the painter and sculptor were exposed to public view. Groves and gardens surrounded these shady retreats, and invited the distracted devotee to refreshing and salubrious exercise. Gaily decorated boats sometimes transported him to breathe, amid rural concerts, the pure breezes of the Nile. In short, all his time was taken up with some pleasurable occupation, or by a system of diversified amusements enhanced and sanctioned by a pagan religion.[5]

Unfortunately this rhapsodic, romantic picture of the treatment accorded the insane has little basis in real fact. Nevertheless, it has been accepted as veritable by many eminent writers on psychiatry, including the most famous of all, Philippe Pinel, whose own description of Egypt's treatment of mental illness is paraphrased in the above quotation. The "golden age" myth probably originated at the time archaeologists first began to disclose the true wonders and glories of the long-lost Egyptian civilization to an astonished world, swinging the pendulum of historical opinion to the extreme of over-estimation of certain aspects of that civilization. Mistranslations, misinterpretations, and corruptions of ancient texts have also played a part in furthering this legend. Its main flaw lies in the imputation that insanity was recognized by the ancient Egyptians as distinct from other kinds of disease, and was specifically treated as such, an assumption without the slightest foundation in authenticated evidence. On the contrary, the eminent Egyptologist, Sir John Gardner Wilkinson, indicates that insanity was not distinguished by the ancient Egyptians from other diseases, nor could it have been given specific treatment, and subsequent medical evidences bear him out.[6]

In early Greece, as in Egypt, mental disorders were looked upon as divine or demoniacal visitations. There are numerous references in Greek mythology to madness sent down upon human beings by angry and displeased deities. "Whom the gods would destroy, they first make mad," runs a popular

Greek saying. Perhaps the best-known instance of insanity in classic myth is that of Hercules, whom the goddess Hera causes to be seized by Madness (literally, Lyssa, a personal demon). In the midst of this seizure, which would today be diagnosed as epileptic furor, Hercules goes on a murderous rampage, slaying his own children, and also those of his brother. Not always, however, did insanity indicate the ill-will of a god. In some cases, where mental illness was characterized by certain forms of religious delusions, the afflicted one was looked upon as being favored by the gods, and in communication with them, and consequently was revered as a holy man or prophet. There is, indeed, reason to believe that the far-famed oracles at Delphi may have been partly recruited from this category of the mentally ill.

Therapeutic measures in mental illness were based on the prevailing theory of causes. Greece, like Egypt, had her healing shrines, the temples of Aesculapius, god of healing, whose emblem was a serpent coiled round a staff. At the height of influence of the Aesculapian cult, these temples numbered more than three hundred, the most renowned of which were located at Epidaurus and Cos. They were presided over by the Asklepiads—priest-physicians who claimed descent from the god himself, and through him the power of healing. Here, too, ritual and incantation served at first as the only forms of curative treatment, to which pharmaceutic remedies were gradually added.

Undoubtedly mental sufferers were brought to these shrines along with other ailing persons, and were subjected to the same mystical ministrations of the Asklepiads. After undergoing an elaborate and impressive ritual of purification, the diseased were taken to the temples at night to partake of the famous "temple sleep", for which cots were provided. Here they awaited the god who would appear to them in their dreams, tell them the nature of their ailments, and deliver instructions for treatment and cure. Customarily, an attendant, dressed as a god, would walk slowly and sedately through the temple as morning approached and, by touching the ailing devotees, indicate where their ills were seated, and perhaps bend down to whisper a remedial formula in their ears. To the tense, excited and anticipatory minds of the sick, it was not difficult to believe that they were being visited by a *bona fide* divinity.

It cannot be doubted that the salubrious and stimulating environment in which these temples were usually located had the effect of sending many a sick sojourner home cured. On the other hand, lest we draw an incorrect corollary from the fact, it should be kept in mind that these environmental influences on prospective patients were most probably never taken into consideration when the temples were built, and that their location was purely accidental in its effect on the sick. The central idea in therapeutic theory and practice was the appeal to supernatural agents. Ritual was paramount, and the curative role of nature was deemed insignificant, if it was recognized at all. Moreover, if the unlucky patient did not respond, within a short period, to the priestly rites and incantations, he was unceremoniously cast out from the temple as one accursed and unworthy of cure, since the gods, in failing to expel the disease from his body, had unmistakably signified their displeasure with him. By this device, incidentally, the wily priests created an iron-bound alibi for all failures, for successful treatment depended not only on their potency, but on the patient's own standing with the gods.

Thus, at first, the healing art was inextricably bound up with religion, and in truth served only as an adjunct of the latter; the priest and physician were one. Gradually, however, medicine freed itself from the domination of religion. With the development of the Greek spirit of inquiry, which burst into full flower in the fourth century B.C., the general theory and practice of medicine, and its psychiatric application, made tremendous strides forward. The contributions of the Greek physicians and philosophers (there was a close relationship between the two) to our subject during this period consist mainly in (1) the recognition of natural phenomena as the causes of mental diseases; (2) attempts, however crude, to classify the various mental afflictions; (3) location of the brain as the center of intellectual activity; and (4) the formulation of specific remedies in the treatment of mental illness.

It was an Asklepiad of Cos, Hippocrates (460–370), known as the father of medicine, who laid the basis for the rational and scientific treatment of diseases, including those comprehended under the term insanity. Born into that great age of Pericles, which saw perhaps the finest flowering of genius the world has ever known, Hippocrates earned the gratitude of future generations in stripping medicine of much of its supernatural trappings, although superstition and magic were to play an important, if not dominant, role in therapeutics for centuries after his time. He ridiculed the current notion that mental diseases were supernaturally induced. Discussing epilepsy, then commonly known as the "sacred disease", he wrote: "The sacred disease appears to me to be no wise more divine nor more sacred than other diseases; but has a natural cause from which it originates like other affections. Men regard its nature and cause as divine from ignorance and wonder, because it is not at all like other diseases." He also attacked the popular notion that cure could be effected merely by the rites of purification and incantation, remarking with wisdom that "they who first attributed this disease to the gods seem to me to have been just such persons as the conjurors, purificators, mountebanks and charlatans now are."[7] With remarkable acumen (when we consider that even that expert anatomist, Aristotle, regarded the brain as a mass of inert, functionless matter), Hippocrates said: "Men ought to know that from nothing else but the brain come joy, despondency and lamentation . . . and by the same organ we become mad and delirious, and fears and terrors assail us, some by night and some by day." A sharp observation for that age, even if falling short of complete accuracy.

Hippocrates explained mental illness according to his system of humoral pathology, whereby all diseases were caused by disproportions of the four humors—black bile, yellow bile, mucus and blood—affecting the heat, cold, dryness and moistness of the body.

Purging and blood-letting came into general use about this time in the treatment of mental diseases, and were to continue as popular remedies well into the nineteenth century. Hellebore was the most widely used drug in the treatment of the insane, and great healing power was attributed to it. Among the Greek physicians who made important contributions to the advance of psychiatric knowledge and practice was Asclepiades of Prusa (born B.C. 124) who prescribed diet, massaging, bathing and exercise for mental patients under his care. He berated his contemporaries who placed their patients in dark chambers on the supposition that darkness was conducive to peace and quiet of mind, and prescribed light, sunlit rooms for his own patients, reasoning that their delusions and fears could be dispelled by the perception of concrete reality.

To Aretaeus the Cappadocian, who lived in the second century A.D., we are indebted for progress in the field of classification. In pointing out the relationship between mania and melancholia, he anticipated Kraepelin's classification of manic-depressive psychosis by nearly two thousand years. He also differentiated between cerebral and spinal paralysis, and described accurately the symptoms of epilepsy, apoplexy and hysteria. This was a long step forward from the simplified classification of the pseudo-Plato, author of *Alcibiades II*, who thus classified the "different kinds of unsoundness of mind": "Those who are afflicted by it in the highest degree are called mad. Those in whom it is less pronounced are called wrong-headed, crotchety, or—as persons fond of smooth words would say—enthusiastic or excitable. Others are eccentric, others are known as innocents, incapables, dummies. . . . All these kinds of unsoundness of the mind differ from one another as diseases of the body do."

Soranus of Ephesus (fl. 2nd century) adopted many of the beneficial aspects of Asclepiades' theory, and added a number of original contributions which, for humane understanding of mental illness, were barely approached until the time that Pinel struck off the chains from the insane at the Bicêtre. Some of his directions could serve even today as the basis of an attendants' manual in the most modern mental hospitals. He advised that patients be placed in light rooms with regulated temperatures, under conditions of utmost sanitation and comfort. They were not to be irritated or exasperated by rough handling or unnecessarily harsh commands; frequent comings and goings of strangers were to be strictly forbidden. Sixteen centuries before John Conolly caused a furore by preaching his "new" and daring doctrine of "non-restraint", the gentle Soranus observed: "Means of restraint, employed without management, increase and even originate fury instead of calming it."

In his footsteps walked a worthy successor, Caelius Aurelianus (fl. 5th century), a Roman physician whose writings are now regarded as consisting mainly of paraphrases of lost originals by Soranus. The following specimen passage, in which Aurelianus bitterly arraigns the methods of some of his contemporaries, is remarkable for its humane insight:

> They seem mad themselves, rather than disposed to cure their patients, when they compare them to wild beasts, to be tamed by deprivation of food and the tortures of thirst. Doubtless led by the same error, they want to chain them up cruelly, without thinking that their limbs may be bruised or broken, and that it is more convenient and easier to restrain them by the hand of man than by the often useless weight of irons. They go so far as to advocate personal violence, *the lash,* as if to compel the return of reason by such provocation.

Truly, here were sentiments that would have seemed far more advanced than the practices existing little more than a century ago! Would that they had never been neglected by later generations, as they were fated to be.

To infer, however, that the therapy advocated by Soranus and Caelius Aurelianus was representative of their times would be hardly less misleading than to conclude from a reading of Jesus' sermon on the Mount that it summed up the ethics of His time. More likely the methods against which Aurelianus hurled his sharp lance in the passage just quoted were the very ones receiving widest application.

Furthermore, even the methods advocated by pioneers like Asclepiades, Soranus and Aurelianus comprised in effect a leisure-class therapy for that time, a therapy available to only a small, insignificant portion of the population. Surely, in a land where the majority of people were destitute not only of comfort, but of what would today be considered the barest necessities of life, the elaborate and costly treatment of Soranus, which included theatrics, music, and leisurely voyages, could hardly have found universal application. It is more reasonable to conclude that the methods advocated by Celsus (fl. 1st century) in his epitome of the medical thought and practice of his day were the ones in general vogue. Celsus, who was otherwise a keen and enlightened observer, advocated chains, flogging, semi-starvation diet and the application of terror and torture as excellent therapeutic agents.

In both Greece and Rome the slaves invariably constituted the great bulk of the population. In view of the extreme cruelty and indifference with which this class was treated generally, it is inconceivable that the insane among them would receive enlightened care. The great majority of insane persons had little or no opportunity for cure, except through the inexpensive *vis medicatrix naturae*. There is, indeed, a strong suspicion, corroborated by early Christian writers, that among the poorer classes of Greece and Rome, mentally diseased persons were frequently put to death as undesirable or intolerable burdens, in the absence of public provision for their care.

Two notable names stand out in the centuries immediately following the fall of Rome—Alexander of Tralles (525–605) and Paulus Aegenita (c. 630), both of whom carried on the humane traditions of Soranus, although neither made any important contributions to psychiatric practice. Some of the recorded "sympathetic" cures of Alexander are amusing. He tells us, for example, that one of his patients who suffered under the delusion that his head had been cut off by order of the king, was cured when the good doctor fashioned for him a leaden hat, the great weight of which convinced him that his head had been restored to his shoulders. Another patient thought she had swallowed a serpent which she could feel wriggling about in her stomach. After racking his brains for a remedy, the doctor finally gave her an emetic, and deftly slipped a snake into the vomit basin. He convinced her that it was the one she had swallowed, and thus (so he claims) effected a complete cure.

Fantastic as the aforementioned therapeutical methods may appear in the light of modern knowledge, they seem remarkably rational when compared with the general attitudes toward insanity, its causes, and cure, that prevailed during the middle ages and succeeding centuries. Certainly, if the sound foundations of inquiry and practice laid down by the pagan apostolate of mental medicine had been built upon by their Christian successors, a mighty bulwark could have been erected against the appalling wave of primeval superstition which swept over European civilization for a millennium and more. The physician once more surrendered his art to the priest; science was submerged by superstition, operating under the convenient guise of religion. While recording this melancholy fact, we have no desire to further the erroneous impression that the middle ages represent a totally static interlude in the general advance of civilization. The contributions of the medieval era to such fields as practical invention, geographic and astronomical discovery, commerce and statecraft, were of lasting importance: imperceptibly they laid the bases for many of our modern institutions. But it is also true that a wide area of scientific endeavor was overshadowed by the dark clouds of superstition. In that field of medical science which treats with mental illness, particularly, the tide of progress was not only halted but washed back. A long period of retrogression set in that lasted not only through the middle ages, but for centuries afterward.

During this period the natural therapy of earlier centuries was succeeded by a superstitious mixture of astrology, alchemy, and a retreat to theology, magic rites and exorcism, with the accompanying belief in demoniacal possession.

A tenth century prescription for insanity, cited in that excellent collection, of *Leechdoms, Wortcunning and Starcraft of Early England,* by the Rev. Oswald Cockayne, reads as follows: "In case a man be lunatic; take a skin of mereswine (sea-pig) or porpoise, work it into a whip, swinge the man therewith, soon he will be well. Amen." From the same source, we obtain the following prescription:

> A drink for a fiend-sick man, to be drunk out of a church bell; githrife, cynoglossum, yarrow, lupon . . . flower de luce, fennel, lichen, lovage; work up the drink off clear ale, sing seven masses over the worts, add garlic and holy water, and let the possessed sing the psalm, Beati Immaculati . . . then let him drink the drink out of a church bell and let the mess priest sing this over him, Domine, Sancte Pater Omnipotens.[8]

As a cure for epilepsy, Peter of Spain, a prominent physician of the 13th century, who became Pope John XXI, prescribed the liver of a vulture drunk for nine days, "or the gall still warm from a dog who should have been killed the moment the epileptic fell in the fit."[9]

The astrological influence whence came the term lunatic (i.e., "moonstruck") may be perceived in this medieval remedy for the same disease:

> For the falling sickness (epilepsy) take berries of this wort, which we name asterion, administer it to be eaten when the moon is on the wane, and let that be when the course of the sun is in the constellation named Virgo; that is, in the month which is called August; and let him have the same wort hung on his swere (neck); he will be cured.[10]

In England of the 16th century, a favorite prescription for "gathering the remembrance of a lunatic" was to beat and cudgel him until he had regained his reason. The efficacy of scourging as a remedy is affirmed by no less a personage than the gentle Sir Thomas More. Relating the case of a man who, after apparently recovering, had relapsed into insanity, Sir Thomas writes with satisfaction: "I caused him to be taken by the constables and bound to a tree in the street before the whole town, and there striped him till he waxed weary. Verily, God be thanked, I hear no harm of him now."

In harmony with the spirit of the times, healing wells and shrines were scattered throughout Europe, some of which claimed miraculous curative powers for the mentally diseased. Treatment for mental illness at special holy wells was popular in Great Britain, where St. Fillan's and St. Ronan's wells, St. Winifred's in Wales, and Great Nun's Pool were among those widely known for the healing potency of their waters.

On the continent were shrines dedicated to various saints, the miraculous cures of which were likewise famed in medieval times. The most famous of the shrines consecrated to the cure of mental illness was located at Gheel in Belgium, and was dedicated to St. Dymphna. According to tradition, the princess Dymphna had been driven insane by the behavior of an incestuous father, and had fled to Gheel, where she was martyred. Large numbers of lunatics were brought to this shrine to partake of its cure, and thousands were reputed to be healed by its miraculous virtues. That many of these cures were real can hardly be doubted; the efficacious influence of that intangible something variously known as faith, the will to believe, auto-suggestion, etc., in mental therapeutics is no longer considered a matter of mere credulity, but a scientifically demonstrated fact. From its "miraculous" beginnings, the village of Gheel has become a world-famous colony, to which mentally ill from many lands come to avail themselves of the family system of treatment for which it is noted.

However absurd were the remedies mentioned above, it must be admitted that they were at least characterized by tolerance, and even sympathy, toward the insane. These characteristics stand out prominently in the earlier centuries of the medieval period. In the great 14th century poem, *The Vision of Piers Plowman,* lunatics are referred to as "God's True Minstrels." The violent insane were commonly thrown into prison, heavily manacled, and treated generally as criminals, but the mildly insane were often permitted to roam about the countryside. Though uncared for, they were at least unmolested, and were allowed to live on the fruits of nature and the occasional charity of their fellow men. Indeed, some whose mental aberrations were manifested by religious exaltation were placed upon pedestals as "divinely inspired" saints or prophets, as in former ages.

Here and there monasteries were open for the reception of lunatics, and the first asylums for their exclusive custody sprang up during this period. As early as 1369 a certain English chaplain, Robert Denton, obtained a royal charter to found a hospital in honor of the Virgin Mary in the parish of All Hallows Barking. It was intended to house "priests and others, men and women, who suddenly fell into a frenzy and lost their memories, until such time as they should recover." There is no record that this hospital ever materialized, however. Lunatics were probably being treated in Bethlehem Hospital, London, in the late 14th century. At least six male lunatics were in confinement there in 1403. In that year the porter, Peter Taverner, absconded with "2 pairs of stocks, 4 pairs of iron manacles, 6 chains of irons with 6 locks" and other items which ominously reveal the type of treatment afforded the inmates.[11] Bethlehem, originally founded in 1247, became in later centuries (under its corrupted name of Bedlam) a byword for cruelty to the mentally ill.

Nowhere during the medieval period did the mentally ill find more understanding and better treatment than at the hands of the "heathen" Moslems. In Western Europe the spirit of inquiry which had motivated the ancient Greek physicians, philosophers and scientists was almost dead; the medical man, for the most part, had surrendered his craft to the theologian and witch-doctor. But in the Mohammedan East the torch of medical science lit by Hippocrates was still held aloft, dispelling the darkness of superstition in the treatment of mental and physical diseases. While the insane in Europe were being sent to churches and monasteries to be exorcised of possessing demons, the great Arab physician-philosopher, Avicenna, was insisting that they were simply suffering from mental maladies, and should be treated as sick persons.

Quite probably, the first asylums for the insane in the world were built by the Moslems. (The claim that such an institution was built at Jerusalem in the fifth century is without substantial foundation in history. The legend that a *morotrophium,* or house for lunatics, existed at Constantinople as early as the fourth century is likewise unverifiable.)

Benjamin of Tudela, the famous Jewish traveler of the twelfth century, gives us a very interesting account of an asylum for the insane that he saw in the city of Bagdad, where poor patients were maintained and treated at the expense of the Caliphate. Notwithstanding the mention of iron chains, his description speaks well for attitudes of the Arabs toward insanity, as contrasted with their contemporaries in Christian Europe:

> Here [in Bagdad] is a building which is called Dar-al-Maristan, where they keep charge of the demented people who have become insane in the towns through the great heat of the summer, and they chain each of them in iron chains until their reason becomes restored to them in the winter-time. Whilst they abide there, they are provided with food from the house of the Caliph, and when their reason is restored they are dismissed and each of them goes to his house and his home. Money is given to those that have stayed in the hospices on their return to their homes. Every month the officers of the Caliph inquire and investigate whether they have regained their reason, in which case they are discharged. All this the Caliph does out of charity to those that come to the city of Bagdad, whether they be sick or insane.[12]

The first European asylum devoted exclusively to the care of the insane of which we have indisputable record was that built at Valencia, Spain, in 1408 by Fray Gope Gilaberto. A number of other asylums were established in various parts of Europe during the sixteenth century.[13] It should be remembered, in connection with these early asylums, that the ministrations to their inmates were more likely to be featured by ceremonial rites than by medical attention, and that severe chastisement rather than gentleness was the rule in treatment. Since the monks and priests to whom the therapeutic functions were usually entrusted did not hesitate to scourge their own persons mercilessly whenever they sensed even partial surrender to the wiles of the great Tempter, they were hardly calculated to entertain kindly sentiments toward their charges, who were felt to be completely possessed by the Evil One.

The belief in demoniacal possession, in its old forms and

some newer and more frightful ones, captured the imagination of the medieval mind to a degree seldom approached before. Properly to comprehend its scope, and its profound effects on prevalent attitudes towards the insane, it is necessary to dip into the dominant theological speculations of the time. An integral part of this theology was the principle of dualism, which had spread into Europe from the East through the medium of neo-Platonism. To its exponents the world was seen as a huge battle-ground over which two antagonistic powers, good and evil, light and darkness, God and Satan, were engaged in a struggle for mastery. It was quite consistent with the anthropomorphic conception of the universe to believe that the immortal souls of men were the chief prizes sought in this cosmic conflict. Everywhere Satan and his infernal demons were at work striving to gain possession of human souls by every ruse possible. Just as the theology of the time surrounded God with choirs of angels, so did it credit Satan with legions of devils and imps, who lurked in every chimney and corner watching for an opportunity to jump into human bodies in unguarded moments and "possess" them.

Since the insane were usually thought to be possessed, they were brought to the priest rather than to the physician for treatment. Amid elaborate ceremonies that outdid the ancients for impressiveness, the rites of exorcism were performed. Filthy and rank-smelling drugs were frequently made use of. At times, reasoning and coaxing were employed in ridding the victim of the possessing devils. More often the demons were driven out with frightful epithets and curses. *The Treasury of Exorcisms,* a widely used work of the 17th century, contains hundreds of pages of the vilest epithets imaginable, to be hurled at the devil in expelling him. Great wonders were often claimed for the power of exorcism. For instance, a certain bishop of Beauvais exorcised with such skill that he not only forced five demons to relinquish possession of a victim, but actually made them sign an agreement not to molest him again! Likewise, some holy men of Vienna, in 1583, announced that they had that year cast out 12,652 living devils.[14]

Such were the lighter aspects of the treatment of the insane; a blacker side existed that degraded European civilization for centuries, and left in its wake a huge sea of human blood.

According to the prevalent superstition, a favorite device of the devil was to induce human beings to sell their souls to him in exchange for supernatural powers enjoyed over a stated number of years. Witches, who thus entered into league with Satan, could work all deeds of the black art. They could make themselves invisible, fly through the air, foretell the future, transform themselves and others into animals, and visit misfortunes upon their enemies. If the devil could not obtain souls through bargaining, he was ever alert to seize them by stealth. Popular belief had the earth teeming with witches and bewitched, purchased or captured by Satan, whose presence was a constant danger to the community. Neighbor suspected neighbor, and even a brother might be denounced should he be seen to act queerly.

To seek out and eliminate witches became not only a social but religious duty. The method of punishment was plainly prescribed in that terrible passage in the Bible: "Thou shalt not suffer a witch to live." (Exodus, xxii, 18.) How many lives were sacrificed through the literal translation of this text will never be known with any degree of accuracy, but the most conservative estimates cannot place at less than 100,000 the total of those executed as witches between the middle of the fifteenth century and the end of the seventeenth, when the mania raged at its worst. Twenty thousand "witches" are said to have been burned or otherwise executed in Scotland alone during the seventeenth century. Tens of thousands more were put to death in England, France, Germany and elsewhere in Europe. Five hundred were burned at the stake in Geneva within three months in the year 1515. Such heights of intensity did the delusion reach, that witch-finding became a lucrative profession. One charlatan, Matthew Hopkins, who bore the imposing title, Witchfinder-general, was alone instrumental in having one hundred "witches" executed in 1645–47 in England.

PROPHETS, DEMONS AND WITCHES 19

Of this period, which has frequently been termed psychopathic, the historian Lecky writes:

> Never was the power of imagination . . . more strikingly evinced. Superstitious and terror-stricken, the minds of men were impelled irresistably towards the miraculous and the Satanic, and they found them upon every side. The elements of imposture blended so curiously with the elements of delusion, that it is now impossible to separate them . . . Madness is always peculiarly frequent during great religious and political revolutions; and in the 16th century, all its forms were absorbed in the system of witchcraft, and caught the colour of the prevailing predisposition.[15]

It is a significant commentary on the unbalanced progress of the revival of learning that the witch mania, far from being confined to the middle ages, not only raged undiminished through the Renaissance but actually reached its most intense form during the latter period. Unfortunately, the rediscovery of classic learning did not extend to those humane Greek medical pioneers who taught the rational treatment of mental illness. Nor did the concurrent religious revolution known as the Reformation bring about an abatement in the persecution of "witches." On the contrary, it had the effect of throwing added fuel on the witch-pyres, as Protestant vied with Catholic in bringing the Devil's agents to judgment. The belief in witches and demoniacal possession was by no means confined to the ignorant and vulgar. It was implicitly accepted by scholars like Erasmus and Melancthon, jurists like Matthew Hale and Blackstone, and scientists like Kepler, Tycho Brahe and Robert Boyle. Martin Luther, who was subject to all sorts of fantastic hallucinations, became quite used to having the Devil follow him around. He tells us that he was one night awakened by a noise, but upon finding out that it was only Satan, he turned back and went to sleep. A black stain on the wall of a room in the Wartburg castle at Eisenach still marks the spot where Luther is said to have hurled an ink-well at the Devil. His own illnesses, and for that matter all diseases of the human body, were in Luther's opinion entirely due to the nefarious machinations of the Evil One.

But what of the medical men of the time? Did they cry out against the superstition which was heaping up this terrible toll in human lives? Did they snatch the insane from the stakes where they were being burned as witches? Did they recognize the symptoms of insanity, and treat it as a naturally caused illness? Sad to tell, so great was the pressure of the prevailing superstition that even the most reputable physicians subscribed to it wholeheartedly. As late as 1664, Sir Thomas Browne, eminent doctor and author of *Religio Medici,* by giving "expert" evidence against two unfortunate women accused of witchcraft, was instrumental in convicting them and sending them to their death.[16] Mr. Robert Burton, speaking of witches and magicians in his classic *Anatomy of Melancholy* (1621), writes: "They can cure and cause most diseases . . . and this of melancholy amongst the rest." In support of his thesis he cites the case of a young man, who by eating cakes that a witch gave him "began to dote on a sudden, and was instantly mad." He also mentions a doctor of Hildesheim who, consulted about a "melancholy" man, thought that his disease was "partly magicall, and partly naturall, because he vomited pieces of iron and lead, and spake such languages as he had never been taught."[17] In the words of Maxime du Camp ("Les aliénés à Paris." *Revue des Deux Mondes,* 1872, v. 101, p. 788):

We may say that doctors shared the insanity of the maniacs. The lunatic was no longer a patient, he was no longer even a man, but a kind of wild and formidable beast, half animal, half demon. In the horror that he inspired, they declared him to be possessed of Satan, and threw him into the flames.

The records of witch trials that have come down to us offer convincing evidence that a large percentage of those accused and convicted of witchcraft were really insane. Many were burned in consequence of their suspiciously "queer" behavior, for which the dominant ideology of the time offered no natural explanation. Of those who confessed voluntarily without the application of torture, and they constituted a large number, many reveal themselves unmistakably to us by their testimony as victims of various psychoses—dementia praecox, manic-depressive psychosis, paranoia, etc.—usually accompanied by self-accusatory and guilt delusions, and a consuming desire for expiation. Too often did these unfortunate deluded individuals implicate other persons in satanic plots that existed only in their own fevered imaginations, and draw these persons to the stake with them. What percentage of the victims of the witch mania were mentally unsound is of course beyond calculation, but on the basis of the records it would seem no exaggeration to judge that they comprised at least one-third of the total executed.

Here and there the voice of reason and science was raised against the witchcraft belief, but for the most part it was a voice crying in the wilderness, lost on the winds of delusion that swept over Europe.

Here and there men of science could be found groping through the thick fogs of ignorance, fear and superstition that enshrouded in mystery the phenomena of mental disease. Imperceptibly they were piling up contributions to the knowledge of the subject for future generations to build upon.

Among the earliest of these was that strange genius, Paracelsus, dabbler in alchemy and astrology, an eccentric and braggart—and a great physician. Before meeting death in a tavern brawl in 1541, Paracelsus had rendered medical science a great service by repudiating Galenism and the humoral pathology that had dominated medical practice for more than fifteen centuries. He ridiculed the notion of demoniacal possession. "Mental diseases," he declared, "have nothing to do with evil spirits or devils; the individuals who are mentally sick merely drink more of the 'astral wine' than they can assimilate. The experienced [doctor] should not study how to exorcise the devil, but rather how to cure the insane . . . The insane and the sick are our brothers. Let us give them treatment to cure them, for nobody knows whom among our friends or relatives this misfortune may strike."[18] These were surely wise and courageous words for those days, the mystic aroma of the "astral wine" notwithstanding. Why, we might even say that Paracelsus was almost as modern as Soranus. His therapeutics, however, was unfortunately not quite as admirable as his kindly sentiments. For Paracelsus, like many of his successors of the eighteenth century, placed his whole faith in bloodletting as the cure of cures. "What avails in mania," he wrote, "except the opening of a vein? Then the patient will recover. This is the arcanum: not camphor, not sage and marjorum, not clysters, not this or that, but *bleeding.*"

In 1564, Dr. Johann Weyer of Cleves published a vigorous, if cautiously worded, polemic against the cruel consequences of the prevailing witch mania and pleaded for gentler and more rational treatment of the insane who were among its chief victims. He artfully paid lip service to the belief in demoniacal possession, going so far as to classify with meticulous care the legions of demons,* but held that the possessed were blameless and entitled to sympathetic treatment; it was the demon who should be punished. To combat the generally accepted notion that nails, stones and the like were introduced into possessed bodies by demons he demonstrated that lunatics, when unattended, are sometimes irresistibly inclined to swallow these indigestible objects.

Reginald Scot, a progressive and fearless soul, published in 1584 his famous *Discoverie of Witches* in which, with consummate skill, he laid bare and ridiculed the childish impostures and absurdities involved in the witchcraft superstition. Many of the poor creatures accused of witchcraft, he wrote, required relief from disease rather than chastisement for supposed sins; physicians to help them rather than executioners or torturers to hang and burn them. However, as Lecky records, his work had no appreciable influence.

Samuel Harsnett, Archbishop of York, showed himself to be surprisingly free of the delusions that seized most of his brothers in the cloth when he wrote in 1599: "They that have their brains baited and their fancies distempered with the imaginations and apprehensions of witches, conjurors

---

*In this book, *De praestigiis daemonum,* Weyer placed the total number of demons at 7,405,926, these being divided into seventy-two companies, each headed by a demonic captain.

and fairies, and all that lymphatic chimera, I find to be marshalled in one of these five ranks: children, fools, women, cowards, sick or black melancholic discomposed wits."

Daniel Sennert of Wittenburg (fl. 1572–1637) found it possible to accept the current belief in witches, and to state quite seriously that maniacs evacuated stones, iron and living animals placed in their bodies by demons, and yet, at the same time, to record some keen observations on the behavior of the insane. He also made an attempt to classify the mental diseases, dividing them into two major groups—mania and melancholia. Far more scientific than his observations and classifications were those of his contemporary, Felix Plater of Basle (1536–1614). Plater was one of the few who dared lift his voice in an appeal for a more humane and enlightened attitude towards the insane.

The late seventeenth century witnessed a growing revolt, participated in by philosophers and physicians, against the superstitions of witchcraft and demoniacal possession and their cruel effects on the insane. But all this outcry reached a stage of real effectiveness only in the following century. As late as 1716 a woman and her nine-year-old daughter were hanged at Huntingdon, England, after being convicted of selling their souls to the devil. It was not until 1736 that the laws against witchcraft were repealed in the United Kingdom, and local persecutions against the insane suspected of practicing witchcraft and sorcery continued intermittently for a long time thereafter. We shall have occasion to note in the next chapter the spread of the witchcraft mania to the newly-settled soil of America, and of its consequences on attitudes toward, and treatment of, the mentally ill in this land.

CHAPTER II
Colonial America: the Old World Heritage

THE early colonists who set sail from Europe to find fresh paths of life in the New World carried over with them, along with their worldly possessions, the assorted cultural accumulations of the lands of their nativity. This body of culture, comprising social, economic and political attitudes, they transplanted to the virgin soil of America, where it was subjected to the modifying influences of a new and vastly different environment.

The seventeenth-century Europe that the colonists left behind was passing through a period of turbulent transition. The walls of the feudal order were crumbling; on its ruins the modern capitalist era was rising toward its place in the historic procession of social systems. Western civilization was experiencing all the birth pains attending the incoming of a new order. Europe was being racked by religious wars, political upheavals and profound economic changes, conflicts that were to find their synthesis in the following century. The pace of progress was very uneven and, as always, cultural change lagged far behind the material advances that serve as its spearhead. In its dominant attitudes toward existence, the seventeenth century still lay within the penumbra of medieval thought. It was weighed down by the same superstitions and haunted by the same specters of the supernatural world that seemed so strangely intertwined with the world of every-day events.

Toward the phenomenon of mental illness, as we have indicated, it exhibited an even harsher and more ignorant attitude than the centuries that preceded it. Demoniacal possession was the common explanation of most forms of mental disorder, and the scourge, the rack, the stake and the gallows were the common methods of treatment. The fate of the mentally ill who managed to escape the accusation of being witches or bewitched was hardly better. If "violent," they were thrown into prison dungeons like common criminals; if "harmless," they were sometimes permitted to wander about the country aimlessly, with never a public thought for their welfare. Shakespeare gives us a vivid glimpse of these wandering "Toms o' Bedlam" when he speaks of "poor Tom, that eats the swimming frog, the toad, the tadpole, the wall newt and the water newt, that in the fury of his heart, when the foul fiend rages, cats cow-dung for sallets, swallows the old rat and the ditch dog, drinks the green mantle of the slimy pool; who is whipt from tything to tything, and stocked, punished, and imprisoned . . ." (*King Lear,* Act III, Scene 4.) In the isolated instances where cure was sought, the mentally ill were more likely to be taken to the clergyman for exorcistic treatment than to the physician for medical care. Moreover, so low was the estate of medicine, that it is problematical whether the ministrations of its practitioners were more effective than the clergy's.

To the European physician of the time, Hippocrates and Galen were the omnipotent authorities in *materia medica.* Few dared to dispute the dicta handed down by the ancients. Those who did were frowned upon as heretics, and ostracised. It was truly ironic that the two great figures who had done most to advance medicine in antiquity were thus fated to serve as checks to progress centuries later in an age that paid slavish, even fanatical, homage to their teachings.

True, the seventeenth century witnessed some great medical discoveries—discoveries that were to lay the foundations for modern medicine—but these were largely isolated from the main stream of contemporary practice. In 1628 Harvey published to the world his discovery of the circulation of the blood. During the same century, Jean Baptiste van Helmont was applying chemistry to the study of physiology with highly beneficial results. Characteristic of the age was his curious blend of mysticism and science, which led him to propound the doctrine of an *anima sensitiva motivaque* (sensitive motive soul) residing in the pit of the stomach whence it directed the entire system. Sanctorius Sanctorius, with that infinite patience which enabled him to carry on a painstaking thirty years' experiment upon himself in bodily weight changes, was paving the way for the modern science of metabolism. The great Thomas Sydenham was contributing to medical progress through his acute powers of observation, and earning the right to the title "master of clinical medicine." Lesser luminaries were building solidly on the foundations laid in a preceding century by the great anatomist, Vesalius.

But the influence of these pioneers on the general medical theory and practice of their day was almost nil. Harvey, in setting forth his theory of blood circulation, brought down upon his head the ridicule of his contemporaries, who accounted him "crack-brained" for daring to assert that he had discovered something unknown to Aristotle. We are told that his own practice "fell mightily" as a result. For the general practitioner medicine remained static. It was still held in the thrall of Galenism, that confused blend of scientific fact and travellers' tales, careful clinical observation and demonological lore, sound pharmacology and "grandmother" remedies.

Panaceas, confidently set forth to cure all ills, were plentiful. Mithridate was widely supposed to cure not only madness and epilepsy, but all the ills that flesh was heir to. The antimonial cup and Oriental bezoar stone were among the other universal antidotes of the time. The most widely consulted pharmacopoeias included among the favorite remedies such delectable items as crab's eyes, frog's spawn, powder from dog's lice, human perspiration and saliva, earthworms and viper's flesh. The most curious remedy of all, perhaps, was the famous "powder of sympathy" for wounds, concocted from sixty-one strangely assorted ingredients, including some of those we have just mentioned. This was applied, not to the wound itself, but to the weapon or implement that had inflicted it, in the confident expectation that the wound would thereupon heal in sympathy. As for attitudes toward mental illness and its treatment, we have noted in the preceding chapter how it was generally attributed to demoniacal

COLONIAL AMERICA

possession, and treated accordingly. Such, then, was the state of medicine in the world from which our early settlers journeyed.

In the colonies medical practice was on an even lower plane, for several obvious reasons. For one thing, there was little incentive for the skilled European-trained physician to chance the practice of his profession in America. The thin, scattered settlements discouraged hopes of a large clientele, while the poverty-stricken inhabitants, comprising the great majority of the population, could ill afford the luxury of physicians' fees. Throughout most of the colonial period there existed no opportunity to study medicine in halls of learning: not until 1765 was a medical school established in America.* The colonial physician rarely earned the academic right to the title "doctor." Ordinarily his art was learned through apprenticeship and the dubious benefits which the medical books of the time afforded. Dipping into one of the popular treatises on *materia medica* of his day, he would likely as not find the famous "Spirit of Skull" described as a potent remedy for epilepsy. Spirit of Skull was concocted from an elaborate preparation of "moss from the skull of a dead man unburied who had died a violent death," mixed with wine. It is a noteworthy fact that this was one of the last remedies administered to King Charles II of England in his fatal illness. Thirty drops of the Spirit were prescribed for "convulsive fits, epilepsy, vapours and pains in the head." The inquiring colonial doctor might find a similar formula for epilepsy, somewhat more difficult to compound, originated by Paracelsus and named by him *Confectio Anti-Epileptica*. The Paracelsan cure required no less than three human skulls of unburied men who had met violent death, which were to be dried and pulverized, and mixed with several liquids.[1] Other gruesome cures for epilepsy that might be suggested to the colonial physician by contemporary pharmacopoeias had for their bases pulverized human hearts, "brains of a young man under 24," and human blood. The last-named substance had been a favorite prescription in Roman times when, according to Celsus, some

*Founded at Philadelphia College, later the University of Pennsylvania.

were cured of epilepsy by drinking "hot blood taken from a gladiator who had just been slain."

Handicapped by the rigors of environment, isolation, and the lack of communication, the average colonial men of medicine fell far below the most backward country doctors in England in medical skill and knowledge. The works of the great medical discoverers and reformers of their day reached the colonial physician but seldom, and influenced him even less. In accordance with time-old tradition, he still diagnosed by the rule of the four humors—black bile, yellow bile, phlegm and blood. Diseases were still attributed to too much moisture, dryness, heat or cold. Mental diseases, when treated as medical problems, which was seldom, were commonly regarded as the result of an excess of bile. By looking into his *Gerard's Herball* (first published in 1597), which was considered a fairly indispensable item in every practitioner's library, the colonial physician would find, as a sure remedy for mental diseases, that favorite cure of the ancient Greeks, black hellebore (also known as melampode, because tradition ascribed its discovery to Melampos, who cured his mad daughters with it). "A purgation of Hellebore," counseled Gerard, "is good for mad and furious men, for melancholy, dull and heavie persons, and briefly for all those that are troubled with the falling sickness, and molested with melancholy."[2]

Like their European fellows, the colonial physicians were inclined to judge the efficacy of their prescriptions largely by the complexity and nauseating character of the ingredients involved. Venesection was universally applied: ill persons of all ages, from the infant to the octogenarian, were bled freely and often. Almanacs of the day recorded for their convenience the phases of the moon most favorable to bloodletting. All the vile and noxious remedies prescribed by their European fellows were imitated here. Many simples were administered. Some of these remedies were truly effective, as attested to by long experience; others, while not beneficial, were quite harmless, while still others had little more effect than to speed the unfortunate patient to his last rest.[3]

However poorly versed in his craft the average physician might be, there was yet a dearth of the profession in colonial America. Medicine was commonly administered by amateurs —mainly clergymen, barbers, civil officers, and plantation owners. Thus we find Michael Wigglesworth, the noted clergyman-poet of the 17th century, described by a contemporary as attending the sick "not only as a Pastor, but as a physician too."[4] Cotton Mather called this fusion of minister and physician an "angelical conjunction."

Of the seventeenth-century public officials skilled in the practice of physic, none was more renowned than John Winthrop, Jr., governor of Connecticut Colony and fellow of the Royal Society. Possessing a wealth of intellectual curiosity, he was fond of dabbling in alchemy, astrology and other mystic sciences, which he mixed generously with his medicine. He had in his repertory several remarkable remedies, among them this "infallible" cure for all sorts of agues: "Pare the patient's nails when the fever is coming on; and put the parings into a little bag of fine linen or sarenet; and tie that above a live eel's neck, in a tub of water. The eel will die and the patient will recover."[5]

Governor Winthrop enjoyed a wide reputation as an administrator of medicine, and was constantly deluged with requests for remedies from all corners of his colony. He was frequently referred to as Dr. Winthrop, and he used that title himself on occasion. So great was his interest in the healing art that he kept in touch with the most respected London physicians in order to avail himself of contemporary knowledge of curative treatment. Of interest to our particular study is a message received by Winthrop in 1643 from Dr. Edward Stafford of London, informing him of many remedies. It begins:

For my Worthy Friend Mr. Winthrop:
For Madnesse: Take ye herbe Hypericon (: in English St. John's Wort) and boile it in Water or drink, untill it be strong of it, and redd in colour; or else, putt a bundle of it in new drinke to Worke, and give it ye patient to drinke, permitting him to drinke nothing else. First purge him well with 2 or 3 seeds (; or more, according to ye strengthe of the partie;) of Spurge. Let them not eat much, but

keep dyet, and you shall see Wondrous effects in fewe dayes. I have knowne it to cure perfectly to admiration in five dayes.⁶

St. John's wort was a favorite remedy for mental illness in those days. Its herbs, after being blessed, were wrapped up in a "hallow paper" and commonly carried about "to be smelled at against the invasions of the devil." In addition to his wondrous remedy for madness which could cure in five days, Dr. Stafford lists a cure for "ye falling sickness." For this ailment he prescribes the ancient and revered remedy, black hellebore, to be prepared in the same manner as St. John's wort was for madness. However, his expression of faith in his treatment for epilepsy is somewhat more cautiously worded: "Use it as above, and God willing he [the patient] shall be perfectly cured in short or longer time, according as the disease hath taken root." In his communication Dr. Stafford reveals to Winthrop his *chef-d'œuvre,* a panacea consisting of live toads boiled outdoors in the month of March and then pounded into black powder, which can be used both to prevent and cure many diseases.

The astrological note was sounded very frequently in medical prescriptions of colonial times, and it is not surprising that we find it mentioned in the treatment of epilepsy as late as 1764, in a case administered by Dr. James Greenhill of Virginia. After describing the unsatisfactory results obtained from the usual bleeding and purging applications to his epileptic patient, Dr. Greenhill tells of "blistering" the latter on the nape of the neck. "This succeeded," he continues somewhat ungrammatically, "and the next Change of the Moon expecting the fit, as usual, he missed them. The Medicines has been continued and he has missed the fits this last full moon again. The blister is almost dry but I intend . . . to draw a fresh one. It is something remarkable that the fits has Usually returned when the Moon was in the Sign of Capricorn even when it was a week before or after the full or change."⁷ This was evidently quite beyond the comprehension of the worthy doctor, who had been taught to expect epileptic recurrences only at the full of the moon!

Several colonial doctors seem to have gained reputations

as specialists in the treatment of mental illness. Among these was Dr. Thomas Kittredge of North Andover, Massachusetts. Toward the end of the colonial period we find him treating as many as ten or twelve mentally ill patients at a time. These he boarded out with two or three families in Andover, where they were closely supervised by members of each family. Apparently little restraint was applied, although the patients were subjected to occasional bloodletting in order to weaken them and thus render them more manageable.[8]

Few of the colonial doctors were acquainted with the real nature of mental disorders, or of positive methods of care and treatment. Not untypical of the absurd conceptions of mental illness is the case cited in John Hale's *Modest Inquiry into the Nature of Witchcraft,* published in 1702. A man "afflicted with hallucinations" sent for a physician some miles away. The doctor was unable to come but sent a diagnosis and remedy by messenger. "The vapours ascending from his sore Legg" ran the diagnosis, "caused a water in his Eyes, and disturbance in his Braines, by means whereof he was troubled with such Visions." To treat the disturbed brain, the doctor sent "an eye water to wash his eyes with, and a cordial to take inwardly; upon the use of these, this disturbance vanished in half a quarter of an hour." A miraculous feat indeed, albeit our own skeptical age would attribute this "cure" less to the remarkable eyewash than to the commentator's credulity. With true Puritanical zeal Hale draws a moral lesson from this case, for he ends his narrative with the observation: "If a disease may do this, what may Satan, working upon bodily distempers and vapours, impose upon the Imagination?"[9]

Here was a significant sentiment that was entertained as widely in the colonies as it was in contemporary Europe. The belief in demoniacal possession was practically universal in seventeenth-century America. It reached its apogee in the famous Salem witchcraft mania of 1692, and died down thereafter, although witch trials continued to recur throughout the first half of the eighteenth century. The common tendency of the time to identify mental illness with diabolical possession is well illustrated in Cotton Mather's biographical sketch of William Thompson, a New England divine who died in 1666. "Satan," he writes, "who had been after an extraordinary manner irritated by the Evangelic Labours of this Holy Man [Thompson], obtained the Liberty to *sift* him; and hence, after this Worthy Man had served the Lord Jesus Christ in the Church of our New England Braintree, he fell into that *Balneum Diaboli,* a *black melancholy,* which for divers years almost wholly disabled him for the exercise of his Ministry."[10]

The name of Cotton Mather is commonly identified with the Salem witchcraft craze of 1691–92. Upon him, as the most influential member of the community, has been placed the burden of responsibility for the twenty-two lives that were sacrificed at Salem. This narrow judgment lacks historical perspective, although we cannot hold Mather free of all blame for the part he played in the tragic episode. In his firm conviction in the reality of diabolical possession, Mather was merely sharing a dogma that was adhered to by most of the educated and advanced men among his contemporaries. The witchcraft mania had raged before his time elsewhere in New England. The first of the two well-defined periods of epidemic witch hunting in America had taken place in 1647–63 (the second being that of 1688–93, in which Mather played so prominent a part). The earliest recorded execution for witchcraft had occurred in Connecticut in 1647, when Mary Johnson was hanged under the law enacted five years before: "If any man or woman be a witch, that is hath or consulted with a familiar spirit, they shall be put to death."[11] Persecution of persons suspected of being witches or "familiars" was of common occurrence in most of the other colonies as well, although nowhere did the delusion reach such a pitch of intensity as it did in Puritan New England.

Puritanism, with its stern repression of healthy human instincts, its abnormal orientation around religion, and its exaggerated expressions of alternate suspicion and credulity, offered a fertile soil for the development of this mania. Any variation from the norm in nature, however trivial, was looked upon by the Puritan mind as a supernatural manifestation. Comets, thunderstorms and meteorites were regarded as solemn signs direct from either God or Satan. They were full of portent for New England, which was prone to regard itself as the special concern of the spiritual powers at war. Deviations from the norm in human behavior were likewise looked upon as suspicious. The causes of strange or irregular conduct (such as a mentally ill person might manifest) were sought in the supernatural, and the answer was commonly found in demoniacal possession.

Such was the atmosphere in which the Salem witchcraft mania originated. Before it had run its course, it was to seize a whole community in its terrifying grasp. It cannot be said that all the witchcraft cases are attributable to insanity on the part of the accused or the accusers. Undoubtedly, many were due to the maliciousness of persons impelled to accuse troublesome or undesirable neighbors. Others resulted from rank imposture, or sheer ignorance and superstitious credulity. But, as the records of the trials impressively show, there were unmistakable manifestations of diseased minds among a large number of the participants—accusers, accused, and witnesses.

The case of Mary Glover of Boston, who was tried and executed in 1688, served as a fitting prologue to the great Salem drama. In microcosm it illustrates very clearly the presence of mental illness in both accused and accusers. Mrs. Glover, a laundress in the Goodwin household, was accused by the four children of the family of having bewitched them. The children all exhibited well-marked evidences of hysteria. At different times they would appear to be deaf, dumb and blind. Their tongues would sometimes be drawn down their throats or hang down their chins. Their bodies were spotted with anaesthetic and hyperaesthetic areas. They were subject to all sorts of convulsions and contortions. They would shriek with pain and cry out that they were in turn being suffocated, burned, pricked and bitten by devils. At least one of the children continued to have "fits" long after the case had been concluded with a witch-hanging.

As for the accused woman, far from denying the accusation, she readily confessed to being in league with the devil. She is described by a contemporary historian as being a "wild Irish woman," and the circumstances of the trial strongly indicate that she was mentally unbalanced. Cotton Mather, narrating the trial and execution in his *Memorable Providences* (1689), tells us that among the items found in her home were "several images, or puppets, or babies, made of rags and stuffed with goat's hair," articles not infrequently found in the possession of insane women. When asked by the judges whether she had any one standing by her, she replied that she had, but "looking very pertly into the air, she added, 'No, he's gone.'" She acknowledged that the Devil was her "Prince" and paramour, and stated that he had served her so basely and falsely that she had decided to confess all. Her absurd and incoherent statements, instead of revealing to her judges the illness which she suffered, were, on the contrary, accepted by them as indisputable evidences of her guilt.

The witchcraft mania in Salem grew out of the quite innocent frolics of a group of young girls who used to gather at the village minister's house. Here they were wont to play at fortune-telling and palm-reading and to discuss the supernatural. Ghosts, devils and witches were favorite subjects of their discussions. In the tense, repressed atmosphere of Salem, where the "invisible world" seemed even to the soberest adults as immanent and real as the visible world, the over-wrought imaginations of these sternly repressed children began to break through the bounds of sanity. They started to see strange things, hear preternatural voices, and dream strange dreams. Their condition soon came to the attention of the village elders, who investigated and solemnly concluded that the girls were "afflicted," or bewitched.

Stimulated and excited by the attention they had attracted—the craving for attention is a common cause of hysteria in young girls—the children began to manifest in heightened degrees all sorts of hysterical symptoms; they barked and mewed, they went into frequent "fits" of catalepsy and convulsions, they jumped and screamed, uttered wild gibberish (this was called "speaking in tongues"), leaped on tables and crawled under them, and cried out that they were being choked, weighed down, pricked and slashed by the devil and his witches.

Pressed for the names of those who were casting evil spells over them, they named first one, then another, of the inhabitants of Salem until it seemed that fully half the village had signed their souls over to the devil. Terror seized the villagers. The hysteria became contagious, and others were soon exhibiting the same symptoms and hurling wild accusations against their neighbors.* In that one year (1691–92), 250 persons were arrested and tried in Salem on witchcraft charges: fifty were condemned; nineteen were executed; two died in prison; and one died of torture.

The type of testimony that was accepted as truth by the unbelievably credulous judges, and that was instrumental in sending a score of innocents to their death, is exemplified in the interrogation of Sarah Carrier, eight, whose mother Martha was hanged as a witch. Awed by the solemnity of the inquisitors, her mind excited by fears and fancies intensified by leading questions, the child testified in this vein:

'How long hast thou been a witch?'
'Ever since I was six years old.'
'How old are you now?'
'Near eight years old.'
'Who made you a witch?'
'My mother. She made me set my hand to the book.'
'You said you saw a cat once. What did the cat say to you?'
'It said it would tear me to pieces if I would not set my hand to the book.' [that is, the "Devil's Book."]
'How did you know that it was your mother?'
'The cat told me so, that she was my mother.'[12]

*Epidemics of demoniacal possession such as that at Salem were of frequent occurrence during the middle ages, notably the dancing manias that occurred throughout Europe following the Black Plague. In fact, such epidemics have been experienced in quite recent times. One of the best known instances of so-called demonomania is that which seized the town of Morzines in Savoy during 1857–62. Here, too, the epidemic was begun by hysterical children and spread rapidly to their elders. For five years intermittently, scores of inhabitants went madly about the town, certain that they were possessed of devils and that their souls were irretrievably lost. It is interesting to note that occasional clerical attempts to exorcise the victims of demons

As for the accused, many of them were first suspected, naturally enough, because of strange behavior and antics on their part. We gain an insight into the mental state of many of them through the testimony of Samuel Wardwell, who himself confessed that he was guilty of covenanting with the devil. He related that some years before he "had fallen into a discontented state of mind because he was in love with a maid named Barker who slighted his love." While in this state of melancholy, he continued, he saw one day "some cats together," one of which assumed the form of "the black man." The latter promised him that "he should live comfortably and be a captain" if he would sign the Devil's Book, after which Wardwell was induced to affix his signature to it.[13] The hapless man later retracted his confession, but his explanation that he was not in his right mind when questioned went for naught, and he was hanged, along with seven others, on September 22, 1692.*

We can readily comprehend the mental state of women who confessed at Salem to riding broomsticks through the air; consorting with devils and having carnal relations with them, pinching and otherwise annoying their neighbors abed by means of their "specters", and visiting illness and death upon others through their black magic. The records include a revealing statement signed by six women, renouncing their confessions of having practiced witchcraft. Residents of Andover, they had been arrested as witches and brought to Salem, where they were all tried and convicted. "By reason of that sudden surprisal," their repudiation reads, "we were

---

resulted only in fanning the flames of the mass hysteria to a still higher degree. It subsided only after psychiatric knowledge and treatment were applied to the town's ailment.

*Incidentally, Cotton Mather, who kept a kind of clinic for the "possessed" at his home, where he might keep them under close surveillance and offer up therapeutic prayer for their release, presents us with a remarkable case history of hysteria in a little-known work of his: *A Brand Pluck'd from the Burning* (1693). In this work, he describes the "bewitchment" of Mercy Short, a maid-servant who testified in several of the witch trials at Salem, and was taken to Mather's home for observation and possible cure. Her actions, which are minutely and faithfully described by Mather as the workings of possessing demons, offer a very interesting, if unintended, contribution to psychiatric lore.

all exceedingly astonished and amazed, and consternated and affrighted even out of our reason . . . Our understanding and our faculties almost gone, we were not capable of judging our condition, but said everything they (the judges) desired."[14]

The mental illness aspect of the witchcraft delusion, the aspect to which our particular interest is drawn, is perhaps best summed up by Thomas Brattle, a contemporary eyewitness to the Salem tragedy. Brattle was one of the very few who managed to keep his common sense clear of the mental storm that swirled all about him. Significantly enough, he was constantly under suspicion of being an infidel and apostate because of his enlightened views.

In a letter sent by him to an anonymous clergyman in October, 1692, at the height of the witch-hunt hysteria, Brattle gives a minute description of the goings-on at Salem. Of the fifty-five persons held in jail under the charge of witchcraft at the time, he states that "some of them are known to be distracted, crazed women." Brattle could not escape completely the current superstitions, and in his letter he affirms his general belief in sorcery, witchcraft and evil demons. But having carefully observed the particular "witches" who had confessed to horrible deeds at Salem, Brattle remarks:

"They are deluded, imposed upon, and under the influence of some evil spirit; and therefore unfitt to be evidences either against themselves, or any one else. These confessours (as they are called) do very often contradict themselves, as inconsistently as is usual for any crazed, distempered person to do."

Turning to the accusers—the "bewitched"—Brattle finds reason to doubt their mental soundness also, and offers these keen observations:

Many of these afflicted persons who have scores of strange fitts in a day, yet, at the intervals of time are hale and hearty, robust and lusty as if nothing had afflicted them. I strongly suspect that the Devill imposes on their brains, and deludes their fancye and imagination; and that the Devill's Book (which they say had been offered them) is a mere fancye of theirs, and no reality.[15]

The horrors and absurdities of the witchcraft trials, with their involved tragi-comic contradictions, finally registered on the public mind and ultimately a halt was called to the proceedings. The wholesome reaction was indubitably hastened by the fact that, with the mounting hysteria, some of the "afflicted" were beginning to point accusatory fingers at prominent and substantial citizens. This personal danger quickly frightened the latter into their senses, and impelled them to suppress the mania. In May, 1693, Governor Phips of Massachusetts Colony issued a proclamation releasing from custody all persons, numbering about 150, still confined in prison on witchcraft charges. Thus ended the most intense phase of the delusion of demoniacal possession, with its consequent persecution of the insane. And with it—though witchcraft trials occurred sporadically in the colonies for some score of years thereafter—a dramatic chapter in the treatment of the mentally ill in America passed into history.

CHAPTER III
Colonial Provision for the Mentally Ill: Punishment, Repression and Indifference

NEITHER the cultural nor material conditions of early colonial America offered fertile ground for the introduction and development of a liberal, well-integrated system of social welfare that would include special provision for persons handicapped by physical, mental and economic ills. The settlements were generally sparse and scattered, populated for the most part by an impecunious people who lived on the ragged edge of existence, engaged in constant struggle to wrench a bare living from the soil. In these circumstances, they were too likely to be burdened with their own immediate problems of existence to give much thought to the welfare of their more needy neighbors. A certain degree of communal stabilization and a relatively close gathering of people in large groups are indispensable requisites for the development of a permanent welfare system of well-rounded proportions: in the colonial settlements these were lacking.

In accordance with the dominant ideology at home and abroad, the sufferings of the handicapped members of the community were looked upon as the natural consequences of a stern unbending Providence, meting out judgment to the wicked and the innately inferior. Contempt, cold and narrow, rather than sympathy and understanding, characterized the attitudes towards the destitute and dependent classes. Public provision for the latter was based not so much upon humane considerations as upon social expediency and economy. The individual in need of assistance was apt to receive public attention only when his condition was looked upon as a social danger or a public nuisance—and he was then "disposed of" rather than helped.

These general attitudes and conditions were reflected and accentuated in provisions for the insane. We may conveniently divide these provisions into two categories: private and public. Mentally ill persons who had relatively well-to-do families or friends were usually cared for in their own homes. In the rare instances when the affliction was recognized as a disease produced, not by supernatural intervention, but by natural causes, and hence amenable to curative measures, they received whatever medical treatment was available (such as has been described in the preceding chapter). If violent or troublesome, even the propertied insane were without compunction locked up and chained by their families in strong-rooms, cellars, and even in flimsy outhouses. In some cases, where the illness manifested itself in a mild and harmless manner, the individual was permitted a degree of freedom of movement. But often enough, even harmless persons were confined for years on end in attic rooms, very much like Sam Evans' aunt in O'Neill's *Strange Interlude,* so that the family "disgrace" might be hidden from the public eye. Until the closing years of the colonial period there were no hospitals where they might be cared for. Not until 1752 was the first general hospital established, while the first asylum for the exclusive reception of the insane was opened two decades later.

The plight of the propertied insane came to the public notice only in so far as their estates were concerned. Significant in this respect is the fact that several of the colonies passed laws regarding the estates of insane persons long before enacting legislation concerned with their personal well-being. This condition harked back to the days of Ciceronian Rome, when elaborate provisions were made for the protection of an insane man's property, while none at all existed for the protection of his person. The responsibility for determining insanity was always placed in the hands of civil officers—never of medical men—and the guardianship of estates was variously entrusted to governors, town selectmen, churchwardens, vestrymen, justices of the peace, and

COLONIAL PROVISION

so on, depending on the civil set-up of the several colonies.

So much for mentally ill persons who were not dependent on the public for economic assistance. As for the dependent insane, their lot was harsher still. By a peculiar twist of logic (which has not been completely dispelled in our day) those afflicted with mental diseases were generally treated as if they had been thereby stripped of all human attributes, together with their rights and privileges as human beings. This pernicious and all-too-prevailing attitude was bluntly summed up by a well-known English jurist of the early eighteenth century who did not hesitate to liken a "madman" to a "brute or a wild beast."

When insanity was publicly recognized, it was usually for the purpose of punishing or repressing the individual; when it was not, indifference to his fate was the dominating note. There was no uniform theory for dealing with the mentally ill. They were disposed of in a number of ways. Provision was of the rough and ready nature that characterized pioneer life: individual cases were considered and decided on as they arose. A number of factors were here involved, among the principal ones being the level of community intelligence and social-consciousness, and the kind and degree of insanity manifested in the patients. The "violent" insane among public dependents were ordinarily treated as common criminals, while the "harmless" were disposed of in a manner differing only in degree of severity from that accorded to all other paupers. The latter cases were hardly more fortunate than the former, for in colonial times and long after pauperism was looked upon as merely a lesser type of crime.

Public provision, in so far as it was extended to the mentally ill, was mainly directed to the problem of safely disposing of violent cases. Incarceration in jail was the common solution. But there were many localities which could not boast the luxury of a jail in the early days, when the pillory, the whipping post and the gallows—all placed convenieniently near the courthouse—afforded simple and inexpensive means for punishing the refractory in short order. Such a lack of institutional accommodation, however, was not likely to deter our ingenious forefathers. Thus, the first known provision for the mentally ill in Pennsylvania, mentioned in the Upland Court records of 1676, took the following form:

> Jan Vorelissen, of Amesland, Complayning to ye Court that his son Erik is bereft of his naturall Senses and is turned quyt madd and yt, he being a poore man is not able to maintaine him; Ordered: yt three or four persons bee hired to build a little block-house at Amesland for to put in the said madman.[1]

To meet the cost of building the block-house and the maintenance of Erik, a small tax was levied on the community. No less enterprising were the inhabitants of the town of Braintree, Massachusetts, who in 1689 voted

> That Samuel Speere should build a little house 7 foote long & 5 foote wide & set it by his house to secure his Sister good wife Witty being distracted & provide for her.[2]

The town obligated itself to repay the said Samuel Speere the expenses of maintaining his sister in this kennel-like habitation. Likewise, in New York, the first "institution" for the insane was a special structure which was ordered to be built in 1677 for the incarceration of Peter Paull, a "lunatick", who was to "bee confined into prison in the hold" pending the completion of the strong-house for his special care.[3] Whether this one-man asylum was ever built, the records do not reveal.

We learn in the later annals of New York City that the city jail was considered quite a satisfactory place for the custody of the insane. In 1725 the town marshal, Robert Crannell, Jr., was paid two shillings six pence a week by the churchwardens "for to Subsist Robert Bullman a Madman in Prison."[4] Not infrequently the unfortunate person spent decades incarcerated like a common criminal. But when some hope was held out for his recovery, only temporary confinement was ordered. In 1720, for example, the same marshal was given the custody of one Henry Dove, "a Dangerous Madman, untill he shall Recover his senses."[5] An earlier instance of this policy toward the "dangerous" insane is contained in the records of York County, Virginia, for 1689. It concerns another "madman", John Stock,

> whoe keepes running about the neighborhood day and night in a sad Distracted Condition to the great Disturbance of the people, therefore for the prevention of his doeing any further Mischeife It is Ordered by the Court that Mr. Robt. Read, High Sherr: doe take Care that the said Stock bee Lade hold of and safely kept in some close Roome, where hee shall not bee suffered to go abroad until hee bee in a better condition to Governe himselfe, and that ye said Robert Read is to pvide such helps as may bee Convenient to Looke after him.[6]

The repressive principle underlying special provision for the mentally ill is explicit in early colonial legislation. For example, the first Massachusetts statute specifically concerned with the insane, enacted in 1676, reads in part:

> Whereas, There are distracted persons in some tounes, that are unruly, whereby not only the familyes wherein they are, but others suffer much damage by them, it is ordered by this Court and the authoritye thereof, that the selectmen in all tounes where such persons are are hereby impowred & injoyned to take care of all such persons, that they doe not damnify others.[7]

This statute, subsequently amended in 1694, served as a model for legislation concerning the insane in other New England colonies.

The fear of "damnification" appears as a prime factor in attracting public interest to the mentally ill in the early days. A singular example of this factor as a stimulus to public action is found in the records of Albany, New York, for 1685, when two gentlemen citizens sent an urgent request to the Common Council that it order "the old Poorman" to be removed from their neighborhood "because of the danger of houses taking fire because of his crazyness."[8]

Special provision for the insane poor, as we have noted, was rare and was chiefly confined to the violent type regarded as social dangers. As for the non-violent dependents, they were ordinarily classified and treated, not as mentally ill, but simply as paupers, one yardstick ordinarily being used for all pauper classes under the poor laws.

The poor relief pattern in the colonies followed minutely the lines set down by the famous Elizabethan Poor Law Act of 1601. Its outstanding feature was the fixing of local responsibility for the support of the poor; its guiding spirit was the repression, rather than relief, of pauperism. An insight into the principle underlying this local relief system may be obtained through a report sent by Governor Dongan of New York in 1686 to the mother country, in which he boasted that "every Town and County are obliged to maintain their own poor, which makes them bee soe careful that noe Vagabonds, Beggars, nor Idle Persons are suffered to live here."[9]

Indeed, the most repressive measures were adopted to keep out poor strangers, including the dependent insane, through the medium of harsh settlement laws. It was no accident that the first legislation respecting the poor were laws of settlement intended to exclude them from the several colonies and local communities. The earliest of the colonial settlement laws was enacted in Massachusetts in 1639. The titles generally given to such acts—"For the Preventing of Vagabonds," "For the Preventing of Poor Persons," etc.—are significant indications of their repressive intent. Strangers arriving in a town were looked upon with suspicion, and were invariably subjected to immediate and searching investigation. Inhabitants were forbidden to lodge strangers without notifying the authorities, so that their economic status might be checked. Parents could not even entertain their own children as guests, nor children their parents, without official permission. A definite term of "quiet and undisturbed" residence in a locality, varying usually from three months to a year, gave a person legal settlement, carrying with it the town's obligation to support him should he thereafter require public relief. Hence, if there seemed the least likelihood of a stranger's becoming a public charge at some future time, he was unceremoniously "warned out." As a further bulwark against dependency, towns usually required newcomers, or inhabitants entertaining them, to furnish bond against the possibility of their becoming public charges. In some colonies, public whippings faced all destitute persons who dared to return to a locality after once having been driven out. In New York, according to a law enacted in 1721, such persons might receive, when caught, "36 lashes on the bare back if a man, and 25 if a woman." In others, still harsher laws provided for the whipping of poor strangers or vagabonds (the terms were used interchangeably) even before expulsion.

The custom of "warning out" was unsparingly practiced in the colonies. Francis S. Drake, the historian of Roxbury, Massachusetts, tells us that warnings were frequent up to the close of the 18th century, and that "Indian stragglers and crazy persons were in the early days often driven from the town."[10] In its application, little consideration seems to have been given to those who had previously held positions of respectability and affluence—men who had "known better days." Witness the sad case of an ex-chaplain who had become mentally ill, as recorded in the Boston Selectmen's Minutes for 1742:

> Complaint being made by mr. Cooke that mr. Samuel Coolidge formerly chaplain of the Castle is now in this Town & in a Distracted Condition & very likely to be a Town Charge, Voted, that mr. Savell Warn him out of Town acording to law.[11]

The dependent insane in particular suffered from the hardships occasioned by the settlement laws. It seems to have been a frequent practice for towns to spirit away mentally ill paupers under the cover of night, and to place them in a distant town or neighboring county in the hope of thus ridding themselves of the burden of supporting them. Frequently, the mentally ill were permitted to wander from place to place, or were hurriedly "passed on" by callous authorities in fear of their "falling on the town." Cast out by unfeeling families and niggardly communities, they strayed on aimlessly, like the Toms o' Bedlam who tramped through England, begging their bread, laying their heads wherever they might do so unmolested, the butts of ridicule of village children and idlers, and more rarely, the objects of charity of some humane individual. The shocking state to which these wanderers were permitted to descend is vividly illustrated in an order of the General Assembly of Connecticut Colony as late as 1756, where it is recorded:

> There is now at Wallingford a strolling woman that has been sometime wandering from town to town, calling herself Susannah Roberts of Pennsylvania, who is so disordered in her reason and understanding that she passeth from place to place naked, without any regard for the laws and rules of decency.[12]

The Assembly ordered the selectmen of Wallingford to clothe the insane woman and to commit her to the care of "some discreet person that she may labour for her support," and agreed to pay the difference between her earnings and the cost of her keep. The town of Wallingford, incidentally, seems to have been lax in assuming legal obligations towards its own dependents, for two years later (1758) we find one of its residents, a "distracted person" named Mary Hall, "allowed to stroll from town to town and place to place, to the great disquiet of many people," and the town is directed to take on her support. If she is thereafter again found wandering outside the confines of Wallingford, the Assembly orders that she be returned at the town's expense.[13]

It sometimes happened that the expense of providing for the insane was too great for one town to bear, as witnessed in an amendment to the Duke of York's law instituted 1665, soon after New Netherland was captured from the Dutch:

> In regard to Conditions of distracted persons, they may be both very chargeable and troublesome and so will prove too greate a burthen for one Towne to bear alone, and each Towne, in the rideing where such person or persons shall happen to be, is to contribute towards the charge which may arise upon such ocasion.[14]

In accordance with the terms of this act, the Court of Sessions for Kings County, New York, in 1695, ordered "that Mad James be kept by Kings County in General and that the deacons of each town within the said county doe forthwith meet together and consider about their propercons for maintainence of said James."[15] This is the earliest recorded instance of county care for the insane that has come to my notice.

In instances where the insane were not punished or repressed for the crime of losing their reason, we usually find that they were treated with an icy indifference. Many localities were not above resorting to scurvy methods in ridding themselves of the responsibility of public care. But here and there, in rare and isolated instances, we do find evidences of sympathetic understanding. It is an interesting fact that the earliest known colonial champion of the right of the mentally ill to humane treatment was Roger Williams, that sturdy fighter for liberty and tolerance in general. In a touching letter to the town council of Providence in 1650, Williams appeals to the latter to minister to the needs of a distracted woman, Mrs. Weston, so that "some publike act of mercy to her necessities stand upon record amongst ye merciful acts of a merciful town yt hath received many mercies from Heaven, and remembers yt we know not how soon our own wives may be widows and our children orphans, yea, and ourselves be deprived of all or most of our reason before we goe from hence, except mercy from ye God of mercies prevent it."[16]

When charity was granted the insane poor, it was usually on a basis identical with that of the other classes of dependents. Since almshouses did not come into general use until the end of the eighteenth century, it was customary to "house" mentally ill paupers in private dwellings at public expense. Here, in embryo, was a form of the "boarding-out" plan. But it was far removed in aim and accomplishment from the system of family care for the mentally ill which later was to achieve such impressive results in Belgium, Scotland and elsewhere in recent times. The term "neighborly" may be applied to this colonial form of relief only in a geographic sense. In essence it was "cold charity"; expediency and not humanitarianism was the determining factor.

Town officers were often charged with the duty of maintaining the mildly insane in their homes. Thus, the colony of New Haven in 1645 made provision for distracted Goodwife Lampson "so far forth as her husband is not able to do it," and committed her to the care of the town marshal.

(Incidentally, this case offers one of many instances where dependent insane were only partly relieved by public funds.) Three years later, finding his charge too burdensome, the marshal begged the authorities to relieve him of his responsibility, whereupon the court ordered Goodwife Lampson's husband either to take her back home or seek another place where she might be kept.[17] Feebleminded dependents were also disposed of in this manner at times. Witness the action of the commissioners of Surrey County, Virginia, in 1661, contracting with Robert House to board John Deanne, an "Iddiott", and to provide him with food and clothing.[18] The latter seems to have earned at least part of his keep, for in the following year he appears in the records in the relation of "servant" to his "master", Mr. House.

Public provision for the indigent insane very seldom included medical treatment. On the rare occasions when it was prescribed it arose more from the motive of economy than of kindness. This calculating approach to the problem is exemplified in the case of Abigail Neal, a distracted woman of Braintree, Massachusetts. For at least a decade following 1697, this woman was boarded out at public expense among several physicians in succession, in the hope that she might be cured and thus relieve the town of her support.[19] The town attempted to wash its hands of a public charge by granting lump sums to each doctor in turn "providing he give the town noe further trouble about her," but in 1707, poor Abigail remained uncured, and the town was still paying for her keep. In 1701 the trustees of the town of Southampton, Long Island, voted that Samuel Barbor's wife "being distracted and out of her reason," be confined in the prison, adding this provision: "We do order Capt. Topping to speak to Dr. Wade to come and see her, and to administer that which is proper for such a Person according to his skill and cunning."[20] How this prisoner-patient responded to Dr. Wade's cunning, history does not reveal, but our survey of medical care for the mentally ill at the time leaves us little room for optimistic conjecture.

During the latter part of the colonial period laws were passed making it mandatory, upon penalty of fine, for relatives within certain degrees of consanguinity to provide for the mentally ill. But in the earlier years it was not unusual for towns to bear the expense of boarding this class of dependents with their own parents, brothers, wives or husbands. For example, at a Providence, Rhode Island, town meeting of November 3rd, 1655, presided over by Roger Williams, it was ordered:

> Since our neighbor Pike hath divers times applied himselfe with complaints to ye towne for helpe in this his sad condition of his wife's distraction, he shall repair to ye Towne Treasurer, who is hereby authorized and required to pay unto ye said Pike unto ye sume of fifteen shillings; and ye Towne promiseth upon his further want and complaint he shall be supplied though to ye value of ten pounds or more.[21]

One method of providing for the dependent insane in colonial times was to grant an individual a lump sum for assuming permanent responsibility for some particular unfortunate, as in the case of Abigail Neal. In this manner the towns sought to rid themselves of the necessity for indefinite provision. In 1699, the town of Braintree ordered the Selectmen

> to treat with Josiah Owen about Ebenezer Owens distracted daughter and give him Twenty pounds money provided he gives bond under his hand to clear the Town for ever of saide girle.[22]

But in this instance, too, the town was unsuccessful in the attempt to rid itself so easily of its proper charge, for further sums were voted to Josiah for Mary Owen's support in 1702 and again in 1706. In the latter year Braintree finally became resigned to its fate, and set aside a definite amount of money to maintain this dependent for the ensuing ten years.

The confused and haphazard nature of colonial relief for dependent insane is manifested in New York City records of the early 18th century. In 1712, for example, we have an instance of provision by indirect loan when the churchwardens were ordered to "lend Phillip Batten, butcher, thirty shillings in order to go on with his trade, (he being reduced to great poverty by reason of his wife being delirious)."[23] Hardly less casual was the aid given to one Susan, "commonly called Mad Sew," in 1721, when she was supplied by order of the Mayor's Court with "a good pair of Shoes & Stockings & other Necessary Warm Clothing. She being Very Old Poor & Non Compos Mentis & an Object of Charity."[24] In 1729, the fear was expressed by the Mayor's Court that Timothy Dally, who "is by intervals perfectly distracted & non Compos Mentis," might lay violent hands upon himself "if no Care be taken to prevent it." Dally's trouble was evidently induced by economic worries, for the Court adopted an unusual solution for warding off the danger of suicide by providing his wife six shillings per week to maintain him at home.[25] Whether this "preventive" measure succeeded in curing him of his suicidal mania, we have no means of knowing.

A sore problem that confronted our colonial fathers was how to dispose of insane persons who committed offenses against the criminal laws. From the historical evidences available we may conclude that in general practice, if not in theory, no differentiation was made between insane and sane offenders, and that the former were held responsible for criminal acts, and were made to suffer the penalties inflicted upon common criminals. Even in relatively advanced communities where the irresponsibility of the insane was recognized, a hazy notion prevailed as to how to deal with their cases. This confusion resulted in decisions that seem strange and inconsistent from our present perspective. In 1674, for example, a case was considered in New York province wherein the defendant was charged with running amok, breaking down doors, setting fire to houses and beating women and children. The judges decided that the defendant, "not being in his right reason", could not be held responsible—an enlightened opinion for those times. But we can only express mystification at the final disposition of the case, for the judges ordered the defendant banished from Flushing to Staten Island, there to be put to work by order of the local magistrate "who is hereby empowered, if the defendant *behave badly,* to *punish* him according as he may deserve."[26] All of which would indicate that although insanity might be considered a mitigating factor in the first offense, it could not save the afflicted person from punishment on future occasions. There is also the curious disposition of the case of one Roger Humphry, a colonial soldier of Simsbury, Connecticut who, in 1757, "became delirious and distracted and in his distraction killed his mother." Humphry was acquitted on account of his manifest insanity, but was ordered confined for life in a "small place" to be erected by his father at his home. The expense for building this home-prison and maintaining its inmate was to be borne by the public treasury.[27]

With the growth and concentration of population in the towns, the need for institutional provision for the criminal and dependent classes became more and more imperative. The haphazard disposition of each individual case on its merits was quite suitable for a thinly populated community where the entire roster of inhabitants could convene on town meeting days to decide public problems, but in a thriving and growing town or city, the old-fashioned methods proved increasingly cumbersome. Gradually corporal punishment by means of stocks, pillories and whipping-posts was supplanted by confinement in jails, bridewells, houses of correction and prisons. Outdoor relief, in the form of individual boarding-out, gave way to workhouses and almshouses— the earliest types of institution exclusively devoted to the custody of dependent classes.

Houses of correction and workhouses sprang up in the more thickly populated districts of the American colonies during the second quarter of the eighteenth century. The workhouse was invariably a combination penal institution and poorhouse, and within its walls petty offenders and paupers were herded indiscriminately. *In theory,* it was a most useful and beneficial institution, fulfilling a number of functions. It was considered as a penal establishment for rogues and vagabonds, idle and vicious; a means for profitably employing the able-bodied poor; a deterrent to those who might not resist the temptation of pauperism were it not for the threat of forced labor and the stigma of workhouse confinement; and an asylum for the impotent poor and the insane.

The first of these institutions to be built in the province of New York (1736) stated its mixed purpose explicitly in the title "Poor-House, Work-House, and House of Correction of New York City." Here the mildly insane were set to work at picking oakum, spinning flax and wool, knitting and sewing, along with the other inmates. For the "unruly" insane, special dungeons were built in "the westermost division of the cellar—to be confined and imprisoned in."[28] Thus were the mentally ill disposed of in a typical workhouse. Needless to say, this all-embracing type of institution, far from realizing the fond hopes of its progenitors, proved a dismal failure.

In some communities, houses of correction were built for the confinement of criminals and misdemeanants. Into these institutions the mentally ill were often thrown, no differentiation being made between them and offenders against the law. For instance, when the act ordering the building of Connecticut's first house of correction was passed in 1727, it provided for the incarceration therein of

> all rogues, vagabonds and idle persons going about in town or country begging, or persons . . . feigning themselves to have knowledge in physiognomy, palmistry, or pretending that they can tell fortunes, or discover where lost or stolen goods may be found, common pipers, fidlers, runaways . . . common drunkards, common night-walkers, pilferers, wanton and lascivious persons . . . common railers or brawlers . . . as also *persons under distraction* and unfit to go at large, whose friends do not take care for their safe confinement.[29] (Emphasis mine—A.D.)

Upon entrance into this house of correction each prospective inmate was automatically whipped on the bare back not exceeding ten lashes, unless the warrant directed otherwise.

This act, grouping the mentally ill with rogues, vagrants and other petty offenders, was by no means an unusual one. Two years earlier, in 1725, a similar law had been enacted in Rhode Island empowering the mainland towns to erect a

COLONIAL PROVISION

common house of correction for the punishment of rogues and vagabonds "and to keep mad persons in."[30]

There remain to be discussed three other types of institutions, and one custom, affecting the mentally ill in the colonial period. The almshouse (as distinguished from the workhouse or house of correction), which was later to become the major custodial institution for the insane, first appeared on the American scene late in the seventeenth century, but did not come into general use until the end of the colonial era. As for the first hospital employed partly as a receptacle for the mentally ill, and the first asylum for their exclusive care, these appeared at the dawn of the American Revolution, as we have already noted. The custom of literally bidding off the insane on the auction block, along with other dependent classes, arose in rural districts just before the birth of the new nation, and was to continue in use for many years after. All these aspects will be described in subsequent chapters.

A summary of the care and treatment of the mentally ill in colonial times cannot but impress one with the hopeless confusion prevailing. We have seen that neither the nature nor proper treatment of mental disease was understood. In the isolated instances when it was recognized as a naturally produced disease and treated therapeutically, the diagnoses and prescriptions given were little less fantastic and ineffectual than the medieval nostrums. During the witchcraft delusions in Salem and elsewhere, the mentally ill were hanged, imprisoned, tortured and otherwise persecuted as agents of Satan. Regarded as sub-human beings, they were chained in specially devised kennels and cages like wild beasts, and thrown into prisons, bridewells and jails like criminals. They were incarcerated in workhouse dungeons, or made to slave as able-bodied paupers, unclassified from the rest. They were left to wander about stark naked, driven from place to place like mad dogs, subjected to whippings as vagrants and rogues. Even the well-to-do were not spared confinement in strong rooms and cellar dungeons, while legislation usually concerned itself more with their property than their persons. Boarding-out the mentally ill with private families or maintaining them at their own homes at public expense did not always result in better treatment, as we have noted in cases where kennel-like structures were attached to homes for their confinement. Whenever public provision was made —usually for the purpose of safeguarding the community from "dangerous madmen"—it generally boded ill for the hapless victim of mental disease. Complete indifference to his lot was in most cases the best he could hope for, since in that event he suffered little more at the hands of a callous society than the taunts, teasings, and the occasional brickbats of village and town bravos.

It is not a bright or cheerful picture to contemplate in retrospect. It must be said, however, in defense of our forebears, that the attitudes and the modes of treatment we have described were by no means peculiar to the American colonies, but grew out of, and reflected, conditions in the Old World. Besides, the men of this period could plead complete ignorance of the nature, causes and cure of mental illness as the root of their harshness, an excuse that could hardly be advanced by authorities of a later century when conditions were hardly improved, and in many respects were even worse.

Thus matters stood on the eve of the Revolution. Meanwhile an upheaval in the concepts of human relationships was shaking Europe, an upheaval that was to have profound repercussions here and was destined to reshape man's treatment of man in general, and the treatment of the less fortunate strata of society in particular.

CHAPTER IV
Rational Humanitarianism: the Beginnings of Reform

MAN is born free, and everywhere he is in chains!"
When Rousseau uttered that despairing cry, in the midst of eighteenth century ferment, he spoke in a figurative sense, having no particular group in mind, least of all the mentally ill. Still to no other dependent class of his time could the latter part of his statement be applied with more tragic accuracy. Everywhere they could be found in chains, in conditions far more miserable than those of the lowest incarcerated criminal.

The jails, workhouses and other receptacles into which the insane were thrown were bad beyond description. Ironically enough the asylums for their special care then springing up in Europe, hailed as great reforms in the treatment of mental illness, were in many respects even worse than the former. Describing these eighteenth century asylums, John Conolly, the famous English advocate of non-restraint, wrote:

> These were but prisons of the worst description. Small openings in walls, unglazed, or whether glazed or not, guarded with strong iron bars, narrow corridors, dark cells, desolate courts, where no tree nor shrub nor flower nor blade of grass grew; solitariness, or companionship so indiscriminate as to be worse than solitude; terrible attendants armed with whips . . . free to impose manacles, and chains and stripes at their own brutal will; uncleanliness, semi-starvation, the garrote, and unpunished murders—these were the characteristics of such buildings throughout Europe.[1]

So far as prolonged physical and mental torture were concerned, the period of repressive confinement, covering most of the eighteenth century, was the worst in the history of the mentally ill. But in the latter part of the century progressive forces were afoot which were radically to influence the trend of social welfare, including that branch concerned with the care and treatment of the insane.

First and foremost among these forces were the political and social revolutions in America and France (1776 and 1789) that acted as liberating agents for a multitude of reform movements. It was at this time, too, that the great Industrial Revolution, destined to bring about tremendous changes in the economic and social relationships of men, was beginning to make itself felt.

In the realm of ideas a new era had dawned. Thomas Paine appropriately termed his period the "Age of Reason"; the most significant intellectual movement of the time was just as aptly called the "Enlightenment." It did not, of course, break upon the world full-blown. It represented, rather, the accumulation of forces that had been gathering for scores of years. But it was in this half-century that the Enlightenment reached its greatest vigor. Its leading apostles took for their text Pope's great maxim: "The proper study of mankind is Man." A restless spirit of inquiry impelled them to examine minutely the world in which they lived. Many went farther; within them burned a desire to change that world for the better. The principal spirits of the movement—men like Voltaire, Rousseau and the Encyclopaedists in France, Goethe, Kant and Lessing in Germany, Hume and Godwin in England, and Franklin, Jefferson, and Thomas Paine in America—refused to have their minds fettered by narrow geographical boundaries. Like Diderot, one of their chief stalwarts, each could proudly declare: "I am a citizen of that town they call the world."

They were truly light-bringers, bearers of a new *weltanschauung,* a new world outlook. Their concern embraced all humanity. They fearlessly penetrated into the darkest corners of society, where an unfeeling civilization had thrust its pariahs—the offenders against its harsh laws, the impotent and poor, the sick in mind and body. In their war on privilege they found effective ammunition in the contrast afforded by ostentatious luxury on one hand and abject suffering on the other, and they were not backward in exposing the latter to the gaze of their fellow men. Paine remarked with bitterness that wherever his eyes fell, he saw "age going to the workhouse and youth to the gallows." Such evidences of man's inhumanity to man were everywhere discernible.

Like the other rationalists of his age, Paine believed that ignorance was at the bottom of all human misery; before the all-conquering light of reason this misery would soon disappear. All that was necessary was to subject social evils to a reasoning-out process and the world would be rid of them. This, briefly, was the spirit of what may be called rational humanitarianism. True, the logic of its representatives was somewhat naïve. The men of reason were generally more sensitive to the existence and effects of social dislocations than they were to their causes. At times, the remedies they proposed proved worse than the ills they sought to cure. But essentially theirs was a most beneficial influence in the upward climb of civilization. They believed in the inherent goodness and nobility of man: the principle of "natural rights" for every living individual was part of their credo. And if they had handed down nothing more to their age and to posterity, their influence in raising mankind —even its lowliest members—to a new plane of dignity, was in itself an epoch-making contribution to social progress. Never after was civilized society to sink to the level of indifference and apathy to human suffering that had existed before. If the social, political and economic revolutions of their time served as liberating forces for social reform, it was their rational humanitarianism that gave guidance and direction to the reforms effected. In some fields of welfare, as in penal reform, they and their disciples managed to achieve immediate and extensive gains. In others, as in the care of the insane, progress was slower, and took the form at first of individual and somewhat isolated experiments.

Noteworthy in this period was the part in reform played by the Quakers, both here and in England. An extremely practical people, they were uncommonly successful in whatever they undertook, whether it were business enterprise or social service. With them theory was never divorced from practice: whatever they believed they tried to carry out, with the moderation that was characteristic of the sect. Good will and good works were principal tenets in their religious belief, and they were not inclined to regard these as dead letters. John Howard, renowned as the father of prison reform, was a Quaker. The great anti-slavery pioneer, John Woolman, was likewise a Friend, and Thomas Paine was the son of a Quaker father. In America, many of the early experiments in social welfare were initiated by Quakers. Appropriately, Philadelphia, the center of the disciples of Fox in this country, was also the chief center of humanitarian reform during the latter half of the eighteenth century. In that historic city, a group of distinguished Friends formed an active nucleus for social welfare work throughout the country.

Not the least accomplishment of this remarkable group was the founding of the first general hospital in America—the Pennsylvania Hospital—where, among other classes of sick persons, the mentally ill were received.* Its claim to prominence in our history is established by the fact that it was the first institution where cure, rather than custody and repression, was the underlying principle in the treatment of the insane. Among its founders two men stand out: Thomas Bond, a distinguished physician of his day; and that most versatile of Americans, Benjamin Franklin.

In an account of the origin and early years of the Pennsylvania Hospital, written by Franklin himself, we learn that it had its beginnings in 1750, at a meeting of citizens who gathered together to consider the advisability of building a "convenient House, under one Inspection, and in the hands of skillful Practitioners," for the reception of the sick, and for persons "disordered in their Senses . . . there being no place (except the House of Correction or Almshouse)

---

*In 1709, at a monthly meeting of the Society of Friends in Philadelphia, the erection of a hospital for such members of the Society as should fall sick or insane had been proposed. This plan did not materialize, however, either because funds were lacking or necessity was not sufficiently pressing.

RATIONAL HUMANITARIANISM

in which they might be confined, and subjected to proper treatment for their Recovery."[2] A proposal for "an Infirmary, or Hospital, in the manner of several lately established in Great Britain" gained general approval, and the launching of a province-wide subscription campaign together with a plea to the Assembly for financial aid was forthwith agreed upon.

On January 23, 1751, a petition drawn up in Franklin's own handwriting was presented to the provincial Assembly. Its opening paragraphs read:

> That with the Numbers of People, the number of Persons distempered in Mind and deprived of their rational Faculties, hath greatly increased in this Province
>
> That some of them going at large are a Terror to their Neighbours, who are daily apprehensive of the Violences they may commit; And others are continually wasting their Substance, to the great Injury of themselves and Families, ill disposed Persons wickedly taking Advantage of their unhappy Condition, and drawing them into unreasonable bargains, etc.
>
> That few or none of them are so sensible of their Condition, as to submit voluntarily to the treatment that their respective Cases requires, and therefore continue in the same deplorable state during their Lives; whereas it has been found, by the experience of many Years, that above two Thirds of the Mad People received into Bethlehem Hospital, and there treated properly, have been cured.*

On May 6, 1751, the Assembly passed an act "to encourage the establishing of a Hospital for the Relief of the Sick Poor of this Province, and for the Reception and Cure of Lunaticks." Its first paragraph, of great significance in the history of the mentally ill, reads in part:

> WHEREAS, the saving and restoring useful and laborious Members to a Community is a Work of publick Service, and the Relief of the Sick Poor is not only an Act of Humanity, but a religious Duty: AND WHEREAS there are frequently in many Parts of this Province poor distempered Persons, who languish long in Pain and Misery,

---

*This estimate of the cures effected at Bethlehem Hospital in London is obviously a gross exaggeration. The error may be attributable to an acceptance of the number of discharges as the actual number of cures. It is known that many were discharged from Bethlehem uncured.

under various Disorders of Body and Mind, and being scattered abroad in different and very distant Habitations, cannot have the Benefit of regular Advice, Attendance, Lodging, Diet and Medicines, but at a great Expense and therefore often suffer for Want thereof; which Inconveniency might be happily removed by collecting the Patients into one common provincial Hospital, properly disposed and appointed, where they may be comfortably subsisted, and their Health taken Care of at a small Charge, and where by the Blessing of God or the Endeavours of skillful Physicians and Surgeons, their Diseases may be cured and removed.[3]

The Assembly offered material aid to this worthy project in the form of a grant of £2,000 for the initial expenses of the institution, provided that a like amount were raised by private subscription. Thanks largely to the energy and prestige of Franklin, this was soon accomplished.

Pending the erection of a suitable building, a "temporary hospital" was set up in a private home hired for that purpose. Of the first two patients received there in February, 1752, one was a "lunatick" sent by the city Visitors of the Poor. The insane patients were relegated to the basement of the house, where makeshift cells were provided for them, so damp and unwholesome as to result in a number of deaths from pulmonary diseases among the patients.

When the Pennsylvania Hospital proper was completed in 1756, it seemed but natural that the mentally ill should again be consigned to the cellar. There they were subjected to medical treatment which, however dubious its benefits, constituted the best that the time afforded. As succinctly stated by Morton, "Their scalps were shaved and blistered; they were bled to the point of syncope; purged until the alimentary canal failed to yield anything but mucus, and in the intervals, they were chained by the waist or the ankle to the cell wall."[4] In outward appearance their condition differed but little from that of the insane in prisons.

"Cell-keepers" was the term appropriately applied to the attendants of that day. Their duties more closely resembled those of prison guards than servers of the sick. Their chief task lay in guarding the insane and preventing escapes. They were also expected to perform a variety of menial duties in

RATIONAL HUMANITARIANISM

their "spare" time, such as cleaning the premises, shopping, gardening, and "diverse other services," as stated in a regulation of 1757. Discipline set down for mental patients was rigidly enforced, and those who broke rules were punished with severity. Morton tells us that the insane were often chained in iron rings to the floor or wall of their cells, or were restrained in handcuffs or ankle-irons, and that the strait waistcoat, or "Madd-shirt", was a much used appliance. This "madd-shirt" was "a close-fitting cylindrical garment of ticking, canvas or other strong material without sleeves, which, drawn over the head, reached below the knees, and left the patient an impotent bundle of wrath, deprived of effective motion." In the earlier years, says Morton, "it was not considered improper or unusual for the keeper to carry a whip and use it freely. These methods begat violence and disorder in the insane, who were then, for that reason, a much more violent and dangerous class than they now are, and the keeper's life was neither an idle nor a happy one."[5]

An echo of the clanging chains that Peter the porter purloined from Bethlehem in 1403 is perceptible in the following blacksmith's account against Pennsylvania Hospital in 1752, an impressive sidelight on the manner of dealing with the mentally ill:

> John Cresson, blacksmith, against ye hospital, 1 pair of handcuffs, 2 legg locks, 2 large rings and 2 large staples, 5 links and 2 large rings and 2 swifells for legg chains.

Despite the heroic regimen imposed on the insane in the early days of the Hospital, the important fact was that for the first time in American history—in principle at least—a public institution was receiving the mentally ill, not to be confined as malefactors, but to receive curative treatment as sick patients. A new ideal, a revolutionary departure from the purely repressive traditions of the past, was being introduced although, unfortunately for the objects of concern, the practice lagged far, far behind the principle.

It is difficult, in viewing the barbarities and horrors of a past age, to judge them in the light of a proper historical perspective. In this particular instance it is doubly difficult to realize that, whatever its shortcomings, the treatment of the insane at the Pennsylvania Hospital was approved by the foremost authorities of the period, and that its progenitors were motivated by a spirit of human kindness no whit inferior in degree to ours. In the same sense that we regard with perfect complacency many conditions that a future generation will undoubtedly look back upon with horror, so things that now seem relics of savagery were in those days looked upon as marks of radical progress, and praised accordingly. An interesting illustration of this truth is implicit in the journal notes of a visitor to the Pennsylvania Hospital in 1787, the good Rev. Manasseh Cutler. After describing the wards for the sick, he continues in this vein:

> We next took a view of the *Maniacs*. Their cells are in the lower story, which is partly underground. These cells are about ten feet square, made as strong as a prison. On the back part is a long entry, from which a door opens into each of them; in each door is a hole, large enough to give them food, etc., which is closed with a little door secured with strong bolts . . . Here were both men and women . . . Some of them have beds, most of them clean straw. Some of them were extremely fierce and raving, nearly or quite naked. This would have been a melancholy scene indeed, had it not been that there was *every possible relief afforded them in the power* of man. From this distressing view of what human nature is liable to, and *the pleasing evidence of what humanity and benevolence can do,* we returned . . . etc., etc.[6] (Emphasis mine—A.D.)

Patients were committed to the hospital with an amazing ease and informality, for it was not until some years after Pennsylvania had reached statehood that a general statute providing for the proper commitment of the insane was enacted. All that was necessary was for a relative, a friend —or, perhaps, an enemy—to apply to one of the managers or physicians for an order of admission. A few words hastily scribbled on a chance scrap of paper (such as "Jas. Sproul is a proper patient for the Pennsylvania Hospital"), and signed by one of the physicians, and the deed was done. Should the prospective patient make too vigorous remonstrance, it was a simple matter to place him in chains or irons or otherwise to pacify him effectively.

Apparently, occupational therapy was applied to the mentally ill as well as to other classes of patients at the very beginning. For this innovation the Friends must have been mainly responsible, since their faith in work as a character- and health-building agent was almost part of their creed. The mentally ill who were able to do so were set at some light labor such as spinning wool or flax. In this implicit recognition of the value of occupational therapy, the founders of the Pennsylvania Hospital anticipated modern psychiatry by many years. True, the insane had been put to labor before this time, but for a quite different reason, namely, to get as much return for their keep as possible, and not at all as a therapeutic measure.

In striking contrast to the rigorous regimen that ordinarily governed the hospital routine, there occurred in 1765 a remarkable instance wherein a patient's whim played havoc with the institutional sense of propriety, much to the amusement and wonderment of Philadelphia's populace. In that year, a sailor, Thomas Perrine, was admitted to the hospital as a lunatic, and placed in one of the underground cells. Here he proved very troublesome, quarrelling incessantly with his fellow patients and the keepers. One day he escaped from his basement cell, rushed to the top of the house and barricaded himself in a cupola, where he successfully defied all efforts to dislodge him. Attempts to remove him were finally given up and bedding was brought up to the cupola, which was now transformed into sailor Perrine's private domain. In this small space he lived for *nine years* until his death in 1774. It is recorded that

> He never left these cramped quarters for any purpose; he was also noted for his long nails, matted beard and hair and for his insensibility to cold since he never, in the coldest weather of nine winters, came near to a fire.[7]

A most shocking custom, one continuing at least to the end of the eighteenth century, was that of exhibiting the insane patients to the gaze of curious sightseers for a set admission fee. Strange as it may seem, however, the decision to exact admission fees to the insane wards originated from a desire to protect the mental patients rather than to exploit them. It appears that when the hospital was first opened the public were permitted to enter at will and to wander about the grounds as they pleased. The hospital then stood in an open lot with no fence or wall to set it off. It was customary, particularly on Sundays and holidays, for idlers and thrill-seekers to gather about the cell windows of the insane which stood at ground level and to take turns at "teasing the crazy people," with the aim of rousing them into raving fury.

Gradually the insane department of Pennsylvania Hospital became known as one of the show places of Philadelphia, as contemporary Bedlam was of London. It was quite the thing for inhabitants to entertain their out-of-town guests by bringing them to observe, or to participate in, the sport of baiting the madmen. So great did this evil become that in 1760 the authorities were constrained to curb it by ordering the erection of "a suitable Pallisade Fence, either of Iron or Wood, the Iron being preferr'd, in Order to prevent the Disturbance which is given to the Lunatics confin'd in the Cells by the great Numbers of people who frequently resort and converse with them."

But this device does not seem to have noticeably lessened the scandalous situation, for two years later the managers again complained that "the great crowds that invaded the Hospital give trouble and create . . . much disturbance." They found it necessary to order the building of "a suitable hatch door and get an inscription thereon notifying that such 'persons who come out of curiosity to visit the house should pay a sum of money, a Groat at least, for admittance.'" In 1767, this rule apparently being disregarded, it was again urged that no curious visitor be permitted entry without the payment of a fee, "Four Pence, as formerly agreed upon." But the admission fee proved a poor deterrent to those seeking entertainment at the expense of the mental patients, and the crowds continued to flock to the institution on Sundays in undiminished numbers. Finally, in

1791, in response to complaints of the physicians that the patients were being seriously harmed by the indiscriminate admittance of visitors, the authorities voted that no person be allowed entry to the insane quarters without express permission from one of the managers or physicians or from the steward. However, the practice of exhibiting patients for a price continued in force, and as late as 1822 we read of an order raising the admission fee from 12½ to 25 pence. At Bedlam, where, until the year 1770, visitors paid a fee at the famous "penny gates" to gain entrance to what was considered London's most amusing "raree-show", the practice seems to have been introduced mainly as a means of replenishing the institutional income. It is said that more than £400 were netted in admission fees at Bedlam in one year.*

During the first half-century of the Pennsylvania Hospital's existence, insane patients were quartered in cells scattered throughout the building, underneath the sections where other sick groups were maintained. With the increase of patients this arrangement proved progressively unsatisfactory. A movement was set afoot to obtain separate provision for the mentally ill. A new wing in the western part of the hospital was accordingly erected, to which the insane were removed in 1796. They still remained under the same roof with all other sick persons, however. It was not until nearly another half-century had passed that a separate building was provided for them.†

The Pennsylvania Hospital represented a tremendous step forward in that it was the first American public insti-

---

*Ives gives this interesting account of the practice in England: "In the eighteenth century—up to 1770—and in some places doubtless, even in later times, the mad people were reckoned among the 'sights'. The public paid to go round the asylums, as they do now to gaze upon wild beasts. The baser and more mischievous among them would irritate and purposely enrage the secured patients, as their descendants tease caged animals to this day, and thus reproduced for the ghastly diversion exhibitions of madness which are no longer to be found." (Ives, George C., *History of Penal Methods*. London, 1914. 409 pp., p. 89.)

†In 1841 a new building, called the Department of the Insane of Pennsylvania Hospital, was opened in West Philadelphia, on the outskirts of the city, and the mentally ill were removed thereto from the old building at Pine Street.

tution where the mentally ill were received specifically for the purpose of treatment and cure. It was also the first where a humane approach to the problems of insanity was attempted. But there still remained the problem of providing an asylum exclusively devoted to the care and treatment of the insane. Such institutions were already in existence in Europe long before the eighteenth century although, as we have noted, they were far from being models of perfection.

To Virginia belongs the distinction of having erected the first American asylum exclusively for the mentally ill. It was opened in 1773 at Williamsburg, then the capital of the colony.

Years before the hospital at Williamsburg was established, proposals for erecting such an institution had been discussed in several colonies, particularly in those growing centers of population where the trend toward institutionalization first became manifest. But somehow such plans had never before gone beyond the embryonic stage of development.

On at least two occasions during colonial times, Boston had been on the verge of building a separate institution for the insane. Abortive plans for this purpose date back to 1730. In 1662 Boston had established what was probably the first almshouse in New England. As was the custom (one, incidentally, which was to continue well into the nineteenth century), indigents and petty offenders were herded indiscriminately into this poorhouse—the sick and well, the able-bodied and impotent, the law-breaking and law-abiding, young and aged, "worthy" poor and vagrants, sane and insane. Attempts were made as early as 1716 to achieve some measure of segregation, and a bridewell was built for the housing of the "unworthy" poor and petty offenders apart from the "worthy and pious" inmates of the almshouses. However, another sore problem remained unsolved. The insane in the almshouse were making life unbearable for the others by their cries and antics, and the town selectmen and overseers of the poor were deluged with urgent pleas that the poorhouse be relieved of the presence of this troublesome element. The town authorities seem to have lent a sympathetic ear to these appeals for on the agenda of a town meeting held in 1730, we find this item among others: "to Consider of making Some adition to the Alms House, for keeping Distracted Persons Separate from the Poor."[8] Nothing further appears to have been done, however, until March, 1746, when the overseers proposed to the town inhabitants of Boston that "the Town purchase the Bridewell house &c. for a mad house."[9] Three weeks later the overseers were commissioned to inquire into the practicability of transforming the old bridewell into an asylum for the insane poor. It is worthy of note that the comfort and better care of the insane was not a dominating motive behind this proposal for a separate building to house them, as the suggested use of the bridewell indicates. The proposal sprang from a desire, laudable so far as it went, to afford greater comfort for the *other* classes of almshouse inmates. Apparently the overseers experienced a change of mind regarding the use of the bridewell for this purpose, since their original proposal was never acted upon.

The plan for providing a separate structure for the mentally ill continued to be pressed. By May, 1746, the project had advanced to the stage where a committee was formed at a town meeting to "endeavor to obtain a Subscription for building or purchasing a House proper for Reception of Distracted Persons."[10] The attempt to raise funds in this manner evidently failed, and five years later the complaint was again repeated that the "Distracted, helpless and infirm people" still comprised a majority of the workhouse population, which was primarily intended for the able-bodied.[11]

In 1764 the idea of erecting an institution for the mentally ill was again revived, under such circumstances that its materialization now seemed a certainty. August of that year witnessed the decease of Thomas Hancock, uncle to that John who so boldly inscribed his name to the Declaration of Independence. Hancock's will carried this provision:

> I give unto the Town of Boston the sum of six hundred pounds lawful money towards erecting and finishing a convenient House for

the reception and more comfortable keeping of such unhappy persons as it shall please God in his Providence to deprive of their reason in any part of this Province; such as are inhabitants of Boston always to have the preference . . . And in case said House shall not be built and finished in three years after my decease, I then declare this legacy to be void; or if I should in my lifetime erect it, this bequest then to be void.*

    We may infer, from the wording of the last clause, that Mr. Hancock had intended to build an asylum for the mentally ill before his death, a desire that probably arose from the fact that during his later years he himself was so greatly troubled with "nervous disorders" as to force his almost complete withdrawal from business life.

    Hancock's legacy was gratefully accepted by the town of Boston, and a committee was appointed at once to determine what steps should be taken to comply with its terms. Serving on this committee was James Otis, who played such an important role in the events leading up to the Revolution and who, curiously enough, was himself fated to become a mental case due to a head injury sustained in 1769. The committee's report, which was unanimously adopted by the townspeople, recommended that Hancock's name be inscribed among those of *Faneuil,* Boston's honor roll, in gratitude for his donation. As for the hospital, it voted that "such House when erected shall be called and known by the name of *Hancock's Hospital.* Thus, while the poor Unfortunates therein provided for shall be insensible from whose Hands they derive their only possible alleviation of their miseries in the power of humanity, those in all Ages who may enjoy the inestimable blessing of a sound mind shall rejoice in the bountiful provision for the distressed."[12]

    Although Hancock, in drawing up his bequest, had apparently believed that £600 would closely approximate the cost of erecting the institution, it soon became evident that this sum fell far short of the required amount. An effort

---

*Thomas Hancock was one of the most successful merchants of the eighteenth century. In his will containing the quoted provision he left the bulk of his huge estate, valued at some £70,000, to his nephew, John Hancock, making the latter one of the wealthiest men in the colonies.

was launched to raise the additional funds required for building the "Bedlam" (as the proposed structure was frequently referred to) by means of private subscriptions. But, as had happened a score of years earlier, the campaign did not arouse sufficient interest and was finally dropped. Meanwhile the three-year limit set in the will for the completion of the building was drawing to a close. As a last resort the town authorities decided to petition the provincial Assembly for financial aid, on the ground that the hospital was intended as a sanctuary for all the mentally ill of the province. The petition was presented to the General Assembly on June 20, 1766, but was withdrawn six days later, for an unexplained reason.[13] Was it because Boston was given an unmistakable sign of the legislature's disapproval? At any rate, the Hancock legacy was finally rejected by the town selectmen, who adopted what was in all probability a face-saving reason: "There are not enough insane persons in the province for the erection of such House." By such narrow margins did Boston twice miss the distinction subsequently gained by Virginia.

The first American hospital exclusively for the insane had its beginnings in November, 1766, when the governor of Virginia Colony, Francis Fauquier, made an earnest appeal for such a hospital in an address to the House of Burgesses. It is interesting to note the striking resemblance that the phrasing of his appeal bears to the Philadelphia petition of 1751:

> It is expedient I should . . . recommend to your Consideration and Humanity a poor unhappy set of People who are deprived of their Senses, and wander about the Country, terrifying the Rest of their Fellow Creatures. A legal Confinement and proper Provision ought to be appointed for these miserable Objects, who cannot help themselves. Every civilized Country has an Hospital for these People, where they are confined, maintained and attended by able Physicians, to endeavour to restore to them their lost Reason.[14]

Within two weeks the legislature, acting upon the governor's humane recommendation, passed a resolution favoring the erection of a hospital for "the reception of persons who are so unhappy as to be deprived of their reason," and ordered a committee to bring in a bill embodying this proposal. But a delay ensued: the House was embroiled in weighty affairs of state. There was serious trouble with the mother country; the first soft mutterings of revolution were swelling into ominous rumblings; the rafters of the House of Burgesses were ringing with the fiery speeches of Patrick Henry and others. In the swirl toward the decisive conflict, reform in the treatment of the mentally ill was temporarily thrust aside. But Governor Fauquier seems to have been determined on action. On April 11, 1767, he again brought before the assembled delegates in the House the "case of the poor lunaticks." Expressing his disappointment at the failure of the House to frame a bill for the establishment of an insane hospital, he declared that this was "a measure which . . . I was in hope humanity would have dictated to every man, as soon as he was made acquainted with the call for it." He pointed out that, because of the lack of proper provision for the mentally ill, he had been forced to authorize the confinement of lunatics in the Williamsburg jail, against both his conscience and the law. "As a point of some importance to the ease and comfort of the whole community, as well as a point of charity to the unhappy objects," he again urged the enactment of a suitable bill on the subject.[15]

Despite his strong plea nothing further was accomplished by the legislature until 1769 when it passed an act "to make Provision for the Support and Maintenance of Ideots, Lunatics and other persons of unsound Minds."[16] It was set forth in the act that "whereas several persons of insane and disordered minds have been frequently found wandering in different parts of this colony, and no certain provision having been yet made toward effecting a cure of those whose cases are not become quite desperate, nor for the restraining others who may be dangerous to society," the "Public Hospital for Persons of Insane and Disordered Minds" (incorporated the preceding year) was ordered erected for their future care and treatment. It authorized the purchase of a piece of ground at or near Williamsburg—"the most healthy in situation that can be procured"—by the trustees of the newly-established hospital. On this plot a "commodious house or houses" was to be built. Among the original trustees were such distinguished citizens as John Blair, George Wythe, Thomas Nelson, Peyton Randolph, John Randolph, Robert Carter, John Tazewell, Dudley Digges and Benjamin Waller. Several of these men became signers of the Declaration of Independence a few years later.

An appropriation of £1,200 was voted to defray the initial cost of building the institution for the insane, and provision was made for personnel consisting of a keeper, a matron, guards, nurses and visiting physicians. Determination of insanity was left to the judgment of three magistrates; no provision was made for examination by a physician.

The hospital was opened for the reception of its first patients October 12, 1773. John de Sequeyra, a leading doctor of Virginia, served as the first visiting physician, retaining his post until 1795. James Galt was appointed the first keeper. The functions of keeper and physician remained distinct until the year 1841, when they were combined in the person of Dr. John M. Galt, the first superintendent. Incidentally, the Galt family was connected with the Williamsburg institution for nearly a century after its inception, resembling somewhat the long and memorable record of the Tukes in the history of the York Retreat in England.

Unfortunately, no record of the early methods of treatment has come down to us, but Wyndham B. Blanton, the historian of medicine in Virginia, ventures the opinion that "undoubtedly the old reliance on chains and confinement in cells prevailed here as elsewhere,"[17] and he is probably correct.

Not the least distinctive feature of this, the first separate institution for the insane in America, is the fact that for a period of fifty years, until the Eastern Lunatic Asylum at Lexington, Kentucky, was opened in 1824, it remained the only state hospital of its kind in the country.

CHAPTER V
Benjamin Rush—the Father of American Psychiatry

THE year 1783, which witnessed the climax of the Revolution and the transition of a rebel people to a sovereign nation, was also portentous in the history of American psychiatry. In that year Dr. Benjamin Rush joined the staff of physicians at Pennsylvania Hospital, beginning a thirty-year period of service that was fraught with great significance to the mentally ill in America. Armed with those indispensable tools of science—a capacity for assimilating knowledge, keen observation and inductive reasoning—he was able to cut away thick layers of superstition, hearsay and ignorance, and to raise the study and treatment of mental diseases to a scientific level for the first time in this country. He was the first American teacher to institute a comprehensive course of study in mental disease; he was the first American physician to attempt an original systematization of the subject. The theoretic structure that he erected was decidedly unsteady, as we shall see, but it marked a real beginning, and an honest one. He wrote the first general treatise on psychiatry in America, and it is no mean tribute to his genius that it remained the only American work of its kind for seventy years after publication. He fully earned the title by which he was known to later generations—"the Father of American Psychiatry."

Rush was no ordinary innovator. He was one of the most remarkable men of his time. In many respects his varied career paralleled that of his illustrious townsman, Benjamin Franklin. His accomplishments in diverse fields were outstanding even in that age which probably produced the most

Courtesy of the Pennsylvania Hospital

BENJAMIN RUSH,
FATHER OF AMERICAN PSYCHIATRY

(*Portrait by Thomas Sully*)

brilliant constellation of versatile geniuses the world has ever known. As with Franklin, there was hardly a reform movement of his day which did not bear the impress of Rush's personality. A glance at a bibliography of his published writings reveals at once the wide range of this man's interests: his works included dissertations on politics, finance, medical theory and practice, ethics, war and peace, slavery, philosophy, philology, anthropology, religion, immigration, penology and criminology, education, agriculture, meteorology, etc., etc.[1]

Rush was born at Philadelphia in 1745 of Quaker parents, although oddly enough, both his father and his grandfather were gunsmiths by trade. A precocious child, he graduated from Princeton (then New Jersey College) before reaching the age of fifteen. Six years of medical apprenticeship followed, after which Rush journeyed to the University of Edinburgh, at that time the chief center of medical education, where he received his M. D. degree in 1768. Following an additional year's stay in Europe, the young doctor returned to Philadelphia, where he set up practice and rose rapidly to prominence. A few months after his return he was made professor of chemistry at America's first medical school, founded at Philadelphia College in 1765, and later became professor of theory and practice of medicine there. Here he attracted a larger number of students than any other medical teacher during the last quarter of the century. His teachings were carried to every part of the country by his pupils. He was the fifth member of a distinguished faculty that included Drs. John Morgan, William Shippen, Adam Kuhn, and Thomas Bond. Upon the outbreak of the Revolution he became a member of the Continental Congress and (at the age of thirty) a signer of the Declaration of Independence. Congress appointed him surgeon-general and later physician-in-chief of the middle department of the continental army. Differences arose and he resigned, resuming his private practice at Philadelphia.

An original thinker, and a reformer by nature, Rush soon involved himself in the various humanitarian movements then being carried forward on the crest of the revolutionary wave. To these movements he lent not only his name, but his time, money and seemingly inexhaustible energy. He was imbued with that sense of rational humanitarianism characteristic of the period's leading reformers, fortunately coupled with a will-to-do and backed by a tremendous store of physical and mental vitality. Optimism, the fruit of a newly born and lusty social order, he had in abundance—a valuable adjunct to a person of his pursuits, since it served as a constant stimulus to action.

Benjamin Rush was a member of the famous reform group in Pennsylvania which included Benjamin Franklin, Roberts Vaux, Caleb Lownes, William Bradford, and other pioneers in American humanitarianism. It was this group which formed the first prison reform society in America,* and succeeded in having the death penalty in Pennsylvania abolished for all crimes except murder in the first degree. They also brought about improvement in the treatment of imprisoned poor debtors who at that time were made the victims of barbaric laws, and laid the foundations for the famous Pennsylvania prison system, which for many years served as a model for penal institutions in America and Europe.

In the field of education Rush was one of the earliest advocates of free public schools for the poor. He championed the then radical cause of higher education for women, and was largely instrumental in the founding of Dickinson College in western Pennsylvania. Like many of the advanced thinkers of his day he was an ardent advocate of temperance, and vigorously preached against spirituous liquors as being harmful not only to the body, mind and morals of individuals, but to society itself. He was a principal founder of the first free dispensary in America (the Philadelphia Dispensary for the Poor), established in 1786. From 1799 to his death in 1813 he was treasurer of the United States Mint. He passionately favored the abolitionist cause, and served as president of the Society for the Abolition of Slavery.

*The Philadelphia Society for Alleviating the Miseries of Public Prisons, organized in 1787.

Rush was fond of literature, as evidenced by the liberal—too liberal, one might say—use of quotations from the classics throughout his writings. Although his own style was too ornate and discursive for modern tastes, he was no mean literary man himself, his publications comprising scores of books, pamphlets, articles and addresses. Besides, his correspondence alone fills some "43 stout volumes." In truth, he wielded his pen with the same facility as he did his lancet, if not with quite the same degree of skill. His works were widely read in his time, and gained him a reputation as a leading man of letters.

In every movement he championed he proved an able propagandist, as attested by his numerous reform pamphlets. A masterful polemicist, he never shrank from a fight, a trait that nearly proved his undoing on several occasions. Few of his contemporaries were engaged in such bitter debates and none, perhaps, over so wide a front. Right or wrong (and he was by no means always right) he was a man of strong convictions. Having once formed an opinion on a subject, he felt no hesitancy in bringing forward his views to the public and denouncing in no uncertain terms those who held opposite views. Naturally, this characteristic earned him many enemies, particularly in his own profession. During and after the great yellow fever epidemic which decimated Philadelphia's population in 1793, Rush (who was at the time probably the busiest physician in the country, visiting upward of 150 patients on many days) found time to engage in one of the most acrimonious medical controversies in American history, on the subject of the proper cure for yellow fever. A principal point of dispute was the efficacy of calomel, which Rush prescribed in copious quantities for fever victims. He called this favorite remedy his "Samson" because of its supposed potency, although his unkind critics said it was aptly named because it "had slain its thousands."

The medical system built up by Rush fell far short of modern standards, and in some respects was more harmful than curative. Nonetheless, it can scarcely be denied that he provided more impetus to medical progress in America than any of his contemporaries, above whom he towered like a giant. Through his original methods and theories and his ability to stimulate interest and discussion in medical problems, he raised the practice of medicine in his country to a far higher plane than it had ever known before.

His own practice was largely based on the teachings of the two most eminent medical theorists of the period—the Hollander, Herman Boerhaave, and the Englishman, William Cullen, under whom he had studied in Edinburgh. From the former, he derived an abounding faith in the efficacy of depleting agents in treating diseases; from the latter, the necessity for simplifying medicine and freeing it of the mystical trimmings with which it had become enshrouded. He was also influenced by the celebrated clinician of a preceding century, Thomas Sydenham, whose emphasis on the superiority of observation and experience over abstract theory became a distinctive feature of Rush's own methodology. In effect then, Rush's medicine represented a synthesis of the teachings of these men, together with many original contributions of his own. He showed no hesitancy in discarding accepted theories when he felt that personal experience had disproved them, and his characteristic indifference to authority several times brought him into violent conflict and disfavor with his fellow practitioners.

Although he showed the greatest respect for Cullen throughout his career, he regarded his teacher's system of classification as too elaborate. His emendations of Cullen were generally beneficial, but in his quarrel with the latter's methods he was not always consistent. For example, as a substitute for Cullen's simple definition of hydrophobia, Rush suggested a complex classification of phobias based on the names of each object exciting fears and aversions—thunder-phobia, ghost-phobia, cat-phobia, rat-phobia, etc. Some of his comments on other phobias are so refreshingly ironic, in contrast with his usually serious approach to such problems, that they are worth quoting:

> Solo-phobia is the dread of being alone. This distemper is peculiar to persons with vacant minds and guilty consciences . . . Rum-

phobia is a rare disease. I have known but five instances of it in the course of my life . . . Doctor-phobia is complicated with other diseases . . . It might be supposed to be caused by the terror of a long bill, but that excites terror in few minds, for who ever thinks of paying a doctor's bill while he can use his money to advantage in another way? . . . Church-phobia . . . has become an epidemic in Philadelphia, hence we see half the city flying in chariots, phaetons, chairs and even stage wagons, as well as on horseback, from the churches in summer as soon as they are opened for Divine worship. In winter they drown their fear of church in plentiful entertainment.[2]

When Rush entered upon his duties in the Pennsylvania Hospital in 1783 he was already the most famous physician in Philadelphia. He immediately centered his attention on the mentally ill, firmly convinced that "the patients afflicted by madness should be the first objects of the care of a physician of the Pennsylvania Hospital."

Rush divided mental diseases into two principal groups: general intellectual derangement, and partial intellectual derangement. His remedies for insanity were likewise placed in two general categories: remedies applied to the mind through the medium of the body, and remedies applied to the body through the medium of the mind.

Depleting agents (bloodletting, purgatives and emetics) held a primary place among his remedies. Venesection he applied to an excess that is truly appalling. He tells us that he once extracted two hundred ounces of blood from one patient within a few months, and from another 470 ounces in forty-seven bleedings.* In passing, it should be said that to judge Rush's therapy merely on the basis of isolated passages and statements would not be fair either to his genius or to his hard-earned reputation. For a full appreciation of his place in mental therapy his methods must be examined in the light of the psychiatric level of his time, both in America and abroad. It is in this light that Rush's therapy and prac-

*Rush was the foremost proponent of venesection in America. In his *Medical Inquiries and Observations,* published in 1809, he included a rather lengthy treatise "In Defence of Blood-Letting." (Philadelphia, 1809, v. 4., p. 285-382).

tice reveal themselves, on the whole, as far in advance of his age.

Bloodletting was approved as a major therapeutic device by nearly all of Rush's contemporaries. Boerhaave, the most influential medical teacher of the time (and before him, Sydenham), had constantly stressed the efficacy of venesection for all ills, including mental ones. Dr. Bryan Crowther, a surgeon at Bethlehem Hospital, London, claimed in 1811 to have bled 150 insane patients in one day without untoward result. Esquirol, the successor to the great Pinel at the Salpêtrière in Paris, wrote in 1816: "On the discovery of the circulation of the blood, it was believed that we had discovered the cause of every disorder and a remedy for all ills. Blood was shed abundantly. The blood of the insane was the more freely shed, as by bleeding them to faintness it was believed that they were cured. This treatment was extended to all the insane." The principle generally adopted in asylums, says Esquirol, was that "the blood being too abundant or too much heated, ought to be evacuated or cooled."[3]

As for Rush, his own liberal recourse to venesection was in harmony with his theory that "madness" is mainly an arterial disease, having its primary seat in the blood vessels of the brain. He held that the disease represented "a great morbid excitement or inflammation of the brains; that an unrestrained appetite caused the blood vessels to be overcharged with blood; and that it is important to relieve the brain before obstruction and disorganization takes place."[4] Since the remedies flowed naturally from the supposed causes, Rush also advocated low diet, purges, emetics and hot and cold showers as measures affecting the circulation of the blood.

Enlightened though he was as a practitioner, Dr. Rush could not entirely free himself from certain ideas representing curious survivals from a previous epoch. Strongly reminiscent of the seventh century "snake-cure" of Alexander Trallianus, described in Chapter I, is Rush's stratagem for ridding patients of their delusions. "Cures for patients who suppose themselves to be glass," he says, "may easily be performed by pulling a chair upon which they are about to sit from under them, and afterwards showing them a large collection of pieces of glass as the fragments of their body."

Rush was the inventor of two curious mechanical devices, the therapeutic values of which he prized highly. One, named by him the "tranquilizer", consisted of a chair to which the patient was strapped hand and foot, together with a device for holding the head in a fixed position. This mechanism was intended to reduce the pulse through lessening the muscular action and motor activity of the patient's body. Although it would be viewed by moderns as a device of fiendish torture, it was really invented by Rush out of humane considerations. In a letter dated 1810, describing the purpose of his invention, he writes: "In attending the maniacal patients in the Pennsylvania Hospital, I have long seen with pain the evils of confining them, when ungovernable, by means of what is called the mad shirt, or straight waistcoat." After relating the sufferings and inconveniences the latter appliance caused the patients, he continues: "To obviate these evils, and at the same time to retain all the benefits of coercion, I requested . . . an ingenious cabinet-maker . . . to make for the benefit of the maniacal patients, a strong arm-chair, with several appropriate peculiarities. . . . From its design and effects, I have called it a Tranquilizer."[5]

The second of Rush's machines was called the "gyrator", and was a modification of a circulating swing introduced in England by Dr. Cox, who attributed its original invention to Erasmus Darwin, grandfather of the famous biologist. The gyrator consisted of a rotating board to which patients suffering from "torpid madness" were strapped with the head farthest from the center. It could be rotated at terrific rates of speed, causing the blood to rush to the head, and thus producing an effect opposite to that of the tranquilizer.

Kindly and humane though he was, Dr. Rush accepted without question the necessity of coercion by mechanical restraint and of certain forms of corporal punishment, even advocating whippings in extreme cases. The controversy over mechanical restraint and its complete abolition was a matter for a later generation to discuss: in his time the question was merely, "How much mechanical coercion is necessary?" Cullen, the teacher of Rush, was like the latter an advocate of gentler forms of mechanical restraint than the brutal ones then in general use, but he nevertheless taught the efficacy of inspiring fear in mental patients. When Rush declared that "terror acts powerfully on the body through the medium of the mind, and should be employed in the cure of madness," he was merely echoing the universally accepted doctrine of his age. Among the terror-inspiring devices recommended by Rush were his own tranquilizer, a cold shower bath continued for fifteen or twenty minutes, and "pouring cold water under the sleeve, so that it may descend into the arm pits and down the trunk of the body"—a mode of treatment that sends a chill down one's spine merely in the reading. If these methods should fail in their intended effects, declared Rush, it would then be proper to resort to the fear of death. To illustrate the efficacy of the latter stratagem he cited the case of an insane woman who had been frightened into her wits, so to speak, by being warned by her doctor that he was preparing to drown her.

And yet Rush's suggestions for "mild and terrifying modes of punishment" were truly gentle when compared with the methods sanctioned by many of his most celebrated contemporaries. It should be kept in mind that even at that advanced day, the insane, particularly the violent cases, were commonly looked upon as creatures who had descended to the level of wild beasts. In this condition it was thought necessary to "tame" them, to "break their spirits," in the same manner that wild animals were subdued. Significantly Rush himself recommended the total deprivation of food in some cases of insanity, citing as his reason the fact that in India, when wild elephants were captured, they were always tamed by depriving them of food until they were greatly emaciated and hence more amenable to domestication.[6] Elsewhere he recommends for violent patients the same treatment used in "breaking" wild horses.

So deep-rooted was the trust in fear-inspiring methods that it often took no account of the patient's rank or station.

George III of England, in one of his periods of insanity* was struck down with impunity at least once by an attendant, apparently with the approval of his physician, Dr. Willis. The king was frequently placed under restraint in straitjackets during these periods. Strangely enough, tortures and terrors that had been applied as outright punishments in previous ages received in this particular age the blessings of respectable medical theory as praiseworthy therapeutic measures. Thus Cullen wrote: "Fear, being the passion that diminishes excitement, may therefore be opposed to the excess of it, and particularly to the angry and irascible excitement of maniacs."[7] It was necessary to awe them, he declared, and "sometimes it may be necessary to inspire [awe] even by blows and stripes."

Physicians specializing in the care of the insane outdid themselves in devising ingenious mechanisms for terrorization. Burdett[8] tells us that one doctor invented a pump, worked by four men, which projected a stream of water with terrific force down the spine of the wretched patient. This treatment usually continued for four minutes, although one physician who had the humanity to try it on himself declared that it was so agonizing that he could not endure it for sixty seconds. Another form of excruciating torture, playfully called the "bath of surprise", consisted of a trap-door which suddenly opened under the unsuspecting patient who had been induced to tread upon it, plunging him precipitately into a pool of cold water, from which "he was frequently extracted more dead than alive." Still another monument to human ingenuity (which, incidentally, seems to excel itself in inventing inhuman and destructive devices) was the well-cure; the hapless patient was chained to the bottom of an empty well, into which water was slowly poured to instill in him the terror of approaching death.

*Beginning with his 27th year, in 1765, King George III was visited by no less than five attacks of mental illness. From the last one, which occurred in 1810, he never recovered. The brutal treatment to which even the sovereign was subjected, as brought out in parliamentary investigations into his condition, had some effect in attracting public attention to the plight of the mentally ill generally, and exerted indirect influence on protective legislation for the insane.

The American psychiatrist, Isaac Ray, tells of a Dr. Willard, who, about the beginning of the 19th century, maintained a private establishment for the mentally ill "in a little town on the line between Massachusetts and Rhode Island."[9] One of the fundamental tenets in his therapy was to break the patient's will by any means possible. On his premises stood a tank of water, into which a patient, packed into a coffin-like box pierced with holes, was lowered by means of a well-sweep. He was kept under water until the bubbles of air ceased to rise, after which he was taken out, rubbed, and revived—if he had not already passed beyond reviving! One wonders whether this "water-cure" was not a direct descendant of the old witch-finding water test, whereby suspected witches were bound and dragged through water in the belief that if they floated, they were guilty, and if they sank—let God have mercy on their souls!

Conolly describes a weird, though romantic, mode of alarm and torture proposed by certain German physicians of this period. A patient, just arrived at an asylum (which, we may infer, was built like a castle) was to be drawn across a bridge spanning a moat, then suddenly hoisted to the top of a tower, and as precipitously lowered into a dark and subterranean cavern. If the patient could be made to alight among serpents, they averred, the result would prove still more satisfactory.[10]

Up to the year 1808, according to the English physician, John Haslam, lunatics (who were still supposed to be under lunar influence) were bound, chained and even flogged at particular phases of the moon, to prevent the accession of violence.* Rush himself subscribed to the belief in lunar influence on the insane, with qualifications. Characteristically, he once set the attendants at the Pennsylvania Hospital to observe the behavior of patients through the night under various phases of the moon, in order to test its influence. From the reports he received he thought it possible to give

---

*More than seven centuries earlier, Giraldus of Wales (b. 1147) had written: "Those are called lunatics whose attacks are exacerbated every month when the moon is full." (*Topographica Hibernica*, v. 5, p. 79. Quoted by D. H. Tuke in his *History of the Insane in the British Isles*, p. 9.)

a scientific explanation of the lunar hypothesis. "There are few cases in which mad people feel the influence of the moon," he concluded, "and when they do, it is derived chiefly from an increase in its light." He added, however, that "the *absence* of its light may be attended with equal commotions" in patients afflicted with "tristimania" (a term Rush substituted for melancholia).[11]

If we have digressed somewhat, it has been with the intention of describing Rush's inadequacies in their proper light, that is, against the background of the theory and practice of his time. So much for the negative aspects of his teaching and practice. On the positive side, he advanced the humane and intelligent treatment of the insane at the Pennsylvania Hospital to a degree that earned him a position side by side with Chiarugi in Italy, Pinel in France and Tuke in England, in the treatment of the mentally ill.

Rush's advanced ideas and his sympathy with his patients impelled him to champion at the hospital many innovations of a far-reaching character. Upon joining the hospital's staff his attention had been drawn to the total lack of heating and ventilating arrangements for the cells in which the insane were housed. As a result he addressed in 1789 a communication to the managers complaining that it was impossible for physicians to improve the condition of the mentally ill while they remained in their existing quarters:

> These apartments are damp in winter and too warm in summer. They are, moreover, so constituted, as not to admit readily of a change of air; hence the smell of them is both offensive and unwholesome.
>
> Few patients have ever been confined in these Cells who have not been affected by a cold in two or three weeks after their confinement, and several have died of Consumption in consequence of this cold.
>
> These facts being clearly established, I conceive that the appropriating of the Cells any longer for the reception of mad people will be dishonourable both to the Science and Humanity of the city of Philadelphia.[12]

This criticism of Rush's stands out in bold contrast to the then widely prevalent theory that the insane were insensible to cold and heat alike, and that it was unnecessary to protect them against the extremities of the weather. This belief, which sanctioned the exposure of mental sufferers, ofttimes naked, to the harshest rigors of winter, persisted for decades after Rush's time.

Largely because of Rush's personal agitation for an additional wing to house the insane apart from the other classes of patients and his success in marshaling public opinion behind the plan, the Pennsylvania legislature voted an appropriation in 1792 for an extension to the hospital for this purpose. Upon its completion in 1796, the mental patients were transferred to the new west wing. Though far from perfect, it represented a decided improvement over the old quarters.

In 1798 Rush again addressed a plea to the managers "for the Benefit of the Asylum for Mad People" (i.e., the insane ward), consisting of two principal recommendations. First, he advocated the installation of two warm and two cold baths, together with an adequate water supply system. This recommendation was favorably acted upon. His second proposal, which indicates that the original plan of the founders for the employment of patients had fallen into neglect, urged "Certain Employments to be devised for such of the deranged people as are capable of Working, spinning, sewing, churning, &c., might be contrived for the Women: Turning a Wheel, particularly grinding Indian Corn in a Hand Mill, for food for the Horse or Cows of the Hospital, cutting Straw, weaving, digging in the Garden, sawing or planing boards, &c., &c., would be Useful for the Men."[13] Commonplace as these words may now seem to us, living as we do in an age when occupational therapy is accepted as an indispensable feature in all modern well managed institutions for the mentally ill, it is only necessary to recall that Rush's proposal seemed startlingly novel to his American contemporaries, in order to appreciate its historic importance.

Kind treatment of mental patients was a major rule in Rush's practice. From the first he insisted that the cells and persons of his patients be kept as neat and clean as possible. If he advocated the use of terror as a therapeutic agent in certain cases, he also taught that the insane should generally be approached with the respect and deference that would be accorded them in ordinary social intercourse, and insisted that doctors be perfectly honest at all times with their patients. He stressed the value of little acts of kindness toward them, such as presents of fruit and sweet-cakes at frequent intervals.

Recognizing the evils arising from the universal practice of hiring ill-paid, coarse and often brutal attendants for the insane, he recommended, in 1803, the employment of "a well-qualified person . . . as a friend and companion to the lunatics, whose business it shall be to attend them . . . ," a request that was acceded to. It is significant that he listed "kind treatment" as one of his principal rules in ministering to the mentally ill.

Anticipating in a sense the "mental catharsis" (purging of obsessions, inhibitions, etc.) that plays such an important role in modern Freudian therapy, Rush believed in having patients write down all that troubled their minds, and then reading what they had written. One of his patients, says Rush, after reading what he had set down, was so disgusted with his ugly thoughts that he rid himself of them and doubtless was greatly relieved thereby. Rush speaks also of the evil effects of repressed emotions on the mental processes.[14]

His thoroughly practical nature, combined with his humane outlook, is rather amusingly illustrated by a long and eloquent appeal to the hospital authorities urging, as an act of kindness to the patients, the substitution of a newly-invented stool pan for the chamber pots then in use. "The inventor of this delicate and healthful contrivance," he exclaims, "deserves more from humanity and Science than if he had discovered a new planet!"

Together with this request, made in 1810, Rush proposed a series of improvements constituting sweeping and unheard-of reforms for that time. These included: (1) the erection of separate buildings to house those in a "high and distracted state of madness" in order to protect the others, including convalescents, from the possibility of sympathetic reaction or loss of sleep; (2) separation of the sexes; (3) the introduction of labor, exercise and amusements for the patients "which shall act at the same time upon their bodies and minds;" (4) the hiring of an intelligent man and woman to attend the different sexes, to share their activities, and to read and discourse with them; (5) the rigid exclusion of all visitors—even near relations—likely to have a disturbing effect on the patients; (6) furnishing the cells of pay patients with feather beds and hair mattresses.[15]

In 1812 there appeared Rush's *magnum opus* in the field of mental diseases, *Medical Inquiries and Observations upon the Diseases of the Mind,* the first American general treatise on the subject, and the only one of its kind up to 1883.* Based mainly on his thirty years of observation of mental patients at the Pennsylvania Hospital, it was hailed as a classic upon its publication, both here and abroad, and for decades remained a primary textbook for American students of mental diseases.

Perhaps the most impressive tributes paid to Rush the man, upon his death in 1813, came from two ex-Presidents, both of whom he had numbered among his dearest friends. Even discounting the possible exaggeration arising from a deeply stirred emotion, this characterization of Rush by John Adams retains a high degree of significance: "As a man of science, letters, taste, sense, philosophy, patriotism, religion, morality, merit, usefulness, taken all together, Rush has not left his equal in America; nor that I know in the world. In him is taken away . . . a main prop of my life."[16]

No less significant a personal tribute is that contained in a letter of Thomas Jefferson to Adams: "Another of our friends of seventy-six is gone, my dear Sir, another of the co-signers of the Independence of our country. And a better man than Rush could not have left us, more benevolent, more learned, of finer genius, or more honest."[17]

In evaluating the place of Dr. Rush in psychiatric history, it is only fair to accept his shortcomings as the shortcomings

---

*The latter year witnessed the publication of William A. Hammond's *A Treatise on Insanity in its Medical Relations* and Edward C. Spitzka's *Insanity.*

of his age; as for his progressive principles and practices, these were largely original with him. None of his contemporaries exercised a greater influence than he did on American medicine in general and psychiatry in particular. It is true that that influence was not altogether wholesome. Some of his teachings were correctly discarded by his pupils and successors as either ineffective or injurious, but the good that remained was enough to make his influence on the whole a decidedly beneficial one. In the scientific aspects of his therapy for the mentally ill he surpassed the generally accepted authorities of his day, Cullen and Boerhaave; on the humanitarian side he was of a stature approaching, if not quite equaling, his great chain-breaking contemporaries in Europe—Chiarugi, Pinel, and Tuke.

CHAPTER VI
The Rise of Moral Treatment

1792. The French Revolution was at its height. The tercentenary of the discovery of a new world was being celebrated. And a new epoch in the care and treatment of the insane was being ushered in. The opening salvos were fired on two different fronts simultaneously—at Paris, France, and at York, England—and were heard and heeded across the Atlantic.

Paris in 1792 was seething with revolutionary fervor. The heads of a king and queen were about to roll into baskets, and with them a whole class was falling. Old forms and traditions were being discarded; in their place new ones arose with breathless rapidity. The time was ripe for social experimentation. And, as always when the time for social change has come, there were men prepared to effect it.

Two principal institutions for the mentally ill had been established in Paris; the Bicêtre, where male lunatics were kept, and the Salpêtrière, for female lunatics. They were indifferently called "hospitals" and "prisons" for the insane. Of the two terms the latter best expressed their purpose, which was purely custodial, and their regimen, which was sternly repressive. The Bicêtre, particularly, owned a questionable distinction: it ranked with the worst asylums in the world. There the patients, or rather, inmates, were loaded down with chains and shackled to floors and walls with irons, at the mercy of cruel attendants armed with whips and the authority to use them freely. Many of the attendants were convicts serving out their sentences in this horrible way. Since the inmates were prejudged incurable, therapeutic treatment was entirely lacking. In 1792, thanks

THE RISE OF MORAL TREATMENT 89

to the efforts of a hitherto obscure physician who dared to introduce an original method, this institution was suddenly and dramatically transformed in a manner that opened a new era in the history of mental illness.

The man was Philippe Pinel; the method was that later designated as "moral treatment." Pinel had come to Paris in mid-life, after having failed to establish himself as a practitioner in a town of modest size. Some years before, a young friend of his in the throes of a mental breakdown had rushed off into the woods where his body was later found torn to pieces by wolves. This tragedy profoundly impressed Pinel, and drew his attention to the subject of mental diseases. An erudite scholar, he delved deeply into the available literature on insanity, particularly the long-forgotten works by and about the ancient apostles of mild and kindly treatment—Asclepiades, Aretaeus, Soranus, Caelius Aurelianus, and the rest. The conviction grew upon him that their precepts were sounder therapeutically, and much more desirable from the viewpoint of humanity, than the brutal methods everywhere prevalent in his day.

At Paris Pinel had become connected with a small private asylum, the Maison de Santé Belhomme. When the French Revolution broke out, it found him occupied here in furthering his observations on mental diseases. He was still unknown to all but a small, though select, circle of friends which included such distinguished men as Condorcet, Helvetius, D'Alembert, Halle and Lavoisier. To these acquaintances he revealed his theories respecting the treatment of insanity. His arguments were very convincing. Consequently when two of them, Thouret and Cabanis, were elevated by the revolutionary government to a triumvirate at the head of Paris's hospital system, they immediately thought of Pinel. Here was a chance to test his theories. Here was the man who could clean these Augean stables, the miserable asylums for the insane. They appointed Pinel physician to that notorious hell-hole, the Bicêtre.

The asylum looked like a circle of the Inferno when Pinel entered upon his duties. The lunatics lay all about, raving, riveted with chains and irons. They were regarded as desperate, dangerous animals* on a lower plane than criminals, for the latter were not stripped of all their human attributes as the insane were supposed to be. And in truth, the inmates of the Bicêtre had the appearance of wild animals—beards and hair were matted with straw and infested with lice; their clothes were tattered, their nails grown long like claws, their bodies encrusted with dirt and filth. They presented pictures of complete neglect. Their cries of anger, agony and frustration induced by intolerable confinement, mingled with the endless clanging of chains and the crack of keepers' whips.

Pinel proposed a radical change. He planned to strike off the chains from these miserable creatures and to inaugurate a regimen based on kindness and sympathy. Couthon, chief aid of Robespierre, came to the Bicêtre to learn at first hand what Pinel was about. "Citizen," he exclaimed, "are you yourself mad to wish to unchain such beasts?" Pinel patiently explained his ideas. Couthon's scepticism vanished. "Do as you please," he said finally, and departed.

Pinel was now free to put into practice the theories inspired by his classic predecessors. Almost his first act was to strike off the chains from fifty-three lunatics, many of whom had been weighed down with fetters for years in the belief that they were exceedingly dangerous. A large proportion of those released proved to be perfectly harmless and mild. Their violent behavior had resulted quite naturally from the oppressive tortures inflicted on them. One whose chains were thus removed, previously regarded as the most dangerous of all, afterward became Pinel's trustworthy and devoted servant. A new regimen based on a minimum of mechanical restraint and a maximum of intelligent understanding was at last in force at the Bicêtre. The results were most encouraging.

Three years after his dramatic entrance into the Bicêtre, Pinel's ministrations were extended to the Salpêtrière, the

---

*This conception was heightened by the occasional murders of keepers by patients within the Bicêtre's walls. Maddened by the tortures inflicted by brutal attendants, inmates were sometimes driven to kill as a means of revenge.

second largest asylum in Paris, where supposedly incurable women lunatics were kept. It was this event that inspired Robert Fleury's famous painting, "Pinel à la Salpêtrière", which depicts the good doctor superintending the removal of chains and fetters from the insane while a patient, whose manacles have just been struck off, kisses his hand in gratitude. By his demonstrations at the Paris asylums Pinel proved conclusively the fallacy of harsh treatment, and opened up new paths along the lines of sympathy and humanity dreamed of by the founders of the Pennsylvania Hospital some forty-odd years before and later partly realized by Benjamin Rush. It was Pinel who first formulated "moral treatment" into a system so soundly conceived and dramatically presented that it caught the attention of the public. Imperfect though his own system was, it served as a cornerstone upon which further psychiatric progress was built.

In the medical aspects of his therapy Pinel hewed rather closely to the line set down by Cullen, whose work he had translated into French. But he frankly expressed his scepticism of prevailing medical methods in the treatment of the insane, and sharply criticized the excessive use of bloodletting and drugs indulged in by most of his contemporaries. He himself used medication very sparingly, placing his main reliance on moral therapy. His system of moral treatment is expounded in his epoch-making *Traité médico-philosophique sur l'aliénation mentale,* published in 1801. Based on sound observation (Pinel was a thoroughgoing clinician), and a scholarly acquaintance with classic and contemporary literature on mental diseases, this treatise exerted a tremendous influence, not only in France, but in Germany, Great Britain and America.

What was the essence of this "moral treatment?" In a little dissertation published in 1811, Dr. T. Romeyn Beck of New York presented such a concise summary of this aspect of treatment, that we quote it in full:

MORAL MANAGEMENT. This consists in removing patients from their residence to some proper asylum; and for this purpose a calm retreat in the country is to be preferred: for it is found that continuance at home aggravates the disease, as the improper association of ideas cannot be destroyed. A system of humane vigilance is adopted. Coercion by blows, stripes, and chains, although sanctioned by the authority of Celsus and Cullen, is now justly laid aside. The rules most proper to be observed are the following: Convince the lunatics that the power of the physician and keeper is absolute; have humane attendants, who shall act as servants to them; never threaten but execute; offer no indignities to them, as they have a high sense of honour; punish disobedience peremptorily, in the presence of the other maniacs; if unruly, forbid them the company of others, use the strait waistcoat, confine them in a dark and quiet room, order spare diet . . .; tolerate noisy ejaculations; strictly exclude visitors; let their fears and resentments be soothed without unnecessary opposition; adopt a system of regularity; make them rise, take exercise and food at stated times. The diet ought to be light, and easy of digestion, but never too low. When convalescing, allow limited liberty; introduce entertaining books and conversation, exhilarating music, employment of body in agricultural pursuits . . .; and admit friends under proper restrictions. It will also be proper to forbid their returning home too soon. By thus acting, the patient will "minister to himself."[1]

The same year (1792) that Pinel's chainbreaking reforms were introduced at the Bicêtre in the midst of white-heat revolution, a similar step, less dramatic but just as far-reaching, was being inaugurated by a layman in a more placid environment among the Quakers of York, England.

At the time the two principal English institutions for the insane were Bethlehem Hospital (or Bedlam) in London, and the Lunatic Asylum of York. The horrible conditions then prevailing in these asylums were proverbial: in both institutions the patients were, quite appropriately, termed prisoners. In the year 1791 a Quakeress named Hannah Mills was admitted to the York Asylum. Some friends who came to visit her were denied permission to do so, on the ground that she was in no condition to be interviewed. A few weeks later this patient died. In the minds of her Quaker friends in York there was a strong suspicion that cruel treatment had caused or at least hastened her death. Among them was William Tuke, who, like so many of his sect, was a "practical idealist." It occurred to Tuke that it would be well for the Friends to establish an institution of their own where fellow-believers who fell prey to mental illness might find gentle and wholesome treatment.*

Tuke presented his idea before a gathering of Yorkshire Friends in March, 1792. Three months later a special meeting was held "for the purpose of taking into consideration the propriety of providing a retired Habitation, with necessary advice, attention, etc., for members of our Society, and others in profession with us, who may be in a state of Lunacy, or so deranged in mind (no idiots) as to require such provision."[2] The proposal met with some stiff opposition, but Tuke was a strong-willed man and pushed his project forward with such determination that it was finally accepted. His staunchest supporter was Lindley Murray, a noted grammarian, who had migrated from his native America some years before to make his permanent home among fellow Quakers at York. Murray, as we shall see, was to form an important link connecting reform movements in old York, his new home, and New York, his old home.

A building was erected on a site near York, and was opened for the reception of patients in 1796. The institution was named "The Retreat," to avoid the stigma associated with the common terms *asylum* and *madhouse*. The name was intended "to convey the idea of what such an institution should be, namely, a place in which the unhappy might obtain a refuge; a quiet haven in which the shattered bark might find the means of reparation and safety."

Among the principal objects of the founders were these: to provide a *family* environment for the patients, as manifested in the non-institutional aspect of the building and its surroundings; emphasis on employment and exercise as conducive to mental health (a principle put into practice from the very start); and the treatment of patients as guests

*An abortive step at founding such an institution had been taken more than a century earlier (1671) when it had been resolved at a meeting of London Quakers: "That Friends seek some place convenient in and about Ye Citty where they may put any person that may be distracted or troubled in mind that soe they may not be put among ye world's people or run about ye streets."

rather than as inmates. Kindness and consideration formed the keystone of the whole theoretical structure. Chains were absolutely forbidden, along with those resorts to terrorization that were still advocated in varying degrees by eminent medical men. The maxims of the institution were taken from ancient texts: Solomon's "A soft answer turneth away wrath," and Aeschylus' "Soft speech is to distemper'd wrath, medicinal." Mechanical restraint was not completely abolished, however. Violent patients were sometimes bound with broad leather belts which secured the arms while permitting the free use of hands; in extreme cases, the straitjacket was used, together with solitary confinement.

The founders and early managers of the Retreat evinced a decided distrust of medicines. In the light of the generally ineffective, if not actually harmful, medical treatment of mental sickness then prevailing, their attitude was not without justification. One positive advance introduced at the Retreat was the complete abolition of bloodletting, that bane of centuries. In their minimization of medical therapy the managers swerved too far to the extreme. Nevertheless, their direction probably represented, on the whole, the best to be found anywhere during the first two or three decades of the Retreat's existence.

Thus in different places, unknown to each other, two men were instituting similar reforms in the "moral" treatment of mental illness—one a layman whose approach was mainly humanitarian; the other a physician who had reached the same conclusion by way of scientific study. The work of both had far-reaching effects on mental hospital administration and practice.

In paying homage to these two pioneers, however, we should keep in mind that the idea of ameliorating the condition of the insane did not originate with them as sparks of pure inspiration. All the elements of a reform movement in this field were already present, waiting only to be fused by the proper leaders. If Pinel and Tuke had never lived, it is quite probable that the same reforms would have been achieved by others about the same time. We have already spoken of the progressive steps taken by Rush in America

THE RISE OF MORAL TREATMENT 95

several years before the transformation of the Bicêtre or the founding of York Retreat. In Italy, too, another great humanitarian, Vincenzo Chiarugi, had struck off chains from his patients and freed them from other torturesome restraints years before Pinel or Tuke. His name is less celebrated than theirs only by virtue of the fact that he operated at a distance too remote from the flow of contemporary streams of thought to permit his work to become widely known, or to exert an appreciable influence on the practice of his day.* Joseph Daquin, a close friend of Pinel, introduced important humanitarian reforms when he became director of the insane department of the hospital at Chambéry in 1787, five years before Pinel came to the Bicêtre. It was Pinel, however, who formulated, systematized and dramatized moral therapy.

The influence of Pinel and Tuke ran along strange geographical divisions. While Pinel was to exercise the stronger influence on psychiatric practice on the European continent, largely through the wide circulation of his classic work on the subject, Tuke's work played the more important role in America. Of the eight mental hospitals that sprang up in the United States during the first quarter of the nineteenth century, the establishment of two was directly inspired by the successful operation of the York Retreat, and the administration of at least two others was patterned after that in effect at the Retreat.

The direct influence of Tuke and the Retreat was clearly manifested in the establishment of the second special institution for the mentally ill to be built in America, and the first built in the 19th century. This was the Friends' Asylum, opened at Frankford, Pennsylvania, in 1817. Its inception dates from 1811, when a proposal to erect an asylum "for such of our members as may be deprived of their reason" was brought before the Spring Quarterly Meeting of the

---

*Chiarugi introduced a number of sweeping humanitarian reforms at the Hospital of St. Boniface in Florence during the years 1774–88. He abolished chains and fetters, encouraged occupational therapy, enforced sanitary measures, and insisted that the mentally ill be treated as human beings.

Philadelphia Society of Friends.* There is good reason to believe that the original proposal came from Thomas Scattergood, a minister of the Quaker faith. Scattergood had previously spent six years (1794–1800) traveling through Great Britain on a religious mission. During this time, he had visited the Retreat near York (January, 1797), conversed and dined with its founder, and had evidently been greatly impressed by what he saw and heard of the institution.[3]

A constitution was drawn up in 1813, and a corporation formed under the name, "Contributors to the Asylum for the relief of persons deprived of the use of their reason." A subscription campaign was then launched, a notable feature of which was the wide circulation among prospective donors of an abridged version of Samuel Tuke's *Description of the Retreat near York,* orginally published in London in 1813. This little book, with its account of the moral treatment practiced by the York Friends, its general atmosphere of kindness and sympathy, and its note of optimism, proved an important factor in raising money. Not only money was solicited, but donations in kind as well. In a pamphlet issued 1816, it was urged that: "In order to lessen the expense of furnishing the house, Friends in the country are informed that any articles of feather bedding, bed and table linen will be very acceptable. Donations in household furniture are expected from Friends in this city."[4]

The institution was opened in 1817 at Frankford, some five miles north of Philadelphia. This site, comprising about fifty-two acres, was chosen because of its retired and sheltered location, where the mentally ill could be protected from the gaze of the idly curious. The building was three stories high, and accommodated forty patients. The charge for the latter ranged from $3.50 per week up, depending on ability to pay, comforts required, etc. At first reception was restricted only to members of the Society and professors with the Society, but in 1834 it was made a non-sectarian institution.

The Philadelphia Quakers placed great emphasis on pro-

*As early as 1709 Philadelphia Friends had considered building a hospital for their sick and insane members, but the project fell through.

THE RISE OF MORAL TREATMENT

viding a proper religious atmosphere, which they believed to be inextricably bound up with the ultimate recovery of the patients. The constitution expressly stated that the asylum "is intended to furnish, beside the requisite medical aid, such tender sympathetic attention and religious oversight, as may sooth their agitated minds, and thereby, under the divine blessing, facilitate their restoration to the enjoyment of this inestimable gift."[5]

"To fetter strong madness in a silken thread" was the ideal observed from the start, and its managers could proudly boast two-score years later that no chain had ever been used there for the restraint of patients. In the minds of the founders the patients were not to be considered either as sub-humans or social pariahs, but as "men and brethren." The system of moral treatment instituted at the York Retreat was here closely followed in its essentials.

A crude attempt was made at classification, the importance of which was becoming generally recognized. The upper stories of the building were reserved for mild and convalescent cases, while the "violent, the noisy and the incurable" were quartered in the lower story. The prevailing confusion concerning proper classification is evidenced in an early description of the Frankford Asylum, in which it is stated: "It is obviously disadvantageous to mingle the furious and the melancholy, the imperious and the fearful, the vociferous and the peaceful, the villainous and the religious, the clean and the unclean, the curable, incurable, and convalescent, together."[6]

Another of the early American institutions for the mentally ill directly influenced by the Retreat at York was the Bloomingdale Asylum. Opened in New York in 1821 as a separately operated institution, the origins of Bloomingdale may be traced back to the founding of the New York Hospital nearly fifty years earlier. In 1771 a royal charter had been granted to the Society of the New York Hospital, the second general hospital established in America.* Erection of the institution was delayed by a disastrous fire, the

*The full title of the incorporated institution was: "the Society of the Hospital in the city of New York in America."

Revolutionary War, and the turbulent years of the postwar period, and it was not until 1791 that the hospital was finally opened.

The original building committee of the hospital had been authorized in 1774, "to appropriate the cellar part of the North wing [of the projected hospital] or such part of it as they may judge necessary into wards or cells for the reception of lunatics."[7] The first mental patient was received into the hospital September, 1792, some twenty months after its opening. As in the early years of the Pennsylvania Hospital, the mentally ill were confined in cells in the basement of the building. But by 1806 this arrangement had revealed itself as so glaringly inadequate and unwholesome that it was decided to erect on the hospital grounds a separate structure for the insane. This building, called the "New York Lunatic Asylum", was opened in 1808, a generous grant having been made by the state legislature toward its construction and maintenance.

In 1809 an act of the legislature authorized the overseers of the poor in towns and counties throughout the state to contract with the governors of the New York Hospital for the maintenance and care therein, at special rates, of lunatics chargeable to such communities. This was the first legislative provision in New York recognizing the pauper insane as a distinct class entitled to hospital care and treatment.

But the new building erected at a cost of $56,000, soon was crowded far beyond its capacity. The proposition was now raised: why not remove the institution to a more spacious site some distance from the city? The leader and guiding spirit behind this plan was Thomas Eddy, a Quaker merchant who was then treasurer and served subsequently as vice-president and president, of the New York Hospital.

In many respects Eddy ranked among the most remarkable reformers of his day. Like Rush in Pennsylvania, he was actively associated with most of the progressive movements in his state, and was the acknowledged leader and initiator of many of them.

Together with most social reformers of his day, Eddy

THE RISE OF MORAL TREATMENT

kept in constant touch with reform developments abroad, particularly in England. Considering the lack of means of communication and the slowness with which news traveled —remember that the historic Battle of New Orleans in 1815 was fought a fortnight after the treaty of peace had been signed due to the primitive means of transmitting messages—Eddy and the others managed to keep astonishingly well informed of contemporary European events in the field of social welfare. Many of the humanitarian reforms introduced in the early period of our country's growth were communicated to us from the British Isles through the interchange of pamphlets and letters. In Eddy's case, scarcely a letter passed between him and his correspondents abroad which did not contain a list of pamphlets or books being forwarded to him by the same mail. Quite probably it was in this wise that a copy of Samuel Tuke's *Description of the Retreat* fell into Eddy's hands.

In April, 1815, Eddy placed before the governors of the Hospital an important plan, outlining his ideas for a new establishment, which was admittedly based on Tuke's work. "In pursuing this subject," he said, "my views have been much extended, and my mind considerably enlightened, by perusing the works of Doctors Creighton, Arnold and Rush; but more particularly, the account of the Retreat near York. . . . The great utility of confining ourselves almost exclusively to a course of moral treatment is plain and simple, and incalculably interesting to the cause of humanity; and perhaps no work contains so many excellent and appropriate observations on the subject as that entitled, *The Account of the Retreat.*"[8]

Eddy laid down for the governors' consideration an eleven-point program, incorporating the ideas of moral treatment which we have already described. He called for the complete elimination of corporal punishment, chains, and the rule of terror prescribed by such authorities as Cullen and Rush. All possible appeals, he urged, should be made to the better intellectual and moral sensibilities of the patient in therapeutic work.

One of the most interesting features of Eddy's plan was

his emphasis on the necessity for keeping case histories.[9] This was in marked contrast to the prevailing disregard for recording even the barest essentials of data concerning patients. (Some institutions did not even trouble to set down dates of admission and discharge, cures or even deaths of patients.)

In concluding his *Hints,* Eddy recommended that a site be purchased in a retired situation, a few miles from the city, large enough to contain walks, gardens, a farm, etc., for the exercise, employment and amusement of the patients.

Eddy's proposals were favorably received by his fellow governors, whose interest in the plan was further aroused by the startling details of barbaric abuses in public and private asylums in England then being exposed by parliamentary investigating committees.* A great deal of attention was thereby attracted to the problems of the insane and the need for improvement in their care and treatment, as evidenced by the flood of pamphlets on the subject circulated at the time.

Meanwhile Eddy had written his friend, Lindley Murray, who was then residing near York, informing him of the plan to build a new institution, and requesting any advice Murray's connection with the York Retreat might suggest. In his reply, dated July 20, 1815, Murray wrote:

> I am pleased to perceive by thy letter, that many of you at New York are deeply interested in promoting the recovery and relief of insane persons, and I hope you will be encouraged in the pursuit of this benevolent and good work.
>
> I did not know how I could better answer thy views and wishes than by putting thy pamphlet [evidently Eddy's *Hints*] and letter into the hands of my benevolent and zealous friend, Samuel Tuke, who has paid great attention to this subject; and I am gratified with introducing you to the acquaintance of each other.[10]

---

*An inquiry into conditions at Bedlam in 1815 uncovered the famous case of William Norris, a patient who had been chained in a manner producing indescribable torture for twelve years. When found he was encased hand, foot and neck, in iron bands and rings, and these in turn were firmly secured by chains to an iron bar fastened to the wall of his cell. The reason given for this punishment was that Norris, twelve years before, had struck a drunken keeper, who had driven him to violence by wanton cruelty.

THE RISE OF MORAL TREATMENT

With this communication Murray sent a pamphlet that had lately been written by Tuke, entitled *Practical Hints on the Construction and Economy of Pauper Lunatic Asylums*. The comprehensive plan contained in this pamphlet had been awarded first prize in a competition for a model design for a public asylum to be built at Wakefield, England.[11]

Simultaneously, Eddy received a personal letter from Samuel Tuke. This contained modifications of the pauper asylum plans to conform with the requirements of the proposed institution in New York, which Tuke correctly judged to be intended primarily for middle-class patients who could afford to pay moderate fees for their maintenance. The letter, among other things, included an interesting discussion on the theory and value of occupational therapy:

> I observe with pleasure that one leading feature of your institution is the introduction of employment amongst the patients, an object which I am persuaded is of the utmost importance in the moral treatment of insanity . . . The employment of insane persons should, as far as is practicable, be adapted to their previous habits, inclinations and capacities and, though horticultural pursuits may be most desirable, the greatest benefit will, I believe, be found to result from the person being engaged in that employment in which he can most easily excel, whether it be an active or a sedentary one . . .[12]

Thus fully equipped with theory concerning the planning and administration of the new hospital for the mentally ill, it now only remained to construct it. A site was selected along the Bloomingdale Road (now Broadway) upon Eddy's recommendation. The asylum, when completed, comprised several tracts of land totalling about 77 acres. The main building stood on the spot now occupied by the Columbia University Library, at 116th Street and Broadway.*

The Bloomingdale Asylum (so named from its location on Bloomingdale Road) was begun in 1817 and was com-

---

*The purchase of this land for about $31,000 proved an excellent investment. When the pressure of New York's rapidly-growing population forced the retreat of Bloomingdale to its present location at White Plains, a suburb of New York, the original site was sold piecemeal at tremendous profits.

pleted in 1821. On May 10, 1821, the governors of the New York Hospital drew up and circulated an *Address to the Public,* announcing that the asylum would open the following month with accommodations for two hundred patients. "This institution," ran the statement, "has been established with the express design to carry into effect that system of management of the insane, happily termed *moral management,* the superior efficacy of which has been demonstrated in several of the Hospitals of Europe, and especially that admirable establishment of the Society of Friends, called 'The Retreat,' near York, in England."[13]

None but pay patients were received into the institution (which remained a department of the New York Hospital) although paupers sent by poor relief authorities from various towns, cities and counties throughout the State were maintained at very low rates. The executive direction of the hospital, except for medical treatment, was entrusted to the lay superintendent, Laban Gardner, who was the first to serve in that post. Dr. James Eddy was appointed resident physician and Dr. John Neilson attending physician. The latter supervised the general medical aspects of care and treatment of the patients. Through the ensuing years this institution, now known as the Westchester Division of the New York Hospital, has maintained a leading place among mental hospitals in America.

Like Bloomingdale, the McLean Asylum of Massachusetts (opened in 1818) developed as part of a general hospital.

In Chapter IV we have described the early efforts to found a hospital for the mentally ill in Boston, which had nearly reached a successful culmination in the 1760's through the bequest of Thomas Hancock. In 1804 William Phillips, another notable citizen of Boston, left $5,000 to the city towards the building of a hospital for the sick poor and insane of the Commonwealth. Unlike the Hancock bequest, this one carried no time-limit specification. Interest in the project was again awakened, but it took several years to mature into an active movement. However, one rising

THE RISE OF MORAL TREATMENT 103

young physician of Boston, Dr. John Collins Warren,* was determined that the erection of a public hospital should no longer be delayed. In assaulting the ramparts of public indifference, Dr. Warren trained his guns first on Governor William Phillips of Massachusetts, the son and heir of the donor. His enthusiasm proved infectious. In a letter dated July 31, 1810, the governor wrote him:

> I am impressed with the importance of the subject upon which we have repeatedly conversed—that of establishing in this town an hospital for the reception of lunatics and other sick persons. To place such an institution in a respectable and permanently useful situation, a large sum will be required.[14]

To this end Phillips offered to contribute $15,000 in addition to the $5,000 left in his father's will, of which he was executor, provided that $150,000 in subscriptions be raised. Taking up this challenge Warren enlisted his friend and colleague, Dr. James Jackson, in the cause. Together they drew up a circular letter addressed to the most influential and richest men in the Commonwealth. The letter—a very lengthy one—pointed out that the only public receptacles open for the sick and insane in the State were the almshouses and jails, where confinement and safekeeping, with no opportunity for curative treatment, were all that could be hoped for. It stated further that:

> The virtuous and industrious are liable to become objects of public charity, in consequence of the diseases of the mind. When those who are unfortunate in this respect are left without proper care, a calamity, which might have been transient, is prolonged through life. The number of such persons who are rendered unable to provide for themselves is probably greater than the public imagine; and of these, a large proportion claim the assistance of the affluent . . . Even those who can pay the necessary expenses would perhaps find an institution such as is proposed, the best situation in which they could place their unfortunate friends. It is worthy of the opulent men of this town, and consistent with the general character, to provide an asylum for the insane from every part of the Commonwealth. But if funds are raised for

---

*Warren was to become one of the most renowned of Massachusetts' medical men. He performed the world's first operation employing ether as an anesthetic, in the very hospital he helped to found.

the purpose proposed it is probable that the legislature will grant some assistance, with a view to such an extension of its benefits.[15]

This circular met a speedy and generous response. The following year (1811) the State legislature incorporated James Bowdoin and fifty-five others under the name, "Massachusetts General Hospital," and subsequently made liberal grants of land, money and the free use of prison labor for the project.[16] The War of 1812 slowed up the progress of the hospital, but it was taken up with renewed vigor in 1816, when a house-to-house canvass was started. Within one week $100,000 in pledges was obtained, about half of which was specifically subscribed for the erection of the "insane hospital." It had been understood from the beginning that the hospital was to consist of two departments—one for mental, and the other for general diseases—and that each would occupy a separate building. In view of the fact that most of the ear-marked contributions were for the insane department, its construction was begun first, on a site at Charlestown, about two miles from Boston, and it was opened for the reception of patients on November 23, 1818. Dr. Rufus Wyman was appointed resident superintendent, this being the first occasion when a medical man was placed in such a post in America.

The theory of treatment adopted by Dr. Wyman followed in general that advanced by Pinel and Tuke, as can be ascertained from his early reports. Denouncing the cruel practices of the past, he wrote, in 1822: "It is too true that such treatment [whips, chains, etc.] in time not long past, has been approved and often advised by medical men. An entire revolution of opinion respecting the treatment of lunatics has been produced . . . Kindness and humanity have succeeded severity and cruelty."[17]

It is interesting to note that the first patient admitted to the asylum was a young man believed to be "possessed of the devil." His father had labored mightily to exorcise him by regular whippings before he was brought to the institution. Superstition dies hard! Incidentally, this first patient was completely cured, became a pedlar and, thanks to a

EIGHTEENTH-CENTURY HOSPITALS FOR THE
MENTALLY ILL

A. Sketch of the Pennsylvania Hospital, 1752—the first hospital in this country to admit mental patients for curative treatment.
B. An early print of the Eastern Lunatic Hospital at Williamsburg, Virginia—the first public hospital in America exclusively for the treatment of the mentally ill.

THE RISE OF MORAL TREATMENT

native Yankee shrewdness, amassed a modest fortune before retiring.

In 1821, a Boston merchant, John McLean, bequeathed a sum of $100,000 to the Asylum for the Insane. In gratitude for this liberal gift the name of the institution soon after was changed to McLean Asylum, and later to McLean Hospital. The asylum was managed on a modest scale during its early years: at the end of 1820 it housed only 23 patients.

Meanwhile, in 1797, six years after the opening of the New York Hospital, a general hospital had been founded in Maryland through an act of the State legislature "to Encourage the establishing of a Hospital for the Relief of Indigent Sick Persons and for the Reception and Care of Lunatics." A charter for the hospital was given to a group of Baltimore citizens, headed by Capt. Jeremiah Yellott. With an initial fund of $26,000 raised by state and city grants and through private subscriptions, a building was begun in 1798 and was opened for the reception of its first patients, including the mentally ill, the same year. Unfortunately, however, funds for the completion of the hospital were lacking, and it soon fell into a state of sad neglect, although continuing to receive patients. In 1808, two enterprising physicians, James Smythe and Colin Mackenzie, proposed to undertake the maintenance and direction of the uncompleted institution, and to make necessary repairs and additions, providing they were granted a lease of fifteen years. Their proposal was accepted and they thereupon took over the institution on the basis of private control. Aided by two legislative grants totalling $48,000, and granted permission to raise an additional $20,000 by lottery (which, incidentally, was a favorite means of raising money for social welfare projects at that time), Drs. Smythe and Mackenzie enlarged and improved the hospital. A handsome profit was realized from their joint endeavors. When finally completed, the hospital accommodated 190 patients, of whom about forty were mental cases.

In 1815 the lease of Drs. Smythe and Mackenzie was extended until 1834. Both the lessees died some years before the expiration of the contract, however, and the control of the hospital passed into the hands of Mackenzie's son, Dr. John P. Mackenzie. A storm of protest had by this time arisen over the surrender of the institution to private enterprise, and in 1828 its character as a public hospital was resumed by a legislative act. The new statute incorporated a group of representative laymen and physicians under the name, "The Maryland Hospital," to supersede Mackenzie at the expiration of the private lease. This group took over control in 1834. Five years later an act was passed directing that thenceforth the hospital should be devoted exclusively to the reception, care and treatment of the insane. This law carried an appropriation of $30,000 for the changes required to adapt the institution to its new purpose, and provided that one-half of its accommodations be set aside for pauper lunatics sent there by various counties in the state, to be maintained at the rate of $100 each per year.*

The years 1821 and 1822 witnessed the founding, in four different states, of four new hospitals devoted wholly or in part to the reception of mental cases. Of these, two were founded as state asylums, one as an incorporated asylum, and the other as a general hospital admitting lunatics together with other classes of patients.

To Kentucky and South Carolina belongs the honor of opening the second and third state institutions exclusively for the mentally ill, although in both cases custody rather than cure was the dominating motive.

Kentucky's asylum was established by a legislative act of December 7, 1822.† At that time it was customary in Kentucky, as in several other states, for the insane poor to be boarded out with individuals at public expense, by order of magistrates or justices of the peace. In a message to the legislature early in 1821, Governor Adair stated that this

---

*In 1852 selection of a new site for the Maryland Hospital was authorized by the legislature. Spring Grove, Maryland, was chosen as the most favorable location but for various reasons—notably the Civil War—the new institution was not opened until a score of years later.

†Called at first simply the "Lunatic Asylum", and then the "Eastern Kentucky Lunatic Asylum", its name was eventually changed to "Eastern State Hospital."

THE RISE OF MORAL TREATMENT

system of boarding out lunatics was wasteful from the financial viewpoint,* and unsound from the social angle since it provided no opportunity for curative treatment. He proposed the erection of a state asylum, such as that in Virginia, to which Kentucky had occasionally sent her lunatics during her existence as a territory. "If only one out of twenty of those unfortunate beings laboring under the most dreadful of all maladies should be restored," he asked rhetorically, "would it not be a cause of great gratulation to a humane and generous public?" He also pointed out that such an institution would be of great value in affording practical experience to students at the medical school of Transylvania University. Following Governor Adair's suggestion, the legislature in 1822 established a state asylum, and appropriated $10,000 to cover the expense of building and outfitting it. This sum proved quite inadequate, particularly in view of the fact that the statute specified that accommodations for as many as *200 patients* be provided. A tract of land near Lexington was selected, comprising about 17 acres. On this site stood an imposing, partly-completed brick edifice which had been begun some years before as the Fayette Hospital, intended for "diseases of every character."† The new institution was opened for the reception of patients May 1, 1824, as the Eastern Kentucky Lunatic Asylum.

Rigorous exclusion of the feebleminded—those who were "imbecile only"—from the institution was ordered by the legislature. Only the "lunatic" were to be admitted.[18] Even among this class, a distinction was made between "maniacs, or persons who are dangerous," and "such as are quiet and peaceable," it evidently being intended to confine only the former group in the asylum, and to continue to provide for the latter by boarding them out as before. Dr. T. O. Powell seems fully justified in stating that the institution, during its

---

*The state expended $18,000 for this purpose in 1823. This sum was regarded as a considerable outlay in that day.

†The Fayette Hospital had been a group venture in public service that collapsed soon after its inception, leaving the building unfinished and unoccupied.

first two decades, "was a madhouse for the safe-keeping of lunatics rather than an asylum for their care."[19] It appears, however, that the second superintendent (the first having resigned soon after entering upon his duties) at least attempted to put into practice the system of moral treatment then in force at the Friends' Asylum at Frankford, as evidenced by this quotation from a letter written by him about 1826:

> When I first entered on my charges, several [inmates] wore chains, and some straps with lock-buckles, &c. At present the same are now freed from those manacles, and are peaceable. The only model presented to me for the internal government of this institution is a small pamphlet published by the trustees of the Friends' Asylum near Frankford.[20]

The South Carolina State Asylum, erected at Columbia, was established in 1821, but was not opened until 1828. In one interesting respect the founding of this institution was unique. It appears that a clamor for an asylum for the insane and a school for the deaf and dumb reached the ears of the state legislature about the same time, and the solons conceived the idea of combining both services in one institution. An act was forthwith passed, in 1821, authorizing "the erection of a suitable building for a lunatic asylum and a school for the deaf and dumb."[21] An appropriation of $30,000 was voted for an institution with this twofold object. Fortunately, however, a commission appointed to study and draw up plans for the project reported that the association of the two groups in one institution was impracticable, and the entire appropriation was therefore expended in building an asylum for the mentally ill. It was opened at Columbia, in 1828, under the management of nine trustees, or regents, appointed by the legislature.

The asylum received both pay patients and paupers, the maintenance of the latter being paid for by the counties to which they were chargeable. It was expressly provided that "idiots, lunatics and epileptics" were to be admitted alike to the asylum.*

---

*It is interesting, in this respect, to note that nearly all the early mental hospitals received these three groups indiscriminately. The first institution in

THE RISE OF MORAL TREATMENT 109

Another public institution receiving mental patients was founded in 1821, when the Ohio legislature passed a statute establishing "a Commercial Hospital and Lunatic Asylum for the State of Ohio" to be erected at Cincinnati. This statute, like that enacted in South Carolina the same year, carried an unusual provision. It directed that the proposed institution, besides furnishing "safe-keeping, comfort and medical treatment of such idiots, lunatics and insane persons of this State as may be brought to it," should also accommodate free of charge all sick boatmen of Ohio, together with those of neighboring states reciprocally offering free hospital treatment to boatmen who were residents of Ohio.[22]

The inception of this institution is credited to Dr. Daniel Drake, one of the best known physicians of his day. A short time before Dr. Drake had founded the Ohio Medical College, of which he was president, and had set about immediately to have a hospital established in connection with the Medical College as a means of affording clinical experience to his students. He embodied this idea in a petition and presented it to the legislature, which acted favorably upon it. Ten thousand dollars in depreciated currency (which netted $3,500 in all) in addition to one-half of the State's auction duties collected in Cincinnati, was appropriated by the state toward the erection of the hospital. Its management was placed in the hands of the trustees of Cincinnati Township. The faculty of the Ohio Medical College were directed to render services gratis to the mental patients, and in return their students were given free entry into the hospital for purposes of observation.

Although the Commercial Hospital was finished in 1823, it was not until four years later that the other department, the Lunatic Asylum, was opened for the reception of patients. The latter was a three-story building. The first story contained cells for the male patients, the second accommodated female patients, and the third was fitted out as a lecture hall for the students of the medical school. When finally completed, it had accommodation for 160 patients. Despite its

America exclusively for the feebleminded dates from 1846, and the first for epileptics as recently as 1891.

promising connection with the Ohio Medical College, we are told by Cincinnati's historians that the asylum was "designed rather as a place of confinement than a hospital for the cure of the insane."[23] This estimate seems to be substantiated by the tenor of a resolution passed by the legislature in 1831, appointing a committee to visit the institution and to observe "whether the cells and apartments of the lunatic asylum are sufficiently separated from one another by thick walls to prevent the inmates from communicating with each other, and whether means of restraint and comfort . . . have been provided."[24] Comment on this resolution would be superfluous.

More closely allied to the progressive ideals enunciated at the turn of the century by Rush, Pinel and Tuke was the Hartford Retreat, incorporated by the Connecticut Legislature in May, 1822. The name, Retreat, was adopted from the Quakers' institution at York, England, along with many of the principles practiced there.

In 1821, a committee was appointed by the Connecticut State Medical Society to obtain data on the need of a public lunatic asylum within the state, and also ways and means of building one.* In its report the committee cited statistics indicating that there were more than one thousand insane persons residing in the state, which still lacked a single institution to afford them curative treatment. A hospital for the insane was undoubtedly necessary, and the committee proceeded to give a detailed description of the architecture and management of the proposed institution, based on the best models then available. Among the recommendations contained in the report were the following:

> Such an asylum should be the reverse of everything which usually enters into our conceptions of a mad house. It should not be a jail, in which for individual and public security the unfortunate maniacs

---

*The movement for an asylum in Connecticut dates back to 1814, when Dr. Nathaniel Dwight, the geographer and physician, sent a communication on lunatic asylums to the Medical Society. In 1814, the Society appointed Dr. Mason F. Cogswell to gather information on the number of insane in the state, and on methods of providing for them, but a questionnaire prepared and circularized by him failed to elicit the desired information.

are confined. Nor should it be merely a hospital, where they may have the benefits of medical treatment—for without moral management, the most judicious course of medication is rarely sucessful . . .

Its exterior should not exhibit the aspect nor even the faint resemblance of a prison; and at the same time, in its formation the safety of its inmates should not be overlooked.[25]

As a model for the architectural design of the institution, the Committee pointed to the Lunatic Asylum at Wakefield, England (which, as we have noted, was built on plans submitted by Samuel Tuke). The York Retreat was praised as a model of asylum management, although, being composed of medical men, the Committee took exception to the extreme minimization of medical treatment at the Retreat.

Among the public advantages accruing from the proposed establishment the Committee enumerated these: it would diminish the number of the insane in the State through curative measures; it would relieve the public of a source of danger; it would furnish an opportunity for recovery to the curable, and afford comfort and sympathy to the others; it would provide an economical means of maintaining lunatics at public expense. Last, but not least, it would serve as a valuable school of instruction for Connecticut's medical men.

When, we ask, did Crowther, Haslam and Coxe become familiar with the diseases of the mind? Bethlehem hospital was the great school in which they were instructed. To what source do we owe the masterly sketches of Pinel and Rush? The public charities of Paris and Philadelphia, which furnished the subjects of their observations, have been perhaps of more utility to the world at large than to their respective patients.[26]

The report of the committee—which included Drs. Thomas Miner, Eli Todd, Samuel B. Woodward, William Tully and George Sumner—was approved by the Medical Society at its convention in October, 1821, and a constitution for a "Society for the Relief of the Insane" was drawn up and adopted. The following year a charter, together with a grant of $5,000 toward the erection of the institution (with the proviso that $15,000 additional be raised by subscription) was obtained from the legislature. The subscription campaign proved highly successful. A site was selected at Hartford, and the institution was opened April, 1824, under the name, "The Retreat." Dr. Eli Todd, who had played an active part in founding the institution, was chosen its superintendent.

To the foregoing institutions, established during the first quarter of the century, we should add the Western Lunatic Asylum for the Insane at Staunton, Virginia, established in 1825. Designed to relieve the pressure of overcrowding at the Eastern State Hospital at Williamsburg, and to accommodate mentally ill persons in the western part of the state, to whom the eastern hospital was all but inaccessible, the Staunton asylum was opened July 25, 1828. Virginia was thus the first state to boast of more than one state hospital for the insane. Hardly was the asylum at Staunton opened for the reception of patients when it was filled to capacity, with a large number of applications pouring in, with the result that the authorities were forced to issue an order restricting admission only to those cases "who are either dangerous to society from their violence, or who are offensive to its moral sense by their indecency, and to those cases of derangement where there is reasonable ground to hope that the afflicted may be restored."

In summing up the movement for special institutions for the insane during the first quarter of the nineteenth century, we find such institutions being established in eight different states for the first time. Of these, six were founded as semipublic institutions by incorporated groups, and two were completely under state auspices. A ninth state, Virginia, established its second state hospital during this period. The initiative of laymen was mainly responsible for the establishment of some, and the enterprise of medical men for others.

While these institutions represented great strides forward, they could accommodate but a small fraction of the total number of persons suffering from mental diseases throughout the country. The dependent insane remained almost entirely neglected, although nominal provision for their reception at low rates was made in all existing public and semi-public asylums. In practice most poor law officials

THE RISE OF MORAL TREATMENT

were loath to send their insane charges to these special institutions, being actuated by a sense of narrow-minded economy. In New York State, for example, while the weekly rates offered by the Bloomingdale Asylum for pauper lunatics were as low as two dollars, the dependent insane were being maintained in almshouses and jails throughout the State at costs ranging from fifty cents to a dollar a week per person. In some communities the cost per individual was as low as twenty-five cents weekly; in others, as we shall see, they were disposed of by the barbaric custom of bidding them off on auction blocks to private individuals, sometimes bringing actual profit to towns and communities in exchange for their labor value. Hence, parsimonious communities often refused to send their pauper lunatics to hospitals, even though cure might await them there. On the other hand, too, hospital authorities were frequently reluctant to accept pauper patients at low rates while pay patients were applying for admission.

What of the dependent insane, who remained beyond the pale of hospital treatment?

CHAPTER VII
Retrogression: Over the Hill to the Poorhouse

PROGRESS in social institutions and services seldom, if ever, travels in a straight, unbroken line of ascent. Rather does it follow a tortuous, spiral curve, registering checks and declines, in the road upward toward human betterment. In microcosm, this truth is abundantly reflected in the history of reform in the care and treatment of the mentally ill.

We have noted the centuries-long period of decline that followed the splendid psychiatric pioneering of the Greek and Roman physicians of antiquity. Fifteen hundred years later history was to repeat itself, though on a greatly-reduced scale, when a downward curve checked the progressive trend ushered in by those titans of psychiatry—Pinel, Tuke and Rush. They had supplied a theoretical and practical groundwork sufficient for the building of a vigorous progressive movement. It seemed certain that this movement would be quickly carried forward on an extensive scale. The institutions for the insane established in nine states of the Union during the first quarter of the century, augmenting the two 18th-century hospitals for the mentally ill, seemed to bear out this promise. But the small-scale experiments that they afforded, instead of being immediately carried into general practice, actually remained isolated amid a scene of widespread stagnation, and even retrogression.

The main streams in public provision for the mentally ill continued to flow along the lines of least resistance, their courses determined principally by the dictates of expediency. A general trend toward institutionalization, a natural outgrowth of the increase and centralization of population, manifested itself during this period. The construction of special asylums for the mentally ill was but one minor aspect of this institutionalizing movement which, on the whole, was to take a quite different turn. For the great majority of the insane it meant participation in the long trek over the hill to the poorhouse—that dreary abode which drew all classes of dependents to itself like a magnet.

Most of the states were still without special institutions for the mentally ill in the first quarter of the century. The few that made such provision could accommodate but a pitifully small proportion of the total insane (and a still smaller proportion of the pauper insane) residing within their respective borders. For example, while there was an estimated total of 1,000 insane persons in Connecticut, when the Hartford Retreat was built, the latter institution (which remained the only one of its kind in Connecticut until 1881) had provision for only forty patients upon its completion in 1824. It seems, too, that the dependent insane reaped but little benefit from the existence of corporate institutions such as the Hartford Retreat. Although nominal admission was usually provided for the pauper class, their reception was not encouraged. This general attitude is explicitly stated in the annual report of the Hartford institution for 1830, wherein the medical visitors declare:

> We are glad to learn that the funds of the Institution are gradually augmenting, and we do most anxiously hope that ere long they will enable the Managers to admit a class of recent cases from amongst the poor at a lower rate. This class, however, should not be numerous, as it is by no means desirable that the admissions to the institution should be gratuitous or even fixed for the generality of patients at very low rates. The inevitable consequence of this would be, that towns would crowd into the Institution pauper lunatics in numbers sufficient to fill it, and all other classes would be excluded. This would lower the character of the Institution and greatly diminish its usefulness.[1]

In other states, too, most insane persons who were reduced to the status of public dependents were denied even the meagre curative treatment then available. Besides, cases considered chronic or incurable were invariably excluded from the benefits of hospital treatment. Because of the extremely limited facilities in most institutions only acute, or recent, cases were admitted as subjects for remedial treatment, while some public asylums (like that in Kentucky) frankly existed only for the confinement of "dangerous" persons whose liberty constituted a public menace. It was not until many years later that the question as to whether the chronic insane were entitled to medical treatment was even advanced as a matter meriting serious consideration.

It is a melancholy fact that the great majority of the mentally ill who were public dependents remained unaffected by the great psychiatric reforms of the time. As far as they were concerned time stood still. They were subjected to substantially the same methods of care and treatment existing in the late colonial period. These methods had changed but little in essence, although shifts in emphasis had taken place, corresponding to changing social conditions.

For purposes of public provision, the insane poor were still commonly divided into two categories: the "dangerous and violent" on the one hand, and the "harmless and mild" on the other. As of yore, the dangerous insane were treated little better than criminals, while the harmless were regarded simply as "paupers" indistinct from other classes of public dependents, and dealt with accordingly.

To obtain a true picture of the general treatment of the dependent insane during this period, it is necessary to comprehend the conditions of paupers as a whole. Sick poor, old poor, able-bodied poor, infant poor, insane and feebleminded—all were grouped together under the same stigmatizing label, "paupers", and all were treated in very much the same manner. If, then, we present in this chapter a rather extended analysis of the pauper system as it prevailed in the early decades of the nineteenth century, it is with the understanding that the care of the dependent insane was inseparable from that system. Because of the prevailing lack of classification, and therefore of identity, this important and dramatic phase in the history of the insane has hitherto been generally overlooked or understressed.

Four principal methods of caring for paupers existed at the time: (1) provision in their own homes, usually granted when only partial or temporary public support was required; (2) auctioning off the poor to the lowest bidders, that is, to the person or persons willing to undertake their support at the lowest cost to the community; (3) contracting the support of all paupers to a single individual at a fixed price; (4) support in a public almshouse.

The custom most shocking to modern thought, undoubtedly, was that of placing the poor on the auction block like so many chattel slaves—the only difference being that they were sold to the lowest, instead of the highest, bidder. However barbaric it may appear in our eyes, the system was at that time generally accepted with quite the same complacency that the average Southerner then showed toward the institution of slavery. As a matter of record, the custom of bidding off the poor persisted over a wide area throughout the 19th century and survives to this day, in modified form, in at least one southwestern state. The guiding principle underlying this practice was to get rid of public charges at the lowest possible cost and the least amount of trouble to the community. The custom seems to have originated in the northeastern states, since it was popularly known as the "New England System."

Let us try to picture a typical auction of "town's paupers." The event takes place at the annual town meeting, usually held at the tavern. The "sale" has been widely advertised in advance, and many are present to participate in the diversion. After other business has been disposed of, a town official (sometimes several took turns) mounts the rostrum as the auctioneer. Huddled on the auction block is a ragged, unkempt group—paupers on sale. Men, women and children are there, ranging through all ages. Among them may be seen one or two insane persons. The "town idiot" is in all likelihood present, standing side by side, perhaps, with an epileptic.

In front of the block stand the prospective bidders. They survey the unhappy group of humanity with shrewdly-appraising eyes, calculating the potential labor value of the human chattels about to be auctioned. For it is clearly understood that the successful bidder is entitled to as much work from his charges as he might be able to extract from them. This factor is important. The insane and the feebleminded are often most eagerly sought after, for "strong backs and weak minds" make good farm laborers—and the bidders are invariably farmers. (Remember, the auction system was almost completely confined to rural districts.) Two classes of bidders are usually represented: middling prosperous farmers in search of free labor, and a little sum besides; and men themselves dangerously close to the line of destitution, hoping to get enough funds from the public purse to sustain not only their charges but themselves and their families as well.

The sale commences along lines contrary to ordinary auction procedure, since the bidding progresses downward. But the usual bag of tricks of the auctioneer is not neglected. The amount of potential labor represented on the auction block is artfully set forth as bait, the auctioneer permitting himself a comfortable degree of exaggeration. A plentiful supply of liquor is usually at hand to stimulate the bidding by offering a free drink to the person lowering the price of the previous bidder.

In some communities the system of disposing of the poor at auction did not operate with quite this degree of callous brutishness. At times bond was required of the successful bidder to ensure "decent" treatment to his charges. Incompetent persons and those of dubious character were barred in many instances from participating in the bidding. Too often, however, the posting of bond was regarded as a mere formality. The town authorities breathed a sigh of relief upon seeing a responsibility lifted from their shoulders for another year, and willingly closed their eyes to whatever conduct the purchaser might display toward his charges. Their duty had ended with the successful completion of the auction sale.

Whole families, pauperized through one circumstance or another, were frequently torn apart, as exemplified in the case of the Upton family, the members of which were "vendued" to the lowest bidders at Gardner, Massachusetts, in 1789. A "committee to draw the conditions of sale" was chosen, and Ebenezer Eaton was appointed "vendue master." The rest of this doleful story is contained in the town records of Gardner:

> Oliver Upton and wife bid off by Simon Gates, at ten shilling per week. Oldest child bid off by Simon Gates, at one shilling per week. Second child bid off by John Heywood at ten pence per week. Third child bid off by Andrew Beard, at one shilling, two pence per week. Fourth child bid off by Ebenezer Bolton, at one shilling, nine pence per week.[2]

The poor were usually auctioned off on a yearly basis, though sometimes (as in the above instance) at weekly rates. Some towns sold them *en masse* to one bidder; others bid them off individually at varying prices per person. In the latter case the reckoning depended on how much labor might be extracted from the individual, or how much trouble he might occasion through disability of one kind or another.* At times a particularly robust man or woman might actually be sold at a profit to the town, as witnessed in the records of Fitchburg, Massachusetts, for 1815, when the Selectmen voted to "let out the collection of Taxes, & the Poor, to the lowest bidder:"

> Ephraim Smith, bid off to Benja. Fuller, at 90¢ per week . . . Samuel French, bid off to David Baldwin, for whom, said Baldwin is to give one Cent per week . . . Mary Wares, bid off to Abial Holt, at 60 Cts. per week . . . Rebeccah Smith, bid off to Jos. Carter at 20 Cts. per week . . . Jonas Spaldwin, bid off to Jona. Wheeler at 70 Cts. per week . . . Oliver Upton [the same individual sold a quarter-century earlier at Gardner] bid off to Joseph Phelps at 85 Cts. per week . . . Putnam Perley, bid off to Jona. Thurston, for whom Said Thurston is to give five Cents per week, and is not at liberty to dispose of him to any other person.[3]

*It is stated in the records of the Orphans Court of St. Clair, Indiana, for March, 1808, that "the insane boy Lemay was cried down to Francois Turcotte, for sixty-nine dollars for one year from that date." The custom of farming out insane paupers was practiced in Indiana for many years. (Evelyn C. Adams. "The Growing Concept of Social Responsibility . . . in Indiana." *Indiana Magazine of History,* 1936. v. 32, pp. 1–22.)

The bidding-off system extended throughout the rural districts of the country, and was a dominant form of poor relief for a half-century and more following the birth of the nation. Commenting on this custom, Field, the historian of Rhode Island, makes this pointed remark: "Practically it was offering a reward to the avarice and inhumanity of the man who would consent to neglect them more flagrantly and to inflict upon them a worse abuse than any other man in town could be induced to practice. It was useless to resolve that only the bids of good men should be taken, and that overseers should visit them from time to time, and that bonds should be required from the successful bidders for their proper treatment. Then as now, a bad man was often a good politician . . ."[4]

Another mode of disposing of the poor was the contract system, whereby paupers were placed with individuals—at large, singly, or in families—at fixed prices for their upkeep. This method was far less humiliating than auctioning them off, but probably involved the same amount of routine misery for the poor.

In Kentucky and neighboring states, as we have noted, it was the custom to confine in institutions only those mental cases who were deemed too dangerous to remain at large. As for the "mild" insane, they were usually boarded out with private families at rates set by judges in deciding individual cases, and paid for out of local relief funds. The opening of the Eastern Kentucky Lunatic Asylum at Lexington in 1824 did not seriously interfere with this custom, since the asylum received the "violent and dangerous" insane almost exclusively.

In other states, where almshouses had been established for the reception of insane paupers among others, such a strong prejudice existed against sending dependents to these institutions that public bodies in certain instances were constrained to give official recognition to this deep-rooted prejudice, and to provide alternatives to meet it.

In 1793, for example, one Julian Fowler petitioned the Maryland legislature for monetary aid in supporting her daughter, Rebecca, who was described as "having convulsion fits, is blind, and . . . has in a great measure been deprived of the use of her senses, and that she, her mother, is no longer able to take care of her, but desires to keep her out of the almshouse."[5] The twenty pounds required to keep Rebecca out of the poorhouse was duly appropriated by the obliging legislature. About the same time another petition was presented to the same body by an aged couple, who requested an annual pension so that they could continue to support at home their four imbecile children, "Solomon, aged 30, Sarah and Mary, aged 28 (twins), and Eliza, aged 26."[6]

The pattern of poor relief was still loose and multicolored, but the threads were gradually being drawn together in one direction. The general trend was leading inexorably to institutionalization—toward the poorhouse. The young nation was growing rapidly: new and thriving centers of population were springing up. The old, haphazard ways of communal life, suitable enough for the rough patchwork existence of a pioneer people, were proving vexatious and inadequate in the settled areas. Closer population groupings demanded greater centralization and uniformity in the operation of social services.

To the class exercising its newly won authority, economy and thrift were generally considered as the major virtues in public and private life. Those in public office were constantly striving to attain these desiderata through the introduction of newer mechanisms. Searching inquiries were launched in leading states with the view of ferreting out and eliminating weaknesses in the poor relief structure, and to devise and substitute more efficient methods in their stead.

This tendency in America was greatly stimulated by contemporary affairs in Great Britain, which was still the "mother country" as far as social influences were concerned. There the whole system of poor relief (and this included the care of the dependent insane) had stirred up a great deal of discussion. Indeed, it had become the most disturbing social problem in the land. The great Industrial Revolution, causing sudden changes in the economic relationships of the people and drawing tens of thousands of laborers from the countrysides into the newly-created industrial centers, was leaving in its wake a wide swath of pauperization among the working class. The old poor laws were found to be utterly inadequate in coping with the new conditions and needs. Authorities became distressingly conscious of sharp increases in expenditures: relief was in a hopeless state of confusion. So great became the alarm occasioned by mounting expenses that many leading social welfare theoreticians (quite unaware of the real roots of growing pauperism) called for the total abolition of public poor relief, charging that it created paupers in the process of relieving them. They demanded that charity be restored entirely to private hands, where it had reposed in earlier times. Others, while not subscribing to the extreme view that the poor laws be abandoned *in toto,* felt a need for radical changes. It was inevitable that this clamor (which finally found expression in the famous poor law reforms of 1834) should be reflected across the Atlantic, though the conditions in America were not quite analogous as yet to those prevailing in Great Britain. Demands for investigations into the poor laws, similar to those instituted abroad, were raised in the larger centers of population in the United States.

In 1820 the first state-wide inquiry into the subject was launched in Massachusetts. A legislative committee, headed by Josiah Quincy (who later served as Mayor of Boston and President of Harvard University), was delegated to "consider of the pauper laws of the Commonwealth," and to prepare recommendations for improvement based on their findings. The committee submitted its report the following year. Chief among its recommendations was the erection, on a large scale, of local almshouses equipped with means for providing their inmates with employment. In support of this plan, the committee cited similar conclusions reached by investigating commissions in England, urging the universal establishment of poorhouses as the most satisfactory solution of the pauper problem.[7] This recommendation received the enthusiastic endorsement of many localities in the Commonwealth.

Two years after the Massachusetts investigation into

poor relief was ended, a similar project was initiated in New York by the state legislature, commissioning Secretary of State Yates to direct the inquiry and to prepare a report with a view toward legislative action. This report, submitted in 1824, contains a thorough description of prevailing relief methods, a discussion of abuses, and recommendations for their correction. It is a document of great value.[8] Not only does it present a comprehensive picture of poor relief as it was practiced in New York State more than a century ago, but it also contains interesting accounts of methods employed in other states. Among its important features are the many communications forwarded to the Secretary of State by local poor law officials, describing their methods of administering relief and presenting frank comments on the subject. Documents such as this one, too often underestimated by historians, may shed more light on the social life of a particular period than thousands of generalizations. Since it embodies contemporary trends and views on poor relief generally, together with some direct accounts of the care of the insane, we shall examine this document in some detail.

Many shocking practices were revealed in the report. Among these was the widespread custom of "passing on" unsettled paupers, in health and in illness, from town to town and constable to constable, until they reached their supposed places of settlement. It was usually the policy of officials engaged in this passing-on to rid themselves of their unwelcome charges as quickly and as inexpensively as possible. In the process the least degree of humanity was exercised. The 1824 report dolefully remarks that this barbaric procedure in vogue throughout the states often brought "untimely dissolution" to paupers subjected to it. The mentally ill in particular were victims of the passing-on system, since they could offer little or no defense against the abuses likely to be inflicted upon them by irresponsible individuals.

Another cruel custom was that of "dumping" paupers on other towns by resorting to gangster methods of taking the victim "for a ride." This practice was almost entirely confined to feebleminded and insane paupers. The latter were spirited away in the dead of night and left in strange towns in the hope that their inability to give coherent accounts of themselves would make it difficult, if not impossible, to trace them back to their original places of settlement. This disgraceful method of relieving a town of its proper charge was resorted to with surprising frequency. Often enough a town, itself imposed on through this practice, would show no compunction in repeating it on another, with no concern for the miserable central figure of the drama. Such towns usually found balm for their conscience in the argument that they were justified in rejecting the role of scapegoats.

Complaining bitterly of this practice, the overseer of the poor of Albany, in his communication to Secretary Yates, related the following incident:

> A poor unfortunate lunatic, of the age of eighteen or twenty years, was left in our streets in the winter, and in the night, whose feet were in consequence badly frozen: he could give no intelligible account of himself, but from all circumstances, there was too much reason to believe that this was one of the tricks frequently resorted to by towns, to free themselves of paupers. This young man was of necessity sent to the almshouse, where he remained several months and by the mere accidental admission of a stranger, his residence was ascertained.[9]

A still more revolting example of the shameful custom is described in a letter from a poor law official of Franklin, in Delaware County. Significantly enough, while the account shows the writer to be a humane person, dismayed by the barbarity entailed in "dumping" human stock, he nevertheless accepts the practice as an unavoidable matter of course. Several years previously, he states, an aged stranger traveling through Franklin fell sick and "was partially deranged." He could give no coherent information about himself or his place of residence. Acting on inspiration, however, the officials decided that he might belong to the town of New Berlin, and he was forthwith "dumped" on that town. But New Berlin would have none of him, and litigation was started over the unfortunate lunatic.* After some costly court

---

*Incidentally, these disputes over settlement often proved to be very expensive matters, and represented one of the most glaring evils of the poor relief

procedure, the old man was returned to Franklin. But this failed to weaken the town fathers' determination to lay the stranger at some other town's doorstep, by hook or crook. After another mysterious train of reasoning, the authorities arrived at the "thought"

> that he might belong to the town of Williamstown, in Massachusetts, and their existing laws laying heavy penalties on any person bringing poor persons to that place, gave rise to the propriety of taking him there in a clandestine manner. He was decoyed there in the night, and left, the Lord knows where, *old, deranged* and infirm![10]

In a communication to Yates from the enterprising village of Danville, the authorities reported that a "pauper lunatic" was now ensconced in a small house erected in the public square "for the express purpose of containing the pauper aforesaid." One suspects that the idea of exhibiting the unfortunate person to the gaze of the curious might have been uppermost in the minds of those who built the one-man institution right in the public square. How else can this strange selection of site be explained? One can almost see the village bucks whiling away an idle hour by "teasing the loon" so temptingly at hand.

Most of the rural localities answering the Secretary of State's questionnaire on methods of poor relief stated that they were auctioning their poor to the lowest bidder. The larger communities had already established poorhouses, which they declared with one voice to be far less expensive than the other relief methods. It was also claimed that poorhouses afforded more comfort to the paupers. Among the smaller towns many favored the abandonment of the old methods and the adoption of the poorhouse plan on a county scale. Both economic and charitable arguments in favor of the plan were presented, with the former motive predominating in most replies.

The town of Fairfield favored the establishment of a

system of the period. One town (Ancram) reported in 1824 that it had spent $338 on a single appeal (sufficient to support a pauper for ten years at current rates), while another town (Austerlitz) reported an expenditure of well over $300 on one law suit involving settlement.

poorhouse for these reasons, among others: "The *infirm* could be more readily healed—the *idiot* more humanly provided for—the *lunatic* more securely kept, and the *youth* better prepared for society." In this argument, more humane than most of the others, we nevertheless find expressed the all-too-common tendency of the day to consider the secure confinement of the insane to be the sole end of institutionalizing them.

Not all the towns looked with favor upon the proposal to institute the almshouse system on a universal scale, however. Some were quite satisfied with the alternatives then in use. The town of Chazy, for instance, stated that it had for four years past "sold at public sale all the poor of the town; this mode of proceeding has been the means of lessening the expenses for the support of the poor, from the year 1817, at least two-thirds. For none, except those that are objects of charity, will apply to the town for assistance, and be exposed for sale and liable to labor." Curiously enough, this very argument of deterrent relief was one of the most effective advanced by the advocates of the poorhouse system. The overseer of the poor at Coeymans also found the practice of bidding off the poor a satisfactory one, stating that "we find no method of supporting our poor so *easy* as we now have adopted." A whole social philosophy is implicit in these simple words—a tenacious clinging to the line of least resistance.

From the town of Ghent, where paupers were disposed of under the contract system, came this pointed defense of rugged individualism: "We are informed that the legislature have it in contemplation to pass an act to build a poorhouse in each county. To this we are *decidedly opposed,* as the plan we have adopted to support our poor is the best we can devise. We find that our poor tax is reduced annually . . . We wish to retain our present privilege, that is to support our poor in our own way and not to be associated with any other towns, or the county."[11] Several towns reported that they had already experimented with poorhouses, but had returned to former methods as being less expensive. Hampstead, for example, stated that "this town formerly had a poor-house, but our overseers of the poor found by experience that it cost the town more money than to sell the poor to the freeholders of the said town."*

We have dealt with the views of these representative communities at some length in the belief that they comprise a fair cross-section of the prevailing methods and theories, and also a significant index to the mental approaches of poor law officials to their problems. To them was entrusted, in the final analysis, the fate, safe-keeping, comfort and perhaps cure of the great majority of the mentally ill throughout the country. Whatever the abstract theories formulated during their time may have been, in their hands rested the practical matters of providing for dependents—the insane poor among them. In the opinions of these lowly officials are revealed actualities of existence that too often escape us in evaluating the social patterns of a given period.

On the basis of the partial returns received in answer to his questionnaire, Secretary Yates estimated that there were in New York State more than 21,000 paupers, of whom 6,896 were "permanent," as distinguished from "occasionals," or those who sought only temporary relief. Of the permanent paupers, 446 (more than 6%) were classified as "idiots and lunatics." Yates was emphatically of the opinion that the prevailing poor relief methods were very imperfect, causing great hardship and involving much waste. Like the Quincy committee in Massachusetts, he strongly urged the introduction of a state-wide system of poorhouses as the best medium for administering relief. Each county, he felt, should have at least one such institution, to be maintained at local expense. Requisite to the success of these poorhouses was an adequate provision for employing all its

---

*The general trend to the poorhouse was reversed in a number of localities, both in New York and other states. The town of Dover, Massachusetts, went through an interesting cycle within a short period. Having started by boarding out paupers with private families at fixed monthly allowances, it next adopted the poorhouse system. This method proved unsatisfactory and the building was sold. Dover then turned to the auction system, which was also discarded, and the town returned to the old practice of boarding-out, completing the cycle. (See: Frank Smith's *History of Dover, Massachusetts.* Dover, 1897. 354 pp., p. 245-46.)

inmates able to do some work. "From these general views," he said in summation, "it will be perceived that the adoption of the poorhouse plan in every county is recommended . . . and it may be safely affirmed, that wherever that plan has been fairly tried, the expense of supporting paupers has decreased 33, and in many instances, 50 per cent." In support of this statement the Yates report cited the confirmatory opinions of many officials of other states.

Acting upon the recommendations embodied in the reports of 1821 and 1824, both Massachusetts and New York enacted laws encouraging the erection of poorhouses. As a result of these acts, such institutions soon sprang up in many of the towns and counties of these two great states. In Massachusetts, for example, there were in 1800 only 35 almshouses throughout the state: by 1830 there were more than three times that number, built for the most part in the decade following the Quincy report of 1821.[12]

In New York the legislature passed a far-reaching law in 1824 which made it mandatory for each county not already possessing at least one poorhouse to immediately set about establishing one.[13] Indigent persons applying for relief were to be sent to these poorhouses, where the authorities might demand of them any labor that lay within their capability. The law also provided that individuals convicted as "disorderly persons" might be committed to the poorhouse to serve out their sentences—a provision that clearly indicates the prevailing confusion concerning the proper purposes of a poorhouse.

In the remaining states, too, the trend toward the poorhouses was strong and unmistakable. The events in Massachusetts and New York marked only the culmination of a general and gradual turn to the institutional ideal, the beginnings of which could be traced back to colonial times. In fact, the poorhouse system had become the dominant form of poor relief in several states even before the advent of the nineteenth century. As far back as 1791 Delaware had enacted a law providing for the establishment of almshouses in all its counties. By the terms of this act, support of the poor in any other manner than by confinement in these institutions was proscribed.* By 1830 nearly every state had encouraged the erection of poorhouses, if not actually prescribing this move as mandatory.

At this time the poorhouse system was envisaged as a panacea, where paupers of all grades and classes could be made happy by honest toil; where the more able could shoulder the support of the impotent; where the morale and health of all would soar to new heights—while the taxpayer could regard with satisfaction sharply reduced poor-rates. But, unfortunately for these fond hopes, the poorhouse system, as planned by its early nineteenth century advocates, proved a dismal failure. Designed as a receptacle for all paupers (and frequently petty offenders, too) with no classification or differentiation, its inherent contradictions doomed it to failure from the very first. An institution admitting all ages of paupers who ran the full gamut of physical and mental health (or more correctly, ill health) could scarcely minister successfully to the needs of any one class of inmates, let alone all of them.

The 1820's—that great decade of almshouse planning and building—had hardly passed into history before these catchalls, which were also expected to serve as cure-alls, gave rise instead to even greater evils than those they were supposed to eliminate. For example, the Boston House of Industry, erected in 1823, and generally regarded as the perfect model of the new type of labor-providing poorhouse, was described just ten years later in these disillusioned terms, contained in a report to the Massachusetts legislature:

> When this establishment was commenced, it was intended for the reception and employment of the able-bodied poor, who should claim the charity of this city; hence it was called the *House of Industry* . . . Instead of being a House of Industry, the institution has become at once, a general Infirmary—an Asylum for the insane, and refuge for the deserted and most destitute children of the city. So great is the proportion of the aged and infirm, of the sick insane, idiots and helpless children in it, that nearly all the effective labor of the females,

---

*One county (Sussex), however, was given the privilege of contracting for the support of part of its paupers, provided that the latter recourse proved substantially cheaper than poorhouse care.

and much of that of the males, is required for the care of those who cannot take care of themselves.[14]

The evils inherent in the catch-all almshouse are further revealed in a report, submitted to the New York legislature in 1838, which described conditions in a typical county poorhouse where the superintendent of the poor, far from being more cruel or narrow-minded than his fellows in other counties, actually displayed a degree of intelligence and humaneness above the average. Of 174 inmates in this poorhouse, according to the report, there were ten lunatics and eight idiots. Distribution of the inmates proceeded along the following lines: in one unheated garret room twenty-five men and boys, two of them insane, shared eleven beds between them. Another garret room, likewise without protection against inclement weather and neither lathed nor sealed, contained twelve women and children, including "one female lunatic who has sufficient sense of propriety to keep herself clothed." All occupants of this room were crowded into five beds. Ten women and children were crammed into three beds in one tiny room (17 feet by 9), while another chamber with ten beds was occupied by nineteen persons of all ages and conditions, namely: "two married men and their wives, and one aged colored woman, two male idiots, one very old man, and eleven children." In still another chamber two mentally ill men lay chained to the floor at opposite corners of the room. The institutional officials, in forwarding their report, freely admitted and deplored the unwholesome and inhuman conditions involved in the operation of the almshouse, particularly the impropriety of permitting "idiots and lunatics to occupy the same room with females and children," but added that they were powerless to eliminate or mitigate these evils. "They [the insane and the feebleminded] were sent to us, and the law compelled us to receive them, but neither the law nor any authority under it provided us the place to keep them in a proper manner."[15]

"They were sent to us." These words were fraught with profound significance. The fault was not that of individual keepers or officials or of individual institutions, but of a society that, at best, was indifferent to such conditions, and at worst, actually put the seal of approval on them in the name of that fetich of government—Economy.

Of course, we would get a distorted picture of the almshouse of this period if we were to use dark pigments exclusively in painting it. There were some institutions that overcame, in varying degrees, their initial handicaps by virtue of decent treatment and intelligent management. Many had infirmaries providing medical aid to the inmates suffering physical or mental illness. From almshouse infirmaries like these some of our greatest hospitals developed. Bellevue Hospital in New York, the Philadelphia General Hospital ("Old Blockley"), and the New Orleans Charity Hospital all trace their origin to early poorhouses in those cities. Here and there some system of segregation was attempted by placing the mentally ill in buildings separate from those housing other classes of paupers.

But on the whole, the road that led over the hill to the poorhouse proved to be a *Via Dolorosa* for those unfortunate creatures driven along it. And of the congeries that made up the population of the average poorhouse, the group receiving the brunt of its manifold evils was the group at the very bottom—the mentally ill. Nor was their condition improved during the decades following the fateful '20's. On the contrary conditions grew progressively worse until, in the 1840's and '50's, that remarkable woman, Dorothea Lynde Dix, brought them to the attention of a shocked nation, and then galvanized the nation into constructive action. What she saw in these poorhouses, and what she did about it, will be described in a later chapter.

CHAPTER VIII

The Cult of Curability and the Rise of State Institutions

THE second quarter of the nineteenth century witnessed a remarkable phenomenon in the theoretical approach to insanity. I refer to the introduction and rise of a "cult of curability," involving an astonishing revolution in psychiatric theory in America, with tangible influences on the erection of state mental hospitals during the period of its ascendancy.

Up to the third decade of the century the general attitude regarding the curability of mental disease was dominantly pessimistic. Despite the encouraging experiences of men like Rush in this country, and the Chiarugis, Pinels and Tukes abroad, it was widely believed that insanity was an incurable affliction. "Once insane, always insane," went the popular adage. About 1830, however, the pendulum of opinion on this subject swung violently to the opposite extreme. The old notion that none, or at best very few, of the mentally ill could be cured was suddenly discarded. In its place, the conviction took root that all, or nearly all, were curable. Wild claims on the probabilities of recovery in mental cases were widely circulated and given full credence. "Insanity is the most curable of all diseases," it was dogmatically declared. "At least ninety per cent of all cases of insanity can be cured," it was solemnly asserted. Extravagant claims indeed, when compared with the cold statistics of our time!* These, regrettably enough, indicate that even with our vastly improved methods of care and treatment,

---

*Of course no inference is intended here that 90% curability in mental disease is unattainable in the future. The terms "cult of curability," and

THE CULT OF CURABILITY 133

about 18 per cent of all cases admitted into State mental hospitals may be expected to recover, with an additional 30 per cent improved sufficiently to warrant discharge.

Around the aforementioned over-optimistic notions there grew up a veritable cult of curability, numbering among its devotees not only laymen but most of the superintendents of institutions for the insane. Indeed, it was the latter who contributed the major stimuli to the spread of the fallacy of easy curability. It is a fact that many among the psychiatric fraternity were fully conscious of the error of the doctrine they were advancing, or at least supporting. It may be said in extenuation that some who knew better paid lip service to the idea of large-scale curability in the sincere belief that they were promulgating a "white lie." They hoped thereby to hasten the establishment of more and better institutions for the mentally ill. Others deliberately doctored their statistics, crediting themselves with staggering recovery records, in order to stay abreast of their fellow practitioners who were doing the same thing. A vicious cycle of fallacies was thus kept in motion, fed by the mutual desire, if not necessity, on the part of institutional heads to "keep up with the procession."

For the origins of this significant phenomenon we must turn back to old England, the source of many practices and theories (not all equally commendable) adopted in America. Let us go back to King George the Third whose reign, in certain broader respects, was of great importance in the historical development of the American nation.

George the Third, as we know, experienced periodic attacks of mental illness, the last of which ended in his death. In his early attacks he was attended by a remarkable person, Dr. Francis Willis. The latter was a minister turned physician who specialized in mental disorders and maintained a private asylum, from which he received very lucrative re-

---

"curability myth" used in this chapter refer strictly to the extravagant claims and over-optimistic beliefs, as contrasted to extremely modest actual achievements, of the period under discussion.

The figures on expectation of recovery and improvement are based on the *U. S. Bureau of the Census, Patients in Mental Institutions, 1942* (U. S. Printing Office, Washington, D.C., 1944.)

turns. The monarch reposed great confidence in him and made him chief attendant, over the protests of the regular staff of royal physicians. In the course of the famous parliamentary investigation into the King's illness in 1789 Dr. Willis advanced the startling claim that he cured nine out of every ten mental patients he treated. His assertion had a startling effect on a generation brought up in the belief that lunacy was, with few exceptions, incurable. When asked to furnish proof of his claim he could offer no definite figures on either the total number of patients he had treated or the number that had been cured. When further pressed for specific data he replied that his claim was based mainly on the grounds that the first fifteen patients treated by him had recovered, and that subsequently as many as ten patients at a time had been discharged as cured from his private asylum. His statement was ridiculed by most contemporary physicians, who suspected, not without reason, that Dr. Willis was somewhat of a charlatan. But the boast had an element of dramatic force which left a deep impression.

In 1820 the question of high-percentage recoveries was again brought forward by Dr. George Man Burrows of England in a pamphlet entitled *An Inquiry into Certain Errors Relative to Insanity*. It was one of the major theses of this little work that mental illness was far more amenable to therapeutic treatment than people supposed at the time. To consider insanity incurable was a pernicious error, Dr. Burrows declared. On the contrary, it was highly curable. As proof, he asserted that he himself had cured 81 per cent of all mental patients, including those in "a state of fatuity, idiocy and epilepsy," in his private asylum. Of "recent" cases (meaning cases of less than one year's duration) he claimed to have cured an average of 91 out of a hundred. Dr. Burrows had treated 296 patients, a total which would hardly seem sufficient to draw any generalizations from even if the alleged percentage of recoveries in this particular instance were substantiated. Dr. Burrows' book was widely read at home and abroad, and his contentions seem to have been uncritically accepted by many of his fellow practitioners.

THE CULT OF CURABILITY

Another book written by an Englishman proved a strong stimulus to the spread of the idea of large-scale curability in America. Curiously enough, the author was a man whose interest lay far afield from the subject of insanity, and the book was a tale of personal travels. In the years 1827–28 Captain Basil Hall, a retired officer of the Royal Navy, made a tour through North America. Upon his return to Great Britain he wrote a book on his travels which excited a great deal of interest and discussion.[1] In America he had visited a number of benevolent institutions, including the Retreat at Hartford, Connecticut, and had set down his impressions in his book. Both the Retreat and its superintendent, Dr. Eli Todd (then recognized as the foremost American superintendent of a mental hospital), received his unstinted praise. He spoke of the "noble establishment" as "a model, I venture to say, from which any country might take instruction."[2] In substantiation Captain Hall quoted a startling passage from the report of the Retreat for 1827, to the effect that "during the last year, there have been admitted twenty-three recent cases, of which twenty-one recovered, a number equivalent to $91\frac{3}{10}$ per cent." This phenomenal record was then compared with statistics of the "most ancient and celebrated institutions in Great Britain" which could boast of only 34 to 54 per cent cures of recent cases. Furthermore, the figures in two "highly respectable institutions" in America showed average recoveries in recent cases of only 25 and 31 per cent.

The remarkable claims of the Hartford Retreat very likely would have been buried in the dust-gathering pages of the original report were it not for the adventitious visit of Captain Hall and the remarks made in his widely read book. America had not yet thrown off the yoke of the "colonial complex" which bound her to Britain culturally: opinions of English visitors on American manners, customs and institutions, favorable or otherwise, were still given exaggerated respect. Moreover, in this instance, the commendation from Captain Hall was particularly impressive since his general notes on American life and institutions were so contemptuous as to arouse great indignation on this side of the Atlantic.* Hall's remarks on the Hartford Retreat were repeatedly quoted in the American newspapers and periodicals. Largely because of the publicity received in this roundabout manner the Retreat soon gained the reputation of being the most successfully operated institution for the mentally ill, not only in the United States, but in the whole world. Its unprecedented record of cures became a mark for the other institutions to aim at. A rivalry was thus set afoot which led to a fantastic race for high recovery rates. The immediate effect of the "curability craze" was beneficial in that it proved a potent impetus to the building of mental hospitals in the United States. But from the long-range point of view the fallacy proved to be decidedly injurious. It led to an unhealthy competition among heads of mental hospitals that lasted many years. Grotesque methods of compiling institutional statistics were resorted to in order to keep alive the fiction. Finally, as we shall see, the reaction following the exposure of the fallacy had a decidedly harmful effect on the cause of the mentally ill.

The claims of Willis and Burrows and the impressive record of the Hartford Retreat, founded though they were on the treacherous sands of unscientific statistics, were accepted at face value by an uncritical generation. Skillfully exploited as major arguments for the erection of mental hospitals, they constituted indeed a powerful factor in the asylum-building movement during the 1830's and '40's. Of course there were other factors favoring this trend, some of which have already been described. Not the least among them were the really solid achievements of the early corporate hospitals (Frankford, McLean and Bloomingdale asylums, and the Hartford Retreat itself). These institutions afforded impressive demonstrations of the truth that a fair proportion of the mentally sick *could* be cured. Their exist-

---

*It is interesting to note that when Mrs. Frances Trollope's famous essay in derogation of the American people, *Domestic Manners of the Americans*, was published several years later (1832), it was at first widely attributed to Captain Hall in the belief that he was the only foreigner unjust enough to cast such aspersions on the social life of the country. A saying of the time ran: "Either Captain Hall is Mrs. Trollope in breeches, or Mrs. Trollope is Captain Hall in petticoats."

THE CULT OF CURABILITY

ence did much to dispel the hopeless atmosphere then surrounding the subject of care and treatment of the insane, and contributed to the optimism necessary to the advancement of the hospital idea.

About 1830 a vigorous movement having for its object the erection of suitable state hopitals for the insane manifested itself simultaneously in several states. This movement found its first concrete expression in Massachusetts with the opening, in 1833, of the State Lunatic Hospital at Worcester.

In 1828, following a stirring plea by Horace Mann in which he enunciated the principle that "the insane are the wards of the state," the Massachusetts legislature had appointed a committee to inquire into prevailing provisions for the insane throughout the state. In its report, submitted in 1829, the committee revealed that an intolerable state of affairs existed. Most of the mentally ill were still confined in jails, houses of correction, poorhouses and workhouses, suffering incredible cruelty and neglect. Many who were innocent of any crime had been incarcerated in prisons like common felons for periods ranging up to forty-five years, robbed of all opportunity for therapeutic treatment. This situation, according to the committee, could be properly corrected only through the erection of a state hospital.

The legislature, with unusual promptness, acted favorably on the report. A site was selected at Worcester and a legislative commission was appointed to oversee the building and organization of the projected hospital. In 1832, the commissioners presented a report, drawn up by Horace Mann, which reflected the growing optimism regarding the curability of mental disease. "Until a period comparatively recent," it stated, "insanity has been deemed as an incurable disease. The universal opinion has been that it was an awful visitation from Heaven, and that no human agency could reverse the judgment by which it was inflicted. During the prevalence of this inauspicious belief, as all efforts to restore the insane would be deemed unavailing, they of course would be unattempted . . . It is now abundantly demonstrated that with appropriate medical and moral treatment insanity yields with more readiness than ordinary diseases."[3] This cheering doctrine had passed beyond the realm of mere theory, the commissioners proclaimed. It was already "established by a series of experiments, instituted from holier motives, and crowned with happier results, than any ever recorded in the brilliant annals of science." Where was their proof? They triumphantly pointed to the claims advanced by Willis and Burrows, and to the records of the Hartford Retreat, indicating, cumulatively, that fully 90 per cent of recent cases of mental illness could be cured. Note the extreme to which the pendulum of opinion had swung, in its oscillations between pessimism and optimism! The Worcester State Hospital was opened in 1833, under the superintendency of Dr. Samuel B. Woodward. In accordance with the recommendation of the Mann Committee the first patients were drawn largely from the correctional institutions of the state.

Simultaneously with the agitation for a state hospital in Massachusetts, a similar drive was being pressed in New York. The movement in the latter state was initiated by the liberal governor, Enos T. Throop, in 1830 when he recommended in his annual report the appointment of a legislative committee to study the conditions of the insane. The legislature complied and, after a year of investigation, a committee turned in a long and learned report, ending with an urgent plea for a state hospital such as the one established in Massachusetts that year. The argument of near-perfect curability was again effectively put forward, in terms even bolder than in the Massachusetts commission report. Basing its claims on the statements of Willis, Burrows and the Hartford Retreat—this trinitarian authority was invoked in state after state by the proponents of mental hospitals— the committee sweepingly declared that every case of mental disease was curable, "unless there be some structural defect, some malcomformation of the cranium or the brain."

Knowing the ways of legislators, and the arguments best calculated to sway their judgment, the committee brought forward the argument of easy curability not only on humanitarian grounds, but on the even stronger basis of economy.

As long as custody rather than cure remained the uppermost purpose of institutionalizing the insane (it was argued) hundreds of mental cases were condemned to life confinement, with no opportunity for curative treatment, at the expense of the public treasury. Now, if these persons were provided with hospital attention their stay in institutions, in a large number of cases, would be greatly shortened. In the long run such a situation would result in considerable savings for the state. Moreover, those discharged recovered from a hospital could thenceforth take their places as producing members of society, with further economic benefits accruing to the state.

Condemning the prevalent methods of selling the insane poor at public auction or incarcerating them in jails and in the strong rooms of county almshouses, the committee charged that "the whole system as to pauper lunatics and idiots is radically defective. It makes no provision for recovery. It does not effect the best mode of confinement. It does not sufficiently guard the public from the consequences of furious madness. And it is the most expensive method of providing for them."[4] The legislature, however, was slow to respond to the eloquent plea of the committee, supplemented though it was by the repeated recommendations of Governor Throop and his successor, Governor Marcy. Important material factors were involved in the delay, namely, the financial crisis of 1834 and the severe economic depression of 1837, which turned the attention of the lawmakers to the problems of raising money rather than spending it on "newfangled projects." It was not until 1843 that the first state hospital was finally opened at Utica, with Dr. Amariah Brigham as the first superintendent.*

In the decade between the opening of the hospitals at Worcester and Utica, nine new public hospitals for the mentally ill were opened in various parts of the United States. Seven of these were either state-owned or state-supported institutions. The Tennessee Lunatic Asylum at Nashville

---

*"An Act to Authorize the Establishment of the New York State Lunatic Asylum" was passed March 30, 1836, but the ensuing depression of 1837 delayed its building, and it was not completed until 1843.

was established in 1832 and opened in 1840. The Maine Insane Asylum at Augusta was established in 1834 and opened in 1840. The Vermont Asylum for the Insane at Brattleboro was established in 1835 and opened in 1836. The Ohio Lunatic Asylum at Columbus was established in 1835 and opened in 1838. The Georgia Lunatic Asylum at Milledgeville was established in 1837 and opened in 1842. The New Hampshire Asylum for the Insane at Concord was established in 1838 and opened in 1842. In Pennsylvania, the department for the insane in the first American general hospital was removed to a site in West Philadelphia in 1841 as a separate institution, and was renamed the Pennsylvania Hospital for the Insane, with Dr. Thomas S. Kirkbride appointed as its first superintendent.

All of these institutions were supported either in whole or in part by the several states, although they differed in important essentials in the matters of funding and administration. The state hospitals in Massachusetts, Ohio and New York were built entirely with state funds and administered by state officials. The Vermont Asylum, the name of which was later changed to Brattleboro Retreat, was originally established through a $10,000 bequest of Mrs. Anna Marsh, the state furnishing the additional funds necessary for the completion of the institution.* In pursuance of the terms

*Behind this bequest lies an interesting tale, showing the late survival of the "water-cure" treatment of mental illness. The need for a mental hospital, it appears, was suggested by the death in 1815 of Richard Whitney, a prominent citizen of Vermont who became "mentally deranged" towards the end of his life and who was attended by several physicians, including the husband of Mrs. Marsh. His treatment is thus described by Brattleboro's historian, Henry Burnham: "A council of physicians . . . decided upon trying, for the recovery of Mr. Whitney, a temporary suspension of his consciousness by keeping him completely immersed in water three or four minutes, or until he became insensible, and then resuscitate or awaken him to a new life. Passing through this desperate ordeal, it was hoped, would divert his mind, break the chain of unhappy associations, and thus remove the cause of his disease. Upon trial, this system of regeneration proved of no avail for, with the returning consciousness of the patient, came the knell of departed hopes, as he exclaimed, 'You can't drown love!'

"According to a former version of the story, there was a second application of the drowning process that terminated the life of Mr. Whitney. But Mr. Hooker . . . lately informed us that Mr. Whitney did not pass through a second ordeal by water; the physicians, upon mature deliberation, concluded

THE CULT OF CURABILITY

of the Marsh bequest it was at first operated as a corporate institution, but was reorganized in 1845 as a state hospital. Georgia's first state hospital was founded through a gift of an anonymous "philanthropist from the North." In other states, funds were raised partly by private subscription, by state aid and, in some cases, by contributions from localities chosen as sites for the proposed hospitals. In New Hampshire, for example, the state contributed 30 shares of New Hampshire bank stock, the town of Concord contributed $9,500 to secure the location of the asylum within its precincts, and the rest was raised by private donations. Incidentally, the widespread practice of having towns bid against one another for the privilege and economic advantages accruing from the choice of site proved a serious impediment to the proper location and construction of mental hospitals built on such terms. It happened all too frequently (as in the case of the New Hampshire State Asylum) that a mental hospital would be located in a certain town, not because it offered a salubrious or otherwise advantageous site for such an institution, but merely because it pledged a greater sum toward the erection of the hospital than any other town.

A very unfortunate feature of most of the institutions reared during this period was their cheap and inferior construction. Usually, the building of state institutions was largely controlled by economic considerations. In the desire to keep expenses down to an absolute minimum, essential details of construction and equipment were disregarded. At times the low quality of hospital buildings was attributable to overzealous friends of the insane who, in submitting appeals and plans for new hospitals, presented ridiculously low estimates of cost for fear that adequate estimates would deter the legislators from taking favorable action. A poor institution for the insane, they believed, was

---

they were on the right track, but had not used the proper agent for the stupefaction of the life forces. The next and last resort was opium, and Mr. Whitney died under the treatment." (Henry Burnham, *Brattleboro, Windham County, Vermont*. Brattleboro, 1880. 191 pp., p. 78.)

better than none at all. Furthermore, they often harbored the secret hope that once the ground was broken the state would not be backward in adding to the original appropriations a sum sufficient to assure adequate standards. These men sensed that when proposals for new institutions were being discussed by public officials and legislators the usual determining factor was not how well, but how cheaply, the job could be done.* Another reason underlying the generally poor construction of institutions for the insane was implicit in the prevalent opinion that, since most state hospitals were intended primarily for pauper and indigent patients, the poorest possible accommodations were quite good enough for them. The result was that buildings were often hastily reared, with important therapeutic aids overlooked, and resembled barracks or poorhouses rather than hospitals for the mentally ill. Not that the zeal for economy was in itself a necessarily retrogressive factor: it was the extreme to which that zeal was carried that made poor construction inevitable.† This overemphasis on economy was thus described by one of the foremost mid-century psychiatrists, Dr. Isaac Ray:

> It is regretted that the movement [to induce states to build mental hospitals] has been too much controlled by economical considerations . . . To meet this spirit, estimates of cost have been too low, and, consequently, points have been sacrificed that were absolutely necessary to the perfect attainment of the object. Hence ensued lame and unsatisfactory results calculated to discourage the benevolent and to fill the ignorant with suspicion and distrust. Of course, in undertakings of this kind, economy is not to be disregarded, but when allowed to frustrate or mar an important end, it is no longer a virtue.[5]

*It is a significant commentary on this subject that the architect who planned and designed the Ohio State Insane Asylum (now the Columbus State Hospital) received for his labors the magnificent reward of $35.

†Oddly enough, this period of penny-pinching was followed a generation later by a swirl of wild extravagance, noticeable particularly in the northeastern states. Huge sums were appropriated for mental hospitals. Unfortunately, the greater part of these outlays was used to line the pockets of politically wise contractors and to build ostentatious, heavily ornate façades in the Victorian tradition, with little thought given to suitable interiors or to utility in general. Such public hospitals came to be known as "pauper palaces" and "lunacy cathedrals."

THE CULT OF CURABILITY   143

Of the Worcester State Hospital, which was highly praised for its unusual distinction of having been erected within the limits of the original appropriation, and which was widely followed as a model for mental hospitals, Dr. Ray remarked: "Being intended for the poorer classes, it was unwisely concluded that every subordinate object might be disregarded, provided the principal one—the custody of the patient—were secured. It was the first considerable example of cheap construction, and one, unfortunately, which building-committees have been too ready to imitate."

Besides institutions built by the state, two municipal hospitals for the mentally ill—the first of their kind in America—were built during this period, one at Boston and the other at New York.* The Boston Lunatic Hospital was established in 1837 and opened two years later, in accordance with a legislative statute of 1836, directing the several counties in Massachusetts to maintain "within the precincts of the [county] House of Correction a suitable and convenient apartment or receptacle for idiots and lunatics, or persons not furiously mad." This act grew out of the realization that the Worcester State Hospital could provide for only a small fraction of the mentally ill, and that some sort of provision must be quickly made for the growing numbers of insane poor who could not be admitted or maintained at the sole state institution. Only three counties—Middlesex, Suffolk and Essex—complied with the statute to the extent of building separate receptacles for the mentally ill. The county asylum at Middlesex was soon abandoned; the Suffolk County institution, located in South Boston, was turned over to the city, its name being changed to the Boston Lunatic Hospital; the Essex County Receptacle for the Insane, at-

---

*Before this time, there had been municipal "asylums" connected with local poorhouses, as at Charleston, S. C., Baltimore, Md., Philadelphia ("Old Blockley"), etc. These, however, were merely extensions of the almshouse departments—sometimes separate buildings, more often only wards of wings providing a minimum degree of classification between the mentally ill inmates and the others. The institutions opened in Boston and New York in 1839 were the first of their kind to merit the distinction of mental hospitals, having been built expressly for that purpose.

tached to the local house of correction, remained for many years the only county institution of its kind.

Like the Boston institution, the New York Lunatic Asylum was opened for the reception of patients in 1839. Its beginnings may be traced back to 1826, when separate wards for mentally ill paupers were provided by the city at Bellevue Hospital, then known as "the great pauper institution" of the metropolis. By 1835 the number of pauper insane in New York City had increased to such an extent that the accommodations at Bellevue proved hopelessly inadequate. It was found necessary to provide a structure for this class apart from the hospital. Blackwell's Island in the East River was chosen as a site, and the new city asylum was opened there in 1839.

It may be remarked, in passing, that Charles Dickens, in his historic tour of the United States in 1842, visited both the Boston and New York asylums. His impressions are recorded in the *American Notes,* a book that set the American public aflame with resentment against what was considered "British snobbishness" on the part of its author. For the Boston institution he had naught but the highest praise; of its New York counterpart he painted a dismal and disheartening picture.

Dickens, who made many a careless, and often amusing, slip in his notes, which were written as he ran, referred to the Boston Lunatic Hospital as "the State Hospital for the Insane." Comparing it with the best pauper asylums in England, he characterized the hospital as "admirably conducted on those enlightened principles of conciliation and kindness which twenty years ago would have been worse than heretical."[6] In view of his generally critical attitude towards American institutions, this praise from Dickens was considered praise indeed.

But how differently he described the New York asylum! During his stay in the metropolis, he tells us, he "paid a visit to the different public institutions on *Long Island* or *Rhode Island.*" A slight error may be noted here: the distinguished but geographically-confused visitor was of course referring

THE CULT OF CURABILITY 145

to *Blackwell's* Island! Here is the Dickensian description of the newly opened lunatic asylum:

> I cannot say that I derived much comfort from the inspection of this charity . . . I saw nothing of that salutary system which had impressed me so favorably elsewhere; and everything had a lounging, listless, madhouse air which was very painful. The moping idiot, cowering down with long, dishevelled hair; the gibbering maniac, with his hideous laugh and pointed finger; the vacant eye, the fierce wild face, the gloomy picking of the hands and lips, with munching of the nails: there they were all, without disguise, in naked ugliness and horror. In the dining-room, a bare, dull, dreary place, with nothing for the eye to rest on but the empty walls, a woman was locked up alone. She was bent, they told me, on commiting suicide. If anything could have strengthened her in her resolution, it would certainly have been the insupportable monotony of such an existence.[7]

The general confusion characterizing the construction and management of institutions for the mentally ill during this period was reflected in the methods of reporting statistics on recovery rates and other matters. The science of statistics was still in its infancy, and its application in the various fields of social phenomena was generally of a crude character. The excellent pioneering work of Esquirol (the worthy successor of Pinel at the Salpêtrière in Paris) was particularly effective in demonstrating the value of tabulating mental hospital records. There was, at first, a great deal of stubborn opposition to the introduction of statistical reporting. Many asylum superintendents ridiculed the idea. It was utter nonsense to attempt any kind of "enumeration," they felt. Some authorities based their opposition to statistical reporting on the quite reasonable grounds that real knowledge concerning mental diseases—classification, causes, symptoms, cures, etc.—was still so meagre that no degree of accuracy could be attained through the use of statistical recording. In fact, they said, such reporting could only create misleading impressions. (This actually proved to be the case.) A heated controversy on this score was carried on throughout the 1840's, with Pliny Earle leading the statistical defenders. In an article published in 1849, Dr. Earle vigorously championed the use of enumeration against the attacks of sceptics. Admitting the prevailing weaknesses in statistical reporting on the part of American institutions, he wisely counseled that it was necessary not to abolish the practice, but to raise it to a really scientific level.[8]

A glance at the records emanating from mental hospitals during the period under discussion explains much of the pessimism as to the utility of statistics in this field. Institutional tabulations were generally vague, contradictory and woefully lacking in either uniformity or precision of data. Take the tables of "Causes" of mental cases, which naturally occupied a prominent place in contemporary case reports. In the tabulated report of a famous institution, the ailments of five different mental patients were respectively attributed to "domestic trouble," "jealousy," "infidelity of wife," "ill-treatment of parents," and "abuse of husband." These blurred distinctions, it will be agreed, were hardly calculated to throw light on the individual cases. In some tables, the laconic etiological note, "disappointment," was conveniently used to cover a multitude of ills. Others, with a greater attention to detail, but with hardly less confusion, laboriously enumerated the various types of "disappointments" regarded as the determining causes in many cases of mental illness: "disappointed love," "disappointed affection," "disappointed ambition," "disappointment in business," "frustrated enterprise," etc. Even the term "disappointed expectation" was entered as a supposed cause. Among other vague "causes" listed in contemporary statistics were: "ecclesiastical difficulties," "mental excitement," "mortified pride," "perplexity in investigating scriptural prophecies," "novel reading," "tobacco," "ill health," "repelled eruption," "blasted prospects," "dread of a future state," "close mental application," and "Millerism."*

---

*"Millerism" was the popular name given to the doctrines of William Miller, who founded the Adventist sect in 1831. Miller predicted that the year 1843 would witness the end of the world and the commencement of the millennium. His prediction gained a remarkably wide circulation and acceptance, and many suicides were attributed to the terror induced by belief in its inevitable fulfillment. It undoubtedly was a precipitating factor in many cases of mental illness. In one year, 1843 (the year which Miller had prophesied

THE CULT OF CURABILITY

Another interesting feature found in early mental hospital statistics is an exaggerated emphasis on quantitative data. In general, this insistence on the importance of quantitative analysis was to exert a healthy influence. But in some instances it was carried to strange extremes. For example, the first annual report (1843) of the Utica State Asylum contains a table intended to serve as conclusive proof of the health-promoting effects of the institution, scrupulously measured in terms of masses. We present a specimen item from this table:

Total weight on admission of 276 patients	34,856 lbs.
" " of those discharged and remaining, December 1st	35,825 "
Increase in weight of all received	1,029 "
Total increase in weight of the 53 patients discharged cured	306 "

Still another indication of the prevailing looseness and confusion in statistical reporting may be mentioned. In 1844, Dr. J. R. Allen, a deservedly well-known superintendent of the Eastern Lunatic Asylum at Lexington, Kentucky, set himself the ambitious task of compiling the statistics of the institution for the first twenty years of its existence. After listing an impressive percentage of patients "cured" during this period, Dr. Allen naïvely remarked that a large proportion of these "cures" were not actually so registered on the books, but that he had reported them "recovered" because there was no record of their condition at the time they were discharged!

Shocking though this might be to modern statistical standards, it constitutes but a mild indication of the liberties taken with figures during the heyday of the curability cult.

We have traced, previously, the origin and early development of the cult of curability from Willis to the 1827 report

would witness the destruction of the universe), no less than 32 patients admitted into three different Northern institutions were officially recorded as victims of "Millerism."

of the Hartford Retreat, given wide publicity through the rather extraordinary medium of a light travel book written by a retired British naval officer. The pleasing belief in easy curability which consequently took hold of the popular imagination was strengthened with the years as statistical reports seemed to prove that other institutions for the insane were not only equalling but actually surpassing the Hartford Retreat record of 90 per cent cures. In fact, the climax was not reached until the claim of 100 per cent cures was finally advanced by at least two eminent superintendents of mental hospitals!

To what may we attribute these remarkable records, besides which our modest present-day claims of an average of about 15 per cent recoveries in institutionalized mental cases compare like candles to the sun? Is it because mental diseases were then of a less serious nature than they are today, and more amenable to treatment? Or was the system of therapeutics practiced in that period superior to present-day methods? Hardly. Where, then, may we properly seek an explanation of the phenomenal records of cures rolled up in the decades following 1830? Mainly, I think, in these directions: (1) the irresponsible, artless manner in which statistics on the subject were compiled; (2) the peculiar set of circumstances which encouraged institutional officers to perpetuate a fallacy of which many were conscious; (3) the convenient use of the term "recent" cases (meaning cases of anywhere from three to twelve months duration), upon which most generalizations regarding curability were based; (4) the confused notions as to the meaning of the word "recovery." Even today, the latter term when applied to mental diseases, necessarily lacks the precision that it connotes in most physical diseases. In the middle decades of the nineteenth century, many superintendents of mental hospitals waited only for a temporary return to "sanity" on the part of a patient to discharge him as "cured," and to record him accordingly.

Let us pursue the interesting history of the cult of curability subsequent to the Basil Hall incident. As has been noted, the record of the Hartford Retreat was brought forward by the friends of the insane in many states as a major argument in favor of establishing mental hospitals. To the legislators it proved an impressive point: obviously, great savings would result in building a hospital where the mentally ill could be cured easily and rapidly, instead of placing them in non-curative institutions where they would most likely remain heavy burdens on the public purse for life. Once such a hospital was built, the superintendent was expected to emulate the achievements in high-recovery rates which had been so vociferously brought forward before its founding, or to face severe criticism and perhaps discharge.

Such was the case with the Worcester State Hospital, the first to be erected in the 1830's. It was no accident that the Massachusetts authorities cast their eyes in the direction of the Hartford Retreat in seeking a suitable head for the new institution. Their choice fell first on Dr. Eli Todd, superintendent of the Retreat, who was forced to decline the offer because of ill health. (Dr. Todd died in 1833.) Dr. Samuel B. Woodward, active in the founding and management of the Retreat, was then appointed. This proved to be a fortunate choice. From his ascendancy to the head of the Worcester institution to his retirement in 1846, Dr. Woodward was generally regarded, both at home and abroad, as the leading American authority on mental diseases.

Statistically, however, the attempt to emulate the Hartford Retreat record of cures got off to a poor start in the first year. Even with some loose handling of statistical data, the institution's first annual report showed less than 50 per cent recoveries of recent cases in relation to admissions. The hospital authorities expressed their apologies for this supposedly low proportion of cures, explaining it on the grounds that many incurables had been transferred from jails and poorhouses to the institution during the first year. In the second year, however, the officers found an ingenious device for stepping up the statistics of recovery to a respectable level. They adopted the simple but quite effective expedient of calculating the percentage of cures, not on the basis of the total number of patients *admitted* during the year, but of the total *discharged*. Thus, they were able proudly to declare in their annual report to the legislature:

> During the past year 119 patients have been received into the hospital; of these, fifty-five were old cases, and sixty-four, recent ones. In the same period 115 have been discharged; of these, forty-nine were old cases and sixty-six recent ones. Of those discharged, sixty-four were cured . . . The cures amount to 55¾ per cent . . .
>
> Of the forty-nine old cases discharged during the year, ten have been cured, sixteen improved, fourteen are stationary, four have died, and one has eloped—the cures amounting to 20½ per cent.
>
> Of the sixty-six recent cases, fifty-four have been cured, six improved, two stationary, and four have died—*the cures amounting to 82¼ per cent.*[9] (Emphasis mine—A.D.)

This method of computing the percentage of cures on the basis of discharges instead of admissions naturally resulted in figures bound to impress. Average cures amounting to more than 55 per cent, and cures of recent cases to more than 82 per cent, compared very favorably even with the vaunted Hartford Retreat. They overshadowed by far the more cautiously compiled records of eminent European institutions, and the authorities were not backward in pointing out this element of apparent superiority in their report. Of course, they conveniently neglected to explain the different techniques employed in arriving at these ratios. The observant eye, to be sure, could apprehend the unorthodox tabulating devices of the Worcester Hospital, but to the untrained and casual general reader the proportion of cures claimed was accepted at its face value.

During the next few years, the recovery percentages at Worcester mounted steadily until, in 1840, Dr. Woodward announced that the cures in recent cases (in proportion to the total discharged) had reached the awe-inspiring point of 90 per cent.

The belief, based on the reports of cures of recent cases, that insanity was easily curable if treated early enough, rapidly impressed itself on the public and professional mind and soon reached the plane of established, immutable dogma. But what of the psychiatric profession as a whole?

THE CULT OF CURABILITY

Did it raise any objections to the spread of this fallacy? On the contrary: except for a very few instances, it not only subscribed wholeheartedly to the current misconceptions but stimulated and strengthened them as best it could. Let us cite a few representative opinions from the most eminent medical superintendents of the day as an indication of the lengths which the delusion reached. As early as 1835, Dr. Woodward made this categorical statement, which was widely quoted for many years after: "In recent cases of insanity, under judicious treatment, as large a proportion of recoveries will take place as from any other acute disease of equal severity."* Two years later Dr. Amariah Brigham, who soon after became the first superintendent of the Utica State Asylum, declared in an article appearing in the *North American Review:* "It is gratifying to be able to state that no fact relating to insanity appears better established than the general certainty of curing it in its early stage." Quite as optimistic was the declaration of Dr. Luther V. Bell, head of the McLean Asylum in Massachusetts, who, in his annual report for 1840, averred: "The records of this Asylum justify the declaration that *all cases, certainly recent*—that is, whose origin does not, either directly or obscurely, run back more than a year—recover under a fair trial. This is the general law; the occasional instances to the contrary are the exception." Even the famous superintendent of the Pennsylvania Hospital for the Insane, Dr. Thomas S. Kirkbride fell victim to the infectious cult of curability. In his report for 1842 we find this grave assertion: "The general proposition that truly recent cases of insanity are commonly very curable, and that chronic ones are only occasionally so, may be considered as fully established." Dr. Pliny Earle, who later did more to explode the curability fallacy than any other individual, wrote in his report for

---

*Eight years later, Dr. Woodward's optimism regarding curability progressed sufficiently to permit him to go even beyond this comparison. In his annual report for the Worcester Hospital in 1843, he states: "I think it not too much to assume that insanity, unless connected with such complications [epilepsy, paralysis, or general prostration of health], is *more* curable than any other disease of equal severity; *more likely* to be cured than intermittent fever, pneumonia, or rheumatism." (Emphasis mine—A.D.)

1845 as attending physician of the Bloomingdale Asylum in New York: "When the insane are placed under proper curative treatment in the early stages of the disease, from 75 to 90 per cent recover."*

The significance of these quotations is enhanced when we realize that all those we have cited were among the founders of the American Psychiatric Association, organized in 1844; that they were all prominent in their profession; and that their views were substantially endorsed by all their contemporaries in America. In some of the general declarations of easy curability advanced by medical superintendents, cautious qualifications appeared, but even in such instances the qualifying words were lost on the general reader whose attention was usually focussed on the high-percentage recovery figures to the exclusion of all else.

Meanwhile, institutions for the insane continued to engage in a fierce, if concealed, rivalry with one another in setting up impressive recovery tables. Higher and higher rose the claims of cures, reaching fantastic heights, even dwarfing the claims of Willis and Burrows and the record of 1827 which had suddenly catapulted the Hartford Retreat into world prominence. Well into the 90's soared the percentages of cures claimed in recent cases. It only waited for some enterprising superintendent to ring the bell at 100 per cent. In his 1842 report as head of the Eastern Asylum for the Insane at Williamsburg, Virginia, young Dr. John M. Galt made a conditional claim to this ultimate result. Of thirteen cases of recent insanity which had been admitted to the institution during the preceding year, he declared, twelve, or 92.3 per cent of the total, had been discharged cured. The thirteenth patient had inconsiderately died, apparently causing the hospital to fall just one short of the perfect goal. But with the characteristic intrepidity of the time, our youth-

*In his first report as medical head of the Bloomingdale Asylum (1844) Dr. Earle had written: "It appears to be satisfactorily proved that, of cases in which there is no eccentricity or constitutional weakness of intellect, and when the proper remedial measures are adopted in the early stages of the disorder, no less than eighty of every hundred are cured. There are but few diseases from which so large a percentage of the persons attacked are restored."

THE CULT OF CURABILITY

ful superintendent was resolved not to let this factor stand as a serious obstacle in the way of the perfect score. With disarming naïveté, he dismissed the demise in this fashion: "If we deduct this case from those under treatment, the recoveries will amount to 100 per cent!"* Carried away by the achievement thus obtained, he concluded: "From such facts as the above, I am led to believe that there is no insane institution, either on the Continent of Europe, in Great Britain or in America, in which such success is met with as in our own."

However, this remained a conditional record. The maximum unconditional claim was yet to be pronounced. It was not long in forthcoming. In the very next year, 1843, Dr. William M. Awl of the Ohio State Lunatic Hospital at Columbus announced the attainment of the *ne plus ultra* in a laconic finale to his statistical report: "Per cent of recoveries on all recent cases discharged the present year, 100." Note the fact that here, as in the case of Woodward of Worcester, the ratios are based on *discharged* cases, and not on admissions. Howbeit, the record advanced by Dr. Awl, the distinguished head of the Ohio institution, gained him the sobriquet, among contemporary wits, of "Dr. Cure-Awl."

By this time, however, voices of protest were beginning to be raised against the excesses of the cult of curability. These voices were feeble and cautious at first, but gained strength and numbers with the passage of time. Dr. Isaac Ray, in his first report as superintendent of the Maine Insane Asylum in 1841, voiced his dissatisfaction with the misleading and wholly arbitrary practice of separating the mentally ill into "recent" and "old" cases, a practice which formed one of the main pillars in the structure of mathematical curability. "I have adopted this classification," he said, "in deference to the practice now somewhat common

*Dr. Galt was by no means lacking in precedent for making this deduction from his computations. It was not unusual for institutional heads to put aside the dead in figuring the proportions of cures, in order to give their statistics a more impressive dressing. Carried to its ultimate conclusion, this practice would permit institutions listing one recovery and ninety-nine deaths out of 100 recent cases to claim 100 per cent cure!

in New England hospitals; but I must be allowed to express my conviction that the distinction is without any precise, well-marked difference, and had better be abandoned." In his next report he added: "Nothing can be made more deceptive than statistics; and I have yet to learn that those of insanity form any exception to the general rule." So strong, however, was the current of the curability mania that Dr. Ray felt constrained to swim along with the tide as far as his statistical reports were concerned, employing under protest the methods of his contemporaries in achieving high recovery rates. About 1850, a number of critics of the prevailing statistical fallacies arose among asylum superintendents. Prominent among these early protestants were Dr. James Bates, successor of Ray at the Maine Insane Asylum, Dr. S. Hanbury Smith of the State Asylum at Columbus, Ohio, and Dr. Andrew McFarland of the New Hampshire Asylum at Concord.

In 1845, Dr. John Thurnam, resident medical superintendent of the York Retreat in England, published a book entitled *Observations and Essays on Statistics of Insanity*, wherein he came to rather gloomy conclusions regarding the curability of mental diseases. Basing his remarks on a study of case histories of 244 persons treated at the York Retreat, he formulated this generalization:

> In round numbers, of ten persons attacked by insanity, five recover and five die, sooner or later, during the attack. Of the five who recover, not more than two remain well during the rest of their lives; the other three sustain subsequent attacks, during which at least two of them will die.

This conclusion, based on painstaking statistical research, had a chastening effect on institutional "enumeration" not only in Great Britain (where the tendency to exaggerate recovery rates also prevailed, though to a lesser extent) but in the United States as well. Superintendents began to tone down curability statistics, or to drop them from their reports entirely. (Dr. Kirkbride of the Pennsylvania Hospital was among the first to adopt the latter course.) The cult of curability, which had reached its peak between 1840

THE CULT OF CURABILITY

and 1850, experienced a gradual deflating process. The pendulum began to swing back to the opposite extreme. So far backward did it swing, in fact, that Dr. Luther Bell, whose confident belief in 90 per cent curability we have quoted, expressed this radically different point of view in 1857: "I have come to the conclusion that when a man once becomes insane, he is about used up for this world."

The curability cult lingered on for many years, however. To Dr. Pliny Earle, who was one of its early devotees, must be given the credit for dealing the fallacy its deathblow. Possessing an inquisitive and thoroughgoing turn of mind, Dr. Earle began to question the validity of contemporary statistics on curability. His doubts deepened with time, and finally led him to enter upon a comprehensive study of the matter. He spent years of intensive research, going far beyond the limits of Dr. Thurnam's work. The complete records of many American institutions for the insane were carefully combed by the indefatigable Earle. The first results of his many years of investigation were published in the annual report of 1875 for the Northampton State Hospital in Massachusetts, of which Dr. Earle was then superintendent. Additional installments appeared in later reports, and were finally gathered together in a book, *The Curability of Insanity,* published in 1887.[10] The revelations contained in these studies had a profound and healthy influence on the subsequent course of statistical reporting in American mental hospitals.

A major factor in the apparently high ratio of cures in institutions for the insane, Dr. Earle found, lay in the abuse of the word "recovered," and in the failure to distinguish properly between the words "case," "patient," and "person." In many instances, the same person was discharged "recovered" from an institution a number of times within a few years, or even in the space of one year. In the statistical reports of the time, the reader was given no intimation that the same *person* might appear as several "recovered *cases*" in the record. Thus, Earle relates, one woman was discharged recovered six times at the Bloomingdale Asylum, and another seven times at the Worcester Hospital, each within the space of one year. Incidentally, the woman who contributed six "recoveries" to the record of Bloomingdale in one year was reported cured no less than *forty-six times* before her death—which took place in an insane asylum! Dr. Earle also discovered that the obliging woman who recovered seven times in one year for the greater glory of Worcester had been discharged as cured nine times in the two preceding years, making sixteen recoveries in three years.

The records of other institutions were replete with similar cases. In five asylums the records of which were examined by Dr. Earle, *forty* persons were reported cured no less than *484* times, averaging more than twelve recoveries each. Three women alone were admitted as patients into mental hospitals an aggregate of 118 times, and were discharged recovered, and placed in the records as such, 102 times. Two of these finally died insane. In one institution, seven women were reported recovered a total of ninety-two times. Naturally, the uninitiated reader took it for granted that the number of cases was identical with the number of persons admitted, and since the statistics were very seldom accompanied by explanations pointing out this vital difference, he readily fell victim to the fallacy. No wonder that the English medical superintendent, Sir James Coxe, in discussing institutional statistics on the insane, wrote of "that spirit of inflation which is a too prevalent characteristic of writers of this branch of medicine." No wonder that the American, Dr. James Bates, dryly noted that "they [statistical reports of cures] were received with wondrous admiration by that portion of the public who are better pleased with marvellous fiction than with homely truth."

But the myth of easy curability lasted long and died hard. Its tenacious survival is indicated by the fact that, when Dr. Earle began publishing his epochal studies on recovery statistics in 1875, most establishments for the mentally ill in America still subscribed to the hypothesis that insanity was easily curable. His findings were bitterly attacked (with more emotion than reason) by many of his contemporaries, including some leading medical superintendents. The wealth of evidence he brought forward, based on years of exhaustive research, created an impregnable wall of proof. But this fact did not save Dr. Earle from the calumnies of men who found offense in conclusions tending to destroy a convenient, comfortable and long-standing hypothesis, erroneous though it may have been.

Once the cult of curability was dealt its death-blow, however, a period of reaction set in, the unfortunate effects of which are still observable today. Disillusioned, the public cast off the cloak of false optimism that had been woven with the warp of error and the woof of short-sighted opportunism. Instead, popular opinion respecting the curability of insanity became mantled in extreme pessimism. And long after a real basis for optimism was established with the firm materials of scientific knowledge, the ancient saying, temporarily discarded during the curability craze, once more echoed a dominant attitude: "Once insane, always insane!"

CHAPTER IX
Dorothea Lynde Dix—Militant Crusader

ON A winter's day in the year 1841, a young theological student knocked hesitantly at the door of the home of Miss Dorothea Lynde Dix in Boston. He was ushered in. Embarrassed, he stood in the presence of Miss Dix, quietly dominant, a retired school teacher nearing forty, her raven-black hair combed back and knotted. The young man immediately plunged into the business that had brought him to her house. His class at the seminary had been assigned Sunday-school instruction at the East Cambridge jail, and he had been chosen to conduct a class among the women inmates. He felt unsuited to the task, too self-conscious. His mother had advised him to solicit Miss Dix's counsel. After pondering for a few minutes, Miss Dix replied with quiet decisiveness: "I will take them myself." The bewildered theologue protested, but in vain.

The next Sunday found Miss Dix at the East Cambridge jail. She was shocked by the filth and dirt, the evidences of negligence and brutality, that she saw all about her. Particularly did she notice the presence of insane persons locked up in cells. What were they doing here, these innocents, in a place intended not for cure or even for care, but for punishment? It was the dead of winter, yet no warmth at all was provided for these insane inmates. They lay huddled in their unheated cells, the cold piercing them like knives. To most others, the sight might bring a sigh of sympathy and a shrug of impotency: no more. But this woman was made of rarer stuff. She raged at the denial of elementary shelter to the insane. She approached the keeper and demanded that heat be immediately supplied to the helpless inmates.

The answer was contemptuous: "The insane need no heat." (The myth that the insane are insensible to extremes of heat or cold was widespread.) With characteristic thoroughness, Miss Dix carried the issue to the East Cambridge court. Her petition was granted; the insane got heat.

A rather trivial incident, this, but it marked the beginning of a long crusade without parallel in American annals. It transformed a retired New England school teacher, seemingly fated to go through life silently and unknown, into a fiery, world-famous standard bearer in a unique cause. For forty years thereafter she journeyed through the land, this apostle of the insane, spreading the gospel of humane treatment for the mentally ill. She built, instead of churches, hospitals where lost minds might find regeneration. At the end of her unusual career she left more than thirty mental hospitals in her native land and abroad, founded or enlarged as a direct result of her personal efforts—majestic monuments to her crusading genius. World-renowned in her own time, it is surprising that this woman, one of the most remarkable America has produced, is hardly known to her countrymen of the present generation.

Little is known of Miss Dix's early years. The cloak of obscurity which she tried desperately to throw over this period of her life indicates its unhappy character more eloquently than the minutest detail could. "I have never known childhood!" she once exclaimed. And the few recorded facts concerning her child life give meaning to that bitter cry.

She was born April 4, 1802, at Hampden, Maine, her parents removing to Worcester, Massachusetts, while she was yet an infant. Her father seems to have been a ne'er-do-well—shiftless, poverty stricken and irresponsible. He was fanatically religious, with a penchant for writing theological tracts in fits of "inspiration," pointing the way of salvation to an indifferent world. The dull, tiresome task of stitching and pasting these fanatical tracts was assigned to Dorothea and the other children, while father Dix waited for further messages from God. To a nature as intense, life-loving and sensitive as Dorothea's, the stifling, joyless atmosphere in the Dix household became increasingly intolerable. At twelve, unable to endure it any longer, she ran away to her grandmother's home in Boston, where Madam Dix dwelt in fairly comfortable circumstances.

Here she received none of that warm understanding and companionship her hungry soul craved, and for the want of which she had run away. Instead, during the next two character-forming years, Dorothea was subjected to a rigorous Spartan discipline that must have seared the soul of the sensitive girl, but proved invaluable in steeling her for her destined work. Madam Dix had stern ideas about one's diligence to duty. In her Puritan mind, all life was summed up in that one word—Duty. She regarded the least manifestation of emotion as an unmistakable sign of moral weakness, and did her utmost to stamp out every trace of it in her granddaughter. Besides, she saw in Dorothea one of Saturday's children, who was fated to work her own way through life. Let other girls indulge in time-wasting fancies and recreations: this one was marked for heavy burdens, and a sense of realism dictated that she be prepared to assume them as soon as possible. And so, scarcely had she come into her 'teens than maturity was precipitated upon her. If she had never known childhood, neither was she ever to know the glamor of adolescence except for a few stolen moments, hastily snatched.

At fourteen Dorothea returned to Worcester, where she opened a school for little children. To affect a grown-up appearance, the child-teacher took to wearing long skirts, long sleeves, and other outward signs of maturity. These trimmings proved superfluous, however. As her biographer Tiffany points out: "She bore the stamp of authority from the start. Herself brought up in a stern school, she had at that date little idea of any government but the government of the will. Indeed, it is always characteristic of very young people, abruptly forced to play the role of maturity and experience, that they overdo things. . . . Thus, the impression left on the minds of the little girls and boys in Worcester by their fourteen-year old teacher, so far from being that of a half-grown girl they could trifle with, was that of one of whom they stood in fear."[1] Here was a nature born to rule—strong, imperious, assertive—revealing itself at this early date with perfect clarity. Unfortunately, the severe regimen she imposed proved unbearable to her pupils. One by one they dropped out: this first venture ended in dismal failure.

Upon the collapse of her enterprise, Dorothea returned to her grandmother's, where she continued her education under the same Spartan auspices as before. In a few years she felt prepared to resume her pedagogic career, and opened a school for older pupils in Boston. In this project she was markedly successful. Soon the Dix mansion itself was converted into a combined day and boarding school presided over by Dorothea. Although frail and sickly, she seemed to possess an unlimited supply of energy. She was an indefatigable worker—frequently up before dawn to commence her varied and arduous tasks, and keeping at them until the midnight hour. To her combined duties of boarding-school administrator and teacher, head of a household, and mother to her two younger brothers (whom she had taken under her protective wing at the Dix mansion), she added a charity school, conducting classes for poor children in a converted barn.*

Miss Dix must have gained quite a reputation as an educator, for soon the leading families in Boston were sending their children to her school. In 1827 Dr. William Ellery Channing, one of the most influential figures in that cultural movement in New England which was featured by the rejection of narrow Puritanism and the introduction of a new humanism in American thought, invited her to tutor his children during the summer months. The offer was accepted and for several years she spent her summers in the stimulating atmosphere of the Channing household. Dr. Channing was a noble and inspiring humanitarian, and for him Miss Dix conceived an admiration and respect closely bordering on hero worship. His lofty ideals of service to his fellow men did much to awaken her own latent impulses, and helped

*Free public schools were almost non-existent at that time: poor children were wholly dependent for education on privately operated charity schools.

give direction to the career she eventually followed. The influence of Dr. Channing (and the movement with which he was identified) was undoubtedly great.

Until 1836 Miss Dix conducted a model day and boarding school with splendid success, and with an intensity that seemed to belie her frail physical health. But finally the strain proved too great, and she suffered a severe physical breakdown. Death seemed perilously near at that moment. Many of her friends shook their heads sadly and gave her up for lost. But she managed to pull through. When she was well enough to move about once more, her doctors ordered her to give up teaching at once and to seek rest and recuperation abroad. A trip to England followed, and in the ensuing eighteen months, spent at the home of kindly English friends, she experienced for the first time in her life the bliss of complete relaxation.

Miss Dix returned home greatly refreshed, though still weak. Her strenuous life seemed definitely behind her. A generous bequest from her grandmother (who had died several years before), together with accumulated savings, gave assurance of a comfortable income for life. It appeared logical for her, as a New England spinster of modest circumstances, delicate health and pedagogic background, to continue teaching on a greatly reduced scale—as a hobby rather than as a profession—and to indulge in little acts of personal charity so common to her kind. And that is exactly what Miss Dix proceeded to do on returning to her native land. Surely, it seemed, finis had been written to her period of intense activity: now this woman would be content to live the remainder of her life in a narrowing orbit, and pass quietly through the years to the final obscurity of a New England spinster-teacher.

There was up to this time nothing in her past life to indicate the role that lay in store for her. She was nearing forty. How could she sense that all her past was to be but the prelude to a new life? Or that she would yet break new trails in the service of humanity, trails that would carry her far beyond the confines of New England and would lead across two continents? True, she may have been aware of the fire of reform that lay smoldering within her, awaiting only a spark to set it into blazing activity. But where was that spark, would it ever come? It did—and, as often happens in the careers of outstanding men and women, it came in the form of a quite inconspicuous event—at that jail in East Cambridge.

To properly comprehend the course that Dorothea Lynde Dix thereafter pursued, it is well to understand the social factors which conditioned it. Miss Dix was not a "sport" of history. She was the product of a particular environment that shaped both her personality and her ends. The famous feminist, Frances E. Willard, tells us that once, while gathering biographical material about Dorothea Dix, an acquaintance remarked: "It seems to me she was a New England woman." "That goes without saying," was Miss Willard's comment. "In those early days no other woman would have dared attempt what she so gloriously performed."[2]

Yes, she could only have been a product of New England, at a particular stage of its cultural development. It was the time of a great cultural revival which found fullest expression during the thirty years preceding the Civil War, and produced such outstanding figures as Emerson, Channing, Thoreau, Theodore Parker, Nathaniel Hawthorne, John G. Whittier, Margaret Fuller, William Lloyd Garrison and a host of others. It represented a sort of humanized Puritanism, a blending of the old rigid concepts with the rising liberalism and humanitarianism that was making itself manifest throughout Europe—a movement strongly influencing the New England thought of the period.

This new Renaissance retained the old religious intensity of Puritanism, but substituted, in the concept of man's relationship with God, the ideal of love for that of fear. That new ideal was extended into the field of man's relationship with his fellow men. In place of the old notion of man as a base, degraded creature forever branded with the taint of original sin, it raised man to a high plane of dignity and nobility, with a firm belief in his innate perfectability. Like the eighteenth-century Enlightenment, with which it had much in common, the New England movement involved a new sense of duty towards humanity, particularly the weaker and more needy sections of it—a sense of duty that had been hitherto almost exclusively reserved for God. Although Dorothea Dix cannot be counted among the molders of the New England Renaissance, she most certainly was one of its representative products.

Like her famous contemporary, Margaret Fuller, Miss Dix cast off the hampering shackles of Puritan womanhood, and fought her way—in her own field—to the top of a man's world. They had in common, also, a degree of self-confidence that bordered closely on egotism. Margaret Fuller could calmly remark: "I know all the people worth knowing in America, and I find no intellect comparable to my own." Miss Dix's consciousness of superiority was curiously tempered by a genuine modesty in all things unrelated to what she considered her divinely ordained duty—reform in the treatment of the mentally ill. She had an imperious bearing, and when she spoke it was as one with God-given authority.

But here the points of resemblance end: in most other things these two eminent New England women were poles apart. In temperament, Margaret Fuller was of the speculative type, like Emerson, a thinker. For her, life was not so much physical movement as mental unfoldment. Dorothea Dix, on the other hand, was the practical reformer, the doer. Within her burned a crusading instinct that sent her far afield in the active service of her fellow men. She was to be to the insane what her great contemporary, Garrison, was to the slaves. She possessed, like him, an indomitable will-to-do, an impulse to ferret out evil and expose it to the eyes of a shamed society. The historic words which Garrison so feelingly inscribed in the first number of his Liberator might well have been uttered by her on the threshold of her own life-work.

> I will be as harsh as truth, and as uncompromising as justice. On this subject, I do not wish to think, or speak, or write, with moderation . . . urge me not to use moderation in a cause like the present. I am in earnest—I will not equivocate—I will not excuse—I will not retreat a single inch—*and I will be heard*.[3]

We return now to our narrative. With the East Cambridge incident, trivial though it was in itself, Miss Dix stumbled upon the right road. She could nevermore retreat to the quietude of normal New England spinsterhood. She could not rest until an answer was found to this question: Were the conditions in the East Cambridge jail exceptional, or were they typical? She set out to find that answer. Her initial survey occupied two years, and took her through the length and breadth of Massachusetts. It entailed visits to scores of almshouses and jails, many of which offered no more hope to their inmates, especially the insane paupers, than the Dantesque legend over the gates of Hell. Her observations were recorded in a little notebook she carried with her. At the end of two years she had collected an amazing catalogue of miseries and horrors.

Miss Dix had found her answer: East Cambridge was *not* an isolated instance of neglect of the indigent insane. Indeed, it was a model institution compared with many of the others. Having gathered the facts, she proceeded to use them. In lesser hands, they might have served to evoke a lurid nine days' sensation: to prick the public conscience, draw a little blood and some explosive anger, and then to give way to another sensation. But in Miss Dix's hands, facts became the foundation stones on which to build concrete progress. If her labors could not bring about the betterment of the conditions in Massachusetts, she felt, then they were in vain. Carefully, step by step, she mapped out a campaign of action. First she embodied her notes in a memorial to the legislature, which burst in its august halls with the force of a bombshell. It began:

> I come to present the strong claims of suffering humanity. I come to place before the Legislature of Massachusetts the condition of the miserable, the desolate, the outcast. I come as the advocate of helpless, forgotten, insane and idiotic men and women . . . of beings wretched in our prisons, and more wretched in our Alms-Houses.
>
> I proceed, Gentlemen, briefly to call your attention to the state of Insane Persons confined within this Commonwealth, in *cages, closets, cellars, stalls, pens: Chained, naked, beaten with rods,* and lashed into obedience![4]

Her arsenal of facts was presented in a style that startled by its very simplicity. In form, it had the bareness of a stock inventory; in content, the dramatic ring of terrible truth. The results of two years of investigation were summed up in this manner:

Lincoln. A woman caged.
Medford. One idiotic subject chained, and one in a close stall for 17 years.
Concord. A woman from the hospital in a cage in the almshouse. In the jail, several, decently cared for in general, but not properly placed in a prison.
Savoy. One man caged.
Lenox. Two in jail; against whose unfit condition there, the jailor protests.
Dedham. The insane disadvantageously placed in the jail. In the almshouse, two females in stalls, situated in the main building; lie in wooden bunks filled with straw; always shut up. One of these subjects is supposed curable. The overseers of the poor have declined to give her a trial at the hospital [i.e., at Worcester], as I was informed.
Franklin. One man chained; decent.
Taunton. One woman caged.

And so on.

Many harmless idiots and insane persons were unjustly confined when they might be set to useful employment, or at least permitted the free use of their limbs. In one almshouse she saw a perfectly harmless insane youth in close solitary confinement in a dark squalid cell, with straw serving as the only article of furniture. When asked why this admittedly mild person was given no opportunity for fresh air or exercise, the matron replied: "O, my husband [the superintendent] is afraid he'll run away, then the overseers won't like it; he'll get to Worcester [Hospital] and then the town will have money to pay."

She discovered another harmless creature, "crazy" for about twenty years, who, as a pauper, had annually been "sold" at the auction block to the lowest bidder. Several years before, he had been placed by his master-for-a-year in an unheated outhouse, and there had frozen his feet, which were now reduced to shapeless stumps. Despite his inability to walk about, chains were nevertheless fastened about his stumps for fear that he might *crawl* forth from his present cell and do some damage!

In yet another town she learned of a young woman, in a complete state of nudity, confined in a stall in a barn, with no bed but straw. There she remained, alone and unprotected, the helpless prey of profligate men and idle boys who were permitted to visit the place at will. This scandalous situation, Miss Dix was told, had continued unchecked until the repeated remonstrances of an *insane* inmate of the town poorhouse forced the authorities to remove the girl to the presumably safe confines of the institution proper.

Where lay the remedies for such abuses and evils? Certainly not in the replacement of one set of superintendents and jail keepers by another. In many instances these very men had protested most bitterly against the conditions they were forced to tolerate under the law. Even the most shocking abuses were usually the result, not of the cruelty of some individual keeper, but rather of ignorance of better methods of treatment. It was still a widespread tendency, by no means confined to poor law and correctional authorities, to regard the insane as no more than brute beasts, to be treated accordingly. For example, in the course of a conversation with a man whose insane nephew was then confined in an almshouse cell, Miss Dix asked: "Has he the comfort of a fire?" The man looked up incredulously: "Fire? Fire indeed! What does a crazy man need of fire? Red-hot iron wants fire as much as he!"*

---

*Perhaps the most shocking example of cruelty that Miss Dix encountered in her extensive tour of America's infernos involved the treatment of a harmless lunatic at the home of his own sister, who gave as her reason for not sending him to an institution: "We had rather take care of him, than leave him to strangers, because we are kinder, and treat him much better than they would." And here are the comforts provided for this unoffending soul, as described in Miss Dix's memorial to the Legislature of Illinois (in which state the incident occurred):

"He was confined in a roofed pen, which enclosed an area of about 8 feet by 8 . . . The interstices between the unhewn logs freely admitted the scorching rays of the sun then, as they now afford admission to the frequent rains and driving snow, and the pinching frost. He was, said a neighbor, 'fed no better than the hogs.' His feet had been frozen, and had perished; upon the

No, the solution did not lie in reprimanding individual persons and communities. State hospitals for the indigent insane—that was the answer! "Hospitals are the only places where insane persons can be at once humanly and properly controlled. Poorhouses, converted into madhouses, cease to effect the purposes for which they were established, and instead of being asylums for the aged, the homeless, etc., are transformed into perpetual bedlams . . ." Massachusetts must build more state hospitals, or must enlarge the only one existing at the time.

The memorial raised a storm of opposition. Although it showed conclusive evidence of painstaking investigation and a constructive approach, the epithets "sensationalist," "distorter of truth," "meddler," etc., were hurled at Miss Dix, especially by those who had felt the direct thrust of her lance. But far from being deterred, she was only spurred on to greater efforts. She drew into the struggle such influential figures as Samuel G. Howe (who was New England's foremost leader in social welfare), R. C. Waterston, Luther V. Bell, Horace Mann, and others.* These men formed effective rallying points for the mobilization of vitally needed public opinion.

Before this formidable barrage, the opposition crumbled.

shapeless stumps he could, aided by some motion of his shoulders, raise his body partially up the side of the pen. This wretched place was cleansed 'once in a week or fortnight' in mild weather; not so in the wet, cold, wintry seasons. I was told that when the pen was opened for this purpose, the help of neighbors was requisite: 'We have men called, and they go in and tie him strongly with ropes, and lay him out on the ground, and then they clean the place and him, by throwing pails of water.' Of course, no fire is here introduced in the cold winter weather; *but a singular expedient has been adopted, as horrible as it is singular. Beneath the pen is excavated a pit about six feet deep and six on either side. This dreary, ghastly place is entered through a trap-door; neither light, heat, nor ventilation are there; but there is to be found a pining desolate, suffering maniac, whose piteous groans, and frantic cries, would move to pity the hardest heart."* (D. L. Dix. *Memorial to the Legislature of Illinois.* Jan. 1847.)

*Dr. Howe published in 1843 a much discussed article supporting Miss Dix's findings and calling for legislative action in the *North American Review*, 1843. v. 56, pp. 171-91. Simultaneously, R. C. Waterston prepared a pamphlet on the same theme: *The Condition of the Insane in Massachusetts.* (Boston, 1843, 23 pp.) Dr. Howe, who was then a member of the State Legislature, brought Miss Dix's memorial before the House.

Courtesy of Houghton Mifflin Company

DOROTHEA LYNDE DIX

The legislature, by a large majority, passed a bill calling for a generous enlargement of the Worcester State Hospital for the reception of indigent insane.

Having achieved this signal triumph, Miss Dix was now prepared to carry the cause of the mentally ill beyond the borders of Massachusetts. Rhode Island was next to feel the galvanizing effect of her presence. Having made a preliminary investigation, she fired her opening gun in the form of an article in a Providence paper, ironically entitled, "Astonishing Tenacity of Life." It describes the remarkable case of Abram Simmons, an insane pauper who had suffered for several years a living entombment in a small Rhode Island town. He had been incarcerated in a vault, six or eight feet square, built entirely of stone except for a door of iron, heavily-bolted. Not a ray of light nor a breath of fresh air could force its way into this miserable tomb. The interior walls were covered with frost a half-inch thick in some places; the straw thrown across an iron frame serving as a bed was thoroughly soaked; the outer of two comforters calculated to save him from freezing was so wet and hoary with frost as to present the appearance of a sheet of ice. "Thus, in utter darkness, encased on every side by walls of frost . . . has this most dreadfully abused man existed through the past inclement winter."[5] Here was a case that could be compared only to the worst brutalities of the dark ages. The story of poor Simmons would have been incredible to the inhabitants of the state founded by Roger Williams, were it not for the fact that it was fully corroborated by eye-witnesses, including the state's leading humanitarian, Thomas G. Hazard.*

Miss Dix's opening shot had its desired effect: the public was aroused to renewed interest in the plight of the mentally ill. Rhode Island had no mental hospital as yet, although a subscription had been started toward building one, and some funds raised. Miss Dix felt that it might be best

*In 1851 Hazard served as a commissioner appointed to make a state-wide survey of pauperism, with particular regard for the insane poor. His report on poor relief conditions in Rhode Island was a model of its kind. (See: Hazard, Thomas G. *Report on the Poor and Insane in Rhode Island. Made to the General Assembly, 1851.* 119 pp.)

for her, under these circumstances, to apply pressure on wealthy individuals so that the subscription campaign already under way could be brought to a successful conclusion. First on her list of prospects she placed the name of Cyrus Butler, reputedly the wealthiest man in the state and also the most niggardly one: he had never been known to contribute a cent toward charity. Friends warned her that she had better save her time and energy for more hopeful possibilities; that it was easier to draw blood from stone than money from this person. Undaunted, Miss Dix sallied forth to beard Mr. Butler in his own den. Accompanied by a skeptical friend—a minister—she sought him out. She was greeted gruffly and suspiciously by her host. Losing no time in the exchange of empty pleasantries, she immediately plunged into the heart of her subject. So impressed was Mr. Butler by the eloquent appeal poured forth in Miss Dix's remarkable low, musical voice that when the short interview terminated, he had pledged the $40,000 needed to build the hospital. When the Rhode Islanders learned the good news, it seemed to them as if Moses, in smiting the rock and drawing forth water for the Israelites to drink, had wrought no greater miracle than this! So was born the Butler Hospital, named after its principal benefactor, which was to become one of the finest institutions of its kind in America.

If there had been any lingering doubts in Dorothea Dix's mind as to her future course, they were by now completely dispelled. She saw eye to eye with destiny, and it pointed clearly along the path she had stumbled upon in that little East Cambridge jail. For forty years after she was to follow that path, winding through the darkest areas of the land where lay, in hidden misery, society's lowliest pariahs —the pauper insane. She threw her whole soul into her new work; all her hitherto dormant powers awakened to the Herculean tasks she set herself. There was in her a firm strength of purpose, fed by a seemingly inexhaustible supply of energy, and driven by a passionate devotion to a cause. This moral and mental stamina stood out in sharp contrast to her frail physical health, seeming like a Diesel engine operating in a canoe.

Her work now became national in scope. In Massachusetts and Rhode Island, Miss Dix had proved the major instrument in enlarging and improving mental hospitals already established or projected. In the next state she marched on—New Jersey—she was to win a newer and more significant triumph. Here the opposition of parsimonious taxpayers had effectively blocked all efforts to establish a state asylum for the insane, despite the urgent need for one. Aligned against progressive legislation, too, were the ever-present watchdogs of the public purse, and the reactionaries generally. But calmly she went through what was to become for her a fixed routine: state-wide investigation of provision for the mentally ill, the preparation of a memorial and bill, the introduction of the latter in the state legislature, and the rallying of public opinion and the press behind her cause. All this involved bitter struggle, during which she was subjected to the sting of direct attacks and the even more poisonous indirect ones. For a time it seemed as though her efforts were futile. But finally she triumphed; her bill providing for the establishment of a state hospital was passed. That hospital at Trenton was remembered ever after by its founder as "my first-born child." She was to prove a prolific mother of such children as this: during her long period of service she was to bring into being more state hospitals than had existed in all the United States up to the time she embarked on her singular enterprise.

The decade following the New Jersey exploit found this American counterpart of Elizabeth Fry carrying her cause personally to every state east of the Rockies. Her plan of action had been perfected to a high degree of effectiveness. It consisted not only in collecting facts and presenting them to the legislature; it involved their interpretation in the light of progressive action. It was not enough to point out degrading conditions; it was necessary to show how they might be changed. New and better state hospitals! This was her invariable solution for the miserable conditions of the pauper insane in the hundreds of almshouses and jails she visited. (The majority of mentally ill dependents were still confined in these institutions.)

From state to state the crusader journeyed, spreading the seeds of justice for the mentally ill and watching them take root. No sooner was her mission in one state accomplished, than she shifted the scene of her activity to another.

Nearly all her memorials included practical suggestions on the selection of proper sites, the most suitable administration of proposed institutions, etc. These suggestions were based on her truly amazing knowledge of the latest advances in psychiatric practice, with which she maintained constant contact through her personal acquaintance with the foremost medical superintendents in America and England, and her broad reading in the subject. A keen student of politics and politicians, she sensed that the most eloquent appeals to humanity set forth in her memorials would be unavailing without the all-important argument of economy. Therefore she always included in her memorials facts and figures proving the ultimate savings of expenditures involved in the creation of state hospitals. "No fact," she would conclude, "is better established in all hospital annals than this: that it is cheaper to take charge of the insane in a curative institution than to support them elsewhere for life."

In nearly every instance her memorial was followed by the erection of a State hospital, or the enlargement and improvement of an existing one. Not in every case, of course, was this happy culmination due solely to her efforts. In some states agitation for legislative provision had been carried on for years before her appearance on the scene—as in Pennsylvania, for example. Her role in such instances was not so much that of a creator as of a catalytic agent, precipitating an action that otherwise might have been delayed for many years.

When we read of the many thousands of miles covered by this ever-sickly frail woman on her missions of mercy, in that day of backbreaking stage coach travel over the rough, muddy roads of young America, we cannot help but marvel at the sheer power of will that could overcome the terrible hardships encountered. The extent of her labors, and the breathless pace she set for herself, is indicated in this characteristically telegraphic summary of her first three years of reform work, in a letter to a friend:

> I have traveled more than ten thousand miles in the last three years. Have visited eighteen state penitentiaries, three hundred county jails, more than five hundred almshouses and other institutions, besides hospitals and houses of refuge. I have been so happy as to promote and secure the establishment of six hospitals for the insane, several county poorhouses, and several jails on a reformed plan.*

What a wealth of drama is hidden behind those words! Picture this lone crusader doggedly pursuing her circuit of Inferno, without even having a Vergil to guide her through all-too-real circles of hell as Dante had in his imaginary ones. Remember, too, that despite her progressive ideals in her special field, here was one who still clung tenaciously to the conservative sex prejudices of the Victorian age, deeply sensitive to her station as a woman. "I am naturally diffident and timid, like all my sex," she once wrote. So extreme were her notions of lady-like propriety that when the sleeping-car was introduced, with all its promise of easing the hardships of long journeys, she denounced the innovation as "immoral" and a device of the devil after her very first trial, and vowed that she'd never travel in a sleeping-car again!

But compared with the obstructions placed in her path by her opponents, the physical hardships of travel were as nothing. Hers was no path strewn with roses, leading to easy triumphs. Every inch of the way had to be fought for. Everywhere she was faced with a disheartening apathy, and the active antagonism of narrow-minded, selfish taxpayers and petty politicians who did not scruple to make her the

---

*It will be noted that Miss Dix's interest in reform extended to correctional and poor law institutions generally. Her eminent role in the history of penal reform in the United States has been all but obscured by the glory of her work for the mentally ill. She conducted many investigations of prison conditions, and her memorials to state legislatures on this subject were instrumental in effecting important progressive changes. Her *Remarks on Prisons and Prison Discipline in the United States* (Boston, 1845, 104 pp.), embodying the results of personal researches throughout America, is considered one of the great milestones in the history of prison reform in this country. Horace Mann, who followed the career of Miss Dix very closely, once said of this aspect of her work: "It would make as wonderful a record as her more especial work in behalf of the insane."

object of unjust attacks. She had to meet the opposition of town and county officials who greedily fought among themselves for the location of proposed institutions within their own borders because of the financial advantages accruing therefrom, regardless of the suitability of their favorite locations. She had to meet the attacks of rich landed proprietors who desired no "madhouses" to blemish the beauty of the scenery surrounding their estates. She had to contend with the enmity of parsimonious public officials who watched the treasury with eagle eye, and who raised heart-rending cries whenever it was dipped into for humanitarian, non-profitmaking purposes.

Her reception by institutional officials on her rounds of inspection was by no means always a cordial one. Certain of these gentry feared and disliked her because the condition of their institutions gave them good reason to expect criticism. There were others, honest and high-minded persons, who deeply resented the intrusion of one whom they termed "a self-appointed Lunacy Commissioner," a lay person with no professional training for the position she had assumed. This resentment, in many cases, was heightened by the naturally imperious bearing she always maintained in her dealings with others—a part of her personality which was vitally needed for the nature of her task, but which unfortunately led to many misunderstandings.

It was not always possible for this single-handed crusader to beat back the imposing array of antagonists aligned against her and the cause she stood for. Along with the wine of victory she was sometimes forced to taste the dregs of defeat. But like most great social reformers, she thrived on struggle.

Untired by the struggles in behalf of the mentally ill in her own country, she found time and energy to carry the cause to neighboring Canada. There she was instrumental in securing the creation of mental hospitals in Nova Scotia and Newfoundland. Received with mingled suspicion and respect by the Canadian public when she launched on her labors, she retired from that country amid a shower of honors for her noble work in gaining the establishment of two badly needed hospitals, one at Halifax and the other at St. John's. A select committee, reporting favorably on her memorial to the Nova Scotia Legislature, took occasion to express their unstinted praise of Miss Dix, "who, endowed with every quality calculated to advance society, dedicates her time and thoughts solely to the cause of those who cannot appreciate her efforts."[6]

Similar tributes were heaped upon her by a number of other grateful legislative bodies, particularly in the Southern states, where Miss Dix scored some of her most important victories. It was quite customary for the Southern legislatures, following each successive Dix conquest, to tender a vote of thanks to that "chosen daughter of the Republic," that "angel of mercy," "that crown of human nature," as she was variously called. A typical tribute was that proffered by the Tennessee legislature, declaring that "her disinterested benevolence, sublime charity, and unmixed philanthropy challenge alike the gratitude and admiration of our state."[7]

Several of the states that responded to her appeals for mental hospitals desired to name these institutions after her, but in line with her aversion for personal glory, she consistently refused to accept such honors. Only in one instance —the Dixmont Hospital in Pennsylvania, established in 1847 —did she permit her name to be associated with an institution she founded. North Carolina, however, would not be deterred from giving the name Dix Hill to the site of the hospital at Raleigh established through her efforts.

Dorothea Dix was cast in a truly heroic mold. In her was that rare combination of endowments that serve to set off great personalities from the ordinary run of men—an imagination capable of conceiving the "impossible," and the will and courage to achieve it. She stormed the citadels of State—and captured them—when wise men shook their heads and termed her a female Don Quixote fighting a hopeless cause. As her brilliant victories over the obstructionists of progress steadily mounted, her contemporaries stared in wide-eyed astonishment as though they were beholding miracles.

Yet, if we were to choose the one event of her career that

captures our admiration above all others, we must turn to a project that ended in defeat, a defeat doubly bitter because it came when victory seemed certain. We refer to the famous "12,225,000 Acre Bill"—the most ambitious project in behalf of the mentally ill conceived up to the twentieth century. It involved a gruelling six-year struggle: the stakes were the highest played for in Miss Dix's career. Had that bill become law it would have written a new chapter, not only in the history of the insane, but in the history of social welfare generally in the United States. For it contained a new concept of the duty of the *nation* toward dependent classes, a concept that has been recognized, officially, only in recent years.

Having besieged state after state and won them to her cause in varying degrees, Miss Dix in 1848 felt prepared to train her guns on the national capital itself. She had noted that Congress was then making generous grants of choice public land to the several states for use in advancing public education and public works. More than 100,000,000 acres of government land had already been apportioned to the states to aid them in raising funds for educational purposes alone. There still remained many more millions in the hands of the federal government. Why not grant some of these acres for charitable purposes? Why not for the benefit of America's mentally ill? No sooner did she conceive the idea than she acted upon it. A petition to Congress was forthwith drawn up, urging that body to grant to the states, on the basis of population, 5,000,000 acres of land, the proceeds of the sales of which were to be used exclusively for bettering the condition of the indigent insane.

Her memorial was one of the ablest she ever prepared, containing a detailed and vivid record, compiled state by state, of man's inhumanity toward the mentally ill. Not only did it describe existing evils and inadequacies; it pointed clearly to the remedies, offering in illustration already-existing model state hospitals where curable cases might find cure, and the others at least comfort.

The petition was received with mixed feelings, with doubt dominating. Granted, said the sceptics, that the treatment of the indigent insane was far from being what it could and should be—what had the federal government to do with this or any other dependent class? Here Miss Dix essayed her boldest stroke. Exactly twenty years before, her friend Horace Mann had startled his contemporaries by enunciating the doctrine that "the insane are the wards of the State." That doctrine was still far from being generally accepted. Imagine, then, the staggering effect of the unequivocal declaration which ended Miss Dix's memorial:

> I confide to you the cause and the claims of the destitute and of the desolate, without fear or distrust. I ask, for the thirty states of the Union, 5,000,000 acres of land, of the many hundreds of millions of public lands, appropriated in such manner as shall assure the greatest benefits to all who are in circumstances of extreme necessity, and who, through the providence of God, *are wards of the nation,* claimants on the sympathy and care of the public, through the miseries and disqualifications brought upon them by the sorest afflictions with which humanity can be visited.[8]

Wards of the nation! Here was a brand-new concept of governmental responsibility for mentally ill dependents. Many greeted her proposal with ridicule. The plan she proposed was wildly visionary, impossible of attainment. Others frankly wondered whether it would not be best for the memorialist to retire to the confinement of one of the institutions she had founded. A mountain of opposition arose at once. But characters like Dorothea Dix thrill to the "tonic of opposition." To the epithets of "impractical idealist" and "spinner of dreams" Miss Dix paid no heed: she went about her campaign with the usual military precision—enlisting the aid of the press and of influential public figures, and marshalling mass opinion behind her plan, for she was well aware of the sensitiveness of legislators to the pressure of public opinion. The bill formulated around her memorial failed of passage that year. Did Miss Dix give up? Did she lessen her demands? Not at all. With the audacity that knows no retreat, she modified her bill *upward,* asking for a grant of *10,000,000 acres* for the insane—double the amount in the original act—and added, to boot, a request for 2,225,000 acres for deaf mutes, making 12,225,000 acres in all.

The ensuing years were fraught with harrowing suspense for the friends of the cause. Delay followed delay. In one session, the House of Representatives passed the bill, but the Senate did not. In another, the tables were turned, the bill failing in the House after passing the Senate. (To become a law, a bill has to pass both houses in the *same* session.) In 1854 the time was propitious for passage of the bill through both houses—and pass them it did, with comfortable majorities. The impossible seemed accomplished. All that was lacking was the President's signature, and vetoes were very rare in those days. Only one man stood between the cause and victory. It appeared incredible that the bill would be vetoed in the face of the overwhelming public support Miss Dix had rallied behind her. But the incredible happened. With one stroke of the pen, President Franklin Pierce nullified the results of years of arduous labor. He seemed to sense that his action was somehow indefensible, for he took the unusual recourse of preparing a lengthy pamphlet to "explain" his veto.[9] Its very length betrayed its weakness of argument.

The government, maintained the President, could not become involved in granting aid for any humanitarian cause whatever. "If Congress have power," he wrote, "to make provision for the indigent insane *without the limits of this district* [District of Columbia], it has the same power to provide for the indigent who are not insane, and thus to transfer to the federal government the charge *of all the poor in all the States.*"

What a *non sequitur!* Boiled down to its essentials his argument meant only this: No power that may be abused should ever be permitted to exist.

Pierce tried to defend his veto on constitutional grounds, too, although Miss Dix in her memorial had cited two precedents when Congress had made land grants for humanitarian purposes—both times in behalf of deaf-mutes. A grant of land in aid of the Connecticut asylum for the education of the deaf and dumb had been made in 1819, and again for a similar institution in Kentucky in 1826. The constitutionality of these acts had never been contested. Another argument advanced by Pierce for his veto was that of "State's Rights," a point evidently intended to win the sympathy of the Southern states to his stand. (He had been elected as "A Northerner with Southern principles.") In performing a humanitarian service to the poor, he claimed, the federal government would be usurping the powers of the individual states!

So was the great 12,225,000 Acre Bill finally defeated by the penstroke of one man. Miss Dix had thrown all her energy into this fight; the end found her completely exhausted and weighed down with disappointment. In the fall of 1854 she set sail for England for much-needed rest and recuperation. But to a nature like hers there is no contradiction between rest and work. Hardly had she set foot on English soil than she wrote to a friend back home:

> I am still here with dear friends, much occupied with charitable institutions and the meetings of the British Scientific Association. All this tires me sadly, but I shall take things easier in a week. It is my purpose to go to Scotland to see the hospitals in ten days.[10]

Little did she dream at the moment that this casually mentioned visit to Scotland would develop into one of the major struggles of her career, the outcome of which was to change completely that country's lunacy system. A short time after, she was writing to the same friend (Miss Anne Heath) from Edinburgh, referring to the sad state of the institutions for the insane: "Of these none are so much needing quick reform as the private establishments for the insane. I am confident that this move is to rest with me, and that the sooner I address myself to this work of humanity, the sooner will my conscience cease to suggest effort, or rebuke inaction. It is true I came here for pleasure, but that is no reason why I should close my eyes to the condition of these most helpless of all God's creatures."[11]

Humanitarianism knows no national boundaries. Where misery is, there duty calls. And to Miss Dix, that call was inexorable. She set about her work, ferreting out abuses and evils, and forcing them before the public eye. No sooner had she begun than the wolf-pack of reaction was at her heels. Here was an alien meddler, they cried, betraying a country's hospitality by interfering in its internal affairs. "The American Invader," one of her opponents labeled her with contempt, and the epithet won the approval of many others. But Miss Dix cared not how many antagonists were arrayed against her, so long as she felt truth and justice at her side. Then, too, she had the full-hearted support of many individuals who had themselves been trying unsuccessfully for years to institute requisite reforms, and who now welcomed the dynamic presence of this new leader.

A survey of affairs in Scotland convinced Miss Dix that an appeal to the native officialdom would be fruitless. She announced her intention to take the cause of Scotland's insane to the British Home Secretary himself. Apprehending trouble and aware of the advantage of having Miss Dix discredited before her arrival at the Home Office, the Lord Provost of Edinburgh, one of her principal opponents, packed his trunk that very night in readiness to depart for London the next day. Miss Dix, however, was not to be outgeneralled by the canny Scot. Anticipating the Lord Provost's stratagem, Miss Dix hurriedly threw her effects into a little handbag, swung on the night mail train for London, and reached her destination after a sleepless, uncomfortable ride. Before the leisurely Scotch official arrived in London, she had gained an interview with the Secretary of the Home Office, and impressed the latter with her presentation of facts and the necessity for an immediate inquiry.

So conclusive was her evidence that on April 3, 1855, Queen Victoria appointed a Royal Commission to inquire into the condition of the lunatic asylums in Scotland, and the state of the lunacy laws of that country. The report of that Royal Commission's inquiries and recommendations, which revolutionized the lunacy system of Scotland and made it one of the most exemplary in the world, marks a notable milestone in the history of provision for the mentally ill. For her great feat, Miss Dix received the unreserved praise of all progressives in Great Britain. A member of

Parliament, stating that "the Commission was entirely due to Miss Dix's exertion," added that "no one could read the report of the Commission without feeling grateful to that lady for having been instrumental in exposing proceedings which were disgraceful to this or to any other civilized country." The Home Secretary, Sir George Gray, voiced similar sentiment on the floor of the House of Commons, regretting only that the materialization of this long-needed reform should have been achieved by "a foreigner, and that foreigner a woman, and that woman a dissenter!"[12]

Her labors in Europe were not yet over. While recuperating in the home of Dr. D. Hack Tuke at the famed Retreat at York, Miss Dix's attention was called by her host to a pamphlet by a Dr. Van Leuven, describing the deplorable condition of the insane in the Channel Islands, due largely to the location there of private asylums by unscrupulous owners who had been driven from England. Miss Dix lost no time establishing correspondence with the Dutch doctor: before long she was on the spot. Within a month, she had made it so hot for the racketeers who preyed on the misfortune of others that they left the island in precipitate haste. She secured the formation of a constructive commission, and was instrumental in getting a public mental hospital established on the Island of Jersey.

Her mission accomplished, Miss Dix journeyed to the Continent, where she spent many months in a tour of inspection of mental hospitals and other types of humanitarian institutions, covering nearly every European country. Everywhere her name and fame preceded her: she invariably was given *carte blanche* to visit and inspect at will. Her most notable work was performed in Rome, where she brought to the Pope's attention the terrible mistreatment of the insane at his very doorstep, and elicited from him the promise that a new institution for the insane would be erected at once.

Two years had been spent in pursuing the ever elusive "rest" abroad; her thoughts now turned toward home. In September, 1856, she set sail from Liverpool for New York.

The outbreak of the Civil War found her in Baltimore. No sooner had the first gun been fired, than she presented herself before the administration in Washington for any service she might fit into. She was promptly appointed to the post of Superintendent of Women Nurses—the highest office held by a woman during the War—with power to "select and assign women nurses to general or permanent military hospitals, they not to be employed in such hospitals without her sanction and approval, except in cases of urgent need."

Miss Dix entered upon her new task with characteristic intensity. Mobilizing a nursing force at that time, with little or no preliminary preparations, might well be compared to the twelve labors of Hercules. But under her skillful hand, iron will, and infinite supply of energy, the work of organization went on admirably. In the field of administration, however, the results were not quite so happy. She soon found herself embroiled in an endless conflict with the medical and technical men in the hospital service, a conflict that continued unabated to the end of the War. Miss Dix was used to giving commands, and having them obeyed. The professional men who worked beside her, on the other hand, deeply resented what they considered the officiousness of an untrained lay person. It was charged also that Miss Dix, in selecting nurses, placed too much emphasis on the moral background of applicants, and too little on their efficiency. She often showed an overzealousness in her duties that brought on clashes with fellow workers. She herself realized the difficulties of her project, and exclaimed once: "This is not the work I would have my life judged by!" Howbeit, Lossing, in his *Pictorial History of the Civil War,* says of her: "Like an angel of mercy, this self-sacrificing woman labored day and night throughout the entire war for the relief of suffering soldiers . . . The amount of happiness that resulted from the services of this woman can never be estimated."[13]

The War ended, and the nursing service demobilized, Secretary of War Stanton sent her a letter of high commendation, inviting her to choose a suitable official reward in recognition of her work. When she asked for nothing more, he presented her with a stand of arms of the nation's colors.

Miss Dix now turned once more to her special labor of love. She was already sixty-five years of age when she resumed her ministrations to the mentally ill, but she continued her rounds of investigation through the states, and agitated for progressive lunacy legislation for fifteen years longer. Her inspection tours brought her many crushing disappointments, as reflected in the despair frequently voiced in her letters of this period. In state after state she found the very abuses and evils she had set out so hopefully to eliminate years ago again rearing their ugly heads. Had all her work, then, been in vain, she asked herself? Most saddening of all was the discovery that many of her "children"—hospitals founded directly through her labors—exhibited scenes of suffering and neglect little better than those she had so bitterly condemned long before in her reports on jails and almshouses. As Franklin B. Sanborn points out in his *Memoirs of Pliny Earle:*

> Through her it was, campaigning for the neglected insane from State to State and from country to country, that so many new asylums had been built, so many old ones enlarged; but they had in too many instances become centres of intellectual indolence or of semi-political intrigue; to whose busy and well-paid medical men new ideas were irksome, and any forward step in the care of their patients or the guidance of public opinion was a kind of reproach to their imbibed complacency of attained perfection. It was the familiar story of goodness gone to seed and planting the surrounding fields with a growth which was not goodness. . . .
>
> Miss Dix had done her work. The fame of it remained and will not be forgotten. It was, however, a work for a time of ignorance and developing civilization, and by no means a permanent model for all coming time. This fact she hardly recognized, nor was it natural she should. Like all strong natures of her type, she saw what she was appointed to see, wrought her task therein with zeal and swift accomplishment, but she saw little beyond.[14]

Miss Dix had throughout her career played the role of the lone eagle, partly because the stage of humanitarian reform in her time gave rise to the individual crusader of the type she represented, partly through the dictates of her own peculiar temperament. By the sheer force of her personality she had awakened public opinion to the sufferings and needs of the mentally ill to a degree unparalleled by any other individual before her time or for many years after. She had succeeded in forcing on recalcitrant public authorities the acceptance of definite standards of care and treatment. However, to *organize* that enlightened opinion on a permanent basis so as to safeguard adequate standards, in addition to obtaining immediate gains, was beyond the capacity of any individual at that time, even of such a rare person as she was. Consider, too, that her activities belonged to a period when social customs made it virtually impossible for a woman to rise above obscurity, and her success becomes all the more amazing.

What a record she could point back to at the end of her long career! Twenty states had responded directly to her appeals by establishing or enlarging mental hospitals. In several states more than one institution was credited to her personal efforts. She had played an important role in the founding of the Government Hospital for the Insane, at Washington, D.C.* As for her work in other lands—Canada, the British Isles, and the Continent—that phase of her career alone would have been sufficient to secure her a prominent niche among humanitarian reformers. In all, she was directly responsible for the founding or enlarging of thirty-two mental hospitals in the United States and abroad.

---

*This institution, now known as St. Elizabeths Hospital, was founded in 1852 and opened three years later. It is under the direct charge of the U. S. Department of the Interior, and receives patients from the military organizations stationed in the United States, from the District of Columbia, and from our island possessions. Miss Dix drafted the bill organizing the hospital, and also obtained its present beautiful location.

A notable feature in the history of this hospital is that three men have served as its head for a total of eighty-one out of its eighty-five years of existence. Its first superintendent, Dr. Charles H. Nichols (a life-long friend of Miss Dix), was appointed in 1852 and served until 1877. His successor, Dr. W. W. Godding, was superintendent for twenty-two years, 1877-99. Dr. William A. White held the post from 1903, until his death in 1937.

DOROTHEA LYNDE DIX

In this connection, we may mention the little realized, but vastly important role of Miss Dix in the development of psychiatric training in this country. The many institutions created through her efforts later became valuable training schools for specialists in mental disease. As Tiffany states, in reference to the "rapid, Napoleonic victories" of her first ten years of crusading, "there had existed—except in a few scattered places—neither the call nor the opportunity for practically enlisting and employing this special [psychiatric] order of medical talent. Now fast grew up a wide demand for it, a great school of practice in which to acquire and exercise the requisite knowledge and skill."[15]

She had effected a revolution in the care of the mentally ill in a foreign country where native reformers had almost despaired of progressive reform. Her greatest battle—the fight for the 12,225,000 Acre Bill—was lost after coming within a hair's breadth of victory. If that fight had been won, the principle of federal grants to states in aid of the indigent would have been established fully three-quarters of a century sooner than actually happened. On this score, posterity vindicated Dorothea Dix and not Franklin Pierce.

In 1881, when nearly eighty, Miss Dix retired from active work. Broken in physical health (though her mental vigor remained unimpaired to the end) she sought asylum in the bosom of her "first-born child," the New Jersey State Hospital at Trenton, where she spent the remaining years of her life.

She died on July 17, 1887, and was buried in Mount Auburn Cemetery near Boston, Massachusetts, in the presence of a small circle of friends. Among them was Dr. Charles H. Nichols of Bloomingdale Hospital who, apprising Miss Dix's English friends of the event, wrote:

> Thus has died and been laid to rest, in the most quiet, unostentatious way, the most useful and distinguished woman America has yet produced.

"The most useful and distinguished woman America has yet produced." Superlative words, these, but, in large measure, true ones.

CHAPTER X
Mid-Century Psychiatrists

DOROTHEA LYNDE DIX was more than a unique personality; she was the symbol of an epoch. Just as we might characterize the age of Chiarugi, Pinel, Tuke and Rush as one of "rational reform" so we might characterize hers as one of "moral reform." Reform moved forward on the wheels of philanthropy, but it was a reform which found its fundamental impetus not so much in a search for scientific knowledge, as in a vague, sentimental attitude toward mankind, heavily tinged with an impersonal, religious sense of duty.*

All too often sentimental humanitarianism, lacking the vital attributes of science, leads along deceptive roads and into blind alleys from which society later extricates itself only with great pain and difficulty. This truth is well exemplified in certain historical phases in the care and treatment of the mentally sick.

The ideal of institutionalization, as we have previously noted, was peculiarly a product of the nineteenth century. It owed its rise mainly to the industrial revolution, with concomitant changes in the social order, rapidly evolving complexities in social relationships, tremendous expansion of population, and closer grouping of that population in large towns and cities. The simple makeshifts of a simple community living under a simple economy were no longer possible in this increasingly complex world. The first and most logical solution that presented itself in dealing with

---

*In at least this respect, E. Douglas Branch is correct in entitling his historical account of the period 1836–1860, *The Sentimental Years*. (New York, 1934.)

the mentally, physically and economically disabled was to gather them together into centers of custody, care and treatment. This was all very well in so far as the building of institutions represented a radical improvement over the former anarchy and indifference and neglect. But in social processes, what originates as a progressive idea may become rigid, inflexible and anachronistic with the passing of time. It fixes itself on the body of reform like an incubus. While the once progressive idea remains static, changing social forces leap ahead of it; what was once a forward tendency degenerates into retrogressive channels.

During the dominance of the custodial ideal, institutionalization was conceived of as an end in itself. Curiously enough, this conception persisted far into the period when cure superseded mere care as an institutional objective. The asylum or hospital had become a fetish, as it were, with near-magic powers unconsciously attributed to it. It seemed to matter not how ill-equipped it might be for curative treatment; any institution labeled "Hospital for the Insane," was expected to restore the sick mind by simply enveloping that mind within its healing walls. Here we meet with one of those interesting recurrences found often enough in the pages of history. For what was this exaggerated concept of a mental hospital *per se*—what was it but a throw-back to the healing temples of the ancient Egyptians and Greeks, where, it was thought, the sick body and mind could be made whole again by the operation of a mystic power inherent in the temple itself? The prevailing approach to the therapeutic problems of mental illness was a simple one; all the insane, or nearly all, could be cured in institutions; none, except a very few, could be cured outside. Even in the minds of the most eminent practitioners in the field of mental diseases, this over-simplified doctrine received credence over a long period of years.

It is not surprising, therefore, that the main emphasis in treating the insane during this period was placed on the mechanics of institutional arrangement. The problems of organization, administration and methods of therapy were, as a rule, considered to be of relatively small consequence in mental hospitals; the important thing was to build them. It didn't matter that some of the special hospitals and asylums were hardly better than the almshouses and jails where the insane had formerly been confined—the very change in nomenclature seemed to possess a magic potency in itself.

There were, of course, other factors tending to emphasize the *construction* of hospitals rather than their *operation* along scientific principles. As Dr. Walter Channing said forty years ago in defense of his forerunners: "It was not a question of knee-jerk, or ankle-clonus or reaction-time which confronted them, but how to house the then already large numbers of insane, who, as shown by Miss Dix, were suffering the tortures of the damned in almshouses and in their own homes; and from that day to this the pressure has never relaxed for more accommodations. There are still [1894] thousands scattered through the country, kept in the vilest of almshouses, still suffering tortures."[1] The paramount question to the early psychiatrists, then, was to provide state institutions built especially for the insane. It remained for later generations to concentrate on the problems of therapeutic treatment within these hospitals.

It goes without saying that in general the mental hospitals erected in this period were really far superior to the old receptacles where the mentally ill were herded indiscriminately with all classes of sufferers, and made possible many recoveries that might never have taken place in the old days of indifference.

In the examination of history one must always be careful to distinguish between theory and actual practice at any given time. Let us not forget that most of the humane theories that rallied the forces of reform in the late eighteenth and nineteenth centuries (and that are still considered sound today) had been clearly enunciated by Greek practitioners like Asclepiades and Aretaeus many hundreds of years before. It was the gradual development of certain social forces that made possible the *materialization* of some of these ideals after a lapse of many centuries. I say "some of them" advisedly, because many of the barbaric practices that had their origin in the days of demoniacal possession and other superstitious beliefs continued to exist well into the humanitarian period.

Kindness is a relative term, depending for its interpretation upon the elements of time and place. Under a kindly impulse, the Quakers of Pennsylvania, while taking an historic step forward by founding the first state prison, inaugurated therein the system of solitary confinement which, in effect, was far more soul-racking than the types of corporal punishment that had been abolished. We have seen how the great pioneer, Benjamin Rush, in the belief that he was aiding the cause of the insane, invented that instrument of torture, the tranquilizing chair, which continued in use for decades after his time. Likewise, his successors, who were also motivated by the kindliest of impulses and looked with horror upon chains and irons, nevertheless sanctioned the liberal use of other types of restraining devices which, though mild enough in appearance, when applied continuously for long periods (as frequently happened) were even more agonizing than the clanking chains and the whips of yore.

Was it because the men of those days were less humane than we are today? Not at all. The difference lay mainly in this: they were just as kind, but their kindness was not implemented by adequate knowledge. Today we benefit by the greater knowledge accumulated slowly and painfully in the intervening years. Our knowledge of mental illness, its causes and treatment, is still very, very far from being complete, but it is ever so much richer than that of our nineteenth century ancestors. Humanitarianism, groping its way forward along the dark corridors of ignorance, can accomplish but little by itself. It becomes truly effective only when its path is lighted by the beacon of science.

It is significant that the greatest reforms in the care and treatment of the insane in the first half of the nineteenth century lay rather in the substitution of kind for cruel treatment than in scientific therapy. Even the most advanced hospitals of the day resembled well-conducted boarding houses rather than hospitals. They had little more to offer the mentally ill than food, clothing, pleasant surroundings, neat apartments, and perhaps some means of employment and exercise. Not that these factors were unimportant: the environment afforded in these institutions was certainly far more conducive to recovery than that of the almshouse, jail or home-made cage. It was a great step ahead. The pity was that too many felt that the end had been reached once a pleasantly located building was reared.

The heads of institutions were pleased to call themselves "medical superintendents," a term that aptly described their functions. In the mid-nineteenth century they actually differed little from their predecessors, the lay superintendents. Except for a few outstanding leaders, most of them were not so much psychiatric specialists as physicians with executive and business ability.[2]

About the time that Dorothea Dix stumbled upon her great life-work, the care and treatment of the mentally ill was in a more or less chaotic state. Medical care in hospitals for the insane had advanced but little since the days of the venerable Rush. A case in point was the still widespread use of bloodletting as a remedy for mental disorders. Progress in this respect took the negative form of *discarding* therapeutics shown by experience to be unavailing or even injurious, rather than of discovering *better* methods of treatment. The construction, organization, and administration of hospitals differed widely and were patterned upon a rather haphazard, unscientific selection. In other aspects of institutional treatment and care a similar anarchy was evidenced. State hospitals were everywhere springing up. But they were heavily handicapped at the very outset by haste in building and lack of adequate planning, general ignorance as to what the true functions of a hospital should be, and the confusion among experts on the whole subject of hospital building and administration. Many of the new institutions were headed by men who were willing and energetic enough, but who had had little or no previous experience in treating the mentally ill. (This situation is unfortunately true even today in certain parts of the country.) Structures that were launched with high hopes and noble aspirations soon degenerated into mere places of custody instead of cure, to the despair of those who had labored and fought to bring them into being. The more advanced among the medical superintendents of the time were keenly aware of the chaotic situation that confronted them. The time was ripe for forming a body to advance the interests of the mentally ill, to organize the knowledge of psychiatry then available, and to build solidly upon it. Early in 1844 the question of an organization of medical superintendents was discussed by Dr. Samuel B. Woodward, of the Worcester State Hospital in Massachusetts, and Dr. Francis T. Stribling of the Western State Hospital at Staunton, Virginia. Both men were convinced of the timeliness of such a society, and made contact with a number of their confreres to bring it about. Their conversation resulted in a founding meeting held at Jones' Hotel in Philadelphia on October 16, 1844, which was attended by thirteen medical superintendents, thereafter reverently referred to in American psychiatric annals as "The Original Thirteen." Out of that meeting was born the Association of Medical Superintendents of American Institutions for the Insane. Eventually, that ponderous title was changed: the organization founded in that Philadelphia hotel was known from 1893 to 1921 as the American Medico-Psychological Association, and it now bears the title of the American Psychiatric Association. It was the first national society of medical men in the United States. In its special field it was not without precedent abroad, since three years earlier, the first national psychiatric body in the world had been formed in England as the Association of Medical Officers of Asylums and Hospitals for the Insane. Its objects, as set forth in the circular letter of organization, were almost identical with those of the American society: "the medical gentlemen connected with lunatic asylums should be better known to each other, should communicate more freely the results of their individual experience; should cooperate in collecting statistical information relating to insanity, and above all, should assist each other in improving the treatment of the insane."[3]

The names of the Thirteen who sat at the founding meeting in Philadelphia loom large in the pages of American psychiatric history. They were Samuel B. Woodward of the Worcester State Hospital, Isaac Ray of the Maine State Asylum at Augusta, Luther V. Bell of the McLean Asylum, Charles E. Stedman of the Boston Lunatic Asylum, Nehemiah Cutter of the Pepperell Private Asylum (Massachusetts), John S. Butler of the Hartford Retreat, Amariah Brigham of the New York State Lunatic Asylum at Utica, Samuel White of the Hudson Lunatic Asylum (private) at Hudson, New York, Pliny Earle of the Bloomingdale Asylum, Thomas S. Kirkbride of the Pennsylvania Hospital for the Insane, William M. Awl of the Ohio Lunatic Asylum at Columbus, Francis T. Stribling of the Western Lunatic Asylum of Virginia at Staunton, and John M. Galt of the Eastern Lunatic Asylum at Williamsburg, Virginia.

Here were names to conjure with. There was hardly a man among them who did not make some outstanding contribution to his field. The original Thirteen represented a fair cross-section of every type of mental hospital in the country: state-owned, municipal, corporate and private. Not the least striking feature about them was their youth; nearly all had been appointed to superintendencies (or the equivalent) at a very early age. Galt was but twenty-two when he became an institutional head (1841); Stribling was twenty-six (1836); Bell received his appointment at thirty (1836); Kirkbride at thirty-one (1840); Ray at thirty-four (1841); Earle at thirty-five (1844); Butler at thirty-six (1839); Stedman at thirty-seven (1842); Awl at thirty-nine (1838); and Brigham at forty-one (1840). Of the Thirteen, only White, Woodward and Cutter were above forty-five years of age at the time of organization.

A compact group they formed, alive with energy. They were for the most part men of great vitality, forceful will and abounding humanity. Naturally they were not without faults and shortcomings, but their defects originated not so much from a lack of fine aims and ability as from the prevailing scarcity of knowledge. They had at their disposal but few scientific data concerning the needs of the mentally sick and methods of meeting those needs. Despite all that had been done in the humanizing of care and treatment, the scientific side of psychiatric practice had advanced hardly at all. Franklin B. Sanborn, in his biography of one of the most eminent of the Thirteen, succinctly describes the situation in these terms:

> None of these alienists . . . had comprehended the statistical, economic, or even sanatory relations of the public care of the insane. It was still a new matter. Experience was wanting . . . The asylums were few and small, receiving but a portion of the insane, and had no means of determining the exact physical condition of the patients they treated. The microscope had hardly begun to do its work in revolutionizing medicine. The localization of function in the brain was in its rudiments, and was obscured by the charlatanry of phrenology. The classification of insanity by its external manifestations was very little advanced, and had to be the study of each alienist in his own narrow field of observation. They experimented with medical and moral treatment; and, like Dr. Rush, they formed singular notions of what treatment was applicable to the mass of the insane. Still, knowledge advanced under their isolated experiences. They communicated facts to each other and to the public.[4]

Nor was America alone in this backwardness. Take Germany, for instance, which was destined soon to gain the foremost place in psychiatric knowledge and experimentation. As late as 1840 there were many German medical men who still accepted as true Heinroth's theory that insanity and sin were identical, that mental illness was merely the manifestation of demoniacal possession, and that treatment should be based on theological doctrines rather than on science. It was not until William Griesinger published his monumental *Die Pathologie und Therapie der psychischen Krankheiten* in 1845 (the year after the Association of Medical Superintendents was founded in America) that the metaphysical concepts of Heinroth were finally swept into the discard. Incidentally it was Griesinger who, more than any other individual of his century, placed psychiatry on a scientific footing, defining its position in relation to kindred sciences. He was only twenty-eight when his revolutionizing book was published, another indication that his was a period when youth led the way in scientific advancement.

In America, as elsewhere, psychiatry was still in its infancy. The thirteen who met in 1844 were alive to the momentous problems facing them. They wisely sensed that their major task of the moment was to gather the loose, disconnected threads of knowledge pertaining to their craft, and to knit these threads into a unified pattern. It was their job to get their bearings and to direct their course accordingly. It was a gigantic task they undertook, but they attacked it with characteristic vigor. Undeterred by their small number, the group of enthusiasts appointed no less than sixteen committees, embracing well-nigh every phase of their specialty, with instruction to submit reports at the next meeting. The names of these committees afford an interesting index to the topics uppermost in the minds of these men. They included a committee on the moral treatment of insanity, another on medical treatment, a committee on restraint and restraining apparatus, on the construction and organization of mental hospitals, on the jurisprudence of insanity, on the prevention of suicide, on a manual for attendants, on statistics, on support of the pauper insane, on asylums for idiots and the demented, on post-mortem examinations, on the comparative advantages of hospitals and private practice, on asylums for colored persons, on proper provision for insane prisoners, and on the causes and prevention of insanity.[5]

Dr. Woodward was elected first president of the Association, Dr. White vice-president, and Dr. Kirkbride secretary.

Referring to that founding group a half-century later, Dr. W. W. Godding invoked the Biblical text: "There were giants in the earth in those days." And we may well concur in that characterization. When we consider how little they had to start with, and what difficulties they faced in the triple threat of apathy, ignorance and niggardliness, their achievements cannot but win our respect and admiration. Together, they tried to formulate their specialty into an integrated whole, and they worked continuously for its advancement. They eagerly strove to collect the facts and to use them to benefit their stricken fellow men. And more: they endeavored to impart their findings not only to their confreres in the field, but to the public at large, knowing that their progressive efforts would come to naught without the backing of an alert public opinion. They were propagandists in the best sense of the term. If they failed in some of the tasks they set themselves, it was not so much their fault, as individuals or as a group, as it was the restricted social frame in which they were compelled to operate. No generation in any profession pulls itself up from its milieu by the bootstraps.

As has been noted, their duties demanded of them a great degree of versatility. Yet, almost without exception, each of the founding fathers was able to gain a marked distinction in some particular branch of his profession to which he directed his special attention. Their individual accomplishments are inseparably bound up with the general progress of the care and treatment of the mentally ill during their lifetime. Let us briefly examine them, one by one.

Samuel B. Woodward (1787–1850) was a pioneer in his profession in a very real sense. He was most active in founding the Retreat at Hartford, Connecticut, in 1824, and afterwards served as one of its visiting physicians. When the Worcester State Hospital was organized in 1832, he was named its first superintendent. His reports as head of that institution were probably the most widely read in America, being circulated in editions averaging three thousand each. They also evoked much favorable comment in Europe. During the movement toward state-asylum building that may be said to have begun with the establishment of the Worcester Hospital, he was probably the most quoted authority on the subject. His optimistic descriptions of results obtained at Worcester did a great deal to stimulate the movement in other states. He paid particular attention to the question of asylum statistics, as the laboriously prepared tabulations in his own reports show. Although his own methods were seriously erroneous in some respects (such as his computing recovery percentages on the basis of discharges instead of admissions) he succeeded in attracting the attention of his contemporaries to the values inherent in the comparatively new science of statistics. An enthusiastic student of Pinel and Esquirol in the treatment of mental illness, he did much to popularize their methods in America.

Samuel White (1777–1845) conducted a private asylum for the insane at Hudson, New York. Opened in 1830, it gained a wide reputation as the most successful private institution in the country. Dr. White was looked upon as New York State's foremost specialist during the '30's. He was frequently consulted by legislative committees in the steps that led to the establishment of the Utica State Asylum, and was the recipient of high praise in several official reports. He died shortly after the founding of the Association.

The one other among the original Thirteen who operated a private establishment was Nehemiah Cutter (1787–1859). His hospital was located at Pepperell, Massachusetts, where it had developed out of the occasional treatment of mental patients at Dr. Cutter's own home while he was engaged in general practice. His reputation as a healer spread rapidly, with a corresponding increase in patients, so that in a short time he was compelled to add new wings to his home in order to accommodate them all, and finally to erect a large hospital building on the premises. This institution burned down in 1853, and was never rebuilt.

The Virginians, John M. Galt (1819–1862) and Francis Stribling (1810–1874), heads of the Eastern and Western Lunatic Hospitals of Virginia, respectively, were the youngest founding members of the Association. Quiet and unassuming, Dr. Stribling was consistently a staunch advocate of humane reforms in the care and treatment of the mentally ill, and presided over his own institution with consummate skill. Dr. Galt, who was appointed medical superintendent of the Eastern Lunatic Asylum in 1841, was the third member of the Galt dynasty to head that historic institution in succession. The family ruled over the destinies of the hospital without interruption for nearly a century, from its opening in 1773 until 1861—a record unequalled even by the famous Tuke family's connection with the Retreat at York, England. Getting his appointment at twenty-two (only a few months after receiving his medical degree), Dr. Galt soon rose to a leading position in his specialty. Of a brilliant temperament and studious frame of mind, his commentaries on insanity, particularly those embodied in his principal treatise, *Treatment of Insanity* (1846), attracted wide attention. He was a frequent contributor to scientific and learned journals on the subject of insanity, and undoubtedly would have achieved greater renown had not his career been cut short at a comparatively early age.

Luther V. Bell (1806–1862) was a man of varied pursuits, equally active in political life and professional work. While in his late twenties, he served as a member of the New Hampshire legislature. (His father had served as governor of that state.) His able reports to the legislature were mainly instrumental in establishing the state hospital at Concord. In later life, Dr. Bell was several times a candidate for high public office in Massachusetts. In 1826 he was appointed physician and superintendent of the McLean Asylum, where he presided for the next twenty years. Aware of the importance of structural details in hospitals he closely followed developments in this field and was quick to embody the latest improvements at the institution he headed. The McLean Asylum, under his superintendency, was the first institution in America to employ successfully a circulating hot water system for warming a large, inflowing current of air. In 1845 he made a round of inspection of mental hospitals in Europe at the solicitation of the trustees of the newly established Butler Asylum in Providence. His recommendations, together with those of Dr. Isaac Ray (who had been sent on a similar mission) formed the basis of the plans for the proposed asylum. When completed, this hospital was conceded to be one of the finest in America.

Dr. Bell's excellent reports, like those of his leading confreres, teemed with propaganda aimed at the erection of more and better built institutions for the insane. They were frequently and effectively quoted by his close friend, Dorothea Dix, in her petitions to various state legislatures. An acute observer and clinician, he made many valuable contributions to the then meagre knowledge of diagnosis in mental diseases. He wrote the first description of a form of acute mania thereafter known as Bell's Disease. In 1856, he resigned his post at the McLean Asylum due to failing health. But when the Civil War broke out he immediately volunteered in the Union forces, and was brigade surgeon to General Hooker's Division when he died in camp on February 11, 1862.

Amariah Brigham (1798–1849) was occupying a professorship of anatomy and surgery at the College of Physicians and Surgeons in New York City in 1840 when he was called to the Hartford Retreat to serve as medical superintendent. He resigned two years later to accept the superintendency of the newly organized Utica State Asylum in New York, built at a higher cost than any other mental hospital up to that time. Dr. Brigham began his regime under great difficulties. Before the asylum buildings had been completed the doors were thrown wide open for the reception of patients, causing no little confusion. Within a year after opening, it was obvious that the original plans were inadequate to meet the pressure of the increasing stream of patients, and enlargements were begun at once. The entire task of overseeing the structural changes, organizing the asylum staff, caring for and classifying the patients, etc., was borne by Dr. Brigham.

Not content with conducting a mere boarding house for the insane, as was then the vogue, he did all in his power to have his institution function as a real hospital, with cure the ever-present and dominant ideal. He was a firm believer in the efficacy of occupational therapy, and instituted a thorough system of indoor and outdoor labor, to suit the varied needs and backgrounds of the patients.

In 1844, Brigham founded the *American Journal of Insanity,* which represented his most important contribution to American psychiatry. It was published at his own expense, edited by himself and his fellow-officers at the Utica State Asylum, and printed with the help of patients at the asylum print shop. This was the first journal in the English language devoted to mental medicine. (A French publication, the *Annales Medico-Psychologiques* had been established a year earlier in Paris, and the *Allgemeine Zeitschrift für*

Psychiatrie was launched in 1844. The first journal devoted to psychiatric problems had been founded in Germany in 1805 by Johann C. Reil.) In his introductory prospectus to the journal, setting forth its *raison d'être* and its objects, Dr. Brigham wrote:

> The object of this Journal is to popularize the study of insanity—to acquaint the general reader with the nature and varieties of this disease, methods of prevention and cure. We also hope to make it interesting to members of the medical and legal profession, and to all those engaged in the study of the phenomena of mind.
>
> Mental philosophy, or metaphysics [!], is but a portion of the physiology of the brain; and the small amount of good accomplished by psychological writers may perhaps be attributed to the neglect of studying the mind, in connection with that material medium which influences, by its varying states of health and disease, all mental operations.
>
> We regard the human brain as the *chef d'oeuvre* or masterpiece of creation. There is nothing that should be so carefully guarded through all the periods of life. Upon its proper development, exercise and cultivation, depend the happiness and higher interests of man. Insanity is but a disease of that organ, and when so regarded, it will often be prevented, and generally cured by the early adoption of proper methods of treatment.[6]

Obviously, its founder intended the journal to reach the general public quite as much as those engaged in the specialty. He burned with the evangelistic zeal that so sharply characterized his generation. This enthusiasm is also reflected in his institutional reports, a generous part of which was always devoted to impressing upon the general reader the necessity of increasing existing facilities for the care and treatment of the insane. He was also alive to the importance of removing from the subject of insanity the mantle of mingled horror and mystery that popular fancy wrapped about it, and to strike down the surviving superstitions standing in the way of progress. This must have been one of his principal considerations in desiring to keep in close contact with the public.

It is interesting to note in Dr. Brigham's prospectus reflected a significant turn in the professional theory of insanity: in contrast to the former belief that mental disease was wholly psychic in origin, it was at this time generally held to be purely physical, with the seat of mental disorders rooted in the brain. A later age was to effect a compromise between the two extremes.

As far as the budding psychiatric profession of the time was concerned, the journal could hardly have appeared at a more opportune moment. As Dr. G. Alder Blumer once said: "This journal . . . soon becoming the organ of the whole specialty in this country, and reporting the papers and discussions of our Association, served to concentrate and strengthen the scientific spirit of investigation and to give it purpose and consistency; for the science itself, in which so much still remains to be done, was then really at a stage almost elementary and inchoate."[7]

After Dr. Brigham's death in 1849, the journal passed into the hands of the managers of the Utica State Asylum. Towards the end of the century it was taken over by the Association, becoming its official organ, and its place of publication was transferred to Baltimore. In 1921 it underwent a change of title to the *American Journal of Psychiatry.*

Another interesting literary experiment was introduced at Utica with the founding in 1850 of an intramural periodical, *The Opal,* edited and published by the patients themselves at the institutional print shop. It was not the first intramural publication prepared by and for mental patients, but it represented by far the best up to that time, and gained the widest recognition. As early as 1837 a newspaper, the *Retreat Gazette,* probably the first of its kind in America, had been published at the Hartford Retreat. It was edited by a patient who had been a newspaperman before entering the Retreat. Unfortunately, the *Gazette* was a one-man affair and ceased to function after the editor's recovery and discharge from the hospital. The second intramural publication in the United States (*The Asylum Journal*) was founded in 1842 at the Vermont Asylum at Brattleboro. It was issued first as a weekly, then as a monthly.[8] It was established by an enterprising young patient—a seventeen-year-old printer—and discontinued publication after four

THE ORIGINAL THIRTEEN

(1) Samuel B. Woodward, (2) Isaac Ray, (3) John S. Butler, (4) Samuel White, (5) Charles H. Stedman, (6) Pliny Earle, (7) Thomas S. Kirkbride, (8) Luther V. Bell, (9) William L. Awl, (10) John M. Galt, (11) Amariah Brigham, (12) Francis T. Stribling, (13) Nehemiah Cutter.

years due to the discharge of the founder and several other editor-patients from the hospital. The third institutional periodical, *The Opal* at Utica, went out of existence in 1861 for similar reasons.

John S. Butler (1803–1890) and Charles Harrison Stedman (1805–1866) served as first and second superintendents, respectively, of the Boston Lunatic Hospital, the first municipal institution of its kind to be established in the United States. Dr. Butler, who received his earliest training in the care of the mentally ill from Woodward of Worcester, occupied the post of superintendent from its opening in 1839 until 1842. The following year he became head of the Hartford Retreat, where he remained for the next thirty years.

Throughout his active career, Dr. Butler exercised a powerful influence in the Association he had helped organize. He made a particular study of the legal aspects of insanity and was frequently called upon to give expert testimony in important cases involving the plea of insanity. In 1873 he resigned as superintendent of the Hartford Retreat, and retired to private practice. Five years later he was named the first president of the newly created Connecticut State Board of Health, retaining his membership on that Board until his death at the advanced age of eighty-seven.

Dr. Stedman was the recipient of glowing praise from the pen of Charles Dickens, who visited the Boston Hospital for the Insane in 1842 (soon after Stedman became the executive officer there) and recorded his impressions of both the institution and its head in his *American Notes*. Besides his duties at the Hospital, Dr. Stedman was called upon to function as physician and surgeon to the city's various charitable and correctional institutions. He resigned in 1851, and thereafter pursued a dual career as practicing physician and politician. He was subsequently appointed Massachusetts' first medical coroner, served in the State Senate and on the Governor's Council, and was senior surgeon at the Boston City Hospital (established 1864) at the time of his death.

William M. Awl (1799–1876) helped found the Ohio

State Asylum for the Insane at Columbus, and became its first superintendent when it opened in 1838. He continued in that office twelve years, when he was turned out by the prevailing system of political appointment. Subsequently he became physician at the Ohio Institution for the Blind, having played a prominent role in its establishment, also.

Pliny Earle (1809–1892) brought to the specialty a temperate, clear-thinking personality. Possessing a keen-edged mind, he was able to cut through many of the layers of ignorance and pretension that lay heavy on the young body of psychiatry. He was not so much an original thinker as a critical one, and his outstanding contributions were born of his critical ability. After falling a victim to the "curability craze" in his early days of practice, he saw through the delusion and set out courageously to destroy it. He managed to expose many other current fallacies, accumulating a formidable array of enemies in the process, as is the fate of every iconoclast. His critiques of the slipshod, archaic methods of compiling hospital statistics in his time proved of great value in rescuing the reporting of institutional statistics from its low estate. Though he was no innovator himself, he was ever ready to adopt new methods that, in his opinion, had been adequately tested by others. Like Kirkbride and Ray, he was a man of strong convictions and stubbornness of purpose. Once convinced a course was right, nothing could deter him from putting it into practice and seeing it through.

Earle began his professional career in 1840 as resident physician at the Friends' Asylum at Frankford, after he had returned from a two-year study of mental hospitals in Europe. In 1844 he was appointed attending physician to the Bloomingdale Asylum in New York. Here he instituted a strong regimen of manual work, believing it to be a major therapeutic agent in the cure of mental diseases. He never hesitated to force labor on patients who, he felt, would benefit by it, regardless of what protests might be made by the patient or his friends on the basis of social status, etc.

Dr. Earle retained his post at Bloomingdale for five years. Then followed a second tour through Europe, with visits to

MID-CENTURY PSYCHIATRISTS

hospitals along the way. His observations were recorded in a work entitled *Institutions for the Insane in Prussia, Austria and Germany* (published 1853). This brochure did much to familiarize medical men in the United States with the progress in these countries, where psychiatrists were throwing off the metaphysical shackles that bound their predecessors. Previously, American and English observers of continental institutions had seldom penetrated beyond the borders of France. Americans were still prone to think of all German "alienists" (the term adapted from the French, designating specialists in mental diseases) as speculative metaphysicians, still following Heinroth slavishly. Significantly enough, English and American medical men were for many years reluctant to accept the term "psychiatry," which originated in Germany, because of their distrust of its metaphysical associations. They clung to the less definite term, alienism, until very recent years. Earle's contemporaries could hardly believe his statement that he had found in the German-speaking countries "a long list of men eminent in the specialty, who had produced a surprisingly large amount of published matter, both of speculative research into the origin and essential nature of insanity, and of treatises on its practical care and recovery."[9]

After his return to America Dr. Earle resumed the practice of his profession, serving for some time as visiting physician in the New York Lunatic Asylum at Ward's Island, and lecturing on mental diseases at the College of Physicians and Surgeons. In 1864 he was named superintendent of the Northampton Lunatic Asylum, which had opened in 1858 as the third state hospital in Massachusetts. Here he remained until his death, although he resigned from active service in 1885 at the age of seventy-six. The curability myth, against which he waged a long and strenuous fight, was dealt its *coup de grâce* in his chief work, *The Curability of Insanity* (1886), based on painstaking research into the reports and statistical records of scores of American and British hospitals over a period of some fifty years.

Isaac Ray (1807–1881) ranks among the foremost leaders of his period. Like many others in the specialty, he began his professional career as a general practitioner after completing his medical education. While practicing at Eastport, Maine, his attention was attracted to the study of insanity, particularly in its legal aspects. This important juridical area was as yet almost totally unexplored in America. There was a crying need for clarification. The need was supplied in 1837 with the publication of Ray's *Treatise on the Medical Jurisprudence of Insanity*, a work that received wide and well merited attention. It is still quoted and accepted as an authority on many phases of medico-legal practice in the United States and abroad.

In 1841 Dr. Ray was appointed medical superintendent of the State Hospital for the Insane at Augusta, Maine. He continued there until 1845, when he was invited to become head of the Butler Asylum at Providence, then in the process of organization. Together with Dr. Bell, he was solicited by the trustees to make an inspection tour of European institutions for the insane, so that the best features abroad might be synthesized in the contemplated hospital. After his return, he spent two years in supervising its erection. When the Butler Asylum opened in 1847 he assumed charge of its administration and, during his ensuing twenty years of service, raised it to a position of high renown. In 1867 he resigned for reasons of health and thereafter made his residence in Philadelphia, where he carried on a lucrative private practice until his death in 1881.

Ray was a man of wide interests, constantly keeping abreast of developments in the social sciences outside the orbit of his own specialty. His published writings, comprising more than one hundred items, display an excellent literary skill, marked by lucidity of thought and grace of style. In 1863 he published a work entitled *Mental Hygiene,* an admirable exposition within the limits of knowledge then prevailing, of the origins and nature of insanity. It was one of the first treatises in America to present a detailed program for the prevention of mental disorders. His third important work was *Contributions to Mental Pathology* (1873) consisting of a collection of papers and essays touching on nearly every phase of the subject.

He possessed an imposing forensic ability, and used it with devastating effect in pointed attacks on the errors and abuses of his day. Like most of his leading contemporaries he was rather inclined to dogmatism, clinging tenaciously to whatever doctrines he believed in. Although later experience did not confirm the correctness of all his policies and theories, he was usually to be found on the side of progress in his profession. There was hardly a major issue in psychiatry that did not find him in the forefront of the battle, and many a false doctrine was utterly demolished under the pitiless blows of his logic. With Pliny Earle and Edward Jarvis, he led the fight for honest and efficient tabulating in mental hospitals. "Statistics which are not really statistics," he wrote, "are worse than useless; and the reason is that they beguile the student with a show of knowledge, and thus take away the main inducement to further inquiry. Why should he look farther for truth when it already lies before him? Some of the prevalent errors respecting insanity and the insane are fairly attributable to these vicious statistics, for figures make a deeper impression on the mind than the most cogent arguments."[10]

Dr. Ray waged a continuous and courageous struggle for adequate appropriations for mental hospitals. At a time when most friends of the mentally ill deemed it sufficient to obtain from the legislatures funds barely enough to build institutions, with no thought for their maintenance, and when many medical superintendents felt it impolitic or dangerous to protest against legislative niggardliness, he repeatedly pointed out the absurd wastefulness—in the long run—of short-sighted, pinch-penny policies tending to hamper, or even to prevent, sound therapeutic practices in public hospitals. Not the least of his achievements was the conspicuous role he played in creating a sounder and more sympathetic understanding of the mentally ill in both the public and professional mind. His delightful little pamphlet, "Ideal Characters of the Officers of a Hospital for the Insane," written in 1873, might well serve today as a handbook in hospital service, as far as the sympathetic treatment of patients is concerned.

Ray was generally considered the foremost authority of his time on insanity in its relation to the law, and his service as an expert was in constant demand in important criminal cases.

The leading figure in the first four decades of the Association and the most prominent American psychiatrist of his time was Thomas Story Kirkbride (1809–1883). Born of Quaker parents, his psychiatric career was begun as a resident physician at the Friends' Asylum at Frankford. Later he joined the staff of the Pennsylvania Hospital as a surgeon, maintaining a flourishing private practice at the same time. When the new Department for the Insane of the Pennsylvania Hospital was opened as a separate building in West Philadelphia in 1841, he accepted a call to become its first superintendent and physician-in-chief. This post he held for nearly forty-three years—probably a record tenure of its kind. So great was the impress of his personality on the institution he headed that it became popularly known as "Kirkbride's." A prominent British psychiatrist, Dr. T. S. Clouston, recalling a visit he once made in Philadelphia, remarked that a street car conductor whom he approached could not tell him where the Pennsylvania Hospital for the Insane was, but readily directed him to "Kirkbride's."[11]

From the very first Dr. Kirkbride stood out as one of the leading medical superintendents. Even his earliest reports reveal a man who had acquired a splendid grasp of his profession, who saw clearly the requirements of his charges and was determined to meet them. Gentle, kind and considerate in manner, he yet possessed a firmness of conviction that, though sometimes indistinguishable from obstinacy, served as a tower of strength to his fellows in those unsteady days of the specialty. We have already alluded to the pronounced tendency of the time to use mental hospital reports as mediums of beneficial propaganda, addressed to the public in the hope of creating mass backing behind the cause of the insane. The reports of no other medical officer, perhaps, showed this proclivity as markedly as Kirkbride's. His reports fairly teem with general information on the subject of mental diseases, and display a knack for dealing with those phases which were uppermost in public discussion at the moment.

Dr. Kirkbride boldly combatted the popular inclination to regard mental diseases as mysterious afflictions, entirely remote in origin and nature from all other diseases. Depending for ammunition upon his arsenal of hard facts, he constantly bombarded the citadels of superstition and delusion and strove to inculcate in the public mind a rational approach toward the subject of insanity. Here are some representative statements culled from his earliest reports:

> Insanity should be classed with other diseases . . . It should never be forgotten that every individual who has a brain is liable to insanity, precisely as every one who has lungs is liable to pneumonia, or as every one with a stomach runs the risk at some period of being a martyr to dyspepsia . . .
>
> It has been too much the custom to say, without any qualification, that "insanity is the greatest infliction that can befall humanity," and many patients have had their wretchedness vastly increased by this common assertion . . . The proposition just referred to has originated from taking, as a type of the disease, some incurable case, laboring under the most violent and repulsive symptoms, and made hopeless, perhaps, by want of proper care, or by a course of management tending only to prevent recovery.
>
> In a comparison of insanity with other diseases, it must be borne in mind that it presents the greatest diversity of aspect, and that the symptoms are in almost endless variety; that many cases are attended with very little suffering, require but little restraint of any kind, are not disabled from appreciating books, or the society around them, or from enjoying many intellectual and physical comforts.[12]

These were sane words for those days, when even many of the most enlightened benefactors of the mentally ill believed that they could most effectively gain their ends by arousing terror and pity through citing the worst aspects of insanity, thus unconsciously tending to perpetuate distorted views on the subject.

In the matter of hospital organization, Dr. Kirkbride was one of the most vigorous advocates of trained nursing staffs, carefully selected and well paid, and one of the first to issue a printed manual to guide hospital employees in their duties. Long before the idea of training schools became accepted, he announced his intention of personally conducting a training course for attendants under his charge (1843). It appears, unfortunately, that the pressure of his varied labors prevented him from carrying out his design.

Kirkbride's most distinctive contribution to the care and treatment of the insane lay in the field of construction of mental hospitals. For an entire generation his word on hospital building was accepted as law in America. Between the years 1851 and 1880, at least thirty mental hospitals in this country were designed and built on the "Kirkbride plan."

Until Kirkbride's time there had been no uniform system of hospital construction. Many of the earlier institutions, as we have seen, had been merely reconstructed private dwellings, or else public institutions originally built for purposes other than the reception of the insane. Still others were built for this specific purpose, but were designed without any thought being given to the special needs of the mentally ill, and differed but little from ordinary prisons or almshouses.

During the custodial period, when institutions for the insane were regarded as places for the secure keeping of lunatics with the safety of the general public in mind, asylums were built accordingly. Even in the early period of the curative ideal, "insanity" was looked upon as "a disease," a single entity, rather than a general term comprehending a large and varied number of mental diseases. The resultant corollary was that, since all the insane were alike, they required the same treatment and the same surroundings. Hence all were congregated together indiscriminately, with little or no classification in treatment, and usually none in structural arrangements.

In the 1840's more and more thought was being devoted to the special requirements of the mentally ill, and this in turn led to serious consideration of structures of special design. Among those who concentrated on this particular aspect of the care and treatment of the mentally ill, Kirkbride soon assumed a position of leadership and authority.

At the time the Association of Medical Superintendents was formed, the question of construction occupied a paramount place in the minds of its members, as their early discussions prove.* They felt keenly the need of definition and clarification, and it was in this direction that their earliest attention was turned. The Association had been in existence but a few years when Dr. Kirkbride, recognized as the ablest among them in building matters, was delegated to draw up a set of "propositions" or rules embodying, as far as possible, the major structural considerations in a model hospital for the insane. In 1851, after a full and free discussion, the Propositions drawn up by Kirkbride were unanimously adopted by the Association as a permanent guide.

Among the twenty-six rules were these: Each hospital for the insane should be located in the country, not less than two miles from a large town, and easily accessible at all seasons; it should have not less than fifty acres of land, devoted to gardens and pleasure grounds for the patients; every state hospital should have at least one hundred acres; no hospital should be built without the plans first having been submitted to experienced medical men for approval; the highest number that can with propriety be treated in one building is 250 patients, while 200 is a preferable maximum; buildings should be constructed of stone or brick and, as far as possible, made fireproof; every hospital with provisions for two hundred or more patients should contain at least eight distinct wards for each sex, making sixteen classes in the entire building; no underground apartments should ever be provided for the confinement of patients, or as their lodging-rooms; the hospital pleasure grounds should be surrounded by a substantial wall; all rooms should be provided with windows; a large hospital should consist of a main central building with wings, the central building to contain the ad-

*As a matter of fact, it continued to hold its supremacy over other questions right up to the last decade of the 19th century. The change in name of the organization in 1893 to the American Medico-Psychological Association represented in large measure a revolt among the younger members against the emphasis placed on the building side of hospital organization, as symbolized by the inclusion of the term "Superintendents" in the old name. They wished more time devoted to clinical discussions, and less to structural ones. Thus the change in name actually symbolized a profound reorientation in American psychiatry—in its larger implications, a movement away from institutionalization as an ideal.

ministrative office and living quarters of the medical superintendent. Other propositions dealt with proper drainage, adequate and pure water supply, a complete system of forced ventilation and heating, etc.[13]

In 1854, Dr. Kirkbride elaborated these original propositions to form the basis of his famous work, *On the Construction and Organization of Hospitals for the Insane,* which became the standard textbook on the subject in America. The individual features of the Kirkbride plan of mental hospital architecture were not original with Kirkbride. Separately, they had been used before in building. It was he, however, who first united them in the closely integrated system known by his name.

Perhaps the major feature of the Kirkbride plan, partly incorporated in the twenty-six Propositions, was the linear projection of wings from a central administration building (Proposition XIV), in place of the quadrangular construction that had dominated hospital buildings up to that time. Another main feature was the limiting of the number of patients in any mental hospital to a maximum of 250 (Proposition V). Around this latter point there gathered a storm of controversy that gained in intensity with the years and finally grew so fierce as to threaten to break the Association apart on the rocks of dissension.

The Propositions were formulated and adopted at a time when highly exaggerated ideas of curability still prevailed. It was thought that recent cases could be quickly cured and that cases discharged recovered would perpetually balance newly admitted ones. Again, at the time, it was considered the duty of executive medical officers personally to supervise the treatment of each individual case in the institution —making the rounds every day if possible. This intensive personal supervision was considered to be impossible in institutions housing more than 250 patients.

As time went on, the older members of the Association came to regard the Propositions with increasing awe and reverence, and finally very much as if they were as immutable and sacrosanct as the ten commandments. A bitter tug of war took place between the "old guard" and the younger members, the former defending the original Propositions as fundamentalists do the Bible. They refused to permit the change of a single line, a phrase, or even a syllable. Arrayed against them were men who agreed that most of the Propositions remained sound, but that several—particularly the one setting the maximum, and the one that prescribed wings extending from a central building—would have to be modified to keep pace with changing social needs.*

Necessity at last solved the controversy, and brought about the downfall of the Propositions. Undoubtedly, when they had been formulated and adopted, they represented a marked step in advance over previous methods of construction. What the founders failed to realize, however, was the truth of the maxim that the only immutable law is the law of change; it was historical blindness to believe that the whole future could be fitted into the rigid framework of their twenty-six rules. Desirable as most of the features were, they could not withstand the imperious demands of necessity.

The most important factor in the breakdown of the 250-maximum rule was the tremendous growth in population and the concomitant increase in the number of insane, necessitating larger hospitals for their care and treatment. Another factor, of course, was the accumulation of uncured cases in hospitals, an eventuality overlooked by the fathers in their over-optimistic views on curability.

---

*For example, the linear plan, admirably suited to small institutions, could not meet the requirements of the larger mental hospitals, with capacities of 1,000 beds and more. Its limitations were well illustrated in the Buffalo State Hospital where the medical officers had to walk a distance of half a mile from the administration building to reach the farthest ward on either side.

It must be said, however, that some serious defects and shortcomings of asylum architecture during the latter half of the century were unjustly attributed to the Kirkbride plan simply because they occurred in institutions ostensibly built according to the lines laid down in that plan. Thus, many of the so-called "pauper palaces" that sprang up during the 1870's and '80's (of which the Danvers State Hospital in Massachusetts was a notable example), involving extravagant outlays for imposing fronts, ornate roofs, etc., at the expense of essential internal items, were wrongly laid to Kirkbride's influence, whereas they were really children of the Victorian vogue which was then blighting all architectural developments. As a matter of fact, simplicity in design was an outstanding feature of the plan formulated by Kirkbride.

Hence, while the Association affirmed and reaffirmed its abiding faith in the Propositions, the exigencies of reality were playing havoc with them. Driven by the inexorable pressure of necessity, state hospitals increased their capacities to 500, 1,000, and even 1,500 beds. Ironically enough, the Pennsylvania Hospital for the Insane, presided over by the venerable framer of the Propositions, was soon forced to expand beyond the 250-maximum originally set. In 1866, the Association was reluctantly constrained to modify Proposition V to permit a maximum of 600 beds in mental institutions. With this modification, the whole set of Propositions proved unwieldy, since many of them had been premised on the small-hospital idea. Finally, in 1888, at a meeting of the Association at Old Point Comfort, the Propositions were scrapped *in toto* after a bitter debate, and none was substituted thereafter.

By that time the trend toward the so-called "cottage system," based on the grouping of small detached buildings around a central administration building, was already gaining strength, a trend that continues to this day. The cottage system permitted a far better classification of patients, a greater degree of privacy, and elimination of much of the old monotony and other unpleasant aspects of institutionalization, and facilitated administrative control and supervision. While the cottage system is universally accepted as the ideal one in the hospital treatment of mental patients, it has failed to achieve universal adoption largely because of economic pressure. Too many of our legislators, executives and "leading taxpayers" are unwilling to sanction the building of hospitals along the best lines of curative principles while outmoded, inadequate designs are available at less expense.

CHAPTER XI

Conflict of Theories: Restraint or Non-Restraint?

THE rise of psychiatric knowledge, with analysis and synthesis evolving from simple into complex processes, inevitably brought in its wake numerous theoretical controversies. In so far as debate reflected a lively interest in a growing science, these controversies constituted an encouraging sign of progress. In some respects, however, they indicated all too clearly the stubborn resistance of old and outworn practices against the advance of new and better ones, and a growing confusion as to aims and methods.

Of the many questions that stirred American asylum superintendents during the half-century following the organization of the Association, one of the most discussed and heated—and probably the least understood—centered around the doctrine of "non-restraint." Although it seemed on the surface a very simple doctrine, apparently involving merely the abolition of mechanical restraint* in the care and treatment of mental patients, it really was quite complicated, and caused no end of confusion and acrimonious dispute on this side of the Atlantic.

The theory and practice of non-restraint is intimately associated with the name of Dr. John Conolly (1794–1867), who first formulated it into a system, although he was not the first to practice it. Of course, it did not come upon the world full-blown: it experienced a gradual development

---

*Mechanical restraint may be simply defined as consisting of "any apparatus that interferes with the free movement of the patient, and which he is unable to remove easily." (*Handbook of the New York State Department of Mental Hygiene*, 1933, p. 356.)

dating from the first removal of chains and fetters by Chiarugi, Pinel and Tuke toward the end of the eighteenth century. Also in the line of evolution was the celebrated British parliamentary investigation of 1815, which revealed horribly cruel treatment of patients in public and private asylums. It had the effect of arousing public sentiment against coercive methods, and led progressive leaders to seek ways and means of bringing restraints down to a minimum.

In 1829, further impetus to reform was afforded by the tragic death at Lincoln Asylum, England, of a patient in consequence of his being strapped in bed in a strait-jacket during the night. As a result of this incident, the asylum adopted a rule that whenever mechanical restraints were used at night, an attendant should remain with the patient. (Night attendant service in institutions throughout the nineteenth century was very rare, it being the custom to simply lock up the patient in his room or cell until morning.) Much to the surprise of the asylum officials, it was observed that mechanical restraints were seldom needed at night for the pacification of patients. Further experiments proved that they could be dispensed with by day as well as by night with no harmful effects ensuing. Finally, in 1837, under the direction of Dr. Charlesworth and Mr. Gardiner Hill, mechanical restrains were entirely abolished at Lincoln Asylum.

The non-restraint methods introduced by Charlesworth and Hill at Lincoln were closely studied by Dr. John Conolly, who was profoundly impressed by them. In 1839 Conolly was appointed medical superintendent of the Middlesex Asylum located at Hanwell, England, where he proceeded to establish the principles of non-restraint. He extended these new principles and finally formulated them into a complete pattern of mental hospital management. This system he presented to the world in his famous book, *The Treatment of the Insane Without Mechanical Restraints* (1856).

The completeness of the reform effected by Dr. Conolly at Hanwell is most impressively shown in his own description of what he found there upon first assuming direction of the institution: "Instruments of mechanical restraint, of one kind or another, were so abundant in the wards as to amount, when collected together, to about six hundred—half of these being handcuffs and leg-locks."[1] In his first annual report (1840) he was able to inform the managers that within four months after his taking charge, all mechanical restraint had been abolished. "No form of strait-waistcoat, no handstraps, no leg-locks, nor any contrivance confining the trunk or limbs, or any of the muscles, is now in use. The coercion chairs, about forty in number, have been altogether removed from the wards."[2]

The non-restraint system, which involved a great deal more than the mere removal of mechanical restraint, as many willing but unknowing hospital heads were to learn through bitter experience, was widely adopted in England after its successful introduction at Hanwell. But in America it met with an antagonism remarkable for its extreme bitterness. The opposition evinced by most American superintendents of mental hospitals undoubtedly originated from serious misconceptions as to the methods and aims of non-restraint. But the antagonism continued long after the misconceptions were cleared up.

The fact that the subject of mechanical restraint was discussed in nearly every meeting of the Association during its first fifty years of existence indicates the lingering doubts in the minds of its advocates as to the validity of their position, and their constant need for reaffirmation. Through the years every possible argument against non-restraint was desperately put forward, some of them appearing pitifully ludicrous in the light of our present perspective, others meriting more serious consideration.

At the founding meeting in 1844, the Association of Medical Superintendents adopted as its very first rule, or "proposition," the following: "Resolved, that it is the unanimous sense of this convention that the attempt to abandon entirely the use of all means of personal restraint is not sanctioned by the true interests of the insane." One of the thirteen there assembled, Dr. Isaac Ray, was to stand out during the next two decades as the foremost opponent of non-restraint on the American scene.* In that very year (1844), Dr. Ray had presented an extended criticism of the system in his annual report for the Maine Insane Hospital. This critique, which indicated that even at that early date the writer had devoted much attention to the subject, remained the major basis for American assaults on the non-restraint system for years to come.

The arguments originally brought forward by Ray in 1844, and later expanded by others, may be summarized as follows:

1. In the final analysis, the ideal of non-restraint could never be completely realized. Hence, it was idle to even consider putting such a system into operation. Some forms of forcible restraint would always be necessary to the proper discipline of a mental hospital. The very walls and gates were coercive. Institutionalization of the insane *per se* implied coercion, as it was often effected against the will and wish of the patient. As for mechanical restraint proper—that is, limitation on the bodily movements of the patient by means of external devices—it would continue to be required in very special instances, as most "Conollyists" freely admitted. This being the case, it was more honest to champion restraint in principle, rather than non-restraint.

2. The abolition of mechanical restraint meant merely the substitution of another form of coercion—"manual restraint," or force exercised at the hands of attendants—which was hardly more desirable.

3. To supplant mechanical restraint by attendants would necessitate larger staffs and consequently greater expense.

4. Suicidal, destructive and unmanageable patients required some form of personal restraints, of which mechanical appliances were least onerous and most effective.

5. Mechanical restraints were also required for patients who were prone to exhaust their energy and to lower their vitality by excessive physical excitement.

6. The patients in European institutions, accustomed as they were to unquestioned acceptance of authority, might willingly submit to "moral" restraint, but not your liberty-loving American who, sane

---

*His place as leader was later occupied by Dr. John P. Gray, superintendent of the Utica State Asylum, who was for years editor of the *American Journal of Insanity,* and was one of the most influential men in his profession.

RESTRAINT OR NON-RESTRAINT? 217

or insane, would never agree placidly to the imposition of authority by an individual, and hence could be restrained only by mechanical means.

7. In certain institutions where the abolition of mechanical restraint had been tried, it had resulted in dismal failure, and the old restraints had been resumed.

These arguments, together with others of less consequence (conjured up from time to time to bolster the opposition), seemed well-nigh irrefutable to the majority of American superintendents for many years. It must be said, in all frankness, that not many of them sought very diligently to examine the claims of the other side. Until the closing years of the past century, non-restraint remained the *bête noire* of American psychiatry—grossly condemned because its practical applications were little understood. Perhaps in no other aspect of the care and treatment of mental illness were American institutions so backward as in this. Had the opponents of non-restraint sought earnestly enough for answers to the arguments we have just enumerated, they might have found them summarized thus, in their respective order:

1. There are certain exceptions implicit in *every* rule of human conduct that may be laid down as a principle. Rejection of a principle, because it admits of such exceptions, invariably leaves room for the encroachment of all sorts of abuses that are effectively checked when the principle is stated in positive terms and enforced.

Strangely enough, many medical superintendents in the United States were themselves reducing the use of mechanical coercion to an insignificant minimum while they went about belaboring non-restraint in principle. Thus, Dr. Kirkbride, who consistently opposed the doctrine laid down by Conolly, was nevertheless characterized by one of its most prominent defenders as "one who advocated restraint but never used it."[3] Kirkbride himself wrote in one of his early reports:

> Had I felt anxious to make such a declaration, it would have been in my power to have stated that during the past year, no restraining apparatus of any kind had been upon the person of a single patient of

this hospital—but believing as I do that its occasional employment may be conferring a favor on the patient, it has always been resorted to where there existed a proper indication for its use. The only indication for its use that is recognized in this Hospital, is the positive benefit or safety of the patient—never the trouble of those to whose care he is entrusted—and the direct order of the physician or his assistant, the only authority under which it can be applied.[4]

As a matter of sober fact, Conolly himself never conceived of, or tried to practice, *absolute* non-restraint, although several of his more enthusiastic disciples, like Dr. Batty Tuke, advanced it to the extreme lengths of doing away not only with all bodily coercion, but even with locked doors and protected windows in *all* cases. Conolly held that restraint might not only be useful but necessary in exceptional instances, such as in surgical operations. His biographer and friend, Sir James Clark, states in clarification of this point: ". . . it should be understood that there is no such thing as an absolute repudiation of restraint in the treatment of the insane. The warmest advocates of non-restraint admit that cases may occur in which it is proper to resort to mechanical restraint, and by this admission we do not think that we invalidate the principle."[5]

The boundaries of the abolition of mechanical restraint, as first defined by Conolly, might best be illustrated by referring to the rules promulgated by the New York State Department of Mental Hygiene in 1933, covering all state hospitals, which read in part:

Mechanical restraint or seclusion is to be employed only for satisfactory surgical or medical reasons, or to prevent a patient from injuring himself or others.

Mechanical restraint or seclusion shall be employed only on the signed order of a physician, setting forth the reasons for its use; and a physician shall always be present at the first application of restraint. A full record of restraint shall be kept from day to day and shall be subject to inspection by authorized persons.

Mechanical restraint consists of any apparatus that interferes with the free movement of the patient, and which he is unable to remove easily. The only forms of mechanical restraint permissible are the camisole and restraining sheet.

RESTRAINT OR NON-RESTRAINT?

The maximum period in the day time during which a patient may be kept continuously in restraint shall be two hours and such patients shall be visited at least every hour.

A patient shall be considered in seclusion, either in the day time or at night, when in a room alone with closed door which it is not possible for the patient to open from the inside.

The maximum period of continuous seclusion shall not exceed three hours in the day time and the patient shall be visited every hour.[6]

It may readily be seen that the establishment of principles in this positive and precise manner admits of relatively few abuses.

2. The picture drawn by those who held that "manual" restraint was the only effective substitute for mechanical appliances was so overdrawn as to sink to poor caricature. They envisaged, in hospitals operated under the non-restraint system, giant bullies hovering constantly about the hapless patient, ready to pounce upon him and to pummel him into subjection at the slightest manifestation of boisterousness or violent behavior. Rather than resort to this alternative, American superintendents, notably Isaac Ray, favored mechanical restraints. As Ray put it: "I have no hesitation in saying that they [mechanical restraints] are far preferable to the vigilance or force of attendants. The object is gained more surely, more effectually, and with far less annoyance to the patient. A mechanical device performs its office more steadily, uniformly and thoroughly, and is submitted to as something inevitable. The will and strength of an attendant are capricious and variable in their operation."[7]

Dr. Ray was wrong in regarding the physical force of an attendant as the only alternative to mechanical restraints. As we shall see, the system advanced by Conolly and his disciples included carefully designed provisions permitting peaceful and healthful safety-valves in congenial occupations and recreation for the pent-up energies of patients. Furthermore, instead of breeding antagonisms between patient and attendant the non-restraint system, when faithfully followed, expressly provided means for obtaining a maximum amount of friendliness between the two.

3. Although many opponents of the non-restraint system

publicly minimized the importance of the economy factor, it undoubtedly exerted no small influence in determining their attitude. Feeling, as they did, that manual restraint was the only alternative to mechanical means, they concluded that the increased expenditures necessitated by corresponding enlargement of staff would be too burdensome to be borne by most institutions. As early as 1844, Dr. Ray had written:

> When mechanical restraints are entirely disused, the first consideration that presents itself is, that the number of attendants must be much larger than when they are used even in a very limited degree, and thus the expense of the establishment is swelled to a very onerous amount. In many parts of our country, the only alternative is between a cheap establishment and none at all; and certainly, nothing but the clearest and weightiest reasons should be suffered to have the effect of debarring a large number of the insane from receiving the benefit of hospital treatment.[8]

This statement stands in surprising contradiction to others made repeatedly by Dr. Ray throughout his career. He invariably stressed the principles of humaneness and generosity above those of expediency and economy. Time and time again he took sharp issue with those who deemed it sufficient to build institutions for mere custody. The fact that this progressive psychiatrist was forced into such a contradiction in his attack on non-restraint indicates, perhaps, the paucity of real arguments against the system laid down by Conolly.

4. The non-restraint system, as we have seen, made due allowance for the use of mechanical restraint in exceptional and extreme cases where patients were dangerous either to themselves or to others. It did, however (as do the best-conducted institutions today), strictly define the limits, both in type of appliances used and maximum time of duration, within which mechanical coercion might be applied. Wherever possible it substituted the milder, less painful and less humiliating method of seclusion as a means of restraint. On the other hand, where mechanical restraint was adhered to

as a principle, there was a strong tendency to resort to it at the least manifestation of suicidal or destructive (or merely annoying) dispositions in patients, and to keep them confined until "they got over it."

In those days, few recognized the fact that mechanical restraints invariably stimulated and encouraged the very conditions they were supposed to eliminate or to mitigate. "Violence begets violence." If the excitement of the normal individual is increased by a display of needless repression, the excited mental patient, forcibly restrained in a humiliating and often painful manner, is apt to become even more agitated. Violent or noisy outbursts that might, under tactful treatment, be overcome in a few minutes, are frequently protracted indefinitely. Suicidal tendencies are likely to become more pronounced, rather than lessened, through the use of mechanical force, which serves to confirm the patient's feeling that he moves about in a hostile environment.

In institutions where non-restraint was rejected as a principle it was too often the custom to confine the patient in strait-jackets, muffs, handcuffs, etc., over long periods of time, not because of a present emergency, but because of some violent outburst in the remote past, or, perhaps, to forestall one anticipated in the future. Often enough, officials were in the habit of placing patients in mechanical restraints on Sundays and holidays for no other reason than that they found themselves "short-handed" of attendants on such occasions.* In still another sense, economy was an important factor in determining the frequency of restraining "destructive" patients; for example, the desire to save clothes and furniture from being torn or broken. The "non-restrainters" resorted to a more humane, though less simple, method of achieving the same end. Instead of shackling patients who destroyed their clothing, or just letting them run about naked, they recommended the expedient of garbing such persons in clothes that could neither be torn nor cast off.

*With much truth Conolly had written: "Restraints and neglect may be considered synonymous; for restraints are merely a general substitute for the thousand attentions required by troublesome patients."

It was maintained by many superintendents that mechanical restraint not only prevented patients from indulging in destructive inclinations, but had the positive effect of building up their power of self-control, thereby advancing their recovery. This argument was somewhat specious. The humiliation, loss of self-respect, untidiness and pain occasioned by most forms of mechanical restraint actually intensified the very traits—self-pity, moroseness, desire for revenge, resentment—best calculated to retard either self-control or recovery. Obviously, too, the liberal use of forcible restraints had a negative effect on the attitude of attendants towards patients, serving to brutalize them, and to generate a contempt toward patients. In marked contrast, hospitals which reduced restraints to an absolute minimum and substituted well planned "safety-valves" generally presented a picture of more contentment, freedom and comfort, and were troubled with far fewer outbursts of violent behavior on the part of patients. Furthermore, institutional tension diminished when psychiatry advanced to the point where it began to probe into the *causes* of violent and destructive behavior and tried to check them at the root, instead of merely dealing with their *consequences*.

5. It is indeed true that some types of mental illness require continued rest as a major therapeutic measure. But mechanical restraints were hardly calculated to effect this aim; on the contrary, they invariably tended to defeat it. For instance, strapping a patient in bed was once a popular method of enforcing rest. The most widely used mechanical device for this purpose up to about a half-century ago was the "Utica crib," so named because it was first introduced in America at the Utica State Asylum, and there developed. The crib-bed, of which it was a modification, had been invented by Dr. Aubanel of Marseilles, France, in 1845, and was adopted by Dr. Brigham at Utica the following year. It was shaped like an ordinary baby's crib, except that it had attached on its top a hinged lid, like that on a trunk. This could be fastened over the patient at night, thus restricting his freedom of movement. The champions of the Utica crib and similar devices overlooked the fact

RESTRAINT OR NON-RESTRAINT? 223

that the patient usually expended as much energy, and more, in struggling to free himself, as he might if his movements were unrestrained. In addition there was the extreme discomfort occasioned by this mode of confinement. On the whole it created a situation hardly conducive to sleep and restfulness. The abolition of the crib proved that patients could rest as easily in "free" beds. The development of modern hydrotherapy (hot baths, etc.) and "chemical restraints" (sedatives) also proved more effective means of ensuring rest.

6. Inasmuch as every conceivable type of argument was conjured up by opponents of non-restraint, it is hardly surprising that they sometimes branded it as a "foreign" system, and defended mechanical coercion on purely patriotic grounds. Many American officers of institutions for the insane were perplexed to discover, on visiting English hospitals operated under the non-restraint system, that, despite the greater amount of liberty permitted in the latter, the patients were invariably more peaceful, better behaved and neater than in the former. At first they were at a loss to explain this paradox. But possessing true Yankee ingenuity, they did not permit themselves to remain nonplussed for long. A convenient theory was evolved: non-restraint might do for Englishmen, but it would never be tolerated by red-blooded Americans! Dr. Clement Walker, head of the Boston Lunatic Asylum and a prominent psychiatrist of his day, in an address delivered before the Association of Medical Superintendents in 1874, declared:

> I suppose if anything has been settled to the satisfaction of the members of this Association it is that, in this country, our patients, by *original temperament,* or by some inherent quality in the *universal Yankee,* will not submit to the control of any person they consider their equal or inferior as readily as that of mechanical appliances.[9]

Commenting on this belief held by some American medical men, the noted British psychiatrist, John C. Bucknill, remarked: "The essence of the non-restraint system is to lead the lunatic by such remains of mental power and coherence as the physician can lay hold upon, and where there has been the least mind, there would be the slightest means of moral guidance; but to make the men of the United States an exception because they, more than others, have learned how to rule themselves, is a blundering censure upon their culture and their virtues."[10]

The defense of mechanical restraint as being "peculiarly" necessary in America because of the singular nature of its inhabitants was most ingenious, to say the least. It represented an amusing oversimplification of a general truth—namely, that social mores, traditions and institutions are bound to influence individual behavior—employed to cover a situation in which that truth had very little, if any, application.*

Allied to the patriotic defense of mechanical restraint in the United States, was the contention that it was needed in this country because of peculiar climatic and geographic factors. It was a common notion that the relatively equable climate of Great Britain bred a mild and complacent people, while the violent changes that characterize meteorological conditions in America (particularly in the Northern states) developed a correspondingly violent race. This violence was especially manifest in the insane, and hence the frequent recourse to mechanical restraint to subdue them. This outlandish theory requires no comment.

Several American institutions for the insane did indeed make an honest effort to introduce the non-restraint system, only to abandon the experiment after a brief trial, and to revert to the free use of mechanical restraint. Invariably, the failure in these hospitals was attributable to a lack of proper understanding of the system, and of its comprehensive scope. Some superintendents merely removed the mechanical appliances from confined patients and then waited

---

*Significantly enough, this very same "liberty-loving, authority-hating" theory was utilized by German medical superintendents of that time to explain the necessity for mechanical restraint in their own country. They, too, argued that non-restraint succeeded in English hospitals precisely because the Englishman, sane or insane, instinctively feared and obeyed personal authority! In Scotland, it was gravely held by some that the native insane had to be treated like wild beasts because of the wild, untamable nature of the Scots!

idly by to see a miracle happen. They heeded not the warning of Conolly, who, in formulating his principle, wrote:

It is, above all, important to remember . . . that the mere abolition of fetters and restraints constitutes only a part of what is properly called the non-restraint system. Accepted in its full and true sense, it is a complete system of management of insane patients, of which the operation begins the moment a patient is admitted over the threshold of an asylum.[11]

Besides the rejection of mechanical coercion, the system included those intangibles that had first been formulated by the Tukes and Pinels under the name of "moral" treatment. It meant nothing less than the complete *humanizing* of the institution in its entirety. It required kindness, patience, understanding and truthfulness on the part of the hospital staff. It required the careful inculcation and development of confidence, trust, self-respect and hope in the patients, as far as possible. It required the elimination of heavy-walled, narrow "airing courts" and other prison-like aspects that cast oppressive shadows over so many institutions, causing some patients to feel that they were being punished for misdeeds rather than being treated for ailments. It required the planning of healthful recreations and congenial occupations to draw the ill mind from morbid fancies and to help build up a sound body to house a sound mind.

In short, the system of non-restraint did not end with the mere removal of bodily coercion. It involved a complex and all-embracing method of hospital administration and treatment. However great was the obloquy heaped upon the principle of non-restraint in America up to the end of the century, this principle nevertheless exerted a decided and healthy influence here from the first. It had the effect of gradually mobilizing public opinion to the point of forcing the reduction of mechanical restraint, in varying degrees, in institutions for the insane throughout the country. This was true even in asylums the officers of which disagreed most violently with the principle of non-restraint. In several asylums non-restraint was actually practiced within the limits originally defined by Conolly, although for one reason or another, the superintendents clung tenaciously to the negatively stated theory of "mechanical restraint at discretion." In taking this course, they unwittingly left a wide loop-hole for all sorts of abuses in institutions run by men of lesser intelligence and, perhaps, looser conscience, than they. As early as 1857, Pliny Earle had pointed out the danger, saying: "While it is occasionally necessary to employ mechanical restraint, yet I believe that this admission is calculated to favor a tendency to its excessive use."

It is difficult to explain adequately the hostile, often acrimonious, reaction of American hospital superintendents to non-restraint during the third quarter of the nineteenth century. Their attitude was in no small measure due to their undeviating insistence that supreme authority in each institution should be wielded by the superintendent without "outside" interference. Rugged individualists all, they felt that non-restraint, legislated on the statute books, might place the executive officer constantly under the thumb of investigating committees, and deprive him of his jealously guarded authority. I might mention another factor, less direct perhaps, but just as potent in keeping alive the resentment of many American superintendents to the British-born system of non-restraint. I refer to the unbearably patronizing attitude of certain English medical men towards their American cousins in the psychiatric specialty. It was not unusual for English physicians to make a casual and very limited inspection of American asylums for the insane, and, upon their return home, to apply some sweeping derogatory generalization covering all such institutions in the United States. (It was then quite the custom for English literary and professional men to cross the Atlantic with the preconception that they were about to visit a savage people, and they usually managed to return with their prejudgments confirmed.)

The most notorious of the blanket attacks on American mental hospitals appeared in the London *Lancet* of 1875. Referring, in a leading article, to the "ignorance and misconceptions of our brethren in America," the writer categorically declared that the American "Mad Doctors" remained for the most part "in that stage in which the lunatic is simply regarded as a wild and dangerous animal, from which society needed protection, and which might be kept in chains, tamed or destroyed, as convenience should dictate." Then followed these choice characterizations:

> Our friends across the Atlantic have not yet mastered the fundamental principles of the remedial system. They adhere to the old terrorism tempered by petty tyranny. They resort to contrivances of compulsion; they use, at least, the hideous torture of the shower-bath as a *punishment* in their asylums, although it has been eliminated from the discipline of their gaols. And worse than all, if reports that reach us may be trusted, their medical superintendents leave the care of patients, practically, to mere attendants, while devoting their energies principally to the beautifying of their colossal establishments.[12]

While it is undoubtedly true that this biting criticism was applicable to many institutions for the mentally ill in America, it was grossly unfair to men like Butler, Earle, Nichols and Kirkbride who, despite individual shortcomings, were putting into practice the most progressive principles of the time. Such indiscriminate attacks could not but stir up deep resentment on this side of the Atlantic. Unfortunately, but quite inevitably, the counter attack loosed on the self-appointed champions of non-restraint who were guilty of the aforementioned injustice, fell in part on the principle itself. It should be noted in passing that the particular *Lancet* article in question was vehemently condemned by the two leading British psychiatrists, John C. Bucknill and D. Hack Tuke, who were best fitted to judge the American scene, and who forced a partial retraction from the editors.

Among the early advocates of the non-restraint system in America were Drs. Edward Jarvis, Joseph L. Bodine, Alice Bennett, E. C. Seguin, William A. Hammond, Nathan Allen and Charles W. Page.

Today, the non-restraint system is written into law on the statute books of several states (notably Massachusetts, which passed the pioneer non-restraint law, framed by Dr. L. Vernon Briggs, in 1911), and is also prescribed in the rules and regulations in many other states (e.g., the New York State rules referred to earlier in the chapter). Some backward states still lack adequate safeguards against the abuses of mechanical restraint, but it is to be hoped that professional leadership and public opinion will, in the near future, eradicate these relics of a barbaric age. It will be a red-letter day indeed when the last appliance of mechanical restraint passes out of service and takes its place beside the tranquilizing chair and the ball and chain as a museum piece, a memento of a bygone age in the care and treatment of the mentally ill.

CHAPTER XII
The Trend Toward State Care

TIME alters many things, including the meaning of terms.* When, for example, young Horace Mann stood on the floor of the Massachusetts legislature and enunciated the principle that "the insane are the wards of the state," his thought was quite removed from the present-day conception of his words. In Mann's time "state care," as construed even by the progressive elements, implied no more than the duty of the state to see that all the insane requiring institutionalization received it in special asylums. The latter did not necessarily have to be built, maintained or supervised by the state itself. A later generation defined the principle as establishing the state's duty to supervise the care of all the insane within its borders, though contributing to the support of this class only to a limited degree. Today, in such states as New York and Massachusetts, state care includes provision in state-owned hospitals, administered and maintained by the state, for all mentally ill persons in need of public care and treatment.

The evolution of state care followed a long and winding trail before reaching its most significant expression with the passage of the New York State Care Act of 1890. Its beginnings in the United States may be traced back to 1751, when the provincial legislature of Pennsylvania appropri-

---

*As interesting illustrations of this truism, we might point to the etymological origins of such psychiatric terms as *melancholia* (literally, "black bile"), reflecting the humoral pathology of Hippocrates; *hysteria* (derived from the Greek for *uterus*), which stems from the ancient notion that this disorder was caused by the movement of the uterus, conceived of as a living, independent animal roving at will through the body; and *lunacy*, the derivation of which is obvious.

ated several thousand pounds toward the erection of the Pennsylvania Hospital at Philadelphia. The next step came in 1769 with the founding of America's first institution exclusively for the insane—the Lunatic Hospital at Williamsburg, Virginia. This institution marked a tremendous advance toward the ideal of state care. It was built entirely at state expense, and the indigent patients therein were wholly supported by state funds. Its administration and control, however, were left in the hands of a self-perpetuating board of directors acting as a corporate body. The Eastern Kentucky Lunatic Asylum at Lexington, established in 1822, seems to have been the first built primarily for the reception of pauper and indigent insane,* although pay patients were also received. Here, too, the cost of caring for dependent patients was borne by the state alone.[1] Differing from this was the policy pursued in most of the mental hospitals established during the '30's and '40's, such as the Worcester Lunatic Hospital in Massachusetts and the Utica Asylum in New York, where the maintenance of dependent patients was charged to the localities in which these persons had settlement, the state paying only for non-resident and alien insane.†

The opening of the Worcester State Hospital in 1833 marked the beginning of an extensive asylum-building movement throughout the country. At first, in accordance with the prevailing belief that fully 90 per cent of mental cases could be cured, it was expected that one centrally located hospital in each state would afford sufficient provision for all the insane. In several of the sparsely settled states in the West, of course, one asylum was for a long time all that was necessary. But in most states this expectation was soon

---

*We might do well to clarify here the distinction between the terms "pauper" and "indigent." A pauper does not possess any property, and is wholly dependent on public support. An indigent person is one not possessing sufficient property or sufficient income to support himself or his family during illness or disability.

†In Massachusetts, where the local poor relief system prevailed, the dependent insane were charged to the towns and cities; in New York, where the county was the poor relief unit, the insane were charged to the counties of settlement.

THE TREND TOWARD STATE CARE 231

dispelled. Hardly were hospitals opened than their capacities became overtaxed by the never-ceasing flow of patients. Overcrowding soon forced upon authorities the problem of selection. Faced with the necessity of admitting a certain number of applicants and excluding others, authorities naturally favored the admission of recent cases over chronic and incurable cases. Gradually, then, there developed the custom—in some states amounting to an "unwritten law," in others explicitly stated in statutes—of sending only acute cases to institutions for the insane, while the chronics (sometimes euphemistically called the "surplus insane") were confined in poorhouses and jails or else supported in the homes of friends or relatives. Generally, if a dependent patient in a hospital was not discharged recovered within a stipulated period (say, twelve months), he was returned from the hospital to his place of settlement as incurable and was thenceforth maintained at a local institution, usually the poorhouse or jail.

Thus there developed a division between recent and chronic cases in relation to institutional treatment, not so much as the result of a definitely formulated plan as of a more or less haphazard development. For practical purposes, state hospitals maintained only acute and dangerous cases, while all others were relegated to local care.

Far from solving the problem of proper disposition of the insane, this situation created new and more complex problems. For one thing, so rapid was the increase in the number of mental patients that accommodations in many states soon proved insufficient even for the acute cases alone. As a result the proportion of insane persons deprived of proper treatment or care grew alarmingly. The following table indicates the increase in insanity in relation to the increase in the general population of the United States, during the latter half of the 19th century:*

*Because of faulty census-taking methods and the reigning confusion over the terms "insane" and "insanity," the figures on the insane from 1840–1870, inclusive, approached neither accuracy nor reliability. Indeed, Dr. John S. Billings, who compiled the report on the insane and feebleminded for the 11th census (1890), stated bluntly: "The figures for the United States Censuses previous to 1880 are entirely worthless so far as the calculation of

Year	Total Population United States	Estimated Number of Insane	Insane in Hospitals and Asylums
1840	17,069,453	17,457*	2,561
1850	23,191,876	15,610	4,730
1860	31,443,322	24,042	8,500
1870	38,555,983	37,432	17,735
1880	50,155,783	91,959	38,047
1890	62,947,714	106,485	74,028

Remarkable though the growth of the general population was during this half century, the rate of increase in insanity appears by the figures to have been far greater. How much of this apparent acceleration in the rate of insanity is attributable to the actual spread of mental illness, and how much to such factors as more efficient methods of census-taking, greater accuracy in diagnosis and classification, and the steady widening of the concept of mental disease, is a speculative question that defies solution at the present time. Be that as it may, the rise in the known cases of mental illness necessitated continual building of new institutions, and enlargement of existing ones. But these institutions could never quite catch up with the total need.

By 1850, when the curability bubble was beginning to burst, it became apparent that (except for a few thinly populated Western states) a single state hospital could not meet the requirements of a growing population. State hospitals were enlarged; new ones were erected. But still the number of insane deprived of hospital care continued to keep pace with the number who found refuge (in varying degrees) in

ratios of the number of insane to the population is concerned, since the number of insane returned in these censuses was certainly less than half the number actually present."

The tremendous leap in the number of insane in 1880 as compared with 1870 is largely attributable to the fact that in this census, for the first time, the cooperation of the physicians throughout the country was obtained in reporting cases of insanity. Conversely, the apparent drop in the ratio of insane persons in 1890 does not represent a real decrease, but is explained by the fact that in this census the physicians did not supplement the reports of the enumerators.

*This figure includes both the insane and the feebleminded, since census takers at that time made no distinction between the two groups.

THE TREND TOWARD STATE CARE

hospitals and asylums.* In 1854 a lunacy commission authorized by the Massachusetts legislature to make a survey of insanity and feeblemindedness, under the able direction of Dr. Edward Jarvis, found that there were then in the state a total of 2,632 insane persons. Of these only 1,141—less than half—were being maintained in special establishments for the mentally ill. The following year a report submitted to the New York legislature revealed that, of an estimated total of 2,123 dependent insane persons within the state, only 296 were being treated in the Utica State Asylum. Most of the remainder were confined in houses of correction, almshouses and jails. Meanwhile the nation was being stirred by the horrible conditions uncovered by Dorothea Dix in her travels through America. Other investigators, too, were constantly bringing forth new evidences of the terrible treatment of the insane in local poorhouses. Still, the majority of the mentally ill continued to be thrust into these receptacles. What was to be done?

Although enlightened opinion was quite unanimous as to the desirability of removing insane persons from the poorhouses, there was no such unanimity on the question as to how to effect this end. Various solutions were offered, the principal ones falling within these categories:

1. The state should provide for all *recent* cases of insanity, while counties should erect asylums for all chronic cases.
2. The state should provide for *all* the insane in state hospitals.
3. Recent and chronic cases should be maintained in separate institutions, the former in hospitals, the latter in asylums. Chronics, being for the most part beyond cure, require only custodial care and could be accommodated much more cheaply in asylums.
4. Chronic and acute cases should be accommodated in "mixed" hospitals, and all subjected to therapeutic treatment.

*The difference between a hospital and an asylum might be stated thus: the former is an institution intended primarily for curative treatment, while the latter is primarily a place of custody. It must be remembered, however, that the terms have been used interchangeably and indiscriminately: asylums have been called hospitals, and vice versa. An interesting case in point is the first special institution for the insane in America, at Williamsburg, Va.,

These proposals fell into two distinct patterns, which finally developed into the systems that characterize public provision for the insane today: state care and county care. The principle of state care is identified with the plan ultimately adopted by New York; the county care system is associated with Wisconsin. These were the pioneer states in the formulation of the rival plans which were adopted, with slight modifications, by most of the other states. In the following pages the historical development of state care in New York will be emphasized, since it was there that the principle experienced its classic evolution.

The earliest organized movement toward complete state care in New York came from a rather unexpected source. In 1855 the county superintendents of the poor in the state held a convention at Utica, primarily for the purpose of formulating a definite policy of public provision for the dependent insane. The situation must have been very serious to have necessitated such a meeting, the first of its kind in the state and probably in the country.* The question of removing the mentally sick from poorhouses to state hospitals received the greatest attention. At the end of the convention, a series of resolutions on the subject were adopted, including the following:

> Whereas, it is already conceded, and has been adopted as the policy of this State, that insanity is a disease requiring, in all its forms and stages, special means for treatment and care; therefore,
> Resolved, That the State should make ample and suitable provision for all its insane not in a condition to reside in private families.
> Resolved, That no insane person should be treated, or in any way taken care of, in any county poorhouse or almshouse, or other receptacle provided for, and in which, paupers are maintained or supported.
> Resolved, That insane persons considered curable and those supposed incurable should not be provided for in separate establishments.[2]

which was called a "hospital" in its early years when its standard of treatment did not rate it above an asylum, and which afterwards underwent an inexplicable change in title to "asylum" at a time when it had already developed hospital standards!

*In 1874 the county superintendents of the poor were organized into a permanent body, and held conventions annually thereafter for the purpose of discussing general public welfare problems.

THE TREND TOWARD STATE CARE

To this set of resolutions, another was added a month after the Utica meeting, reading as follows: "Resolved, First that the present provision for the insane of the state is defective and inadequate. Second, That their present condition demands immediate attention and relief. Third, That the relief should be commensurate with the demand."

The passage of these resolutions by the county superintendents of the poor stands in remarkable contrast to the subsequent role of these officials. In later years they were to offer the strongest and most inflexible resistance to the state care system. Nevertheless, in this historic instance a state care movement was not only supported, but actually initiated, by its traditional foes. To implement their resolutions, a memorial to the legislature was prepared, setting forth the inadequate provisions for the insane in county poorhouses and recommending "the immediate erection of two State lunatic hospitals, so located that they may accommodate the largest number of insane at present unprovided for, and so relinquish the undersigned the pain of longer continuing a system fraught with injustice and inhumanity."[3]

Acting upon this petition, the state Senate in 1856 appointed a select committee to visit charitable institutions, particularly almshouses, throughout the state, to ascertain the condition of the dependent insane and to make recommendations based on the survey. After a thorough investigation the committee submitted its report, revealing among other things the disheartening spectacle of lunatics chained in cells and dungeons under conditions as dismal as those observed by Dorothea Dix twelve years before.[4] The committee endorsed the recommendations made by the county superintendents for immediate establishment of two or more state asylums. As a result of this investigation, an act was introduced into the legislature providing for two new hospitals to supplement the one at Utica. This bill passed the Senate but the Assembly adjourned before it could be voted upon by that body. It was subsequently laid aside and forgotten.

Nothing further was accomplished until 1864, when the legislature ordered a state-wide inquiry into the care of the insane in local poorhouses. Dr. Sylvester D. Willard, secretary of the New York Medical Society, was appointed special commissioner to direct the investigation. With the cooperation of physicians throughout the state, Dr. Willard was able to collect comprehensive data on prevailing conditions, which he embodied in a report submitted to the Legislature in January, 1865.[5] Once more the old and oft-repeated tale of misery, neglect and cruelty was unfolded. The disheartening truth, as abundantly illustrated in the report, was that the plight of the insane remained as desperate as it had been in 1857, and even in 1845 when Miss Dix made her tour of inspection of the institutions of New York. There were 1,345 insane persons confined in almshouses. Most of these were chronics, although a number of instances were adduced in which recent cases had been sent directly to poorhouses instead of to Utica, because it was cheaper to maintain them there than at the state hospital.

"Let an institution for incurables be established," Dr. Willard recommended. "Let the incurables be there colonized. Take the insane from the counties where they are ill provided for first, and change the law relative to the insane poor, so that counties shall not have the management of them, nor any authority over them."[6]

Behind the drive to get the insane poor out of the almshouses was the pressure of public opinion that had been mounting steadily as inquiry after inquiry brought forth additional evidence of the inhuman treatment of the insane. This public pressure must have been formidable indeed, since it forced legislative action at a time when civil strife was consuming the energy and attention of the war-torn nation almost to the exclusion of everything else. In April, 1865, an act was passed creating a state asylum for the chronic insane. It was named after Dr. Willard, who had died shortly before.

The Willard Act provided for the removal to the Willard Asylum of all chronic insane persons from the county poorhouses. All those discharged as chronic cases from the Utica hospital were also to be sent to Willard. Defining chronic lunatics by inference, the act required local authorities to send to Utica all indigent and pauper insane coming under their jurisdiction "who shall have been insane less than one year." All others were to be admitted and maintained at Willard.

The act provided for 1,500 beds, making the asylum by far the largest institution for the insane erected up to that time in the United States. This was a radical departure from the time-honored limits of 250 beds per institution, set by the Association of Medical Superintendents in its Propositions of 1851. In 1866, largely through the pressure exerted by the establishment of the Willard Asylum, the Association modified its proposition upward to permit a maximum capacity of 600 beds in institutions for the insane.

The founding of Willard marked the introduction of a new principle, explicitly stated, in the care and treatment of the mentally ill in the United States; namely, the creation of two distinct types of state institutions—hospitals for the acute insane and asylums for the chronic cases.*

A flood of discussion within the psychiatric specialty was precipitated by the passage of the Willard Act. The debate, often reaching acrimonious proportions, found its peak at the annual convention of the Association of 1866. This session was probably the most exciting in the history of the Association. It certainly witnessed more heated argument and mutual recrimination than any other.

The opening shot at this conference was fired by Dr. George Cook of Brigham Hall Asylum at Canandaigua, New York, in a paper entitled, "Provision for the Insane Poor in the State of New York." It constituted a vigorous defense of the Willard Act, defying the great majority of the Association membership who opposed separate institutions for chronics and acutes. The major significance of the Willard Act, he maintained, was not that it provided a separate state asylum for chronics, but that it rescued all

*At the time, the principle of treatment in separate institutions was already in operation in England, Germany and France, having arisen out of very much the same conditions of pressing necessity as were responsible for the origin of Willard. (See Henri Falret, in an interesting paper, "On the Construction and Organization of Establishments for the Insane," published in the *American Journal of Insanity*, 1854. v. 10, pp. 218–67.)

the insane from the blighting environment of poorhouses and placed them in a properly conducted institution where they would receive special care. There they could be comfortably supported at a cost per week well within the reach of every county.*

According to Dr. Cook, the creation of the Willard Asylum was an important step in advance, since it recognized for the first time in explicit terms the vital principle that the chronic, as well as the recent cases, were entitled to proper care and treatment in state institutions. He challenged the assertion of those opponents of the Willard experiment who branded it as "a retrograde step," and who maintained that the separation of chronic and acute cases was wrong in principle and led to abuses in practice.

The opposition to the principle of separate care for the chronic insane was led by Dr. John B. Gray, superintendent of the Utica State Asylum of New York, and editor-in-chief of the *American Journal of Insanity*.† The opposition's main arguments might be briefly summed up as follows:

1. All insane persons are essentially sick, and are entitled to therapeutic treatment, whether chronic or recent cases.
2. Chronic cases are not necessarily incurable. Some recover after an illness lasting many years. It would work an injustice on chronic cases who were not beyond cure to remove them from curative institutions.
3. At present, it is impossible for a physician to pronounce with certainty who are, and who are not, curable or incurable. To main-

---

*As has already been noted, the counties of New York were charged with the expense of maintaining dependent insane at the state asylum. The Willard Act fixed a maximum charge upon counties of two dollars per week for each inmate chargeable to them. This rate was later found to be too low, and was raised to three dollars per week.

†Previous to the passage of the Willard Act, Dr. Gray succeeded for a time in persuading Dr. Willard that the latter's proposal for a separate institution was inimical to the interests of the chronic insane. At Willard's suggestion he drew up a substitute bill, providing for two additional state hospitals of the mixed type recommended earlier by the county superintendents and the Senate committee of 1857. For some unexplained reason, however, Gray's bill was suddenly withdrawn after having been introduced in the legislature, and the original bill drawn up by Willard was voted on and passed.

tain two separate types of institutions would render it difficult, if not impossible, to correct an error of diagnosis, and to transfer a patient subsequently found curable from an asylum for chronics to a hospital for acute cases.

4. The stamp of incurability on inmates of asylums for chronics is unnecessarily cruel and painful not only to many patients, but to their close relatives and friends, who are thus robbed of the solace of hope. On the other hand it gives to unkind relatives a pretext for indifference and neglect.

5. "Many that are incurable are monomaniacs. They are deranged on but one or two subjects, and sane on all others. Such surely should not be deprived of any comforts that are afforded the curable class, among the greatest of which is *hope,* which would be destroyed if they were sent to an incurable asylum."*

6. While custodial institutions for the chronic insane might be built and maintained at less cost than hospitals, it would be only at the expense of the inmates, who would thereby be subjected to reduced standards of care and comfort.

7. Vigilance against abuses tends to slacken in institutions where the inmates are regarded as hopeless cases. Separate asylums for chronics, then, would result in lesser safeguards against neglect and abuse.

At the end of the debate in the Association's memorable convention of 1866, several sets of resolutions on provision for the chronic insane were offered by opposing sides to the membership for adoption.

A set of propositions drawn up by Dr. Chipley of Kentucky was finally adopted by unanimous vote.[7] Two of his resolutions were substantially identical with those adopted by the Association in 1851, namely, that the state should make ample and suitable provision for all its insane, and

---

*This argument, quoted by Dr. Gray in his rebuttal to Cook's paper, was originally advanced by Dr. Amariah Brigham in a letter to Dorothea Dix strongly opposing separate institutions for the insane. In an article appearing in the first issue of the *American Journal of Insanity* (July, 1884) Dr. Brigham had written: "We hope never to see such institutions [for the incurable insane only] in this country. On the contrary, let no asylum be established but for the curable, and to this the incurable, the rich and the poor should be admitted; let all have the same kind care; and all indulge the same hope, even if delusive to many, of ultimate recovery, but do not drive any to despair . . . ."

that recent and chronic cases should not be placed in separate institutions. Towards the close of the meeting, Dr. Charles H. Nichols, of the Government Asylum for the Insane at Washington, introduced a set of five resolutions calling mainly for the division of large states into geographical districts where easily accessible mental hospitals could be constructed, and for the enlargement of public hospitals for the insane to accommodate a maximum of 600 patients, "embracing the usual proportions of curable and incurable insane in a particular community." Four of Dr. Nichols' resolutions were adopted without dissent, but the last one, modifying the mooted maximum-capacity proposition of 1851, was passed only after a sharp debate, and by a very close vote.

Despite the Association's emphatic rejection of the principle of separate provision for chronic and recent cases, the establishment of the Willard Asylum had the effect of stimulating movements in that direction in several states besides New York. In 1866 the Massachusetts State Almshouse (now the Tewksbury Infirmary), which had previously received all classes of state paupers, was converted by law into an asylum for the harmless and incurable pauper insane, and also for the crippled, the epileptic, the feebleminded, and "for such other persons who, on account of their infirmities, are unable to support themselves."

In Rhode Island, the Asylum for the Incurable Insane was opened at Cranston in 1870. (This was probably the first and only instance when a state's initial institution for the mentally ill was opened exclusively for incurable cases.) Up to that time the insane poor requiring institutionalization had been sent to the Butler Asylum, a corporate institution where a nominal fee was charged for public dependents, or else to asylums in neighboring states. After 1870 the state continued to send its acute cases to the latter institution, while the "incurables" were sent to Cranston. In 1885 a law was enacted providing that all acute cases, as well as chronic, be thereafter admitted to the asylum at Cranston, thus ending the separation between the two groups in Rhode Island.

In California, a movement was set afoot in 1866 to convert the Stockton State Asylum into an institution exclusively for chronics, but this plan met with decisive defeat. Twenty years later an act was passed by the California legislature creating an asylum for the chronic insane at Agnew but due to the articulate distaste of the public for such an institution, it was soon after converted into a "mixed" hospital. Similarly, the legislature of Connecticut enacted a statute in 1877 converting an abandoned home for soldiers' orphans into an asylum for chronics, but under the weight of public opposition this plan fell through.

Attempts to effect a satisfactory compromise between complete separation and non-separation were largely responsible for the introduction in the United States of the "cottage" and "colony" systems of institutionalization. Both types had existed in European countries long before their adoption in America, where the acceptance of the plans in theory antedated by many years their application in practice.

The cottage plan which, in essence, involved the principle of segregation as opposed to congregation (that is, distributing the patients in a number of small buildings, or cottages, instead of congregating them in one massive building), won wide approval among the early practitioners of psychiatry in America. The earliest approach to the cottage plan in the United States was effected in those institutions, like the Friends' Hospital at Frankford, Pennsylvania, where the classification system of the German psychiatrist, Spurzheim, was put into practice. This system required a large central building for administering treatment to curable cases, and separate lodges for convalescents, disturbed patients, and harmless and chronic cases. In his first annual report as superintendent of the Worcester Hospital, Dr. Samuel B. Woodward had written in 1833: "If to this [the existing large building] could be added a cheap building, as a retreat for incurables (of which this Institution will always have a large share), this establishment would combine all the advantages which could be derived in a Hospital for the insane—a quiet and undisturbed Asylum for incurables; Lodges for the violent and noisy; the great Hospital for the recovery of curable cases, old and recent; and a peaceful and pleasant abode for convalescents."[8]

In 1870 a vigorous, organized campaign for the introduction of the cottage system was initiated in Illinois. The state legislature, in the preceding year, had voted an appropriation for the establishment of two new state hospitals and had left the matter of form and construction to be decided by the Board of State Commissioners of Public Charities, in conference with other officials, including the officers of the existing state hospital at Jacksonville. The secretary of the Board of State Commissioners, Frederick H. Wines, one of the foremost social welfare leaders of his time, had made a comprehensive study of the care and treatment of the insane, and had become convinced that the cottage system constituted a marked improvement over the congregate (usually identified with the Kirkbride) plan then in universal use. Under his dynamic direction a "Conference on Insanity" was called by the Board, to which asylum superintendents of neighboring states were invited. A questionnaire was sent to all known superintendents of American institutions for the insane, soliciting opinions on the cottage system.

At the conference, Mr. Wines, ably seconded by Dr. Andrew McFarland, superintendent of the State Asylum at Jacksonville, urged the adoption of a cottage plan for the two proposed hospitals. His plan was based on the system practiced at the famous colony of Fitz James, a private institution for the insane at Clermont, France, which had been founded in 1847. The conference, however, considered that the introduction of a cottage system *in toto* was too radical a move, and adopted a compromise plan expressed in these resolutions:

> Resolved, That in the judgment of this conference, so far as practicable, a combination, in insane asylums, of the cottage system with that at present in vogue, is desirable.
>
> Resolved, That there are weighty reasons for the belief that such a combination is practicable, and that it would increase both the economy and efficiency of asylums for the insane.[9]

THE TREND TOWARD STATE CARE 243

The result of the compromise was the establishment of the Illinois State Hospital at Kankakee in 1877, incorporating the principle of a group of small buildings, or "cottages," each accommodating about 100 patients, grouped around a large central building. Although construction was not based on a complete acceptance of the cottage plan, the Kankakee State Hospital marked the first practical application of the principle in America, and paved the way for its wider acceptance in the future. The main ends sought in the construction of the Kankakee hospital, as stated by Mr. Wines, were: "(1) the cheapening of the cost of building, in order that a larger number of the insane in the State might, with a given appropriation, be furnished with proper quarters, attendance, and medical oversight, thus relieving the county poorhouses of the pressure upon them; and (2) the application of the principle of graduated restraint, or differentiation in the treatment of the insane, so as to allow to each patient the largest measure of personal liberty of which he is individually capable. Some of the incidental results hoped for were: the introduction of a simpler and more natural mode of life; the disuse, as far as possible, of mechanical restraints; and an increase in the amount of useful labor by patients."[10]

Today, the superiority of the segregate or cottage plan over the old congregate system is a fact generally accepted by leading authorities. Unfortunately, however, due mainly to the failure of legislatures to appropriate sufficient funds to build modern mental hospitals and the general unwillingness to abandon outworn institutions based on the congregate plan, the cottage system has found no application *in practice* commensurate with its acceptance as an institutional ideal *in theory*.

The introduction in the United States of the colony system, which is closely allied to the cottage plan, dates from 1885, when a tract of 250 acres was purchased and added to the State Asylum at Kalamazoo, Michigan, as a "farm colony."

Before that, from time to time, American psychiatrists returning from Europe had opened discussions on the various colonies for harmless and chronic insane that they had visited on the continent. Because of the general antagonism to separation of chronic and recent cases, however, the application of the colony system to America was frowned upon by institutional authorities.

In 1863 Dr. Richard Hills, superintendent of the Central Ohio Lunatic Asylum at Columbus and one of the earliest outspoken advocates of separation, proposed, in his annual report to the legislature, the establishment of a farm colony for the chronic insane.[11] This colony, he suggested, should be planned on a village basis, approximating as closely as possible normal village life, and might appropriately be named the "Hamlet Home for the Chronic Insane." No action was taken on this proposal. At the 1867 convention of the Association of Medical Superintendents, Dr. Benjamin Workman of the Provincial Lunatic Asylum at Toronto, Canada, read a paper on "Asylums for the Chronic Insane in Upper Canada," in which he described how the pressure of overpopulation in the Toronto Asylum had led to the establishment of "branch asylums" for the chronic insane situated about three miles from the parent institution. These "branches," he reported, had proved very satisfactory.[12]

Interestingly enough, the first farm colony in the United States—that at Kalamazoo, Michigan—represented a synthesis of the two ideas we have just mentioned. The Kalamazoo colony for the chronic and harmless insane was based on the village principle of construction advocated by Dr. Hills twenty years earlier. On the administrative side it resembled the Toronto plan in that it was a branch of a parent institution, was located about three miles from the latter, and was under the same administration.

The partial adoption of the "boarding-out" system by Massachusetts in the '80's—which, in effect, represented still another alternative to poorhouse care of the dependent chronic insane—will be discussed in a later chapter.

As we shall see, the final disposition of the problem of maintaining the chronic and acute insane in separate institutions had a profound influence on the development of the

THE TREND TOWARD STATE CARE 245

two rival systems at present operating in America—state care and county care. Meanwhile, an important movement toward centralization of administrative control in state agencies was gaining ground. This general centralizing tendency was to play an important part in the evolution of state care.

CHAPTER XIII
State Care: Exodus from the Poorhouse

IN LARGE measure the movement toward state care was part of a broader, more far-reaching process involving a logical trend toward centralization of public welfare activities. This process had been going on throughout the nineteenth century, but became clearly discernible for the first time in the years following the Civil War. (In at least one important aspect, the end of the Civil War itself symbolized the triumph of centralization over divided authority.)

From the very beginnings of the American colonies, local responsibility had been the keystone on which the structure of public welfare was built. This system operated admirably while the country consisted, more or less, of a patchwork of loosely connected, self-contained communities. But as the nineteenth century—that century of tremendous change in the material conditions of life—advanced towards maturity, the once sufficing policy of exclusively local responsibility in public welfare grew increasingly and painfully anachronistic. It was evident that the governmental superstructure would have to be modified if it were to keep pace with the material changes of life. The chaos and contradictions arising from many-headed, independent authorities had to be reduced to some semblance of order. Uniformity and centralization of authority was the order of the day. Since this centralizing tendency in welfare work profoundly affected the rise of the state care system, it will be pertinent to our study to briefly trace its progress.

The steady increase of charitable institutions and agencies —poorhouses, orphanages, asylums, hospitals, etc.—particularly after 1850, brought in its train a series of vexing problems, most of them arising out of the policy of unsupervised local responsibility. Local officials, together with superintendents and boards of managers in public and semipublic institutions, ruled with absolute authority over their realms. In many instances, to be sure, they were nominally responsible to the governor of the state or to the state legislature. But since the state authorities were invariably too busy with other duties to make inquiries into the stewardship of institutional officials, the latter remained relatively free from higher interference save when they became involved in major scandals forcing executive or legislative action. Private charitable institutions were for the most part entirely unencumbered by governmental restraints of any sort. It is unnecessary to go into details concerning abuses of these well-nigh unlimited powers; it is sufficient to point out that the very existence of unchecked power constituted a constant source of wrongdoing. Moreover, because each institution was governed as a virtually independent entity, there was a complete lack of uniformity in administration. Anarchy was rampant.

Meanwhile, contradictions between policy and practice were placing the various states in an untenable position. More and more, as local facilities and local treasuries found it increasingly difficult to cope with the expanding public welfare needs of a swiftly-changing society, the states were becoming involved in the financing of charitable institutions. They were pouring out funds in larger amounts for the construction and support of such institutions. In return, the state usually required no accounting beyond reports submitted annually to the executive power or legislature. Like as not, these reports would go unread. Thus, while the state served as a heavy subsidizing agent, it was an irresponsible one. The incongruity of this situation grew all too evident.

The solution obviously lay in the direction of greater state responsibility, of a more active role in the supervision and administration of public welfare. By investing supervisory powers in a central authority a potent check could be raised against abuses, and a greater degree of uniformity in the operation of charitable institutions could be attained.

Even more important, in the eyes of many who raised the demand for a central state authority, was the question of economy. A centrally supervised or controlled welfare system, it was believed, would result in greater efficiency and less overlapping of functions, and in definite savings in state expenditures.

Massachusetts was the pioneer state in the establishment of a central public welfare body. In 1858 its legislature appointed a joint committee to investigate the whole system of state charitable institutions, and to formulate recommendations. In its report, submitted the following year, the committee pointed out that there were, at the time, nine state institutions of a charitable nature, three of which were mental hospitals (Worcester, Taunton and Northampton).[1] Of the nine institutions, all save one had been erected during the preceding decade. "Each of these new [state] institutions," it was reported, "has been created without especial reference to others, and in no degree as a part of a uniform system. It happens accordingly that there are anomalies in their organization and management, increasing the expense of conducting them, and impairing their efficiency."*

In its main recommendation, the committee urged the creation of a permanent board of charities empowered to supervise the whole system of public charities within the Commonwealth, in order to secure the greatest degree of usefulness at the least expense. It was proposed that a ro-

---

*Compare this statement with the arguments advanced by Governor Reuben E. Fenton of New York in his annual message to the legislature for 1867, which led to the creation of a board of charities in that year: "For some years past, the State has made annual appropriations in the support of Orphan Asylums, Hospitals, Homes for the Friendless, and other charitable institutions. No adequate provision, however, has been made by law for the inspection of these and other corporations of a like character, holding their charters under the State, or for any effectual inquiry into their operation and management. There are a great number of these institutions, and the amount contributed for their support by public authorities and by public benevolence is large, and so many persons—the aged, the helpless, the infirm and the young—fall under their care, that I deem it expedient that the State should exercise a reasonable degree of supervision over them. To this end I recommend a board of commissioners, in such manner as the Legislature may deem proper, to serve without compensation, but whose actual expenses shall be paid . . ." (*Messages from the Governors of New York.* v. 5, pp. 447-48.)

tating board of five members be appointed by the governor, to serve without compensation, but to be reimbursed for actual expenses. In addition to the five members, the employment of a salaried secretary was suggested.

The recommendation of the committee was favorably acted upon in 1863, when the Massachusetts legislature created the first state board of charities in the country. Other states soon fell in line. During the next decade, ten similar boards were organized: Ohio and New York in 1867; Illinois, North Carolina, Pennsylvania and Rhode Island in 1869; Wisconsin and Michigan in 1871, and Kansas and Connecticut in 1873. The names of these boards varied widely,* but in most of them, the set-up and functions differed but little.

In some instances, the scope of the board's work was limited to charitable institutions; in others, it was extended to the correctional fields also. With one exception the powers of all these early boards were restricted mainly to visitation and inspection of institutions and the right to remove and transfer inmates under certain conditions. Licensing power was added to these functions in some instances. Rhode Island alone, from the beginning, placed in the board's hands the administration and control of state institutions, together with wide supervisory powers. The same act creating the Board of State Charities and Corrections in Rhode Island (1869) provided for the establishment of a state workhouse, a house of correction, a state asylum for the incurable insane, and a state almshouse. All these institutions were to be located in the town of Cranston and were placed under the direct control of the state board.[2]

*"In Massachusetts and Ohio, the authority was called the Board of State Charities; in North Carolina and Pennsylvania it was the Board of Public Charities; and the words 'public charities' were in the names of the New York (State Commissioners) and Illinois (Board of Commissioners of) authorities. Rhode Island alone of these states used the word 'corrections,' while Wisconsin had the idea of 'reform' (State Board of Charities and Reform); and Michigan spelled out the whole purpose in the title, 'Board of State Commissioners for the Supervision of Charitable, Penal, Pauper, and Reformatory Institutions.'" (Breckinridge, Sophonisba P. *Public Welfare Administration in the United States: Select Documents.* Chicago, 1927. 786 pp., p. 243.)

In those states limiting the duties of a board to institutional visitation and inspection, without administrative or corrective powers, this agency was in effect reduced to a mere advisory status. It could ferret out abuses and evils, but lacked the authority to eliminate or alleviate them. It could draw up plans for reforms and improvements, but had no power to put them into practice. It could only recommend such measures to a higher authority. So complicated were the processes leading to remedial action that recommendations often became hopelessly entangled in the involved mechanism, and were lost sight of before reaching the point where progressive action could be applied.

Despite functional handicaps, however, these early boards proved to be very important factors in the progress of public welfare. They were particularly effective in mobilizing public opinion behind reform movements, especially those in behalf of the mentally ill. Several boards were staffed by men who combined remarkable ability and intelligence with a genuine zeal for social service. Unlike some of their present-day successors, they did not regard their offices as merely honorary posts with nominal duties. They took up their tasks with dynamic energy, and worked incessantly for reform. Men like Samuel Gridley Howe and Franklin B. Sanborn of Massachusetts, Frederick H. Wines of Illinois, General Roeliff Brinkerhoff of Ohio, William P. Letchworth of New York—these were keen and articulate critics of the wrongs rooted in the social order. When their searching eyes noted evils and abuses, they dared to point them out, even at the risk of embarrassing people in high places.

So sweeping were the reforms advocated by certain boards on behalf of the dependent classes that they aroused the fierce antagonism of the state officialdom. At times, the politicians retaliated by abolishing a board outright, or else emasculating it by refusing to appropriate funds necessary to its proper functioning. For instance, the North Carolina Board of Public Charities, in its first annual report to the General Assembly (1869), not only vigorously protested against the abominable treatment of dependent insane in

EXODUS FROM THE POORHOUSE 251

public institutions, but arraigned the prevailing system of poor relief *in toto*. "The whole system, or rather want of system, that seems to have grown up by accident and without any benevolent concern for the welfare of the pauper classes, or the reformation of the erring or vicious, needs patient and thorough revision," it declared.[3]

So well did the Board champion the cause of the insane and other dependent classes, and so insistent was its demands for immediate reform, that the harrassed legislature in 1873 abruptly terminated its existence by the simple expedient of neglecting to appoint new members at the expiration of the terms of incumbents, as provided by law. It was not until 1889 that the Board was revived.

The Ohio Board, organized in 1867, experienced a similar fate. It was abolished in 1871, after making repeated exposés of the plight of the pauper insane and others dependent on the public bounty, and calling for drastic changes in the system of public welfare.

The first report of the Illinois Board of State Commissioners of Public Charities (1870), prepared by its dynamic secretary, Frederick H. Wines, included a searching analysis of the whole philosophy and structure of public welfare. It contained many biting criticisms of existing abuses, together with recommendations for reform. We have mentioned, in the preceding chapter, the "Conference on the Insane" called by the board in 1870 as one of its first official acts, and of its influence in introducing the cottage plan of mental hospital construction into the United States.

Also indicative of the progressive tendencies of these early state boards is the fact that in 1870, only one year after its establishment, the Pennsylvania Board of Public Charities adopted a resolution urging the "establishment by the state, within a reasonable time, of sufficient accommodations for the maintenance and treatment of all the insane who may not be cared for in private hospitals."[4]

Reforms in the care and treatment of the mentally ill advocated by these early boards varied somewhat in detail, but on one point they were unanimously agreed: Poorhouses were improper places for the confinement of the mentally ill, and the latter should be withdrawn from such institutions at the earliest possible moment. In those formative years there was also general agreement that *all* the insane requiring public provision should be supported in state-owned hospitals or asylums. This position was perhaps best summed up in the first report of the Wisconsin State Board of Charities and Reform (1871), recommending that all the insane in local institutions "be removed from their present quarters and placed in an insane hospital." With the completion of the State Hospital at Oshkosh, then in process of construction, it was hoped that "sufficient accommodations may be found for them all, but if not, that the state will not stop building and enlarging until this end shall be fully secured."*

In New York the State Board of Charities (as it was known after 1873) was confronted with a most difficult problem in relation to provision for the mentally ill from the very moment of its organization. With the passage of the Willard Act in 1865, it had been confidently expected that the question of providing for the dependent insane with a maximum of humanity, efficiency and economy had been at last satisfactorily solved. Henceforth, it was assumed, all recent cases of mental illness would be sent to Utica Asylum for treatment, while all chronics would be cared for at the Willard Asylum at greatly reduced cost. In this way all the insane of the state would be the beneficiaries of comfortable provision in state-owned institutions, and the ills arising from the confinement of insane persons in poorhouses would forever be avoided.

Alas for these expectations! Hardly was the Willard Asylum opened in 1869 than overcrowded conditions promptly appeared, together with a host of related evils. When it had been established in 1865 as the largest institution of its kind in America, with a capacity of 1,500 inmates, it was expected to comfortably accommodate all the chronic insane

---

*This attitude, be it noted, stands out in sharp contrast to the policy adopted by the Wisconsin Board a few years later, advocating the introduction of the county care system as opposed to state care.

then confined in poorhouses. Had the original intention been carried into effect—that is, the removal of all chronic cases from almshouses and the maintenance thenceforth of all cases of insanity in state institutions (even though counties continued to be charged with maintenance cost)—it would have marked a sizeable step toward the realization of state care. But when the Willard Asylum was opened at Ovid, it was found that the number of chronic insane in the state had increased to such an extent in the years intervening between its creation and completion that its capacity was already inadequate to accommodate them all.

The asylum quickly filled up and overflowed with chronic cases transferred from Utica and from local poorhouses and jails. Within a short time the authorities were forced to cry out "Hold, enough!" and to close the doors to further admissions. Meanwhile hundreds of additional cases of insanity were pouring into the poorhouses. There they remained: there was no room for them in Willard. An embarrassing situation arose. On the one hand, the law required local authorities to send all chronic cases to the new state asylum. On the other, the inability of Willard to receive additional cases compelled these authorities to violate the state laws in spite of themselves.

By 1871 the predicament had become so acute that the legislature was constrained to enact a new law authorizing the State Board of Charities to exempt certain counties from the provisions of the Willard Act. Such exempted counties were permitted to provide for their own chronic insane in local institutions.*

Nominally, counties receiving such exemption were required to meet certain standards of care. But in reality the "asylums" they maintained were usually either part and parcel of the poorhouse proper, or mere appurtenances thereto. There the mentally ill were generally treated in a manner no whit different than the pauper inmates except, of course, in the imposition of greater restraints. No regard

---

*The original Willard Act, as passed in 1865, had already exempted three counties (New York, Monroe and Kings) on the ground that these counties provided satisfactorily for their own insane in special institutions.

was given to their special needs—medical, dietary, occupational, etc.

The Willard Act, in charging the counties with the cost of indigent and pauper insane maintained at Willard, had specified that no more than two dollars per week per inmate should be billed to the county of settlement. However, when it was realized that adequate care could not be rendered at so low a rate, the price of maintenance was raised to three dollars per week. It was subsequently reduced, under county pressure, to $2.75 per week. Many county authorities balked at paying what they considered a high rate, feeling that they could provide for their own insane in the local houses at much less cost. (The cost of maintaining insane charges at county almshouses averaged at the time about $1.50 for each person.) With this thought dominant, county after county applied for, and received, exemption from the Willard Act in accordance with the law of 1871. Before many years had passed, nineteen counties (more than one-third the total) were granted exemption.

Thus was defeated the main purpose of the Willard Act, namely, to remove all the insane from the poorhouses. The new policy of permitting certain counties to care for their own insane, inaugurated as a temporary expedient, proved highly unsatisfactory. The conviction spread among enlightened people that whatever improvements were made, and however honest its management might be, there were inherent evils in poorhouse care of the insane which could never be obliterated. A poorhouse could function well only as a home for the aged and infirm; it could never be successfully blended to serve as an asylum for the mentally ill in addition to its other functions. Dissatisfaction with the prevailing condition of the insane poor mounted steadily.

Meanwhile, with the increasing number of insane persons and the growing complexity in public provision for their care and treatment, it soon became evident that the State Board, burdened with its manifold duties, could not devote sufficient attention to this problem without an organizational change. The need for a separate state authority which could devote full time and undivided attention to the

EXODUS FROM THE POORHOUSE 255

supervision of institutions for the mentally ill was clearly indicated. Besides, the public was growing restless due to periodic scandals involving illegal and unjust commitments of sane persons to asylums. Added to these factors were the ever-recurring revelations of intramural abuses of asylum inmates. A responsible head was required to act in a supervisory capacity and to serve as a liaison officer, in order to maintain public confidence in the institutional care of the insane.

In 1873, New York took a partial step toward solution of this problem by creating a State Commissioner in Lunacy, not as a separate authority, but as an ex-officio member of the State Board of Charities, directly responsible to that body.[5] He was required to examine into the condition of the insane and "idiotic" of the state, to visit and inspect institutions for their custody and treatment, and to report annually to the board. He was also directed to collect information on methods of caring for the mentally ill in other states and countries. No remedial powers were vested in him: his was merely an advisory post. The same act creating this office extended the powers of the State Board to include the right to license all establishments for the insane, public and private, none of which might be operated without such license.

New York was not the first state to create the office of commissioner in lunacy on a permanent basis. As early as 1845, Vermont had appointed a Commissioner of the Insane, whose duties, however, were almost exclusively confined to visiting and inspecting the Vermont Asylum (later the Brattleboro Retreat) and to report yearly on its condition to the legislature. A similar office was created in Connecticut some years later, in connection with official periodical inspection of the Hartford Retreat in relation to public charges maintained there. The New York State Commissioner in Lunacy, limited though his powers were, functioned in a far wider field than any other permanent officer of his kind up to that time.

The voice of the State Lunacy Commissioner soon swelled the chorus raised in criticism of the chaos in the care of the mentally ill.* In the decade 1871–1881, four additional state institutions for the insane were opened,† but the inflow of insane persons into almshouses continued unabated. Their numbers mounted by the hundreds. On the other hand, the drive toward state care was gaining strength. By 1880, the forces of progress had formed a solid united front on this issue. In its report for that year, the State Board of Charities came out categorically against the system of permitting counties to care for their chronic insane. "Unless the state promptly extends its accommodations for this class," it declared, "the work must necessarily be taken up by the counties. That, it is believed, would be a public calamity, as experience has fully shown that the efforts of counties to provide for their chronic insane have in most cases proved failures." In this and in subsequent reports it bombarded the legislature with urgent appeals for a state care system.

An important factor in the final triumph of state care in New York was the work of the State Charities Aid Association, a semi-public welfare body founded in 1872, which carried on an incessant propaganda campaign for the cause during the decade leading up to 1890. Early in its development the Association had formed a standing committee on the insane, which soon became a focal point of activity. At the head of the Committee was Louisa Lee Schuyler, founder of the S.C.A.A., and its outstanding personality. She proved to be a most active agent in pushing to a successful conclusion the fight for state care. From its voluntary visiting committees (which exercised the privilege of visitation and inspection of all public charitable institutions,

*Dr. John Ordronaux, professor of medical jurisprudence at Columbia University, was the first to be appointed to this office. He was succeeded by Dr. Stephen Smith, who held the post until it was superseded by the State Commission in Lunacy in 1889.

†The Hudson River State Asylum at Poughkeepsie was opened in 1871; the Middletown State Homeopathic Asylum, established through the insistence and aid of a group of citizens who wished to see the Hahnemannian method applied to the treatment of the mentally ill, was opened in 1874; the Buffalo State Asylum was opened in 1880, and the Binghamton State Asylum for the Chronic Insane, the second of its kind in New York, in 1881. The latter was converted from a former inebriate asylum originally opened in 1859, but abandoned as a failure twenty years later.

granted by special legislation) the organization received with disheartening regularity reports of terrible treatment of the mentally ill in poorhouses and county asylums throughout the state. At the same time, the committee on the insane was gathering information on the care of the mentally ill in this country and abroad, with a view toward suggesting concrete legislative action on this score. Allied with the forces advocating state care was the National Association for the Protection of the Insane and the Prevention of Insanity, the energetic, though short-lived, reform society which operated mainly in New York. Dr. Stephen Smith, State Commissioner of Lunacy from 1882 to 1889, was an influential figure in the movement, second in importance only to Miss Schuyler. As early as 1884, he had framed a state care bill and approached Miss Schuyler with the suggestion that the S.C.A.A. sponsor it.[6] This bill served as the basis for the one introduced into the legislature under S.C.A.A. sponsorship some years later.

With the approach of the final decade of the nineteenth century, the reform movement in behalf of the mentally ill in New York was advancing in full swing along three parallel fronts. Its main objects were: (1) removal of all insane persons from almshouses; (2) discontinuance of the practice of maintaining separate institutions for the chronic and acute insane; (3) state control and supervision of all institutions for the mentally ill.

In 1887 the State Charities Aid Association sponsored a state care bill that was introduced into the legislative sessions of 1888 and 1889, failing of passage both times. It is noteworthy that the annual convention of the Association of Medical Superintendents held in 1888 unanimously adopted a resolution, drawn up and submitted by Dr. G. Alder Blumer (then assistant physician at the Utica State Asylum), in which it went on record as "cordially endorsing" the principle of state care as embodied in the bill introduced by the S.C.A.A.[7] Simultaneously, the New York Neurological Society passed a resolution calling for the transfer of all insane persons from poorhouses to state hospitals.

Though the state care act failed of passage in 1889, another bill important to the progress of provision for the insane did become law in that session. This was the act creating a state commission in lunacy, consisting of three members, in place of the one-man commissionership established sixteen years before. Curiously enough, this bill was drawn up and vigorously pushed by Dr. Stephen Smith, in face of the fact that it abolished the office he held. The new law provided that the Commission be composed of a physician, a lawyer, and "a citizen of reputable character."* It was constituted as an independent body directly responsible to the governor, instead of to the State Board of Charities as had been heretofore the case with the commissionership. The powers of supervision, licensing, transfer and removal in matters relating to the mentally ill that had been vested in the State Board of Charities were now transferred to the Commission in Lunacy, and considerably extended. Chief among its duties, the Commission was required to meet at least quarterly; to keep records of every insane person admitted and maintained in institutions; to visit and inspect, at least twice each year, "every asylum and institution in which the insane are in legal custody in this state;" to grant licenses to institutions for the insane and to revoke them, if necessary; to supervise the correspondence of institutional-

---

*It should be mentioned that the Association of Medical Superintendents carried on a long and strenuous struggle against the creation of commissions in lunacy. Extremely anxious to maintain independent authority over their institutions, and deeply resentful of any action regarded by them as "outside interference" and "over-snooping," the members of the Association periodically issued broadsides against the commission idea. As early as 1863, an Association resolution had bluntly stated: "The appointment of Lunacy Commissioners, with a view to official visits, etc., or any supervision of State or corporate institutions for the insane, is to be deprecated as not only wholly unnecessary, but injurious and subversive of the present efficient system of control." In 1875 it had again voiced its bitter antagonism towards lunacy commissions in a series of eleven resolutions drawn up by Dr. Isaac Ray, one of which read: "Resolved, That any supernumerary functionaries, endowed with the privilege of scrutinizing the management of the hospital, even sitting in judgment on the conduct of attendants and the complaints of patients and controlling them, directly by the exercise of superior power or indirectly by stringent advice, can scarcely accomplish an amount of good sufficient to compensate for the harm that is sure to follow." (Proceedings of the Association, 1875. *American Journal of Insanity,* 1876. v. 32, pp. 345–54.)

ized insane persons; to afford all such persons opportunities for private interviews to air real or imaginary abuses; to investigate cases of alleged wrongful detention or custody, or cruel and negligent treatment; and to report annually to the governor.

Similar trends toward the creation of lunacy commissions were already evident in other states. In fact, New Hampshire in 1889 passed a law constituting the Board of Health as a Commission in Lunacy besides its other functions. In many states special lunacy committees had been organized within state boards. In Maryland a State Commission of Lunacy was created in 1886, with supervisory powers over all public, corporate and private institutions in which insane persons were kept. The Commission consisted of four members, two of whom were physicians, with the attorney-general of the State serving as an *ex-officio member*. Massachusetts early recognized the growing importance of lunacy supervision. In 1879 the State Board of Charities and the Board of Health were merged into a Board of Health, Lunacy, and Charity—the first time in America that the term "lunacy" was made part of a state board's title. A second reorganization, in 1886, created two separate bodies, one of which was called the Board of Lunacy and Charity. In 1898 a separate Board of Insanity was established in Massachusetts, the first independent board of its kind in the United States. Many of our present state boards and departments of mental hygiene evolved out of such committees and commissions in lunacy.

In its very first report (1889) the New York Commission in Lunacy placed itself on record as unqualifiedly in favor of state care and of non-separation of chronic and acute cases of mental illness.[8] In 1890, thanks to the favorable mass pressure that had been gradually accumulating, and despite the stubborn opposition of certain local authorities in exempted counties, the State Care Act was passed, opening up a new epoch in the care and treatment of the mentally ill.[9] As originally enacted, the statute provided for the division of the state into hospital districts, in each of which a state hospital should be located. All insane persons, acute and chronic alike, within such districts were to be received into the district hospital. The two existing state asylums for chronics exclusively, Willard and Binghamton, were thenceforth to be operated on the same basis as the other state institutions for the mentally ill, admitting all cases within their respective districts. Thus was abolished the system of providing separate institutions for the chronic and recent insane in New York.

The law directed that all the insane in almshouses be transferred to state hospitals as quickly as accommodations could be made for them. Three counties—New York, Kings and Monroe—whose provision for their own insane was regarded as adequate, were exempted from the terms of the act, as they had been exempted from the Willard Act of 1865. In 1895, however, these counties were also brought under the terms of the act, thus completing the state care system in New York. The whole cost of care and treatment was now borne by the state, in contrast to the former policy of charging the counties of settlement with the cost of maintaining the dependent insane in state institutions. By the terms of the act, inexpensive, detached buildings of moderate size were to be immediately erected on the grounds of existing state hospitals, of sufficient capacity and number to provide for all the mentally ill who were then confined in county institutions. The State Commission in Lunacy was authorized to recommend the erection of additional institutions as necessity demanded. In keeping with the progressive spirit of the State Care Act, a statute passed the same year ordered that the term "hospital" be substituted for "asylum" in all state institutions for the insane.

The most important features of the state care legislation of 1890 may be summed up as follows: (1) it provided for the removal of all the insane poor from the poorhouses; (2) it carried the principle of state care to its ultimate conclusion, namely, support of all the indigent insane (except those in private institutions) in state hospitals at state expense; (3) by districting the state, and by obliging each state hospital to admit all the insane in its district, it abolished the legal distinction between chronic and acute cases; (4) by specifically ordering the substitution of the term "hospital" for "asylum" in all public institutions for the insane, it inaugurated a significant change in nomenclature, symbolizing the new ideal of having all such institutions curative in name and intent.

The State Care Act, obviously, was not original in all its provisions: some had been anticipated at least *in principle* in other states long before. For example, the principle of state care seems to have been implicitly stated in the Constitution of North Carolina, as revised in 1868—nearly a quarter-century earlier than the enactment of the New York law. In a clause of the Constitution of 1868, we find this passage: "The General Assembly shall provide that all the deaf, mutes, the blind, and the insane of the State, shall be cared for at the charge of the State." (Article XI, Section 10.) But whatever its original intent may have been, this clause was interpreted by the Assembly as applying only to those insane persons maintained in the existing state hospital at Raleigh. A large percentage of mentally ill dependents continued to be confined in local poorhouses—at local expense.

Michigan, in 1877, took an important stride toward state care with the passage of an act prohibiting the placing of any insane person in a county almshouse after the completion of the Eastern State Hospital at Pontiac, which was opened in 1878. Thereafter, all the insane were to be supported in state hospitals. The act contained this unique feature: pauper and indigent patients maintained for two years continuously at a state hospital were to be supported at county expense; if they remained longer than two years, the burden of support fell upon the state.[10] Although overcrowded conditions in the state hospitals resulted in the practical nullification of some of its provisions, this statute probably constituted the most advanced legislation relative to public provision for the mentally ill up to that time.

We might add one more instance of state care tendencies in states other than New York previous to 1890. In 1886, the legislature of Vermont passed an act, one section of which provided: "Insane persons in any town destitute of the means to support themselves, and having no relative in the state bound by law to support them, shall be supported by the state."[11]

However, it can be said for the New York State Care Act that it truly marked the culminating point of a great movement, and the beginning of a new period. Embodied in it were the most sweeping legislative provisions in behalf of the insane ever enacted in the United States. What is even more important, the law not only stated high-minded principles; it provided the instrumentation for carrying them into practice. It set into motion an impressive exodus of the mentally ill from the poorhouses of the state. It constituted a momentous victory that brought renewed confidence and strength to the forces of progress in the care and treatment of the mentally ill.

The great step taken by New York in 1890 was bound to have a deep influence on other states throughout the country. The principle of complete state care (as well as the creation of commissions in lunacy) was adopted in state after state following its momentous inauguration in New York.

Meanwhile a rival plan, the county care system, had been introduced and developed in several states, notably Wisconsin. So closely was this plan identified with the latter state that it became known (and still is known to this day) as the "Wisconsin system." The county care plan involves county provision for all chronic cases of insanity and state provision for acute cases, with both state and county participating in the costs.

Like nearly all lines of development in the history of the care and treatment of the mentally ill, this system did not arise as the practical result of a definite long-range plan. Rather was it the outgrowth of a pressing need that demanded immediate action, without regard to its ultimate effects. The more or less elaborate body of theory that grew up around the system of county care was in large measure formulated *ex post facto,* as a rationalization of a condition already existing.

In a very profound sense, the county care system was not

"chosen"; it was forced by the exigencies of a desperate impasse. In most instances its main precipitating factor was overcrowding—that chronic ailment of institutionalized care of the insane throughout modern history. In Iowa, for example, a crisis in the care of the insane occurred in 1878, when the two state hospitals became so overcrowded that they were forced to close their gates against many new cases requiring treatment. In desperation the hospital authorities took advantage of a hitherto inoperative statute permitting them to return harmless and incurable patients to their places of settlement. As a result large numbers of dependent insane persons were suddenly loosed upon the county poorhouses. This action had the effect of merely shifting a problem of overcrowding from one type of institution to another. To meet the critical situation, many counties hastily built "asylums"—buildings which were closely connected with the poorhouses and often indistinguishable from the latter. Called into being as temporary expedients to meet an emergency situation, these asylums gradually became permanent fixtures. Their existence had to be reckoned with in all subsequent measures affecting public provision for the mentally ill in Iowa, and played a determining part in most of the legislation that followed. Thus evolved in Iowa the county care system that obtains there to this day.[12]

For the classic development of the county care system, however, one must turn to Wisconsin. In that state, the evolution of county care followed a circuitous and interesting course. Perhaps no single group was more instrumental in deciding its final form than the State Board of Charities and Reform (later the State Board of Control), established in 1871. As in most other states, the problem of public provision for the mentally ill was a major concern of the Board from the very outset. At first, the policies adopted by the Wisconsin Board in relation to the care of the insane were similar to those advocated by nearly all contemporary state bodies of its type. The recommendations contained in its early reports clearly reflected such policies; they insisted that all the insane were entitled to state care, that the poorhouse was not, and never could be, a fit place for the custody of any part of the insane, chronic or acute. As a means of providing suitable maintenance for all the mentally ill, the Board recommended the enlargement of existing state hospitals, and the building of additional ones.

But as fast as additional accommodations could be furnished, the increase of insanity always remained several leaps ahead of the total capacity. Concluding that this situation was due mainly to the steady accumulation of chronic cases, the Board next recommended the erection, on the grounds of one of the existing hospitals, of an asylum large enough to accommodate all the chronic insane found in almshouses. Institutional rivalry, together with the opposition of county officials, prevented the adoption of this proposal. In its annual report for 1876, the Wisconsin Board brought forward still another plan. It pointed out that the two state institutions for the insane were badly overcrowded. A large percentage of the mentally ill were confined in county jails and poorhouses. Of the 1,200 insane persons in the state, it was estimated, nearly 1,000 were chronic cases. Why not build a large separate asylum for the latter group? As a supporting argument, the board cited the alleged success of the Willard Asylum in New York, opened several years before.[13] Again failing to obtain action, the Board in the following year advanced still another compromise; namely, that the state hospital at Madison be converted into an asylum for chronics, leaving the Northern State Hospital at Winnebago to receive recent cases only. Once more the opposition of county officials to any and all forms of state care prevailed, and this proposal also was rejected.

In 1878 the State Board suddenly reversed its longstanding policy and came out in favor of county care for the chronic insane, mainly on the supposition that the average per capita cost of maintenance for this class in a county asylum would be less than one-half the per capita expense in state hospitals. The board cited other reasons for its change of heart. Within the previous six years, the state had almost trebled its mental hospital capacity without materially reducing the number of insane persons still confined in poorhouses. During that time, the Board felt, a noticeable improvement in the condition of the insane in local institutions had been manifested, especially in those counties which owned asylums partly or wholly separated from the poorhouse proper. In view of these and other observations, the Board concluded that it was neither practicable nor desirable to furnish state care for the chronic insane poor. It was deemed more advisable from the viewpoint of expediency and economy to assign the care of this class to county institutions. A bill was accordingly drawn up by the Board providing for the establishment of county asylums for chronic cases, with state hospitals treating only "curable" patients. This bill was passed by the legislature, but in so modified a form as to defeat its original purpose. It permitted counties to build (with the approval of the governor and the State Board of Charities and Reform) their own institutions for the insane. But it contained no proviso stating definitely that this privilege should apply only to chronic cases, as was originally intended.* Under this act, a county hospital for the insane was established in Milwaukee. Opened in 1880, the Milwaukee County Insane Asylum thereafter received all dependent insane persons, chronic and acute, residing within its limits.

In 1881, largely through the efforts of the State Board of Charities and Reform and particularly of its president, Andrew E. Elmore, a statute was enacted which finally crystallized the county care system, thereafter known as the "Wisconsin plan."[14] According to the provision of the new law, counties which, in the judgment of the State Board, "possessed accommodations for the proper care of the chronic insane," would thenceforth upon receiving proper certification be paid $1.50 per week from the State treasury

---

Wisconsin Laws of 1878, Chapter 298. A section of the act did provide that "whenever any insane person, committed to said county asylum ... shall be found to belong to the class defined as acute insane, and to require permanent and special treatment for the purpose of cure, said persons *may* be transferred to the state hospital for the insane." The permissive nature of this clause robbed it of any practical effectiveness.

By the terms of this act, the State undertook to pay half the expense of erecting county asylums, provided that the total cost did not rise above $600 per patient, and to pay eighty per cent of the maintenance cost for each dependent patient.

for each chronic insane person maintained in such institutions. (A later amendment raised this rate to $1.75 per week per inmate.) Conversely, counties to which patients in state hospitals were chargeable were required to share in the maintenance cost to the extent of $1.50 per week, plus clothing costs.

Rules relating to the management of county institutions for the chronic insane were to be prescribed by the state board. Whenever, in its opinion, any county did not properly care for its mentally ill, the Board was authorized to remove insane persons, and to transfer them to other county institutions. There they were to be maintained at the fixed rate of three dollars weekly, the cost to be shared equally by the state and the chargeable county. Regulations concerning restraints, ventilation, heating, proper attendance, the appointment of visiting physicians, etc., were drawn up by the Board to govern county care. Originally, the Wisconsin law was intended to cover only those chronic cases not already cared for in one of the state hospitals. A later amendment to the county care act, however, made it mandatory to remove *all* chronic cases from state hospitals to county institutions. Also, the provisions covering county asylums were so altered as to make counties which maintained their insane in properly certified *poorhouses* eligible for state aid on the same terms as those counties which possessed separate *asylums*.

The Wisconsin plan, as finally developed, provided a safeguard against the possibility of hopeful cases being committed to county institutions. A provision made it mandatory that all new cases of insanity, whether deemed curable or not, be automatically sent by county authorities (except in the case of Milwaukee, which possessed its own hospital) to a state hospital for treatment. If, after a certain period of observation and treatment, the hospital authorities found a patient to be chronic or incurable, they were authorized to transfer him to a county institution where he remained unless other provision were made for his care. Such were the principal features of the county care system adopted in Wisconsin.

As we have noted previously, separate care for chronic

EXODUS FROM THE POORHOUSE 267

and recent cases in county and state institutions, respectively, had been in actual operation in many states long before the passage of the county care act in Wisconsin—often in direct contradiction to existing statutes. But it was Wisconsin which first crystallized the practice into a complete and comprehensive system.

When, in 1890, the State Care Act was passed in New York, the country was confronted for the first time by the spectacle of two opposing systems functioning in two different states in accordance with definite, concrete plans. The issue of county care versus state care was clearly outlined at last, and advocates on both sides entered into a sharp and passionate debate on the merits and drawbacks of the systems. The New York State Board of Charities on the one hand, and the Wisconsin State Board of Control, on the other, became the chief rallying-points for the opposing factions. Arrayed on the side of the former was the Association of Medical Superintendents (which became the American Medico-Psychological Association in 1893). The Association drew the particular fire of the county care defenders, who sharply impugned its motives, declaring that its members favored state hospitals for all the insane mainly out of the selfish desire to protect and extend their "vested interests" in such hospitals. The Wisconsin system did not lack eloquent advocates in other states.*

At any rate, the controversy over the respective systems

*Franklin B. Sanborn, for many years secretary of the Massachusetts State Board of Charities and one of the most influential leaders in social welfare of his time, vigorously endorsed the Wisconsin system. As early as 1865, he had collaborated with Dr. John S. Butler, then superintendent of the Hartford Retreat, in preparing a plan of separate provision for the chronic insane to be laid before the Association of Medical Superintendents for consideration. In 1892, he made the following declaration before the National Conference of Charities and Correction:

"I make the assertion, and I challenge any one to prove the contrary, that the State of Wisconsin comes at this moment nearer to the ideal standard of providing for every insane person the treatment best adapted to his needs than any State in the Union. I have studied this matter for years, have watched and examined the Wisconsin system, and have repeatedly stated (and it has never been disproved) that the insane of Wisconsin are better provided for in all the essentials of treatment than the insane of any other State." (*Proceedings of the National Conference of Charities and Correction*, 1892. p. 364.)

waxed fiercely during the last decade of the nineteenth century. The annual meetings of the National Conference of Charities and Correction (now of Social Work) in particular provided an auspicious forum for the champions of both sides. Let us sum up the advantages claimed for the contending systems, as brought out in the debates. On behalf of the Wisconsin plan of county care, its advocates averred that:

1. It was more economical than state care, resulting in large savings to both state and counties.

2. It was no less humane than state care. It permitted an even greater degree of liberty for the mentally ill. Restraints found necessary when chronics were associated with acute and disturbed patients could be dispensed with in county institutions.

3. It permitted greater opportunities for employment of chronic inmates, profitable to both the public purse and the individual's health.

4. The individual was maintained close to his home environment, easily accessible to relatives and friends who might wish to visit him. The familiarity of his surroundings was certain to be beneficial.

5. The Wisconsin plan was in reality a "system of county care under state control," since county institutions were under the strict and constant supervision of the State Board of Control. The latter body had the power to withdraw certification and to transfer insane persons to other counties if the standards of care fell below the requirements set by the Board.

6. Chronic cases, except for a very small percentage, were beyond recovery and therefore did not require hospital treatment.

7. By removing chronic cases from state hospitals, the Wisconsin system permitted a more concentrated attention to the treatment of recent and recoverable cases.

8. It made possible the care of a large proportion of the mentally ill in small institutions, while state institutions for the insane were invariably constructed on a gigantic scale. In this respect, at least, it came closer to the ideal size urged by the Association of Medical Superintendents itself.

9. It provided a means whereby increase in the insane population of a state could be met easily and inexpensively, and obviated the administrative and legislative complexities attending the establishment of new state institutions.

10. Since the Wisconsin law provided that all cases of insanity be automatically passed through the state hospitals for treatment, it

guaranteed a period of therapeutic treatment to all, precluding the danger of sending recent and promising cases to county asylums first. Insane persons were transferred from state hospitals to county institutions only when certified as chronic by hospital authorities.

11. The constant supervision of the State Board of Control curbed the "proverbial stinginess and political manipulations" popularly associated with county administrations. Conversely, the financial aid rendered by the state acted as a positive stimulus to good care on the part of the county officials.[15]

The case for state care was presented in impressive detail by Oscar Craig, a prominent member of the New York State Board of Charities, in a paper read before the National Conference of Charities and Correction in 1891. The following series of arguments advanced in favor of the state care system is based largely on his paper:

1. The medical supervision of the average state hospital, with daily or even semi-daily inspection of all patients by competent and trustworthy physicians, and the absence of anything resembling such medical routine in the average county poorhouse or asylum, are reasons enough for exclusive state care of the insane. A strong point advanced against county care was the general policy in localities operating under this system of auctioning off the post of visiting physician to the lowest bidder, a policy hardly calculated to attract the best medical talent available in a community. In other localities, which offered more attractive remuneration to the visiting physician (very few had physicians regularly in attendance), the post was regarded as a legitimate link in the spoils system; fitness was based not so much on personal ability as on political loyalty.

2. State hospitals are invariably located in more healthful and beautiful surroundings, and on grounds far more expansive than the average county institution, a factor more conducive to greater comfort and better chances for health and recovery.

3. The small size of county institutions, far from constituting an advantage, actually provides a serious obstacle to the proper classification of inmates—always an important factor in the care and treatment of the mentally ill. Inasmuch as 100 patients require as many classifications as do 1,000, it is obvious that the state institution, with its more abundant capacity, and its relatively large number of wards or buildings has a decided advantage in the matter of adequate classification over even the best-conducted county asylums.

4. The labor of the state hospital patient is usually assigned and conducted under medical supervision with the primary emphasis on its therapeutic effects on the patient, while the labor of the inmate of the county asylums is invariably carried on with economic considerations foremost. The benefit to the patient is only a secondary consideration.

5. In fine, the state institution nearly always, and the county asylum very seldom, treats its mentally ill patients as sick persons, as in fact they are whether their illness is recent and curable or chronic and incurable.

6. The degrading, demoralizing associations of county care, due to the general procedure of placing the insane in the poorhouse or in an adjoining or adjacent building under the control of poorhouse officials, cannot but have a negative effect on the well-being of the chronic mentally ill, a large number of whom retain the capacity to think clearly and react sensitively to many matters affecting their lives.

7. Individual care and treatment is practicable to a greater degree in state institutions despite, or even because of, their larger size, since they afford greater and more varied medical facilities, more extensive and inspiring surroundings, and means for more correct and complete classification. It can differentiate the treatment in accordance with differing cases, and with changes in the same case.

8. Though the idea of placing chronic and acute cases in the same hospital is not essential to state care, it is a characteristic of most state care systems. It has one important advantage in the opportunity it affords for transferring cases back and forth between hospital treatment and custodial or domiciliary care, as occasion requires—a facility seriously lacking under county care systems, where curative and custodial institutions might be widely separated and transfer of patients between the two rendered difficult.

9. The supervision of a lunacy commission or other central authority is greatly facilitated by the existence of a small number of large institutions as far as visitation and inspection is concerned; conversely, it is rendered difficult when a large number of small institutions are scattered through the state.

10. The state care plan is much simpler in its administrative aspects, since it operates mainly among state institutions, while the county care system involves divided authority among county and state agencies. The cumbersome and complicated machinery necessary to the operation of the latter leads to much friction and confusion.

11. County care, for obvious reasons, is more likely to be influenced by the evils of political patronage than state care, where civil service

competition is more apt to be the rule in the selection of institutional staffs. Again, the wider opportunities of the state in the matter of selectivity of personnel constitute a decided advantage over the necessarily narrow range of county selection.[16]

In varied forms and degrees the state care system was adopted by many states following its introduction in New York in 1890. The majority of states now operate under well-defined state care systems. The county care plan persists in a very few states, notably in Wisconsin and Iowa. In still other states, no definite plan of public provision for the mentally ill has ever been formulated. Methods of care and treatment are of a patchwork character, representing merely the accretion of improvised expedients.

The introduction of state care undoubtedly marked one of the great milestones in the history of the treatment of mental illness in the United States. But, as in all progressive movements, there were some over-enthusiastic supporters who believed that with its adoption the trumpets of jubilee would sound the dawn of the millennium for the mentally ill, and these were doomed to deep disillusionment. Many ills, many abuses, still remained. Centuries-old obstacles to progress were yet to be overcome. It was one thing to try to eradicate long-standing evils by decree; it was far more difficult to put an end to them in practice.

CHAPTER XIV
Psychiatry Emerges from Isolation

THE study of the human mind is the noblest branch of medicine." Some three hundred years have passed since the great jurist, Grotius, expressed this conviction at a time when thousands of mentally disordered persons were being burned and hanged as witches. It was only within the past century, however, that general medicine consented to take unto its bosom this "noblest branch" and to acknowledge it as a legitimate child. It is a significant commentary on the long isolation of the profession ministering to the mind diseased that only a score of years ago one of its most prominent members, Thomas W. Salmon, found occasion to say that psychiatry was still "the Cinderella of medicine." So long had the public at large, as well as the general practitioners of medicine, thought of healers of mental disorders in terms of priests, mystics and wonder-workers, that only with the greatest difficulty did it achieve recognition as a scientific specialty. This traditional attitude was not without foundation in fact, because it is indeed only a matter of several decades since psychiatry has risen to a level approaching scientific technique. The isolation of psychiatry until recent years was not entirely the result of the general indifference, neglect and active hostility on the part of society toward the problems of mental disorder and its treatment. It was rooted partly in the narrowness of the specialty itself throughout most of its history, a narrowness due to natural, inevitable conditions and to seclusive tendencies manifested by members of the specialty themselves.

Throughout the nineteenth century the mental hospital had preserved a strange and unhealthy isolation from the main streams of community life. Often situated in rural districts, it was at times difficult of access even by railroad in those days before the advent of the automobile and other modes of rapid transportation and communication broke down distances and drew rural and urban communities closer together. In more than one sense, the typical institution was aptly termed a "monastery of the mad." The fact of this physical isolation from the centers of social and scientific activities tended to create a corresponding feeling of cultural isolation in the medical staffs of mental hospitals, living hermit-like existences for long periods of time.

A newly-appointed medical superintendent might come to his duties fresh with enthusiasm, scientific curiosity and lofty ideals. More often than not, however, he soon found himself swept into a maelstrom of administrative details that demanded most, if not all, of his attention. Inevitably there was the problem of chronic overcrowding to be dealt with, problems of personnel, problems of keeping the physical structure in repair, and the daily problem of feeding and housing his charges. In most instances he was constantly beset with the problem of stretching a niggardly appropriation to its maximum limits in maintaining the institution. (Only in rare cases did a public asylum receive appropriations sufficient to provide elementary comforts for its patients or inmates.) It was a very unusual institutional head who managed to keep his medical identity from being absorbed by the business executive. After some years of the deadening routine of asylum administration, the scientific interest of the average medical superintendent became so dulled that he would not engage in scientific work even if he had the time.

There were outstanding exceptions, of course. Luther V. Bell of the McLean Hospital, one of the founders of the American Psychiatric Association, was constantly engaged in original research of a clinical nature and gained a wide reputation for his description of Bell's Disease, a form of acute mania. Amariah Brigham of the Utica State Hospital, another member of the Association, retained a lively interest in the scientific aspects of the specialty until his death, and was instrumental in introducing the works of some of the most important European psychiatrists to this country, chiefly through the medium of the *American Journal of Insanity,* which he founded. Isaac Ray, while mainly interested in the medico-legal and administrative aspects of his profession, made several valuable contributions to mental pathology, and in 1863 wrote a book on *Mental Hygiene.* Joseph Workman of Toronto regularly contributed papers of clinical and pathological interest to the proceedings of the Association and to the *Journal* during the 1850's and 1860's.

In succeeding decades scientific work was carried on or encouraged, in varying degrees, by men like John P. Gray at Utica, Pliny Earle at Bloomingdale and Northampton, W. L. Worcester at Kalamazoo and Little Rock, S. V. Clevenger at Cook County Asylum and Edward Cowles at McLean.

But these men were exceptions to the rule. In general the scientific aspects of psychiatry absorbed but little of the time and energy of the average medical superintendent and his assistants. This lack of interest and activity is well reflected in the proceedings of the American Psychiatric Association and in the pages of the *American Journal of Insanity* during the first half-century of their concurrent existence. One finds that the dominating subjects of discussion were those dealing with the practical management of institutions rather than with the scientific study of mental disease. Quite naturally so, in an important sense, for the problems of architecture, of plumbing, heating and ventilation, of food supply and of income-producing labor for patients, were problems forced upon the institutional heads by circumstances over which they had little or no control. We have already noted their great contributions to the sound organization of the early institutions.

As for the assistant physicians in asylums, their opportunities for indulging scientific interests, as a rule, were either strictly limited or nonexistent. Understaffing, like overcrowding, has been a characteristic feature of the average state hospital from the very beginning. An understaffed personnel usually signified an overworked personnel. The terrible demon of dull routine stalked the member of the medical staff as it did the superintendent. Harried by his own administrative problems, his own scientific interests frustrated, the latter was seldom inclined to encourage and stimulate scientific work among his assistants. Still other factors which we have not the space to consider contributed to the discouragement of scientific work in the average mental hospital (or, more properly, asylum) of the nineteenth century. The sum total of these factors might be epitomized as follows: isolation, physical and cultural, from the main currents of social and scientific life; the deadly grind of routine; and the fact that psychiatric practice in this and other countries still lacked a sound base of scientific theory.

Until the final decades of the nineteenth century, psychiatric practice was almost entirely confined to institutions for the insane. Extramural psychiatry was all but unknown, and was frowned upon by the leading specialists, who were the medical superintendents of their day. Little thought was given to medical care in most institutions, which were frankly administered along boarding-house principles.

The scientific literature on mental disease from the pens of asylum staffs was very meagre. Writing in 1876 on the state of American medical literature, Dr. John Shaw Billings dolefully remarked:

> Our literature of insanity and the pathology of mental disease is insignificant in comparison with the importance of the subject and the opportunities existing for its study . . . Considering the number and size of asylums for the insane in this country, and the amount of money which has been spent upon them, it is rather curious that the medical officers connected with them should have contributed so little to the diagnosis, pathology or therapeutics of diseases of the nervous system.[1]

The pressures that finally succeeded in forcing American psychiatry to emerge from its institutional boundaries came from a number of directions. Not the least were the expansive forces within the psychiatric profession itself, reaching outward from its narrow base. A nuclear point for the external forces which operated to drive psychiatry into broader pastures was afforded by the infant and very voluble profession of neurology. We might here attempt a distinction between neurology and psychiatry. While there is no clear line of demarcation between the two, neurology may be broadly defined as the medical specialty that deals with the nervous system and its diseases (including those which do not impair mental processes) while psychiatry concerns itself with the study and treatment of personality disorders. There has also developed the borderline group of neuropsychiatrists, who deal with the disorders of both the nervous and mental systems.

Neurology as a profession in America was practically created by the Civil War. That bloody conflict presented medical men with an extraordinary opportunity for studying and treating injuries to the nervous system due to gunshot wounds and other causes. It was to neurology what the World War later was, in a measure, to psychiatry. Many a general practitioner and surgeon who served in the medical department on either side during the Civil War emerged from the conflict as a practicing neurologist. Prominent among these was William A. Hammond, who was appointed United States Surgeon-General and later became one of the foremost neurologists of his time. It was Hammond who introduced the most renowned neurologist of them all, S. Weir Mitchell, into the profession. In 1863 he put Mitchell in charge of a temporary hospital at Philadelphia for soldiers suffering from nervous disorders. This event placed Dr. Mitchell (who had previously dabbled in various types of physiological research while practicing general medicine) in contact with a rich store of neurological material, and changed the course of his career. Mitchell's best known contribution to neurological thought and practice was his "rest cure" for nervous and mental ailments, consisting mainly of complete rest, seclusion, overfeeding and massaging. (This system of rest treatment was first formulated in his *Fat and Blood,* published in 1877.) There were many other neurologists of note who served their novitiate in the Civil War.

During the 1870's, neurology rose rapidly into a position of great influence in American medicine. The New York Neurological Society was established by a distinguished group in 1872. Two years later the *Journal of Nervous and Mental Diseases,* chief organ of the profession in this country, was founded by J. S. Jewell of Chicago. In 1875 the American Neurological Association was organized, with Dr. Jewell serving as its first president.

Between the neurologists and the institutional psychiatrists there quickly developed a feeling of mutual distrust, suspicion and hostility. The study and treatment of mental and nervous disorders seemed to the "old guard" of the Association of Medical Superintendents to be inseparably bound up with the institutions they managed. They were inclined to regard the neurologists as upstarts, as trespassers upon a preserve that was theirs by right of preemption. The neurologists, on the other hand, were outspoken in their criticism of the management of the mental hospitals of the time. They heaped ridicule upon the medical superintendents as persons who were at best merely efficient business executives, without either scientific knowledge or interest, and berated them roundly for their apparent indifference to scientific research. One has only to read the periodicals of the rival professions published during the 1870's and '80's to appreciate the bitterness and animosity between the specialties.

Unfortunate though this intense rivalry of the early years may have been in certain respects, it exercised a decidedly healthy influence in others. Free criticism is invariably a strong factor, even a necessary one, in the setting up and raising of standards in any field of human activity. From the first, certain neurologists placed themselves in the position of prosecutors-at-large who sought out evidences of asylum abuses, exposed them to the public view and demanded retribution of the guilty. Many of these neurologists were actuated by the best of motives in their critical pursuits. They were true reformers, shocked by existing evils and abuses, and striking out for their elimination. Others acted, no doubt, from motives of "enlightened self interest," finding justification in serving the public weal while at the same time enhancing their own reputations. Still others among the critical neurologists were merely self-interested. For what could serve their own practice better than to stir up public suspicion and distrust of the institutional psychiatrists, thus diverting potential clients to their own offices? While nearly all psychiatric practice was carried on within the walls of institutions for the insane, most neurologists at that time were engaged in private practice or in academic posts, or both.

A negative result of the neurological attacks on asylums for the insane was to heighten public distrust and fears of these institutions, buttressing the popular unwillingness to send sick relatives and friends thereto, and thus impeding adequate popular support and the early treatment of patients so essential in many cases. There was an important positive effect, however. Smarting under the blistering and incessant attack of the neurologists,* the institutional psychiatrists, or "alienists" (a term now exclusively applied to the psychiatrist in his role as expert witness in court procedure), were constrained to put their house in order. Conversely, the vigorous counter-attacks of the psychiatrists helped check the frequently overbearing arrogance of some of their self-appointed critics and also did much to aid the latter in overcoming their own weaknesses. Let it be noted here that the "border wars," as Dr. Richard Dewey called them, between both professions are now for the most part only of historical interest. Today a common basis for understanding exists. Many neurologists are members of the American Psychiatric Association and many function as staff members of mental hospitals, while many psychiatrists are members of the American Neurological Association and many are engaged in private practice.

One of the earliest frontal attacks of importance on the

*A significant index to the extent to which these criticisms were prosecuted is afforded by the activities of the New York Neurological Society's "Committee on Asylum Abuses" in the early '80's. This Committee maintained a keen and relentless vigil over asylums in New York State, and its charges against institutional managements (many of them well-founded) led to several legislative investigations, most of which, however, accomplished little good.

institutional superintendents came from the pen of Edward C. Spitzka, a leading neurologist of his day. In an article on "Reform in the Scientific Study of Psychiatry," published in 1878, Dr. Spitzka arraigned the institutional officers for their lack of scientific study on the one hand, and for their evident unwillingness to provide extramural neurologists with material for pathological research on the other.[2]

In 1894 S. Weir Mitchell carried the attack on the institutional medical officers to a climax in a remarkable address delivered at the fiftieth annual meeting of the American Medico-Psychological Association.* Invited by the Association to criticize "boldly and with no regard to persons," Dr. Mitchell took his hosts at their word and proceeded to lecture the assembled phychiatrists in terms stripped of all pretense of polite discourse. Charging the asylum staffs with responsibility for their isolation from general medical practice, he declared: "You were the first of the specialists and you have never come back into line. It is easy to see how this came about. You soon began to live apart, and you still do so. Your hospitals are not our hospitals; your ways are not our ways. You live out of range of critical shot; you are not preceded or followed in your ward work by clever rivals, or watched by able residents fresh with the learning of the school." The annual reports of medical superintendents, Dr. Mitchell continued, contained "too comfortable assurance of satisfaction, . . . too many signs of contented calm born of isolation from the active living struggle for intellectual light and air in which the best of us live." Warming up to the "uncongenial task of being disagreeable," he sharply criticized the asylum superintendents for the poverty of research in their institutions. Admitting the partial validity of the superintendents' defense that they lacked time, money and adequate assistance for sound research, he insisted that they were not wholly free from blame since in many instances they failed to make strong, urgent demands for necessary equipment and personnel in their reports and other writings.

*The name of the organization had been changed in 1893 from the Association of Medical Superintendents of American Institutions for the Insane.

Too many asylums, he said, were still featured by insufficient and ill-planned employment of patients; absence of recreational and exercising facilities; monotony of diet; and too frequent use of mechanical restraint—factors that served to give to the average asylum the appearance of a dismal prison. "There is another function which you totally fail to fulfill," he added, "and this is by papers in lay journals to preach down the idea that insanity is always dangerous, to show what may be done in homes, or by boarding out the quiet insane, and to teach the needs of hospitals until you educate a public which never reads your reports, and is absurdly ignorant of what your patients need."[3] Mitchell's insistence that greater emphasis be placed upon extramural treatment of mental patients reflected a growing movement to expand psychiatric treatment beyond the confines of institutional walls.

Passing on from forthright criticism to positive recommendations for improving the asylum atmosphere, Dr. Mitchell urged the appointment of intelligent assistant physicians who should enjoy periodic vacations of sufficient length to keep them from growing stale on the job. It was the bounden duty of the asylum head (who should be a neurologist) to keep alive the intellectual and scientific curiosity of his staff by constantly inspiring them with his own example. More trained nurses should be introduced into mental hospitals to facilitate individualization of treatment. Many more recommendations did he make in his eloquent and pointed oration, most of which were far better suited to the ideal mental hospital for private upper-class patients than to the practical possibilities of state hospital management. The asylum superintendents suffered his withering blasts with a surprising degree of patience and toleration, although one can well imagine their faces reddening under the scorching fire of reproof.

While, in truth, his criticisms were on the whole basically sound, nevertheless, he did indulge in hyperbole and in some strange speculations that have been negated by the test of time. Some of his views were premised on imperfect knowledge of the real situation, while his recommendations were

PSYCHIATRY EMERGES FROM ISOLATION

largely of an idealistic and impractical nature. The injustice of some of his harsher condemnations of asylum superintendents was pointed out by Dr. Walter Channing in a reply to Dr. Mitchell's charges, published in the *American Journal of Insanity* in 1895, and also in an eloquent defense of the old superintendents delivered some thirty years later by William A. White.[4] Surely, Richard Dewey was justified in comparing certain aspects of Dr. Mitchell's criticisms to that of "a naval commodore who should assail the army for not winning victories upon the high seas." But some of the points raised by Mitchell struck home at vital defects in the existing asylum system.

Beginnings had already been made here and there in the mending of some of the shortcomings pointed out by Mitchell. One of his chief criticisms was directed at the general scarcity of trained personnel in mental hospitals. The first permanent training school for nurses in an American institution for the insane had been instituted by Dr. Edward Cowles at McLean Asylum in 1882.* A similar school was inaugurated at the Buffalo State Hospital the following year, and the training school idea spread slowly to other institutions during the next decade. Incidentally, Dr. Cowles, who was responsible for many progressive innovations in America, was also the first to introduce the use of women nurses in male wards. In the beginning this step aroused the bitter opposition of shocked Victorians, but it proved so successful that it won adoption in many other asylums. Women physicians seem to have been employed first in the state hospitals of Pennsylvania. There the novel experiment of placing a woman in medical control over the female wards was introduced in 1880 when Dr. Margaret A. Cleaves took over the medical direction of these wards at the Harrisburg State Hospital, while Dr. Alice Bennett performed the same function at the newly opened Norris-

---

*It is interesting to note, in this respect, that Dr. Thomas S. Kirkbride had planned to establish a training school for attendants at the Pennsylvania Hospital for the Insane as early as 1843, but was unable to carry through his project. Training schools for nurses in general hospitals date from Florence Nightingale's activities in Great Britain, resulting from her experience in the Crimean War of 1854.

town State Hospital.* In 1890 a law was passed by the New York legislature authorizing the appointment of at least one woman physician in each state hospital.

A sore point touched upon by Dr. Mitchell was the obvious lack of specially trained physicians on the staffs of most mental hospitals. But to place the entire blame for this situation on the shoulders of the medical superintendents was hardly fair. The chief fault lay with the prevailing indifference to the subject of mental disorder displayed in all but a few of the medical schools in this country. Until the 1870's even occasional lectures on mental and nervous diseases, not to speak of systematic courses, were extreme rarities in our medical schools. It appears that no systematic course was given on these subjects anywhere in America from Benjamin Rush's death in 1813 until 1867, when William A. Hammond was appointed professor of nervous and mental diseases at the Bellevue Hospital Medical College in New York City. A year later a lectureship in mental diseases was established at the College of Physicians and Surgeons for Dr. Edward C. Seguin, son of the famous pioneer in the training of mental defectives. Dr. Isaac Ray conducted summer courses in psychiatry at the Jefferson Medical College of Philadelphia during the years 1870–72.[5] Aside from these and a few other courses, the subject of insanity was hardly mentioned in medical lectures, or in medical textbooks of the time.

It is significant that Benjamin Rush's *Medical Inquiries and Observations upon the Diseases of the Mind,* published in 1812, remained the only American systematic treatise on mental disorder until 1883, when two new texts appeared. It is also significant that both these works were written by neurologists—William A. Hammond and E. C. Spitzka.[6]

---

*In 1879 the Pennsylvania legislature had enacted a statute providing that "in all hospitals or asylums now built or hereinafter to be built, and under the control of the State, and in which male and female insane patients are received for treatment, the trustees of said asylums or hospitals may appoint a skillful female physician who shall reside in said asylum or hospital, and who shall have the medical control of said female inmates, who shall report to the superintendent and also to the trustees." (Quoted in the *Sixth Report of the State Committee on Lunacy of Pennsylvania,* 1888. pp. 22–23.)

Cognizant of the appalling lack of psychiatric instruction, the Association of Medical Superintendents early launched a campaign for the inclusion of special courses on the subject, a campaign which it has carried on to this day. As far back as 1871 the Association passed a series of resolutions dealing with this topic, the first of which reads in part:

> Resolved, That . . . it is the unanimous opinion of this Association that in every school conferring medical degrees, there should be delivered, by competent professors, a complete course of lectures on insanity and on medical jurisprudence, as connected with disorders of the mind.[7]

In spite of the continued agitation for more adequate psychiatric instruction, however, the introduction of special courses in general medical schools proceeded at a snail's pace. Among the unfortunate results of this indifference to psychiatric problems was the fact that physicians who took up work in institutions for the mentally ill invariably came without any previous special instruction or training at all. Their knowledge of mental disorders consequently had to be picked up empirically, bit by bit, during the course of a routinized life in the asylum that gave them little time for delving into research problems of their own.

Progress of Research in Mental Disorder. We may gather from the aforementioned facts that up to the time of Weir Mitchell's address, facilities for, or even encouragement of, scientific research in the mental hospitals of this country were all but nonexistent; only in a few hospitals was research even feebly carried on. Many institutions even neglected to perform elementary autopsies on the brains of deceased patients. Most of the original research that was carried on was undertaken on the initiative of neurologists —men like Hammond, Mitchell, Spitzka, Seguin and Dana. As we have indicated, it was largely because of the pressure of this group that research was stimulated among psychiatrists in our mental hospitals.

In 1868 Dr. John P. Gray had a pathologist, Edward S. Hun, installed at the State Asylum at Utica, New York, to carry on systematic research. Commenting on this initial step in organized pathological research in an American asylum, Adolf Meyer expressed the opinion "that this appointment was to quite an extent a gesture to meet the increasingly vigorous onslaughts of outsiders and neurologists and not a response to a compelling need and eagerness for investigation."[8] Dr. Gray recommended the following major lines of pathological research: examination of secretions in all stages of the disease; observing the pulse under the sphygmograph in order to "determine its force and character," and to show influences of medicine on the circulation; ophthalmic examinations; study of the skin, its temperature, color, etc., in the several kinds and stages of the disease; *post mortem* appearances, gross and microscopic; and photographic representations of morbid conditions and specimens. This line of research ultimately proved to be quite barren in results.

The trend of psychiatric thought had by this time begun to shift from an emphasis on "moral" causes (causes that would be included today in the term *psychogenic*) to an emphasis on physiological causes. This trend, incidentally, was largely due to the rise of materialism during the nineteenth century. The old metaphysical speculations concerning insanity were being discarded, and the pendulum of professional opinion was swinging violently in the opposite direction. The causes of mental disorder were no longer being sought in divine dispensations or metaphysical mysteries, but in the anatomy and physiology of the brain. The causes of insanity, said Gray in 1872, "as far as we are able to determine, are physical; that is, no moral or intellectual operations of the mind induce insanity apart from a physical lesion."[9] In a paper read the previous year before the State Medical Society of New York, Gray had presented an interesting indication of the rise of the physiological concept of mental disease. He quoted his predecessor, Amariah Brigham, as having declared in his 1843 report for the Utica State Asylum, that, "with Pinel, Esquirol and Georget, we believe that moral causes are far more operative than physical." (Moral causes were those "acting through the emotions, passions, sentiments and affections;" physical causes were those "producing their effects, through physical impairment, diseases or injuries.") Dr. Gray drew up a table revealing that in 1843 over 46 per cent of the admissions to Utica were assigned to moral causes, while in 1870 over 85 per cent of the cases admitted were ascribed to physical causes and none at all to moral causes, the remainder being listed as "unascertained."[10]

This physiological approach dominated research in mental disease during the last quarter of the century. At the same time the scientific study of insanity was gradually moving out of the ward, where the great clinical observations of Pinel, Esquirol and Griesinger had been made, into the dead house, whence came increasing hundreds of brains to be subjected to pathological study.

The first great step toward organized psychiatric research in this country was taken in 1895 with the establishment of the Pathological Institute of the New York State Hospitals. The Institute was founded as an integral part of the state hospital system organized under the epochal State Care Act of 1890. Located in New York City, its first director was Ira Van Gieson, a neuropathologist. Dr. Van Gieson was an enthusiastic research worker with some original ideas on the correlation of all the sciences, but was more fitted by temperament for the pursuit of independent research than for the direction of fellow researchers.

In the beginning the activity of the Institute was strictly confined to laboratory work. The aims pursued, as stated by Dr. Van Gieson, were: "to carry on studies on abnormal mental life and their neural concomitants, based on psychology, psychopathology, experimental physiology and pathology, cellular biology, pathological anatomy, comparative neurology, physiological chemistry, anthropology and bacteriology."[11] During the early years there were no facilities for clinical observation. Receiving morbid materials from the various state hospitals of New York, the Institute served as a clearing house for pathological study and information for the entire system.

In 1902 Dr. Adolf Meyer, who had already won wide recognition for his outstanding research work at Kankakee and Worcester hospitals, succeeded Dr. Van Gieson as director. Soon after, the Institute was removed from its expensive quarters in the Metropolitan Building in New York City to Ward's Island, where the Manhattan State Hospital was located. This change of site, bringing the Institute into direct contact with a hospital for mental diseases, afforded a splendid opportunity for clinical observation in addition to the regular laboratory research. Exploiting this important advantage to the full, Dr. Meyer soon organized a clinical department of the Institute, and started training courses for staff physicians sent from the state hospitals of New York. We shall have occasion to speak at greater length of the profound changes in American psychiatric study and practice brought about by Dr. Meyer's system of psychobiology, evolved in part during his association with the Pathological Institute. One of the greatest services of Meyer was to free psychiatric research in America from its dependence on the dead house and its almost complete concentration on morbid materials, and to turn its attention to the living material represented by the individual patient, studied as an organism in relation to his environment. Symbolizing this important shift in emphasis, the name of the Pathological Institute was changed in 1908 to the Psychiatric Institute at Dr. Meyer's insistence, in conformity with the expanded aims and methods developed under his leadership.

Psychiatry Enlists Social Work. Meyer's dynamic approach to the problems of psychiatric research and treatment did much to precipitate the long-pending confluence of social work and psychiatry in America. This collaboration had existed in Europe for many years before its adoption in this country. Dr. Meyer, in common with other advanced psychiatrists at the turn of the century, was insisting that it was the patient, and not the disease, that had to be treated and cured. Meyer went further: it was not enough to study the individual as an isolated physical unit, as the mechanical materialists had done; it was quite as important to study the environment whence he sprang and in which he developed. He conceived of the brain not only as an anatomical entity, but as man's *social* organ, acted upon and reacting to external social stimuli. He saw mental disorder as a maladjustment of the *whole personality,* rather than as a brain disease in the purely physiological sense. Until his time, it had been quite common in American mental hospitals to label a newly admitted patient with a one-word disease term, to scrawl the name of the supposed affliction on his case card and to end the diagnosis there. Meyer insisted on complete case records, including data on all ascertainable aspects of the patient's makeup and life-history: social, economic, hereditary, physical, mental and emotional. When he took over the directorship of the Pathological Institute and organized the clinical department in connection with the Manhattan State Hospital, he especially emphasized the value of getting past histories of each case. In other words, to prepare a comprehensive case record of the patient, the mental hospital had to reach out into the community. A contact between hospital and community must be established. Visits had to be made to the patient's home and to his place of employment, to his relatives or friends, for first-hand information concerning the personal and environmental background of the individual's illness. At first the physicians made these visits and worked up the case histories themselves. But it soon became evident that a division of labor was necessary in obtaining these histories. Dr. Meyer states that in 1904 he enlisted the voluntary service of Mrs. Meyer in visiting his patients at Ward's Island and also their families in the city: "We thus obtained help in a broader social understanding of our problem and a reaching out to the *sources* of sickness, the family and the community."[12] Later, the value of utilizing trained social workers to obtain case histories, in addition to after-care work, impressed itself upon institutional psychiatrists until the social service department became recognized as an indispensable part of every modern state hospital system.

In the meantime, while this call for social service was developed from the inner needs of psychiatry, a simultaneous drive had been proceeding *from* the social work profession *toward* psychiatry. From the very beginnings of social work as an organized profession in the 1870's, the subject of mental disorder in its social aspects had taken up a considerable part of the proceedings of the National Conference of Social Work. The social worker constantly came in contact with this problem at several points. To begin with, provision for the indigent insane constituted one of his major tasks. There was also the problem of looking after the families of individuals who had been the breadwinners before being incapacitated by mental illness.

One of the serious questions confronting social workers revolved around the readjustment of mental patients returning from state hospitals to normal community life. It often happened that a patient discharged as cured was unable to readjust himself to communal existence. Such a person, unaided, might break down again under the strain, with consequent readmission to a hospital, perhaps permanently this time. The environmental conditions he met upon returning to society were never quite the same as when he was first hospitalized. He was invariably burdened with new handicaps, one of the heaviest being the "stigma of insanity" with which the ex-patient of a "madhouse" was branded. The patient cured of pneumonia or typhoid or appendicitis might return to take up his affairs at the point where his temporary illness had interrupted his normal routine. But not so the recovered mental patient. He was a marked man. He had been "crazy", and didn't the popular saying go, "once insane, always insane"? His relations with his family or friends thereafter were likely to be strained, at least for some time; his "term" in a mental hospital stood as a serious obstacle to reemployment. Under these added strains many a mind gave way again, rendering the individual socially inadequate.

Another concern of the social worker was the fact that many times a patient in a mental hospital recovered, or at least improved sufficiently to warrant return to the community, but his discharge had to be delayed because of socio-economic difficulties. There might not be any home or family to which he could be sent, or he might find it impossible to get employment at once so that he could start life anew on a self-supporting basis. Often, in such instances, there remained only one of two choices for the hospital superintendent, neither of which could be a satisfactory one: the patient could be retained in the hospital or be transferred to the poorhouse, where he might spend the rest of his life as an unhappy public dependent. There still existed no medium or agency through which the recovered patient could be given the initial help and advice that might start him off on the road to independence. The situation was a serious one, revealing the vicious end-results of a policy of *laissez-faire*. It called for solution, a solution that found its earliest expression in the rise of the after-care movement.

The after-care movement had its beginnings in America during the last decade of the nineteenth century, when it won vigorous champions among psychiatrists, neurologists and social workers. The principle behind this movement was to provide adequate financial, medical and moral assistance to patients discharged from mental hospitals, in order to aid their adjustment to the outer world and to check relapses due to social handicaps. The after-care movement was first introduced in 1829 by Dr. Lindpainter, director of the Eberbach Asylum in Nassau, Germany. In France, a "Société de Patronage" was founded by Dr. Falret in 1841 for this purpose in the Department of the Seine. The idea was gradually adopted on a nation-wide scale under government auspices. A similar society, called the "Guild of Friends of the Infirm in Mind," was established in England in 1871. In this country, prominent psychiatrists and neurologists including Richard Dewey, Peter M. Wise, Frederick Peterson, Adolf Meyer, Henry R. Stedman, Charles L. Dana and F. X. Dercum, joined by many eminent social workers, strongly advocated the forming of after-care associations during the nineties and early 1900's.* In 1896 the State

---

*A paper on this subject was read before the 1893 meeting of the American Medico-Psychological Association by Dr. P. M. Wise. The following year the American Neurological Association appointed a Committee on After-Care consisting of Drs. Stedman, Dana and Dercum. In 1894 and 1895, Dr. Richard Dewey presented papers on after-care before the National Conference of Charities and Correction. Dr. Meyer advocated after-care in several important papers thereafter.

Charities Aid Association of New York (which had played such a prominent part in forcing the passage of the great State Care Act of 1890) authorized its Committee on the Insane "to inaugurate and maintain, for convalescents leaving hospitals, who may be friendless, a system of 'after-care,' whereby they may be strengthened in health, protected and cared for until able to support themselves."[13] The plan was held in abeyance for a decade, however. In January, 1906, a conference attended by members of the State Commission in Lunacy, the superintendents of all but one of the fifteen State hospitals for the insane, and officers of the State Charities Aid Association, adopted several resolutions supporting a plan for the launching of a statewide after-care system, on the basis of private philanthropy, by the State Charities Aid Association. The following month, a subcommittee on after-care of the insane was organized by the Association under the chairmanship of Miss Louisa Lee Schuyler. The subcommittee immediately launched plans for the establishment of after-care committees for each state hospital, to work under the general direction and control of the statewide subcommittee. In the same month the "Manhattan After-Care Committee of the S.C.A.A." was formed—the first functioning committee of its kind in this country. Shortly afterward Miss E. H. Horton, a trained social worker, was engaged as after-care agent in the Association. Her initial assignment consisted of aiding the Manhattan After-Care Committee.[14] Miss Horton in consequence was probably the first psychiatric social worker in America. Other hospital district after-care committees were soon organized, their major purposes being to find suitable homes and employment for needy ex-patients, to render other social services as needed, and to exercise general supervision over them during the period immediately following their discharge.

Such were the beginnings of direct collaboration between social workers and psychiatrists in America. In Boston, about the same time, Dr. Richard C. Cabot was introducing similar innovations in collaborative work between the two professions. The subsequent development of this confluence, which received tremendous impetus in the period following the World War, will be discussed in a later chapter.

Evolution of the Psychopathic Hospital. Another development of major importance in American psychiatry that symbolized the extension of the practice beyond asylum confines was the rise of the first psychopathic hospitals and wards at the turn of the twentieth century. This type of institution was in operation in Germany long before it was finally introduced into the United States. The functions of a modern psychopathic hospital may be briefly described as follows: It is usually located in large towns and cities. It provides first care, examination and observation for persons suffering or believed to be suffering from mental disorder, pending commitment to a general mental hospital. It administers short, intensive treatment in incipient and acute cases. It provides educational facilities for medical students. It functions as a center for clinical and pathological research in nervous and mental disorders. It serves as a clearing house which sorts out those persons whose mental aberrations are not of such kind or degree as to render them socially inadequate from those whose disorder requires commitment to a mental hospital.

There are four major types of psychopathic hospitals: (1) that connected with a university; (2) that connected with a general hospital; (3) that connected with a hospital for mental diseases; and (4) that which operates independently.

While the psychopathic hospital came as a belated innovation in American psychiatric practice, its need was early expressed in this country. The very term, "psychopathic hospital," is of American origin, and was used in the title of a paper by Pliny Earle in 1867 wherein he urged the establishment of separate hospitals for the "acutely insane."

The first strong movement in the direction of psychopathic hospitals in this country was started by the California State Board of Health soon after its establishment. In its second biennial report (1871) this body, composed of progressive individuals with an unusual interest in the problems of the mentally ill, published a paper written by one of its members, Dr. A. B. Stout of San Francisco, advocating the establishment of "probationary asylums" in the large towns for the treatment of "ephemeral attacks of mental alienation."[15] "In an extended meaning of the word," Dr. Stout explained, "probationary signifies tentative, or an institution in which the effort is made to afford relief by quick and prompt intervention in the incipiency of mental disorders." A large percentage of "permanent insanity," he declared, was due to the failure to apply prompt treatment while the disease was in its incipient stage. "Give it [insanity] no foothold; it will fail to hold possession. As things now are, parties interested, in the most loyal faith, rush around for relief, but can only find it after protracted and expensive delay." Dr. Stout drew up a bill providing for a "probationary asylum" to be established in San Francisco. This bill was introduced into the state legislature but went down to defeat. Dr. Stout and his fellow members on the Board of Health continued their efforts in this cause but it was some years before California adopted the idea, and then in a form far removed from the ideal of Dr. Stout.

During the 1870's there was quite a public clamor in New York City revolving around frequent instances in which mentally disordered persons were arrested and brutally beaten by the police, locked up in station houses and sent to the penitentiary or workhouse before their mental condition was discovered—in flagrant violation of a state law prohibiting the detention of insane persons in jails or prisons. Leading neurologists residing in the city were particularly critical about this state of affairs.

In response to the public pressure for better care of mentally ill persons pending commitment, the city constructed an "Insane Pavilion" at Bellevue Hospital in 1879. Formerly, persons brought to the hospital and supposed to be mentally disordered had been detained in the "alcoholic wards" together with cases of acute alcoholism. The new building for the mentally ill was divided into two wards for female and male patients, and contained twenty-four "cells." It was intended "only for patients whose sanity is in question, where they may be kept under observation until proper commitment papers can be made out for their transfer to other institutions."[16]

The "insane pavilion" at Bellevue did not constitute a psychopathic hospital in the modern sense of the term. It was a detention hospital, pure and simple, affording no therapeutic treatment for its patients. Nevertheless, while its functions were restricted to detention and observation, the "insane pavilion" at Bellevue marked an important step forward in the evolution of the modern psychopathic hospital. (Out of this pavilion, in fact, evolved the well known psychopathic hospital of Bellevue.) Similar detention or observation wards were established at the Philadelphia General Hospital ("Old Blockley") in 1890.[17] As with Bellevue, the alleged insane admitted into "Old Blockley" previously had been thrown into the "Drunk" wards. In 1912 the observation wards were reconstituted by legislative enactment into "psychopathic wards," under the supervision of neuropsychiatrists.

The first psychopathic ward in a general hospital in America fulfilling the function of actual therapeutic treatment besides detention and observation was established at the Albany Hospital in 1902. "Pavilion F" was added to the hospital in that year "for the detention and care of persons afflicted with nervous and mental disorders," upon the initiative of Dr. J. Montgomery Mosher, who directed its operation for many years thereafter.[18] Since 1902, psychopathic wards or hospitals have been established in connection with general hospitals in many of the large municipalities.

While the movement for psychopathic wards in general hospitals grew largely out of the desire to provide decent accommodations for doubtful cases of mental disorder in cities pending commitment proceedings, the university psychopathic hospital arose mainly out of the need for adequate psychiatric research and education. The first American institution of this type was founded at the University of Michigan in 1901. For some years previously Dr. William J. Herdman, professor of mental and nervous diseases at the University, had resorted to periodic visits to a state asylum in carrying out the clinical part of his course. The University had also entered into more or less informal agreement with the state hospitals whereby it acted as a center of pathological research for all of them, as was the case with the Pathological Institute in New York. This loose arrangement proved unsatisfactory for several reasons. Dr. Herdman, recognizing the advantages of a psychopathic hospital at the University itself, carried on a persistent campaign toward this end. His efforts were rewarded in 1901 when the state legislature passed an act authorizing the construction and equipment of a psychopathic ward of forty beds at the University Hospital. A sum of $50,000 was appropriated for this purpose.

The psychopathic ward was opened in 1906 under the direction of Dr. Albert M. Barrett, whose official title was Pathologist of the State Asylums. Under an act of 1907, the institution was reorganized as the State Psychopathic Hospital at the University of Michigan, to serve as a "state hospital specially equipped and administered for the care, observation and treatment of insanity and for persons who are afflicted with abnormal mental states but are not insane."[19] The act further provided that "there shall be maintained as a part of the Psychopathic Hospital at the University of Michigan a clinical pathological laboratory for the Michigan state hospitals for the insane, and a laboratory in which research into the phenomena and pathology of mental diseases shall be carried on."

The first psychopathic hospital connected with a state hospital for mental diseases was opened in Boston in 1912. As early as 1900 Dr. Owen Copp, executive secretary of the Massachusetts State Board of Insanity, had urged the establishment of a psychopathic hospital in a special report. The agitation was continued throughout the first decade of the century by that energetic crusader for progressive lunacy legislation, Dr. L. Vernon Briggs. In 1909 the state legislature enacted a statute appropriating $600,000 for the establishment in Boston of a hospital "for the first care and observation of mental patients and the treatment of acute and curable mental diseases and for an out-patient department, treatment rooms and laboratories for scientific research as to the nature, causes and results of insanity." The Psychopathic Hospital was opened in June, 1912, as a department of the Boston State Hospital, which had been transferred from city to state control four years earlier. Dr. E. E. Southard, one of the foremost psychiatric researchers in the United States, was chosen as first director, a position he retained until his death in 1920. In the latter year, the Psychopathic Hospital was separated from the administration of the Boston State Hospital, and functioned thereafter as an independent unit under the control of the State Department of Mental Diseases.

In its report for 1910, the State Board of Insanity of Massachusetts outlined the function of a model psychopathic hospital so fully that I quote from it at some length:

The Psychopathic Hospital should receive all classes of mental patients for first care, examination and observation, and provide short, intensive treatment for incipient, acute and curable insanity. Its capacity should be small, not exceeding such requirement.

An adequate staff of physicians, investigators and trained workers in every department should maintain as high a standard of efficiency as that of the best general and special hospitals, or that in any field of medical science.

Ample facilities should be available for the treatment of mental and nervous conditions, the clinical study of patients in the wards, and scientific investigation in well-equipped laboratories, with a view to prevention and cure of mental disease and addition to the knowledge of insanity and associated problems.

Clinical instruction should be given to medical students, the future family physicians, who would thus be taught to recognize and treat mental disease in its early stages, when curative measures avail most. Such a hospital, therefore, should be accessible to medical schools, other hospitals, clinics and laboratories.

It should be a center of education and training of physicians, nurses, investigators and special workers in this and allied fields of work.

Its out-patient department should afford free consultation to the poor, and such advice and medical treatment as would, with the aid of district nursing, promote the home care of mental patients. Its social workers should facilitate early discharge and after-care of patients, and investigate their previous history, habits, home and working conditions and environment, heredity and other causes of insanity, and endeavor to apply corrective and preventive measures.[20]

Implicit in the last paragraph is an important development in psychiatric history—the adoption of the out-patient department in mental hospitals. This development in America dates back to 1885. In November of that year, a dispensary for the free treatment of persons suffering with "incipient mental disease" was opened in the out-patient department of the Pennsylvania Hospital at Pine Street, Philadelphia. Morton, the historian of the Pennsylvania Hospital, tells us that "the service was regarded at that time as experimental . . . It was undertaken under a conviction that in a city of one million inhabitants, a large number were suffering from premonitory symptoms of insanity as nervous prostration and depression, who might receive timely advice and treatment, and that a further development of mental disorder might thus be arrested."[21] The dispensary was operated by members of the medical staff of the Department for the Insane of the Pennsylvania Hospital under the direction of the superintendent, Dr. John B. Chapin.

A few months later the trustees of the State Hospital for the Insane at Warren, Pennsylvania, of which Dr. John Curwen was superintendent, followed suit by adopting this resolution:

> Resolved, That the Physician-in-Chief and Superintendent be requested to give notice that from two to six o'clock of the afternoon of the second and fourth Wednesdays of each month, he will give advice and counsel to those who may feel that the symptoms of mental disorder are developing in themselves, or in any member of their family.[22]

Such were the beginnings of out-patient departments for mental patients, which were later to become an outstanding feature of psychiatric care and treatment. "Nerve clinics," for the treatment of nervous disorders, had been established earlier in Philadelphia (1867) and Boston (1873).

Now let us return to our account of the rise of psychopathic hospitals. In 1913, the year following the opening of the Boston Psychopathic Hospital, the Henry Phipps Psychiatric Clinic was opened in connection with the Johns Hopkins Hospital at Baltimore. The Henry Phipps Psychiatric Clinic (which has all the features of a psychopathic hospital) has been under the direction of Dr. Adolf Meyer since its inception, and is generally recognized as one of the great centers of psychiatric research and education, not only of this country, but of the world.

Meanwhile a movement for a psychopathic hospital located in New York City (in addition to the psychopathic wards at Bellevue) had been under way for a number of years. In 1904, thanks largely to the efforts of Dr. Frederick Peterson, then president of the New York State Commission in Lunacy, Dr. Adolf Meyer, and officers of the State Charities Aid Association, the state legislature passed a law authorizing the city of New York to "acquire a site and to lease the same to the State for the establishment thereon of a Reception Hospital for the Insane." An initial appropriation of $300,000 was made for this purpose. A site was actually selected but was later found unsatisfactory, and the entire plan was dropped until 1920, when a new plan for a psychopathic hospital to be integrated with the work of the Psychiatric Institute (then on Ward's Island) was adopted, and $700,000 was appropriated by the legislature. By a happy coincidence plans were then in progress for the erection of the great Columbia-Presbyterian Hospital Medical Center in upper Manhattan, and, largely through the efforts of Dr. Thomas W. Salmon and Dr. C. Floyd Haviland, cooperation between the two new institutions was agreed upon and the necessary legislative authorization was obtained. In 1929 the New York State Psychiatric Institute and Hospital was opened under the direction of Dr. George H. Kirby as an affiliated unit of the largest medical center in the world. The control of the Institute remained in the hands of the New York State Department of Mental Hygiene. Rising twenty stories above the Hudson River in a fireproof building of beautiful design, with a bed capacity for two hundred patients and thoroughly equipped with therapeutic, research and educational facilities, the New York State Psychiatric Institute and Hospital ranks as one of the finest institutions of the kind anywhere. It enjoys the dual advantage of affiliation with a great medical school (the College of Physicians and Surgeons of Columbia University) and a general hospital of the first order.

Like the aforementioned Psychiatric Institute, the Payne Whitney Psychiatric Clinic is connected with a great medical center in New York City, the result of an amalgamation between a medical college and a general hospital, in this case forming the New York Hospital-Cornell Medical College Association. Built at a cost of over $2,000,000, the Payne Whitney Psychiatric Clinic was opened October 1, 1932. Notable features of this development are its extensive therapeutic resources in both the in-patient and out-patient services, its visiting and consulting psychiatric service for the medical and surgical departments of the general hospital with which it is connected, and its relations with the long-established Westchester Division of the New York Hospital at White Plains, New York, formerly called Bloomingdale Hospital. The extension of this psychiatric service was made possible largely through the efforts of Dr. William L. Russell, general director of the psychiatric work of the New York Hospital and professor emeritus of psychiatry at the Cornell University Medical School.

Psychopathic hospitals or wards of the four major types have been established in many large cities and university centers throughout the country. The nine psychopathic hospitals maintained under state auspices include: Boston Psychopathic Hospital (opened 1912), Iowa State Psychopathic Hospital at Iowa City (1920), Colorado Psychopathic Hospital at Denver (1925), New York State Psychiatric Institute at New York (1929), Syracuse Psychopathic Hospital at Syracuse, New York (1930), Galveston State Psychopathic Hospital at Galveston, Texas (1931), Illinois Neuropsychiatric Institute at Chicago (1931), Western State Psychiatric Hospital at Pittsburgh, Pennsylvania (1942), and the Langley Porter Clinic at San Francisco, California (1943).

We have traced broadly in this chapter some of the significant advances at the turn of the twentieth century that heralded the coming of age of psychiatry in America. We have seen the process stimulated during this period by the development of new facilities and techniques in psychiatric education, training and research. Of equal significance was the breaking away of psychiatry from its narrow institutional shell by the growth of private practice, the rise of out-patient departments and psychopathic hospitals, and the beginnings of the employment of social case work techniques in the care and treatment of the mentally ill.

CHAPTER XV
The Mental Hygiene Movement and Its Founder

THE opening decade of the present century was extraordinarily rich in the rise of reform movements—political, economic and social.

In the field of social welfare, particularly, there was a striving for new goals, accompanied by inevitable changes in the approach to social problems and their solution. There was a growing conviction that radical measures were required in dealing with the major social ills: poverty, delinquency and disease. The cyclic interaction of these evils was discerned with increasing clarity. Poverty was a prolific mother of both delinquency and disease; disease, in its turn, bred more poverty, and so ran the vicious cycle. To break this cycle, it was now manifest, emphasis must be placed not on therapeutics, not on patching-up, but on the drastic application of preventive measures. Prevention became the keynote in social work and in public health as the new century opened.

The phenomenal rise of the eugenics movement during this decade was in large measure a reflection of the rise of the preventive ideal. While eugenicists were concentrating on problems of heredity, other groups, more aware of the environmental causes of human misery, were devoting themselves to the herculean task of eliminating social and economic conditions unfavorable to the health and happiness of the race.

Developments within the field of public health undoubtedly exerted a decided influence on the growth of the preventive ideal. The epochal discoveries of Pasteur, Koch and the other pioneer microbe hunters had, in a remarkably short period, made possible the prevention of diseases that had hitherto taken huge annual tolls in human life. Man was at last beginning to master his unseen enemies in the microscopic world. One after another, disease-bearing germs were being discovered and destroyed. In a few decades, through the application of sanitation and hygiene, dread scourges like cholera, bubonic plague and typhus all but disappeared from the western world. The dramatic conquest of yellow fever by Walter Reed and his associates at the turn of the century was an important factor in making America health-conscious. If the practical abolition of a number of man's greatest plagues had so quickly followed upon the discovery of their causes, why couldn't the field of exploration and prevention be extended to other diseases?

On many fronts, the fight against disease was intensified. Originating largely with individuals, by the turn of the century this fight was increasingly taking on an organized form. Scientific data concerning the causes, cure and prevention of diseases were piling up at so rapid a pace that organization was necessary to collect and collate such data, to broadcast the information to the public, to awaken that public to the recognition of life factors harmful to the individual and to society, and to stimulate activities leading to the amelioration or elimination of factors injurious to health. Fittingly enough, Fielding H. Garrison, in his *History of Medicine,* refers to this period as the "beginnings of organized preventive medicine." It is no accident that the decade under discussion produced such organizations as the National Tuberculosis Association (established 1904 as the National Association for the Study and Prevention of Tuberculosis); the American Social Hygiene Association (which grew out of the American Federation for Sex Hygiene, organized in 1910); the American Child Health Association (organized 1909 as the American Association for the Study and Prevention of Infant Mortality); and the National Committee for Mental Hygiene, formally organized in 1909, though its inception dates one year earlier.

It was within this framework of developments, which we have hastily sketched, that the mental hygiene movement originated in 1908; it is only with this background in mind that its beginnings and early rise can be properly understood. The social climate was propitious for such a movement. Its rise was an inevitable result of the clear and unmistakable trends of the time. In general, then, it may be freely stated that the mental hygiene movement developed out of the same broad forces that brought into existence similar movements in other fields about the same time. In several important respects, however, this particular movement was unique in origin. Few movements have been founded under such extraordinary circumstances as this one. Few founders of contemporary movements have had careers so unusual as that of Clifford Whittingham Beers.

Born in New Haven, Connecticut, on March 30, 1876, Beers's boyhood and early youth followed a pattern not markedly different from that of the average youngster of his native city. At eighteen he entered Yale University, fired with the not unusual ambition to become a successful business man and make a lot of money after graduation. But during his undergraduate years, a family misfortune occurred that was to affect the whole course of his future. An older brother was suddenly seized with epilepsy. Under the stress of this nerve-racking experience, Clifford Beers became prey to an obsession that he, too, was destined to fall victim to the dread disease. For six years he lived under the darkening shadow of this fear, while his unhealthy mental condition remained unperceived by his companions and elders. His abnormal obsession he revealed to none: none of his acquaintances or mentors even suspected that he was in other than a nervous condition of no serious import.

Graduating at Yale in 1897, Beers entered upon a business career. Three years later disaster overtook him. The fear of epilepsy which had been insidiously growing upon him for six years now seized complete domination of his mind. One sunny noon in June, 1900, he threw himself from the window of his room, located on the fourth floor of his family dwelling, in a suicidal attempt, caused by his delusional belief that he had become an epileptic, to which affliction he preferred death. Thanks to a last-minute whim of a

THE MENTAL HYGIENE MOVEMENT

sick mind, however, he dropped from the window sill by his hands, landing feet first on soft earth a bare three inches from a stone pavement. On that fateful three inches hinged not only the life and death of a man, but the birth of a world-wide movement. As it was, he escaped with no other physical injuries than broken bones in each foot and a sprained but unbroken spine, conditions which were but temporarily incapacitating.

A strange transformation now took place in his mental processes. The obsessive fear of epilepsy that had gradually gained possession of his mind, resulting in the impulse to suicide, was forever dispelled the moment he struck the ground. Instead, the sick mind was now stormed by a train of delusions, alternating from those of persecution to those of grandeur, that ruled over his thought for the next three years. These years he spent as a patient within the walls of three mental hospitals in Connecticut, except for a few months spent in the home of a friendly attendant in a town near New Haven.

A cross-section of the three major types of institutions for the insane was represented by these hospitals; the first to which Beers was committed was a privately owned asylum run for profit, the second a private, non-profitmaking institution, and the third a state hospital. In all three he was treated in the harsh and crude way that was all too prevalent at that time. He was beaten mercilessly, choked, spat upon and reviled by attendants, imprisoned for long periods in dark, dank padded cells, and forced to suffer the agony of a strait-jacket for as many as twenty-one consecutive nights. Once, after a particularly excruciating experience, he scribbled on the wall of his room this ironic inscription: "God bless our Home, which is Hell."

A large measure of this treatment had its source in the prevailing ignorance concerning insanity—ignorance not only of proper therapeutics, but of the very nature of mental disorder. If, here and there, enlightened people were recognizing "insanity" as an illness no more mysterious in essence than physical disease, the popular mind still held it in great awe and dread. It was still regarded less as an illness than as a family disgrace and as a frightful visitation for some evil or sin committed by the victim. There were still institutions where, in *practice,* notwithstanding the encouraging language of their annual reports, many of the insane were being treated as sub-humans, stripped by their disease of all claims to human dignity. Inhuman punishments were inflicted by ignorant attendants upon Beers and other patients for harmless eccentricities or innocent, playful acts directly attributable to the sick state of their minds—actions that they could no more control than a paralytic can control the affected parts of his body. Their reason was acknowledged to be impaired by the very fact of their presence in supposedly curative institutions, yet they were often expected to act like perfectly rational beings and were meted out swift and humiliating punishments for failing to do so.

Liberty-loving, strong-willed, and aggressively independent in spirit, Clifford Beers rebelled against the frequent resort to senseless brutality on the part of attendants and its apparent toleration by some of the physicians. His own keen sensitivity to injustice was touched to the quick; the memory of those scenes remained with him always.

During the first two years of his illness Beers suffered from delusions of persecution or self-reference manifested in the feeling that he had committed some vague, unpardonable crime, and that he was being shadowed by detectives, government agents, and the like. At the end of this time these delusions vanished quite dramatically, never to reappear, and Beers passed from a state of profound depression into one of extreme exaltation. It was during this period of elation, accompanied by definite symptoms of approaching recovery, that the idea of starting a world-wide movement for the protection of the insane took shape in his mind. Such harsh and stupid treatment as he had suffered at the hands of hospital officials and employees must be abolished. He had seen other patients subjected to like brutality and even worse. He had reason to believe that at least one of his fellow patients had been beaten to death. These infamies burned deeply into his soul. There welled up within him an overpowering determination to put an end to all such abuses in institutions for the mentally sick. Burning with indignation, he addressed long letters to the Governor of Connecticut and to other officials, describing the conditions in mental hospitals, and calling for immediate investigation and remedy. His letter to the governor brought no results though it was not entirely ignored.

In his state of elation, the plans he made to bring about sweeping reforms in the management of institutions for the insane took on grandiose forms. Upon recovery, he vowed, he would immediately launch a world-wide reform movement that would forever blot out the abuses inflicted upon himself and his fellow patients. In order thoroughly to familiarize himself with all aspects of asylum life—the better to expose them—he deliberately provoked his attendants to throw him into the worst of the "violent" wards, where patients were kept strait-jacketed in small, bare unventilated cells. There was method in this madness.

During his last months as a patient Beers filled literally reams of paper—standard-sized sheets being too small to compass the unceasing flow of his active imagination, he wrote on long strips of wrapping paper—with accounts of his asylum experiences, together with elaborate programs for reform.

In September, 1903, he emerged from his three-years period of hospitalization a free and healthy man. It might be expected that in the exhilaration of recovery and new-found freedom, the man would be only too glad to forget the painful experiences he had suffered and had seen others suffer, and to set aside the high resolves he had made to bring about radical reforms. But Beers did not forget. On the contrary, the project for reform grew stronger after his return to normal life in the community. Indeed, so enthusiastic did he become over the project that about a year later he experienced a recurrence of mild elation, causing him to return voluntarily to the large private mental hospital where he had formerly been a patient. There he remained for a month, and this time he came out completely recovered.

During the following two years he devoted himself to his

business career with promising results. But his idea of creating a movement in behalf of the mentally ill and for the prevention of mental illness held him in its grip; he could not shake it off even if he would. Possessing a keen foresight and a natural talent for "building up" a project, he began to campaign cautiously and methodically. He was fully aware of the discouraging difficulties to be faced, of the deep-seated prejudices to be overcome. He knew that a slight misstep on his part might well prove fatal to the attainment of his object.

How to begin the movement? Thinking of the tremendous influence of *Uncle Tom's Cabin* in stimulating the antislavery movement, he decided that it would be best to write his projected book. A book about himself, about his experiences in three institutions for the insane, a book with a constructive message and a definite plan. A book that would not merely entertain or instruct, but would rally its readers to action along lines set down by the author.

Obtaining a leave of absence from his employers, Beers began writing the first draft of his story. In January, 1907, he abandoned his business career and gave himself wholeheartedly and uninterruptedly to the task he had set himself. The result was that remarkable classic in American autobiography, *A Mind That Found Itself,* published in 1908, shortly before the author's thirty-second birthday.

Now, books about asylum life written by former patients had appeared before. But here was a book that was different from all its predecessors; it was truly unique. Others had written "exposés" of institutional life, with horrifying details based all too often on reality. But because of warped outlook, a suspicious lack of coherence, inadequate literary ability on the author's part, or some other defect, these books had generally produced little or no tangible effect.

A notable exception was the case of Mrs. E. P. W. Packard, who wrote several "exposés" after spending three years (1860–63) as a patient in the State Insane Asylum at Jacksonville, Illinois.[1] Mrs. Packard claimed that she was committed to and confined in this asylum while perfectly sane, and that other patients she met there were likewise sane.

Her allegations created a national sensation and resulted in a wave of sentiment in favor of legislation providing better safeguards for persons "accused" of insanity. A woman of forceful personality, she succeeded in getting the Illinois legislature to enact, in 1867, a law "for the protection of personal liberty," which prohibited the commitment of any person to an institution for the insane without trial by jury. In this case the remedy proved worse than the condition it was supposed to cure. The requirement of a jury trial did not protect the insane at all, nor the sane for that matter, since it left the decision as to insanity in the hands of a lay jury ignorant of the medical aspects of mental disease. Contrariwise, due to the publicity and humiliation attendant upon open trials as required by law, many families hesitated to go through commitment proceedings for a mentally disordered relative, and thus lessened the chance of recovery that early attention might bring. Needless to say, the Illinois law met with the unanimous opposition of the psychiatric and allied professions.

In addition, there had been occasional exposés of certain insane asylums by reporters seeking sensational material, who managed to "break into" such institutions by feigning insanity. One of the best known of these accounts was written by that amazingly venturesome newspaperwoman, Nellie Bly, who in 1887 had herself committed to the New York City Lunatic Asylum (then on Blackwell's Island). Her story, serialized in Joseph Pulitzer's *New York World,* was entitled "Ten Days in a Mad-House," and bore the revealing sub-titles, "Feigning Insanity in Order to Reveal Asylum Horrors; the Trying Ordeal of the *New York World's* Girl Correspondent."[2] Only rarely did exposés of this kind result in permanent gains in the treatment of the insane. However laudable the motives of individual narrators of asylum horrors might have been, however accurate their facts, few succeeded in bringing about even minor reforms. Their revelations might fill the front pages as nine-day sensations, but, comet like, they usually were lost to sight as suddenly as they had flared up.

Then came *A Mind That Found Itself.* Its author showed

restraint in withholding its publication until he had submitted his manuscript to a number of psychiatrists, psychologists and leaders in other fields for criticism and comment. This was indeed a farsighted move, forestalling the possibility of having the story dismissed by superficial commentators as the vagary of an irresponsible ex-patient. The book was not published until 1908,[3] five years after its author's final emergence from his round of mental hospitals. With an introduction by William James, it won immediate acclaim in America and abroad. Reviews, editorials and articles on the book and its author soon appeared in leading scientific and popular publications in many countries. (The 22nd edition appeared in 1935.) The book was widely recognized for what it really represented: not merely an admirable literary production but an instrument for progressive social action. Its publication heralded the beginning of a great crusade and a new era in the management of mental ills. A masterful indictment of the asylum system of the time, based on personal experiences, it was presented in such a manner that it could not fail to impress the reader with its ring of sincerity and truth. But it did not stop with a mere indictment. It concluded with a concrete program for the amelioration and prevention of the evil conditions it described and condemned.

"I am not telling the story of my life just to write a book," Beers declared, "I tell it because it seems my plain duty to do so." Elsewhere he wrote: *"Uncle Tom's Cabin* had a decided effect on the question of slavery of the Negro race. Why cannot a book be written which will free the helpless slaves of all creeds and colors confined today in the asylums and sanitariums throughout the world? That is, free them from unnecessary abuses to which they are now subjected."

But the betterment of institutional conditions in behalf of the mentally ill was only part of the program put forward by Beers in his book. The circumstances of his own illness had convinced him that mental disease was not only curable in many cases, but also preventable. Several psychiatrists of repute had told him, following his recovery, that his break-

THE MENTAL HYGIENE MOVEMENT

down could have been prevented if his condition had been brought to the attention of a competent specialist in its early stages, particularly during his undergraduate years. Added to this personal element was the influence exerted on him by the prominence given to the subject of prevention in public health and social services during that period—a factor that we have already discussed.

In his book, Beers outlined a plan for the establishment of a national society for the purpose of initiating and furthering reforms in the care and treatment of the mentally ill; for disseminating to the public information designed to create a more humane and intelligent attitude towards this class of sufferers; for encouraging and carrying on research into the causes, nature and treatment of mental disorder; and finally, for the creation of services directed toward the prevention of mental maladies.

A Mind That Found Itself created a profound impression in professional and lay circles. Its rallying cry was heard and heeded. Men and women from all walks of life flocked to the banner flung aloft by the young reformer. The willingness, indeed eagerness, with which persons of prominence lent their names and active support to the new movement is a significant indication that that movement filled a deeply felt need. William James was one of the first to rally to the new cause; his support was enthusiastic and sustained. Other eminent Americans soon followed. Dr. Adolf Meyer proved a tower of strength in the formative years. A supporting letter of his, in which he described Beers and his project in highly favorable terms, served as a valuable open sesame to minds that might otherwise have been locked against ideas expounded by an ex-patient of a "lunatic asylum." It was Dr. Meyer who suggested the apt term "mental hygiene" to designate the new movement and the organization that was to serve as its spearhead. The term was by no means new, having been used in America as early as 1843,* and in Germany a few years earlier. Subsequently, during the nineteenth century, it was employed in a sense

---
*The first known use of the term in the United States occurred in William Sweetster's book, *Mental Hygiene; or an Examination of the Intellect and*

closely approximating its present meaning, embracing the principles of the cure and prevention of mental disorder and the preservation of mental health. Of course, the means of achieving these desiderata were but dimly understood throughout that time, as indeed they were at the turn of the twentieth century. Nevertheless, the ideal was clearly enunciated by these early writers on mental hygiene.

By the time *A Mind That Found Itself* was published, Beers had already enlisted enough support to start a mental hygiene organization. The movement was formally launched shortly after the book appeared. Beers was prepared and eager to organize it on a national scale, but the more cautious among his advisers suggested that the movement be started on a modest state-wide basis to serve as a sort of demonstration project. This advice prevailed. On May 6, 1908, a group headed by Beers established the pioneer Connecticut Society for Mental Hygiene at a meeting held in the founder's native city, New Haven, and he was made its executive secretary. The demonstration quickly proved successful, and on February 19, 1909, the realization of Beers's first major goal was gained with the formal founding of the National Committee for Mental Hygiene, at a meeting in New York City. Beers was made secretary, a position which he has filled continuously ever since. The twelve charter members of the National Committee present at that meeting included, besides Clifford Beers, Lewellys F. Barker, Russell H. Chittenden, Horace Fletcher, August Hoch, William James, Julia Lathrop, Marcus M. Marks, Adolf Meyer, Frederick Peterson, Jacob Gould Schurman and the Rev. Anson Phelps Stokes, Jr.

Here it seems appropriate to describe briefly an interesting historical forerunner of the National Committee, of

Passions, Designed to Illustrate their Influence on Health and Duration of Life. (New York, 1843. 270 pp.) This work, advanced for its age although naïve from the viewpoint of present standards, was intended to demonstrate the unity of mind and body in man, and the interrelationships between intellectual and emotional activities. It stressed the "importance of a judicious exercise of the intellectual powers to health and happiness." The term, mental hygiene, appeared in the titles and texts of many books and articles during the nineteenth century. A book of that title by Dr. Isaac Ray was published in 1863.

which Beers had never heard until two or three years after his project had been launched. Just as the term "mental hygiene" had a history running far back before its adoption to designate a new movement in 1908, so the National Committee itself was not without its nineteenth-century antecedents. As long ago as 1842 a Society for Improving the Condition of the Insane had been organized in London. Lord Shaftesbury, the famous social reformer, served as its first president. Among its most active leaders was Dr. D. Hack Tuke, of the noted Quaker family associated for nearly a century with the York Retreat. The purposes of the London Society were modest in scope, as indicated by the aims set forth in its constitution:[4]

1. The diffusion of practical knowledge concerning the nature, causes and treatment of Mental Disorder, by meetings of Medical Practitioners, and other persons who feel interested in the subject, in London and its vicinity.
2. The institution of Correspondence and Prize Essays on various points connected with the treatment of Insanity, and with the management of hospitals, and public and private asylums for the insane.
3. The advancement of the moral, intellectual and professional education of the immediate attendants on insane patients.*

It is interesting to note that a short account of the London Society written by Dr. Pliny Earle in 1845 for the *American Journal of Insanity* concluded with the challenge: "When will a similar association be formed among the dignitaries of this land?"[5]

Such a society did materialize in the United States a generation later. Like its twentieth-century successor, the National Association for the Protection of the Insane and the Prevention of Insanity was formed during a decade (1872–1882) that witnessed an unusual development of organized social movements in various fields.† Founded in

*This organization gradually declined in influence, and seems later to have been merged in the Lunacy Law Reform Society of London.

†Among the organizations established during this decade were: the New York State Charities Aid Association (1872); the National Conference of Social Work (1874); the American Public Health Association (1872); and the Charity Organization Society movement (1877 *et seq.*).

1880, the existence of this National Association spanned but a brief four years. Short-lived though it was, its origin and activities are of historical interest.

The movement leading toward the establishment of this society received its major impetus from the National Conference of Social Work. The Conference was then in its infancy, but had already become a center from which radiated many important social movements. At the 1878 annual session of the Conference, Dr. Nathan Allen, a member of the Massachusetts Board of State Charities and a leading social reformer of the time, read a stimulating paper on "The Prevention of Disease and Insanity."[6]

The following year (December, 1879) a mass meeting was held at Cooper Union, New York City, for the purpose of discussing various problems of lunacy reform, particularly the need for establishing a state lunacy commission in New York. At this meeting, presided over by George W. Curtis, a resolution was adopted recommending the founding of a protective society for the insane. This society, with the long but expressive title, The National Association for the Protection of the Insane and the Prevention of Insanity, was formally organized in Cleveland on July 1, 1880.* Its initiators consisted mainly of social workers, neurologists, psychiatrists and social-minded laymen.

Dr. Hervey B. Wilbur, superintendent of the New York State Asylum for Idiots at Syracuse, was elected president; Dr. Nathan Allen of Worcester, Massachusetts, was made vice-president; Miss A. A. Chevaillier, a social worker of Boston, was secretary, and Dr. George M. Beard, a neurologist well known for his pioneer work on neurasthenia, was treasurer.

The methods by which the society proposed to attain its ends included the encouragement of special clinical and pathological observations of the nervous system by the

*It is interesting to note that the founding meeting of the National Association occurred in connection with the annual session of the National Conference of Social Work at Cleveland in 1880. A day or two prior to the establishment of the organization, Dr. George M. Beard read a paper before the Conference entitled, "Why We Need a National Association for the Protection of the Insane." (*Proceedings*, 1880. pp. 144-51.)

THE MENTAL HYGIENE MOVEMENT   313

medical profession generally, as well as by those connected with asylums for the insane; education of the public as to the nature of mental disorder, the importance of early treatment, and improved methods of management; the advancement of an enlightened state policy in regard to the insane; the stimulation of legislation aimed at more complete and efficient state supervision of all institutions for the insane; and the allaying of public distrust in relation to the management of insane asylums by placing the latter on the same footing with other hospitals.[7]

During its brief existence, the National Association accomplished much good, particularly in the state of New York, where it was most active. By exercising a keen vigilance in matters of institutional care, and by agitating for legislative inquiries wherever the existence of abuses was known or suspected, the Association undoubtedly exerted a generally healthy influence in preventing and alleviating such abuses. For a little more than one year (April, 1883 to October, 1884) it published a quarterly periodical, *The American Psychological Journal*.

Despite its early promise and usefulness, the National Association came to an untimely end a few years after its founding. Several factors, internal and external, contributed to its disintegration. Not the least important was the fact that from the very first it was forced to contend with the powerful and unremitting antagonism of the Association of Medical Superintendents of American Institutions for the Insane (now the American Psychiatric Association). This animosity arose largely as a reaction to the energy with which the National Association prosecuted campaigns for the exposure of prevalent asylum evils, promoted legislative inquiries into institutional management, and advocated state central bodies with supervisory and control powers over individual insane asylums. At each of these points, the National Association came into direct and violent conflict with the stated policies of the society of medical superintendents. Another factor in the failure of the reform group was the internal conflict, sometimes open, sometimes concealed, between the neurologists and psychiatrists among its members. Most important of all, probably, was the fact that the society, for divers reasons, failed to rally behind itself the public support vital to all such organizations. And so it was that the National Association for the Protection of the Insane and the Prevention of Insanity gave up the ghost about 1886. By the time the mental hygiene movement was founded in 1908, this interesting forerunner was but a dim memory in the minds of a few surviving members.

The conditions that called into being this brave, but short-lived society still prevailed through the land a quarter-century later when Beers founded the National Committtee for Mental Hygiene. Here and there, it is true, progressive innovations had been introduced into agencies for the control, care and treatment of the mentally ill. But such improvements usually took the form of isolated phenomena. The fact that a reform was introduced in a particular institution or a particular state was no indication that it would find immediate application elsewhere. The slow and uneven pace of progress was everywhere sadly evident. At the turn of the century, cruelties savoring of the medieval inquisition were still practiced with sickening frequency not only in the backward areas of America but in institutions located within the compass of the very citadels of American civilization. One has only to turn to contemporary records of legislative investigations of such institutions as "Old Blockley" in Philadelphia and the City Insane Asylum at Ward's Island, New York, to find graphic illustrations of this melancholy state of affairs.

Such was the situation when Clifford Beers launched the mental hygiene movement in 1908. The time demanded the movement, and was favorable to its success.

As outlined in one of the early publications of the National Committee for Mental Hygiene, the chief objects of the new society were:

> To work for the protection of the mental health of the public; to help raise the standard of care for those in danger of developing mental disorder or actually insane; to promote the study of mental disorders in all their forms and relations and to disseminate knowledge concerning their causes, treatment and prevention; to obtain from

every source reliable data regarding conditions and methods of dealing with mental disorders; to enlist the aid of the Federal Government so far as may seem desirable; to coordinate existing agencies and help organize in each State in the Union an allied, but independent, Society for Mental Hygiene, similar to the existing Connecticut Society for Mental Hygiene.[8]

It will be seen from the above quotation that the positive principle of prevention of mental disorder was a primary interest of the mental hygiene movement. The skepticism that had to be overcome in the acceptance of the preventive principle is witnessed by a passage in a review of Beers's book that appeared in *The Nation*. Written from an intelligent and generally advanced viewpoint, the review none the less cast doubt on the preventive aspects of the movement proposed by Beers, while endorsing its ameliorative program. "One is bound to face the fact," the reviewer declared, "that insanity is in the majority of cases an unpreventable and an incurable disease, and nothing short of Utopia itself can make it very much less so. In the meantime, any effort toward the amelioration of the lot of these unfortunates by decreasing their sorrows and increasing whatever joys they can still appreciate deserves hearty commendation and support."[9] This sentiment as to the limitations of the mental hygiene movement was shared by many progressive individuals of the day.

Another important purpose of the National Committee was to combat the still prevalent belief that mental disease, besides being an "incurable" affliction, also carried with it the stigma of disgrace. Alexander Johnson, in a review of Beers's book published in *Charities and The Commons*, indicated the seriousness of this problem:

> The two reasons for failure which are the most far-reaching and injurious in their effects are the lack of belief in the curability of insanity and the sense of disgrace connected with it. To the extent that people, not only the laity, but members of the medical profession, both those in general practice and many of those in charge of the insane, think that "once insane, always insane"—that permanent recoveries are rare exceptions—the insane will receive asylum care instead of hospital treatment. And because people connect a stigma of disgrace with

mental alienation, early symptoms, even if detected, which happens rarely, are neglected, and not until it is impossible any longer to ignore the disease, is application for admission to a hospital made.[10]

While the objectives of the National Committee were clearly enunciated from the first, it took some time for the organization to begin active work toward the realization of these objectives. Beers had quickly gained the enthusiastic support of psychiatrists including progressive superintendents of mental hospitals, social workers, educators and others, to his cause. But, unfortunately, adequate funds, essential to the activity and growth of the organization, were slow in forthcoming. Beers, who had no financial resources of his own, was forced to go heavily in debt during the formative period to keep the organization alive; a contribution of one thousand dollars from his staunch friend and supporter, William James, once came as a godsend.

Not until 1912, shortly after Henry Phipps donated $50,000 to the National Committee, was it able to place its work on an active basis. In that year Dr. Thomas W. Salmon, then connected with the United States Public Health Service, was engaged as director of special studies. This proved to be a most fortunate choice. Dr. Salmon soon showed himself to be an excellent planner, administrator and organizer, and in 1915 was appointed medical director of the National Committee. The primary task of the organization was to initiate a survey of existing mental hygiene facilities in the United States, and this was the nature of the first project undertaken under Dr. Salmon's direction. It was the purpose of this project to obtain a picture of the entire field as a prelude to active constructive work. Since the launching of its regional survey program the National Committee has conducted more than sixty state-wide and local surveys in thirty-five states, concerned mainly with institutional provision for the mentally ill and the feebleminded, financed largely by the Rockefeller Foundation. Many of these surveys resulted in securing increased and expanded services for these groups. Other studies, such as the prevalence of mental deficiency in school children and the prevalence of mental disorder and mental defect in correctional institutions, in the dependent groups, etc., were also engaged in.

The entrance of the United States into the World War in 1917 resulted indirectly in the recognition of the importance of mental hygiene generally, and psychiatry in particular, to the health of the human race. It is one of the grotesque ironies of history that wars, with their frightful carnage in lives lost and wrecked, do tend to give impetus to various health movements. Governments which, in times of peace, gave little or no thought to the problem of protecting and preserving the health of their citizens, turned their attention increasingly to the problems of physical and mental health of the military forces during the World War. Not to make robust citizens, to be sure, but to make more efficient fighting machines of their soldiers, present and potential. The high rate of mental disorder among soldiers had been noticed in the early years of the war. Up to 1917, one of every seven British soldiers discharged for disability was suffering from some nervous or mental disease. The incidence of mental disease in the army was several times greater than that among the civil population.* The various disorders grouped under the name "shell shock" contributed a large proportion of the nervous cases.

One of the first acts of the Federal Government upon entrance into the war was the creation of a division of neurology and psychiatry within the Surgeon General's office. The task of organizing this division was entrusted by the Surgeon General's office to the National Committee for Mental Hygiene. Dr. Pearce Bailey was made chief of the division, with Dr. Thomas W. Salmon and Dr. Frankwood E. Williams of the National Committee's staff serving as

*A preliminary survey by a committee on neuropsychiatry prior to our entrance into the War revealed the following facts, among others: that even in peacetime the incidence of mental disorder was much higher in the army than in the civil population; that out of a group of 1,069 enlisted men discharged from the U. S. Army in 1912 on account of disability from all causes, more than 200, or practically 20%, were found to be mentally diseased or defective; and that the discharge rate for mental diseases in the U. S. Army in 1916 was three times the admission rate for these disorders in the adult male population of New York State.

his principal aides, Dr. Salmon's position being senior consultant in neuropsychiatry in the American Expeditionary Forces. The functions of the division of neurology and psychiatry were mainly (1) to prepare for the examination of recruits in the mobilization camps in order that those unfit for military service because of neuropathic or psychopathic conditions might be discharged; (2) to prepare adequate facilities for the observation, treatment and care of soldiers ill of nervous or mental diseases pending discharge; (3) to prepare for the treatment of soldiers in the American Expeditionary Forces who became incapacitated because of nervous or mental disease; and (4) to prepare for the continued treatment and final disposition of soldiers invalided home.[11]

The war and post-war period witnessed a tremendous development of interest in mental hygiene, arising largely from the serious problems involved in the "war neuroses," and the demonstration of their diagnosis and treatment by the psychiatrists engaged with the military forces. The public's attention was increasingly directed to the problem of eliminating preventable mental disorders and of improving existing methods of treating such disorders. The mental hygiene movement rapidly extended its scope to include many new fields of activity. Within a few years after the World War it was being recognized as an important factor, present or potential, in such varied fields as education, public health, general medicine, industry, criminology, penology, and social work. It was in the field of social work that the influence of the mental hygiene movement was most profoundly felt.

Mental Hygiene and Social Work. The confluence of mental hygiene and social work was quite inevitable. We have already discussed at some length the rise of psychiatric social work in the early years of the present century in connection with the after-care movement (Chapter XIV, p. 286 ff.). We have seen how forces within both psychiatry and social work were then converging toward common objectives. This process continued during the ensuing years.

In both psychiatry and social work there was an increasingly strong trend toward "individualization" of treatment.

In psychiatry this trend was leading to the discovery and rediscovery of broad social factors hitherto obscured from the medical specialist engaged in treating the mentally ill on a mass basis. As it broadened its scope and reached out further into the community, psychiatry felt a deep need for trained social workers who could interpret the environmental factors in mental breakdown and who could aid in the social adjustment of discharged and furloughed patients. The attention of social work, on the other hand, was being increasingly focused on personality in the study and treatment of socially unadjusted individuals. It turned to the psychiatrist more and more to help it interpret the dynamics of personality, particularly in relation to social failure. The individual gradually replaced the family as the unit in social case work. This process emerged partly as a revolt against the impersonal, mechanical methods of relief followed in poor law administration, and partly as a logical continuation of the emphasis on "character-building" in private social service, dating back to the work of George Chalmers in Scotland in the early nineteenth century, and developed by the charity organization movement from its inception in the 1870's.

During the first decade of the twentieth century, when social workers became acutely conscious of the broader environmental factors underlying social ills, they made valiant efforts to ally themselves with the great social reform movements that were sweeping the country at the time. Attempts to change unfavorable environmental conditions dominated the practice of social work. These efforts did not produce the expected results, largely because the social workers of the time were unable to distinguish between fundamental and superficial socio-economic forces, and tried to achieve preventive measures by means that were at best only palliative. At any rate, the failure to arrive at their objective through attempts to change the environment in dealing with problems of social maladjustment was an important factor in bringing about the shift of emphasis upon individual personality rather than upon environmental and social forces. Still another factor in this trend was the appearance of a number of "alarmist" studies of degenerate families, tending to show a causal relationship between mental defect and mental disease and nearly all cases of dependency and delinquency. Now discredited, these studies gained wide credence at the time and made a profound impression upon social workers. The introduction and development of mental tests, especially as applied to dependent groups, also influenced the trend away from sociological to psychological factors.

As social work swerved from its orientation around mass social reform movements, case work rose to an increasingly prominent position in relation to general social work. In 1917, Miss Mary E. Richmond, the leading exponent of social work theory of the period, defined social case work as consisting "of those processes which develop personality through adjustments consciously effected, *individual by individual*, between men and their social environment."[12]

In Miss Richmond's *Social Diagnosis* (1917), and in the works of others, social case work was presented with a theory; it now wanted a technique. Having become self-conscious, it eagerly sought a technique that would place it on a firm professional basis.

Into this scene the mental hygiene movement entered with all the force and éclat of a *deus ex machina*. To many social work leaders, casting about for a methodology, the solution presented itself in a very simple formula: Mental hygiene was mainly interested in developing healthy personality. Social case work, as defined by its leading exponent, was mainly interested in developing healthy personality. Things equal to the same thing are equal to each other. Q.E.D.

The World War also served as an important stimulus to the integration of mental hygiene with social work. As the war drew to a close it became evident that preparations must be set afoot for the treatment and rehabilitation of returning soldiers suffering from war neuroses and psychoses. In the work of rehabilitation it was evident that far more psychiatric social workers would be required than were then available. The training of additional workers became a pressing problem. Until then the only attempt at systematic training for psychiatric social work was being made at the Boston Psychopathic Hospital, where the director, Dr. E. E. Southard, and his chief of social service, Miss Mary C. Jarrett, had been conducting an apprenticeship course since 1914 for six or seven students at a time. The names of these two individuals, incidentally, stand out most prominently in the development of psychiatric social work; the very term was coined by them.

This need for trained psychiatric social workers was particularly felt by the National Committee for Mental Hygiene, immersed as it then was in the problems of mentally disabled soldiers. It proposed the establishment of a training school for psychiatric social work, and formed a subcommittee to accomplish that end. The committee consisted of Drs. E. E. Southard, William L. Russell, L. Pierce Clark, Walter E. Fernald, and W. A. Neilson, president of Smith College. In the summer of 1918 the Training School for Psychiatric Social Work was opened at Smith College, offering an intensive eight-weeks course, under the direction of Miss Jarrett. Operated jointly by Smith College and the Boston Psychopathic Hospital under the auspices of the National Committee, the school proved its usefulness at once, and was transformed from an experimental to a permanent school—the present Smith College School for Social Work.* In order to encourage specialization in psychiatric social work it was emphasized from the first that the need for this profession would not end with the emergency problem of caring for mentally disabled soldiers, but would continue to expand in connection with civilian mental patients.

Thenceforth the application of psychiatric principles to social work techniques progressed by leaps and bounds. It soon outgrew the narrow confines of the special branch known as psychiatric social work, and rapidly permeated the general field of social work. A large part of the National Conference of Social Work held at Atlantic City in 1919 was devoted to a section on "Mental Hygiene" and, in the words of leading social workers present, "mental hygiene

*In the summer of 1917, courses in mental hygiene had been included for the first time in the curriculum of the New York School of Social Work.

and psychiatry swept the conference." In a paper read before the National Conference in 1923, Dr. Jessie Taft, one of the most active proponents of the psychiatric point of view in social work, manifested the enthusiastic reaction of social workers to the introduction of mental hygiene:

> The linkage between mental hygiene and social case work has deepened steadily and almost without opposition since the inception of the mental hygiene movement a few years ago. No other profession or field of work has as yet been so fundamentally affected by it . . .
>
> Social case work has leaped to this new exposition of human behavior [mental hygiene] as something which it had been seeking vainly in the offering of the university curriculum. In mental hygiene, case work found a theory wrought out of the very material in which it was already struggling, and for whose organization it had as yet developed no adequate psychological interpretation. Social case work had been starving for a practical human psychology, and had been fed for the most part on academic husks. The doctrines of mental hygiene and the new psychology came as the fulfillment of a long-felt conscious need . . .[13]

It is interesting to note, in the passage we have just quoted, that the term *mental hygiene* is used as a theory of human behavior, instead of as a movement for improving the care and treatment of the mentally ill, preventing mental disorder, and preserving mental health. This misuse of the term was quite prevalent in that day.

In 1922 two significant books appeared, reflecting the profound influence of the mental hygiene movement on social work. One was Mary E. Richmond's *What Is Social Case Work?* In this volume, the psychological aspects of case work theory were stressed, in contrast to the dominant consideration given to sociological factors in Miss Richmond's *Social Diagnosis,* published five years earlier. The second book was *The Kingdom of Evils* by E. E. Southard and Mary C. Jarrett. "We are entitled to claim for psychiatric social work," the authors declared, "that it employs not only the general stock of human ideas about character, but seeks with some success to employ the new point of view of mental hygiene. Possibly that point of view can best be

THE MENTAL HYGIENE MOVEMENT 323

intimated in a single word by the term *individualization* ... *psychiatric social work in general.*"[14] (Emphasis in original.)

During the next decade the psychiatric approach to social case work gained ground with amazing rapidity. The process was undoubtedly quickened by the tremendous popular interest manifested in psychology and psychiatry during the 'twenties. Courses in mental hygiene became an integral part of the curriculum of social work schools. Indeed, so great was the enthusiasm over mental hygiene, that it led for a long time to a dangerous over-emphasis on the mental factors in problems of social work. The important sociological factors were lost sight of while psychological factors were given almost exclusive attention. Mental hygiene was being "oversold" by over-enthusiastic adherents. The great economic depression that broke upon the country in the fall of 1929 and precipitated millions of "normal" families into the dependent class had the effect of bringing out of obscurity the socio-economic factors in social work problems. At present the over-emphasis on mental hygiene—which has been discouraged by organized mental hygiene—is being eliminated, and there is now a tendency toward a clearer estimate of the economic, physical and mental factors in social work.

Mental Hygiene and the Child Guidance Movement. Although child guidance did not emerge as a distinct movement until 1922, its beginnings may be traced back many years earlier to the pioneer child study experiments undertaken by American psychologists, and the establishment of the first juvenile courts toward the end of the nineteenth century. The development of the preventive ideal in dealing with social ills in the early years of the present century also served to focus attention on the child. It became increasingly clear that many of the ills and maladjustments of adults could be traced back to childhood. In a very real sense, it was recognized, the child is the father to the man. The field of criminology was among the first to stress causal relationship between personality problems in childhood and adult delinquency, and it was in this field that the first practical steps to study the child separately were taken. In 1909 the Juvenile Psychopathic Institute was founded by Dr. William Healy at Chicago in connection with the juvenile court located in that city. This clinic, intended for the study of the juvenile delinquent, was financed by Mrs. William F. Dummer as a five-year project, with the understanding that if the demonstration proved successful, it would be taken over by the public. The patients at the Institute were mainly recidivists and mentally abnormal children. Three years later, independent of the Chicago experiment, a children's clinic was opened at the newly established Boston Psychopathic Hospital. In 1913 the Henry Phipps Psychiatric Clinic opened in Baltimore with a special department for children. At both the Boston and Baltimore institutions, social service became highly integrated with the psychiatric study and treatment of child behavior.

In 1914 Dr. Healy's clinic in Chicago was taken over by the county, and its name was changed to the Institute of Juvenile Research.* The following year witnessed the publication of his epochal work, *The Individual Delinquent*, based on case studies made at the Institute during the preceding six years. In this book Dr. Healy advanced the concept that the causes of delinquent behavior must be sought primarily in the mental life of the delinquent. When the Judge Baker Foundation (now the Judge Baker Guidance Center) was opened in Boston in 1917, Dr. Healy was engaged to act as its director, and there he organized his famous clinic for delinquent and problem children. Meanwhile other juvenile courts had been established in various parts of the country, some of which had psychiatric clinics attached. During this period, the development of separate psychiatric clinics for children was almost entirely confined to work with juvenile delinquents. But in the years following the World War child psychiatric work took on a broader aspect: the emphasis shifted from the juvenile courts to the community at large.

Beginning with 1915, the National Committee for Men-

---
*In 1917 control of the Institute passed from Cook County to the State of Illinois.

THE MENTAL HYGIENE MOVEMENT 325

tal Hygiene had been conducting surveys among school children, especially with reference to mental deficiency. These surveys demonstrated two things: (1) that many behavior problems existed among apparently normal children attending public schools; and (2) that facilities for dealing with these problems were grossly inadequate—in fact, almost non-existent. The need for special psychiatric clinics for children was evident, and the National Committee stood in the forefront of the drive to meet this need. Dr. Salmon was particularly active in this direction, and much of the credit for launching the child guidance movement in the early 'twenties is attributed to him. In 1917 he had expressed the opinion that "the enormous increase of interest in the mental life of childhood is leading to the recognition at a much earlier period than formerly of those factors which endanger mental health."[15] Dr. Salmon was mainly instrumental in organizing a conference on the prevention of juvenile delinquency, held at Lakewood, N. J., in March 1921, under the joint auspices of the Commonwealth Fund and the National Committee for Mental Hygiene. Following this conference, a five-year demonstration program of child guidance clinics was launched jointly in 1922 by these two organizations. The movement was greatly stimulated through this experiment, and many clinics were subsequently established. V. V. Anderson, Lawson Lowrey, Marion E. Kenworthy, Ralph P. Truitt, David Levy and George S. Stevenson have been prominent leaders in this movement.

The child guidance clinic has been described by Dr. George S. Stevenson as "a psychiatric clinic designed to diagnose and treat the behavior and personality problems of childhood. These problems are made manifest by disorders of behavior, such as tantrums, stealing, seclusiveness, truancy, cruelty, sensitiveness, restlessness, and fears. The clinic treats these problems by treating not only the child through whom they become overt but treating as well the family, school, recreational, and other involved factors and persons which contribute to the problem, and whose disorder the problem may really reflect."[16] The nucleus of such clinics follows the classic pattern of all psychiatric clinics: a psychiatrist, a psychologist and a psychiatric social worker. It is estimated that child guidance clinics (known under various names, such as institutes for juvenile research, child guidance bureaus, etc.) constitute from one-third to one-half of all psychiatric clinics in the United States. Included in the general category of child guidance clinics are the habit clinics for pre-school children, devoted to the study and treatment of the behavior problems of infancy. The first habit clinic was established at Boston in 1921, under the direction of Dr. Douglas A. Thom.

A survey made in 1946 revealed that there were, in the United States, a total of 285 psychiatric clinics exclusively for children, together with some 350 serving children along with adults. These clinics were operated by public and private agencies and were mostly connected with juvenile courts, general hospitals, state hospitals, schools, family service agencies, and public welfare departments. Only a fraction of these clinics were functioning on a full-time basis, however.

Mental Hygiene and Prison Clinics. Like the child guidance clinic, the prison clinic developed out of the extension of mental hygiene to the field of delinquency. Under the sponsorship of the National Committee for Mental Hygiene, a psychiatric study of prisoners was instituted in 1917 at Sing Sing Prison in New York State, with Dr. Bernard Glueck directing the project. In connection with this study, a psychiatric clinic was established at Sing Sing headed by Dr. Glueck. From the clinic emanated a series of reports throwing valuable light on the extent of mental disorder among prisoners and on recidivism. These reports included recommendations for more scientific methods of classifying prisoners and for special types of institutions for offenders.

The founding of the pioneer clinic at Sing Sing was followed by the establishment of similar clinics in other correctional institutions. Unfortunately, there has been regression as well as progress in the field of correctional psychiatry. In 1942 the chief of the Sing Sing classification clinic, Dr. Ralph S. Banay, felt constrained to resign his post on the ground that the clinic was so lacking in funds and in personnel that it could not perform even a minimum psychiatric service. At

San Quentin State Prison in California, on the other hand, a modern classification center is being developed under psychiatric direction. All adult males sentenced to state prison are screened through this center for placement in a suitable institution, for occupational and psychological classification, psychiatric diagnosis, and, if need be, for psychiatric treatment. The center also assists in the intramural adjustment of San Quentin inmates. A similar central classification clinic for youthful offenders was established in 1945 at the Elmira Reformatory in New York State.

Among the advantages of an adequately staffed clinic in a penal or correctional institution, the following may be mentioned: (1) it sorts out cases of mental disorder and mental defect which do not properly belong in a general prison; (2) it acquaints the prison authorities with the characteristics and make-up of other mentally abnormal types among the prison population; (3) it aids the prisoners by helping them to make proper adjustments in prison, and occasionally helps in preparing for readjustment in the normal community beyond the walls; (4) it provides a valuable means for carrying on research work into the nature, causes and treatment of delinquency.[17]

It is interesting to note, in this connection, that in 1924 the American Orthopsychiatric Association was founded "to meet the needs for a central organization of those dealing with the psychiatric aspects of delinquency." The scope of the Association was subsequently expanded and its membership now includes psychologists, social workers, educators, criminologists, and other professionals primarily interested in the scientific study and treatment of human behavior and its disorders.

Mental Hygiene in Industry. The application of mental hygiene to the problems of industry grew out of the concept that the psychiatrist, the psychologist and the social worker combined could play an important part in personnel selection, in finding the job for which the prospective worker is best suited, and in raising the level of efficiency and personal satisfaction of the worker by helping him solve his individual emotional problems, to the mutual advantage of both employer and employee. It differs from personnel work and applied psychology in industry in that it goes beyond an exclusive interest in the efficiency of the worker and takes into consideration his personal welfare and happiness. E. E. Southard, who took a leading part in furthering this movement during the post-war years, defined the scope of mental hygiene in industry as including concepts such as the "human element," individualization, character analysis, scientific selection, social significance, moral values, workman's standpoint, workman's ambition, creative impulse, instinct of workmanship, role of habit, fatigue and efficiency, antisocial behavior, wasteful emotions, unemployment and personality, the psychopathic employee, civilian shell-shock analogues, neurasthenia, etc. This aspect of mental hygiene attracted much attention during the years of industrial unrest following the first World War,[18] but the Great Depression of the 1930's witnessed a considerable flagging of interest in industrial psychiatry. It again came into prominence in World War II, but signs of concrete results in the postwar period are not yet in evidence.

Organizational Growth of Mental Hygiene. While the mental hygiene movement was expanding outward, it was also growing in organizational strength. By 1917 the National Committee had grown to a point where it could launch an organ of its own, *Mental Hygiene,* a quarterly which was started under the able editorship of Dr. Frankwood E. Williams, who succeeded Dr. Salmon as medical director of the National Committee in 1922 and remained in that post until his resignation in 1932. In 1917, too, the mental hygiene movement formally entered upon its international phase when a conference between Mr. Beers and Dr. Clarence M. Hincks of Toronto resulted in the organization of the Canadian National Committee for Mental Hygiene. Dr. Hincks became its medical director and, since 1932, has served in a dual capacity, acting also as general director of the National Committee in the United States.

Meanwhile, the pioneer Connecticut Society for Mental Hygiene had been augmented by many similar bodies. By 1918 there were seventeen state societies for mental hygiene

Pirie MacDonald

CLIFFORD WHITTINGHAM BEERS
Founder of the Mental Hygiene Movement

in this country; in May, 1936, there were more than fifty state and local societies, some of which, however, were functioning only on a part-time basis.

In 1928 the American Foundation for Mental Hygiene was founded by Mr. Beers and his associates as a financing arm, in so far as its resources permit, for the carrying forward of mental hygiene activities in the United States, with reference in particular to the work of the National Committee for Mental Hygiene.

The internationalization of the organized mental hygiene movement progressed steadily until in 1936 there were national societies for mental hygiene in thirty countries, representing every continent. A dramatic event in the worldwide movement came in 1930, when the First International Congress on Mental Hygiene was held in Washington, D.C. The congress was attended by more than three thousand persons, representing fifty countries besides the United States and its territorial possessions.

Among the major purposes of the congress were:

1. To bring together from all countries . . . workers in mental hygiene and related fields, for exchange of information and experience, and for mutual consideration of individual and social problems growing out of nervous and mental disease, mental defect, and mental and emotional maladjustments of the individual to his personal and social environment.

2. To consider ways and means of world cooperation and of more effective promotion of mental hygiene in the various countries.[19]

A permanent International Committee for Mental Hygiene was founded (largely through the efforts of Clifford W. Beers) at the Washington congress of 1930; the late Dr. William Alanson White was its first president. A second international mental hygiene congress was held in Paris during the troubled days of 1937, when the clouds of war were already moving over the earth. The third—and by far the most important—was held in London in August, 1948, under the sponsorship of the International Committee for Mental Hygiene. A major outcome of this congress was the birth of the World Federation for Mental Health, to work closely with the United Nations World Health Organization and the U.N. Economic, Social and Cultural Organization. Representatives of more than a score of countries immediately joined as charter members of the Federation, dedicated mainly to promoting "among all peoples and nations the highest possible level of mental health." Dr. John R. Rees of England was elected first president.

These international congresses served as dramatic symbols vindicating the founder of the mental hygiene movement. The "crazy" idea for a world-wide movement in behalf of the mentally ill, originating in the mind of a patient in a mental hospital, had now come to fruition. That idea had encircled the earth, and taken root in many countries, leaving no continent untouched. The dream that had caused skeptics to whisper "delusions of grandeur" when first revealed by its progenitor had been realized within a generation.

The late Dr. William H. Welch, one of the greatest medical statesmen America has produced, collected tributes to Clifford Beers from hundreds of leaders in many fields of activities throughout the world. These tributes were published in 1933 in a volume entitled, *Twenty-Five Years After —Sidelights on the Mental Hygiene Movement and Its Founder*. Among the many fine contributions was one written by the late Dr. George Alder Blumer, then superintendent emeritus of Butler Hospital in Providence, Rhode Island. Dr. Blumer wrote:[20]

.... His temperament, which is not and never has been (happily) one that could be characterized as of equable, commonplace regularity, has proved exactly what was needed to start the Mental Hygiene Movement and keep it going. His eagerness, intensity, pertinacity, untiring energy, geniality, approachableness and ease of approach, fluency of speech—these, as well as other contributory elements in a Pauline make-up—have stood him and his evangel in good stead as an indomitable apostle. Without them his mission would not have been crowned with so quick success or endured to flourish and grow wherever the good seed had been planted. . . .

No "push" for Clifford Beers, save that of his own ardent spirit and high courage; no "pull," save that of might and main to fulfill his humane vision. For he is in the Temple of Fame by inherent right of entry; and in that part of it dedicated to the daughter of Aesculapius his name will stand out in bold relief with those of Philippe Pinel, William Tuke and Dorothea Dix, to mention only three illustrious reformers who wrought with like zeal and effectiveness to save and succour the wretched in whose cause Clifford Beers went forth valiantly to battle twenty-five years ago.

It is an interesting coincidence that Clifford Beers, like his forerunner in crusading, Dorothea Lynde Dix, spent his last days in a hospital administered by a friend of long standing. Mr. Beers died on July 9, 1943, at the Butler Hospital, where, in his last illness, he was the guest of Dr. Arthur H. Ruggles.

CHAPTER XVI

Historical Backgrounds of Mental Defect

LET us interrupt our narrative at this point to pick up the threads of evolution in the care and treatment of mental defect, a subject that has been inextricably bound up with mental disease throughout history.

The study of this subject is unnecessarily hampered by a lamentable lack of uniformity in the use and meanings of key terms. Accepted definitions do not define. Identical words in common usage convey widely divergent meanings in various parts of the English-speaking world. For example, in the United States the term *feebleminded* is used generically to cover the three principal grades of mental defect. In Great Britain it is applied to one grade only (the highest of three grades, equivalent to our *moron*). The British use the term *mental deficiency* in the same sense that feeblemindedness is used here. But in the United States it is rather indiscriminately used, not only in this sense but as a term covering a far wider field, including all persons who are intellectually subnormal whether or not they fall into the category of feebleminded.

There is no precise or universally accepted definition of the term feebleminded or of mental defective. According to the 1929 British Committee on Mental Deficiency, "if a person is suffering from a degree of incomplete mental development which renders him incapable of independent social adaptation and which necessitates external care, supervision and control, then such person is a mental defective."[1] More comprehensive, perhaps, is the definition of a mentally defective (or feebleminded) person contained in the New York State Mental Hygiene Law:

"Mental defective" means any person afflicted with mental defectiveness from birth or from an early age to such an extent that he is

HISTORICAL BACKGROUNDS

incapable of managing himself and his affairs, who, for his own welfare or the welfare of others, or of the community, requires supervision, control or care and who is not insane or of unsound mind to such an extent as to require his commitment to an institution for the insane.[2]

According to the classification of the Subcommittee on Problems of Mental Deficiency of the 1930 White House Conference on Child Health and Protection, the mentally deficient would comprise all those whose mental handicap, whether serious or slight, is at least partially evidenced by low intelligence-test scores. The mentally deficient include: (a) the feebleminded, in whom additional criteria of inadequacy are found, inclusive of social failure; and (b) the intellectually subnormal, comprising all those mentally deficient persons in whom low intelligence-test scores are not *necessarily* associated with additional criteria of inadequacy.[3] The major criterion for identifying the feebleminded, it will be seen, is the social one. In the following pages the term mental defect will be used synonymously with feeblemindedness, as distinguished from the more comprehensive meaning of mental deficiency.

Up to the twentieth century the term idiot, which now denotes but one (the lowest) of the three principal grades of mental defect, was used in the same generic sense represented by *feebleminded* today. In early English law an idiot was regarded as "a natural fool," a person so congenitally deficient in reasoning power as to be incapable of ordinary acts of reasoning or of rational conduct. The term was used in this sense in the English language as early as 1300. In 1590 Swinburne (*Testaments,* II, 39) defined the term as follows: "An idiote, or a naturall foole is he, who notwithstanding he bee of lawful age, yet he is so witlesse that he can not number to twentie, nor can he tell what age he is of, nor knoweth who is his father, or mother, nor is able to answer to any such easie question." Later English law followed this definition with slight modifications.

From the earliest times mental defectives have been commonly regarded as objects of ridicule or disgust. Historical evidence offers abundant proof that the "village idiot"—

traditional scapegoat and butt of practical jokers, adult and juvenile—was already an established institution in ancient days. Like the mentally ill, the fortunes of idiots varied in accordance with the dominant social attitudes and superstitions of each epoch. Among early peoples infanticide was a rather common means of ridding the race of mental defectives. As a matter of fact, infanticide represents man's earliest attempt to practice negative eugenics, i.e., the elimination of the socially unfit and undesirable. The practice of killing physically and mentally defective children was often considered a social duty, and was sometimes made compulsory by law. It was commonly practiced among the ancient Greeks, particularly the Spartans, and the laws of Lycurgus expressly approved the deliberate exposure of defective infants. The regard in which infanticide among the Greeks was held as late as the fifth and fourth centuries B.C. is indicated by the fact that it was sanctioned by Plato and Aristotle—by the former for eugenic, by the latter for economic, reasons.[4] The practice of eliminating mentally defective children by infanticide is still found today among backward and pauperized peoples.

In ancient Rome, as elsewhere in later centuries, it was an established custom for persons of wealth and rank to employ feebleminded individuals as attendants or servants, more for purposes of amusement than of utility.* Until quite recent times, the feebleminded "fool" or jester was a conspicuous figure in nearly every royal household.

Like mental illness, mental defect has frequently been looked upon as a manifestation of demoniacal possession and treated accordingly. Luther regarded idiots as children of the devil. He once advised the parents of a feebleminded child to throw him into the river, and thus rid their house

*A letter from the philosopher-playwright, Seneca, to his friend Lucilius, throws some light on this custom. "You know," he writes, "that my wife's idiot girl, Harpaste, has remained in my house as a burdensome legacy. Personally, I feel the profoundest dislike for monstrosities of that kind. If ever I want to amuse myself with an idiot, I have not far to look for one. I laugh at myself. This idiot girl has suddenly become blind. Now, incredible as the story seems, it is really true that she is unconscious of her blindness and consequently begs her attendants to go elsewhere because the house is dark." (D. H. Tuke's *Dictionary of Psychological Medicine.* v. 1, p. 17.)

of the presence of a demon.⁵ On the other hand, particularly when the defect was of a mild, harmless type, the feebleminded were sometimes regarded as "children of God" and "innocents," who walked on earth while their minds (or souls) dwelt in heaven. In some Slavic countries, it was— and still is—considered sinful to jibe at or harm the feebleminded, who were permitted to roam about at will through the countryside, fed and sheltered by the common folk. At times they were believed to be in direct communion with God or the saints and their muttered gibberish was eagerly listened to and seriously analyzed as inspired prophecies.

In Brazil, we are told, "an imbecile in a family is considered more a joy than a sorrow. Rich and poor alike roam the streets undisturbed, soliciting alms which are never refused; in this way, among the poor, an idiot may be the sole support of a family."⁶ In the Oriental world the feebleminded generally have been treated with a great degree of tolerance and often enough with reverence, as the favored of the gods. The Moslems, throughout history, have shown particular kindness to the feebleminded, as they have with their insane also. The Koran specifically enjoins the faithful to "give not unto the feebleminded the means which God hath given thee to keep for them; but maintain them for the same, clothe them and speak kindly unto them."

In the Punjab, India, there exists a curious religious order supported entirely by the earnings of mental defectives, who are known as Chûhas, or Rat-children. These children are brought to the shrine of the Shah Daula Daryai, patron saint and protector of the feebleminded, where they are trained to beg by the fakirs who control the shrine. Large sums of money are gathered by the begging Rat-children, since tradition has it that anyone who fails to show proper pity and generosity to the Shah Daula's protégés will be punished by having Chûha children born into his own family. The fakirs in the order divide the funds obtained among themselves on a shareholders' basis.⁷

Though the feebleminded do not seem to have shared, to any noticeable extent, the frightful tortures and executions suffered by the mentally ill in the witch hunting periods of medieval and Renaissance Europe, their own lot was generally harsh and inhuman enough. As we have seen, many people (including Luther and Calvin) regarded them with deep hatred as being children of the Devil. When deemed dangerous to society, they were usually thrown into prisons and dungeons; otherwise, they were callously neglected. When their ailment was not explained in the superstitious terms of "children of God," or "children of the Devil," the feebleminded were looked upon as persons doomed from birth to an existence without human emotions, without human mind—without any human attributes—and hence beyond the pale of human sympathy or human aid.

As with mental diseases, the dawn of scientific and humane treatment of mental defect dates from the latter part of the eighteenth century. The movement originated in a curious and quite accidental incident.

In 1798 a group of sportsmen hunting in the forest of Aveyron, France, encountered a boy living in a wild state, roaming naked through the woods, and subsisting on roots and nuts. The lad, apparently about 17 years of age, was captured and brought to Paris by the sportsmen. He showed only the most feeble indications of intelligence. He had no articulate language and appeared to lack the faculty of speech, while his senses of smell and touch also seemed impaired. He tore to shreds all garments that were placed on him, and acted in a generally capricious manner.*

After undergoing a short period of observation by Professor Bonaterre of the Central School in the Department of Aveyron, the lad was turned over to Dr. Jean M. G. Itard, chief medical officer of the National Institution for the Deaf and Dumb at Paris. The discovery of the "savage

---

*To his contemporaries, this lad seemed to be a "natural man," or savage, such as Linnaeus had classified as constituting a distinct and separate variety of the genus *Homo*. Linnaeus had listed ten instances of persons found living in wild states in civilized lands during the sixteenth, seventeenth and eighteenth centuries. To these ten, Bonaterre added an eleventh, *Juvenis Averionensis*—the "savage of Aveyron," found in "the eighth year of the French Republic." It is interesting to note, in this connection, that as late as our own century, an experiment was undertaken at one of the foremost American universities to determine whether the feebleminded *do* constitute a separate species of *Homo!*

of Aveyron" had aroused great interest throughout Europe. The followers of Rousseau, the Encyclopedists, and other leaders of the Enlightenment were engaging in much speculation and discussion on theories of educational reform. A popular subject for conjecture in this field revolved around this question: what would the effect be on a "natural man" or savage, if suddenly placed in the midst of civilized society and subjected to its influences, educational and otherwise? Here, it seemed, in the finding of this wild boy, was a splendid opportunity to test the efficacy of certain educational theories. Bonaterre expressed the belief that "a phenomenon like this would furnish to philosophy and natural history important notions on the original constitution of man, and on the development of his primitive faculties; provided that the state of imbecility we have noticed in this child does not offer an obstacle to his instruction."[8] Itard, too, foresaw important possibilities in the attempt to train the "savage" lad in civilized ways. Despite the pessimistic pronouncement of his friend, the great Pinel of the Bicêtre, that the boy was an idiot (remember, the term was then used in a generic sense) and therefore untrainable, Dr. Itard enthusiastically entered upon the task of devising a system of instruction for his protégé. In common with most men of his time he believed that feebleminded persons were not susceptible to mental improvement. But he was convinced that Victor, as he named the boy, was not an idiot at all, but merely a wild, untutored savage. (A fortunate error it proved, since otherwise Itard might never have launched his history-making experiment.) With this conviction, he set out to determine "what might be the degree of intelligence, and the nature of the ideas in a lad who, deprived from birth of all education, should have lived entirely separated from individuals of his kind."

An advocate of the sensationalist theories of Locke and Condillac, holding that "the faculties of our mind are but our sensations transformed," and that "all simple ideas are the result of sensation alone," Dr. Itard applied to the boy his techniques of physiological instruction, whereby the mind was stimulated and developed through the sensori-motor system. This approach had previously been used with notable success in the education of deaf-mutes by Jacob Rodrigues Pereire, with whose work Itard was familiar. After some time of patient instruction, however, Itard was finally forced to affirm in his own mind Pinel's opinion that his pupil, the "savage of Aveyron," was really an idiot. Nevertheless, having already achieved considerable improvement in his protégé, he continued his ministrations for five years longer, modifying his methods as he went along, placing more and more emphasis on education through the senses.*

At last illness and the pressure of a large practice forced Itard to give up his experiment. He had failed in his original objective—to raise, through the application of his educational theories, a "savage" to a state of normal civilized behavior. But in his seeming failure, he had achieved something quite as important. He had been the first to attempt the methodical training of an idiot. He had been the first to demonstrate that a feebleminded person was trainable. His experiment had marked the beginning of the long drive toward developing the limited potentialities of the feebleminded to a maximum point of efficiency.

Shortly before his death (1838) Dr. Itard handed down the results of his researches and experiment to Edward Seguin, a promising young physician of Paris. Dr. Seguin, who possessed a broad mind and deep humanitarian sympathies, entered upon his new work with great zeal, carrying on intensive research in mental defect—its causes, its nature, and possible modes of treatment.

Meanwhile active interest in the education of idiots was being manifested in other countries. Beginning with 1818, feebleminded children were admitted into the American Asylum for the Deaf and Dumb at Hartford, Connecticut, where instruction was imparted to them, apparently with fair results. Several were taught to communicate in the sign language.

In 1828, Dr. G. M. A. Ferrus of the Bicêtre in Paris

---

*Itard's general approach embraced a three-fold program: (1) the development of the senses; (2) development of the intellectual faculties; (3) development of the affective functions.

attempted the instruction of the more promising idiots maintained at the institution. The same experiment was introduced at the Salpêtrière by Dr. H. L. Falret in 1831. Two years later Dr. Voisin opened a private school for idiots at Paris. These projects, however, were abandoned after short trial periods. In 1837 Dr. Seguin founded his own school on an experimental basis, and five years later went to the Bicêtre to carry on work with the mentally defective there. He returned after a short period to his private institution, where he successfully developed a system of instruction based in part on Itard's methods. In 1846 he published his classic monograph, *Traitement moral, hygiène et éducation des idiots*, the first comprehensive work on this subject and the first to attempt to outline a complete plan for training mental defectives. It remains a basic work in the field to this day.

Seguin's system of training was based on the methodology of physiological education. It was his theory that idiocy (or feeblemindedness, as we term it today) is only a prolonged infancy, and that it could be overcome through the application of proper training methods. For a long time he cherished the belief that mental defect was curable. While later results showed this notion to be untenable, the same results did confirm the great value of his educational methods in improving the condition. His methods are still used today, unaltered in essence. The system of Seguin was predicated on the theory which regards the manifestations of life as the expressions of functions, and all functions as resulting from a certain organism. Education was to proceed with the aim of bringing all the senses and organs to their maximum functional point. Physical training must precede mental training: the perceptual faculties must be awakened before conceptual functions could be developed. Applying this method to the various degrees of feeblemindedness, each function could be trained with particular reference to the peculiarities and deficiencies of the individual, and also in its relation to all other functions, with a view towards achieving an harmonious whole. Important agencies are pure air, proper diet, gymnastic exercise to stimulate the physical development and to correct physical abnormalities, together with imitative instruction, vocational training and farm labor. The significance of Seguin's system, incidentally, is by no means confined to the training of the feebleminded. It has exerted an important influence on general education also. The well-known Montessori system is largely based on the principles formulated by Seguin.

While the activities of Seguin and other French pioneers were attracting the attention of physicians and social reformers throughout the western world, work with the feebleminded was introduced in other countries. In 1842 Dr. J. Guggenbühl established, on a beautiful site on the side of the Abendberg in Switzerland, an institution for the care and training of cretins, who were found in large numbers in the Alpine valleys. In the same year, a school for idiots was established in Berlin by Dr. C. M. Saegert. The encouraging results obtained by Seguin and others in France served as the inspiration for the founding of similar institutions in England. A movement in behalf of the feebleminded in the latter country was led by Dr. John Conolly, of nonrestraint fame, and Mr. Andrew Reed. As a result principally of the efforts of these two men, a private school for idiots was opened at Bath in 1846, followed soon after by the famous public institutions at Colchester (1849) and Earlswood (1855).

In the United States, legislative actions seeking public provision for mental defectives were initiated almost simultaneously in New York and Massachusetts in the year 1846. Up to that time, no special institutional provision had been made for this class in America. Whether they were maintained at home or in general pauper and penal institutions, or left to wander abroad, their treatment was usually characterized by neglect, ignorance, confusion and cruelty. Kentucky was unique in granting regular allowances out of public funds for the maintenance of pauper and indigent idiots in their own homes, in accordance with a series of "Pauper Idiot Acts" dating from 1793.*

*In 1825 a state law specified that a fixed amount of $50 per annum should be paid out of the public treasury towards the support of each pauper and

HISTORICAL BACKGROUNDS 341

Many of the early state institutions for the insane received the mentally defective along with the mentally ill— a custom still to be found today in various parts of the country. Little, if any, legal distinction was made between the mentally defective and the mentally diseased until well along in the nineteenth century.* Both groups were herded in identical institutions. They were indiscriminately coupled in legislative statutes, as if their problems were exactly alike. Furthermore, they were enumerated together in census reports, as in the first two national censuses of the insane (1840 and 1850).

The great majority of institutionalized defectives were to be found in those convenient catchalls of dependency, the poorhouses. Many others were confined in houses of correction and local lockups. In states where provision was made for the custody of defectives in lunatic asylums (which, on the whole, accommodated them more comfortably than other types of institutions), they were invariably removed to the house of correction or poorhouse to make way for the admission of lunatics whenever overcrowded conditions existed.

In the early 1840's, social-minded American visitors to Europe were returning with impressive accounts of the successful work of Guggenbühl, Saegert, and especially Seguin, in the training of mental defectives. Why not open such "idiot schools" in the United States? In 1844 Dr. Samuel B. Woodward included in his annual report for the Worcester Hospital a brief account of the training schools

indigent mental defective maintained in his own home. This sum was later raised to $75 per annum.

*Esquirol is generally credited with having been the first to clearly distinguish mental defect from mental disease. In his *Maladies Mentales* (1828) he wrote: "Idiocy is not a disease but a condition in which the intellectual faculties have never been manifested . . . A man in dementia is deprived of that which he has once enjoyed. He is a rich man become poor. The idiot has always been poor and wretched." (v. 2, pp. 284–85.)

The first distinct separation of the feebleminded from the insane in English law dates only from 1886, when the "Idiots Act" was passed. A British statute of 1845 provided for "insane" persons "in which class are to be included idiots who have had no understanding from their birth, as well as lunatics . . . who have lost the use of their reason." (See the *Oxford Dictionary*, definition of *idiocy*.)

in France, and suggested the possibility of utilizing the experience of the French pioneers in training defectives in their own homes. The following year Dr. Amariah Brigham devoted several pages to the subject of an "idiot asylum" in his report as superintendent of the New York State Lunatic Asylum at Utica. Pointing to the wretched state of the feebleminded in New York (1,600 of whom had been enumerated in the state census of 1845), Dr. Brigham wrote: "We are of the opinion that much may be done for their improvement and comfort; that many, instead of being a burden and expense to the community, may be so improved as to engage in useful employments and to support themselves; and also to participate in the enjoyments of society." Passing on to an enthusiastic description of the work then being carried on in Europe, he concluded:

> Confident in the success of an experiment to improve this class of persons and to render their condition far more comfortable, we cannot but hope that it will soon be made under the direction of the State of New York. We scarcely know of a subject more worthy of the attention of the patriot, philanthropist and Christian.[9]

The first legislative move toward separate provision for the feebleminded was initiated in New York State on January 13, 1846, when Dr. F. F. Backus introduced a resolution in the State Senate setting up a committee to study and report upon that part of the 1845 state census relating to idiots. As chairman of the committee, Dr. Backus presented an able report urging the immediate establishment of a state asylum for this class. A bill embodying this object was drawn up, but unfortunately failed of passage that year and the next by very narrow margins.

Ten days after Dr. Backus submitted his report, Horatio Byington successfully introduced a resolution in the Massachusetts legislature authorizing the appointment of a commission "to inquire into the condition of idiots in the Commonwealth, to ascertain their number, and whether anything can be done for their relief." A commission of three was forthwith appointed, with Samuel Gridley Howe serving as chairman. After submitting a preliminary report in

1847, Dr. Howe drew up and presented an exhaustive document in which he pictured the prevailing state of the feebleminded in Massachusetts as one characterized by appalling ignorance, cruelty and neglect.[10]

Acting promptly on this report the legislature, on May 8, 1848, voted an appropriation of $2,500 annually for three years towards the support of an experimental school where ten pauper and indigent idiots, selected from various parts of the state, were to receive instruction. This, the first state institution for the feebleminded in America, was opened on October 1, 1848, with Dr. Howe as director. It occupied a wing of the Perkins Institution for the Blind, which was also conducted by Dr. Howe. The experiment proved so successful that at the end of the three-year trial period, the legislature doubled the original annual appropriation and placed the institution on a permanent basis, incorporating it under the name, The Massachusetts School for Idiotic and Feeble-Minded Youth. (The term *feebleminded* was introduced about this time to denote higher-grade defectives.) The institution was later moved to Waverley, Massachusetts, and is now known as the Walter E. Fernald State School, named after the great physician who served it for thirty-seven years up to his death in 1924.

In the meantime, Dr. Hervey B. Wilbur had started a private school at Barre, Massachusetts, in July, 1848, the first institution of its kind to be opened in this country. According to its announcement, it was "designed for the education and management of all children who by reason of mental infirmity are not fit subjects for ordinary instruction."

In New York State, after several unsuccessful attempts to obtain legislative action, an appropriation was finally voted in July, 1851, for the establishment of an experimental school at Albany.* Dr. Wilbur, who had attracted much favorable attention through his work in training men-

---

*During the campaign for the passage of this act, Dr. Howe of Massachusetts, upon invitation, gave a demonstration with some of his pupils before assembled New York officials and legislators at Albany. This demonstration proved a valuable aid in obtaining the desired legislative action.

tal defectives at Barre, was summoned to Albany to serve as the superintendent of the newly established institution. In describing the aims of the school in his first report (1851), Dr. Wilbur wrote:

> We do not propose to create or supply faculties absolutely wanting; nor to bring all grades of idiocy to the same standard of development or discipline; nor to make them all capable of sustaining, creditably, all the relations of a social and moral life; but rather to give to dormant faculties the greatest practicable development, and to apply those awakened faculties to a useful purpose under the control of an aroused and disciplined will. At the basis of all our efforts lies the principle that the human attributes of intelligence, sensibility and will are not absolutely wanting in an idiot, but dormant and undeveloped.[11]

With very slight modification, this statement of purposes could proudly stand as a prospectus for the most advanced of our modern training schools.

As in the case of Massachusetts, the New York school was placed on a permanent basis after a successful trial period. In 1853 a bill was passed authorizing the erection of new and suitable buildings for the school, which had been occupying a leased private dwelling. Syracuse was selected as the site for the new institution, and there, in September, 1854, was laid the cornerstone of the first building in the country planned and built specifically for the feebleminded. Of the two prior schools, one had been installed in a wing of an institution for the blind, while the other was conducted in the director's private residence.

Pennsylvania was next to make special provision for the mentally defective. In 1852 a private school was established at Germantown by Mr. J. B. Richards, who had served as the first instructor in Dr. Howe's school at South Boston. It was incorporated the following year as the Pennsylvania Training School for Feebleminded Children, receiving a grant of money from the state legislature towards its partial support, the remainder of the required funds being raised by private subscription. Soon after its incorporation the school was removed to Elwyn, the site of the present well-known institutional village for mental defectives.

HISTORICAL BACKGROUNDS

It is a noteworthy fact that the organization of three of the first four American institutions for the feebleminded owed much of their success to the personal aid of Dr. Seguin. The latter, who was an active Socialist in politics, had departed from France when the accession of Napoleon III to the throne signalized the failure of the 1848 Revolution. Coming to the United States, where he thereafter made his home, he helped Howe organize the Massachusetts School for Idiotic and Feebleminded Youth, and later performed a similar service with Wilbur at Syracuse and Richards at the Pennsylvania School. His influence was strongly felt in the early development of all three institutions, particularly that at Syracuse under Dr. Wilbur. Indeed, his presence and active work in this country did much to vitalize the whole American movement in behalf of the feebleminded. Nearly all the institutions of this class established up to the time of Dr. Seguin's death in 1880 acknowledged in one form or another a deep debt of gratitude for his personal interest and advice.

In 1857 the Ohio State Asylum for the Education of Idiotic and Imbecile Youth was organized as an experimental school at Columbus. In Connecticut, following the report of a commission of inquiry into the conditions of idiocy in the state (1856), the Connecticut School for Imbeciles was established at Lakeville in 1857 as a private institution receiving state aid.

The Kentucky Institution for the Education of Feeble-Minded Children and Idiots was opened at Frankfort in 1860. The state of Illinois established an experimental school for this class in 1865 at Jacksonville. This school was later incorporated on a permanent basis and removed to Lincoln, Illinois, in 1873. In 1866 the first municipal school for the feebleminded, the New York City Idiot Asylum, was opened on Randall's Island.

Thus, up to the year 1866, separate institutional provision for the mentally defective existed in seven states of the Union, accommodating about 1,000 pupils in all.

It is significant that nearly all the aforementioned institutions started as tentative experiments, in the face of a deep-rooted general belief that the feebleminded were beyond all hope of improvement and that efforts at training them were futile. In a biography of her father, Samuel G. Howe, Mrs. Laura E. Richards thus describes the reaction to Dr. Howe's 1848 report recommending an educational institution for idiots in Massachusetts:

> The Report created a profound sensation. There were people who laughed and said to one another: "What do you think Howe is going to do next? *He is going to teach idiots!*" They printed a caricature of him and Charles Sumner [the statesman and social reformer] as twin Don Quixotes tilting at windmills. A friend told my mother that "the Doctor's report was a report *for* idiots as well as concerning them."[12]

Similarly, after listening to the expert testimony delivered by Drs. Howe and Wilbur and the great Seguin himself, at a hearing held prior to the organization of the New York Idiot Asylum, a legislator voiced a widely prevalent sentiment when he declared: "Do not take it as personal, but I must say that I think none but fools would think of teaching fools."[13] In a report submitted in 1856, a legislative committee of inquiry on idiocy in Connecticut,* while recommending the establishment of a school for this class, confessed that it had found "a settled conviction of a large majority of the citizens of the Commonwealth that idiots were a class so utterly hopeless that it was a waste of time even to collect any statistics concerning them."[14]

In his well known treatise on *Idiocy,* published in 1866, Dr. Seguin expressed the hope that an organization be formed among those dealing with the mentally defective. "Every year," he wrote, "the Superintendents of the various schools should meet, to impart to one another the difficulties they have encountered, the results of their experience, and mostly to compare the books containing their orders and

---

*Incidentally, this committee discovered an interesting example of how the selfish desire of one community to unburden itself of a feebleminded girl led to the "manufacture" of feebleminded paupers through public cooperation. "In one instance," the report states, "where a female idiot lived in one town, the town authorities hired an idiot belonging to another town, and not then a pauper, to marry her, and the result has been that the town to which the male idiot belongs has for many years had to support the pair, and three idiot children."

regulations."[15] He further outlined a model agenda for the annual meetings of such an organization. Ten years later, on the occasion of the Centennial Exposition at Philadelphia, an invitation was issued by the officials of the Pennsylvania Training School at Elwyn (then Media) to all officers of similar institutions to meet there for the purpose of discussing common problems. On June 6, 1876, a group of superintendents gathered at Elwyn and decided to form an organization. The following day a constitution was adopted and the name, The Association of Medical Officers of American Institutions for Idiots and Feebleminded Persons, was chosen. This name was changed in 1906 to the American Association for the Study of the Feebleminded, and again in 1933 to the American Association on Mental Deficiency.* Its charter members included Drs. Edward Seguin, H. B. Wilbur, G. A. Doren, Isaac N. Kerlin, H. M. Knight, C. T. Wilbur, George Brown, and Joseph Parrish—all of them outstanding pioneers in the care and treatment of the mentally defective in America.

Like the state hospitals erected during the heyday of the cult of curability (described in Chapter VIII), the early institutions for the feebleminded were launched on a high wave of optimism. Almost without exception these schools were organized along strictly educational lines and were considered to represent, primarily, extensions of the common school system. They were founded on the supposition that most feebleminded children, through proper training, could be improved sufficiently to restore them to the community as self-supporting citizens. Their major purpose, as indicated in their titles, was educational rather than custodial; they were regarded as being truly schools, rather than "institutions." In an address delivered in 1893, Dr. Walter E. Fernald quoted from an early report of his predecessor, Dr. Howe, illustrating this viewpoint. "It [the school

*In 1896 the Association began to publish the *Journal of Psycho-Asthenics* as its official organ, under the editorship of Dr. A. C. Rogers of the Minnesota School for the Feebleminded at Faribault. The *Journal,* which appeared quarterly, was devoted almost exclusively to the proceedings of the annual conventions of the Association. It is now published annually as the "Proceedings and Addresses" of the annual sessions.

for idiots] is a link in the chain of common schools," wrote Dr. Howe, "the last indeed, but still a necessary link in order to embrace all the children in the State."[16] Dr. Wilbur, in his seventh report for the New York State Idiot Asylum, expressed a similar sentiment: "A new institution in *a new field of education* has the double mission of securing the best results, and at the same time of making that impression upon the public mind as will give faith to its object." (Emphasis mine—A.D.)

But with the passage of time, the educational ideal so enthusiastically advanced by the pioneers began to break down under the pressure of a multitude of difficult problems. Gradually it gave way to the custodial ideal, which for many years thenceforward governed institutional provision for the mentally defective.

Nearly all the early schools, as we have noted, were founded on the belief that most feebleminded children could be trained and improved to a degree that would warrant sending them back to the community as self-supporting citizens. With this in mind little, if any, provision was made for permanent custody in these institutions. But time and experience showed this course to be too sanguine. It was found that a certain proportion *could* be restored to community life on a fair plane of economic and social efficiency. Many others, on a lower plane of efficiency, could at least be trained to take care of their immediate personal wants and needs, and to get along quite well under the watchful guidance of family and friends. But there were many more who could not be sent back at all. Included among these were the low-grade defectives, some utterly hopeless and helpless, requiring lifelong care and supervision. Others, who under favorable circumstances might have enjoyed a contented, harmless existence among relatives or friends, had to be institutionalized for life because the impoverished condition of their families was too acute to stand the added burden of their support. Then there were high-grade defectives— "moral imbeciles" as they came to be called—who could be trained to economic efficiency, but who were tainted with hyper-sexual or delinquent tendencies which made it socially unsafe and undesirable to release them into the stream of normal life. What should be done with these persons? This was the problem that now confronted the officers of schools for the feebleminded. Should they be transferred to the degrading, miserable poorhouses? Or to jails and houses of correction? Or to home environments even more unfavorable, perhaps, than these institutions?

A far larger problem revolved around the extramural cases of mental defect. The existing schools were few and small. They could accommodate but an insignificant fraction of the known defectives. Naturally, in view of their limited resources, they followed a rigorous policy of selecting pupils from among those most likely to benefit by the training available. What provision should be made for the great numbers who, for one reason or another, were shut out from the benefits of these educational institutions? Apart from these schools, there existed no public institutions to which they might be sent except the poorhouses, prisons, or mental hospitals equipped with custodial provision for a very limited number of feebleminded.

To an increasing extent, the solution of these problems seemed to lie in the construction of special custodial asylums for the mentally defective. Other factors, too, were moving in the same direction. Not the least of these was the general tendency in the last half of the century toward differentiation and classification of the various classes of dependents and delinquents. It should be emphasized that all the foregoing factors in the swing toward custodial provision for the feebleminded were of a positive and humanitarian character, being determined chiefly by a concern (however misdirected) for the interests of the feebleminded themselves.

There was also a negative factor, however, which exerted an increasing influence on the trend toward separate and permanent institutionalization of the mentally defective. We refer to the rise of the study of hereditary factors in human life, and the application of current theories of heredity to the problems of the feebleminded. The beginnings of this trend may be traced to the publication in 1859 of Darwin's epoch-making *Origin of Species* in which, among other things, he advanced the theories of "natural selection" and "the survival of the fittest." These theories, in the hands of subsequent popularizers, were distorted into convenient rationalizations for the *status quo* and apologies for the aristocracy, together with contempt for, and hostility toward, the less endowed (economically, mentally and physically) members of the human family. Beginning with 1865, Francis Galton, cousin of Darwin and founder of modern eugenics, began publishing his important researches in heredity, tracing the pedigrees of genius in support of the theory of inheritance of mental traits.

We now know that his conclusions on the inheritance of mental characters were greatly overdrawn. Be that as it may, his studies attracted much attention, and his theories many followers, both in Europe and America. It is quite probable that his views inspired the first of a long series of studies in degenerate human stock in this country.

In 1877 Richard L. Dugdale's famous study in family degeneracy, *The Jukes,* was published.[17] Mr. Dugdale, a merchant who had for many years served as a visitor to penal institutions for the New York Prison Association, found in his investigations that a certain family had contributed an unusually large number of members to the prison population. After tracing this family, the Jukes, through five generations, he came to the conclusion that the social ills—crime, pauperism and disease—were somehow transmitted from generation to generation and were closely associated with intemperance, licentiousness, feeblemindedness and mental disorders. Dugdale, in his summary, was careful to stress the important influence of environment in shaping the destinies of this family, and also pointed out that whatever conclusions he had arrived at had relevance only to the very unusual pedigree of the Jukes. This did not prevent many of his readers from jumping to the generalization that social ills were always biologically inherited. Also, in spite of the fact that, of the total of 709 individuals studied, only one case of certified feeblemindedness was found by Dugdale, the conclusion was drawn that the aforementioned social ills were invariably associated with a transmitted taint of

HISTORICAL BACKGROUNDS 351

mental defect. Dugdale's work was widely read and discussed, and exerted an important influence on his own and succeeding generations. (Even today it is still accepted in many quarters as a fundamentally sound and valid study, however unscientific and unreliable it appears in the light of modern standards of research.) It turned many minds to the study of the relationships, real and apparent, between mental defect and crime, pauperism, prostitution, alcoholism, etc.

In the year following the publication of Dugdale's book, Mrs. Josephine Shaw Lowell, a member of the New York State Board of Charities, proposed to the board that a special institution for feebleminded women of childbearing age be established. Mrs. Lowell, who was one of the best known welfare workers of her time, had devoted much attention to the problems of crime and pauperism and was strongly inclined to emphasize hereditary factors as causes of these social ills. A study of feebleminded female paupers had convinced her that such women, when left at large, were invariably licentious, and alarmingly prolific in bearing illegitimate children with the inherited stamp of mental defect and pauperism. She had drawn up an impressive list of feebleminded girls who periodically utilized the poorhouses of the State as delivery stations for casually conceived children, left their offspring in these institutions, and sallied forth on further adventurous expeditions.* A separate custodial institution for this class was urgently needed, she declared, for two principal reasons: (1) to protect female defectives from the myriad evils of society to which they fell easy prey, and (2) to protect society from the burden of supporting tainted progeny by checking their procreation at the source.

In accordance with the suggestion of Mrs. Lowell, who was supported in her aim by Dr. H. B. Wilbur, an experimental branch of the New York State Asylum for Idiots

*Simultaneously, Mrs. Lowell carried on a vigorous campaign for the establishment of a separate reformatory for delinquent women, which culminated successfully in the founding of the House of Refuge for Women at Hudson, New York, the first separate correctional institution of its type in the United States.

was opened in September, 1878, at Newark, New York, for the reception of feebleminded women of childbearing age. The Newark Asylum remained under the direction of the Board of Managers of the Idiot Asylum at Syracuse until 1885, when it was incorporated as a separate institution. The establishment of the Newark Asylum marked an important step in the evolution of the care and treatment of the feebleminded in America. It not only represented the beginning of separate *custodial* care for mental defectives, but was also the first attempt to cut off defective germ plasm through the medium of segregation.

New York State also established the first custodial institution for low-grade defectives. In 1894 the Rome State Custodial Asylum (now the Rome State School) was opened for the reception of helpless and unteachable idiots.

Differentiation of institutions for the feebleminded made another stride forward in 1911 when, largely due to the efforts of Dr. Walter E. Fernald, Massachusetts enacted the first legislation in the United States authorizing separate provision for defective delinquents. Authorities had long been faced with a vexing problem regarding the disposition of this class. Delinquents were a constant source of trouble when placed in the ordinary institutions for defectives; on the other hand, defectives should not be confined in general institutions for delinquents. Obviously, the solution lay in separate provision for the defective delinquents. The Massachusetts law, however, was not put into effect until 1922, when a separate division for male defective delinquents was opened at the Massachusetts State Farm at Bridgewater. A division for female defectives was added there in 1926. Meanwhile New York had established, in 1921, a special state institution for male defective delinquents at Napanoch, which was opened the same year.

While this development in differentiation was going on, a far more important change affecting the status of the feebleminded was in process. Far-reaching reorientations in attitudes were afoot, premised in large measure on the factors previously described. Seguin, Howe, and other pioneers had preached the gospel of sympathetic understanding toward the mental defective. The latter was pictured as a weaker member of the human family who had to be protected from gross abuse at the hands of society. At the turn of the century, through a swift metamorphosis, this picture was completely changed: the feebleminded person was looked upon as a parasite on the body politic who must be mercilessly isolated or destroyed for the protection of society. For a period of two decades and more the man of science and the man on the street, with almost unanimous accord, regarded him as the most potent, if not the sole, source of all social evils. He was a sinister force threatening the very foundations of civilization itself. The mental defective, by general consent, was nominated to the position of Social Menace Number One.

This period of pessimism and alarmism, and its aftermath, will be described in the following chapter.

CHAPTER XVII
Changing Concepts in Mental Defect

THE first two decades of the present century have been aptly referred to as the alarmist period in the study and treatment of mental defect. Four major factors combined to create the dominant attitudes and approaches during this period:

1. The invention and development of mental tests, and their application to the diagnosis and grading of feeblemindedness.
2. The rediscovery of Mendel's laws of heredity.
3. The rise of the eugenics movement, with its emphasis on hereditary factors, especially in relation to mental defect.
4. The publication and widespread influence of genealogical studies of degenerate and defective stock.

In 1905 the French psychologists, Drs. Albert Binet and Thomas Simon, invented their famous scale for measuring the mental age of individuals. As Binet explained, the scale was "composed of a series of tests of increasing difficulty, starting from the lowest intellectual level that can be observed and ending with that of average normal intelligence."[1] This scale was introduced into the United States in 1908 by Dr. Henry H. Goddard, director of the Research Laboratory at the Training School for the Feebleminded at Vineland, New Jersey. As an experiment, Goddard tried it on the children at the Training School and found, to his surprise, a very close correspondence between the results of the test in rating mental age and the actual grading of the children based on institutional experience. Encouraged by this initial success, Goddard continued to employ the mental test as a means of grading the defectives at Vineland. By

1910 he had formulated a system of classification which he presented to the American Association for the Study of the Feebleminded. Under this system, as adopted by the Association, the mentally defective were divided into three grades: (1) *idiots,* comprising defectives with a mental age up to two years; (2) *imbeciles,* having a mental age of three to seven years; and (3) *morons,* having a mental age of eight to twelve years.* Goddard arbitrarily fixed the top mental limit of feeblemindedness at twelve years because he had found it to be the highest reached by the pupils at Vineland. The term, moron, was derived by him from the Greek word, *moros,* meaning stupid or foolish.

Mainly through Goddard's sponsorship, the intelligence-test idea gained ready acceptance and was soon widely employed throughout the country in the detection and grading of mental deficiency. Revisions of the Binet-Simon test were subsequently made by Lewis M. Terman, Fred Kuhlmann, R. M. Yerkes, and others. Most important, probably, was the modification made by Dr. Terman, known as the Stanford revision. In place of the scale that measured intelligence only in terms of mental age, the Stanford revision introduced the Intelligence Quotient, originally invented by Dr. William Stern and based on the ratio of chronological age to mental age. The I.Q. in children is obtained by simply dividing the latter by the former.

*Compare this classification, based on psychological criteria alone, with that employed sixty years before by Dr. Howe, based solely on language criteria. Dr. Howe also divided feeblemindedness (or idiocy, as it was then called) into three grades. Beginning with the highest grade, the simpleton, he explained: "The *simpleton* is very backward about learning to talk. During a long time he uses only nouns and verbs; but at last he learns to make simple sentences. He comes to use all the principal parts of speech and to express himself with tolerable correctness about simple matters of fact but he cannot make or understand involved sentences or those expressive of abstract ideas ... The idiot of the second class, or the *fool,* learns to speak still more tardily and imperfectly. While a child he uses only names of things. When a youth he may perhaps master two principal parts of speech, nouns and verbs. Pronouns, conditional verbs, adverbs, etc., are incomprehensible signs to him ... The *idiot of the lowest class* utters only a few simple sounds, or interjections, which are expressive of his appetites, or strong emotions, and which are not peculiarly parts of human speech, for animals also use interjections." (Samuel G. Howe. *Report on Idiocy, 1850.* Massachusetts Senate Document No. 38, 1850. p. 35.)

Despite some serious shortcomings, the development of mental tests represented a great stride forward in the study and treatment of mental deficiency. It provided not only standardized methods for measuring intelligence, but also standard coefficients for approximating the intellectual capacities of individuals. Thus, classification of the feebleminded, which formerly had depended entirely on personal empirical opinions, with no basis for uniformity, was now placed on a solid foundation approaching, though not reaching, scientific exactness. Unfortunately, however, as often happens when a new theory or a new technique is introduced in some particular branch of study, the early advocates of the mental tests in America, in the first flush of enthusiasm, claimed for it an importance far out of proportion to its true relevance and value.

A point was soon reached where every person who tested twelve years or less in an intelligence test was pronounced, *ipso facto*, to be feebleminded. With the extension of the use of mental tests to groups outside of institutions for the mentally defective, startling "discoveries" were made and alarming conclusions were drawn therefrom. Among the first groups to whom mental tests were applied were the "social debtors"—persons in prisons, poorhouses and other places for the delinquent and the dependent, as well as prostitutes, drunkards, etc. And when it was found that a large proportion of these groups tested twelve years and less, it was immediately inferred that an organic connection existed between feeblemindedness on the one hand, and crime, pauperism and social degeneracy on the other.

Further shock and alarm came when the tests were extended to school children and others in "normal" environments. To the dismay of many it was found that tens of thousands of children who had been considered normal, or merely dull, tested under the top mental age set for feeblemindedness. The moron was being discovered on a vast scale. Surveys undertaken in various states brought forth evidence indicating that mental deficiency was far more prevalent than had ever been dreamed of before. The climax came with the application of mental tests to drafted men during the World War. When the statistical results of these tests were compiled, it was shown that fully 47.3 per cent of the white drafted men had mental ages of twelve years and less. According to the accepted system of identification and classification, nearly half of the drafted men were feebleminded! Statisticians' pencils moved swiftly into action. Taking the results of the Army examinations as a basis, it was calculated that some 50,000,000 Americans—nearly half the total population—came under the category of mentally defective. Pessimistic computations were made on every hand showing how, in a short time, the country would be composed entirely of feebleminded citizens. The situation seemed dark and doleful. Meanwhile other factors were at work contributing to this pessimistic picture. These factors revolved mainly around the relationship between heredity and mental defect.

In 1900 the laws of heredity formulated by the Austrian monk, Gregor Mendel, and forgotten since their publication in 1866, were rediscovered simultaneously and independently by three botanists—DeVries, Correns and Tschermark. Interest in the study of human heredity was increasing rapidly at the time. Hardly were the Mendelian principles made known than the law governing the transmission of "dominant" and "recessive" characters was applied to the study of feeblemindedness. Was it not possible that this condition was a recessive character inherited in accordance with Mendel's law? No sooner was the problem posed than it was considered solved. In what was perhaps the most authoritative work of the alarmist period, the author confidently claimed: "It is clear from the data already presented that feeblemindedness is hereditary in a large percentage of the cases, and that it is transmitted in accordance with the Mendelian formula."[2]

About the same time that Mendel's long-lost laws were being resurrected, the modern eugenics movement was launched. The term *eugenics* (from the Greek meaning "well born") was coined by Sir Francis Galton in 1883, and was defined by him as "the study of the agencies under social control that may improve or impair the racial qualities of future generations either physically or mentally."* As early as 1865 Galton had urged the study of the inheritance of mental and physical characters as a means for improving the human breed. The movement he founded was formally launched in 1904, three years after he had laid down its guiding principles in a paper entitled, "Possible Improvement of the Human Breed," published in the scientific journal, *Nature*. The movement spread rapidly, especially in Great Britain and the United States, and exerted a profound influence on contemporary sociologists and economists, as well as biologists. Its practical aim was twofold: (1) "positive" eugenics, that is, the encouragement of biologically fit and socially desirable stocks, and (2) "negative" eugenics, that is, discouragement of inferior and subnormal stocks. It was the latter purpose, naturally, that brought the eugenist face to face with the problem of feeblemindedness.

The rediscovery of the Mendelian laws and the rise of the eugenics movement combined to create a considerable interest in the subject of heredity in its relation to problems of human life. Very soon, thanks largely to the propaganda assiduously spread by eugenic enthusiasts, it became an established custom to trace the majority of social, physical and mental ills (feeblemindedness among them) to hereditary influences. As for the feebleminded, estimates of the proportion of cases attributable to heredity ranged to 90 per cent and more.

Among the factors tending to emphasize heredity in the causation of mental defect was the profusion of published studies tracing the pedigrees of "royal families" of de-

---

*The aim of eugenics, thus defined, would of course include the study of all factors in the improvement of the human breed, hereditary and environmental alike. With this aim none could disagree. However, the eugenics movement as a whole has tended to stress the importance of heredity in human development while at the same time minimizing the environmental factors, and to insist that the betterment of the race—socially, biologically, etc.—depends mainly on the control of heredity rather than environment. While there are many scientific eugenists, including H. S. Jennings, H. J. Muller, Julian Huxley and Lancelot Hogben, opposing this tendency, it is nevertheless true that the eugenics movement has become identified with the belief in the dominance of heredity over environment. It is mainly in this sense that the movement is referred to in the pages following.

generate stock, along the lines of Dugdale's *The Jukes*. These were influential in heightening the prevalent spirit of pessimism and alarmism in the approach to the problem. The most widely read as well as the most significant of these studies was Goddard's *The Kallikak Family*, published in 1912. In this work Goddard traced the genealogy of two lines, one "good" and the other "bad," both tracing their descent from Martin "Kallikak,"* a soldier of respectable parentage and position who fought in the Revolutionary War. The "bad" strain resulted from an unconventional alliance between Kallikak and a presumably feebleminded servant girl. A heavy taint of inherited degeneracy seemed to run through this family, with mental defect casting a dark shadow over the entire line down through the generations. The "good" strain, owing its descent to a quite respectable marriage contracted by Kallikak after being mustered out of the army, stood out in sharp contrast to the other, and comprised for the most part well-respected, useful members of the community. At the end of his study, Goddard felt justified in drawing this conclusion:

> The Kallikak family presents a natural experiment in heredity. A young man of good family becomes through two different women the ancestor of two lines of descendants—the one characterized by thoroughly good, respectable, normal citizenship, with almost no exceptions; the other being equally characterized by mental defect in nearly every generation . . . On the bad side we find paupers, criminals, prostitutes, drunkards and examples of all forms of social pest with which modern society is burdened.
> From this we conclude that feeblemindedness is largely responsible for all these social sores.
> Feeblemindedness is hereditary and transmitted as surely as any other character.[3]

During the period 1912–1916, a number of other pedigrees of defective stock were published. Among the more prominent were: *The Nam Family* by Arthur H. Estabrook and Charles B. Davenport (1912); *The Hill Folk*, by Charles B. Davenport and Florence H. Danielson (1912);

*The name *Kallikak* is a pseudonym representing a telescoping of Greek words meaning "good-bad."

The Pineys, by Elizabeth S. Kite (1913); *The Jukes* in 1915,* by Arthur H. Estabrook (1915); and *The Family of Sam Sixty,* by Mary S. Kostir (1916).

Without exception, all these studies arrived at the same basic conclusions: mental defect was mostly hereditary; it was a principal, if not the most important, cause of many of the social evils. These views were subscribed to by practically all the specialists engaged in the study and treatment of mental deficiency during this period, in Great Britain as well as in America.

All the aforementioned circumstances merged together to generate a steadily mounting phobia of the feebleminded. A period of social hysteria set in, comparable in many respects to the witch-hunting mania of yore. It was generally agreed that mental defect was "the mother of crime, pauperism and degeneracy." Civilization was in imminent danger of being overrun by defective stocks, who were already eating it away like internal parasites. "The Menace of the Feebleminded" significantly graced the title-page of dozens of papers and pamphlets on the subject. The voice of authority, which in an earlier generation had been raised in behalf of sympathetic understanding and treatment of the mental defective, now rang out sternly against him. Said one of the leading authorities of the time, in 1915: "For many generations we have recognized and pitied the idiot. Of late we have recognized a higher type of defective, the moron, and have discovered that he is a burden; that he is a menace to society and civilization; that he is responsible in a large degree for many, if not all, of our social problems."[4] Said another:

> The feebleminded are a parasitic, predatory class, never capable of self-support or of managing their own affairs. They cause unutterable sorrow at home and are a menace and danger to the community. Feebleminded women are almost invariably immoral, and if at large usually become carriers of venereal disease or give birth to children who are as defective as themselves. . . . Every feebleminded person, especially the high-grade imbecile, is a potential criminal, needing only

---

*This was a follow-up study of Dugdale's famous investigation, tending to confirm the latter's conclusions.

the proper environment and opportunity for the development and expression of his criminal tendencies.[5]

A few years later, the author of the foregoing remarks, Dr. Walter E. Fernald, experienced a complete change of mind and heart, and was honest and courageous enough to admit his previous errors. Looking back in 1924 at the alarmist period, Fernald referred to it as the classic age of the "Legend of the Feebleminded," in which a composite portrait of a mythical person, embodying all the worst qualities (everything that was immoral, vicious, degenerate, criminal) of the worst types of defectives, appeared as "hero."

Mental defect was raised to the first rank among social problems, the source of most of the others. The question was naturally posed: What to do about it? Dependence on therapeutic devices seemed hopeless. Even the "harmless" cases were considered to be constant menaces to society. There was no corrective to their "inherent" lack of self-control, and none could foretell what anti-social outbursts on their part might occur.

Since attempts at cure or improvement were deemed futile, the only solution to the problem seemed to lie in the direction of preventive measures. Significantly enough, the 1915 National Conference of Charities and Correction devoted a large section of its proceedings to the discussion of "Prevention of Mental Defect." The keynote of this session was sounded in a paper read by Dr. M. W. Barr of the Pennsylvania Training School at Elwyn, entitled "Prevention of Mental Defect, the Duty of the Hour," which opened with these words: "That the prevention of the transmission of mental defect is the paramount duty of the hour, is a truism not to be questioned."[6] This note was elaborated in an address by Dr. Goddard before the same conference, in which it was categorically declared:

> Thanks to the investigations already made, we now know that in two-thirds of the cases, feeblemindedness is caused by feeblemindedness, that is to say, feebleminded parents transmit their mental defect to their offspring. It therefore follows that if we could prevent re-

production among the feebleminded, we could reduce mental defect to one-third of its present proportions.[7]

Such were the approaches and conclusions adopted in the period of alarmism. Let us not lose sight of the positive contributions to the knowledge of mental deficiency during this period. New and far-reaching discoveries were being made. It was largely the pioneering attempts to evaluate and apply these discoveries that produced the grosser errors. It remained for a more scientific and analytical period, marked by advances in the field of genetics, sociology, and psychiatry, to separate the wheat from the chaff, as well as to prick some of the bubbles blown to fantastic proportions during the heyday of the alarmist outcries.

If the first two decades of the century represented a period of uncritical acceptance of hasty theorizing based on partial and distorted truths, the years that followed witnessed a great deal of searching analysis and self-criticism, of important revaluations of former values. Under the light of this analysis and criticism, essential errors in alarmist theories and conclusions have been revealed.

Critique of the mental test. The scope and importance of the mental test, though representing a major advance in the development of classification, was greatly over-emphasized in its early application. While it was, and still remains, an essential factor in the diagnosis of mental status, those who introduced it in the United States erred gravely in spreading the impression that it could serve as the *sole* determinant, not only in grading feeblemindedness, but in identifying it.

In contrast to its action of 1910, the American Association on Mental Deficiency, in adopting a new classification system in 1934, was careful to differentiate between *identification* of the condition of mental deficiency and its *grading*. Separate groups of criteria were formulated for determining the condition and the grade, and it was pointed out that "the *grade* of mental deficiency is to be understood as applying only after the *condition* has been established."[8]

The alarmists who hastily concluded, upon publication of the Army mental tests of drafted men during the war, that

CHANGING CONCEPTS IN MENTAL DEFECT 363

nearly half of the population were mentally defective failed to differentiate between intellectual subnormality and feeblemindedness. Analysis of the Army tests revealed another flaw: there was something fundamentally wrong with a test indicating that the average person was below average in mentality. This was a contradiction in terms. If nearly half fell below the top mental-age line for feeblemindedness, that line has been set too high and was in need of modification.*

Furthermore, there were serious imperfections inherent in the very nature of the intelligence tests themselves. No mental test thus far devised has proved itself a perfect measuring scale for intelligence. None has universal validity, being necessarily based on definite cultural patterns, which vary from country to country, from section to section, and from community to community. For example, the statement, "Silence must prevail in churches," used in at least one well-known intelligence test, would naturally evoke an affirmative answer in the normal New York child, but would a child with a southern "shoutin' Methodist" background be wrong in answering negatively in perfect accordance with his or her environmental experiences?

All psychometric tests invented to date have definite limitations. Those based on language (such as the Binet-Simon test) have been unable to overcome completely the problem of language difficulties in individuals which may have nothing to do with their innate intelligence. The non-

*In 1934, the American Association on Mental Deficiency adopted this important modification of the psychological criteria for grading mental defect:
"An idiot is a mentally defective person usually having a mental age of less than three years, or if a child, an intelligence quotient of less than twenty. An imbecile is a mentally defective person usually having a mental age of three years to seven years, inclusive, or if a child, an intelligence quotient from twenty to forty-nine inclusive. A moron is a mentally defective person usually having a mental age of eight years or upwards, or if a child, an I.Q. of fifty or more."
Note that no upper limit of mental age is placed on the moron. As for the I.Q., the Association states: "As a rule the upper limit for a diagnosis of mental deficiency should be an I.Q. of sixty-nine, but this limit should not be adhered to in cases where medical, social and other factors clearly indicate that the patient is mentally defective." The I.Q. used in the Association's grading system is based on the Stanford-Binet test, with the mental age divided by sixteen for adults, with sixteen years as the upper limit of average mental age.

language, or "performance," tests also have inherent limitations. Many a person scoring a relatively high mental rating in language tests shows a low rating in performance tests, and vice versa. Then, too, the same individual may respond quite differently at different moments to the same test, because of highly variable conditioning factors. Environmental factors, emotional make-up and attitudes of the person tested all enter as important though concealed factors in mental tests.

In short, the mental test is a helpful and essential, but by no means infallible, index to intelligence, not to speak of mental status generally.

Changing criteria of mental defect. It is now recognized that feeblemindedness must be diagnosed on the basis of the *whole* personality, of which the psychological factor, though essential, forms but one part. Even should the perfect mental test be invented, it would be considered absurd from the scientific viewpoint to employ it as the sole determinant of feeblemindedness.

Dr. Fernald introduced, in the diagnosis of feeblemindedness, ten "fields of inquiry" for determining mental status which are now generally employed in Massachusetts and other states. These fields of inquiry include: physical examinations; family history; personal and developmental history; school progress; examination in school work; practical knowledge and general information; social history and reactions; economic efficiency; moral reactions; and mental examination.

In 1934 the American Association on Mental Deficiency adopted the report of its committee on statistics which set up the following standards:

> The condition of mental deficiency or the diagnostic mental status is to be determined by a combined consideration of all clinical data relating to the patient; that is, his present mental condition, as to intelligence level and emotional reactions in relation to his anatomical, physiological and neurological constitution; his general behavior and social adjustment, his background in biological and social heredity; and his genetic developmental history, including particularly events affecting his physical, social and emotional development. In short, all

those data which are necessary in order to evaluate the present status of the individual.[9]

Inherent in every definition of feeblemindedness is the recognition that the main criterion for diagnosing the condition is not the psychological but the social one. The Army test, for example, proved that a great many individuals who tested far below twelve years of mental age were none the less socially and economically efficient. A man might show a mental age as low as eight years and still be a respected, socially useful member of his particular community. To be rated feebleminded, social and economic inadequacy must be present.

Feeblemindedness itself is not a fixed, but a variable condition, depending on time, place and circumstance. Since urban life is more complex than rural, and makes greater demands on the individual, social adjustment and economic efficiency are more difficult to attain there. A large proportion of urban dwellers who are thrust into the ranks of the feebleminded because they are unable to respond sufficiently to the demands and needs of their environment might, despite their limited mental capacity, find adequate adjustment in a simple rural environment. Binet summed up the situation neatly when he said of a native of a rural province who was seeking his fortune in the French capital: "He is feebleminded in Paris, and normal at home." To repeat, the only satisfactory criterion for mental defect is the social one.

Mendelianism and Mental Defect. The extreme hereditarians, whose influence was overwhelmingly dominant in the period of eugenic alarm, have been forced to drop some of their most important claims in the light of recent findings in genetics and the rising challenge of the environmentalists. The theory, early propounded by Davenport, Goddard and others, that feeblemindedness is a simple Mendelian recessive, is held to be utterly untenable today. Only in a few rare clinical groups, such as amaurotic idiocy, has heredity been definitely traced as the source, and even here the application of the simple Mendelian formula is questionable.

Defective Pedigrees. The genealogies of defective and degenerate stock which appeared in such profusion during the second decade of our century, and which contributed so much to pessimistic alarmism, have been in large measure discredited by subsequent critical analysis of their methods and conclusions. Commenting on the reckless speculations indulged in by genealogists of degeneracy, the distinguished English geneticist, Lancelot Hogben, declares that their elaborate compilations of ancestries "demonstrate very little beyond the fact that extreme poverty can often be demonstrated in several successive generations of a given family."[10] Another eminent geneticist, T. H. Morgan, writes: "The numerous pedigrees that have been published, showing a long history of social misconduct, crime, alcoholism, debauchery, and venereal diseases, are open to the same criticism from a genetic point of view, for it is obvious that these groups of individuals have lived under demoralising social conditions that might swamp a family of average persons. It is not surprising that, once begun, from whatever cause, the effects may be to a large extent communicated rather than inherited."[11]

As was the case with Dugdale's study of the Jukes, published in 1877, the later pedigrees of defective stock were generally characterized by thoroughly unscientific methods of investigation. In the most famous of these studies, *The Kallikak Family,* the author tells us that field workers engaged in tracking down the descendants of the Revolutionary soldier and the servant girl were permitted to ascertain feeblemindedness in a person by merely "looking at" him or her. Evidence of feeblemindedness (and other defective and degenerate traits) was largely based on hearsay: in many cases it was deemed sufficient proof of mental defect if a person, deceased two or more generations perhaps, was reported to have been "a wild, immoral fellow," or a "plodding, dull, and drinking fellow." And how, in the first instance, the author was able to ascertain that a "nameless girl" living in Revolutionary times, a poor servant maid unknown but for her genealogically convenient *affaire d'amour,* was feebleminded, is not revealed.[12]

A large measure of the bewilderment in the alarmist period is attributable to the prevailing tendency to confuse low cultural level with mental defect. As Fernald pointed out, the "legend of the feebleminded" current during the alarmist period was based partly on studies of defectives in institutions for dependents and delinquents. These were precisely the ones who *had* got into trouble and were *in* institutions, and *had* behaved badly and *were* shiftless and lazy. It seemed entirely logical at the time to assume that *all* mental defectives had similar histories and tendencies. One important factor was overlooked, namely, the large number of mental defectives living as harmless and even useful members of their respective communities, and displaying no antisocial, immoral or degenerate traits. As for the evidence of the large percentage of feeblemindedness among dependents and delinquents, triumphantly brought forward by certain groups as proof of the inseparable association between the one and the others, Fernald wisely remarked: "It would be equally logical to describe an iceberg without a reference to the 87 per cent of the bulk invisible below the surface of the sea."[13] From the data already available at the time (1924)—impressively verified by subsequent investigations—Fernald felt justified in concluding that "there are good defectives and bad defectives" and that "the good vastly outnumber the bad."* So much for feeblemindedness being "the mother of crime, pauperism and degeneracy."

But whatever modifications in attitude were occasioned by subsequent research, the following notions regarding mental defect dominated the first twenty years of the century: (1) this condition represented a major menace to civilization;

---

*A research project recently carried on in Great Britain offers interesting findings on the relation between mental defect and crime. We quote from *Mental Welfare* (London), October, 1934, p. 111, describing the contents of the 20th annual report of the British Board of Control for 1933:

"A review of the figures of persons found guilty of criminal offences and dealt with as mentally defective is given for the three years 1931–33, inclusive . . . For this period the total of persons found guilty of indictable offences was nearly 170,000 and the number of these offenders found certifiable as mentally defective was only 728. Even allowing for cases in which mental defect is not recognizable when they first come to Court, the proportion of defective offenders to the total number remains very small."

(2) it was mainly hereditary in origin, and probably transmitted in accordance with the Mendelian formula; (3) drastic action was required to check its incidence; (4) a preventive program must be sought in cutting off the defective germ plasm from the human race; (5) segregation and sterilization afforded the two principal means for attaining this end.

Segregation. This was earliest to win wide support as a large-scale eugenic measure. At first, as we have noted, the ideal underlying institutional custody of the feebleminded was to protect the inmates from the dangers of society. The turn of the century witnessed a complete revolution in the custodial ideal; the main object now was to protect society from the menace of mental defectives. A sharp rise in institutional construction occurred during the first decade of the century. Many existing asylums were enlarged. Still others, which had previously been operating on a training-school basis, were converted in whole or in part to custodial establishments with the aim of permanent confinement. The "school" of an earlier generation was now the "institution"; the "pupil" of yesterday was now the "inmate." While the growth of the custodial ideal was in large part due to the general feeling of pessimism regarding the possibility of training feebleminded persons for satisfactory adjustment in the community, it gradually became more and more identified with the idea of eugenic segregation. Addressing the annual session of the American Association for the Study of Feeblemindedness in 1906, Dr. Alexander Johnson crystallized this very point: "I believe that every member will agree that the segregation and even permanent detention of at least a great majority, if not all of the feebleminded, is the proper procedure." In a splendid retrospect of work in America, Dr. Fernald wrote in 1924: "For nearly two decades all our knowledge of the feebleminded indicated that the obvious and logical remedy was life-long segregation, and this became the policy in nearly every state."

But in time the futility of segregation as a eugenical panacea became apparent even to its most enthusiastic proponents. A few significant figures may serve to indicate the

CHANGING CONCEPTS IN MENTAL DEFECT 369

failure of isolation as a solution to the problem. In 1904 the total number of patients in institutions for mental defectives was 14,347. By 1910 the total had increased to 20,731. In 1923 it rose to 42,954. Today, with the total number of mental defectives conservatively estimated at 1,250,000 (about one per hundred of the whole population), less than 80,000 are accommodated in special institutions for their care and treatment.* It may be seen that, in spite of the fact that the special institutional population trebled between the years 1904 and 1923, and has doubled again since then, at no time has there been provision for more than one-fifteenth of the estimated total of feebleminded persons.

To build institutions that could house all mental defectives, or even a considerable proportion of them (assuming that such a procedure were really desirable), would require gigantic financing that no administration or legislature would be willing or able to undertake. But even should it be possible to surmount the tremendous economic and administrative difficulties involved in such a step, our present knowledge of the operation of hereditary factors in mental defect clearly indicates that segregation as a eugenic measure is quite futile. Goddard, who once estimated that two-thirds of feeblemindedness would disappear in one generation by preventing procreation among known defectives, recently stated that even if it were possible to segregate all of them the proportion of defect thus prevented would amount to but a small fraction of the total.

Sterilization. The relative efficacy of sterilization in the prevention of mental defect has been, and still is, a most hotly contested issue. Unlike the idea of isolation, it still attracts to its banner a large and influential number of supporters.

Sterilization of the feebleminded had been urged as a preventive measure in America even before the present century was ushered in. As early as 1897 Dr. M. W. Barr, in his presidential address before the American Association for the Study of Feeblemindedness, strongly advocated it as the

*Several thousand additional mental defectives are scattered in general institutions for dependents and delinquents and in mental hospitals.

most practical step in a preventive program. In the same year the first human sterilization bill in this country was introduced in the Michigan legislature, but failed of passage. Indiana was the first state to enact a human sterilization law. This pioneer statute, passed in 1907, provided for the compulsory sterilization of "confirmed criminals, idiots, imbeciles and rapists." The operation was to be performed after a committee of experts and institutional officials had decided that procreation was inadvisable and that there was no probability of the subject's mental improvement.* Later laws in Indiana modified the administrative details of the original statute, and extended the scope of sterilization to non-institutional mental defectives upon the recommendation and approval of the proper authorities.[14]

State after state followed the lead of Indiana. In some, the laws were later repealed or declared unconstitutional as violating the "due process of law" clause in the 14th Amendment to the Constitution. Other acts, which provided for sterilization as a punitive measure (as applied to various types of criminals), in addition to eugenic purposes (as applied to defectives), were voided as constituting "cruel and unusual punishment" in contravention of state constitutions that embody the Bill of Rights. In 1927, the U. S. Supreme Court handed down the famous *Buck v. Bell* decision upholding the constitutionality of the Virginia sterilization statute. An unusually brief opinion, lacking legal citations or expert sociological and psychiatric support, was drawn up by Justice Holmes, and ended with the well known words: "The principle that sustains compulsory vaccination is broad enough to cover the cutting of the Fallopian tubes . . . Three generations of imbeciles are enough." The Supreme Court decision eased the way for subsequent sterilization legislation, and was followed by the passage of a number of such laws. On July 1, 1936, twenty-five states had eugenic

---

*Even before 1907, superintendents of institutions in several states were secretly sterilizing feebleminded persons. Several hundred males were sterilized secretly and illegally by Dr. H. C. Sharp of the Indiana State Reformatory before the passage of the pioneer law. It was Dr. Sharp, incidentally, who first devised the surgical operation known as vasectomy which is today most often used in sterilizing males.

CHANGING CONCEPTS IN MENTAL DEFECT

sterilization laws on their statute books. Operations producing sterilization for surgical purposes such as treatment of pathologic conditions in the genito-urinary tract are usually legal, and widely practiced. This therapeutic aspect of the problem of sterilization does not enter into our discussion. Neither does the question of voluntary sterilization for economic reasons. We are concerned here only with *eugenic* sterilization.

All the existing state eugenic statutes include mental defectives among the groups subject to sterilization. Many also include persons suffering from mental diseases believed to be hereditary. Other classes included in various laws are habitual criminals, rapists, sexual perverts, drug addicts and epileptics. Most laws authorize compulsory sterilization for selected feebleminded persons; others authorize only voluntary sterilization, that is, with the consent of the patient or his legal guardian.

The two most widely used sterilizing operations are vasectomy (section of the seminal ducts in the male) and salpingectomy (section of the Fallopian tubes in the female). The former is a minor, the latter a major, operation. Neither interferes with the desire for sexual intercourse or with its gratification. Of the more than sixty sterilization statutes that have been passed in the United States since 1907, only one (Oregon, 1917) permitted castration, and that law is no longer in effect.

While eugenic sterilization laws exist in twenty-eight states today, only in a few states are they operative. This situation is due principally to strong popular, religious and scientific opposition to sterilization, besides constitutional and administrative difficulties in enforcing these laws. A survey made in 1926 showed that such statutes were functioning effectively in only four states, with moderate efficacy in eight more, while in the remaining states, operations were performed only sporadically if at all.[15]

From 1907 to January 1, 1946, according to a report published in *Eugenical News* (March, 1946), a total of 45,127 sterilizations had been performed in 30 American states. (The sexual sterilization laws of two states—Alabama and

Washington—had been nullified as unconstitutional after some operations had been performed.) California was by far the most active state in this regard, accounting for a total of 17,835 sterilizations. The sterilizing activity in California is largely attributable to the effective pro-eugenics propaganda carried on in that state for years by the now defunct Human Betterment Foundation in Pasadena, founded and financed by the banker, E. S. Gosney, and directed by Paul Popenoe. The California statute, dating from 1917 (an earlier law having been repealed), authorizes compulsory sterilization of selected patients of the state institutions for the mentally ill, the feebleminded, the dependent or the delinquent, prior to parole or discharge. Feebleminded persons at large may be sterilized with the written consent of their legal guardians. The organized movement for eugenic sterilization in this country is now led by Birthright, Inc., Princeton, N.J.

Of the 45,127 persons operated upon in the United States under the sterilization laws since 1907, a total of 21,311 were in the "insane" category, 22,153 were feebleminded and 1,663 belonged to other categories.

It may be readily seen that the number of mental defectives sterilized over a period of four decades represents but a small fraction of 1 per cent of the present total of mental defectives in the country. Assuredly, then, sterilization has thus far proved a striking failure as a large-scale measure for cutting off defective stock.

Meanwhile the pros and cons of sterilization continue to be debated on the biological, sociological, religious, and more recently, the political fronts. Major arguments for eugenic sterilization of the mentally defective, besides those discussed on preceding pages, may be summed up as follows:

1. If all the feebleminded could be sterilized, the total would be greatly reduced in one generation and might in several generations be practically rooted out of the human race.

2. It is a more practical and effective method of preventing procreation among the feebleminded than segregation; it is less expensive, and thus would result in considerable financial savings to the state. Furthermore, it can be applied on a far wider scale than segregation.

3. The fear of procreation thus eliminated, it permits a more liberal

system of parole and discharge from institutions, and also marriage and better social adjustment of the individual operated upon.

4. Feebleminded persons make unsatisfactory parents, and create unfavorable home conditions for children.

5. Contrary to popular notions, sterilizing operations such as vasectomy and salpingectomy do not involve the loss of desire for, or ability to perform, the sex act (as castration does).

Eugenic sterilization found its most active expression in this country until the coming to power of the Nazis placed Germany in the lead. Among its leading American exponents are Paul Popenoe, C. B. Davenport, E. S. Gosney, E. M. East, H. H. Laughlin, A. H. Estabrook, together with such general "race alarmists" as Madison Grant, Ellsworth Huntington, A. E. Wiggam and T. L. Stoddard. In 1930 the American Association for the Study of Feeblemindedness endorsed selective sterilization and in the same year the Mental Deficiency Committee of the White House Conference on Child Health and Protection approved it in principle.

In spite of its influential, if not always scientific, advocates, there has been a growing opposition to the practice of sterilization of mental defectives and other socially inadequate classes on theological, moral, social and scientific grounds. On the latter two grounds, the opposition is generally not directed against the principle as such, but against its application at the present time.

In summarizing some of the principal objections to sterilization as applied to the mentally defective, we may immediately dismiss those based on religious or moral grounds such as the "divine and natural rights of the individual to his procreative powers," since they are founded on faith rather than reason, and are therefore removed from the realm of logical debate.

The scientific objections are far more formidable, particularly in the light of recent findings in genetics. It is argued that we have not, as yet, sufficient scientific knowledge of hereditary factors in mental defect to warrant the application of eugenic sterilization to any appreciable extent. By far the greatest proportion of inheritable mental defect is transmitted by normal "carriers," that is, persons who are not themselves defective. It is estimated that about 89 per cent of inheritable mental defect is transmitted through such carriers. We have at present no means of discovering who these carriers are. Even should all the feebleminded be sterilized at once, it would reduce the number in the next generation only about 11 per cent. In later generations, according to Jennings, preventing the propagation of the feebleminded would have little further effect save to keep the number down to that already reached. The hope of sterilization enthusiasts that this measure would result in immediate wholesale elimination of the condition from the human stock has no scientific basis. Part of the exaggerated hopes placed in this and other eugenic measures based on hereditary factors lies in a persistent tendency to regard mental defect as a single clinical entity, an approach that is superficial and very misleading. It is now recognized that mental defect covers a heterogeneous group of entities having widely varying causes and calling for widely different methods of prevention and treatment. As Hogben points out, genetic analysis of these extremely complex entities has hardly been attempted yet. Assuredly, a great deal more scientific research, and less speculation, is required before sterilization can be scientifically employed on a considerable scale.

The fond hope that checking the procreation of mental defectives would result in the rapid disappearance of dependency, delinquency and many (if not all) other social problems is likewise based on an inadequate conception of the modes of transmission of heredity and of the role of environmental influences.

Besides the present lack of scientific knowledge concerning hereditary factors in feeblemindedness, there are grave social objections to sterilization at the present time. It is not only a question of who shall be sterilized, but who shall do the sterilizing? For example, the primary criterion in judging feeblemindedness is the social one. But *who* is to determine the standards of social fitness and desirability? Many prominent eugenists themselves doubt the wisdom of en-

CHANGING CONCEPTS IN MENTAL DEFECT

acting sterilization laws on any appreciable scale under present social conditions. They feel that, desirable though eugenic sterilization may be when scientifically employed, there is too much danger at present of its being converted from a useful tool into a perilous weapon. Professor Hogben, an active member of the Eugenics Society of London, has ably commented on present proposals for eliminating the feebleminded through sterilization and like measures:

> A rationally planned society might easily be persuaded to take this course. The sympathy with which such proposals are at present greeted by some students of social problems is not enhanced by the fact that they are almost invariably put forward by those who are most anxious to perpetuate forms of parasitism more costly and disastrous than feeblemindedness. To the writer it seems that the selfishness, apathy and prejudice which prevent intellectually gifted people from understanding the character of the present crisis in civilization is a far greater menace to the survival of culture than the prevalence of mental defect in the technical sense of the term.[16]

Certain it is that our legislatures as constituted today are not happily suited to the task of enacting sound eugenic laws. This is indicated by the extreme carelessness and confusion, the abuse of elementary terms, the lack of precision and definition, and the failure to prescribe adequate administrative details and safeguards, that characterize most of our present legislation on the subject. The lack of uniform standards as to the proper persons qualified to judge which defective individuals are fit subjects for sterilization is impressively mirrored in these laws. Some states confer this responsibility on institutional officials, others on physicians, or psychiatrists, or psychologists or neurologists, and still others (somewhat more wisely) delegate this power to committees composed of several of these professional categories.

Legislators generally have shown an amazing ignorance of the purposes and utility of eugenic measures. In enacting laws on sterilization, they have frequently rushed in where scientists fear to tread, and have claimed a knowledge of laws of heredity far beyond the reaches as yet attained by the humble scientist. The heights to which such ignorance can soar is illustrated in a bill introduced in the Missouri legislature as recently as 1929. It provided that

> Whenever a person shall have been convicted of murder (not in the heat of passion), rape, highway robbery, chicken stealing, bombing, or theft of automobiles, the judge trying the said case shall immediately upon disposition of the case, if conviction is upheld, appoint a competent physician, resident of the county in which the conviction was had, to perform on said convict the operation known as vasectomy or oophorectomy for the purpose of sterilizing such convict, so that the power to procreate will be forever destroyed.[17]

How the learned legislator who devised and introduced this bill (which fortunately was defeated) obtained the knowledge that chicken stealers and auto thieves are defective types and proper subjects for sterilization, remains an esoteric secret.

Under the unstable conditions prevailing throughout the world, sterilization looms as a frightful weapon in the hands of unscrupulous politicians coming to power. Sober social scientists point to the terrible example of Nazi Germany as an extreme case in point. Nine vaguely-defined categories of human beings, including the mentally defective, were subject to sterilization under the Nazi laws. The term "feebleminded" was stretched by some Nazi officials to include all political enemies of the totalitarian state. One government edict sanctioned sterilization for the "slightly feebleminded." What were the criteria, one wonders, for determining what citizens were "slightly feebleminded"? Sterilization of certain racial and religious "non-Aryan" groups as representing biologically inferior and undesirable stock received grave consideration before the question was finally resolved by the official Nazi policy of outright extermination, or genocide, of whole peoples—resulting in the slaughter of millions of innocents. It was revealed at the war-crime trials of Nuremberg in 1947 that more than 275,000 insane, feebleminded and physically handicapped Germans were put to death under the official Nazi euthanasia program. The danger of placing sterilizing power in the hands of men filled with hatred against individuals and groups on racial, religious, political or merely personal grounds, is too obvious to require further elaboration.

Today, in view of our scant scientific data on the laws of human heredity in respect to defective stock, and the socially dangerous uses that can be made of too little knowledge, it is well to hold ambitious schemes such as eugenic sterilization in abeyance until a more opportune time. For the present, many scientists feel, the most effective means of coping with the problem of eliminating mental defect is to concentrate upon the environment. Thus, Dr. Frank Douglas Turner, Medical Superintendent of the Royal Institution at Colchester and an outstanding authority on mental deficiency, declared in his presidential address before the British Royal Medico-Psychological Association in 1933: "Do what you will, sterilize whom you will, you will still fail and are bound to fail to eliminate the normal people with somewhat below average intelligence who cannot react successfully to their environment and whom, therefore, we label mentally defective. The only hope for the future lies in tackling the environment instead of . . . the method of cure by wholesale surgical operations."[18]

Marriage laws. Besides sterilization and segregation, the prohibition of marriage of the feebleminded has been urged as a preventive measure against hereditary defect. Most states in this country have enacted laws of this type, but thus far these laws have invariably proved worthless, chiefly because of the lack of adequate provision for the identification or diagnosis of the mental status of applicants for marriage licenses.

Since all three major measures proposed for the prevention of propagation among the mentally defective have failed (at least thus far) as large-scale solutions to the problem, more and more emphasis is being placed on other types of social control, mainly extramural in character. A modern program would include these major provisions:

1. *Early identification and registration of the mentally deficient.* These measures, undertaken on state-wide bases, would facilitate the planning and operation of broad com-

munity programs for the prevention and treatment of mental deficiency.

2. *Special Classes: Differentiated Education.* The first special class for the mentally handicapped was established in Providence in 1896. Since then the idea of maintaining classes for "retarded" and "backward" children has spread throughout the country. New Jersey (1911), Minnesota (1915), New York (1917), Wisconsin (1917) and Massachusetts (1918) were among the first states to enact laws making such provision. Some of these laws are permissive, others mandatory. Unfortunately, due to the lack of cooperation and coordination among those responsible for carrying out their purposes and the inadequacy of funds, the mandatory statutes have remained largely inoperative. This is true, for example, in New York State, where the mandatory provisions of one of the best-framed special class laws have never been enforced during the nearly twenty years of the statute's existence.[19]

The public school has become the central point in modern programs for the control of mental deficiency. It has been estimated that some 550,000 mentally subnormal children of school age, or about 2 per cent of the total school population, are in need of special class instruction. Thus far, the program has fallen far short of meeting the needs. Present provision accommodates only about one-tenth of the estimated total of mentally handicapped children of school age.*

Besides special classes, an effective school program for the mentally subnormal (only a very small fraction of whom are feebleminded) should include specially trained teachers, modification of curricula with special emphasis on manual and vocational training for the handicapped groups, visiting teachers, nurses, educational counselors, parent guidance and adequate follow-up work.

On the whole, even where special class programs have been introduced, they have thus far failed to reach an effec-

---

*A survey undertaken by Dr. Arch O. Hack in 1927–28 showed a total of 2,552 special classes in 266 cities of the U.S. with an enrollment of 46,625 subnormal children.

tive plane of operation. Besides the general apathy and indifference of key officials, inadequate funds and insufficient clarity of method and purpose have combined to cause a large proportion of failures in maintaining a fair standard of efficiency. Until all mentally handicapped children in need of special attention are provided with proper educational facilities within the public school system, universal education will not have attained its goal.

3. *Mental Hygiene Clinics.* The establishment of mental hygiene clinics within, or connected with, the public school system is an important factor in a workable program for the social control of mental deficiency. In Massachusetts, a state-wide system of mental clinics is operated under the auspices of the State Department of Mental Diseases. Under the Massachusetts plan, each of the state hospitals for the mentally ill and the state schools for the mentally defective maintains a traveling clinic consisting of a psychiatrist, a psychologist and a social worker. Each traveling clinic unit provides service to all public schools in a given district, aided by the school nurse and a selected teacher.[20] Similar clinic units have been organized in Connecticut, Minnesota, New York, New Jersey, Ohio, Pennsylvania and Wisconsin.

A number of public and private schools now employ educational counselors, visiting teachers with psychiatric training, or child guidance clinics treating the behavior problems of children, including those mentally subnormal. Adequately staffed and well-equipped child guidance clinics, such as are fostered by the National Committee for Mental Hygiene, are valuable assets in the solutions of mental deficiency problems.

4. *Institutional Care and Treatment.* Since the alarmist period there has been a noticeable swing away from the concept of the institution as a place for mere custody or permanent confinement. There has been a gradual closing of the cycle back to the ideals of Seguin, Howe and Wilbur, who envisaged the institution as a training school intended to return the patient or pupil to a place in the normal life of the community. Of course, there are still (and probably will always continue to be) many hopeless and helpless cases who

require more or less permanent institutionalization. But there are a great many more mentally deficient children who, because of unfavorable home environment, lack of special provision for them in common schools, etc., require only temporary institutional care and training with the intention of eventually returning them to the community.
According to U. S. Census Bureau figures, there were 114,-800 mentally defective patients on the books of institutions for their special care at the end of the year 1944; 98,969 were resident in these institutions, while the remainder were either in family care or in other extra-mural care. First admissions of mental defectives in all institutions for their special care totaled 9,163 in that year; 8,262 were admitted to public institutions and 901 private institutions. Overcrowding in public institutions averaged 7.5 per cent above rated capacity. The Census Bureau listed 183 institutions for mental defectives and epileptics in the United States; 86 were state institutions, two were city institutions and 95 were privately controlled. Of the 118,534 mental defectives and epileptics in residence at these institutions in 1944, 112,375, or 94.8 per cent, were in public institutions while 6,159 were in private institutions. A total of $39,777,794 was spent for maintenance in all public institutions for these patients in 1944, representing a per capita expenditure of $365.20 a year. It has been estimated that only one-fifteenth of the nation's mental defectives were accommodated in institutions for their special care.

The training ideal, as contrasted with the custodial, has received impetus from various follow-up studies of persons discharged from institutions for the feebleminded. Through these studies it has been discovered that a gratifying proportion of mental defectives make a satisfactory adjustment in normal community life after a period of training.

5. *Colony System.* To facilitate the work of preparing mentally deficient patients for a return to normal social life, some institutions have adopted the colony system. The White House Conference Subcommittee on Problems of Mental Deficiency defined a colony as "a number of mentally deficient persons, living together under supervision and control,

outside of, but in affiliation with, an institution and supported more or less by group earnings." Until 1906 colonies for mental defectives were operated on practically the same basis as those for the mentally ill. Their major purposes were to relieve the parent institution of overcrowded conditions, to provide a less restricted and more congenial environment for patients fit for colony life, and to utilize their labor profitably.

In 1906 Dr. Charles Bernstein, Superintendent of the Rome State Custodial Asylum (now State School) at Rome, New York, introduced the policy of establishing small "mobile" colony units distributed in outlying communities to serve not merely as custodial labor centers, but as training centers. The colony is a sort of half-way house between the institution and the community. Under this plan, the more promising cases in the central institution are assigned to small, carefully-supervised colonies in selected outlying districts. They are placed at employment—agricultural, industrial or domestic, as the case might be—with the primary object of providing a practical training for the patients under conditions as far as possible approaching the normal. A large proportion of boys and girls may thus be rehabilitated and paroled or discharged on a basis of fair social and economic efficiency. Others, unable to make the grade to the point of being returned to the community, stay in these colonies, where they are more contented than they would be in institutions. Still others, after a trial period, are found unfit even for this half-way life, and are sent back to the institution. Of the 3,446 patients on the books of the Rome State School in 1935, 1,154, or one-third of the total, were living in colonies.

The major arguments favoring the mobile colony plan are: it relieves overcrowding, provides better living conditions than central institutions, prevents deterioration of the more hopeful cases, yields greater content, promotes mental hygiene and is cheaper to organize and maintain. It is also a trying-out place to determine to what degree the patient can stand increased responsibilities and greater freedom under community conditions which, while sheltered, closely approach the normal. The small mobile colony plan introduced by Dr. Bernstein has been adopted in a number of institutions in the United States and Great Britain, with very promising results.

An outstanding example of the "stable" colony plan, as contrasted with the mobile colony, is afforded by Letchworth Village at Thiells, New York. Established in 1909 and opened two years later, it was at first intended to serve as a purely custodial institution (its name having been, originally, the Eastern New York Custodial Asylum). It now receives all grades of mental defectives. Splendidly located, and planned to resemble as closely as possible a real village with little of the institutional atmosphere, Letchworth Village ranks among the most famous institutions of its type in the world. In connection with this subject, it is worthy of note that the stable colony plan has been adopted in several states as the best plan for providing public care for the epileptic. Until the last decade of the nineteenth century, there was no separate provision for this group anywhere in the United States. They were confined in general institutions for dependents and delinquents, for the insane and the feebleminded. While there were some epileptics who were mentally diseased and others who were mentally defective, there were many who suffered no observable mental impairment at all. To force the latter into constant association with either the insane or the feebleminded was detrimental to their health and to their happiness.

The need for separate provision for the epileptic was expressed as early as 1863 by Dr. James Rodman in his annual report as superintendent of the Western Kentucky Lunatic Asylum at Hopkinsville. His plea for a separate institution for these unfortunates, then quartered at the insane asylum, went unheeded, however. In 1868 the Ohio State Board of Charities launched a campaign for separate provision that culminated more than two decades later in the establishment of the first public institution exclusively for epileptics in this country.

In the latter part of the century the attention of American psychiatrists was attracted to this problem by the success

CHANGING CONCEPTS IN MENTAL DEFECT 383

of the Bethel Colony for Epileptics established in 1867 near Bielefeld, Germany. Patterned as closely as possible along normal community lines, affording varied pursuits, recreation and occupation for the patients, the colony at Bielefeld gained almost instantaneous success and soon grew into a large community numbering several thousand patients. This example greatly stimulated agitation for similar colonies in America.

The first separate American institution for epileptics was established in 1891 at Gallipolis, Ohio, as the "Asylum for Epileptics and Epileptic Insane." Modeled after the Bielefeld colony plan, this institution was opened in 1893, its name having been changed the preceding year to the "Ohio Hospital for Epileptics."

New York was the next state to establish a separate colony for epileptics. As early as 1874, Dr. John Ordronaux had recommended such a step in his first annual report as State Commissioner in Lunacy. Agitation for a state hospital for epileptics was continued by Dr. Frederick Peterson, following the latter's visit to the Bielefeld colony in 1886. Others who were prominent in the movement were Dr. George W. Jacoby, and Oscar Craig and William P. Letchworth, members of the New York State Board of Charities. The unremitting pressure exerted by these individuals and others resulted in the establishment of Craig Colony for Epileptics in 1894 at Sonyea, New York. It received its first patients in 1896. This colony, beautifully situated and boasting a ramified system of amusements, entertainments, occupations, education facilities and therapeutic equipment, has become one of the best known in the world.

Among the major advantages of separate care for the epileptics in colonies are the following:

1. The model colony provides the patient with an environment from which many of the dangers he faces in normal community life, as well as stresses injurious to his mental health, are eliminated. It is planned as closely as possible along the pattern of normal community life, with features adapted to his individual needs.
2. It provides him with constant medical care and supervision.
3. It relieves society in some measure of a source of potential dan-

ger to the public safety, since certain types of epileptic seizures are often accompanied by homicidal impulses.

4. It removes the patient from a general institution where he is forced into close contact with various groups of dependents (the mentally ill and defective, etc.) under conditions highly unsatisfactory to himself and his fellow-patients or fellow-inmates.[21]

While the separate colony idea is generally accepted as offering the best institutional provision for epileptics, it has received actual adoption but slowly.* There are barely a dozen public institutions exclusively devoted to the care and treatment of epileptics. Many sufferers from this ailment are placed in institutions for mental defectives. Others are maintained in state mental hospitals, and several thousands are still to be found in almshouses and penal institutions throughout the country.

The U. S. Bureau of the Census reported that, at the end of 1944, there were 20,838 epileptics on the books of all institutions for mental defectives and epileptics, of whom 18,443 were actually in institutions and the rest in family care or other types of extramural care. Of those in institutions, 17,739 were in public and 684 in private institutions. First admissions of epileptics (the Census Bureau statistics do not contain a breakdown of these types of institutions) totaled 1,603 in 1944.[22] Of all epileptics under public care, only one third, approximately, are maintained in separate institutions.

Several years ago Dr. William T. Shanahan, then superintendent of Craig Colony, justly noted that:

> More separate institutions to care for epileptics are needed. There is no particular objection to having insane or markedly feebleminded epileptics placed in the institutions provided for patients with similar mental conditions, but the considerable number of epileptics who do not show mental impairment suffer greatly from the enforced contacts

---

*With the development of effective drugs for the control of epileptic seizures, together with newer knowledge of the nature of epilepsy, there has been a decided trend away from institutionalization toward normal life in the home, save in exceptional cases. The American Epilepsy League, Inc., with headquarters at Boston, Mass., has conducted an extensive educational campaign which has done much to improve public attitudes toward epileptics and the treatment of epilepsy.

which are almost inevitable if they are placed in institutions for the mentally disordered or mentally defective.[23]

6. *Parole.* The practice of provisional and extended parole was developed chiefly through the efforts of Dr. Bernstein of the Rome State School and Dr. Fernald of Massachusetts. The parole period is designed to determine the feasibility of non-institutional life under supervision. The Mental Deficiency Subcommittee of the 1930 White House Conference recommended that parole periods be divided into two classes: (1) the "short vacation" of about four weeks, which affords sufficient time to determine probable success under non-institutional conditions; and (2) the "long vacation" lasting a year or more, granted when results of the short vacation have proved satisfactory. The Subcommittee strongly condemned the practice, restored to by many state institutions, of paroling mentally defective persons who have not been adequately trained, or who cannot be properly supervised, as a means of solving problems of overcrowding and insufficient funds. It pointed out that in many cases the advantages of institutional and colony training have been lost because of premature release and failure to provide adequate safeguards of parole and aftercare. On December 31, 1945, according to the U. S. Census Bureau, about 15,000 mental defectives were on parole from public institutions for their special care. This total represents more than four times the total paroled twenty years ago.

7. *Boarding out.* Several states provide for the placing-out of dependent mental defectives in foster and boarding homes. To date, boarding out of this class has not been practiced on any extensive scale in the United States.

Besides those mentioned above, social agencies utilized in dealing with the mentally deficient include juvenile courts, vocational guidance clinics, and general social work organizations.

It is generally agreed, however, that all the aforementioned agencies can afford at best only a partial solution to the problem of mental defect. The ultimate, large-scale solution lies in prevention, rather than in therapy. Here we return again to the controversy between the hereditarians and the environmentalists. Where can the greater gains be made, at least in the immediate future: in tinkering with the germ-plasm or in seeking more satisfactory environmental conditions? The answer provided by the distinguished biologist, H. S. Jennings is so penetrating that we may be pardoned for quoting it at some length:

> The great difficulty about this is that bad living conditions often produce the same kinds of results that bad genes do. . . . So long as living conditions are bad, we do not know what ills are due to poor genes. We must therefore correct the bad living conditions, not only for their directly beneficial effect, but also for the sake of eugenics. When this is done, it will be possible to discover what defects are primarily the result of defective genes, and then to plan measures for getting rid of these genes: measures for stopping the propagation of their carriers. That is, as a preliminary to the effective work of eugenics other reforms must be carried through. Measures of public health must be carried out, overwork and bad conditions done away with, faults of diet, both quantitative and qualitative, corrected; economic ills conquered, grinding poverty abolished. When the human plant is given conditions under which it unfolds its capabilities without stunting, poisoning and mutilation by the environment, then it will be possible to discover what ills are due primarily to defective genes, and to plan such measures as are possible for their eradication. Acting on such precise knowledge, far more rapid results may be hoped for than from the present blind action in merely encouraging the propagation of certain classes, discouraging that of others . . .
>
> To join with energy in present attempts to correct environmental evils of society is one of the two most important steps for the advance of eugenics. Until the preventable environmental ills are largely corrected, what eugenics can do is relatively little. The other important step toward increased efficiency of eugenic measures is to promote the advance of genetic science, that the normal carriers of defective genes may become identifiable.[24]

With these objectives attained, says Dr. Jennings, feeblemindedness may be brought rapidly to disappearance. Then, and then only, humanity may have in its hands the power to suppress hereditary feeblemindedness and a host of other ills within a generation.

CHAPTER XVIII

Insanity and the Criminal Law

"... *to define true madness, What is't but to be nothing else than mad?*"——

HAMLET, Act 2, Scene 2.

STANDING on the floor of the House of Commons some fifty years ago, Lord Blackburn, a noted English legal authority, declared: "I have read every definition [of insanity] which I could meet with and never was satisfied with one of them, and I have endeavored in vain to make one satisfactory to myself. I verily believe it is not in human power to do it."[1]

Except for the rather pessimistic note struck in the last sentence, that statement might be uttered with the same degree of justification today. Definitions there are in abundance—too many, in fact—with a generous variety of interpretation attesting to a confusion twice confounded. Indiscriminately used in both a medical and a legal sense, the word *insanity* lacks scientific sanction or precise meaning in either.[2] As a medical or psychiatric term, fortunately, it is fast falling into disuse, having been discredited by the great majority of psychiatric authorities. In medical parlance, it has been superseded by the more apt terms, "mental disease," "mental disorder" and "mental illness." Although the use of *insanity* is obsolescent in medical terminology, however, it is not yet obsolete and is still loosely used in a generic sense covering all mental diseases.

In its socio-legal sense, insanity might be broadly defined as a state of mental disorder of such kind or degree as to render a person socially inefficient and to make it necessary to place him under social control. But this definition is admittedly inadequate and does not cover all the usages of the term, particularly in its legal relation. In law, the only meaning of the term universally accepted is "unsoundness of mind." Unfortunately, this phrase is just as vague and nebulous as its synonym, insanity. What does "unsoundness of mind" consist of? Weighty and learned dissertations have been written around this question but these remain, for the most part, inconclusive.

It is a significant commentary on the backwardness and general inflexibility of our legal mechanisms that, though life and death frequently hinge on the proper understanding of insanity in its relation to law, one finds only chaos and contradiction where one has every right to expect precise definition. The interpretation of insanity, or unsoundness of mind, varies greatly in different jurisdictions, and often enough within a single jurisdiction. It is sometimes employed in a very comprehensive sense to include not only mental disease, but also mental defect.

In English and American law, insanity is sometimes used interchangeably with "lunacy." At other times it is used in a broader sense, while "lunacy," in turn, is held to mean only "intermittent" insanity occurring between lucid intervals—a concept that goes back to the time when mental disease was supposed to be influenced by certain changes of the moon.*

Broadly speaking, however, the legal concept of insanity may be stated as including that kind or degree of mental disorder that:

1. Exempts a person from responsibility for crime, or limits such responsibility.
2. Affords ground for preventing or delaying the trial, sentence, or punishment of a person accused of a criminal act.
3. Invalidates or voids legal acts, such as contracts, wills, etc.
4. Affords grounds for depriving a person of the control of his person or property, or both, by due process of law.
5. Affords grounds for depriving a person of his liberty, and placing him under restraint.

*Thus the seventeenth century jurist, Sir Matthew Hale, in describing "permanent" and "interpolated" dementia, wrote: "The latter is that which is usually called *lunacy,* for the moon hath a great influence in all diseases of the brain, especially in this kind of *dementia;* such persons commonly in the

INSANITY AND THE CRIMINAL LAW

The first two points apply to insanity in its relation to the criminal law, the last three to the civil law. This chapter will deal mainly with the criminal law as it affects the insane. The subject is vast and complex. Only a rough sketch can be attempted here, tracing the major lines of development and eschewing medico-legal niceties.

Insane and Criminal Responsibility. From early times, the legal irresponsibility of persons suffering from certain forms of mental disease or mental defect was recognized by law. In Roman law the insane person, being held to lack free will and hence incapable of voluntary action, was regarded as being unable to assume civil rights and responsibilities, and was therefore stripped of both. His person and his property were usually placed under the control of a guardian, or curator. The law, however, suspended the condition of guardianship during lucid intervals of persons believed to suffer only intermittent attacks of insanity.

During the middle ages the legal interest in the insane person was confined mainly to the disposition of his property. In England the lands and estates of idiots and lunatics were annexed to the crown through the law of the king's prerogative, which was in force before the time of Edward II, though a specific statute establishing that rule (*De Prerogativa Regis*) was first enacted in the latter's reign (1307–1321). Little or no legal consideration was given to insane persons possessing no estates. In certain regions of medieval Europe, insanity was expressly barred as a defense in criminal trials. For example, at the Council of Worms held in the year 868 a synodal resolution declared that penance should be imposed on every insane offender, on the ground that his very disease was a product of his sins.[3] Incidentally, this tendency to regard mental disease as a manifestation or result of sin persisted in Germany well into the nineteenth century.

Seldom was the insane person given special consideration in criminal cases. Perhaps the most striking example of the

---

full and change of the moon, especially about the equinoxes and summer solstice, are usually at the height of their distemper." *History of the Pleas of the Crown.* v. 1, p. 30. (1st American ed., Phila., 1847.)

fate of an insane offender is afforded by the case of Robert François Damiens, who suffered in the year 1750 what was perhaps the most barbaric execution meted out to any man in modern times. Damiens, a palpably insane man who mixed various fanciful delusions with real complaints, pricked Louis XV of France slightly with a pen-knife as the king was leaving his palace. It was his hope, he later explained, to "warn" the king to mend his oppressive ways. Damiens offered no resistance to seizure and made no attempt to escape. He was immediately accused of attempting to assassinate the king. After suggestions had been solicited from all parts of France as to the most fitting mode of executing the poor demented wretch, the following refined procedure was adopted: the flesh of Damiens was torn with red-hot pincers; boiling oil and molten lead were poured into his wounds; the hand that wielded the pen-knife was burned off with lighted sulphur; his tongue was torn out at the root; and finally he was drawn and quartered. When four powerful horses pulling in opposite directions failed to rend the quivering body of the still-conscious victim after an hour of tugging, a merciful executioner ended the agony by cutting the body in quarters with a knife. This spectacle was witnessed and enjoyed by many of the Court ladies. One or two expressed sympathy—for the struggling horses. Such was the fate of one offender; such was the mercy meted out to him because of his insanity.

In English common law, insanity began to be recognized as a defense in criminal cases in the early fourteenth century, although it did not save the offender's property from being forfeited to the crown even when the defendant was found insane. It was then the practice not to acquit an accused person on the ground of insanity but to render, together with a verdict of guilty, a special verdict of insanity, which was invariably followed by the king's pardon.

Beginning with the seventeenth century a succession of jurists and legal commentators took turns at devising "tests" for determining the kind and degree of insanity that excuses a person from criminal responsibility. Coke used *non compos mentis* as a generic term synonymous with insanity, stating that *"Non compos mentis* is of four sorts: 1st. Idiota, which from his nativity, by a perpetual infirmity is *non compos mentis.* 2nd. He that by sickness, grief, or other accident wholly loseth his memory and understanding. 3rd. A lunatic, that hath sometimes his understanding and sometimes not *aliquando gaudet lucidis intervallis;* and therefore he is called *non compos mentis* so long as he hath no understanding. 4th. He that by his own vicious act, for a time depriveth himself of his memory and understanding, as he that is drunken."[4] Elsewhere he wrote: "Of a lunatic, all acts which he doth during his lunacy are equivalent to acts done by an ideot, or he who is utterly *non compos mentis:* but acts done by him *inter lucida intervalla,* when he is of sound memory, shall bind him." This theory of "lucid intervals," utterly discredited by the findings of modern psychiatry, was long recognized in law as valid and caused much confusion in subsequent criminal trials involving insanity. Coke, it should be noted, did not himself subscribe to any particular test of insanity, as did later jurists and commentators, but held that the general requirement for responsibility in criminal cases was "guilty intent" on the part of the accused, and that a person of unsound mind could have no such intent.

Sir Matthew Hale, about 1680, attempted a clarification of the subject of insanity in relation to criminal law, but only succeeded in creating still greater confusion for those who followed him. Hale made a distinction between "total" and "partial" insanity, and described the latter type in these terms: "Some persons that have a competent use of reason in respect to some subjects, are yet under a particular dementia in respect to some particular discourses, subjects or applications; or else it is partial in respect of degrees." This partial insanity, he continued, "seems not to excuse them in the committing of any offence for its matter capital."[5]

Although Hale warned against the practice of accepting any single "test" for determining responsibility, he himself suggested a "best measure for total insanity" which should exempt an accused person from punishment. According to his test, "such a person as labouring under melancholy distempers hath yet ordinarily as great understanding, as ordinarily a child of fourteen years hath, is such a person as may be guilty of treason, or felony."* In this fourteen-year-old-child test for determining mental responsibility, we have an interesting precursor of the modern mental-age test idea. Hale's test was widely used in English criminal cases for many years after his time.

The next great writer on the subject of insanity and the criminal law was Hawkins, who formulated the "good and evil" test in these words:

> Those who are under a natural disability of distinguishing between good and evil, as infants under the age of discretion, ideots and lunaticks, are not punishable by any criminal prosecution whatever.

In 1724, Judge Tracy laid down what was subsequently known as the "wild beast" test. In his charge to the jury in the case of Arnold, tried for shooting Lord Onslow, Judge Tracy attempted to define the kind of mental unsoundness that excuses from criminal responsibility, as follows:

> If a man be deprived of his reason, and consequently of his intention, he cannot be guilty . . . It is not every kind of frantic humor or something unaccountable in a man's actions, that points him out to be such a madman as is to be exempted from punishment; it must be a man that is totally deprived of his understanding and memory, and doth not know what he is doing, no more than an infant, than a brute, or a *wild beast;* such a one is never the object of punishment.

Surely one of the strangest cases involving the plea of insanity was that of Lord Ferrers, tried in 1750 before his peers—the House of Lords in august assembly. Arraigned on a charge of murdering his steward, Lord Ferrers pleaded insanity as a defense. In accordance with the old English common law, he was permitted no counsel, but was obliged to plead his own case before the jury. He argued his case with marked talent—so skillfully, in fact, that the jury was

---

*In his *History of the Criminal Law of England* (London, 1883), Sir James FitzJames Stephen aptly observed, in criticising this test: "Surely no two states of mind can be more unlike than that of a healthy boy of fourteen and that of a 'man labouring under melancholy distempers.' The one is healthy immaturity, the other diseased maturity, and between them there is no sort of resemblance." (v. 2, pp. 150–51.)

INSANITY AND THE CRIMINAL LAW

convinced that so intelligent a man could not possibly have been insane, and they sent him to his execution.

The case of Hadfield in 1800 ushered in a new concept of criminal responsibility, namely, the presence of delusion as a decisive "test." Hadfield, who was tried for shooting at George III, suffered under the delusion that he was fated to sacrifice himself for the salvation of the world, like Christ, and chose this dramatic method of achieving martyrdom. He was defended by Lord Erskine, one of the greatest criminal lawyers in history. With consummate eloquence and skill, Erskine shattered the hitherto unquestioned authority of Coke and Hale, both of whom had insisted that "total insanity" was essential to excuse from responsibility. There were extreme cases, Erskine admitted, in which "the human mind is stormed in its citadel, and laid prostrate under the stroke of frenzy." But such cases were very rare, he claimed. "In other cases, reason is not driven from her seat, but distraction sits down upon it along with her, holds her, trembling upon it, and frightens her from her propriety." There were often cases of delusion, he continued, where imagination holds the most uncontrollable dominion over reality and fact, and these are the cases which frequently mock the wisdom of the wisest in judicial trials, "because such persons often reason with a subtlety which puts in the shade the ordinary conceptions of mankind; their conclusions are just, and frequently profound; but the premises from which they reason, when within the range of the malady, are uniformly false . . . Delusion, therefore, where there is no frenzy or raving madness, is the true character of insanity."[6]

Erskine's eloquent defense resulted in a favorable verdict, with the judge charging the jury to find the defendant mentally irresponsible. We have no means of knowing how much this course was influenced by the real conviction that "delusion" was a better test than "good and evil" and how much was attributable to Erskine's irresistible rhetoric, but his "delusion" test was thereafter adopted far and wide as a precedent.*

*For example, in a very similar case occurring in the United States in 1835, that of Lawrence for shooting at President Andrew Jackson, the jury

Although Erskine did a good turn in destroying the "total insanity" measure of Coke and Hale, he nevertheless fell into the same error of advancing a single symptom of mental disorder, in this case "delusion," as a final and perfect test of criminal irresponsibility. In effect, Erskine raised to a new level of dignity the "partial" insanity scorned by earlier commentators as insufficient to excuse, and upheld it as the only true test. Based on the theory that a person may be insane on one subject or in one direction, and perfectly sane on all others, this test presaged the rise of the "monomania" concept which enjoyed wide credence during the nineteenth century.

In the Bellingham Case, tried in 1812, the presiding judge revived the "good and evil" test, swept aside in Hadfield's Case, as the sole test of responsibility. A notable feature of this case is the despatch with which it was disposed of. Bellingham, a decided paranoiac, killed a man on May 11, 1812. He was tried on the 15th and executed on the 18th—all within one week.

The most important trial in the history of legal tests was M'Naghten's Case, held in 1843. Daniel M'Naghten, a paranoiac laboring under the delusion that he was being hounded by his enemies, killed the secretary of Prime Minister Sir Robert Peel, in the mistaken belief that the victim was Peel himself. Mental unsoundness was introduced as a defense, and the evidence plainly indicated a highly systematized train of delusions of persecution. M'Naghten was acquitted by the jury on the ground of insanity. The verdict proved highly unpopular. Such a stir was created that the House of Lords called the fifteen judges of England before it to answer a series of five questions on insanity in relation to irresponsibility, in an effort to clarify the subject for all time.

Instead of the expected clarification, however, the answers of the fifteen judges tended only to pile further confusion on the already chaotic structure of the criminal law.

was advised by the judge to base their verdict on the principles laid down in Hadfield's Case. (*Niles' Weekly Register,* 1835. v. 48, pp. 119–125.) Lawrence was acquitted.

INSANITY AND THE CRIMINAL LAW

The high point in the Answers of the Judges is contained in the following passage:

> The jury ought to be told in all cases that every man is to be presumed to be sane, and to possess a sufficient degree of reason to be responsible for his crimes, until the contrary be proved to their satisfaction; and that, to establish a defence on the ground of insanity, it must be clearly proved that, at the time of committing the act, the party accused was labouring under such a defect of reason, from disease of the mind, as not to know the nature and quality of the act he was doing, or if he did know it that he did not know he was doing what was wrong.[7]

The "nature-and-quality" and "right-and-wrong" tests thus laid down have served as the rule in all subsequent cases involving criminal responsibility in England, and have been generally accepted throughout the United States; not without protest and dissatisfaction, however. With mounting intensity, criticism after criticism has been leveled at the rule laid down in M'Naghten's Case. As Sheldon Glueck points out (*Encyclopedia of Social Sciences*, v. 8, p. 65): "Almost every phrase in this classic judicial utterance has been subjected to criticism from both the legal and psychiatric points of view." Elsewhere, Professor Glueck has succinctly summarized some of these criticisms. From the angle of legal interpretation alone, he states, "this fountainhead of the modern right-and-wrong or knowledge tests has created more problems than it has solved. One or more elements of the originally vague and questionable answers of the judges have been seized upon by different courts at various stages and emphasized out of their setting. . . . Some decisions today speak of knowledge of right and wrong in general, some of right and wrong as to the particular act involved, many employing these concepts interchangeably and indifferently. Some states have adopted the right-and-wrong test from the point of view of knowledge of moral wrong; some from that of knowledge of legal wrong; some include both. Some cite the nature-and-quality elements in the test disjunctively with the right-and-wrong feature, some conjunctively. Many decisions jumble all these elements together, throwing in other scraps of expert and inexpert opinion and dictum for good measure. . . ." ("Psychiatry and the Criminal Law." *Mental Hygiene*, 1928. v. 12, p. 575.)

From the point of view of psychology and psychiatry, Professor Glueck declares:

> It is evident that the knowledge tests unscientifically abstract out of the mental make-up but one phase or element of mental life, the cognitive, which, in this era of dynamic psychology, is beginning to be regarded as not the most important factor in conduct and its disorders. In brief, these tests proceed upon the following questionable assumptions of an outworn era in psychiatry: (1) that lack of knowledge of the "nature or quality" of an act (assuming the meaning of such terms to be clear), or incapacity to know right from wrong, is the sole or even the most important symptom of mental disorder; (2) that such knowledge is the sole instigator and guide of conduct, or at least the most important element therein, and consequently should be the sole criterion of responsibility when insanity is involved; and (3) that the capacity of knowing right from wrong can be completely intact and functioning perfectly even though a defendant is otherwise demonstrably of disordered mind. (*Ibid.*, p. 580.)

However cogent and valid the criticisms of the rule laid down in M'Naghten's Case may be, the fact remains that the law pertaining to criminal responsibility in the United States rests mainly on this rule. We may sum up the present status of the tests of criminal responsibility in this country as follows:

1. The right-and-wrong test is the *sole* criterion of criminal responsibility in 29 states of the Union, as it is in England.* In 17 additional states it is one of the rules followed. This test is variously phrased. In many states, the rule specifies that a person is excused from responsibility if, at the time of committing the act, he was laboring under such a defect of reason as not to know the "nature and quality" or the "nature and consequences" of the act he was doing, or that he was doing "wrong."

*These states are: Arizona, California, Florida, Georgia, Idaho, Iowa, Kansas, Maine, Maryland, Minnesota, Mississippi, Missouri, Nebraska, Nevada, New Jersey, New York, North Carolina, North Dakota, Oklahoma, Oregon, Pennsylvania, South Carolina, South Dakota, Tennessee, Texas, Utah, Washington, West Virginia and Wisconsin.

2. The "irresistible-impulse" test, embodying the idea that the accused person had not sufficient will power to resist the impulse to commit the act, by reason of mental unsoundness, is a rule recognized in seventeen states of the Union and in the District of Columbia, together with the right-and-wrong test.* In these jurisdictions, as Weihofen points out, "a person is excused if he is incapable of knowing the wrongfulness of the act, or, even if he does know that it is wrong, if he is incapable of controlling the impulse to commit it."[8]

The latter rule, though imperfect, is a decided improvement over that laid down in M'Naghten's Case, since it recognizes the conative as well as the cognitive mental processes.

In New Hampshire, both of the aforementioned tests have been rejected by the court. The rule followed in this state is that "there is no legal test of irresponsibility by reason of insanity. It is a question of fact for the jury in each case whether defendant had a mental disease, and if so, whether it was of such character or degree as to take away the capacity to form or entertain a criminal intent."†

In the remaining state, Rhode Island, the question of the legal test has never been passed upon.

The "irresistible-impulse" test originated in America. The earliest recorded case in which the test was laid down was tried in Ohio in 1834 (*State v. Thompson*). In this case Judge Wright instructed the jury that if the defendant "at the time could discriminate between right and wrong, and

---

*The states in which the irresistible-impulse test is employed as a rule are: Alabama, Arkansas, Colorado, Connecticut, Delaware, Illinois, Indiana, Kentucky, Louisiana, Massachusetts, Michigan, Montana, New Mexico, Ohio, Vermont, Virginia and Wyoming.

†The New Hampshire rule, first established by Judge Doe in 1866, was best formulated by Judge Ladd in the famous case of *State v. Jones* in 1871, in which it was stated:

"At the trial where insanity is set up as a defence, two questions are presented—First: Had the prisoner a mental disease? Second: If he had, was the disease of such a character, or was it so far developed, or had it so far subjugated the powers of the mind, as to take away the *capacity to form or entertain a criminal intent?* Now, the entertaining of a criminal intent includes the volitional capacity; if this is pathological, the criminal intent is incomplete."

was conscious of the wrongfulness of the act, *and had power to forbear or to do the act,* he was responsible."

In addition to the aforementioned tests of responsibility, some states accept the "mistake-of-fact" test. According to this rule, an accused person suffering from insane delusions must be judged by the supposed facts presented by the delusion. This rule, first suggested by Erskine in Hadfield's Case was enunciated by the fifteen judges in M'Naghten's Case in answer to Question Four propounded by the House of Lords. It was asked of them, "If a person under an insane delusion as to existing facts commits an offence in consequence thereof, is he thereby excused?" To which the learned judges gave answer:

> The answer must of course depend on the nature of the delusion: but, making the same assumption as we did before, namely, that he labours under such partial delusion only, and is not in other respects insane, we think he must be considered in the same situation as to responsibility as if the facts with respect to which the delusion exists were real. For example, if under the influence of his delusions he supposes another man to be in the act of attempting to take away his life, and he kills that man, as he supposes in self-defence, he would be exempt from punishment. If his delusion was that the deceased had inflicted a serious injury on his character and fortune, and he killed him in revenge for such supposed injury, he would be liable to punishment.[9]

The main fallacy in the rule thus laid down arises from the arbitrary insertion by the judges of an assumption that did not appear in the original questions, namely, "that he labours under such partial delusion only, and is not in other respects insane." Such a condition of mind that this statement presupposes does not exist, nor has it ever existed. As Mercier remarks, "There is not, and never has been, a person who labours under partial delusion only, and is not in other respects insane."*

---

*Dr. Isaac Ray, one of the "Original Thirteen," offered a brilliant criticism of this answer of the judges from still another angle. "This (Answer IV) is certainly very plain," he wrote, "and it must be reasonable, too, *if insane men would but listen to reason!* . . . This is virtually saying to a man, 'You are allowed to be insane; the disease is a visitation of Providence, and you cannot help it; but have a care how you manifest your insanity; there must

INSANITY AND THE CRIMINAL LAW

In no jurisdiction in the United States is mental disease or mental defect considered in itself sufficient grounds for excusing a person from criminal responsibility. The New York State Law declares, in this respect (Section 1120 of the State Penal Law):

> A person is not excused from criminal liability as an idiot, imbecile, lunatic or insane person, except upon proof that, at the time of committing the alleged criminal act, he was laboring under such a defect of reason as:
> 1. Not to know the nature and quality of the act he was doing; or
> 2. Not to know that the act was wrong.

Quite as confusing as the legal tests are the modes of procedure governing trials that involve the plea of insanity. Oppenheimer[10] has drawn up the following summary of the basic principles on which such trials rest:

> 1. Everybody is presumed to be sane.
> 2. Everybody, even one proved to be insane, is presumed to be responsible; in other words, even the raving lunatic is presumed to come up to the law's standard of responsibility, i.e., to distinguish right from wrong.

A prisoner who sets up the plea of insanity has to prove:

> 1. That he is of unsound mind. Having satisfactorily established this, he must show further
> 2. That he fulfills that condition under which alone the law excuses a madman who has done an act otherwise criminal.

The observation made by Dr. Isaac Ray many years ago to the effect that the law respecting mental responsibility lags hopelessly behind the development of scientific knowledge regarding mental disorder is still applicable today. Bound

be method in your madness. Having once adopted your delusion, all the subsequent steps connected with it must be conformed to the strictest requirements of reason and propriety. If you are caught tripping in your logic; if in the disturbance of your moral and intellectual perceptions you take a step for which a sane man would be punished, insanity would be no bar to your punishment. In short, having become fairly enveloped in the clouds of mental disorder, the law expects you will move as discreetly and circumspectly as if the undimmed light of reason were shining upon your path." (Ray's *Medical Jurisprudence of Insanity*. Boston, 1860. 4th ed., pp. 46–47.)

securely by the shackles of archaic traditions, the law gives little heed to the advances made in the study of mental phenomena in normal and abnormal manifestations. The actual question in cases involving mental responsibility, it would seem, is how far the various elements of that responsibility have been affected by the presence of disease. To answer it correctly there is implied not only some knowledge of the constitution of the mind in its normal condition, but also a thorough knowledge of its manifestations under the influence of disease. Here lies a fundamental error of the courts, in supposing that the question of responsibility may be determined without the aid of scientific research and observation. It further presumes, as Dr. Ray has pointed out, "that men who, never in their lives perhaps, observed very closely a single case of insanity; who know nothing of its various forms, nor of the laws which govern their origin and progress, are qualified to lay down general principles touching the measure of responsibility which is left after reason has been driven from her throne, or reduced to share a divided empire with the caprices and impulses of disease."[11]

Psychiatric Expert Testimony. A great deal of the criticism of the criminal law in its relation to insanity has been directed toward the present methods of utilizing psychiatric testimony in court trials. In the popular mind, the procedure of expert testimony has become identified with the spectacle of three dignified gentlemen solemnly testifying that the defendant in a criminal case is insane and irresponsible, only to be followed by three equally solemn gentlemen testifying that the defendant is sane and responsible. Thus the witnesses tend to cancel one another, and it is quite probable that members of the jury often throw out the expert testimony of both sides and rely wholly on their own judgment in framing their verdict. The practice of placing medical men in the position of paid partisans in a "battle of experts," open to the stigma of bias to the side paying the fee, has tended to cast serious discredit on their testimony in insanity trials, and to bring the ridicule of the public on the heads of psychiatrists. While it is true that the major blame for this situation rests upon the current rules of criminal practice, and while it is equally true that psychiatrists have been incessantly criticising those rules, it must be admitted that the latter are not wholly free from blame, since they permit themselves to become parties to this procedure.

The Hypothetical Question. A major target of criticism by medico-legal authorities is the use of the "hypothetical question" in expert testimony. In accordance with the rules of the game, the expert is called upon, not to testify directly as to the mental condition of the defendant as it appears to him, but to answer a series of hypothetical questions based on facts *assumed* to be proved by the defense or prosecution, as the case may be. The expert witness may have made no personal observation of the defendant, or he may even doubt the truth of the assumed facts involved in the evidence, but his testimony is valid so long as his answers are based on the *assumption* that these assumed facts *are* true.* It is the universal opinion of psychiatric authorities that the hypothetical question in court trials should be abolished, and that the expert be permitted to testify directly on the condition of the defendant. The employment of the hypothetical question has been clearly shown to be wrong in theory and ineffective in practice.

Another serious objection raised by psychiatrists to the procedure generally followed in criminal trials is that the question of insanity is usually left to the judgment of a lay jury. It is argued that a group of twelve laymen can scarcely be expected to pass accurate judgment on the complex and highly technical problems involved in the relationship be-

*Commenting on the absurd situation created when the psychiatric expert is forced to testify on "a hypothetical monstrosity created by the method of legal procedure," Dr. White points out that while the witness formally answers the hypothetical question, "his answer refers to the defendant, it is his opinion of the defendant from all he has been able to learn of him; and what is more everybody knows that his opinion refers to the defendant and so the whole complex, illogical, unreasonable, artificial structure that has been so carefully reared through days perhaps of the examination and cross-examination of witnesses, through the intricacies of innumerable objections, arguments, and exceptions, all based upon years of tradition built up of decisions—this whole complex structure comes tumbling down like a house of cards with the utterance of a single word." (W. A. White. *Insanity and the Criminal Law.* New York, 1923. 281 pp., p. 87.)

tween mental disorder and irresponsibility. Even the court itself, with its lack of special psychiatric knowledge, is hardly capable of deciding justly on this question without expert aid.

An instance frequently cited as indicating the futility of placing the determination of insanity in the hands of twelve laymen, however good and true they may be, is the notorious Remus case tried in Cincinnati in 1927. Remus, a millionaire bootlegger on trial for murdering his wife, conducted his own defense. He dug up for himself a bizarre type of mental disease, "transitory maniacal insanity." The only psychiatric experts testifying at the trial declared that the defendant was sane, and had been sane at the time of the killing. But Remus delivered a tearful, sentimental summation in his own behalf; pictured himself as a worn, long-suffering victim; ended by wishing the jury a merry Christmas; and won acquittal on the ground of insanity. He was thereupon committed to a mental hospital, but gained his freedom a few months later through a writ of *habeas corpus*. A member of the jury is reported to have explained the verdict in this wise: "He [Remus] did not have any Christmas last year, and we wanted to see him have one this year."

Limited Responsibility and Mitigation of Punishment. At times cases occur where the mental unsoundness of the defendant does not come within the legal tests of irresponsibility, but where a plea for mitigation of punishment (or of the offense) is entered on the ground of "limited responsibility." It is argued that there is a class of "semi-insane" or "semi-responsible" offenders who, while their mental disorder does not entirely exculpate them, should not be made to suffer the same penalties imposed on sane persons.

The courts of several states recognize the rule that punishment should be reduced when the defendant is mentally disordered, though he may be capable of understanding the quality and nature, or wrongfulness of his act, or of controlling his impulse to commit it. However, it has not been accepted as law in any state in the Union, except possibly Nebraska. There, feeblemindedness and mental disease have been held to afford grounds for mitigating punishment under a statute giving the Supreme Court power to reduce a sentence which it deems excessive.

In certain cases where the mental disorder of a defendant is not deemed sufficient to excuse him from responsibility, the accused may plead guilty and throw himself upon the mercy of the court with the plea that his mental condition be taken into account as a circumstance in mitigation of punishment. The best known case of this kind was the Leopold-Loeb hearing held in Chicago in 1925. The two youngsters, Leopold and Loeb, defended by the astute criminal lawyer, Clarence Darrow, pleaded guilty to the slaying of little Bobby Franks, but asked for mitigation of punishment on the ground of mental disorder. After a hearing in which eight of the most prominent psychiatrists in America testified, the plea for mitigation was granted, and the defendants received terms of life imprisonment instead of being sentenced to death. This hearing, which found some of the most eminent psychiatric authorities arrayed against one another, in sharp disagreement on diagnosis and general principles, served more than any other case, perhaps, to bring popular discredit upon the practice of psychiatric expert testimony. Unfortunately, the fact that the experts for the defense, and several of those for the prosecution, tried unsuccessfully to place the proceedings on a dignified plane by urging common consultations between the experts on both sides, failed to get the public notice it deserved.

Mental Examination of Defendants. Procedure relating to the mental examination of defendants pleading insanity varies widely throughout the United States. A number of states have laws providing for the appointment of experts (not exceeding three) by a trial court to examine the defendant when the question of mental responsibility is at issue, and to testify on their findings during the trial. In most instances, the appointment of such experts is discretionary with the court. In California and Indiana, however, this step is made mandatory in all cases where insanity is pleaded as a defense.

In Louisiana, when the plea of insanity is made, the trial judge notifies the parish coroner and the superintendents of the two state hospitals, who constitute a Commission of Lunacy. If they find the defendant insane, proceedings against him are dropped, and he is forthwith committed to the "criminal ward" of a hospital for mental diseases. If the commission finds the defendant sane, a judicial hearing is held on the issue, either before a court without a jury (in misdemeanor cases), or with a jury of five (felony cases) or twelve (capital cases). Should he again be found sane in this hearing, the defendant may then be tried upon the plea of not guilty.

In Maryland and California the issue of insanity is also tried separately. This issue is usually tried *before* the trial on other issues, but in California it is decided in a separate trial *after* the other issues.

In a number of states, the law provides for the appointment of a physician, or of a commission composed of physicians, or of physicians and lawyers, to examine the defendant, and to report on his mental state to the court. In most cases, the physicians called need not be specialists in mental diseases. In some states (New York, Colorado, Rhode Island, Vermont, Wisconsin) the appointment of such a commission when insanity is at issue is permissive with the court; in others (California, Indiana) it is mandatory. Usually, the commission acts only in an advisory capacity, and final judgment as to the insanity of the defendant rests with court or jury.

Several states (Colorado, Maine, Massachusetts, Ohio, Vermont, Wisconsin) have statutes providing that when criminal responsibility or "present insanity" is at issue, the court shall have the power to commit the defendant to a mental hospital for a certain period, usually not exceeding thirty days. There the hospital authorities or experts appointed by the court may examine him and report to the court on his condition. In Colorado such commitment for observation by the court is mandatory whenever the plea of insanity is set up.

In rapidly increasing numbers, courts are utilizing the services of psychiatric clinics of their own in the examination of persons accused of crime, or are availing themselves

INSANITY AND THE CRIMINAL LAW 405

of accessible clinics of a public or semi-public nature. A survey conducted by the National Crime Commission in 1927 and 1928 indicated that nearly 10 per cent of the criminal courts in this country were being served regularly by a psychiatrist employed by the court on a full-time or part-time basis, or furnished by some other public agency. In an additional 6 per cent of the courts a psychologist's services were being regularly utilized.[12] Examinations are made by such clinics which submit reports to the court, aiding the latter in understanding the personality makeup of the individual. More and more, psychiatric clinics are being regarded as indispensable adjuncts to juvenile courts and courts of domestic relations.

The best law governing the procedure for determining the mental responsibility of defendants now in effect in the United States is the "Briggs Law" of Massachusetts. This statute, named after Dr. L. Vernon Briggs, a psychiatrist who framed the bill and fought for its passage, was enacted in 1921. The Briggs Law provides that any person indicted for a capital offense, or any person indicted or bound over to the Superior Court who is known to have been indicted for any other offense more than once, or to have been previously convicted of a felony, shall be reported to the Massachusetts Department of Mental Diseases for examination, "to determine his mental condition and the existence of any mental disease or defect which would affect his criminal responsibility." Two psychiatrists are assigned by the Department of Mental Diseases, and are paid a nominal fee for their services. Their report is filed with the clerk of the court in which the trial is to be held, and is made accessible to the court, the probation officer thereof, the district attorney, and to the attorney for the accused.

The significant features of the Briggs Law are: (1) the examination is conducted by neutral, impartial experts; (2) these experts are selected by a professional department of the administrative branch of government, namely, the State Department of Mental Diseases; (3) the examination is applicable to *all* defendants falling within certain clearly-defined legal categories, and is not dependent upon the supposed "recognition" of mental disease by the judge, defense attorney, or some other non-psychiatric participant in the proceedings; (4) the examination is made, and the psychiatric report is submitted, before trial.

The report of the examining psychiatrists is not admissible as evidence. Its only purpose is to inform the court and counsel as to the defendant's mental condition and as to the advisability of trying him on criminal charges. The report usually serves as a decisive factor, since it is generally regarded by all parties as a fair, competent and impartial study. While the Briggs Law does not abrogate the right of either prosecution or defense to introduce other experts, this right is rarely exercised, and the report of the psychiatrists attached to the Department of Mental Diseases is usually accepted as final by all concerned.

The advantages of the Briggs Law has been summarized as follows by Dr. Winfred Overholser, former Commissioner of the Massachusetts Department of Mental Diseases:

> By providing an impartial and competent mental examination of certain legal classes of persons accused of crime in advance of trial, it has furnished to court, prosecution and defense information as to the defendant's condition, and by so doing has avoided the expense of numerous costly trials; it has reduced to a negligible number the "battles of experts" which have in the past brought discredit upon psychiatric expert testimony; it has protected the rights of the psychotic or otherwise mentally incompetent accused who might without it have gone unrecognized; it has served in numerous cases to indicate a disposition which was more desirable socially and more in accord with justice and fairness to the defendant than would ordinarily have been meted out; finally, it has aided in the process of educating judges, prosecutors, and the bar generally to a realization of the value of psychiatry as an aid to the individualization of justice.[13]

Though it is the most practical and efficient statute of its kind in operation in this country, the Briggs Law is not without its minor weaknesses. Perhaps the most pronounced of these is the fact that the law applies only to certain types of offenders, namely: (1) those indicted for a capital offense; (2) those who have been indicted more than once for an offense; and (3) those who have been previously convicted of a felony. The law would certainly have far greater effectiveness were it liberalized in scope to include a wider range of offenders. Why not, indeed, make a routine, impartial psychiatric examination before trial for *all* offenders before the law? The advantages of such a procedure in the prevention and lessening of crime and the rehabilitation of offenders are obvious.

"Present Insanity" and the Law. We have thus far considered the relation between the law and insanity at the time an offense is committed. Other important aspects of insanity in relation to the criminal law deal with the question of "present insanity," that is, insanity before or at the time of indictment or trial or after sentence is pronounced, or before execution. For centuries the common law has held that no person known to be insane can be indicted, tried, sentenced or executed. In Blackstone's words:

> If a man in his sound memory commits a capital offense, and, before arraignment for it, he becomes mad, he ought not to be arraigned for it; because he is not able to plead to it with that advice and caution that he ought. And if, after he has pleaded, the prisoner becomes mad, he shall not be tried: for how can he make his defense? If, after he be tried and found guilty, he loses his senses before judgment, judgment shall not be pronounced; and if, after judgment, he becomes of nonsane memory, execution shall be stayed.[14]

The tests for determining "present insanity" are quite different in character and purpose from those governing the determination of insanity and irresponsibility at the time the act was committed. The kind and degree of mental unsoundness deemed sufficient to prevent the indictment, trial, sentence or execution of a person has been stated thus by Weihofen: "Has the defendant capacity to understand the nature and object of the proceedings against him, to comprehend his own condition in reference to such proceedings, and to make a rational defense?"

The procedures employed in the several states of the Union for determining present insanity fall into four major categories: (1) the means of inquiry are left to the discretion of the court; (2) lunacy proceedings in chancery must be instituted; (3) a jury is held to render judgment of insanity; (4) inquiry is made by two or more qualified physicians, or by a commission of physicians and lawyers.

If found insane while awaiting arraignment, or before or during trial, the accused person is usually remanded to jail or committed to a hospital for mental diseases until such time as he recovers, when the proceedings against him are continued. If the defendant becomes insane after conviction, judgment cannot be rendered or sentence pronounced so long as he remains in that condition. If he becomes insane after sentence of death has been pronounced, execution is stayed until he recovers. If recovery ensues, he is liable to the punishment to which he has been sentenced, unless he be pardoned or his sentence commuted in the interim.

It seems to have been a practice, in the early days of the Republic, to pardon persons who became insane after sentence of death was passed upon them. Thus, Benjamin Rush tells us of an individual condemned to die for treason in 1794 against the Federal government in western Pennsylvania. President Washington appointed Rush and two other physicians to constitute a commission to investigate the man's mental condition. Although his two fellows were inclined to dismiss the case as one of feigned insanity, Rush insisted that the person was really insane and held up as "indisputable" proof the fact that the man's pulse was twenty strokes per minute above normal. Rush's opinion prevailed, the commission rendered a verdict of insanity, and the man was pardoned by the President.[15]

Another early instance of a pardon granted because of insanity occurred in 1800 when the New York legislature, by special act, pardoned one John Pastano who had been sentenced to death for murdering a woman, on the condition that he be deported to Madeira, where his relatives resided.[16] This case affords an interesting example of the difficulties encountered in dealing with the insane in those early days, when there was a general absence of proper legislation relating to this subject. The governor of New York being at that time powerless to grant pardons in such cases, and

INSANITY AND THE CRIMINAL LAW

there being no suitable institutions in the state within which insane convicts could be confined, the legislature was the only tribunal to which an appeal could be taken for clemency, and a special act had to be passed for that purpose.

Disposition of the Criminal Insane. The proper disposition of persons acquitted on grounds of mental irresponsibility has ever afforded a problem of great complexity, and remains without satisfactory solution to this day. We have described, in an earlier chapter, two incidents illustrating the haphazard methods adopted by the colonial fathers in disposing of the criminal insane. In the year 1674 a case was decided at Flushing in New York province wherein the defendant was charged with "running amok, breaking down doors, setting fire to houses, beating women and children" and sundry other offenses. The defendant was acquitted, "not being in his right reason." But the court's disposition of the defendant merits remark: he was ordered banished from Flushing to nearby Staten Island, there to be put to work by order of the local magistrate, who was "hereby empowered, if the defendant *behave badly,* to *punish* him according as he may deserve." It might be deduced from this decision that insanity might excuse a person's offense once, but not a second time. Then there was the case of Roger Humphry, a colonial soldier of Simsbury, Connecticut, who in 1757 murdered his mother in a paroxysm of mania. Humphry was acquitted by reason of insanity, but the court ordered him confined for life in a "small place" to be erected by his father. The expense of building this home-made prison and maintaining its solitary inmate was to be borne by the colonial treasury. (*Public Records of the Colony of Connecticut.* v. 11, p. 313.)

The confusion regarding the disposition of this class of mentally ill persons has by no means been cleared away in our time. The laws of the various states on this subject reveal great disparities.

It may be well, before we proceed further, to distinguish between the "criminal insane" and "insane criminals." The criminal insane are those whose anti-social acts or tendencies are directly attributable to their mental disorder. This class includes accused persons who are acquitted by reason of insanity. The insane criminals, on the other hand, are criminals whose mental disorder is only incidental. This class includes convicts who become insane while serving terms in prison. A third group, the "dangerous insane"—that is, mentally ill persons who are not known to have committed an offense but are believed to be potential criminals—are often included among the criminal insane. Of course, there is no sharp dividing line between the two major classes. Often enough, the terms criminal insane and insane criminals are used indiscriminately as if they were identical. At times, even where the distinction is recognized, as in the state of New York, a man who is criminally insane is treated like an insane criminal because his mental disorder, which may have existed over a long period of years, is discovered only after he has been convicted of a crime and is already serving a sentence in prison.*

With the exception of four states (Georgia, Tennessee, Texas and Wyoming), all states have statutory provisions for the commitment, as insane persons, of defendants acquitted on the plea of mental irresponsibility. The manner of disposing of such cases falls mainly under the following categories:

1. The court upon acquittal, automatically orders the defendant committed to a mental hospital without enquiring further as to his present mental condition. This procedure is followed in Kansas, Minnesota, Nebraska, Nevada, Ohio, Oklahoma and Wisconsin. In Massachusetts the procedure is employed only in murder and manslaughter cases.

2. The court, upon presentation of a verdict of not guilty by reason of insanity, exercises permissive power to order commitment to a mental hospital or other suitable institution. This is the rule in Arkansas, Connecticut, Delaware, Maine, New Mexico, Pennsylvania and South Carolina.

*Dr. Rudolph Schwarz of the Dannemora State Hospital presents a number of cases wherein the insanity of an accused person was overlooked by the trial court and was recognized only after he began serving a prison sentence, hence being treated as an insane criminal instead of a criminally insane person, as he should have been considered. (See Dr. Schwarz's article, "The Criminal Insane under Jurisdiction," in *Mental Hygiene*, 1934. v. 18, pp. 452–461.)

INSANITY AND THE CRIMINAL LAW 411

3. The court may order such commitment if, after investigation, it is satisfied that the defendant is still insane. (Alabama, Indiana, Kentucky, Michigan, New Jersey, North Carolina.)

4. The court may order such commitment if it deems the defendant's discharge dangerous to the public peace or safety. (Florida, Iowa, New Hampshire, New York, North Dakota, Oregon, South Dakota, Vermont, Virginia, West Virginia.) In Massachusetts this rule holds in other than murder and manslaughter cases.

5. The governor, or other official, may order such commitment upon certification of insanity by the court. In the District of Columbia, commitment may be ordered by the United States Secretary of the Interior upon such certification. In Rhode Island the governor is given power to perform this function.

6. A second jury trial is required to determine whether a defendant acquitted by reason of insanity at the time of the offense is still insane. (Arizona, Idaho, Montana, Utah.)

7. In those states where the jury decides not only the question of irresponsibility at the time the act was done, but the present mental condition of the defendant, the court is required to order commitment if the jury finds that the defendant was, and continues to be, insane. (Illinois, Maryland, Mississippi, Washington. In Missouri, the court *may* order commitment after such verdict is rendered by the jury.)

Place of Confinement. During colonial times, as we have previously noted, insane offenders against the law were usually disposed of in the same manner as sane criminals, being mutilated, whipped, imprisoned or executed, as the case might be. In the few instances when their insanity and irresponsibility were recognized, the manner of dealing with them was characterized by loose and haphazard measures.

With the rise of state prisons after the establishment of the republic, persons acquitted on grounds of insanity were usually incarcerated with common felons when their discharge was deemed dangerous to society. Sometimes special strong-rooms were built in almshouses for their reception. These measures led to protests on the part of institutional heads and friends of the insane, who condemned the practice of treating innocent persons like common criminals by confining them in general prisons, or of treating them like common paupers by placing them in almshouses.

With the opening of the first public hospitals for the

mentally ill, several states enacted laws providing that persons acquitted by reason of insanity should forthwith be committed to such institutions. Massachusetts made this provision as soon as the Worcester State Hospital was opened in 1832, and New York in 1843 with the opening of the Utica State Asylum. In several states, including the two aforementioned, laws were passed forbidding the confinement of *any* insane persons in institutions for criminals. The state hospitals and almshouses became the only legal places of confinement for the criminal insane, although the laws were never strictly observed and this class continued to be frequently incarcerated in prisons and jails.

The commitment of the criminal insane to state hospitals on the same terms as the civil insane raised another vexing problem. Now the friends and relatives of the civil insane in state hospitals protested against the enforced association of this class with persons having criminal traits and tendencies. Added to this problem was the chronic overcrowding in public hospitals for the mentally ill, which aggravated the situation considerably.

New York State was the first to attempt a solution of the problem of properly disposing of the criminal insane and insane criminals by providing a separate institution for their custody and care. Until 1859 convicts who became insane were regularly transferred either to the Utica State Hospital or else to special wards or buildings of penal institutions. In that year the State Lunatic Asylum for Insane Convicts was opened at Auburn, on a site adjoining the Auburn State Prison. As its name implies, it was originally intended only for the reception of insane convicts, but in 1869 the institution began to receive criminally insane persons committed directly from the courts, as well as insane criminals transferred from general penal institutions. The asylum for these groups at Auburn soon became intolerably overcrowded, and in 1892 it was removed to Matteawan. The following year, its name was changed to Matteawan State Hospital.

In 1900 the Dannemora State Hospital was opened at Dannemora, New York, adjoining the site of the Clinton

INSANITY AND THE CRIMINAL LAW 413

State Prison. The organic law of this hospital limited admissions to persons declared insane while confined in a penal institution for felony. At the present time the criminal insane in New York State are committed to Matteawan, and the insane criminals to Dannemora.

Meanwhile separate institutions for the criminal insane and insane criminals were established elsewhere. Besides New York, there are now such hospitals in Illinois, Indiana, Kansas, Massachusetts, Michigan, Ohio, Pennsylvania, Wisconsin and other states. Most of these institutions receive both insane persons committed directly from the courts and those transferred from prisons. Admissions usually are drawn from the following groups:

1. The "dangerous insane," that is, mentally ill persons who have not yet committed an offense against the law, but are believed to have dangerous criminal tendencies.
2. Persons acquitted by reason of insanity.
3. Persons found to be insane while awaiting trial or judgment.
4. Insane persons previously convicted of a crime.
5. Insane convicts.[17]

Some of these institutions admit both insane misdemeanants and felons; others only the latter.

In many states, the criminal insane are segregated in hospital wards or buildings in general prisons, or in criminal wards or buildings of state hospitals. In Florida, the court may commit a defendant acquitted by reasons of insanity to jail, or to the custody of friends on condition that the latter furnish satisfactory security for his proper care. The court in New Hampshire may commit such person to prison or to the state hospital. In Vermont, he may be ordered confined in the state prison, the state hospital, "or some other suitable place." In West Virginia, the court may order him committed to jail until he can be sent to the hospital for the insane. Three states besides Florida provide for custody in the care of friends upon receipt of proper security, as an alternative to institutional commitment.

Release after Recovery. In nearly all the states, a person committed to an institution after acquittal on the grounds of mental irresponsibility may seek release upon recovery through procedure provided by statutory law, or by securing a writ of *habeas corpus*. About two-thirds of the states, in 1935, had statutory provisions governing this procedure. The question of recovery and the right to release is usually determined by one of the following agencies: (1) the superintendent of the institution where the person is confined; (2) an administrative board (Board of Commissioners of State Charities, etc.); (3) a court, ordinarily the one by which the person was committed; (4) by the concurrence of two of these agencies (e.g., the institutional superintendent and the court).

In two states, Kentucky and Washington, a jury trial is required to determine the question of recovery. In Georgia and North Carolina persons committed after acquittal by reason of insanity in capital cases can be released only by special act of legislature; in cases other than capital, a warrant or order of the governor is required. Persons acquitted of murder or manslaughter on the plea of insanity in Massachusetts can be discharged only by the governor, with the advice and consent of the council, if it appears, after investigation by the State Department of Mental Diseases, that they may be released without danger to others. It is provided in New Hampshire that when a defendant is committed to prison after acquittal by reason of insanity, he may be discharged upon recovery by the governor and council, or by the Superior Court. If committed to an asylum after such acquittal, he may be released by either the commission of lunacy or a justice of the Superior Court.

Habeas Corpus. In nearly all the states, an individual confined in an institution as an insane person has the right to have the question of his recovery determined by *habeas corpus* proceedings, under the constitutional guarantee against restraint of personal liberty without due process of law. Procedure in *habeas corpus* cases, on the issue of recovery after commitment of the criminal insane, varies widely in the several states.

Suggested Reforms. The modern psychiatrist approaching the criminal law is faced with a number of vexing problems. Some of these appear to be hopelessly insoluble under the present state of affairs. Several basic concepts of criminal practice and psychiatric theory are seemingly in irreconcilable conflict. For instance, the whole structure of the criminal law rests on the metaphysical concept of freedom of the will, while the psychiatrist in pursuing his profession ignores the doctrine of free will and thinks and acts mainly along deterministic lines.* In spite of the new *theories* of progressive criminologists, the fact remains that the criminal law as *practiced* today is still guided by the idea of punishment and deterrence. Rehabilitation and reformation of the individual offender is secondary and incidental to the main function of the law, as leading jurists frankly avow. The psychiatrist, on the other hand, sees the problem of crime not as one of punishment but of treatment; he approaches the offender as a patient, not as a prisoner; he is interested in the individual, rather than the criminal act. Dr. White aptly sums up the approach of the progressive criminologist and psychiatrist in these words:

> The principles of criminology dictate that the criminal and not the crime should be the matter of prime consideration and that the sentence, or better the decision of the court, should be calculated to cure the social illness as it has been shown to exist in the conduct of the defendant. The situation is analogous to the relation between physician and patient, only that the disease is not individual but social and the place of the physician is taken by the state. Under the operation of these principles a defendant who was only charged with a minor offense might well have to spend the rest of his life more or less restricted in his liberty if an analysis of his makeup and a study of his behavior showed that he never sufficiently improved or profited by his experience to warrant discharge as a free citizen into the community. In the same way a person who had committed a serious offense might be ultimately discharged after a comparatively brief internment. It is the same here as in the practice of medicine. All cases of pneumonia

*Dr. William Healy, in his monumental work, *The Individual Delinquent* (Boston, 1915), renders the sober opinion that "the criteria of responsibility involve so much that is intricate, uncertain, metaphysical, and are themselves properly subject to variations by reason of environmental and disease conditions, by reason of innate defects and differences in social suggestibility, that, for the purposes of general discrimination and the development of a practical standardization, they are thoroughly impracticable." (p. 20.)

are not treated alike just because the disease happens to be labeled pneumonia . . . The patient is treated and not the disease and it is as illogical to sentence a person who has committed a certain offense to a specific term of imprisonment as it would be to decide when a patient is admitted to a hospital, the day upon which he shall be discharged.[18]

This concept, of course, does not imply the complete abolition of all unpleasant forms of dealing with offenders. Disciplinary measures, such as prolonged restraint in institutions, etc., would still be necessary under the best of systems, but such measures would be imposed primarily not with the object of punishment for the individual's offense against the law, but because such measures would be deemed necessary for his own welfare or for the welfare of society.

A number of proposals for the reform of criminal procedure in line with our present-day sociological and psychiatric knowledge have been formulated by various bodies such as the American Psychiatric Association, the American Bar Association, and the American Medical Association, acting individually and collectively. Among the principal reform proposals advanced thus far are the following:*

1. That there be available in every criminal and juvenile court a psychiatric service to assist the court in the disposition of offenders.
2. That in all cases of felony or misdemeanor punishable by prison sentence the question of responsibility be not submitted to the jury. The latter will thus be called upon to determine only that the offense was committed by the defendant.
3. That the disposition and treatment (including punishment) be based on a study of the individual offender by properly qualified and impartial experts cooperating with the courts.†

*Some of these proposals were embodied in resolutions adopted in 1929 by the American Bar Association; others have been recommended by the American Institute of Criminal Law and Criminology.

†Sheldon Glueck and others have long advocated a complete separation of the "guilt-finding" and "sentence-imposing" phases in court trials. Decisions involving treatment (i.e., sentence) should be made by a broad tribunal specially qualified in the interpretation and evaluation of psychiatric, psychological and sociological data. Each case, Glueck suggests, should be reconsidered at stated intervals. The treatment originally proposed could thus be modified from time to time in the light of scientific reports of progress. To make this system effective, two conditions are required: first, a flexible,

4. That psychiatric boards or commissions, chosen preferably from university and major hospital staffs, be permanently attached to the courts, receiving adequate annual remuneration from no private individual or corporation but from the State and the State alone.

5. That the indeterminate sentence system be extended to all types of criminal cases involving prison sentences, thus making more efficient the individualization of treatment.

6. That there be a psychiatric service available to every penal and correctional institution.

7. That there be a psychiatric report on every prisoner before he is released.

8. That there be established in each state a complete system of administrative transfer and parole, and that there be no decision for or against any parole, or transfer from one institution to another, without a psychiatric report.

One finds encouragement in the fact that psychiatric programs for the reform of the criminal law in harmony with modern scientific findings are receiving increasing attention, instead of being dismissed as wild vagaries as was formerly the case.[19] More and more states are adopting these programs in part, while increasing numbers of lawyers, judges and bar associations are adding the weight of their influence to the advancement of these modifications.

Of course, psychiatry can offer no panacea for the solution of fundamental problems in the criminal law. Truly basic solutions wait upon profound changes in the whole socio-economic structure of society. In the meantime, the progressive psychiatrist and the criminologist can join forces in carrying forward a program bringing closer to fruition the idea of the criminal court as a clinic dedicated to the scientific solution of problems of social maladjustment, replacing its present function as a blind, retributive tribunal.

indeterminate sentence, and second, a sufficient control of institutional and extramural treatment facilities by the board to guarantee the efficient carrying out of its recommendations. (See Sheldon Glueck's "Mental Hygiene and Crime." *Psychoanalytic Review*, 1932. v. 19, p. 30.)

CHAPTER XIX

Our Commitment Laws

THE plight of the perfectly sane individual "railroaded" to a "madhouse" by villainous relatives, friends, or business associates scheming to separate him from his fortune or his sweetheart, has long been a favorite theme in our melodramatic literature. According to the familiar story, the unfortunate hero finds himself "buried alive" in the "Bastille of lunatics" among "raving maniacs and gibbering idiots," pining away while he "vainly beats against the iron bars of his cage." If the romance has a sad ending, our hero winds up hopelessly "crazy," driven mad by the sight of these multiple horrors; in the happy ending he is rescued in the nick of time just as he totters on the brink of a "fate worse than death."

Behind the popularity of this timeworn theme lies a deeply significant aspect of our national tradition—the jealous regard of the people for the rights of personal liberty. Few constitutional questions have evoked such discussion as the guarantee in the Bill of Rights that no person shall be deprived of "life, liberty, or property without due process of law."

The imposition of restraint upon a person convicted of a criminal offense is simple to understand. But when we approach the subject of depriving an insane person of his liberty, often against his will or without his consent, it immediately becomes much more complicated and difficult, for it involves forcible restraint of a person who is guilty of no crime, but is merely sick.* What could be more indicative

*It should be understood that this entire chapter deals with the *civil* insane—that is, mentally ill persons charged with no crime, as contrasted with the *criminal* insane dealt with in the preceding chapter.

of the complexity of this question than the chaotic state of our present laws respecting the commitment of the insane?

Of all the social problems arising out of the phenomenon of mental disease, perhaps none has captured the popular imagination during the past century as the possibility of confining sane persons in "insane asylums." Let thousands of mental patients in the public hospitals of a state exist under terrible conditions of overcrowding; let them be fed with bad food; let them be placed under all sorts of unnecessary restraints; let them lack adequate medical care due to poor therapeutic equipment or an understaffed personnel; let them be housed in dangerous firetraps; let them suffer a thousand and one unnecessary indignities and humiliations, and more likely than not, their plight will attract but little attention. The newspapers will maintain a respectful silence; the public will remain ignorant and indifferent. But once let rumor spread about a man or woman illegally committed to a mental hospital, and newspaper headlines will scream; the public will seethe with indignation; investigations and punitive expeditions will be demanded. Now, it is indubitably true that there have been instances where sane persons have been committed to institutions for the insane, sometimes through honest error, sometimes through the machinations of intriguing relatives, "friends," or unscrupulous owners of proprietary hospitals. This state of affairs must have been particularly true during the first century of our nation's existence, when safeguards against illegal commitment (especially in private hospitals) were either entirely absent or inadequate. But that this aspect of the history of the mentally ill in America has been greatly exaggerated is no less true.

In colonial times, as we have seen, there were no statutory provisions respecting commitment of the mentally ill. However, the common law which the colonies inherited from the mother country upheld the right to deprive insane persons of their liberty. Anyone could arrest a "furiously insane" person, or one deemed "dangerous to be permitted to be at large," and confine him for the duration of his dangerous condition, provided that this were done in a humane manner. It was permitted to "confine, bind and beat" him if his condition rendered it "necessary." Insane persons recognized as such (namely, the violent and the dangerous) were dealt with by the police powers.

Until the last quarter-century of the colonial period there were no hospitals in all the land to which the mentally ill might be sent. Generally they were not considered as a special class, but were disposed of as criminals or as paupers, as the case might be. They were ordinarily confined in jails, workhouses, poorhouses, or in private pens, cages and strong-rooms. The object of public provision was frankly repressive or custodial; no thought was given to therapy.

During the early years of the Republic, the only insane persons provided for by special legislation were those deemed "furiously mad" or dangerous to themselves or to society. For example, the first New York State law providing for the insane, enacted in 1788 and copied almost verbatim from an English law of 1744, read:

Whereas, There are sometimes persons who by lunacy or otherwise are furiously mad, or are so far disordered in their senses that they may be dangerous to be permitted to go abroad; therefore,

Be it enacted, That it shall and may be lawful for any two or more justices of the peace to cause such person to be apprehended and kept safely locked up in some secure place, and, if such justices shall find it necessary, to be there chained. . . .[1]

Similar statutes were enacted about the same time in a number of other young states. Massachusetts passed an almost identically worded act in 1797, significantly entitled, "An act for suppressing Rogues, Vagabonds, Common Beggars and other idle, disorderly and lewd Persons."

When the early hospitals and asylums for the mentally ill sprang up, commitment could be effected with the greatest of ease. No specific legislative safeguard existed for the protection of the personal liberty of the supposedly mentally ill person. No special laws concerning commitment procedure were enacted in America until the second quarter of the nineteenth century. The pauper and indigent insane might be summarily committed to the poorhouse, prison or hospital by friends or relatives or by order of public officials (such as superintendents or overseers of the poor), police authorities, or courts.

During the progress of the humanitarian movement in behalf of the mentally ill in the early decades of the nineteenth century, several states enacted laws making it illegal to confine the mentally ill in penal institutions, except for short periods. A New York statute of 1827 forbade the detention of lunatics in any prison, jail or house of correction, or "in the same room with any person charged with or convicted of any criminal offense." The act provided that indigent insane persons must be sent by the county superintendents of the poor to the Bloomingdale Asylum in New York City, which was under contract to receive pauper patients at public charge, or else to almshouses "or other places provided for the reception of lunatics."[2] Interestingly enough, the same law stated that relatives able to do so were to pay for the support of mentally ill persons maintained in the asylum or a public place of custody, but added that no relative was liable for support if he provided a suitable place of confinement at his own cost, and maintained the lunatic there in a manner agreeable to the local overseer of the poor. If the latter course were adopted, it was held unlawful to remove the lunatic from the custody of his relatives. This provision led to many abuses on the part of parsimonious relatives who cooped up their unfortunate kin in pens, cages and strong-rooms under conditions unfit for animals, to save the cost of maintenance at a public institution.

Some states, however, gave specific sanction to the commitment and confinement of the insane in penal institutions. Thus Virginia, which had earlier taken the lead in progressive legislation for the insane, enacted a law in 1806 providing that when, for want of room or other causes, the directors of the state hospital at Williamsburg refused to admit an "idiot or lunatic," the latter was to be brought back to his place of settlement. There, if it should be deemed expedient, he or she was to be confined in the county jail and the "jailor thereof shall be compelled to receive such person and shall be paid for each day's maintenance of him or her, in the same manner as jailors are now paid for prisoners confined for offenses."[3] On the whole, however, the trend was decidedly in the direction of removing the insane from penal institutions, as it was later to take the form of removing them from almshouses.

With the increase of state hospitals during the 1830's and 1840's the serious consequences of the total lack of legislation defining commitment procedures became more and more manifest. Insane persons were still being committed to mental hospitals and poorhouses without any formal procedure. There was yet no central supervision or control over either private or public institutions. Shocking instances of abuses in institutions unencumbered by legislative restraints and restrictions were seeping through to the public. Most of the states had already enacted more or less elaborate laws regarding the disposition of the property of the insane. Was it not high time to place safeguards around their *personal* rights?

During the first three decades of the nineteenth century, commitment remained on about the same level of informality as when Benjamin Rush authorized the admittance of a patient by scrawling "James Sproul is a proper patient for the Pennsylvania Hospital" on a chance scrap of paper and appending his signature.

Two prominent suits instituted in the 1840's by persons claiming to have been wrongfully committed attracted much attention to the problem of personal liberty in connection with civil insanity.

In 1845 Josiah Oakes was brought before the Massachusetts Supreme Court on a writ of *habeas corpus*. Oakes sought his discharge from the McLean Asylum on the ground that he had been illegally committed by his family. In denying the petition of Oakes, Chief Justice Shaw laid down the following rule:

> The right to restrain an insane person of his liberty is found in that great law of humanity which makes it necessary to confine those who, going at large, would be dangerous to themselves or to others. And the necessity which creates the law creates the limitations of the law . . .
> The question must then arise in each particular case, whether a pa-

tient's own safety, or that of others, requires that he should be restrained for a certain time, and whether restraint is necessary for his restoration, or will be conducive thereto. The restraint can continue as long as the necessity continues. This is the limitation, and the proper limitation."[4]

Here was one of the most important decisions affecting the civil insane in the history of American jurisprudence. It defined the justifications and limitations implicit in the common law concerning restraint of the insane. More: Chief Justice Shaw ruled that restraint of the insane was legally justified not only by regard for public or personal safety, but by considerations of remedial treatment. This was probably the first time that the therapeutic justification for restraint was explicitly stated in a decision handed down by an American court.

The second important case during this decade was that of Hinchman, tried in Philadelphia in 1849. Dr. Isaac Ray summed up this case as follows: "A man named Hinchman who was placed in the Friends' Asylum for the Insane at Frankford because, as the evidence showed beyond a doubt, he was violently and dangerously insane, brought an action of conspiracy against every individual the least concerned in the measure—his mother, sister, cousins, the sheriff, a passing traveler, the physicians of the asylum and the physicians who signed the certificate and others—and he succeeded in obtaining heavy damages!"[5]

The Hinchman case served to emphasize the necessity for legislation clarifying and extending the common law to conform more closely to the requirements of an increasingly complex social order. Such legislation, it was now obvious, was needed not only for the protection of the patient, but for the protection of institutional officials and others concerned in the commitment and custody of the insane.

In the 1860's two important events, of a somewhat different character from the cases we have just described, exerted profound influence on subsequent lunacy legislation in the United States. One was the first appearance in this country of Charles Reade's novel, *Hard Cash*.[6] This story, by the "sensation" novelist who then enjoyed a popularity second only to that of Charles Dickens, was built around the illegal commitment of the sane young hero to a private asylum through the infernal machinations of business associates seeking to separate him from his modest fortune. Based on an actual incident in which Reade himself had been instrumental in effecting the release of a young man wrongfully committed to an asylum, this book was widely circulated in England and in America. It dramatically brought to the fore the appalling weaknesses of the existing commitment laws in both countries.

A second event which occurred in the 1860's had a still greater influence on the development of commitment laws in this country. I refer to the case of Mrs. E. P. W. Packard, a *cause célèbre* that provoked nation-wide discussion for many years. In 1860 Mrs. Packard was committed to the Illinois State Hospital at Jacksonville upon petition of her husband, the Rev. Theophilus Packard. She gained her freedom three years later, claiming that she had been perfectly sane when committed and confined in the state hospital, and that she had been the innocent victim of her husband's dastardly plot to get rid of her.

No sooner was Mrs. Packard, a middle-aged woman possessing courage, energy and ability, discharged from the hospital than she launched a crusade for more effective protection of allegedly insane persons. Her cause was greatly aided by the fact that the Illinois law under which she had been committed was so grossly discriminatory and unjust as to arouse the resentment of all fair-minded people. Enacted in 1851, the statute read:

> *Married women* and infants who, in the judgment of the medical superintendents of the state asylum at Jacksonville are evidently insane or distracted, may be entered or detained in the hospital at the request of the husband of the woman or the guardian of the infant, *without* the evidence of insanity required in other cases.

Mrs. Packard pushed her cause with tireless vigor, and attracted a great deal of public attention and sympathy.*

---

*Whether Mrs. Packard was mentally sound or not at the time of her commitment or confinement is a moot question. It appears to be established

OUR COMMITMENT LAWS 425

She wrote several books based on her "railroading" to a state hospital and her confinement therein, and describing her discharge, triumphant public vindication, and the setting in motion of her crusade for better commitment laws. Incidentally, these books enjoyed huge sales from which she cleared many thousands of dollars.[7] She also journeyed from state to state addressing public meetings and legislative bodies on the need for better protective laws for the mentally ill, or, more accurately, for the protection of mentally sound persons alleged to be insane. Her efforts resulted directly in the enactment of new commitment laws in three states (Illinois, Iowa and Massachusetts), and indirectly influenced lunacy legislation in a number of other states.

Mrs. Packard's crusade began in her native state, Massachusetts, where, in 1865, she presented two bills for the consideration of a legislative committee. The first read: "No person shall be regarded or treated as an insane person or a monomaniac simply for the expression of opinions, no matter how absurd these opinions may appear."[8] This bill, she explained with much reason, was intended to protect reformers and progressive thinkers from being adjudged insane merely because their ideals might seem too "queer" to their more backward contemporaries. Her second bill read as follows: "No person shall be imprisoned (*sic*) and treated as an insane person except for *irregularities* of conduct, such as indicate that the individual is so lost to reason as to render him an unaccountable moral agent." By these bills she hoped to establish general *behavior* rather than particular *opinions* as a criterion for determining insanity. Neither of her bills was adopted, but her agitation resulted in a new commitment law providing that a petitioner for the admission of an allegedly insane person to a mental hospital in Massachusetts must henceforth submit, along with his application, a

that she suffered from certain delusions, and had been a patient at the Worcester State Hospital in Massachusetts for a brief period when a girl. She expressed the belief at one time that she was the third person in the Holy Trinity and the mother of Jesus Christ. On the other hand, her behavior following her discharge from the state hospital at Jacksonville was so intelligent, and her ability so striking, as to lend weight to her charge that she had been "railroaded."

list of the patient's nearest relatives, not exceeding ten in number, all of whom were to be notified by the superintendent of the institution within two days after admission or commitment. Notice was also to be sent to any other two persons named by the patient.[9] This law was intended to render secret frameups more difficult by informing a number of interested persons of the event.

In 1866 Mrs. Packard returned to Illinois, where she submitted to the legislature a "personal liberty" bill. This bill, which became law in March 1867, provided that no person should be committed to an insane asylum without a trial by jury, and that all patients then in the state hospital at Jacksonville must be given a jury trial to ascertain their mental condition. In 1872 Mrs. Packard succeeded in having a similar "personal liberty" bill enacted by the Iowa legislature. Strenuous efforts on her part to effect the passage of personal liberty bills in other states failed, but there can be no doubt that her agitation gave impetus to a strong wave of sentiment throughout the country that resulted in many new commitment laws in subsequent years.

The passage of Mrs. Packard's personal liberty bill, requiring a jury trial in every commitment proceeding, is a classic example of the harm that good men (and women) can do when their admirable zeal is misdirected. Far from proving beneficial, this law exercised a most deleterious effect during the twenty-five years it remained on the statute books of Illinois. The same is true of laws adopted in other states making jury trials mandatory. Richard Dewey, who was superintendent of the Kankakee (Illinois) State Hospital for many years, rendered this sober judgment on the personal liberty law:

> The entire annals of the insane in the state of Illinois furnish no greater evidence of cruelty to the insane and their friends than this so-called "reform" so zealously promoted by Mrs. Packard. As a matter of fact, more sane persons were found insane by jury trials, as shown by the reports of institutions from year to year, than were ever wrongfully committed under the earlier system. The effect upon the patient was frequently detrimental, arousing in his mind the idea that the court proceedings were for the purpose of substantiating

OUR COMMITMENT LAWS 427

some charge against him, and when found insane he believed himself innocently condemned.[10]

The trial was usually held in open court, where the condition of the mentally ill person was exposed to public view, with consequences harmful not only to himself but to his family and friends. Rather than go through this trying ordeal relatives often would leave a patient for months and even years without proper treatment. Many who might have been restored to health by prompt attention, sank into hopeless mental conditions because of such delays.*

A great deal of the lunacy legislation enacted in many states in the 1870's is attributable to the pressure arising from the public distrust of mental hospitals. In his report as a lunacy commissioner to the Massachusetts legislature in 1874, Nathan Allen noted that "there has grown up and existed for some time an antagonism of feeling and interest between hospitals, the superintendents and trustees as a body, and the general public." Dr. Allen quoted one hospital trustee as remarking: "It seems as if the public believed that every man connected in any way with a hospital for the insane had entered into a conspiracy to deprive the patients of all their rights and to do violence to all the relations of life."[11] In his report Dr. Allen referred with approval to the first permanent state commission in lunacy established in New York in 1873. Both he and his fellow-commissioner, Wendell Phillips, recommended the founding of a similar commission by the Commonwealth of Massachusetts.†

The lead of New York was soon followed by the establishment in Massachusetts and other states of state supervisory bodies, tending to allay somewhat the fears of the public concerning the personal rights of the insane and the possibility of illegally committing or detaining sane persons. As time passed, the scope and powers of these commissions

*The compulsory jury trial law of Illinois was repealed in 1893, though a modified jury system still obtains.

†It was largely in response to the public clamor we have noted that the first permanent commissions in lunacy were organized to ensure stricter supervision of individual institutions by central state bodies. Other factors in the rise of lunacy commissions have been discussed in Chapter XIII.

were gradually extended in many states from supervisory functions, such as mere visitation and inspection of mental hospitals, to complete administration and control over the state hospital system. Coincident with the extension of powers over state hospitals, came closer supervision over private institutions for the mentally ill, which had hitherto been beyond the restraining power of any public authority. In some states, as this process continued, commissions on lunacy were elevated to state boards and then to state departments.*

The development of commitment laws followed devious paths throughout the country. Today commitment procedures vary widely in the several states. Broadly speaking, however, the methods of judicial commitment of the insane in the United States fall into four major categories:

1. Commitment by court upon the findings of a commission in lunacy.
2. Commitment by court upon findings of one or more medical examiners.
3. Commitment by court following a trial by jury.
4. Commitment by a commission in lunacy empowered by law with judicial authority.

At present the steps taken in committing the insane follow this general pattern:

1. *Petition.* An application for commitment of the alleged insane person is sworn to and filed with the proper authority. Usually the petition may be made only by a certain person or persons specified by law—near relatives, friends, legal guardians, or public officers, such as overseers of the poor or county superintendents. In some states any reputable citizen may make such petition. In Florida the application must be signed by at least five reputable citizens, only one of whom may be related to the person concerned.

The petition is usually filed in a specified court of record. In Michigan it may be filed in any such court. The New

---

*In New York State, this authority passed through three evolutionary stages: a one-man commission in lunacy (1873); a three-man commission in lunacy (1889), which became a state hospital commission in 1912; and the present-day State Department of Mental Hygiene (1927).

OUR COMMITMENT LAWS

York State law specifies that application for commitment may be made to a judge of a court of record of the city or county, or a justice of the supreme court of the judicial district in which the allegedly insane person resides or is found. In other states, the petition may be filed in the district court (Louisiana, New Mexico, Utah), circuit court (Virginia, Illinois), probate court (Indiana), superior court (California), or with the town officers (Maine and Vermont), justices of the peace (Maine), the board of commissioners (Nebraska), etc. In Delaware the procedure is unusual in that the petition, accompanied by a certificate signed by two physicians, is made directly to the state hospital.

2. *Notice.* In most states, legal notice of commitment proceedings must be served on the person alleged to be insane, within a specified time. The laws of some states require that near relatives or friends of the person concerned must also be notified of the proceedings. In New York notice must be served upon the allegedly insane person at least one day before application is formally filed unless the judge to whom application is made decides that such service would be ineffective or detrimental to the person's health, in which case legal notice upon the person concerned is dispensed with.

3. *Certificate.* Generally a certificate of insanity, signed by one or more reputable physicians, must accompany the petition. Most states provide that examining physicians may not be related by marriage or blood to the person concerned, or connected in any way, financial or otherwise, with the institution to which it is proposed to admit him.

4. *Hearing.* A hearing may then be held, generally by a court of record, sometimes by a lunacy commission acting as a judicial body, to determine the question of insanity and issuance of a commitment order. This commission may consist of two or three physicians, or of a physician together with a psychologist, a lawyer or a reputable layman. In some states, commitment proceedings do not require a hearing, thus saving the patient from an embarrassing and often painful experience.

In most states the court appoints two qualified physicians to examine the mental condition of the person concerned, and issues a commitment order if it is convinced that the findings contained in their report show that the person is insane. A few states still have statutes making jury trials obligatory in every case of commitment. In nearly all other states the law requires a trial by jury when demanded by the allegedly insane person, a relative or a friend, or when the court believes such trial to be expedient. A jury may consist of five, six, twelve or twenty-three persons. In other states where trial by jury in the determination of insanity is not specified by law, it is commonly recognized that such trial must be granted upon request. In most states the presence of the allegedly insane person at the hearing is required by law, exception being made if the court or the commission decides that the presence of the respondent may have an adverse effect on his health. In some instances when trial by jury is specified, the court is given the discretion of ordering a new trial if dissatisfied with the verdict. Fortunately, where archaic laws are still on the statute books, they are seldom enforced.

In certain states the law provides for the establishment of permanent district commissions in lunacy with power to determine insanity and to issue commitment orders. In Iowa, for instance, each county has a commission on insanity consisting of three members: the clerk of the district court, a reputable practicing physician and a reputable practicing lawyer. The latter two members are appointed by the district court for terms of two years. The commission acts as a judicial body with full power to commit, subject to appeal to the district court.[12]

5. *Commitment order.* After a "verdict" of insanity is handed down by a jury, commission or judge, the court of jurisdiction issues an order authorizing the commitment of the patient to a state, county or private hospital or private sanitarium, as the case may be. A number of states are divided into state hospital districts and a person adjudged insane must be committed to the hospital in the district wherein he resides, with special exceptions allowed. In sev-

OUR COMMITMENT LAWS

eral states, as we have noted, the court may reject the findings of the jury or commission and order a new trial or hearing. In certain instances the court may commit the insane person to the custody of a relative, or friend, or a committee in the district where the patient resides. In committing a person, the court or commission sometimes appoints a guardian, a conservator, or a committee to manage his property and other interests. Generally, however, appointment of a guardian is separated from commitment proceedings.

6. *Transportation.* The cost of transporting the insane person from his home to the mental hospital is usually borne by the county or town of settlement. Sometimes the state is charged with transportation expenses. The patients or their relatives are obliged to pay it themselves if they can afford it. Generally the patient is sent to the institution in the custody of police officers—sheriffs, constables, etc. Due to the recurrent scandals arising out of transporting women patients in the custody of male officers, an increasing number of states now make it obligatory that each woman patient be accompanied by a female attendant or nurse, unless accompanied by her father, brother, husband or son. In New York State nurses from the state hospitals transport the patients.

Voluntary and Temporary Commitment. It is quite obvious that the judicial procedure generally followed in commitment cases involves much pain and humiliation to the patient and his family, not to speak of the serious effect on the patient's mental health often resulting from the delay entailed in the tortuous process. One of the most perplexing problems in the historical development of the care and treatment of the mentally ill has been to find ways and means of reducing to a minimum the judicial process of commitment without infringing on the constitutional safeguard against the deprivation of personal liberty without due process of law. The rise of voluntary admission and temporary commitment laws have done much to bring this problem closer to solution. In Massachusetts, about half the admissions to mental hospitals are now made under the temporary care law. In this connection we may trace an interesting instance of the oscillations of the historical pendulum. Up to the middle of the nineteenth century, commitment of the insane was accomplished with the greatest facility, accompanied by little formality or none at all. Then the pendulum began to swing violently in the opposite direction; commitment procedures became so enmeshed in restrictive laws that the barriers raised in the path of admission to mental hospitals were well nigh insurmountable in many states.

In the last quarter of the ninteenth century, the pendulum started to swing backward toward a median point between the two extremes. While retaining their vigilance against improper commitment and confinement, the more progressive states enacted laws facilitating admission so as to encourage early and prompt treatment. A most important step in this direction came with the passage of voluntary admission laws permitting, within certain limits, the admission of patients into mental hospitals upon their own applications. Massachusetts enacted the first voluntary admission law in 1881. (*Chapter 272, Acts of 1881.*) In the beginning this form of admission was restricted to pay patients only, but eventually its benefits were extended to all who desired and needed institutional treatment. The laws generally provide that no voluntary patient may be detained in a mental hospital beyond a specified period, usually from five to ten days after he has given written notice of his desire to be discharged.

The passage of "emergency" or "temporary" commitment statutes in some states marked another important advance in the care and treatment of the mentally ill. Such laws provide that in certain cases where prompt treatment or immediate restraint is necessary, mentally ill persons may be admitted for a limited period, usually from ten to thirty days, without going through the complete legal procedure ordinarily required.

The introduction of the psychopathic hospital was in part a response to the need for providing prompt attention to mental patients without red tape entanglements. In turn, the growth of psychopathic hospitals greatly stimulated the practice of commitments without legal proceedings.

Dr. Frankwood E. Williams has summarized the beneficial results of voluntary and temporary commitment systems as follows: (1) They tend to express in legal form the modern conceptions of mental disease, without endangering the personal liberty of any individual; (2) they at the same time emphasize the patient's cause as a patient; (3) they make it possible to provide early treatment, which is the most hopeful treatment; (4) they afford protection to the patient both from himself and from unprincipled members of the community quick to take advantage of his illness; (5) they afford protection to the family and community against the acts of the patient; (6) they obviate in a large number of cases the delays, legal exactions, and semi-publicity of having been declared insane; (7) they remove the hospitals from the isolation they have suffered in the community and make it possible for them to take their place as hospitals in fact as well as in name, a more integral part of the social fabric; (8) they make possible a wider cooperation between the hospitals and the lay and medical public . . .; (9) and finally, by means of a wider understanding of the more fundamental facts in regard to mental disease on the part of physicians, cooperating with the hospitals, through the more frequent use of these laws, it may be possible to prevent certain forms of mental disease.[13] It may be added that they also avoid the need for confining mental patients in lockups and jails while waiting for the court to act.

The practice of voluntary admission, together with the rise of psychopathic hospitals, has proved of great value in the humanization of the care and treatment of mentally ill persons. Today, in many instances, persons alleged to be insane are sent for observation to psychopathic or general state hospitals on temporary commitments for a period usually limited to thirty days to determine their mental condition before final commitment is made. This procedure has saved large numbers of mentally ill persons from the "stigma" of being declared legally insane. One of the best statutes tending to minimize judicial processes in commitment is that in effect in Delaware, to which we have already alluded. There the petition, with a certificate of two physicians, is made directly to the state hospital. The person concerned is placed in the hospital for thirty days' observation and the facts of insanity are determined by the institutional board of trustees, the patient retaining the right of appeal to the courts. The Mental Hygiene Law of New York declares that, upon a certificate signed by a health officer, "the superintendent or physician in charge of any state hospital, except the Matteawan and Dannemora state hospitals [for the criminal insane], or of any licensed private institution for the care and treatment of the insane may . . . receive and care for in such hospital or institution as a patient for a period not exceeding thirty days . . . any person who needs immediate care and treatment because of mental derangement other than drug addiction or drunkenness." When a patient is admitted through a petition accompanied by a certificate of one qualified examiner, he may be detained indefinitely unless he, or any person in his behalf, makes written request for release.

With the development of more enlightened ideas in the care and treatment of the mentally ill, a growing tendency to open the doors of mental hospitals to voluntary patients has been discernible.

It is a sad commentary on the uneven pace of progress that many states in the Union are still without voluntary or temporary commitment laws. Worse still, there are yet some states that permit commitment of mental patients to *prisons* and *jails* in civil procedure. While the statutes in such cases usually specify that persons adjudged insane may be confined in penal institutions only when the state hospitals are crowded to capacity or overcrowded, and then only for limited periods, the fact is that in some backward states mentally ill persons, guilty of no crime or offense, are detained in such institutions for many months and even years at a time.

A related problem is the detention of persons alleged to be insane pending commitment. Throughout the United States, especially in rural districts, it is quite common to confine mental patients in jails, lockups and police stations pending their commitment to state hospitals. This is true even in states which strictly prohibit the confinement of a mentally ill person in any place intended for the custody of offenders against the law.

New York's law prohibiting such detention dates back to 1827. Yet, as late as 1909, Dr. William L. Russell estimated that fully 18 per cent of the persons admitted into the state hospitals during the preceding year had been detained in jails, lockups and station houses pending their commitment. Dr. Russell presented many instances of terrible treatment accorded to insane persons in such places of temporary detention.[14]

In 1925 Stanley P. Davies, then executive secretary of the New York State Committee on Mental Hygiene of the State Charities Aid Association, conducted a survey of detention of the insane pending commitment, and made the following comment on his findings: "In New York State, especially outside the larger cities, such local care has all too commonly consisted of confinement in a jail cell (in specific violation of the Insanity Law), in a cell in a municipal or county building, or in an uncomfortable, unsafe, cell-like room in quarters rented for the purpose, often over a store or factory. Proper medical and nursing care have been lacking, and hospital care, which should be the rule, has been the rare exception. Much unnecessary suffering has thus been forced upon these mentally sick persons and their mental ills have been often so aggravated through improper handling as seriously to hamper their later treatment and their chances for recovery."[15] While these conditions no longer prevail in New York, they still exist elsewhere, as shown by the fact that in 1933 the laws of fourteen states permitted the detention of persons alleged to be insane in jails pending commitment, while six permitted such detention when the patient was violent.[16] Surely, such conditions cry for immediate correction in the name of justice and humanity, in states where they still obtain.

Discharge and Parole. Intimately bound up with the problems of commitment are the processes of discharge and parole, for which latter word there is now a tendency to substitute "provisional release" and "trial visit." In ordering commitment, the court cannot decree a definite term of custody for the patient. The term of restraint depends solely upon the condition of the patient. As Chief Justice Shaw pointed out nearly a century ago, restraint of the insane is justified in law only so long as it is socially necessary or beneficial to the patient. "And the necessity which creates the law creates the limitations of the law." Commitment must end when the condition of "insanity" ends. Detention thereafter may be terminated by *habeas corpus* proceedings. It is the generally recognized rule that a committed person (or a relative, friend, or other party) has the right to apply for a writ of *habeas corpus* to determine the legality of his confinement.[17]

Besides *habeas corpus* proceedings, a patient may be removed from a mental hospital (a) by being discharged as recovered, improved or unimproved; (b) by transfer to another institution; or (c) by parole. Commitment is terminated only by discharge. A person is discharged when he has recovered, or when institutional care and treatment is no longer considered necessary or beneficial. The laws of some states provide that when a state hospital is filled to capacity, patients whose condition is deemed incurable or harmless must be discharged to make room for the admission of recent, hopeful and dangerous cases. Once officially discharged, a person cannot be readmitted without a repetition of the legal procedure governing the original commitment, except in cases of voluntary admission or temporary commitment.

Authority to discharge patients may be vested in (a) the superintendent alone; (b) the hospital board of trustees or managers, upon the recommendation of the superintendent; or (c) a central state authority, such as a lunacy board, mental hygiene department, or board of control. In a few states eligibility for discharge is determined through an examination by the hospital physicians in staff session.

Transfer to another institution within the same state is made under the original commitment, and merely transfers custody from one superintendent or institutional board to another. A patient sent out on parole remains under the legal custody and supervision of the institution to which he was committed, and the original commitment remains in force.

Parole, or furlough, constitutes a trial visit of the patient from the hospital to a private home, as a test of his ability to resume his place in normal community life. Nearly every state in the Union has a parole system for mental patients. The period of parole in the several states ranges from three months to one year; some states authorize renewal after its expiration. A patient on furlough is always subject to return under the original commitment.

If his adjustment to the outside world is deemed satisfactory, the patient is automatically discharged; if not, the parole period is extended or he is returned to the hospital for further care and treatment. During the period of parole, the patient usually must report for examination to the hospital at periodic intervals.

The entrance of the social worker into the scope of state hospital work greatly facilitated the practice of parole. The social worker could keep in constant contact with the patient through visits at his home or his place of employment, observe the degree of his rehabilitation in a community setting, and help him with advice and with social services such as financial aid and job placement. The rise of the psychiatric clinic also proved an important stimulus to the parole system. Many patients find it difficult and unpleasant to return to the state hospital at regular intervals for medical advice and treatment. It is far more convenient and less irritating to attend a nearby mental clinic where they may receive the aid and counsel of psychiatrists and social workers.

Dr. Thomas H. Haines aptly described the parole system as "a means of finishing off the rehabilitative processes begun under medical supervision in the hospital. From the point of view of rehabilitation of character and reestablishment of the individual in society, it is the only logical means of safely bridging the gap between hospital care and self-directed life in the community. From the point of view of the hospital management, it does serve to reduce population and thus it diminishes the public expense for the maintenance of the insane. For many patients can be released under supervision under these conditions when it would be unsafe to discharge them absolutely from hospital supervision."[18]

The parole or furlough system has developed steadily in the United States in recent years. According to U. S. Census Bureau statistics, 68,118 of the 582,626 patients on the books of mental hospitals at the end of the year 1944 were listed under the category "extramural care" apart from the 2,164 under family care.[19]

Unfortunately, there are some states in which the practice of parole is grossly abused and perverted. In several backward states the parole system is nothing more than a mockery and a sham. Patients are "paroled" without any adequate supervision, or follow-up care and protection. Little or no effort is made to follow the progress of the patient after removal from the hospital. Lacking continued psychiatric treatment and advice or the helpful guidance of competent social workers in the critical early period of attempted rehabilitation many a patient who, under proper supervision, might have found adjustment in society, fails to do so and has to be returned to the hospital.

Recommendations. The disparities and shortcomings in our commitment laws have long been the subject of criticism on the part of progressive psychiatrists and others interested in the welfare of the mentally ill. The feature in commitment proceedings that has attracted the most concentrated attention and criticism is the trial by jury which is made obligatory in the laws of several states, and frequently resorted to in others. The disgraceful legal attitude toward the mentally ill which still persists in many parts of the country—and which has contributed in no small degree to the stigma attached to mental disease—is evidenced in the terminology still widely used in commitment procedure in states requiring jury trials. The mentally ill person is referred to as a "suspect"; he is "arrested" or "apprehended"; he is "accused" and placed on trial on a "charge" of insanity; he stands trial in the position of a *quasi* criminal, with lawyers on both sides using the customary methods of

OUR COMMITMENT LAWS

attack and defense to prove the "guilt" or "innocence" of the "defendant"; the jury or court pronounces a "verdict" on his condition, and he is "convicted" of insanity! (Remember, we are discussing here the procedures governing the commitment of the *civil* insane, and not of persons pleading insanity in *criminal* trials.)

Drs. Winfred Overholser and Henry Weihofen thus described the type of courtroom scene witnessed in the District of Columbia up to 1938, when the mandatory jury trial for insanity was finally abolished:

"The trappings are those of the criminal court room, with the judge on the bench and the jury in the box, the defense attorney and the prosecutor in court. The hapless patient is brought in, the charge is read to him, testimony is given by the doctors, the latter are cross-examined by the 'defense' attorney, and the jury, who may never before have seen a mentally ill person, are called upon to say whether the patient is of unsound mind or not."[20]

The general requirements of modern practice in the commitment of the mentally ill are stated in the recommendations submitted by the Committee on Legal Measures and Laws to the First International Congress on Mental Hygiene, held in Washington, D.C., in 1930. The recommendations follow:

1. Admission to a mental hospital for treatment should be made as informal and easy as the constitution and the laws of the country will permit. To this end, we further recommend that jury trials on the issue of insanity for commitment be abolished; that the presence in court of the patient to be committed be not required, but within the discretion of the judge; that the voluntary admission of patients who are seeking treatment and who are competent to make such applications be encouraged, and that those countries and states which do not have such laws be urged to adopt them. Laws also should be adopted as speedily as possible for the temporary care and study without formal commitment of patients upon the recommendation of a physician, as well as for provision for the commitment of patients for a period of observation.

2. We recommend that provision be made, wherever it does not now exist, for the release of patients on parole and supervision during a period of convalescence, such patients to be allowed to return to

the hospital without further legal proceedings should their condition necessitate return. We recommend further, that provision be established for the discharge of recovered patients without their needing to have recourse to legal proceedings for this purpose.[21]

Out of the confusion that has so far characterized the development of our commitment laws, one encouraging factor stands out: the growing trend toward commitment without judicial process. For instance, it was estimated in Rhode Island that one-half of the mental patients admitted to hospitals in 1933 were committed by non-judicial methods. The more progressive states now provide a number of procedures other than judicial for committing the mentally ill to mental hospitals. Of the five principal methods for commitment authorized by the Mental Hygiene Law of New York, four are non-judicial. These methods are: (1) admission on voluntary application, under which the patient may be detained not more than ten days after he gives written notice of his desire to leave; (2) admission on petition of relative or friend and certificate of one physician, valid for a period not exceeding thirty days after notice, etc.; (3) admission upon request of a health officer, valid for thirty days only; (4) emergency admission for a period not exceeding ten days; (5) regular court commitment.

Another encouraging tendency has been the gradual change in terminology in the commitment laws of certain states, by substituting medical for legal terms. In Pennsylvania, the word "insane" has been taken out of the state laws and supplanted by "mentally ill."

But there is no ground for complacency in viewing the present state of our commitment laws. Progress still moves with the pace of a sloth. Obstructionist forces of all kinds still place barriers in the path of progress. In 1933 a bill humanizing the commitment laws of California passed both houses of the legislature, only to be vetoed by the governor upon the request of the California Sheriffs' Association. The latter organization objected to the bill because it contained a clause which removed the function of transporting mental patients from the hands of sheriffs, thus depriving them of a source of liberal fees!

Let us not be satisfied with the fact that the trend toward more humane commitment laws is evident: it is necessary to mobilize our forces for the rapid acceleration of that trend.

CHAPTER XX

Modern Trends in Institutional Care and Treatment

"IT IS a fact," said Thomas W. Salmon thirty-five years ago, "that every stage in the long and painful history of the care of the insane from 1247, when the first institution for the insane in England was provided, could actually be witnessed in some American community this afternoon."

With very little modification, that observation might well be made today, a generation later. Progress in institutional care has been extremely irregular. Over-optimistic historical accounts have tended to concentrate on the peaks of progress that arise here and there, overlooking the lowlands and the valleys which still comprise the general level. This melancholy truth impressed itself deeply upon the author during a recent journalistic survey of state mental hospitals across the nation.

The introduction of a progressive therapeutic technique or the enunciation of an advanced idea, while marking a milestone in history, does not necessarily attain immediate or universal adoption, even though its soundness might be demonstrated beyond all doubt. There are often great time-lags between the introduction of a workable theory, its acceptance as valid, and, finally, its transmutation into general practice. Again, standards of institutional care and treatment may be poles apart in different states or even in hospitals within the same state. The present-day institutional pattern might be likened to a crazy quilt—with some bright new patches and a plenitude of tatters.

There was, to be sure, a gradual development from the custodial to the curative ideal, symbolized by the change in

MODERN TRENDS IN INSTITUTIONAL CARE 443

official institutional nomenclature from "asylum" to "hospital." Newer institutions tended to cast off the forbidding external appearances that characterized most nineteenth-century asylums. High, ugly walls were eschewed. Depressingly close "airing courts," reminiscent of penal institutions, were replaced by expansive lawns and shaded walks. Heavy iron bars, casting deep shadows over the cell-like rooms of patients, gave way to lighter bars, then to hardly perceptible steel traceries worked into artistic patterns in window panes. In the more progressive states, the use of mechanical restraint and seclusion ("solitary confinement") were rigorously proscribed by law in attempts to reduce them to a minimum. The statutes in New York and Massachusetts, for instance, allowed mechanical restraint to be used only in surgical cases and similar emergencies, and then only for limited periods of time, with the knowledge and consent of the chief officer. "Chemical restraint," or sedation by drugs, which once included the free use of opium and other narcotics for pacifying disturbed patients—with the effect of speeding them along the road toward premature deterioration and death—was drastically minimized in many modern hospitals. Again, where patients of all kinds, in every degree of mental sickness and defect, had once been herded in a single building, the gradual advance of classification and diversification brought about separate wards for the disturbed, and the quiet, the acute and the chronic, the young and the old.

The establishment, here and there, of farm colonies connected with state hospitals permitted the employment of selected patients under conditions of greater freedom and contentment than they otherwise could enjoy. Differentiation of institutions made it possible, in some states, to remove the mentally deficient from mental hospitals to colonies and institutions for their special care. Separate colonies for the epileptic, institutions for defective delinquents, and special hospitals for the criminally insane were established in the more advanced states.

Meanwhile, desirable changes were taking place in institutional personnel. Under the stimulus of the nineteenth-century humanitarian movement, "cell keepers" had been replaced by custodial attendants. Later, attendants were supplemented by trained nurses, whose functions included participation in therapy. The systematic training of nurses for mental hospitals, introduced by Dr. Edward Cowles at the McLean Hospital in 1892, proved a powerful factor in the extension of the hospital idea.* Another factor, as previously noted, was the gradual use of female nurses on male wards. In most states, the choice of mental hospital superintendents narrowed down to physicians with at least some special training in psychiatry. Qualifications for other medical personnel were also raised. Competitive civil service examinations were increasingly made the basis of personnel selection in public mental hospitals.

Three familiar types of mental therapeutics—psychotherapy, occupational therapy, and hydrotherapy—gradually evolved from their crude forms in classic times to more precise institutional techniques.

Psychotherapy,† the earliest form of treatment, has gone far since Alexander of Tralles placed a leaden hat on one patient's head and a snake in the "vomit basin" of another, to cure the former of the delusion that he was headless and the latter that she had writhing serpents in her stomach. Present-day psychotherapy parallels in large degree the rise of the psychogenic concept—that is, that psychic or emotional disturbances can produce mental illness. But its range has extended far beyond the confines of psychiatry proper, and is fast becoming a recognized form of treatment in many non-psychiatric medical cases. A large number of physicians are now specializing in this form of treatment, while at the turn of the century there were only a scattered few. Psychotherapy comprehends a variety of methods and techniques. As explained by Dr. George H. Kirby, these fall into two main groups: "the first depends chiefly on the influence of so-called suggestion, while the second utilizes some form of mental analysis, although there also suggestion apparently plays an

---

*In 1946 there were 23 active basic schools of psychiatric nursing in mental hospitals. Twelve of these were in New York State, leaving only eleven for the rest of the country. (Report of American Psychiatric Association's Committee on Psychiatric Nursing, 1946.)

†Psychotherapy includes all forms of treatment of disease by mental influence.

MODERN TRENDS IN INSTITUTIONAL CARE

important role. In the first group are found such procedures as suggestion in hypnotic or waking states, persuasion, reeducation, progressive relaxation, discipline, isolation, rest, etc. In the second group fall (1) the method of personality analysis and psychiatric interview as developed by Adolf Meyer; (2) the psychoanalytic technique of Freud; (3) other methods which are variants of modifications of the psychoanalytic."[1]

Occupational therapy, like psychotherapy, was practiced by the ancient Greeks.* As we have seen in a previous chapter, it occupied an important place in the therapeutics of the early hospital superintendents in America. While the old psychiatrists believed labor of any kind to be beneficial in itself—and agriculture was the only form of work available to the patients of most mental hospitals—modern psychiatry has developed highly individualized forms of occupational therapy, which aims to fit the work to the needs of the individual patient.

Among the fundamental principles of occupational therapy formulated by Dr. Hermann Simon and presented at the 1930 International Congress on Mental Hygiene in Washington, D.C., are the following:

> Every achievement expected from the patient must remain within his capability, which must be determined exactly by his physician and nurse. All components of the total personality must here be considered.
>
> The work must always be kept at the highest level of the patient's work efficiency, because the available energy can be strengthened only by its full utilization.
>
> The constancy of the work assigned facilitates the adjustment through practice and habituation which are powerful allies of therapy.
>
> The work must be serious—no pastime or joke, no "occupied idleness." All deviating and pathological behavior must be corrected whenever it manifests itself during the activity.
>
> As many diverse forms of activity as possible should be available in all institutions, especially in the supervised wards for the difficult patients.[2]

---

*As defined in the *Memorandum on Occupational Therapy for Mental Patients,* issued in 1933 by the British Board of Control, occupational therapy is "the treatment, under medical direction, of physical and mental disorders by the application of occupation and recreation with the object of promoting recovery, of creating new habits, and of preventing deterioration."

Among the advantages of occupational therapy we might list the following: The patient's mental attitude is favorably influenced; good habits are induced and maintained; the "socializing" process which prepares the patient for life in the normal community is accelerated; and, incidentally, substantial economic savings for the institutions are effected. Unfortunately, the last consideration is too often the predominating one in the application of occupational therapy.

Gymnastics, sports, rhythmic exercises, and other forms of recreation and amusement are carefully planned in our better hospitals in accordance with the needs of the patients, as an integrated part of occupational therapy. Music therapy—dating back to the time when David cured Saul's melancholy by playing on his harp—has been experimented with in a number of hospitals.

Hydrotherapy has also traveled far through the centuries, though the basic principles remain much the same as those originally formulated by the Greeks. The crude "water-cures" of a few centuries ago—including the "bath of surprise" whereby the luckless patient was sent hurtling through a trapdoor into an icy bath below in an effort to shock him into his senses—has been superseded by a system of hot air, vapor and saline baths, sitz baths, various forms of douches, hot and cold wet packs, etc., which now comprise the hydrotherapeutic department of every modern hospital. It is doubtful whether hydrotherapy is in itself curative; its efficacy lies largely in its use as a sedative, tonic or stimulating agency with temporary benefits. Wet sheet packs are often used as sedatives for excited patients instead of the old forms of mechanical restraint; in some quarters it is claimed that these packs are in themselves but a disguised form of mechanical restraint.

The Great Economic Depression that started with the stock market crash in 1929 and lasted almost a decade sharply reversed the generally upward trend in mental hospital standards witnessed during the previous half century. When state budgets were drastically curtailed, institutions for the mentally handicapped felt the pinch first and worst. Construction projects were scrapped for years. A bright spot in an otherwise total gloom was the Federal Public Works Administration, created by the Roosevelt Administration to help revive employment through public building. The PWA in one year (1933–34) allocated $12,000,000 for state hospital projects. Four-fifths of these federal funds, however, went to only three states which were best prepared to match the grants on a 50–50 basis, in accordance with PWA regulations.[3] A report on "State Hospitals in the Depression," prepared by the National Committee for Mental Hygiene in 1934, revealed that three-fourths of 104 institutions included in the survey were overcrowded and that one-fourth had been forced to close their doors against new admissions. Long waiting lists were found in a number of states, while in some states many men and women patients were confined for lengthy periods in jails because of mental hospital overcrowding.

The grave overcrowding problem during the economic depression stimulated a movement toward wider adoption of the "family care" system, first inaugurated in this country in Massachusetts in 1883 and continued there on a modest scale since that time. Many experts regarded this system as a potentially major means of relieving overcrowded institutions. It had operated successfully for many decades in Scotland, where mild "chronic" and convalescent cases were boarded out with suitable selected families in scattered communities. The New York State Legislature in 1935 authorized adoption of the plan on a small scale by making a maximum sum of $20,000 available to every institution operating under the State Mental Hygiene Department for placing out patients in families. It was stipulated in the enabling act that the rate for boarding out each patient should not exceed four dollars a week; the rate has been increased since, but is still too low to attract wide participation.

Dr. Horatio M. Pollock, a leading proponent of the family care system, listed four benefits in his book on the subject:

1. Patients placed in suitable families resume a measure of community life with a natural environment and with more freedom than could be possible in a state hospital.

2. The families receiving patients have an outlet for their altruistic sentiments and acquire a secure economic status.

3. The state hospital, relieved of many of its custodial cases, can devote more of its energies to the scientific treatment of acute and recoverable patients.

4. The state conducting an extensive system of family care could be relieved of the necessity of building new hospitals and would have a better opportunity to treat its mental patients in accordance with their individual needs.[4]

Despite the impressive arguments in its favor, the family care system has not been adopted on a considerable scale in New York or other states.

The persistence of the economic crisis throughout the Thirties continued to wreak havoc with state hospital standards. Plans for needed expansion were scrapped for want of funds. Existing institutions underwent serious deterioration; for years in some states not a penny was appropriated for repairs. Budgets for personnel, food, and upkeep were cut to the bone. Staffs were demoralized; patients despaired; curative ideals were forgotten in the desperate push for mere physical survival.

The low estate of the state hospital system was fully documented during the course of a three-year nation-wide survey of state hospitals launched in 1937 by the U. S. Public Health Service and the National Mental Hygiene Committee, with the co-operation of the American Psychiatric Association and other interested groups. The field work was undertaken mainly by Dr. Samuel W. Hamilton and his two associates, Drs. Grover A. Kempf and Victor H. Vogel. Their detailed findings, set down in confidential reports on individual institutions and states, revealed conditions of inhumanity and neglect in many places such as few dreamed possible in a civilized country. The published final report on the survey, considerably "softer" than the confidential reports, nonetheless provided a most depressing picture of general deterioration of standards throughout the public mental hospital system on the eve of World War II.[5]

Shortly after the end of World War II in 1945, the writer started on a journalistic survey of state mental hospitals that, during the next two years, carried him through more than two dozen institutions from coast to coast. Most of them were located in or near great centers of culture in our wealthier states such as New York, Michigan, Ohio, California, and Pennsylvania. In some of the wards there were scenes that rivaled the horrors of the Nazi concentration camps*—hundreds of naked mental patients herded into huge, barnlike, filth-infested wards, in all degrees of deterioration, untended and untreated, stripped of every vestige of human decency, many in stages of semi-starvation.†

The writer heard state hospital doctors frankly admit that the animals of near-by piggeries were better fed, housed and treated than many of the patients in their wards. He saw hundreds of sick people shackled, strapped, strait-jacketed and bound to their beds; he saw mental patients forced to eat meals with their hands because there were not enough spoons and other tableware to go around—not because they could not be trusted to eat like humans. He saw them crawl into beds jammed close together, in dormitories filled to twice or three times their normal capacity. He saw, in institution after institution, cold unappetizing food placed before patients at mealtime—food that patients either wolfed down to get the ordeal over quickly or else left untouched.

He saw black eyes and bruises which were reported to the writer to have been received at the hands of fellow patients or attendants. He saw court records and hospital accident lists indicating that brutality against patients, while not as common as occasional newspaper exposés might suggest, was of shocking frequency. Occasional accounts of fatal beatings of mental patients attested to the end-results of some of this treatment.

There were signs of medical neglect, of possibly curable cases sinking into chronicity, although if modern psychiatric treatment had been available it might have restored them to their homes. There were wards upon wards of patients sitting

---

*The Editorial Committee interprets this as figurative language rather than a literal comparison.

†To avoid possible misunderstanding the author wishes to make it clear that the statements in this paragraph and the three that follow are not based exclusively or even mainly on his eye witness observations, but are in each case supported by documentary evidence and/or the supporting statements of the institutions.

in idleness, day after day, and retreating farther and farther into their private worlds until they were, it seemed, completely out of touch with reality. No state hospital met all the minimum standards for adequate operation established twenty years earlier by the American Psychiatric Association. Everywhere there were various stages of overcrowding and understaffing, with underpaid and overworked employes laboring under discouraging handicaps.[6]

The institutions were gravely depleted of professional and lay personnel during World War II; institutional morale and standards of care and treatment deteriorated still further. It was inevitable that the war would have a negative effect on prevailing standards. But in most states the protective organizational structure surrounding these institutions proved so weak that war's impact was not merely damaging; it was disastrous. Criticism of institutional care and treatment of mental patients appeared with increasing frequency in the press.

Here and there, official investigations revealed shocking conditions. A New York State Senator in 1943 made public serious charges against a particular hospital after a personal visit. The Governor then appointed a Moreland Act Commission to investigate the management and affairs of the State Mental Hygiene Department and the institutions operated by it. The Commission's resulting report, published in 1944,[7] was a severe indictment of long-standing defects in the entire system that shocked the people of a state that had prided itself on its pre-eminent place in mental hygiene. While it was obviously "slanted" to place preceding state administrations under a rival political party in the worst possible light, the report nonetheless did expose effectively many real defects and abuses that had existed long before they became aggravated by the war emergency.

The report of the state investigating committee presented the following criticisms of what had been considered to be one of the best, if not the very best, of state mental hygiene systems:

> The outstanding deficiency in the mental hospitals in New York State is that the Department of Mental Hygiene in past years has allowed them to become principally custodial institutions rather than

hospitals in the true sense of the word. Progress in these hospitals has not kept pace with that shown in general hospitals.

The war has accentuated some of the problems arising from inability to provide adequate curative care. The war has not caused them. . . .

The real problem is not one of active mistreatment of the patient as much as it is of the lack of adequate professional care of the patient. . . .

The emphasis in all the institutions has been on administration, at the expense of clinical medicine. . . .

Visits to many wards in many of the hospitals revealed huge, overcrowded, dreary units with masses of patients, some in bed receiving a minimum of nursing care, others up and, except as they were assigned to assist with the work of the institution, inactive for many hours of the day. The majority seemed apathetic, some restless, and many unhappy. . . .[8]

During the war, some three thousand conscientious objectors were assigned to state mental hospitals as attendants under the Civilian Public Service program. Scores of these persons—sensitive to the suffering of the patients under their care—kept careful notes of incidents and observations in diaries and reports. These notes were later collected by a central group in Philadelphia and published in various forms by the National Mental Health Foundation, which was organized in 1945, primarily by idealistic ex-attendants.[9]

At its annual meeting in May, 1946, the American Psychiatric Association took frank and official cognizance of the public exposure of bad institutional conditions. The Council of the Association gave full approval to a report by its committee on psychiatric standards and policies, headed by Dr. Mesrop A. Tarumianz, superintendent of the Delaware State Hospital at Wilmington. The statement put the Association on record as urging "its entire membership, including state mental hospital superintendents, to call forcefully to the attention of the public and their legislators all of the shortcomings and deficiencies in state hospitals, and to demand the assistance and backing necessary to maintain mental hospitals in fact as well as in name."

The Association's Council stated further:

"It is estimated that not more than 25 per cent of present-day medical knowledge is made available to patients in state mental hospitals, and the Council calls to public attention the fact that in some cases it has been all too vividly revealed that these wards of the State are not even receiving good board and room."

The report of the committee on standards noted that institutional psychiatric service had never been provided on the same basis as the services of other medical branches in general hospitals. It urged that costs of care and treatment in mental hospitals be brought up to prevailing rates in general hospitals. The Committee concluded its report with these words:

> The American public will not consider psychiatry as a legitimate scientific branch of medicine as long as mental patients are treated in institutions with a cost of a minimum 65 cents per diem and a maximum of two dollars per capita per diem.
>
> The Committee believes the American Psychiatric Association should become more realistic and demand that every state mental hospital consider a minimum of five dollars per capita per diem for the care and treatment of acute, sub-acute and convalescent cases and two dollars and fifty cents per capita per diem for the care of various types of chronic cases.[10]

The Committee also urged the American Psychiatric Association to establish a permanent system of inspecting and rating mental hospitals, such as the American Medical Association maintains with respect to general hospitals. This recommendation was approved by the APA's Reorganization Committee, headed by Dr. Karl Menninger, and concrete steps toward the creation of a permanent rating system were taken when Dr. Daniel Blain became the first medical director of the American Psychiatric Association in 1948.

The APA in 1945 approved a revised set of standards for psychiatric hospitals drafted by Dr. Tarumianz's committee. The committee's report on standards, promulgated as an official APA document, included a ten-point program of minimum standards, as follows:

1. All hospitals should have a small unit or department which will take the place of the present receiving ward, where patients upon admission will remain a brief period (usually not to exceed two weeks) to be classified and housed according to their condition. This unit will require the services of a psy-

MODERN TRENDS IN INSTITUTIONAL CARE

chiatrist for every 30 patients under observation; a graduate nurse for every 4 patients and a trained attendant for every 6 patients under observation.

2. Approved hospitals should have a special unit or department for acutely mentally ill, where a patient will receive individual medical, psychiatric, nursing care and treatment, and individual services in the field of occupational, recreational and allied therapy. Intensive psychotherapy, in conjunction with physio-hydrotherapy, as well as modern organic therapy must be considered as indispensable in each case. The size of such a unit should accord with the admissions within a three- to six-months' period. This unit will have a small sub-unit for disturbed acutely ill individuals who will receive the same individual care and treatment.

All cases in the unit for acutely ill should be housed either in single rooms or in small dormitories. Such a unit will require a psychiatrist for every 30 patients; a graduate nurse for every 4 patients; a trained attendant for every 6 patients; a physio-hydrotherapist, an occupational therapist, and a recreational therapist for every 30 patients requiring such treatment, and any other service indicated.

3. Hospitals should have a unit or department for a convalescing group where a patient will receive somewhat similar care, although not requiring as intensive treatment as in the unit for acutely ill. The size of such a unit will be determined by the number of home convalescing patients during a period of six months. Such a unit will require a psychiatrist for every 50 patients; a graduate nurse for every 10 patients; a trained attendant for every 7 patients, an occupational therapist for every 30 patients; a recreational therapist for every 50 patients, and any other service indicated.

4. Hospitals assuming responsibility for patients with a favorable prognosis but who require intensive prolonged treatment and care should have a unit or department for such patients. Such a re-educational service will require a psychiatrist for every 75 patients; a graduate nurse for every 25 patients; a trained attendant for every 8 patients; a trained physio-hydrotherapist, an occupational therapist and a recreational therapist for every 75 patients, and any other service

indicated. This unit will have a special sub-unit for chronic disturbed patients.

5. Hospitals receiving patients who require continued treatment should have a special unit or department. Such a unit will need a psychiatrist for every 200 patients; a graduate nurse for every 40 patients; a trained attendant for every 6 patients; a physio-hydrotherapist for every 200 patients; an occupational therapist for every 50 patients; a recreational therapist for every 100 patients, and any other service indicated.

6. Hospitals receiving senile and arteriosclerotic patients should have a special unit or department for such patients. Such service will require a psychiatrist for every 200 patients; a graduate nurse for every 50 patients; a trained attendant for every 8 patients; an occupational-recreational therapist for every 100 patients; and any other service indicated. This department will also include a special infirmary section with a graduate nurse in charge.

7. Hospitals should have a special unit known as a medical and surgical department for patients who are actually physically ill, requiring either medical or surgical treatment. This unit will require well-trained physicians, who have had adequate experience in general medicine and general surgery, with some psychiatric background. This unit should meet minimal standards of the American College of Surgeons.

8. Mental hospitals receiving children under 16 years of age will require a special unit or department known as the children's unit. Such a unit will require the services of a psychiatrist, who has had training and experience in a child guidance clinic, and preferably pediatrics, for every 30 children; a graduate nurse for every 10 children; a trained attendant for every 7 children; a teacher for every 20 children; an occupational-recreational therapist for every 30 children; a physio-hydrotherapist for every 30 children; and any other service indicated.

9. If a mental hospital receives alcoholics and/or other drug addicts, it should have a special unit or department for their care and treatment. Such a unit will require a psychiatrist for every 25 patients; a graduate nurse and a trained at-

MODERN TRENDS IN INSTITUTIONAL CARE 455

tendant for every 8 patients; a physio-hydrotherapist for every 25 patients; an occupational therapist for every 50 patients; a recreational therapist for every 30 patients; and any other service indicated.

10. Mental hospitals should have a special unit or department for tuberculous patients. Such a unit will require the services of a physician experienced in the field of tuberculosis for every 75 patients and a psychiatrist for every 100 patients; a graduate nurse for every 5 patients; a trained attendant for every 6 patients; an occupational therapist for every 25 patients, and any other service indicated.

No institution can be considered a modern hospital unless it has adequate facilities for all types of physical examinations and tests required by the American College of Surgeons, including well-organized clinical and pathological laboratories under competent direction; a roentgenological department; and a medical library under supervision of the clinical director.

The APA report on standards also recommended that every approved mental hospital should have as its superintendent an experienced psychiatrist with administrative ability; that every staff member should be encouraged to devote some hours each week to research or scientific study; that it should have a well-organized department of clinical psychology, adequate training courses for psychiatric nurses and attendants, a minimum of one social worker for every 100 annual admissions, and adequate dental, pharmacy, and library departments.

The report also contained a strong recommendation that every state permit by law voluntary commitment of patients to mental hospitals.[11]

Mental Hospital Statistics. The annual report of the U. S. Census Bureau on *Patients in Mental Institutions* for 1945* showed a total of 517,989 patients in mental hospitals for permanent psychiatric care at the end of that year, representing 371 persons out of every 100,000 in the general popula-

---

*The duty of compiling statistics on institutions for the mentally ill and the mentally defective was transferred in 1948 from the U. S. Census Bureau to the Mental Hygiene Division of the U. S. Public Health Service.

tion of the United States. These census figures do not include psychopathic hospitals, psychiatric facilities in general hospitals, or station hospitals maintained by the armed forces. They cover 190 state mental hospitals,* 33 veterans hospitals maintained by the U. S. Government for psychiatric cases, 95 county and city hospitals and 192 private hospitals. There were 592,454 patients on the books of these hospitals at the end of 1945, including 21,191 under family care and 72,274 under other types of extramural care. Of all institutionalized patients, 505,100 were on the books of state hospitals, 47,300 in U. S. veterans hospitals, 25,591 in county and city hospitals, and 14,463 in private hospitals. The number admitted to these institutions in 1945 totalled 193,894.[12]

Total expenditures for maintenance of the 190 state hospitals in 1945 amounted to approximately $165,750,000.

Many states, during the war years, established postwar planning commissions which included in their scope the rehabilitation of existing state hospitals and the building of new ones. High building costs and scarcity of building materials in the years immediately following the war greatly impeded these construction programs, however.

Dr. Samuel W. Hamilton in 1944 listed sixteen institutions for mental and nervous disorders operated by church bodies; the oldest is the Seton Institute in Baltimore, opened in 1840. Twenty-nine institutions operated by non-profit secular associations were listed by Dr. Hamilton, the oldest being the Pennsylvania Hospital, West Philadelphia Department, opened in 1752.[13] Since Dr. Hamilton's list was compiled, the Menninger Sanitarium in Topeka, Kansas, has been converted into a non-profit institution, operated by the Menninger Foundation. The rated capacity of these non-profit mental hospitals ranges from 50 to 500 beds.

The ideal size for mental hospitals is still as much debated a question as it was back in 1866, when the issue threatened to split the American Psychiatric Association. Some psychiatrists advocate the small-sized hospital as affording a better setting for individualization of treatment and close

---

*The federally operated St. Elizabeths Hospital in Washington, D.C., is included in the state-hospital category for census purposes.

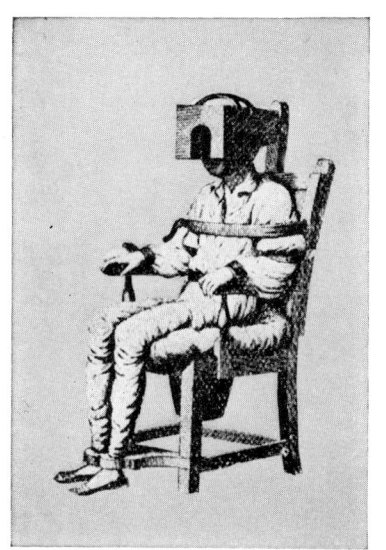

OLD METHODS OF RESTRAINT AND A MODERN SUBSTITUTE

A. Benjamin Rush's Tranquilizer (See p. 79).
B. Norris in Chains, 1815 (See p. 100 n.).
C. Recreational therapy in a modern state hospital, a positive factor in curative treatment.

rapport between patient and staff members. Others are in favor of large-sized hospitals of 3,000 to 5,000 bed capacity as permitting better patient classification and diversification, and finer therapeutic equipment, the cost of which is spread over a larger population. Central Islip State Hospital in New York has a patient population of over 7,000; the Pilgrim State Hospital, not far distant, has a capacity for 10,000; the Georgia State Hospital at Milledgeville is a crowded city of 9,000 patients and hundreds of employes. The consensus in psychiatric circles is swinging back to the ideal set forth by the pioneers of a century ago—the small institution where patients can be persons instead of vaguely remembered numbers on the regimented wards.

CHAPTER XXI
Psychiatry in World War II

THE GREAT DEPRESSION of the 1930's, with its impact on the emotional health of many Americans, was hardly over when mental hygienists were confronted with an even greater crisis—the war emergency. Prolonged economic crisis, with its attendant insecurities, gradually gave way to an attenuated world political crisis precipitated by Nazi Germany in its bold drive for global conquest. The diplomatic capitulation of 1938, which led deluded statesmen to sign the Munich Pact with Hitler in the hope that it would guarantee "peace in our time," actually set the stage for the impending conflict. As the shooting war developed, following the Nazi invasion of Poland in September, 1939, Americans in increasing number realized that the United States would inevitably be drawn into the bloody maelstrom. Some Americans saw the need for preparation earlier than others.

Among the far-visioned ones were some psychiatrists and mental hygienists. They were eager to have the costly psychiatric lessons of the first World War promptly applied to the second. They hoped, particularly, that the failure of early psychiatric screening of military recruits in World War I would not be repeated this time. Their hopes were realized, in substance, only toward the end of the war, after a succession of costly blunders in this and other aspects of wartime mental hygiene.

As the war crisis grew more acute, these major objectives of mental hygiene in wartime became manifest:

1) Maintenance and strengthening of civilian morale on the home front;

2) Formulation of techniques for psychiatric selection of recruits for the armed forces, and for separation at the earliest possible moment of bad military risks, from a psychiatric viewpoint, who had escaped detection at selective service and induction centers;

3) Prompt and efficient treatment of psychiatric casualties in the armed forces;

4) Maintenance of optimum mental health and furtherance of good morale among men in the military ranks;

5) Rehabilitation of rejected draft registrants and of military men returned to civilian life as psychiatric casualties of war;

6) Maintenance of minimum mental hospital standards.

It cannot be said, in truth, that psychiatry and mental hygiene rose nobly to the challenge posed by these objectives. The leadership in this field, as in many others, was handicapped by indecision, excessive timidity in an emergency demanding boldness of purpose and methods, confusion and jealous rivalries. Most important of all inadequacies, however, was the pitiable shortage of psychiatric personnel in every field of activity, a shortage that became more and more apparent as the war situation developed. There were less than 3,000 trained psychiatrists in the entire country when war broke out—a fraction of the number needed to meet the monumental crisis adequately. Shortages in auxiliary professions were likewise acute.

The hesitation of psychiatric leadership to assert itself in the war crisis was matched by the profound indifference of civil, military, and selective service officials toward calling upon the profession for help. The National Committee for Mental Hygiene, which in 1917 was promptly invited to provide leadership for the organization of psychiatric services in the armed forces, was ignored by responsible authorities in the early period of World War II. The Committee's chronic lack of financial resources hampered its efforts to arouse active public interest in the problems of wartime mental hygiene. Lastly, but not least, the tremendous gaps of scientific knowledge in the etiology, prevention, and treatment of emotional disorders, individually and in the mass, was an inhibiting factor in the early development of a sound mental hygiene program for the civilian and military populations.

Home Front Morale. Even before the United States was precipitated into World War II by the bombing of Pearl Harbor, it had become obvious that the country was due for a considerable amount of social disorganization that might affect the emotional health of civilians. The "national defense emergency"—as the period between the Nazi invasion of Poland and the Pearl Harbor attack was commonly called—saw the start of a mass migration of unprecedented character in this country. Hundreds of thousands of Americans and their families pulled up stakes to converge in the many "boom towns" created by expanding war industries. The sudden mass-scale dislocation quite naturally produced lively discussion in professional and lay circles as to its impact on mental health and social stability. There was confusion and disorder as a nation in crisis girded itself for still greater crisis. Great industrial centers sprang up virtually overnight on hitherto barren prairies. Another and greater migration began when the military draft was voted by Congress—the migration of millions of young men, and young women, first toward the induction centers and army camps, then overseas toward the war fronts. Millions of families were disrupted. New orientations became imperative. Fears and anxieties seized masses of Americans after the stunning blow at Pearl Harbor. Tension was particularly high during the first bleak months of actual warfare, when repeated defeats and disasters brought the fear of actual invasion or bombardment distinctly within the realm of possibility.

There was much discussion in the lay and professional literature on buttressing civilian mental health, known more popularly as home-front morale. Sporadic efforts were undertaken toward morale-building propaganda. The U. S. Office of Civilian Defense was a main spearhead of such efforts. In general, however, the official and professional counsel on this subject was rather weak, confused, and contradictory.

As the war progressed, attention of the civilian morale-builders was concentrated on the "teen-age problem"—war's impact on adolescents—and especially on the increase in juvenile delinquency in war-industry areas. In the end, the mental and emotional stamina of the American masses proved much tougher than had been anticipated. The favorable turn of the war, after the first few months of our participation, greatly relieved general tensions. War prosperity made it possible for millions of American families to eat more and live better than they ever had before. It appears that civilian psychoses actually decreased during the war years, and there is no concrete evidence that there was any increase of the milder mental disorders as a result of the wartime tensions. Some psychiatrists feel that war-created motivations, and the general sense of belonging involved in participation of common defense, actually strengthened the emotional fibre of many people.[1]

Psychiatry and Selective Service. The problem of psychiatric screening for military service was widely discussed early in the emergency, but it was not until late in the war that an adequate screening system was put into effect. Organized psychiatry, in this respect as in others dealing with the war emergency, was slow to press home to the proper authorities and to the public the importance of psychiatry in the general screening process. Individuals and groups were, it is true, early alerted to the psychiatric emergency precipitated by the war crisis, but their voices were lost in the general hue and cry for many precious months and even years.

The most alert single psychiatric group in the pre-war period was the William Alanson White Psychiatric Foundation, established in 1937 as a memorial to the great American psychiatrist who died that year. Barely a year after its founding, the Foundation's trustees, concerned with the war clouds that gathered ominously after the Munich fiasco, prepared a memorandum on the role of psychiatry in the armed forces.

The February, 1939, issue of the Foundation's journal, *Psychiatry,* published a report by Captain Dallas G. Sutton of the U. S. Navy Medical Corps on military psychiatry. Captain Sutton, in his paper, observed that psychiatric screening played a negligible role in peacetime recruitment procedures, and stressed its importance in the anticipated large-scale recruitment for a potential war.

The Council of the American Psychiatric Association, at the annual meeting in May, 1939, recognized the impending crisis by creating a Committee on Military Mobilization to confer with Federal authorities on the role of psychiatric personnel. This Committee's contribution to the war effort was a very modest one.

The Southern Psychiatric Association, at its October, 1939, meeting—only a few weeks after the Nazis invaded Poland—framed a memorial to the Federal Government on the potential values of psychiatry in national defense. At its next meeting, in 1940, a report was presented by a special committee dealing mainly with the psychiatric aspects of the Selective Service Act, passed by Congress in September, 1940.[2]

The William Alanson White Psychiatric Foundation, meanwhile, had been actively preparing plans and materials concerned with the war crisis. In October, 1940, it published an outline for the psychiatric examination of draft registrants which became the basis for the Selective Service System's Medical Circular No. 1, promulgated November 7, 1940.[3] The circular was aimed at helping the examining physicians at the 6,403 local draft boards throughout the country to recognize symptoms of disabling personality disorders. But in the haste and confusion that attended the early period of the military draft, the task of orienting already hard-pressed general practitioners to quick detection of psychiatric symptoms proved most difficult. The acute shortage of trained psychiatrists in the face of the overwhelming need to recruit a huge military force speedily was another great barrier to adequate psychiatric screening of draft registrants. Selective service officials refused to heed the lessons of World War I and tended grossly to underestimate the value of psychiatric screening. Dr. Harry Stack Sullivan, then president of the William Alanson White Psychiatric Foundation, was appointed psychiatric consultant to the Selective Service Administrator shortly after the draft was begun. But differences arose between administrator and consultant, and Dr. Sullivan resigned his post. He had thrown himself enthusiastically into the task of preparing adequate screening procedures, only to have his plans ignored or poorly handled. Proposals for psychiatric selection that seemed eminently feasible during the first months of the military draft became obviously impossible of attainment after the accelerated draft process following Pearl Harbor.

It had been recommended that one psychiatrist be assigned to draft examining boards for every fifty registrants, and that a minimum of fifteen minutes be devoted to every psychiatric examination. When the many millions began to pour through selective service centers, however, these proposals became scraps of paper on the wind. Instead of fifteen minutes, an average of barely two minutes was devoted to the psychiatric examination of Army recruits. It was not unusual for a single psychiatrist to examine 200 men daily. The course of psychiatric screening throughout the war was highly irregular. In some states and in some centers, men with long mental hospital records were rushed into the armed forces; in many centers, no effort was made to ascertain institutional histories for psychotic episodes; at others, men with histories of very mild emotional disorders were summarily rejected. The pendulum of directives swung from one extreme to another during the war; at one period, practically everybody not obviously psychotic was accepted for service; at another, nobody with the slightest trace of neurosis passed the examining board.

A significant development in psychiatric screening was the official adoption in October, 1943, of the "medical survey" program, wherein the volunteer services of several thousand social workers were enlisted. The program is described by one of its progenitors. Dr. Luther E. Woodward, field consultant, National Committee for Mental Hygiene, as "a device for obtaining health, work, social and educational histories of registrants and for making the same available to the induction boards as aids in their examination and evaluation of registrants."* Dr. Raymond Waggoner, psychiatric consultant to the Selective Service System at the time, was mainly instrumental in getting the program adopted after it had been tried experimentally in several states. During the fiscal year

*For details of program, see Medical Circular #4, Selective Service System, October 18, 1943, U. S. Government Printing Office, Washington.

1945, when the Federal Government appropriated $1,000,-000 to subsidize the medical survey program in 37 states, a total of 365,000 names were cleared through social service exchanges and 483,000 social histories were compiled.

The figures on the percentage of draft registrants rejected for psychiatric disabilities or defects, as revealed toward the end of World War II, shocked the nation and had the effect of greatly accelerating the wartime interests in mental health. Testifying before a Congressional Committee in August, 1945, Major General Lewis B. Hershey, Director of the Selective Service System, stated that of the 4,800,000 men, aged 18 to 37, who had been rejected for military service (out of approximately 15,000,000 examined) up to August 1, 1945, no less than 1,091,000 had been turned down for neuropsychiatric disorders. Of these, 856,000 had been rejected for mental ills and 235,000 for neurological conditions. If, to these figures were added the rejectees for mental and educational deficiencies, the total amounted to 1,767,000 out of the 4,800,000.[4]

General Hershey estimated that about 80 per cent of the psychiatric rejectees were deemed to be suffering from psychoneuroses or psychopathic personalities, while the rest were afflicted with "more serious mental disorders." He added that others among the 4,800,000 rejected men had neuropsychiatric disorders, although these were not listed as the main reasons for rejection.

Even though it was repeatedly explained that most of the men found unfit for military duty on neuropsychiatric grounds were leading independent and even successful lives in the normal civilian community, the realization that about 17 per cent of Americans in the prime of life were deemed unfit for military service on those grounds had a sobering effect on the public and gave great stimulus to the mental hygiene movement.

Psychiatry in Armed Forces. If psychiatry, traditionally, was the Cinderella of civilian medicine, its estate in military medicine was even lower when the war crisis broke upon the world. Disregarding the patent lessons of World War I, the

PSYCHIATRY IN WORLD WAR II

Army Medical Corps had not even set up a special psychiatric section. In spite of the obvious shortages of trained psychiatrists, flagrant instances of misuse of scarce specialists accumulated during the early period of the second World War. Psychiatrists, in many cases, were assigned to general medical duty while general practitioners were put in charge of psychiatric wards in military hospitals.

The first significant step toward adequate recognition of psychiatry in American military medicine during World War II came in February, 1942, when the Surgeon General of the Army Medical Corps created a neuropsychiatric branch in his office. Col. Roy D. Halloran was named chief of the Branch in August, 1942. A school for training military psychiatrists was established at the Lawson General Hospital in Atlanta under the direction of Col. William C. Porter. (It was later transferred to Brentwood, New York, in affiliation with the Mason General Hospital there—the best known of Army psychiatric installations in the United States.) Neuropsychiatric consultants were gradually appointed to each of eight service commands; ultimately, a divisional psychiatrist was appointed to each Army division.

A notable innovation in the development of wartime military psychiatry was the establishment of mental hygiene clinics at Army replacement training centers. The first of these was organized in 1943 at Fort Monmouth, New Jersey, under Major Harry Freedman.

Colonel Halloran, in a paper prepared in collaboration with his assistant, Lt. Col. Malcolm J. Farrell, described the rationale for these camp mental hygiene clinics as follows:

> It is inevitable that even under the most exacting induction examination, some individuals will be missed who cannot adapt themselves to military life. Every attempt, therefore, must be made to weed them out during the early training period. It soon became evident that the ideal place to accomplish this is the replacement training center. Here the new soldier is given basic training and here the hazards of Army routine begin to manifest themselves in emotionally unstable and intellectually inadequate individuals. The Army has established, therefore, special mental hygiene units in eighteen replacement training centers, under

the direction of specially selected and qualified neuropsychiatrists. More will be established as qualified specialists become available.* This medical officer is assisted by a psychologist and a psychiatric social worker furnished by the American Red Cross. In some instances, psychiatric social workers among enlisted personnel are available.

The purpose of these clinics is to aid the adjustment of normal individuals and those with minor difficulties, and to detect and eliminate the mentally unstable who are or may become a distinct liability to military training.[5]

The raising of camp morale became increasingly a part of the psychiatrist's job in the Army. One of the best morale programs was worked out by psychiatrists at the Ordnance Replacement Training Center at Aberdeen Proving Ground, Maryland. A fresh variant in military morale work was introduced later by Major Julius Schreiber, chief psychiatrist at Camp Callan, California, who prepared a regular column for the camp weekly newspaper, *The Range Finder*. This weekly column, a unique venture in military journalism, explained in simple and lively language such issues as the basic conflict between democracy and fascism, everyday personal problems of camp life, and the like.

Morale [Major Schreiber wrote] is a state of mind which enables a soldier to carry on and persevere in his mission in spite of the most adverse conditions. It can come only when he fully understands the very fundamental issues at stake—only when he feels that he is an integral part of everything he is fighting for.[6]

Colonel Halloran died suddenly in 1944. He was succeeded as chief psychiatrist in the Army by Lieutenant Colonel, later Brigadier General, William C. Menninger. Under General Menninger the prestige and importance of the Army psychiatric service increased steadily, and by the time the war ended psychiatry was equalized within the Army Medical Corps on the same plane with medicine and surgery. In a paper summarizing the psychiatric experiences of World War II, read at the 1946 annual meeting of the American Psychiatric Association, Dr. Menninger cited these interesting statistics:

*Mental hygiene units were subsequently established at all Army training camps.

During the period of January 1, 1942, through December 30, 1945 . . . there were approximately one million patients with neuropsychiatric disorders admitted to army hospitals. This represented a rate of 45 admissions per 1,000 troops per year and constituted 6 per cent of all admissions.

Seven per cent of the neuropsychiatric admissions were for psychoses; 64 per cent were for psychoneuroses, and the remaining 29 per cent represented diagnoses of psychopathic personality, mental deficiency and other psychiatric or neurological disorders. Of the one million neuropsychiatric admissions, 40 per cent were among troops overseas and 60 per cent among troops on duty in the United States. The peak load of neuropsychiatric patients occurred in April, 1945, with approximately 50,000 in Army hospitals.

From January, 1942, through December, 1945, there were 380,000 men who were granted medical discharges from the Army because of neuropsychiatric disorders, which represented 39 per cent of all medical discharges. In addition 137,000 men were discharged administratively for personality disorders which included mental deficiency, psychopathic personality, enuresis and other conditions which, according to army procedure, are not given medical discharges. This makes a total of over 500,000 men discharged for personality disturbances.

The evacuation figures also are significant during the four-year period of 1942–1945. Nearly 19 per cent of the number of army patients evacuated from overseas were neuropsychiatric. This figure broken down shows that 31 per cent of the patients who were returned in 1942 for medical reasons were psychiatric, and following the great increase of battle wounded, this fell to 15 per cent in 1945.[7]

In a review of wartime psychiatry at the same session, Captain Francis J. Braceland, Dr. Menninger's opposite number in the U. S. Navy, presented these summarized statistics:

In the U. S. Navy from January 1, 1942, to July 1, 1945, a period which roughly covers the war years, there were 149,281 patients admitted to various naval hospitals and dispensaries throughout the world for all reasons which could be subsumed under the heading of psychiatric diseases. This comprehensive category includes everything from mild emotional instability to malignant schizophrenia. Of this number of patients, 76,721 individuals had to be separated from naval service, and this figure represents roughly 32.4 per cent of the total naval medical separations during the entire war.

During the war years, 91,565 enlisted and inducted recruits were separated from naval training centers because of neuropsychiatric difficulties. These discharges for neurologic and psychiatric reasons were also all inclusive. They included the mentally deficient, the patients with organic central nervous system diseases and epilepsy, as well as those with behavior disorders and all other forms of psychiatric illnesses.[8]

A total of 2,400 physicians—992 of whom were members of the American Psychiatric Association—served in the Army's neuropsychiatric services during the war; in the Navy, these activities were undertaken by 693 naval medical officers "with varying degrees of psychiatric training."

In the early part of the war, it was customary for the Army to discharge all psychiatric casualties who did not respond to rapid, more or less makeshift, treatment. This policy was later changed to provide maximum hospital benefits save for cases of chronic psychotic reactions and degenerative neurological disorders. General Menninger, in his review of the Army experience, observed that patients were concentrated in 28 specially designated general hospitals for the treatment of psychotics and severe neurotic reactions; neurological centers were established in 18 general hospitals. Elaborate treatment procedures developed at convalescent hospitals resulted in the return of from 15 to 25 per cent of psychiatric casualties to duty, although these hospitals received only those soldiers not considered salvageable through treatment in overseas hospitals. The majority of the other convalescent hospital patients were returned to their homes much improved.

In 1942, General Menninger noted, about 80 per cent of the Army's psychotic patients were transferred to veterans hospitals or state hospitals for further care, while in 1945—after the treatment program had been effectuated—about 75 per cent were recovered sufficiently to return directly to their homes.

Wide interest was evoked in the latter years of the war in the rather extensive use of group psychotherapy, psychotherapy through sedation (especially the form known as narcosynthesis), and hypnotic techniques.

General Menninger expressed particular satisfaction with the treatment program developed for combat casualties. At the outset of hostilities, there was no plan at all, beyond sending psychiatric casualties to rear-area hospitals, with only 5 to 10 per cent salvaged for duty. When the program was organized, treatment centers were set up near the front line, utilizing division psychiatrists and others borrowed from evacuation hospitals. With prompt treatment, General Menninger stated, 60 per cent of psychiatric casualties were returned within 2 to 5 days to duty for combat or service in the forward area. The hospitals farther in the rear salvaged an additional 30 per cent for non-combat duty in the theater.[9]

As the war progressed, increasing use was made of psychiatrists in Army disciplinary procedures; they participated in the examination and rehabilitation efforts of about 45,000 military offenders.

Certainly one of the most significant achievements of American military psychiatry during the second World War revolved around development that attracted little outside notice at the time. This was the revolutionary change in official psychiatric nomenclature effected under General Menninger. The traditional existing standard nomenclature was vague in definition, lending itself to widely variant interpretations, and was heavily weighted in the listing of psychotic ailments as compared with the psychoneuroses. It closely resembled civilian state hospital nomenclatures in its emphasis on the psychoses. This was an anomaly in the Army, where only 7 per cent of the neuropsychiatric casualties were psychotics. With the help of outstanding civilian psychiatrists, the Army psychiatric authorities revised the nomenclature, giving great weight to the more prevalent neuroses and clarifying many diagnostic listings.[10] In its revised form, the official Army nomenclature proved of great benefit to post-war civilian psychiatry in the clarification of diagnostic concepts and procedures.

The revised nomenclature broke down mental and emotional disorders, as observed in the military service, into five major categories, namely:

1) Transient personality reactions to acute or special stress (including combat exhaustion and acute situational maladjustment);

2) Psychoneurotic disorders (including anxiety reaction, dissociative reaction, phobic reaction, conversion reaction, somatization reaction, obsessive-compulsive reaction, and hypochondriacal reaction);

3) Character and behavior disorders (including pathological personality types, addiction, immaturity reactions, passive-dependency, passive-aggressive and aggressive reactions, and immaturity with symptomatic "habit" reaction);

4) Disorders of intelligence (including mental deficiency and specific learning defects);

5) Psychotic disorders (including schizophrenic, paranoid and affective disorders, and psychoses with demonstrable etiology or associated structural changes in the brain, or both).

Army psychiatry, notwithstanding its impressive achievements, by no means progressed uninterruptedly from one triumph to another. Many obstructions along the path were never surmounted; and there were disturbing failures. Some individual medical officers in the psychiatric service returned to civilian life with critical, sometimes bitter, accounts of defects and failures.[11]

General Menninger, in a retrospective view of the Army experience, gave free vent to significant short-comings. He wrote:

> We must admit many failures. Many of our difficulties arose from the lack of planning. There was no psychiatric screening of the national guard and other units, including the medical officers, that came into the Army by any means other than through the induction center and not even gross misfits in these groups were eliminated. On the other hand, we expected far too much from the induction center screening, and fell in with the overselling of what psychiatry could do at that level, even to the point that some people assumed there would be no psychiatric casualties because we had screened them out. We never were successful in applying psychiatric principles to the selection of officers.
>
> The Army policy did not retain psychiatric patients for treatment until we changed the policy two years after the war began; we knew most neurotic patients were not helped by hospitalization, but it was nearly three years after war began that we were able to get them into convalescent facilities. . . . We often failed in orienting our own

medical officers, including psychiatrists, in the specific needs of the military, in which one must accept the group aim and needs as of paramount importance instead of that of the individual. . . .

None of us in the military feel that we more than scratched the surface of many possibilities and we were never in a position to do much more than attempt to meet the more pressing demands for our services.

The most severe indictment that can be made must be laid at the feet of the psychiatric profession as a whole—we permitted the military to forget almost all the lessons that we learned in the last war. As a consequence we began this war with hospital treatment forbidden, with no plan of treatment for combat troops, no unit to provide such, no plans for training, no psychiatrist in combat divisions, and not even a psychiatrist in headquarters when war was declared.[12]

On the whole, Dr. Menninger concluded in his review, psychiatry in the Army did a "reasonably creditable job primarily because of the devotion, integrity and ability of a small group of men." Its many defects can be attributed mainly to the failure to select and train new and better psychiatrists, and to the marked inarticulateness of the psychiatric profession in terms of pressing for the military goals possible of attainment.

Psychiatric drive was not lacking in the Army Air Forces where, under the virtually autonomous Air Surgeon's Office, a small group of younger psychiatrists fought hard against inertia and even hostility at the top to get the best available services for their men. The AAF psychiatrists, in general, manifested an extraordinary sense of dedication to the men under their care. Frequently braving the displeasure of their superiors in the Air Surgeon's Office, they pressed constantly for adequate hospital facilities for psychiatric casualties, for a sound mental hygiene program in the AAF, and for extensive briefing of flight surgeons in the special psychiatric hazards of flying.

A carefully prepared treatment-teaching program of on-the-job training for AAF psychiatry was recommended to the Air Surgeon's Office, but gained only partial acceptance. A treatment-teaching center—organized around "psychiatric teams" consisting of psychiatrists, junior psychiatrists, personal physicians, psychiatric social workers and clinical psychologists—was set up at Fort Logan, Colorado, under Col. John Milne Murray, and another at Don Ce-Sar Hospital, St. Petersburg, Florida, under Col. Roy R. Grinker.

During the war, wide and favorable publicity was given to the achievements of psychiatry in the AAF. Much of this publicity was fully merited. But at war's end, in an unusually frank and critical review, Colonel Murray summed up as "decidedly limited" the contribution of AAF psychiatry to helping make the Forces more effective in their military tasks and in alleviating the sufferings of psychiatric casualties.

"It will ever be thus," Colonel Murray said, "until men in authority, with whom rests the ultimate power of decision, have breadth, vision and courage behind their desire to help those in the lower echelons who are hurt by war."[13]

At one time during the war, the feud between the Air Surgeon and the Army Surgeon General, who was nominally his superior, took on such fantastic proportions that it seriously affected the medical care of sick and wounded flying men. Human values seemed to be lost as the two officers jockeyed for greater power and prestige. Dr. Edward A. Strecker, who held the unique wartime distinction of serving simultaneously as psychiatric consultant to the Army Medical Corps, the Air Surgeon's Office, and the Surgeon General of the U. S. Navy, referred briefly but significantly to this fantastic feud at the 1946 American Psychiatric Association meeting:

"I would be remiss if I did not mention that amazing inner conflict between the medical departments of the Army and the AAF. I will say nothing of its merits but it did not help psychiatric effectiveness and it must never happen again."[14]

Psychiatry in the Merchant Marine. A special problem of wartime psychiatry arose in the early years of the war as a result of the emotional hazards of merchant shipping. An effectively destructive campaign was conducted by Nazi submarines and bombing planes against our ships which served as the life lines of supply between us, the allied nations, and our troops overseas. American seamen experienced extraordinary hardships in the course of long voyages through dangerous waters in blacked-out ships, with unseen dangers apt to strike at any moment. Survivors of torpedoed or bombed ships often had to undergo prolonged tortures and sufferings surpassing those encountered by front-line soldiers. The psychiatric toll resulting from these perils was naturally very high. The acute manpower shortage in the merchant marine, together with the vital need to keep the life lines of supply operating, put a premium on reducing psychiatric casualties to a minimum and on returning as many as possible to duty as soon as possible.

Most of the psychiatric casualties among merchant seamen took the form of what was known as "shell shock" in the first World War and as "combat fatigue" in the second. To the seamen themselves, it was commonly called "convoy jitters." Greatly distressed by this drain on marine manpower, the U. S. War Shipping Administration requested Surgeon General Thomas Parran of the U. S. Public Health Service to furnish medical services to the victims. A program was set up under the direction of Dr. Daniel Blain, who later served as chief of neuropsychiatry in the Veterans Administration. It was sponsored jointly by the War Shipping Administration and the United Seamen's Service, a wartime welfare agency which provided necessary but long-neglected services to merchant mariners.

The medical activities for merchant seamen, as outlined by Dr. Blain, were manifested in three main phases: (1) survivors of torpedoed or bombed ships were given emergency care as they returned to American shores; (2) those with medical and surgical conditions were referred to appropriate hospital and clinic facilities; and (3) a series of convalescent centers or hospitals were operated to care for those suffering from traumatic war neuroses.

While the centers admitted somatic convalescents, their programs were mainly psychiatry-oriented, with the interests of victims of traumatic war neuroses primarily stressed. The centers were set up in or near convenient ports of call along the Atlantic, Pacific, and Gulf coasts.

The gravity of the problem of "convoy fatigue" among American seafarers was underscored by the convening of a special conference on "Traumatic War Neuroses among Merchant Seamen" at The New York Academy of Medicine in

January, 1943. The conference was attended by leading military and civilian psychiatrists of the United States and Canada. Out of this conference came many valuable suggestions for the rehabilitation not only of merchant seamen, but also of military personnel suffering from combat fatigue.[15]

Shortly after the war ended, the convalescent centers for seamen were abandoned, and the rest of the psychiatric program was terminated. The merchant seamen, who had been the "forgotten men" in pre-war years, then suddenly glorified during the early war period (there were more fatal casualties among merchant seamen in the first war year than in the Army and Navy combined), slipped back into obscurity. The war-created services for them disappeared with the loss of public interest.

Veteran Rehabilitation. As the war wore on, much concern was manifested among professional and lay groups in the adjustment problems of returning servicemen. Many articles, pamphlets, and even books were published giving counsel to families and communities on how to help the "normal" veteran hurdle the expected emotional upsets upon his return to the civilian milieu after extended subjection to military regimen. It was anticipated that large numbers of the 16,000,000 men and women who passed through the wartime military services would experience various degrees of emotional maladjustment following their release. Thanks mainly to generally favorable economic conditions persisting through the period of mass demobilization—with conditions of "full employment" prevailing—the civilian readjustment of the average veteran proved surprisingly smooth.

But until late in the war, psychiatrically disabled veterans and others requiring medical attention encountered serious obstacles along the road to rehabilitation. The Veterans Administration, charged with the duty of providing hospital and out-patient care and treatment for veterans with service-connected disabilities, was ill-prepared at the outbreak of war for its monumental task. In 1944 this writer conducted an extensive journalistic survey of the Veterans Administration medical services, with special attention to hospital and out-patient facilities for psychiatric cases. His findings, published in a lengthy newspaper series beginning in January, 1945,* revealed general administrative demoralization and disorganization, bureaucratic inertia and red tape, apathetic disinterest in medical services at the top echelons of the Veterans Administration and the rule of repression and mediocrity at the lower echelons. Psychiatric facilities were isolated from the mainstreams of modern medicine. They were staffed in large part by inadequately trained personnel cut off from the stimulating medical communications required for professional progress. Out-patient psychiatric treatment often consisted of routine prescriptions of sedatives doled out at stated intervals. In a number of communities, psychoneurotic veterans were getting into serious trouble for lack of adequate attention. The dispensing of psychiatric services within the Veterans Administration was generally sluggish and dispirited.

A Congressional committee investigation was launched in the spring of 1945 into the V.A.'s medical services following the published revelations by this writer and other journalists, notably Mr. Albert Maisel. In August, 1945, Brigadier General Frank T. Hines, was replaced by General Omar Bradley as Administrator of Veterans Affairs as a result of a directive from President Truman. General Bradley instituted what amounted to a revolution in the V.A. medical services. He appointed as medical director Major General Paul R. Hawley, a vigorous exponent of first-grade medicine. Dr. Hawley, in turn, appointed Dr. Daniel Blain as chief of the V.A. psychiatric division. Dr. Blain succeeded in attracting to V.A. service many outstanding psychiatrists, some of them recruited directly from the military forces.

Resident and intern programs were introduced into V.A. psychiatric facilities, or hospitals, for the first time. Younger men, inspirited with modern psychiatric methods and ideals, were drawn into the program. Social workers, psychologists, psychiatric nurses and attendants (who began to be called "psychiatric aides") were given more dignified status and salaries more commensurate with their important duties in restoring mentally disturbed veterans to the community. The walls of isolation were steadily broken down; staff members

*In the newspaper *PM*, New York.

were encouraged to maintain contact with civilian medicine; V.A. psychiatric programs, wherever possible, were oriented around or near large medical centers; leading civilian psychiatrists were employed as part-time consultants and were otherwise prevailed upon to help raise existing standards. New psychiatric clinics were established in the community to serve veterans requiring out-patient treatment, with well-rounded programs of activity. These clinics never approached adequacy for the amount of service needed, but the quality of the available service generally surpassed by far the standards prevailing before the "Bradley-Hawley-Blain" revolution. For a time, in the period following the war, veterans with service-connected psychiatric ailments requiring out-patient care were permitted to place themselves under the care of private psychiatrists of their own choice, with the V.A. footing the bill. High financial costs, together with occasional abuses of the program, led to the termination of this experiment in 1946, and ambulatory patients were thereafter required to visit V.A. clinics for out-patient treatment.

The Winter Veterans Hospital at Topeka, Kansas, under the direction of Dr. Karl Menninger, stood as an institutional symbol of the progressive "psychiatric revolution" in the V.A. Dr. Menninger, a top-ranking psychiatrist, developed this former Army hospital into one of the nation's leading psychiatric centers, comparable with the best of civilian mental hospitals.

Of the 91,224 patients in Veterans Administration hospitals on June 30, 1947, more than half—51,907— were neuropsychiatric cases. Of the 101,273 operating beds in V.A. hospitals, 55,513 belonged in the neuropsychiatric category. Of the 367,079 patients admitted to veterans hospitals during the fiscal year 1947, neuropsychiatric cases accounted for 54,-731. A total of 588,175 out-patient treatments was furnished by the V.A. for neuropsychiatric conditions during the same year. The Veterans Administration, on June 30, 1947, was operating 123 hospitals, 33 of which were neuropsychiatric hospitals. The operating cost per patient-day in these neuropsychiatric hospitals during fiscal 1947 averaged $5.38. Bed occupancy in NP facilities averaged 92 per cent.[16]

In February, 1948, Dr. Blain was able to summarize the following developments, among others, in his two years' stewardship of the V.A.'s neuropsychiatric program:

Neuropsychiatric hospitals of the Veterans Administration were being converted into general hospitals, with well-established general medical and surgical sections. At the same time, neuropsychiatric units were being organized in general hospitals, making possible more complete facilities for the general patient and allowing intensive early treatment of acute psychotic and other psychiatric patients.

Modern treatment methods of demonstrated validity were being increasingly utilized in veterans hospitals for psychiatric patients. Medical rehabilitation procedures were being intensified.

Improved treatment methods were leading to "an enormous increase in hospital discharges over the past two years." Actual neuropsychiatric beds had been increased 14 per cent during this period, but monthly discharges had increased 68 per cent and admissions 53 per cent. "These figures indicate not only the spread of hospital treatment among greater numbers of veterans, but also that many veterans can and are being returned to their homes in a much improved state and able to readjust to normal life." On November 30, 1947, Dr. Blain reported, the V.A. was operating 55,767 neuropsychiatric beds. Admissions in 1947 averaged 5,500 monthly; discharges averaged 5,400 a month.

The V.A. psychiatric services were developing the "teamwork" approach to the treatment of the patient—with physicians, nurses, attendants, clinical psychologists, social workers, medical and vocational rehabilitation workers and others pushing as a team toward the goal of the patient's recovery.

The V.A. psychiatric division had established affiliations with 38 medical schools in the development of a residency training program in V.A. hospitals. Within the short span of two years, many veterans psychiatric hospitals had become teaching centers, with a total of 21 residents in neurology and 408 residents in psychiatry.

At the end of 1947 the V.A., which could boast few certified specialists in neurology or psychiatry two years earlier, had more than 270 of its fulltime staff doctors certified by the American Board of Psychiatry and Neurology.

In breaking down the isolationist tradition of the veterans hospitals, the psychiatric division had greatly stimulated the utilization of volunteer workers in hospital programs, and the participation of hospital staff members in community and professional activities outside the institution.

Within two years, V.A. psychiatric clinics had increased from five or six (operated on a more or less casual basis) to 38 V.A. mental hygiene clinics and 53 contract clinics in full operation, handling a total of 1,000 new cases a month. In September, 1947, more than 15,400 veterans received almost 45,000 treatments in these 91 clinics.

A radical re-orientation had taken place in the attitudes toward research in the V.A. psychiatric program. Previously, there had been virtually no psychiatric research worthy of the name in veterans hospitals. Now, an intensive research program was being developed and encouraged in all hospitals and clinics. "Contracts have been let with various institutions for research in the causes of war neuroses, in the treatment of epilepsy, schizophrenia, group psychotherapy, and on methods of selection of psychiatrists and clinical psychologists for training," Dr. Blain reported. "Within the V.A. installation itself such subjects as shock therapy, prefrontal lobotomy and effectiveness of various other types of therapy are being studied. Special laboratories have been provided for certain neuropsychiatric hospitals for studies in pathology and psychosomatic disorders."[17]

Dr. Paul B. Magnuson, successor to Dr. Paul R. Hawley as chief medical director of the Veterans Administration, was careful to note, in a preface to Dr. Blain's report, that "while there is general improvement, the high standards toward which we have worked have been actually reached in only a very few instances. Much remains to be done to give veterans all the aid that is available within our present knowledge."

No millennium had been reached, but the psychiatric program for veterans had advanced to an impressively high level. The question for the future is whether that advance will continue with time, or again be allowed to regress through general indifference and neglect.

Civilian Lessons from War Psychiatry. During the course of World War II, the American public was frequently regaled with stories in the popular press and in widely circulated magazines purporting to describe "sensational" new discoveries in the therapy of mental and nervous disorders made by military psychiatrists. The sober fact is that the war created no new psychiatric treatment. But the war experience did add considerably to the scientific knowledge not only of war neuroses, but of the psychiatric ills of civilians. Its contribution to the development of psychiatric skills and techniques was not inconsiderable. Among the psychiatric advances stemming from the war experience, the following may be mentioned:

1. The condition known in World War I as "shell shock" and as "combat fatigue" in World War II was studied intensively. Progress was made in the treatment of situational neuroses, which carried over into civilian psychiatry.

2. New stimulus was given to the further development of modern therapeutic methods. Experiments in military psychiatry reawakened wide professional interest in hypnosis as a tool in psychiatric procedure. New values were found in group psychotherapy, which consisted mainly of having groups of patients gather periodically to share their experiences and reactions and to gather common insight into their problems under the guidance of the therapist. Thus a virtue was made of necessity—the acute shortage of trained psychiatrists. Psychotherapy under sedation, sometimes known as *narcoanalysis* or *narcosynthesis*—featured by the use of injected drugs such as sodium pentothal or sodium amytal to stimulate articulation of repressed experiences or emotions—was extensively used, with apparently good results, by some military psychiatrists. Doctors Roy R. Grinker and John P. Spiegel describe the development of this technique in their book *Men under Stress* (New York, 1945), as used by them in the U. S. Army Air Forces.

Reviewing the lessons from military psychiatry, General Menninger declared:

The army in its necessity developed a system that promptly detected the soldier who was unable to adjust and early referred him to a psychiatrist. This system prevailed from basic training camp to combat.

The net result and lesson from this experience was that intensive, effective treatment could be and was instituted for a large number of psychiatric patients. It would seem that army psychiatry proved without a doubt that even with limited personnel the treatment job could be done, if the attitude prevailed that this was the chief aim. It served to prove the theory that psychiatric patients, if treated early, have an infinitely better chance to recover. Our experience revealed the relative effectiveness of treatment for even a comparatively short period. . . .[18]

3. The vital importance of morale in the maintenance of mental health—in civilian as well as military populations—was realized in World War II as it never had been before. The war experience brought new insight into such morale factors as motivation and incentive as pillars of mental health. Morale-building became a recognized procedure in preventive psychiatry.

4. The successful operation of several mental hygiene units in military installations gave dramatic affirmation to the value of the psychiatrist-psychologist-social worker team in this kind of setup. The value of auxiliary professional personnel, underscored by the Army experience, was not lost on postwar civilian psychiatry.

5. The drastically revised Army nomenclature of psychiatric disorders had a wholesome influence on civilian psychiatry; it tended to reduce the exaggerated stress on psychosis in standard nosologies and to focus more attention on the commoner neuroses so often seen and so little understood in the psychopathology of everyday civilian life. The new nomenclature also helped sharpen the diagnostic terms and tests in American psychiatry.

6. The recognized need to conserve trained military manpower, as the war progressed, led to intensified efforts at maximum rehabilitation of psychiatrically disabled soldiers, instead of merely casting them out like used-up material. All-out rehabilitation efforts, wherever they were undertaken, gave gratifying results in terms of more men returned to military duty or to useful places in the civilian community.

7. Psychiatric examination of draft registrants furnished impressive evidence of the usefulness of social histories in evaluating mental and emotional fitness. Toward the end of the war, the practice of obtaining the social histories of registrants (such as any history of institutionalization for mental disease) through central clearing agencies became standard procedure in a number of states.

8. The war experience revealed grave deficiencies in psychiatric knowledge on the part of many military medical officers who had been in general practice before joining the armed forces. These gaps in knowledge were traced, in large measure, to inadequacies in medical school curricula; the revelation led to a strong movement toward obtaining more time for improved psychiatric teaching in medical schools.

9. The observations of military psychiatrists provided the basis for a remarkable stimulus to postwar study of the social aspects of mental disorders. As General Menninger put it:

Psychiatric observations led to a renewed appreciation of the importance of stress from social forces as a major factor in the causation of psychiatric casualties. The major adjustments that were required of the average soldier could be measured in their effect in terms of how the same stress effected one individual as compared with others in this group. In evaluating the stress—or, more specifically, the causes of breakdowns —the picture became complicated by the numerous influences that strove to maintain the man's functional integrity. Contributions to disintegration of the personality were the effect of fear, the tremendous importance to the ego of the secondary gain in illness, the strain of isolation, physical discomfort and privation, negative influences reflected from the home front, and a host of other difficulties. Factors that aided integration were effective leadership, identification with the group, motivation or conviction as to the importance of the job, the confidence gained from training and belief in the weapons.[19]

10. As had happened in the period following World War I, it became apparent that many of the techniques of psychiatric selection of draft registrants might be applied to personnel selection in industry, and that the lessons of military morale could be applied to plant morale. There was, in consequence, widespread discussion of a new era in industrial psychiatry,

although the concrete manifestations of this discussion have thus far failed to appear in significant amount.

11. A great stimulus was provided to the study and treatment of psychosomatic diseases by observation of the causative factors in peptic ulcers and other ailments in military men under conditions of stress. It was learned that many ailments heretofore considered organic in nature were actually precipitated by emotional factors. Although a great deal of research had already been done in psychosomatic medicine, it was largely the war experience which brought this branch of medical research and therapy to the fore.

Yes, there were many valuable lessons of military psychiatry in World War II that could be learned with profit by postwar civilian psychiatry. Will those lessons be impressed on our minds, or will they be dissipated as were the main lessons of the first world war? Dr. Alan Gregg, director of the medical sciences division of the Rockefeller Foundation, in an eloquent paper on this theme, concluded on this note:

"The lessons of the war are clear enough. They are so nearly trite that it will take special effort if they are not to be neglected, ignored and forgotten. Many of the lessons are humiliating—a powerful reason for repressing them. Many call for unremitting work if the mistakes are not to be continued and repeated. Circumstances make a schizoid reaction all too easy for us—a flight from reality and an escape from responsibility. The greatest unpleasant surprise of the war for medical men was the importance of psychiatry and psychology. And yet so inconstant, evasive, or preoccupied are the majority of men that this greatest lesson can be disputed, evaded, and soon forgotten."[20]

CHAPTER XXII
Towards Mental Hygiene

IN A given field of human endeavor, progress sometimes may be measured not so much by the problems it has solved, as by the new types of problems it produces. This rule might be applied to the changing problems of twentieth century psychiatry in America. At the beginning of the century, Dr. Adolf Meyer took occasion to note the lack of diversity in the approach to psychiatry. "For some reason," he remarked in 1904, "there is rather a striking uniformity and an absence of definite schools of research which could not only bring out contrasts, but also would prompt individuals to concentrate on special fruitful topics in preference to endless generalities."[1] Exactly thirty years later (1934) the problem, as stated by a committee of distinguished scientists participating in a symposium on mental disorder, had become one of unifying the divers schools of psychiatry that were struggling for dominance: "When we consider the tremendous inherent difficulties of coping with the [mental] disorders," declared the editors, "then add the wide involvement of institutions and interests, and finally take into account the deep temptation in human affairs to speculate, to invoke magical agents, and to form sects, schools and parties, we shall not wonder either at the complexities of the entire situation or at the contentions and contradictions still to be found among schools and practitioners."[2] It is evident that profound transformations in American psychiatry had taken place in the three decades intervening between these two observations to change the problem from one of too much uniformity to one of creating harmony out of existing diversity.

We can present in this chapter little more than the barest

description of the various schools in present-day psychiatric practice and theory. In general, these schools fall into two major methods of approach—the neurological and the psychological.

It was the neurological approach that dominated American psychiatry at the beginning of the century. "Insanity is a brain disease," was the dogmatic statement—meaning that there could be no mental disorder without a corresponding brain lesion. Research in mental disease was confined almost exclusively to the anatomy and pathology of the nervous system. The microscope and the sectioning knife were still the chief instruments of research, and they were being applied to thousands of brains in post-mortem examinations. The structure of the brain was explored and carefully charted, down to its minutest observable portion. A great deal was thus added to our knowledge of mental mechanisms. For example, laboratory experiments in cerebral physiology had brought about such important discoveries as that certain fields of the brain, called the "motor areas," control many activities of the limbs and the head, and that deterioration, impairment or removal of part of this area would result in paralysis of the corresponding part of the body it controls.

With the increase in knowledge of the structure of the brain and some of its functions in relation to the rest of the human organism, it was firmly believed by many brain investigators that the microscope would soon reveal the great secret of the nature and causes of mental disease. It was the golden age of "brain mythology." Although the neurological attack was carried on vigorously, it failed to fulfill the over-optimistic anticipations of its devotees. Reluctantly the admission came that, in most mental disorders, even the most powerful microscopes could not discover any clear distinction between the appearances of diseased and normal brains. So unpropitious was the outlook that Dr. Peter M. Wise, in his presidential address before the American Medico-Psychological Association in 1901, quoted with approval a contemporary's opinion that "our knowledge of the essential nature of insanity, of the causes which foster and produce it, of the means by which it might be prevented and cured, is scarcely greater today than it was a hundred years ago."[3]

The clinical attack gained toward the end of the nineteenth century, when Emil Kraepelin, the last and greatest of the descriptive psychiatrists, introduced a new system of classification that served as an important stepping-stone to further progress. For centuries students of mental disorder had been trying without success to formulate a workable nosology. Hippocrates, we may recall, divided mental illness into two main groups: mania and melancholia. His successors for hundreds of years down through Felix Plater, Boerhaave, Cullen, Pinel and Esquirol, had improved but little upon his original classification. The lack of a comprehensive and clear-cut nosological system contributed largely to the general chaos in the study of mental disorder. So slow was progress in this field that as late as 1892, Dr. D. Hack Tuke could write in his *Dictionary of Psychological Medicine:* "The wit of man has rarely been more exercised than in the attempt to classify the morbid phenomena covered by the term insanity. The result has been disappointing."

But Kraepelin was already formulating his new system of classification, which was to give to psychiatry a much-needed point of reference. When Kraepelin came into the picture, psychiatry was dominated by the loose, over-simplified classification of Pinel, which divided mental diseases into mania, melancholia and dementia. (Pinel's inclusion of idiocy as an entity in mental disease had been discarded by Esquirol, who showed it to be a defect and not a disease.) Mental illness was still diagnosed on the basis of a symptom or group of symptoms at a particular moment, without reference to the cause or the course of the disease. While Kraepelin's classification was like those of his predecessors based on symptoms rather than causes, it did take account of the whole course of a disease, even when characterized by changes in syndromes. He noted the tendency for extremely diverse symptoms to manifest themselves at different periods in the development of a single case. While the alternation of melancholia and mania (formerly considered distinct disease entities) in a patient had been noticed long before, Kraepelin made psychiatric history by using this observation as the basis of a new disease concept which he called manic-depressive insanity. Even more important was his development of the concept of dementia praecox, a disease group which accounts for about one-half of all patients in mental hospitals. Bleuler later substituted the concept schizophrenia (meaning "split personality") for dementia praecox; the terms are now interchangeably used. Together, dementia praecox and manic-depressive cases comprise at present over 65 per cent of our mental hospital population and about 35 per cent of new admissions. Many psychiatrists regard both as "functional" psychoses, that is, diseases without any known physical cause, in contrast to the "organic" psychoses.

Kraepelin's new system was introduced into the United States by Adolf Meyer and others. In 1896 the Worcester State Hospital, with which Meyer was then connected, adopted it in modified form. Worcester was probably the first institution in the world to do so, next to Kraepelin's own clinic at Heidelberg. Kraepelin's system was far from perfect; it was rigidly circumscribed by descriptive psychiatry; it led to static conceptions of mental disorder; it reflected the extreme dogmatism of its formulator; but it still serves as the basis for the classification used in most mental hospitals in America.

Kraepelin fell far short of his aim to create order out of the existing chaos in psychiatry. He did, however, provide new points of orientation from which psychiatry could advance at an accelerated pace. Classification is an essential factor in the development of any science; in a large degree, Kraepelin was to psychiatry what Linnaeus had been to botany. Another distinct service rendered by Kraepelin was to help shift the emphasis in psychiatric research from the pathological laboratory to the clinic—from the dead to the living. The same service, as we have previously noted, was performed in this country by Adolf Meyer. Though differing profoundly in other things, both Kraepelin and Meyer stressed the need of basing diagnoses on the patient accumulation of facts, rather than on vague, loose and hasty generalizations.

Kraepelin's contributions provided a valuable key to the understanding of the *what* and the *how* in mental disorder. But the greatest question—the *why*—still remained wrapped in deep mystery. The study of mental disorder was ready to pass from the realm of the purely descriptive to the dynamic phase.

While Kraepelin was making his epochal observations in the clinic upon which he based his new nosology, a Viennese physician, Sigmund Freud, was attacking the problem of mental disorder from another approach. It is still too early to evaluate accurately the contribution of Freud and psychoanalysis to the understanding of mental disorder. Controversy still rages fiercely around the man and the theories he has developed. Opinions vary from that of a number of psychiatrists who hold that Freud's theories are entirely valueless, if not actually harmful, to that of the fervid admirers of Freud who regard him as the greatest figure not only of his generation, but of all time.

Born in 1859, Freud studied at Paris with Charcot, who was demonstrating that hysteria could be produced by psychological means, and could be made to disappear through hypnotic suggestion. Returning to Vienna, Freud collaborated for some years with an older colleague, Joseph Breuer. The latter, in 1880–82, had had occasion to treat a young woman suffering from a certain form of hysteria. Under the influence of hypnotism, the patient had recalled many hidden occurrences that she could not remember in her conscious state. The recollections were often attended by manifestations of intense emotion, as if the long-forgotten experiences were being lived over again. As these hidden portions of the past emerged from the unconscious, the nervous symptoms disappeared one by one until a complete cure was effected. Breuer discontinued this method for about a decade, when Freud persuaded him to resume it on a collaborative basis. In 1895 Freud and Breuer published their *Studien über Hysterie,* in which they advanced their observations on hysteria as a psychogenically produced phenomenon, and their treatment of it by psychotherapeutic methods. Their work, as Freud points out, had many forerunners; it was by no means startlingly original. The use of hypnotic suggestion in therapeutics might be traced back to the "personal magnetism" of Paracelsus in the sixteenth century, to Mesmer and "mesmerism" in the eighteenth century, and to the experiments of Bertrand and Braid (who coined the word "hypnotism") in the middle of the nineteenth century.

At the time that Freud entered upon his monumental work, Charcot and Bernheim had already carried on signal experiments in the application of hypnosis to the treatment of hysteria—the former emphasizing the physiological, the latter the psychological, approach. But Freud, first working with Breuer and then independently, had hit upon the germ of an idea that developed into his system of psychoanalysis, which has profoundly influenced the study and treatment of mental disorders. Freud early discarded the use of hypnosis as an unsatisfactory method of inquiry and substituted for it the method of "free association," which involves the conscious cooperation of the patient in the "talking out" process, and the bringing back to the realm of consciousness long-forgotten events of the past. Freud discovered that many of these events had a causal relationship to the patient's nervous disorder and had been purposely forgotten, or "repressed." It became the major object of psychoanalytic therapy to bring these repressions to conscious acknowledgment. While Freud did not "discover" the unconscious, he delved deeper into the reservoir of primitive, infantile instincts than anyone had ever done before. He brought to light vast areas in the mental life of man hitherto unexplored. As his exploration of the unconscious continued, he formulated the startling theory that the major portion of man's mental processes goes on outside the sphere of his awareness; that the unconscious is not an inactive, but a dynamic—and even a determining—factor in human life, ever present, ever active, always demanding expression; that the sex life of the individual actually begins

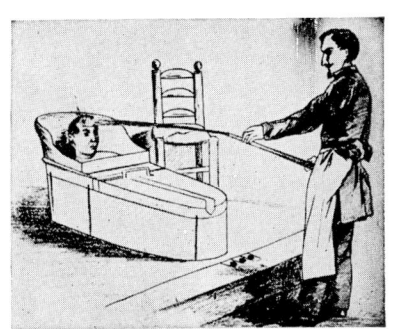

HYDROTHERAPY, OLD AND NEW

long before puberty; and that the most significant factors in mental and nervous illness are to be found in disturbances in the erotic sphere. He ascribed many, though not all, mental disorders to repressed emotions dating back to early childhood. Freud saw a hidden significance in dreams, as keys to the unconscious. The interpretation of dreams, together with the technique of free association, became a vital part of psychoanalytic therapy.*

It was inevitable that the daring theses developed by Freud would meet with terrific resistance and opposition. Seldom in the past century has any doctrine encountered so antagonistic a reception as psychoanalysis received. There were elements in the new theory that were so diametrically opposed to prevailing ideas, popular and scientific, that an avalanche of criticism could easily have been prophesied for it. The notion that the more important processes of man go on outside the field of consciousness was so novel when it was first expressed by Freud that it evoked incredulity. The dominant emphasis that Freud gave to sex, especially his concepts of the Oedipus complex and infantile sexuality, shook the structure of Victorian morality to its very foundations, and raised a storm of bitter detraction. The important place accorded to dream interpretation appeared to his contemporaries as a fantastic compound of biblical mysticism and gypsy lore. Freud's system was referred to as the "psychoanalytic plague." Certain individuals declared that only the gay, frivolous atmosphere of Austria's capital could have produced such a system as psychoanalysis. "Perhaps one dreams such things in Vienna," was the disparaging remark made in reference to the Freudian interpretation of sex symbolism in the dream content.

In 1909 Freud, together with his disciple, C. G. Jung, came to America at the invitation of G. Stanley Hall, to deliver a series of lectures on his new doctrines in connection with the twentieth anniversary celebration of Clark Uni-

---

*In this connection, Freud insisted that the ravings and rantings of the mentally disordered were not merely meaningless gibberish, as had hitherto been supposed, but represented in a significant sense "the language of their disease." Psychiatrists now listen to and note carefully the utterances of mental patients as possible clues to their disorder and its cure.

versity, over which Dr. Hall presided.[4] His visit here aroused tremendous interest in his theories, which was reflected in the large output of literature on psychoanalysis at the time.* The antagonism displayed in this country toward psychoanalysis was quite as violent as that abroad. As late as 1916 Theodore H. Kellogg, a prominent American psychiatrist of the day, confidently expressed the following verdict in the *Reference Handbook of the Medical Sciences:* "Psychoanalysis, as now known, will not become of general use in mental disorders and a decennium hence will probably only be referred to as an interesting phase in experimental psychiatry. It has not even the tangible basis of hypnotism, which as a psychiatric remedy has had its day, and is passing into merited oblivion."[5]

However, the Freudian theories did gain the support of a small but vigorous and talented group of American psychiatrists, including A. A. Brill (who translated most of Freud's early works into English), Smith Ely Jelliffe and William A. White. Besides, it gained the sympathetic interest of leaders in other fields, such as G. Stanley Hall, the psychologist, and the neurologist, James J. Putnam. In 1911 the Freudian movement was formally launched in this country, with the establishment of the New York Psychoanalytic Society. (An American Psychoanalytic Society was formed later.) In 1913 the *Psychoanalytic Review* began publication here, with Drs. Jelliffe and White as editors. At the 1914 annual meeting of the American Medico-Psychological Association, a heated discussion took place between the defenders and the opponents of psychoanalysis that almost rivalled in intensity the historic controversy over the Kirkbride plan at the 1866 meeting.[6]

The argument over the relative value of psychoanalysis still continues. But this body of doctrine has steadily gone forward against a strong current of opposition. Originating as a therapeutic technique, it has developed into a threefold system; (1) it is a tool for treating mental disorders, as it was in the beginning; (2) it is a method of research

---

*See, for example, the symposium on psychotherapy and psychoanalysis published in the *Journal of Abnormal Psychology*, 1909, v. 4, pp. 69–199.

into mental processes, normal and abnormal; (3) it is a theory of human personality. Assuming an ever-expanding scope, it has influenced not only psychiatry, but such diverse disciplines as philosophy, psychology, sociology, anthropology, criminology, pedagogy, art and social work. It has thus far successfully withstood not only opposition from without but discord within. Several historic split-offs from the parent body of doctrine have taken place, notably those led by two of Freud's most prominent pupils, C. G. Jung and Alfred Adler. The former has created a school of "analytical psychology" while the latter's school is known as "individual psychology." On the other hand, not a few of Freud's disciples have adopted an attitude toward psychoanalysis comparable to that of fanatical adherence to a religious creed, as if it were an immutable body of dogma, although the master himself has been constantly modifying his theories in accordance with new findings. They look upon their teacher as a veritable Moses and his doctrines as a Mosaic code which may be elaborated but not deviated from. Those who dare adopt the latter course are regarded as ungrateful backsliders. Thus, in a sense, is confirmation given to Huxley's observation that "it is the customary fate of new truths to begin as heresies and to end as superstitions."

As a therapeutic technique, psychoanalysis undoubtedly has proved of great benefit in the neuroses or psychoneuroses. Its application to the major psychoses, however, is still in an experimental stage. Some encouraging results have been reported in the analytic treatment of certain types of schizophrenia. Dr. John Nathaniel Rosen, a former pathologist who turned to psychiatry some years ago, has reported on 37 cases of "apparently successful treatment of deteriorated schizophrenics by a method known as 'direct analysis.'" Dr. Rosen, a New York practitioner, has impressed a number of high-ranking psychiatrists who have studied his methods and his results. His technique may be briefly described as making contact with the patient's unconscious—driving into his psychosis—by first participating in the patient's fancies and activities on the latter's own terms, then gradually drawing him toward the plane of reality. Each of Dr. Rosen's 37 cases was diagnosed as severely schizophrenic by other physicians before coming under his care. They represented all three major types of schizophrenia—hebephrenic, catatonic, and paranoid. Duration of psychosis ranged from seven months to 21 years before Dr. Rosen commenced treatment; many had been intensively treated with other forms of therapy. Duration of Dr. Rosen's "direct analysis" leading to apparent recovery ranged from three days to eleven months.[7]

Dr. Frieda Fromm-Reichmann is reported to have obtained impressive results also by means of similar role therapy at Chestnut Lodge, Maryland.

A serious shortcoming of psychoanalysis to date is the apparent failure to apply it on a mass basis in psychiatric cases. Several major obstacles to its application in large-scale therapy may be mentioned: it involves, usually, a long and expensive process, requiring from several months to several years of intensive treatment at rates prohibitive for the average patient (fees in private practice average about $10 to $15 per hour, with three to five sessions weekly); its efficacy, at least up to the present, depends largely on the age, educational level and cultural background of the patient; it requires in the physician, besides skill, a personality suitable for the "transference" phase of psychoanalytic therapy.

Psychoanalysis plays an important therapeutic role in a number of private mental hospitals, where intensive individualized treatment is possible. Modifications of the technique have been introduced in a growing number of public mental hospitals; younger doctors entering the state hospital system and the veterans psychiatric hospitals are, to an increasing extent, equipped with knowledge of the methods and concepts of Freudian analysis. Curiously enough, some of the bitterest attacks against the use of modified psychoanalysis in mental hospitals come from fundamentalist Freudians of the "all-or-nothing" school of therapy. In spite of the Freudian purists, on the one hand, and the antagonism of the extreme anti-Freudians on the other, psychoanalytic concepts are gradually being integrated into general psychiatric practice. Dr. Eugen Bleuler was especially instrumental in effecting this synthesis.

In contrast to Freud's psychological approach to mental disorder, there are many organic or somatic concepts in psychiatry, drawn largely from the allied sciences such as anatomy, bacteriology, physiology, psychology, biochemistry, pharmacology, neuropathology, endocrinology. The difference between the psychological and the somatic approaches is mainly that of emphasis. The Freudians do not deny, of course, that certain mental diseases are organic in origin and are more amenable to treatment by physical agents rather than by psychotherapy. Conversely, most adherents of the somatic schools in psychiatry freely admit the existence of psychogenic disorders and the value of psychological treatment in many cases.

Psychosomatic medicine is a term of recent vintage, although the recognition of emotional components in many "physical" diseases is as old as the medical art itself. Many cases have been reported of successful treatment of bronchial asthma, ailments of the heart and blood systems, allergies, and other "organic" diseases through psychotherapeutic techniques. The Psychoanalytic Institute in Chicago has conducted intensive research into the nature and treatment of supposedly physical diseases having a basis mainly or largely in emotional problems. Drs. Edward Weiss and O. Spurgeon English, in their *Psychosomatic Medicine* (Philadelphia, 1943), and Dr. Flanders Dunbar, in her *Psychosomatic Diagnosis* (New York, 1943), have furnished extensive discussions of this subject.

While the concept of psychosomatic medicine is by no means new, the rapid development of scientific research and therapeutic approaches has greatly stimulated teamwork between psychiatrists, general practitioners, internists and others in a common attack on psychosomatic disorder. Psychiatrists, in some hospitals, are being introduced on the general medicine wards for the first time. It is estimated that perhaps 70 per cent of all patients in general hospitals have emotional problems that are either causative or complicating factors in their illness.

As for somatic attacks on mental disorder, one of the most successful has been applied to the treatment of general paralysis, or paresis, which accounts for nearly 10 per cent of all new cases admitted to state mental hospitals. Paresis had been described as a disease entity in insanity as early as 1822 by Bayle. With the introduction of the Wassermann test, it was shown that the blood tests of paretics were frequently, and their spinal fluid always, positive in untreated cases. Further study indicated that paresis was the end result of many syphilitic cases; that it usually appeared after the venereal disease had run its course for five or more years; and that it was characterized by progressive deterioration of the mentality terminating in certain death within a short period. Paul Ehrlich's salvarsan, the savior of many syphilitics, proved ineffectual in the treatment of most paretics. In 1903 Dr. Frederick Peterson could state categorically that there were no recoveries from paresis, and that the average duration of life of paretics after admission to a mental hospital was from three to five years. A few years later (1913) the great bacteriologist, Hideyo Noguchi, along with J. W. Moore, discovered the presence of the syphilis germ—the spirochete—in the brains of paretics. The cause of general paralysis was thus definitely ascertained; it remained to find a remedy. A promising remedy was supplied in 1917, by a Viennese psychiatrist, Julius Wagner-Jauregg. Some years earlier, Dr. Wagner-Jauregg had noticed a remarkable improvement in one of his paretic patients following an attack of erysipelas, which produces a high fever. Now, fever treatment (that is, inducing a high fever to destroy a disease), had been used many centuries ago by Hippocrates. The possible link between the fever and the improvement in his mentally disordered patient was not lost upon Wagner-Jauregg. Why not try "fever therapy" in paresis? In 1917 he found an opportunity to test his theory with paretic soldiers serving on the Italian front. He injected two of them with malaria bacteria. It was a dangerous experiment, but it succeeded. The two patients went through the period of fever which burned out the deadly spirochete in the brain, and gradually the paresis symptoms disappeared. A cure for many cases of this hitherto incurable disease had been found. For this epochal achievement, Wagner-Jauregg received the Nobel Prize in 1927.

Fever therapy for paresis is now practiced in many of our mental hospitals. But, instead of malaria treatment, some hospitals utilize a recently invented "fever machine," which produces and controls high temperature by means of electricity. The drug tryparsamide is also used in the treatment of paresis, often in addition to malarial therapy. It is estimated that approximately one-third of these cases, formerly considered hopelessly incurable, are now sufficiently improved to resume their normal social life. According to a recent report on ten years of malarial therapy at the Marcy State Hospital in New York, more than half of the paretics admitted since malarial therapy was introduced into the hospital in 1925 were discharged as "much improved" or "improved" and able to return to work, within three years of admission; the majority of these were discharged within six months. As Dr. Hutchings points out, "this is an impressive picture of the advances in the treatment of this disease since malarial therapy was introduced."[8] In recent years, penicillin has been added to fever therapy in the treatment of paresis, with encouraging results.

From the physiological laboratories of Pavlov, Sherrington, Cannon and others, have come significant contributions to the study of mental disease. The celebrated Russian reflexologist, Pavlov, built up a theory of the functional mental disorders based on his principle of the conditional reflex. In his well known experiment for producing neurosis in dogs, the animal is trained to differentiate between two tones of different pitch. In the beginning only one tone is given, and it is always accompanied by food. Then a new tone is introduced, which is not accompanied by food. After learning to differentiate between tones one and two, the dog develops a reflex of inhibition to the latter, while retaining his reflex of excitement toward the former. Then tone two is gradually brought closer and closer to tone one. As the tones near the same pitch and it becomes increasingly difficult to differentiate between the two, the dog begins to show restlessness and pain.

Finally he develops a new reaction; he refuses to take food, and manifests the inhibitory reaction to tone one as well as to tone two. The dog goes to pieces; he experiences a "nervous breakdown." He develops stereotypy, reacting to all the conditioned stimuli in nearly the same way, even to those not connected with the original differentiation.[9]

As Dr. W. Horsley Gantt notes, both Pavlov and Freud make use of the principle of conflict in their theories of mental disorder. But while Freud's conflict is a psychic one, Pavlov's is mechanical and physiological—a conflict between the inhibitory and excitatory reflexes. Pavlov's theory requires further experiment before it can be properly evaluated. His demonstration that a neurotic condition may be produced through the food reflex alone, without any reference to the sex drives which Freud considers of primary importance, may lead to interesting consequences on psychiatric theory.* The experimental work of Pavlov and his school so far as research in mental disorder is concerned, is seriously limited by several considerations: it deals with dogs and not with human beings; besides, the dogs exhibit the symptoms of "nervous breakdown" only under the condition of laboratory experiment; outside the laboratory they lead the normal dog life.

From another quarter has come the theory of focal infections as a primary cause of mental disease. In 1922, Dr. Henry A. Cotton, late superintendent of the New Jersey State Hospital at Trenton, and one of the most active psychiatric researchers in this country, advanced the theory that focal infections—mainly of the teeth, tonsils, and intestinal tract—were responsible for nearly all cases of mental disorders. He held that the toxic substances arising from focal infection reached the brain, causing actual physical changes in the brain cells and leading to mental abnormality. "If the control of insanity is to make any real headway," he wrote in 1933, "heredity, environmental defects, personality and improper training must be subordinated to the study of infections which can be attacked directly by resort to surgical

---

*Freud has laid down the well-known dictum: "In a normal *vita sexualis* no neurosis is possible." It should be noted that not all psychoanalysts accept this thesis.

methods, and eliminated."[10] Dr. Cotton performed many tonsillectomies and appendectomies upon his patients, extracted their teeth, irrigated their sinuses and intestinal tracts on a grand scale, and claimed as a result that the recovery rate of the hospital had doubled. Unfortunately, other investigators were unable to duplicate this claim. Although focal infection is still recognized as a factor in some mental disorders, the theory attributing most mental cases to this source has been discarded.

The chemical attack on mental disease also includes methods based on theories of brain toxicity. Not many years ago Professor Wilder D. Bancroft of Cornell University formulated a theory that all functional psychoses are due to disturbances of the brain proteins, and that the specific type of psychoses produced depends upon whether the proteins are "over-coagulated" or "over-dispersed." (Coagulation is the process of thickening a colloid; dispersal is the process of thinning.) Bancroft believed that mental disorders may be cured by sending coagulating or dispersing agents to the brain through the blood stream, as needed. He divided the psychoses into two classes: one was improved by administering sodium amytal (a coagulating agent) and aggravated by sodium rhodonate (a dispersing agent), while the other reacted in reverse manner. Experiments conducted by the U. S. Public Health Service in 1932 failed to confirm Bancroft's theory, and it has found no general acceptance in psychiatry.

Nearly every drug has had its day in psychiatric practice. But the field of pharmacology still furnishes some interesting and valuable experiments toward the understanding and treatment of mental disorder. Bulbocapnine and other chemicals have been used to produce psychotic states in cats, dogs, and other animals that show a marked similarity to the symptomatic manifestations of human psychoses. The science of psychiatry, of course, is not so much concerned with producing psychoses as in curing them. Tridione, dilantin, and other drugs have proved effective in the control of epileptic seizures, and their administration has enabled many epileptics to pursue normal lives without harrowing fears. Sodium amytal and sodium pentothal have been used with impressive results in psychiatric therapies known as "narcoanalysis," "narcosynthesis," and, more popularly, as "twilight sleep." Administration intravenously of amytal or pentothal often has a dramatic effect in producing temporary periods of clarity and accessibility in mental patients who have been deeply withdrawn from reality. Nobody has yet offered a generally acceptable explanation of what, exactly, the drug does to produce the temporary alterations in the patient's personality. Its practical effects in clearing away, momentarily, the clouds of unreason are twofold: it brings to the surface repressed material, often of value to the therapist's understanding of the case; it makes the patient accessible to psychotherapeutic procedures. Whether the mechanism of improvement in sodium amytal or sodium pentothal treatment is psychological or biochemical is still a question of lively debate. The rationale is not yet clearly understood; the therapy is not yet standardized; the efficacy awaits decisive evaluation.

A somewhat similar procedure is the use of various drugs, including amytal, to induce prolonged and deep narcosis, or sleep, ranging up to ten days. Patients who have been mute and otherwise inaccessible often speak freely and clearly while emerging from this state of prolonged coma. As in narcoanalysis or narcosynthesis, much significant repressed material is often brought to the surface, providing valuable clues to the nature of the illness. Here, too, as in the other narcosis therapies, many theories have been advanced as to the nature and effectiveness of prolonged narcosis (the procedure dates back at least to 1870), but no generally satisfactory rationale has yet appeared.

Shock Therapies. In recent years three major forms of shock therapy for psychotic patients have flared across the psychiatric skies, created sensations of longer or shorter duration as a result of astonishing recovery claims made in their behalf, only to be countered by increasing skepticism. Most extraordinary results were claimed for hypoglycemic, or insulin shock, therapy soon after it was introduced by Dr. Manfred Sakel of Vienna in 1933. The application of insulin shock treatment to schizophrenics and other psychotics developed quite accidentally from Dr. Sakel's original use of insulin in the treatment of morphine addicts. The aim is to induce a state of hypoglycemia (which is a condition of sugar deficiency in the blood) through injections of insulin. The doses of insulin are increased daily until the so-called shock dose is reached, whereupon the patient lapses into a state of coma of deepening intensity. This coma is terminated after several hours by the administration of a neutralizing sugar solution. (A variant of this therapy is called insulin sub-shock, in which the patient is given only enough insulin to put him in a light coma.) Frequency and duration of insulin shock treatment varies with the condition of the patient, his rate of improvement and the therapist's personal opinions. Usually a coma is induced daily for five or six days in a week; the average course of treatment may run to 50 or 60 comas.

The psychiatric world was astounded by the early claims made for insulin shock therapy. A report by Sakel and his coworker, Dussik, published in 1936 and covering 104 insulin-treated cases indicated that three-fourths of the patients ill less than half a year made apparently complete recoveries, with an additional 18 per cent sufficiently improved to return to their normal pursuits in the community. Of patients whose illness had endured more than six months, nearly 50 per cent were reported to have made a good social recovery, while about 20 per cent were discharged as completely recovered. These optimism-laden figures, compared with the disheartingly low recovery rate for schizophrenia in our mental hospitals, were certain to create a sensation. In 1937, Dr. Sakel went to the Harlem Valley State Hospital on the invitation of the New York State Mental Hygiene Department to demonstrate his treatment there. Insulin shock therapy was adopted in other hospitals, although the need for high ratio of doctors and nurses to patients proved a serious handicap to its speedier spread.

In 1944, an impressive statistical report on the results of insulin shock therapy was made public by the New York State Temporary Commission on State Hospital Problems. The report was based on a study made by the Commission of 1,128 insulin-treated dementia praecox patients at the Brooklyn State Hospital over a five-and-a-half year period and a comparable "control group" of 876 non-treated patients admitted to state hospitals in the New York metropolitan area. The figures indicated that 79.5 per cent of the insulin-treated patients were able to leave the hospital as compared with 58.8 per cent of the non-treated group. It also appeared that the average hospital stay of the insulin-treated patients was shorter than that of the control group, and that those who were discharged adjusted better than the discharged non-treated group.[11]

The immediate impact of this report—the first effort at a large-scale scientific evaluation of insulin shock therapy—was later dissipated when critical checks of the study's methodology revealed serious defects in the validity of its findings. Meanwhile, the shortage of trained personnel together with the appearance of two cheaper and more easily executed forms of shock therapy tended to turn interest to other directions.

Ludwig von Meduna of Budapest—who, like Sakel, later became a United States resident—reported in 1935 on the treatment of schizophrenic patients with artificially induced epileptic convulsions. He had noticed, as had several others, an apparent antagonism between epileptic fits and the schizophrenic state. He experimented in artificial production of epileptic convulsions by using camphor or metrazol (a camphor-like product that acts like a camphor upon the heart). While the reported results were not as optimistic as those from the use of insulin, they were encouraging enough to give metrazol convulsive shock therapy a wide vogue for a period of years. A high proportion of fractures to the skeletal system was one of the factors dampening the early enthusiasm for this therapeutic procedure.

Electric shock treatment, first demonstrated in Rome in 1938 by U. Cerletti and L. Bini, has had by far the most extensive application of any of the shock therapies—mainly because it is cheapest and easiest. Many thousands of mental hospital patients in the United States have undergone this form of treatment, with results that are still the subject of furious debate in psychiatric circles. Many sober psychotherapists regard electric shock treatment, along with the other shock therapies, as merely twentieth-century analogues of the old terror treatments for mental disease designed to frighten patients into their wits. There is no doubt that the ease of administering electric shock therapy in its crude form has led to widespread abuse. It has been widely applied in private practice to ambulatory neurotics, in spite of the repeated observations of some experts that it has no effect on the milder mental disorders except to change moods temporarily. There have been many avoidable injuries due to clumsy use, although these have been sharply reduced in recent years. The early claims of very high recovery percentages have been considerably scaled down, as apparently recovered patients have had relapse after relapse following repeated courses of electric shock treatments. The average course runs to about 20 convulsions, although some therapists stop at three or four while others go on to as many as one hundred.[12]

The abuse of electric shock therapy by ill-trained and poorly oriented physicians took so serious a turn in 1947 that the Group for the Advancement of Psychiatry issued a statement strongly condemning its indiscriminate use, especially in the case of treatment of ambulatory patients out of private offices. It has been repeatedly stressed by authorities that electric shock is effective only when used in conjunction with psychotherapy. Yet it cannot be denied that it is frequently used as an exclusive therapeutic procedure, with no semblance of psychotherapeutic follow-up.

Neurosurgery, more recently, has assumed a prominent place on the psychiatric horizon. Prefrontal lobotomy or leucotomy, consisting of the severance or removal of certain parts of the brain, was introduced in 1936 by Egas Moniz of Lisbon, Portugal. The procedure was introduced in the United States later that year by Drs. Walter Freeman and J. W. Watts of Washington, D.C. Since then, over 5,000 prefrontal lobotomy operations have been performed on mental patients in this country. The operation has been limited mainly to chronic mental patients, usually schizophrenics, with long records of institutionalization. The early enthusiasm for this operation has lately been succeeded by growing skepticism and by deepening concern about the irreversible brain damage and personality impairments resulting from lobotomy. In March, 1948, a group representing staff members of the Columbia University College of Physicians and Surgeons and the Greystone, New Jersey, State Hospital, reported on a modified operation called topectomy, in which a smaller part of surface brain tissue is cut away with what has appeared to be considerably less brain damage and a more satisfactory personality structure in the patient. It is too early to evaluate the contribution of the newer neurosurgery as applied to mental diseases.

The study of mental disease, its causes and cure, continues along many fronts. However, as Dr. Arthur H. Ruggles aptly observes, "no single school of thought can explain the variety of conditions arising in mental disorders and the great need of the present day is for soundly trained physicians who will be able to apply a variety of methods of study to the complex phenomena of mental maladjustments."[13]

Since Lombroso, many researchers in mental disorder have sought to find a significant correlation between bodily constitution and particular types of psychosis. Ernst Kretschmer made extensive investigations into this subject. In his *Physique and Character* (New York, 1925), he attempts to prove, with a wealth of supporting statistics, that a mutual relationship exists between temperamental types (schizothymic and cyclothymic) and physical types (asthenic and pyknic, with an intermediate type termed athletic). Statistics indicate that nearly 85 per cent of the cases of manic-depressive psychosis belong to the *pyknic* type, distinguished by middle height and rounded figure, with large broad skull, rounded shoulders, short and thick neck, barreled chest, and other characteristics. Nearly half of the schizophrenic cases belong to the *asthenic* type: lean, narrowly built, long and narrow face, angular profile, narrow shoulders, long arms and legs, etc. Although there are many exceptions, Kretschmer's general observations regarding constitution types have, on the whole, been verified by other students of mental disorder.

In another field of research, studies are being made of the endocrine glands as predisposing or precipitating causes of mental disorder, and their possible utilization in therapeutics. The causal relationship between thyroid deficiency and certain types of mental defect (particularly cretinism) has long been known. But glandular research into mental diseases has thus far produced no conclusive results. The eminent endocrinologist, Professor R. G. Hoskins, concludes, "the psychoses may be importantly determined by antecedent or concurrent endocrine abnormalities, but that none of the evidence compels that conclusion."[14] Similarly, gland therapy in psychiatry is still in an experimental stage.

Dr. Hoskins, in his Thomas W. Salmon Memorial Lectures on *The Biology of Schizophrenia* (1946) urged a radical change in emphasis regarding research into the causes and mechanisms of this psychosis, which accounts for half of all hospitalized mental patients and more than 20 per cent of whole hospital populations in the United States.

"If the psychosis represents primarily failure of maturity," Hoskins observes, "then the fundamental problem becomes one of the biology of the maturing processes. That implies, among other things, that the next and most fundamental research in schizophrenia should be made not in the mental hospitals but in the biology laboratories. The work of the comparative biologists on maturation in the lower marine forms and the lower vertebrates should be extended to the higher mammalian forms. . . . Such studies might be addressed to the influences of the various amino acids and especially glutamic acid and proline."[15]

Studies in the effect of nutrition on mental processes have shown an indubitable coexistence of undernutrition and certain psychic abnormalities. Pellagra, a disease of malnutrition, was directly responsible for 0.5 per cent of the psychotic patients admitted to state hospitals in 1934. Dr. L. Emmett Holt has asserted that "most of the neuroses of childhood entirely depend upon disorders of nutrition." Further research in nutrition promises to reveal some interesting relationships between diet and mental disorder.

While research is being carried on in a number of particular fields, attempts are being made to find a synthetic basis for a comprehensive psychiatric theory. Adolf Meyer's formulation of his system of psychobiology probably represents the foremost step in this direction. Essentially a synthetic system, psychobiology repudiates what Meyer calls the "deadly parallelism" which artificially divides the physical and psychic processes of man. Defining mind as "sufficiently organized living being in action and not a peculiar form of mind stuff," he asserts that "mental activity is really best understood in its full meaning as the adaptation and adjustment of the individual as a whole, in contrast to the simple activity of single organs." According to Meyer, "psychobiology starts not from a mind and a body or from its elements, but from the fact that we deal with biologically organized units and groups and their functioning. It occupies itself with those entities and relations that form, or pertain to the he's or she's of our experience—the bodies we find in action, as far as we have to note them in the behavior and functioning of the 'he' or 'she' . . . It is behavior, overt, and internal or implicit, that concerns us, so far as it works as the 'he' or 'she.'" [16] He interprets mental disorder as a maladjustment of the entire personality rather than as a specific mental or physical complaint. Properly to understand the nature of the disorder, it is necessary to consider the individual as a whole in all his aspects—hereditary, environmental, constitutional, physical, social and economic, etc. All available facts must be determined and evaluated in an attempt to create an adequate adjustment between the patient and his environment, which constitutes a cure. Dynamic in its conception, psychobiology insists on study of the living, functioning man in his environmental setting. "We are quite sure," Meyer says, "that man undissected is more real and important to us than the paradox of a divided individual. We are more inclined to focus and train our methods on our facts as the facts need them, instead of trimming our facts to suit mere methods."

Meyer developed an elaborate method of examining the patient and obtaining a life history which has been widely adopted in America. The first to introduce the Kraepelinian system of classification into America, he has since formulated a classification of his own, based on the term *ergasia* (from the Latin, *working*), which Meyer describes as "actions and reactions and attitudes of the 'he' or 'she' or 'you' or 'I.' " In several important respects Meyer's system is distinctly American as in its functionalistic basis, its pragmatic emphasis on common sense in the study and treatment of mental disorders, and its pluralistic approach to the subject.

The encouraging advances recently made in psychiatric study have done much to dispel the fatalistic attitude toward mental disease that has hitherto served as a brake on progress. At the other extreme are some enthusiasts who tend to over-rate the extent of current psychiatric progress. A careful perusal of the latest statistics leaves little room for either ebullient optimism or for deep pessimism as to the present state of psychiatric knowledge and treatment. The average rate of recoveries in American state hospitals in 1944 was 18 per cent, while an additional 31 per cent were discharged as improved. The rate of recovery and improvement in the endowed hospitals is much higher. However, this is due in large measure to the fact that a greater degree of selection of hopeful cases is possible in the latter type of mental hospital.

Of the twenty definite groups of psychoses listed in the standard classification of mental disease, by far the greatest problem is presented by the dementia praecox (schizophrenia) group, which occupies more than half the beds in our mental hospitals and nearly a quarter of all hospital beds in the United States. As its name implies, dementia praecox is mainly a disease of early life; about one-half of such cases occur between the ages of fifteen and thirty. According to the federal census, 29,010 cases of dementia praecox entered our mental hospitals in 1944 out of a total of 128,475 first admissions and re-admissions, constituting 22.6 per cent of the total. They are among the youngest patients to be admitted, and they usually stay the longest. Of the patients who died in American state mental hospitals, the dementia praecox group showed a median length of hospital life of 14.9 years, as compared with a median length of 6.2 for the manic-depressive group. The recent development of the shock therapies and other forms of treatment has stimulated more hope for the eventual outlook of this large class of patients, but it still presents the greatest single challenge in the field of institutional psychiatry. While many hypotheses have been forthcoming, particularly in recent years, the nature, cause and specific therapy for this category of psychosis remain shrouded in mystery. The conquest of schizophrenia, or dementia praecox, will surely rank among the greatest of medical triumphs when it is accomplished.

Although the nature of that other great functional disease, manic-depressive psychosis, is also unknown, it presents a more hopeful picture in terms of prognosis. Manic-depressive patients accounted for 9.2 per cent of all cases admitted to mental hospitals in 1944.

The so-called organic psychoses, which are known to have physical causes, constitute about 46 per cent of total mental hospital admissions. Psychosis with cerebral arteriosclerosis accounts for 11.8 per cent of all admissions annually, senile psychosis for 9.9, general paralysis for 5.1 and other forms of syphilis of the central nervous system for 0.9 per cent, and alcoholic psychosis for 3.3 per cent, according to 1944 census figures.

An impressive array of figures could be presented to show the magnitude of the mental disease problem in modern society. We need cite only a few. There were about 635,000 patients on the books of mental hospitals at the end of 1945. It is estimated that if the same facilities for recognition and treatment as exist in New York and Massachusetts were to be adopted in all other states, there would be nearly twice as many patients in mental hospitals. The mental hospital population is increasing at the rate of about 20,000 a year, with over 125,000 new patients entering these institutions annually. According to statistics compiled in New York State, about one out of every twenty persons may be expected to spend some part of his life as a mental hospital patient. If the present rate of mental breakdown continues, about one million children now in our public schools will be admitted to mental hospitals in later life. One out of every 272 Americans is now a patient in a state hospital; in New York and Massachusetts, which afford greater psychiatric facilities, the ratio is about one out of every 185. It is estimated that the economic cost of mental disease to the nation—in terms of maintenance, loss of wages and business, etc.—reaches the staggering total of one billion dollars annually. The cost in terms of human misery—of broken homes, the mental anguish of sufferers, their relatives and friends—is beyond computation.

This leads us to an interesting question: Is mental disease increasing and if so, at what rate? This aspect of the problem of mental disorder has occasioned much gloom and alarm in certain quarters. United States census figures for the past fifty years or more would seem to afford considerable cause for concern, since they indicate that the rate of mental disease has been rising by leaps and bounds. In 1880 the total number of patients in public mental hospitals was less than 41,000;* in 1910 it was about 188,000; in 1944 it was 507,383. While the population of the United States is now slightly more than twice that of 1880, the number of patients in state hospitals has increased twelvefold in the same period. To put it another way, in 1880, the number of patients in state hospitals was 63.7 per 100,000 of the general population; in 1944 the comparative figures were 366.7 or more than five times as high. Does this mean that the rate of increase in the incidence of mental disease is five times that of fifty years ago? On the surface this would appear to be true.

Yet there are a number of important reasons for doubting that the *real* rate of incidence in mental disease has been increasing to any great extent. The major explanations for the *apparent* increase in the rate of mental disease would include the following points:

1. The concept of "insanity" has widened considerably in scope during the past half-century; mental disease is more readily recognized. Mental hospitals have increased rapidly in number, have expanded in size, and have become more accessible to the community. Experience has shown that the rate of increase in the number of patients tends to follow the increase in hospital accommodation and the proximity of the hospital to the community served. Federal statistics show that the incidence of mental disease in Massachusetts and

---

*There were, in addition, about 50,000 insane persons in poorhouses, prisons, under home care, etc.

New York is about 593 per 100,000 of the general population, while in Alabama, Tennessee and Mississippi it is about 200 per 100,000. Does this indicate that the former states have nearly three times as many mentally ill persons as the latter? Not at all. The explanation is to be found partly, if not entirely, in the wide difference in hospital facilities for the mentally ill.

2. As mental hospitals have improved, and education has gradually diminished vague fears, superstitions and suspicions on the part of the public toward "crazy houses," the mentally ill are more readily committed to hospitals by their friends and relatives. In other words, increased public confidence in state hospitals has been a factor in the increase of patients.

3. A steady improvement in standards of hospital accommodation and treatment has prolonged the average length of hospital life of patients, resulting in a progressive accumulation of the latter.

4. A most important factor has been the prolongation of the average span of life in the general population. Thanks to the great advances in medical science, sanitation and hygiene, the average expectancy of life has been raised from forty to sixty-seven years in the past half-century. Larger numbers of people are growing into old age. As a consequence, a larger proportion of the population is becoming susceptible to those mental diseases that are associated with maturity and senility. About 20 per cent of patients admitted to mental hospitals suffer from the two major psychoses of advanced age, senile psychosis and psychosis with cerebral arteriosclerosis.

In a statistical analysis of the alleged increase in the incidence of major psychoses, published in 1934 and based on a study of statistics in Massachusetts and New York, H. B. Elkind and Maurice Taylor arrived at the conclusion that there has been no real increase in the rate except for the psychoses associated with advanced age, which show a distinct rise.[17] Some authorities, however, believe that there has been an actual increase in the rate of incidence in the major psychoses, due in part to the increased stresses and strains of the progressively complex society we live in.

What of the milder mental disorders—the neuroses or psychoneuroses? Are these disorders increasing? A study of the available literature on this subject leads one to believe that the rate of incidence in the neuroses is certainly on the rise. The neuroses, it seems, are to a far greater extent than the major psychoses attributable to socio-environmental influences. Among the important contributing factors in the causation of the neuroses are social tension, fear, uncertainty, anxiety, and insecurity. No one can doubt that we live today in a world where these factors are present in an abnormal degree. In a recent work on schizophrenia, Dr. C. Macfie Campbell declared that "there are circumstances which destroy self-confidence, which foster a feeling of inferiority, which stifle independence, which give rise to a feeling of guilt, of inner corruption, of impending doom. It is on factors which touch such topics as the above that we lay emphasis when we are considering the external factors which may contribute to the development of the schizophrenic psychoses."[18] If these factors are important in the incidence of schizophrenia, they are far more so in that of the common neuroses.

Here we come to an interesting question: What was the effect of the Depression Decade, 1929–1939, on the mental health of the American people? Its full impact could never be accurately measured, but the subject is of more than academic or historical interest because of its possible significance for future economic crises. A survey of state hospitals during the depression, conducted in 1934 by the National Committee for Mental Hygiene, indicated that, while the crisis had exercised no *dominant* influence, it had been a *contributing* factor in the rate of increase in state hospital patients.[19]

That the economic depression of the Thirties had an unwholesome effect on the mental and emotional life of long-time unemployed workers and their families was obvious to most students of the problem. While disaster in some instances brings out the best in man, increased family tensions, anxieties, insecurities, disillusionment and loss of hope, lowered standards of living, malnutrition—all these factors that arise from a prolonged depression took a toll in terms of mental health, a toll that became manifest when the "depression children" in large numbers were rejected as psychiatrically unfit at World War II induction centers.

Colonel (later Brigadier General) William C. Menninger, in testimony before a U. S. Senate Committee holding hearings on a "Full Employment" Bill in September, 1945, urged passage of the measure and vividly described the disastrous effects on family life and on human personality should the nation again experience chronic mass unemployment such as it did during the Great Depression. He was particularly concerned with its effects on children.

"A healthy family relation," Menninger noted, "is essential to the development of 'normal' children. When that family is plagued with unemployment, it is impossible to conceive of the children maturing without some degree of warp in their personality structure and, consequently, difficulties in their relations to people and to the community—evidence of mental ill health."[20] Colonel Menninger called for a national program of maximum job opportunities together with a realistic social-security and public relief system that would not injure the morale of the temporarily unemployed and would serve as a strong buttress against the hazards of increased psychiatric disorders.

It is evident from the foregoing facts that measures to prevent the recurrence of cyclic depressions are at the same time measures pointed toward the ultimate goal of mental hygiene.

To what extent is the control of mental disease possible? It has been estimated that at least 40 per cent of mental disease could be prevented if we utilized to a maximum degree the knowledge of certain disorders already at hand. The organic psychoses, comprising about 46 per cent of all mental diseases offer the most hopeful immediate field for preventive work, since the causes are already known. Syphilis and alcohol together are responsible for over 11 per cent of admissions to mental hospitals. Both of these causes could be eliminated through an effective program of social control. Two lines of action for the immediate future are indicated in the struggle against these disabling factors: education and effective legislation. In the case of syphilis, a vigorous unrelenting fight must be waged against prevailing ignorance and the outworn superstitions and prejudices that stand as stubborn bulwarks against health and enlightenment. Besides, we need greatly increased facilities for the early treatment of this disease. In the case of excessive consumption of alcohol, often leading to psychosis as an end-result, preventive steps would include a vigorous, co-ordinated campaign of education, buttressed by intelligent legislation and resolute enforcement of measures of social control.

Pellagra, which still accounts for a number of cases in our mental hospitals, can be eradicated by affording a sufficient and well-balanced diet to the lower-income groups who are particularly susceptible to the ravages of this disease, which occurs mainly in certain sections of the South. Other types of psychosis, attributable to such factors as physical exhaustion, general debility, and poisons introduced into the body, could be eliminated through the constant application of preventive measures. A large percentage of the traumatic psychoses are caused by injuries to the brain and nervous system sustained in avoidable accidents. As for the mental diseases primarily associated with advanced age, which account for about 20 per cent of admissions to state hospitals, our knowledge of the processes of senescence and arteriosclerosis must progress further than it has today before a specific preventive campaign can be planned.

What of functional psychoses—those without known physical causes? How can these be prevented? There can be no doubt that such agencies as habit clinics, child guidance and adult psychiatric clinics and psychopathic hospitals have been instrumental in preventing incipient cases of mental disorder from developing into frank psychoses. The after care movement, in which psychiatric social work has played an important role, has also served in a preventive capacity. Successful adjustments have been made for many discharged patients who might have failed to find their way back to normal community life unaided.

The field of functional disorders has become an active battleground on which the old controversy over heredity and environment, nature and nurture, is being fought. The extreme hereditarians hold that most, if not all, mental disorders are fundamentally hereditary in nature, and propose ambitious plans for mass sterilization of the "unfit" as the only solution to the problem. However, recent studies made in this country and abroad have failed to confirm the belief that mental diseases—functional or organic—are primarily due to hereditary factors. The report of the American Neurological Association's Committee for the Investigation of Sterilization, published in 1935, pointed out that while heredity is a factor in certain mental disorders, the mechanism of heredity is entirely unknown; that the inheritance of these conditions is not classically Mendelian; and that probably some environmental factor is at work as well as the hereditary one. The attempt to sterilize people who, though not mentally sick themselves, are believed to be "carriers" of mental disease, would be futile. Furthermore, sterilization of those actually suffering from mental illness with a hereditary basis would not greatly reduce their incidence.[21] The Committee of the American Neurological Association, while recommending a circumscribed policy of voluntary, selective sterilization, urged that strong safeguards be erected around such a program, and counseled extreme caution in enacting legislation at this time. "The crying need of eugenics," declared Abraham Myerson, chairman of the Committee, "is not legislation, but real research."

It is a significant commentary on our approach to the problem of mental disease in general that over $200,000,000 of public funds is spent annually on the care and treatment of mental patients in this country, while only a relatively small amount is appropriated for research. Aside from the question of humanity, this is shortsighted from the point of view of economy alone. A well-planned, liberally financed program of research into the causes and cure of mental disorders might well result in incalculable financial savings to society, not to mention the results in terms of the prevention of human suffering.

The passage of the National Mental Health Act by Congress in 1946 marked a notable milestone toward the attainment of these ends. It brought to fruition the idea of federal aid that Dorothea Lynde Dix had advanced a century earlier —but on a far greater scale than she had dreamed. It made possible for the first time an organized, nation-wide long-range program for controlling mental disease. The Act authorized a three-pronged attack on the problem with the aid of federal funds to be administered and supervised by the United States Public Health Service. Dr. Robert H. Felix, director of the Public Health Service's mental hygiene division, was placed in immediate charge of the program. The National Mental Health Act contained three main provisions:

1) Authorization of federal grants to aid in the training of desperately needed psychiatric personnel for the care, treatment, and prevention of mental illness;

2) Authorization of federal grants to non-profit institutions and agencies, public and private, for the conduct of scientific studies on the nature, cause, and treatment of mental ills;

3) Authorization of federal grants, up to $10,000,000 annually, for aid to community psychiatric services. The grants were to be made to states on a matching basis—two federal dollars for every state dollar. No federal funds, under this Act, were to be used for operating in-patient services in mental hospitals.

The Act also authorized the establishment of a National Institute of Mental Health to be operated by the Public Health Service as a research and training center. It was decided later to locate this center at Bethesda, Maryland, as a part of the new Clinical Center of the National Institutes of Health now being built for the Public Health Service.

The Act also set up a National Advisory Mental Health Council, consisting of six outstanding leaders in the field, to advise the Surgeon General of the Public Health Service on research, training and community service programs. The first Council appointed by Surgeon General Thomas Parran included Drs. David M. Levy, William C. Menninger, John Romano, George S. Stevenson, Edward A. Strecker and Frank F. Tallman. The program initiated under the National Mental Health Act is probably the greatest single episode in the progress of the mental hygiene movement during the past generation.

Another great stimulus to the movement occurred with the creation in May 29, 1946, of the Group for the Advancement of Psychiatry during the Chicago annual meeting of the American Psychiatric Association. The organization of this group reflected a growing impatience within the psychiatric profession of the slow pace of progress in their specialty. The Group for the Advancement of Psychiatry—which became known as the GAP—comprised about 150 psychiatrists, all members of the American Psychiatric Association, and including many of the most prominent men and women in the field. The GAP meets twice a year to discuss the most pressing problems of psychiatry and mental hygiene, with a view toward formulating sound programs and principles and thus speeding up the pace of psychiatric progress. Dr. William C. Menninger was elected chairman of the group at the organizing meeting, and Professor Henry W. Brosin of the University of Chicago was elected its secretary. The Group has about fifteen active committees. The titles of these committees reflect the scope of the GAP's interests: medical education, preventive psychiatry, therapy, public education, social work, cooperation with federal agencies, state hospitals, cooperation with lay groups, social issues, industrial psychiatry, clinical psychology, forensic psychiatry, research, international relations and child psychiatry. It is the hope of the Group's founders and participants that its activities may eventually be transferred to the American Psychiatric Association; the GAP then will be disbanded.

The GAP, in its deliberations, has devoted much attention to the relations between psychiatric problems and the social environment, carrying forward the gradual development of psychiatric interest in this relationship. In an address delivered in 1926, William Alanson White pointed out the mutual advantages in an alliance of psychiatry with the social sciences. "Mental disorder as we ordinarily meet it," he said, "is a disorder of the individual as a social unit. It is not a purely individual affair like an infection, for instance, but is a disorder of the individual at the level of social adjustment."[22] An interesting example of the interplay between a medical and a social art is afforded by the insight into individual personality which was psychiatry's great gift to social work, a contribution that was amply repaid by the insight into the cultural conditioning of personality supplied by social workers to psychiatrists. Anthropology, too, has recently made important contributions to psychiatry through studies of the variations in mental disorder in different cultural settings.

From the study of psychiatric problems in relation to the social background has developed a new group of specialists in mental disorders—the social psychiatrists, who are trying to deal with abnormal behavior as it affects groups rather than individuals, and who stress the environmental factors involved. The late Frankwood E. Williams was an outstanding advocate of this approach to mental disorder. Williams formulated a "hygiene of society" which he believed to be a necessary basis for a well integrated program of mental hygiene. He continually pointed out that some psychiatrists, together with social workers coming under their influence, have tended to lay too great emphasis on individual defects in personality maladjustments, without giving proper consideration to the play of environmental factors.

It is worthy of note that a similar instance of the recognition of socio-economic factors in mental disorder was made by the predecessor of Williams in the directorship of the National Committee for Mental Hygiene. In 1917, Thomas W. Salmon wrote: "Unemployment, overwork, congestion of population, child labor, and the hundred economic factors which increase the stress of living for the poor are often contributing factors in the production of mental disease. Weaknesses in constitutional makeup are discovered under the stress of such conditions, that might have remained undiscovered under happier circumstances . . . Everything which makes for the betterment of those upon whom the stress of living falls heaviest will save many from mental disease."[23]

It was the opinion of Dr. Williams that an effective mass application of mental hygiene must rest on a frank and objective revaluation of present-day society, with a view toward changing that society so that the factors inimical to mental health might be eradicated, while those favorable to the promotion of mental health could be retained and developed.

It was the writer's pleasure to be present at one of the most inspiring psychiatric addresses of our generation. On October 22, 1945—two months after hostilities ceased in World War II—Dr. G. Brock Chisholm, who had served with distinction as director of general medical services in the Canadian Army (the equivalent of our Army Surgeon General), delivered the annual William Alanson White Memorial Lecture in Washington, D.C. The subject of his lecture was "The Psychiatry of Enduring Peace and Social Progress." In the course of an address pregnant with insight and courage, Dr. Chisholm presented the following observations and challenge to his fellow psychiatrists:

> We are all now, perforce, citizens of the world, whether or not we are sufficiently mature adequately to carry that responsibility. In the face of this new status as world citizens we must accept the uncomfortable fact that we are the kind of people who fight wars every fifteen or twenty years. We always have, for as far back as we know anything of the race, and if we go on being the same kind of people it is to be supposed that we will continue to fight each other. . . .
>
> Can we identify the reasons why we fight wars or even enough of them to perceive a pattern? Many of them are easy to list—prejudice, isolationism, the ability emotionally and uncritically to believe unreasonable things, excessive desire for material or power, excessive fear of others, belief in a destiny to control others, vengeance, ability to avoid seeing and facing unpleasant facts and taking appropriate action. These are probably the main reasons we find ourselves involved in wars. They are all well known and recognized neurotic symptoms. . . .
>
> We have never had a really peaceful society in the world, but only short intervals of forgetting and then frantic preparation between wars. Can the world learn to live at peace? I think so, but only if individual psychiatrists and psychologists can live up to Strecker and Appel's definition—"Basically, maturity represents a wholesome amalgamation of two things: one, dissatisfaction with the status quo, which calls forth aggressive, constructive effort; and two, social concern and devotion." If we cannot, the job will be left to what survivors there may be after the next war, or to intellectually more honest and braver people who may get a chance some generations later. With the other human sciences, psychiatry must now decide what is to be the immediate future of the human race. No one else can. And this is the prime responsibility of psychiatry.[24]

Later, in his role as general secretary of the United Nations World Health Organization interim commission, Dr. Chisholm helped stimulate the development of the International Congress on Mental Health, held in London in August, 1948. The inspiration for the Congress came mainly from a group of British psychiatrists and social scientists led by Dr. John Rawlings Rees, wartime chief of the British Army's psychiatric services. It was sponsored jointly by the International Committee for Mental Hygiene, founded by Clifford Beers, and by the World Health Organization's interim commission. The theme selected for the Congress was significant: Mental Health and World Citizenship. Also significant were the main topics chosen for the Congress: Problems of world citizenship and good group relations; the individual and society; family problems and psychological disturbances; planning for mental health—organization, training, propaganda; mental health in industry and industrial relations. Americans chose as their main subject for preparation the problems of mental health as they affect the child.

And now we come to the end of our study of the mentally ill in America. We have traced their history from the days when they were believed to be possessed and elaborate rites of exorcism were performed over them to drive out the devils, down through the times when they were chained in cages and kennels, whipped regularly at the full of the moon, and hanged as witches in New England. We have seen how the only public institutions provided for them in early America were the almshouses and prisons; how they were sometimes "bid off" as paupers on the auction block, like common chattels; how they were exhibited like animals in a menagerie before crowds who paid admission fees in our earliest mental hospitals, how our early psychiatrists drained them of pints of blood in the hope of cooling their fevered brains. We have traced the gradual evolution of the modern state hospital, and the rise of the state care system. We have sketched the origin and rise of the mental hygiene movement, and the consequent raising of standards of care and treatment for mental patients, the encouragement of psychiatric research, and the beginnings of an organized drive toward the prevention of mental disease. Three great personalities stand out in the story of the mentally ill in America, each one pioneering along a new path of progress. Benjamin Rush, the father of American psychiatry, made the first groping efforts to raise the study and treatment of mental disease to a scientific level. Dorothea Lynde Dix traveled the length and breadth of this land for forty years in a crusade to humanize the treatment of the insane, to transfer them from the poorhouses and prisons in which they were then incarcerated into hospitals for their special care and treatment. Clifford Beers, in launching organized mental hygiene, brought about a synthesis of scientific and humanitarian reform in a single movement, and promoted the application of the twentieth century ideal of prevention to the field of mental illness.

We have traveled a long road upward from the ideal of repression to the ideal of prevention, from manacles to mental hygiene. But the contemplation of past triumphs leaves no room for a complacent attitude toward present conditions. We are too often inclined to ignore a present evil by recalling still greater evils of the past. Progress is achieved not by the philosophy of "things have been worse," but by the philosophy founded on the premise that "conditions could be made better." A mantle of mystery still hangs over a large area of mental disorder. Psychiatric researchers and experimenters in the supporting sciences, greatly handicapped in their work by a woeful lack of funds, are striving manfully to tear apart this mantle, to bring light upon the nature of mental disease, so that we may the better grapple with it.

In the last analysis, the problem of mental health cannot be divorced from the general problem of the public health. Nowhere has this principle been stated more impressively, perhaps, than in the charter of the United Nations World Health Organization, which defines health as "a state of physical fitness and of mental and social well-being; not only the absence of infirmity or disease."

Among the goals listed in the WHO charter are the following:

"Satisfactory individual and collective emotional health is essential to the harmony of human relations.

"Healthy development of the child toward world citizenship is of paramount importance."

A world of peace and freedom, from which the twin specters of war and insecurity will be banished, a world of equal opportunity, where people will be freed from stunting inhibitions and "guilt feelings" arising from outworn prejudices and taboos, a world where children may lead healthy, happy lives and grow into useful, well adjusted citizens, where the personality is permitted to develop naturally and freely, where the individual is given a sense of personal worth and dignity, and where his activities and ambitions are integrated with the development of group life—such is the goal toward which mental hygiene must strive.

BIBLIOGRAPHY

CHAPTER I

1. Tuke, D. Hack. *Insanity in Ancient and Modern Life.* London, 1878. 219 pp., p. 8.
2. Williams, Charles. *Demoniacal Obsession and Possession as Causes of Insanity.* London, 1911. 51 pp.
3. Dawson, Warren R. *Magician and Leech.* London, 1929. 159 pp., p. 72.
4. Coriat, I. "An Ancient Egyptian Medical Prescription for Hysteria." *Annals of Medical History,* 1921. v. 3, pp. 12–16.
5. Lord, Henry W. "Hospitals and Asylums for the Insane." *Proceedings of the National Conference of Charities and Correction,* 1879. p. 84.
6. Tuke, D. Hack. *Dictionary of Psychological Medicine.* London, 1892. v. 1, p. 3.
7. *The Genuine Works of Hippocrates.* (Translated by Francis Adams.) London, 1849. v. 2, p. 843.
8. Cockayne, Oswald. *Leechdoms, Wortcunning and Starcraft of Early England.* London, 1864–1865. v. 2, pp. 137–39.
9. Thorndike, Lynn. *A History of Magic and Science During the First Thirteen Centuries of our Era.* New York, 1923. v. 2, p. 496.
10. Cockayne, *op. cit.,* v. 1, p. 165.
11. O'Donoghue, E. G. *The Story of Bethlehem Hospital from its Foundation in 1247.* London, 1914. 427 pp., p. 79.
12. Benjamin of Tudela. *Itinerary of Rabbi Benjamin of Tudela.* (Translated by Marcus N. Adler.) London, 1907. p. 39.
13. Burdett, Henry C. *Hospitals and Asylums of the World.* London, 1891–93. v. 1, p. 39 ff.
14. White, Andrew D. *History of the Warfare of Science with Theology in Christendom.* New York, 1896. v. 2, p. 109.
15. Lecky, W. E. H. *History of the Rise of the Spirit of Rationalism in Europe.* London, 1872. v. 1, p. 82.
16. Lloyd, James H. "Sir Thomas Browne and the Witches." *Annals of Medical History,* 1928. v. 10, pp. 133–37.
17. Burton, Robert. *Anatomy of Melancholy.* London, 1660. (Seventh edition.) 723 pp., p. 56.
18. Quoted by Gregory Zilboorg in *The Medical Man and the Witch During the Renaissance.* Baltimore, 1935. 215 pp., pp. 92–93. For a learned and extremely interesting account of psychiatric development in this and succeeding periods, see Dr. Zilboorg's *A History of Medical Psychology,* prepared in collaboration with Dr. George W. Henry (New York, 1941. 606 pp.)

CHAPTER II

1. Thompson, C. J. S. *Mystery and Art of the Apothecary.* London, 1929. 287 pp., p. 206.

BIBLIOGRAPHY 521

2. Gerard, John. *The Herball.* (Thomas Johnson, ed.) London, 1636. 1630 pp., p. 977.
3. The preceding medical résumé is based principally on Garrison's *History of Medicine;* Packard's *History of Medicine in the U.S.,* v. 1; and O. W. Holmes' *Medical Essays.*
4. Quoted in O. W. Holmes, "The Medical Profession in Massachusetts." *Mass. Historical Society. Lowell Lectures on the Early History of Massachusetts, 1869.* p. 272.
5. Wertenbaker, Thomas J. *The First Americans.* New York, 1927. 358 pp., p. 169.
6. Letter from Edward Stafford to Gov. John Winthrop, Jr., 1643. *Proceedings of the Massachusetts Historical Society,* 1862. v. 5, pp. 379-80.
7. Letter of Dr. James Greenhill to Col. Theodore Blank, 1764. Quoted by W. B. Blanton in *Medicine in Virginia in the Eighteenth Century.* pp. 6-7.
8. Gundry, Richard L. "Non-restraint in the Care of the Insane." *Proceedings of the National Conference of Charities and Correction,* 1885. p. 124 ff.
9. *Danvers Historical Society. Historical Collections.* v. 4, p. 85.
10. Mather, Cotton. *Magnalia Christi Americana; or The Ecclesiastical History of New England.* London, 1702. Book III, p. 119.
11. Taylor, John M. *Witchcraft Delusion in Colonial Connecticut.* New York, 1908. p. 24. Incidentally, the witch laws in some of the New England states were copied verbatim from the Bible (*Leviticus,* xx, 20, and *Exodus,* xxii, 18).
12. Upham, Charles W. *Salem Witchcraft.* Boston, 1867. v. 2, pp. 209-10.
13. Bailey, Sarah L. *Historical Sketches of Andover.* Boston, 1880. 626 pp., p. 212.
14. *Narratives of the Witchcraft Cases, 1648-1706.* New York, 1914. pp. 374-76.
15. Brattle, Thomas. "Letter to a Clergyman, October 8th, 1692." Reprinted in *Narratives of the Witchcraft Cases,* p. 169 ff.

CHAPTER III

1. *Upland (Delaware County, Pa.) Court Records, 1676-1681.* (*Memoirs of the Historical Society of Pennsylvania.* v. 7, pp. 102-3.)
2. *Braintree, Mass., Town Records, 1640-1793.* p. 26.
3. *Minutes of the Mayor's Court of New York City,* Nov. 20, 1677. (MS.)
4. *Ibid.* April 5, 1725.
5. *Ibid.* July 5, 1720. Incidentally, sixteen years later we meet with a Henry Dove who is pronounced "wild, ungovernable, and Non Compos Mentis" by selectmen of Boston delegated to determine his sanity. (*Boston Town Records,* 1736. v. 13, pp. 313, 315.) Can it be the same Dove whose conduct so belied his peaceful name?
6. *York County, Virginia, Records.* v. 8, p. 363. Quoted in W. B. Blanton's *Medicine in Virginia in the Seventeenth Century.* Richmond, 1930. 337 pp., p. 131.
7. *Records of the Colony of the Massachusetts Bay.* v. 5, p. 80.
8. *Minutes of the Common Council, Albany, N.Y.* January 6, 1685. (MS.)
9. O'Callaghan, E. B. *Documents Relating to the Colonial History of the State of New York.* New York, 1853-87. v. 3, p. 415.
10. Drake, Francis S. *Town of Roxbury, Mass.* Roxbury, 1878. 475 pp., p. 383.
11. *Boston Selectmen's Minutes.* v. 15, p. 366.

12. *Public Records of Connecticut*, February, 1756. v. 10, p. 464.
13. *Ibid.*, March, 1758. v. 11, p. 111.
14. *Colonial Laws of New York.* v. 1, p. 79.
15. Furman, Gabriel. *Notes Relating to the Town of Brooklyn.* Brooklyn, 1824. 116 pp., p. 101.
16. Field, Edward. *State of Rhode Island and Providence Plantations at the end of the Century.* Boston, 1902. v. 3, p. 390.
17. *New Haven Colony Records.* v. 1, pp. 203, 414. Cited in E. W. Capen's *Historical Development of the Poor Law of Connecticut.* pp. 23, 47.
18. *Surrey County Records.* v. 1, p. 203. Quoted in W. B. Blanton's *Medicine in Virginia in the Seventeenth Century.* p. 129.
19. Adams, Charles F. *Three Episodes of Massachusetts History.* Boston, 1893. v. 2, pp. 725-26.
20. *Records of the Town of Southampton*, April, 1701. v. 5, pp. 161-62.
21. Field, *op. cit.* v. 3, p. 391.
22. *Records of the Town of Braintree.* pp. 41, 43, 46.
23. DeVoe, Thomas F. *The Market Book.* New York, 1862. v. 1, p. 91.
24. *Minutes of the Mayor's Court, New York*, October 10, 1721.
25. *Ibid.* May 13, 1729.
26. O'Callaghan, *op. cit.* v. 2, pp. 689-90.
27. *Public Records of the Colony of Connecticut.* October, 1759. v. 11, pp. 313, 590.
28. *Minutes of the Common Council of New York City*, 1675-1776. v. 4, p. 310.
29. *Public Records of Connecticut Colony.* v. 7, p. 127. Cited in H. W. Capen's *Historical Development of the Poor Law of Connecticut.* p. 63.
30. Arnold, S. G. *History of the State of Rhode Island and Providence Plantations.* New York, 1859-60. v. 1, p. 80.

CHAPTER IV

1. Conolly, John. *Treatment of the Insane without Mechanical Restraints.* London, 1856. 380 pp., pp. 4-5.
2. Franklin, Benjamin. *Some account of the Pennsylvania Hospital, from its first rise to the beginning of the Fifth Month, called May, 1754.* Philadelphia, 1754. 40 pp., p. 4.
3. Morton, Thomas G. *History of the Pennsylvania Hospital.* Philadelphia, 1897 (rev. ed.). 591 pp., p. 10. I am indebted to this valuable work for much information concerning the early history of this institution.
4. *Ibid.* p. 125.
5. *Ibid.* p. 147.
6. *Life, Journals and Correspondence of Rev. Manasseh Cutler.* Edited by William P. and Julia P. Cutler. Cincinnati, 1888. v. 1, pp. 280-81.
7. Quoted in Morton, *op. cit.* p. 134.
8. *Boston Selectmen's Minutes*, March 2, 1730. v. 13, 6. 194.
9. *Boston Town Records*, March 10, 1745-46. v. 14, p. 77.
10. *Ibid.*, May 28, 1746. v. 14, pp. 89, 101. This bridewell, which seems to have fallen into disuse, stood near the workhouse established in 1737.
11. *Ibid.*, May 14, 1751. v. 14, p. 198.
12. *Boston Town Records*, March 25, 1765. v. 16, pp. 139-40.
13. *Journal of the House of Representatives, Massachusetts*, 1766. June 20 and 26, 1766. pp. 105, 127.

BIBLIOGRAPHY 523

14. *Journals of the House of Burgesses, Virginia.* November 7, 1766. v. 1766-69, p. 12.
15. Governor's Message, April 11, 1767. (*Journals of the House of Burgesses. Virginia.* v. 1766-69, p. 131.)
16. Hening's *Statutes at Large of Virginia.* v. 8, pp. 378-81.
17. Blanton, Wyndham B. *Medicine in Virginia in the Eighteenth Century.* Richmond, 1931. 449 pp., p. 293.

CHAPTER V

1. A complete bibliography of Rush's writings may be found in Nathan Goodman's *Benjamin Rush: Physician and Citizen.* Philadelphia, 1934. 421 pp.
2. Quoted by Charles K. Mills, *Benjamin Rush and American Psychiatry.* (A paper read before the American Neurological Society, Dec. 1886.) 36 pp., p. 27.
3. Tuke, D. Hack. *The Insane in the United States and Canada.* London, 1885. 264 pp., pp. 21-22.
4. Morton, *History of the Pennsylvania Hospital.* p. 163.
5. Mills, *op. cit.* p. 15.
6. *Ibid.* p. 19.
7. Quoted in George C. Ives's *History of Penal Methods.* London, 1914. 409 pp., p. 85.
8. Burdett, Henry C. *Hospitals and Asylums of the World.* v. 1, p. 63.
9. Cited by Richard Gundry, "Non-restraint in the Care of the Insane." *Proceedings of the National Conference of Charities and Correction*, 1885. p. 126.
10. Conolly, John. *Treatment of the Insane,* p. 12.
11. Rush, Benjamin. *Medical Inquiries and Observations upon the Diseases of the Mind.* Philadelphia, 1812. 367 pp., pp. 171-72.
12. Morton, *op. cit.* p. 144.
13. *Ibid.* pp. 145-46.
14. Lloyd, James Hendrie. "Benjamin Rush and his Critics." *Annals of Medical History*, 1930. v. 2, p. 473.
15. Morton, *op. cit.,* p. 148 ff.
16. Goodman, *op. cit.* p. 348.
17. *Ibid.* p. 349.

CHAPTER VI

1. Beck, T. Romeyn. *An Inaugural Dissertation on Insanity.* New York, 1811. 40 pp., pp. 27-28.
2. Hunt, Harold C. *A Retired Habitation: A History of the Retreat, York.* London, 1932. 144 pp., p. 7.
3. *Memoirs of Thomas Scattergood.* Compiled by W. Evans and T. Evans. London, 1845. 464 pp., p. 382.
4. *An Account of the Present State of the Asylum for the Relief of Persons Deprived of the Use of Their Reason.* Philadelphia, 1816. 24 pp., p. 5.
5. *Ibid.* p. 7.
6. Waln, Robert, Jr. "An Account of the Asylum for the Insane established by the Society of Friends, near Frankford in the vicinity of Philadelphia."

Philadelphia Journal of Medical and Physical Science. 1825. v. 10, pp. 238-39.
7. *Minutes of the Society of the New York Hospital, Board of Governors,* October 25, 1774. (MS.)
8. Eddy, Thomas. *Hints for introducing an improved mode of treating the Insane in the Asylum. Read before the Governors of the New York Hospital . . . Fourth-month, 1815.* New York, 1815. 18 pp., p. 4. (Reprinted 1916 by the Bloomingdale Hospital Press.)
9. *Ibid.* pp. 15–16.
10. Knapp, Samuel L. *Life of Thomas Eddy.* New York, 1834. 394 pp., p. 231.
11. Tuke, Samuel. *Practical Hints on the Construction and Economy of Pauper Lunatic Asylums.* York, 1815. 55 pp.
12. *Letter of Samuel Tuke to Thomas Eddy, on Pauper Lunatic Asylums,* July 17, 1815. (Published by Governors of New York Hospital, N.Y., 1815.) 11 pp., p. 7. For further correspondence between Eddy and Tuke, see Knapp's *Life of Eddy.*
13. *Address of the Governors of the New York Hospital to the Public Relative to the Asylum for the Insane at Bloomingdale, New York.* May 10, 1821. 8 pp.
14. Warren, Edward. *Life of John Collins Warren.* Boston, 1860. v. 1, p. 99.
15. Bowditch, Nathaniel I. *History of the Massachusetts General Hospital.* Boston, 1851. 442 pp., pp. 6–7.
16. *Massachusetts General Hospital: Address of the Board of Trustees to the Public.* Boston, 1814, 14 pp.
17. *Massachusetts General Hospital: Report of the Trustees,* 1822. 34 pp., p. 24 ff.
18. *Chapter 703, Laws of 1824, Kentucky.* "An Act to carry into operation the Lunatic Asylum."
19. Powell, T. O. "A Sketch of Psychiatry in the Southern States." (Presidential Address.) *Transactions of the American Medico-Psychological Association,* 1897. v. 4, pp. 96–98.
20. *State of the Asylum for the Relief of Persons Deprived of the Use of their Reason.* Phila., 1826. 30 pp., p. 5.
21. *South Carolina. Statutes at Large,* 1821. v. 6, p. 168.
22. *Chapter 36, Laws of 1821, Ohio.*
23. Ford, Henry A., and Mrs. Kate B. Ford. *History of Cincinnati, Ohio.* Cleveland, 1881. 534 pp., p. 206.
Not long after its completion, the basement of the asylum was converted into a poorhouse, and was also used as an orphanage.
24. Quoted in Hurd's *Institutional Care of the Insane.* v. 3, p. 298.
25. *Report of a Committee of the Connecticut Medical Society, Respecting an Asylum for the Insane.* Hartford, 1821. 16 pp., p. 9.
26. *Ibid.* p. 12.

CHAPTER VII

1. *Annual Report of the Medical Visitors of the Hartford Retreat,* 1830. pp. 5–6.
2. Quoted in William D. Herrick's *History of the Town of Gardner, Worcester County, Mass.* Gardner, 1878. 535 pp., pp. 238–39.
3. *Old Records of the Town of Fitchburg, Mass.* Compiled by Walter A. Davis. Fitchburg, 1902. v. 5, pp. 85–86.

BIBLIOGRAPHY 525

4. Field, Edward. *History of the State of Rhode Island.* v. 3, pp. 407–8.
5. Hurd, Henry M. *Institutional Care of the Insane.* v. 2, p. 510.
6. *Ibid.* v. 2, p. 511.
7. *Report of Committee to whom was referred the consideration of the pauper laws of the Commonwealth. Submitted to the Massachusetts legislature, 1821.*
8. *Report on the Relief and Settlement of the Poor in the State of New York, 1824.* Submitted by the Secretary of State, J. V. N. Yates. 154 pp.
9. *Ibid.* p. 4.
10. *Ibid.* pp. 17–18.
11. *Ibid.* p. 61.
12. Sanborn, Franklin B. "The Public Charities of Massachusetts." Boston, 1876. Published as a supplement to the *Twelfth Annual Report of the Massachusetts Board of State Charities,* 1876.
13. *Chapter 331, Laws of 1824, New York State.*
14. "Report of the Commissioners on the subject of the Pauper System of the Commonwealth of Massachusetts, 1833." *House of Representatives Documents, 1833.* No. 6, p. 44.
15. *New York State Assembly Documents, 1838.* v. 6, No. 310, pp. 11–15.

CHAPTER VIII

1. Hall, Captain Basil. *Travels in North America in the years 1827 and 1828.* Philadelphia, 1829. 2 v.
2. *Ibid.* v. 1, p. 314.
3. *Report of the Commissioners appointed to superintend the erection of a Lunatic Hospital at Worcester, January 4, 1832. (Massachusetts Senate Documents, 1832.* No. 2, p. 19.)
4. *Report of the Select Committee on Bloomingdale Hospital and the propriety of building a new establishment for the Insane. (New York State Assembly Documents, 1831.* v. 3, Document 263, p. 29.)
5. Ray, Isaac. "American Hospitals for the Insane." *North American Review,* 1854. v. 79, pp. 67–90.
6. Dickens, Charles. *American Notes for General Circulation.* London, 1842. v. 1, pp. 105–11.
7. *Ibid.* v. 1, pp. 221–23.
8. Earle, Pliny. "Statistics of Insanity." *American Journal of Insanity,* 1849. v. 6, pp. 141–45.
9. *Second Annual Report of the State Lunatic Hospital at Worcester,* 1834. pp. 5–6.
10. The finding of Dr. Earle on statistics of insanity may be found in condensed form in a paper read by him before the National Conference of Charities and Correction in 1879 (*Proceedings of the Sixth Annual Conference, 1879.* pp. 42–50), and in his article on "Curability" in the *Dictionary of Psychological Medicine,* edited by D. Hack Tuke. (London, 1892. v. 1, pp. 321–24.)

CHAPTER IX

1. Tiffany, Francis. *Life of Dorothea Lynde Dix.* Boston, 1891. 392 pp., pp. 12–13.

2. Willard, Frances E. "Dorothea Dix." *The Chautauquan*, 1889. v. 10, pp. 61–65.
3. Garrison, W. P. and F. J. *William Lloyd Garrison*. Boston, 1885. v. 1, p. 225.
4. *Memorial to the Legislature of the State of Massachusetts*. Submitted by D. L. Dix, January, 1843.
5. *Providence (Rhode Island) Journal*, April 10, 1844. Quoted by Tiffany, *op. cit.* pp. 96–98.
6. Hurd, Henry M. *Institutional Care of the Insane*. v. 4, p. 108.
7. Hamer, Philip M. *Tennessee: A History, 1673–1932*. New York, 1933. v. 1, p. 333.
8. *Memorial of D. L. Dix, Praying a grant of land for the relief and support of the indigent insane in the U.S.*, June 27, 1848. (*U. S. Senate, Miscellaneous Documents*. No. 150.)
9. *Special Message of President Pierce to the Senate of the U.S.*, May, 1854. 16 pp.
10. Tiffany, *op. cit.* p. 205.
11. *Ibid.* p. 231.
12. *Ibid.* p. 239.
13. Lossing, Benson J. *Pictorial History of the Civil War*. Philadelphia and Hartford, 1868–72. v. 1, p. 576.
14. *Memoirs of Pliny Earle*. Edited by Franklin B. Sanborn, Boston, 1898. 409 pp., p. 306.
15. Tiffany, *op. cit.*, p. 155.

CHAPTER X

1. Channing, Walter. "Some Remarks," etc. *American Journal of Insanity*, 1895. v. 51, p. 171.
2. Quoted by Edmund B. Whitcombe in his Presidential Address before the British Medico-Psychological Association, 1891. *Journal of Mental Science*, 1891. v. 37, pp. 501–14.
3. *Memoirs of Pliny Earle*. p. xi.
4. "Official Account of the Meeting of the Association of Medical Superintendents of American Institutions for the Insane." *American Journal of Insanity, 1844.* v. 1, pp. 253–258.
5. Quoted in obituary of Dr. Brigham, *American Journal of Insanity*, 1849. v. 6, p. 189.
6. Blumer, G. Alder. "A Half-Century of Literature of Psychiatry." *Transactions of the American Medico-Psychological Association*, 1894. v. 50, p. 146.
7. "Periodical Literature of Lunatic Asylums." *American Journal of Insanity*, 1845. v. 2, pp. 77–79.
8. *Memoirs of Pliny Earle*. p. 164.
9. Ray, Isaac. "Statistics of Insanity." *Contributions to Mental Pathology*. Boston, 1873. 558 pp., p. 67. (Reprint of an article in the *American Journal of Insanity*, 1849. v. 6, pp. 23–52.)
10. *Journal of Mental Science*, 1881. v. 27, p. 66.
11. *Pennsylvania Hospital for the Insane: Report for the Year 1883*. pp. 127–29. This report contains a memorial of Dr. Kirkbride, with many quotations from his reports extending over forty-two years.
12. "Propositions Relative to the Construction of Hospitals for the Insane." *American Journal of Insanity*, 1854. v. 11, pp. 160–62. In 1852 another set of

propositions, fourteen in number, relating to the organization of mental hospitals, was drawn up by Kirkbride and adopted by the Association. The principles contained in this second set were of a general and noncontroversial nature, and never aroused the interest evoked by those on construction.

CHAPTER XI

1. Conolly, John. *The Treatment of the Insane without Mechanical Restraints.* pp. 189–90.
2. *Ibid.* p. 194.
3. *Report of the Pennsylvania Hospital for the Insane,* 1883 (Containing a Memorial of Dr. Kirkbride). p. 80.
4. *Report of the Pennsylvania Hospital for the Insane for the Year 1842.* p. 41.
5. Clark, Sir James. *Memoir of John Conolly.* London, 1859, 298 pp., p. 160.
6. *Handbook of the New York State Department of Mental Hygiene,* 1933. pp. 356–57.
7. *Annual Report of the Maine Insane Hospital, Augusta,* 1844. p. 32.
8. *Ibid.* pp. 31–32.
9. *American Journal of Insanity,* 1874. v. 31, p. 182.
10. Bucknill, John C. "Notes on the Asylums for the Insane in America." *American Journal of Insanity,* 1876. v. 33, p. 158.
11. Conolly, *op. cit.,* p. 35.
12. *The Lancet,* London. November 13, 1875. pp. 705-7.

CHAPTER XII

1. *Chapter 703, Kentucky Laws of 1824.*
2. *Report and Memorial of the County Superintendents of the Poor of this State on Lunacy and Its Relation to Pauperism and for relief of Insane Poor,* 1856. (*New York Senate Documents,* 1856. v. 1, Document 17. 20 pp., p. 1.)
3. *Ibid.* p. 16.
4. *Report of Select Senate Committee to Visit Charitable and Penal Institutions,* 1856. (*New York Senate Documents,* 1857. Document 8, 217 pp.)
5. *Report of Syvester D. Willard on the Condition of the Insane Poor in the County Poorhouses of New York,* January 13, 1865. 70 pp.
6. *Ibid.* p. 15.
7. "Proceedings of the American Association of Medical Superintendents of Institutions for the Insane, 1866." *American Journal of Insanity,* 1866. v. 23, p. 127 ff.
8. *First Annual Report of the State Lunatic Hospital at Worcester,* 1833. p. 20.
9. *First Biennial Report of the Board of State Commissioners of Public Charities of the State of Illinois,* 1868–70. p. 95.
10. Wines, Frederick H. *Provisions for the Insane in the United States.* Springfield, 1885. (Reprinted from the *Eighth Biennial Report of the Illinois State Commissioners of Public Charities,* 1885.) 28 pp., p. 23.
11. *Twenty-fifth Annual Report of the Board of Trustees and Officers of the Central Ohio Lunatic Asylum,* 1863. pp. 18–23. Also see the annual report for 1864.

12. This paper was published in the *American Journal of Insanity*, 1867. v. 24, pp. 42–51.

CHAPTER XIII

1. *Report of the Special Joint Committee appointed to investigate the public charitable institutions of the Commonwealth of Massachusetts*. (Senate Document No. 2, 1859.) pp. 3–4.
2. *Acts of the State of Rhode Island*, 1869. Chapter 814, Section 4.
3. *First Annual Report of the North Carolina Board of Public Charities*, 1869. p. 8. It is interesting to note, in passing, that one of the three original members of the Board was Dr. Eugene Grissom, superintendent of the State Insane Asylum at Raleigh and one of the most prominent hospital heads in his day.
4. *A Plea for the Insane in the Prisons and Poorhouses of Pennsylvania: Report of the Board of Public Charities*. Written by George D. Harrison, president of the Board. Philadelphia, 1873. 103 pp., pp. 7–8.
5. *Laws of New York, 1873, Chapter 571*. "An Act further to define the powers and duties of the board of State Commissioners of Charities." This Act, incidentally, changed the name of the central authority to State Board of Charities.
6. Smith, Stephen. *Who Is Insane?* New York, 1916. 285 pp., pp. 221–23.
7. "Proceedings of the Association of Medical Superintendents of American Institutions for the Insane, 1888." *American Journal of Insanity*, 1888. v. 45, p. 148 ff.
8. *First Annual Report of the New York State Commission in Lunacy*, 1889. pp. 78–79.
9. *Chapter 126, New York Laws of 1890*.
10. *Michigan Laws of 1877, Public Act No. 194*. Sections 23, 26 and 34. Later, this provision was modified, reducing the period of county support for patients in state hospitals from two years to one.
11. *Acts and Resolves of the State of Vermont, 1886. Public Act No. 42*, Section 8.
12. See John L. Gillin's *Poor Relief Legislation in Iowa*. Iowa City, 1904. 404 pp. Also: *First Biennial Report of the Iowa State Board of Control of State Institutions*, 1897–99. pp. 122–29.
13. *Sixth Annual Report of the Wisconsin State Board of Charities and Reform*, 1876. pp. 8–12.
14. *Chapter 233, Laws of Wisconsin, 1881*.
15. For favorable interpretations on the Wisconsin system, see:

    Giles, H. H. "County Care of Insane Paupers." *Proceedings of the National Conference of Charities and Correction*, 1882. pp. 97–102. (Discussion on pp. 102–19, 231–40, 253–61.)

    Giles, H. H. "Wisconsin System of County Care." *Ibid.*, 1891. pp. 78–84. (Discussion, pp. 319–24.)

    Heg, James E. "County Care of the Insane Under State Provision." *Ibid.*, 1896. pp. 181–90.

    Bullard, Ernest L. "The Wisconsin System of County Care of the Chronic Insane." In Hurd's *Institutional Care of the Insane*, v. 3, pp. 824–849. In the same work may be found a critical discussion of the Wisconsin plan. (See: "The Wisconsin System of County Care," v. 1, pp. 168–75.)

BIBLIOGRAPHY 529

A Report to the Pennsylvania Board of Public Charities from the Committee on Lunacy on the County Care of Indigent Chronic Insane, Dec. 2, 1896. 13 pp. This report, based on an extensive survey of the Wisconsin plan in operation, presented an enthusiastic account of the system, and was largely responsible for its adoption by the State of Pennsylvania in the following year, 1897.

It is an interesting experience to compare the aforementioned report with the scathing indictment of the Wisconsin plan, likewise based on personal observation, presented by Dr. C. B. Burr about the same time. See Dr. Burr's "A Winter Visit to the Wisconsin County Asylums," published in the *American Journal of Insanity,* 1898. v. 55, pp. 283–99.

16. For literature favoring the state care system see:

Craig, Oscar. "The New York Law for the State Care of the Insane." *Proceedings of the National Conference of Charities and Corrections,* 1891. pp. 85–96.

Dewey, Richard. "Some Outlines of State Policy in the Care of the Insane." *Ibid.,* 1892. pp. 125–41.

"Report of the Special Committee on Legislation for the Insane." *Annual Report of the State Charities Aid Association of New York,* 1890. p. 21 ff.

Wise, Peter M. "State Care of the Insane." *American Journal of Insanity,* 1898. v. 54, pp. 373–84.

MacDonald, Carlos F. "State Care and State Maintenance for the Dependent Insane in the State of New York." *Transactions of the American Medico-Psychological Association,* 1896. pp. 207–40.

Folks, Homer. *The State as Alienist.* New York, 1915 (?). 20 pp.

CHAPTER XIV

1. *A Century of American Medicine, 1776–1876.* Phila., 1876. 366 pp., p. 319.
2. Spitzka, Edward C. "Reform in the Scientific Study of Psychiatry." *Journal of Nervous and Mental Diseases,* 1878. v. 5, pp. 201–29.
3. Mitchell, S. Weir. "Fiftieth Anniversary Address." *Transactions of the American Medico-Psychological Association,* 1894. p. 116.
4. Channing, Walter. "Some Remarks on the Address ... by S. Weir Mitchell, M.D." *American Journal of Insanity,* 1895. v. 51, p. 171 ff.

    White, William A. "Presidential Address before the American Psychiatric Association." *American Journal of Psychiatry,* 1925. v. 82, p. 1 ff.
5. Weisenberg, T. H. "Neurologic Teaching in America." *Transactions of the Section of Nervous and Medical Diseases of the American Medical Association,* 1908. pp. 9–24.
6. Hammond, William A. *A Treatise on Insanity in its Medical Aspects.* New York, 1883. 767 pp.

    Spitzka, Edward C. *Insanity: Its Diagnosis, Causes and Treatment.* New York, 1883. 415 pp.
7. "Proceedings of the Association of Medical Superintendents of American Institutions for the Insane, 1871." *American Journal of Insanity,* 1871. v. 28.
8. Meyer, Adolf. "Presidential Address before the American Psychiatric Association, 1928." *American Journal of Psychiatry,* 1928. v. 85, p. 3.
9. Gray, John P. "Thoughts on the Causation of Insanity." *American Journal of Insanity,* 1872. v. 29, p. 277.
10. Gray, John P. "The Dependence of Insanity on Physical Disease." (A paper

read before the Medical Society of New York State, February, 1871.) *American Journal of Insanity*, 1871. v. 27, pp. 378–79.
11. Quoted by George H. Kirby in "The New York Psychiatric Institute and Hospital: A Sketch of its Development from 1895 to 1929." *Psychiatric Quarterly*, 1930. v. 4, p. 151.
12. Meyer, Adolf. "A Historical Sketch and Outlook of Psychiatric and Social Work." *Hospital Social Service Quarterly*, 1922. v. 5, p. 22.
13. Quoted in the *Thirteenth Annual Report of the State Charities Aid Association*, 1905. p. 25.
14. First Annual Report of the Sub-Committee on After Care of the Insane, p. 10. (*S.C.A.A. Publications, No. 96.*)
15. Stout, A. B. "Report on Probationary Asylums." *Second Biennial Report of the State Board of Health of California*, 1871–73. pp. 97–102. See also his "Second Report on Probationary Asylums in Large Cities," in the Board's *Third Biennial Report* for 1874–75. pp. 70–72.
16. Carlisle, Robert J., editor. *An Account of Bellevue Hospital*. New York, 1893. 381 pp., p. 90.
17. Stouffer, J. F. "History of the Psychopathic Hospital at Old Blockley." *Medical Life*, 1933. v. 40, pp. 270–74.
18. Mosher, J. M. "Pavilion F: A Department for Mental Diseases of the Albany Hospital." *Proceedings of the National Conference of Charities and Correction*, 1907. pp. 422–33.
19. Hurd, H. M. *Institutional Care of the Insane*. v. 2, p. 820.
20. *Annual Report of the Massachusetts State Board of Insanity*, 1910. pp. 29–30.
21. Morton. *History of the Pennsylvania Hospital*. p. 186.
22. *Annual Report of the Committee on Lunacy of the Pennsylvania Board of Public Charities*, 1886. pp. 49–50.

CHAPTER XV

1. *Mrs. Packard's Prison Life* (Chicago, 1867, 450 pp.) and *The Prisoners' Hidden Life; or Insane Asylums Unveiled* (Chicago, 1868, 2 v. in 1). The latter work was republished in a revised edition, under the title, *Modern Persecution* (Hartford, Conn., 1885–87, 2 v.). The books are written in a highly sentimental and melodramatic vein.
2. New York, 1887. 120 pp. (Bound together with "Nellie Bly as a White Slave.")
3. Beers, Clifford W. *A Mind That Found Itself*. New York, 1908. (Revised, 1935. 434 pp.)
4. *American Journal of Insanity*, 1845. v. 2, p. 91.
5. *Idem.* p. 92.
6. *Proceedings of the National Conference of Charities and Correction*, 1878. pp. 79–90.
7. *Constitution, By-Laws, Papers, etc., of the National Association for the Protection of the Insane and the Prevention of Insanity*, 1880. Boston, 1880. p. 4.
8. Origin, Objects and Plans of The National Committee for Mental Hygiene. *The National Committee for Mental Hygiene: Publication No. 1.* New York, 1912. 15 pp., p. 2.
9. *The Nation*, 1908. v. 86, pp. 265–66.
10. *Charities and The Commons*, 1908. v. 20, pp. 536–37.

BIBLIOGRAPHY 531

11. *The Medical Department of the United States Army in the World War:* v. 10, *Neuropsychiatry.* Edited by Col. Pearce Bailey, Lieut. Col. Frankwood E. Williams, Sergt. Paul O. Komora, and others. Washington, D.C., 1929. pp. 10-11.
12. Richmond, Mary E. *Social Diagnosis.* New York, 1917. 511 pp.
13. Taft, Jessie. "Progress in Social Case Work." *Proceedings of the National Conference of Social Work,* 1923. pp. 338-39.
14. Southard and Jarrett. *The Kingdom of Evils.* New York, 1922. 708 pp., p. 378.
15. Salmon, Thomas W. "Mental Hygiene." In Rosenau's *Preventive Medicine and Hygiene.* 2nd ed., 1917. p. 351.
16. Stevenson, George S. "The Child-Guidance Clinic—Its Aims, Growth, and Methods." *Proceedings of the First International Congress on Mental Hygiene,* 1930. v. 2, p. 215.
17. Baker, Amos T. "The Psychiatric Clinic of Sing Sing Prison." *Psychiatric Quarterly,* 1928. v. 2, pp. 464-65.
18. For a detailed account of mental hygiene in industry, see V. V. Anderson's *Psychiatry In Industry.* New York, 1929. 364 pp.
19. *Proceedings of the First International Congress on Mental Hygiene,* 1930. Edited by Frankwood E. Williams. v. 1, pp. 9-10.
20. *Twenty-Five Years After: Sidelights on the Mental Hygiene Movement and Its Founder.* Edited by Wilbur L. Cross. New York, 1934. 564 pp., p. 40.

CHAPTER XVI

1. *Report of the Mental Deficiency Committee: being a Joint Committee of the Board of Education and the Board of Control of Great Britain,* 1929. Part 1, p. 13.
2. *Handbook of the Department of Mental Hygiene, State of New York,* 1933. p. 94. (Quoted from Mental Hygiene Law, *Chapter 426, Laws of 1927.*)
3. *The Handicapped Child: Report of the Committee on Physically and Mentally Handicapped Children of the White House Conference on Child Health and Protection,* 1930. Section IVB, p. 332. (Report of Subcommittee on Problems of Mental Deficiency.)
4. Fisher, R. A. "Evolution of the Conscience in Civilized Communities in Special Relation to Sexual Vices." (*Scientific Papers of the Second International Congress on Eugenics,* 1921. v. 2, p. 315.)
5. Lecky, W. E. H. *History of the Rise and Influence of the Spirit of Rationalism in Europe.* v. 1, pp. 61-62.
6. Barr, Martin W. *Mental Defectives: Their History, Treatment and Training.* Philadelphia, 1904. 360 pp., p. 25.
7. Rose, M. A., and A. C. Elliott. "The Chûhas, or Rat-Children, of the Punjab." *Indian Antiquary,* 1909. v. 38, pp. 27-32.
8. Quoted by Edward Seguin in his *Idiocy: And Its Treatment by the Physiological Method.* New York, 1866. 457 pp., p. 19.
9. *Third Annual Report of the New York State Lunatic Asylum at Utica,* 1845. p. 59.
10. *Report of the Commissioners appointed to inquire into the Conditions of Idiots of the Commonwealth,* 1848. (*Massachusetts General Court. Senate Document No. 51,* 1848.)
11. *First Annual Report of the New York Asylum for Idiots,* 1851. pp. 15-16. (*New York Senate Document No. 30,* 1852.)

12. Richards, Laura E. *Samuel Gridley Howe.* New York, 1935. 283 pp., p. 172.
13. Quoted by F. Kuhlman: "A Century of Progress." *Quarterly of the Minnesota State Board of Control.* September 21, 1933. v. 33, p. 14.
14. *Report of the Commissioners appointed to inquire into Idiocy in Connecticut, 1856.* New Haven, 1856. 76 pp., p. 1.
15. Seguin, E. *Idiocy: And Its Treatment by the Physiological Method.* p. 289 ff.
16. Fernald, Walter E. "History of the Treatment of the Feebleminded." *Proceedings of the National Conference of Charities and Correction,* 1893. p. 209.
17. This study had originally been published in 1875 as an appendix to the thirty-first annual report of the New York Prison Association under the title, "A Record and Study of the Relations of Crime, Pauperism and Disease." (This appeared as the sub-title when the study was published separately in 1877.)

CHAPTER XVII

1. Quoted in Stanley P. Davies' *Social Control of the Mentally Deficient.* New York, 1930. 389 pp., p. 50. Dr. Davies' excellent work contains a thorough discussion of the "alarmist period."
2. Goddard, H. H. *Feeblemindedness: Its Causes and Consequences.* New York, 1914. 599 pp., pp. 560–61.
3. Goddard, H. H. *The Kallikak Family.* New York, 1912. 117 pp., pp. 116–17.
4. Goddard, H. H. "The Possibilities of Research as Applied to the Prevention of Feeblemindedness." *Proceedings of the National Conference of Charities and Correction,* 1915. p. 307.
5. Fernald, Walter E. "The Burden of Feeblemindedness." *Journal of Psycho-Asthenics,* 1913. v. 17, pp. 90–91.
6. *Proceedings of the National Conference of Charities and Correction,* 1915. p. 361.
7. *Ibid.* p. 308. In fairness to Dr. Goddard, it should be noted that he repudiated this conclusion less than a year later.
8. *Statistical Manual for the Use of Institutions for Mental Defectives,* 1934. (Prepared by the Committee on Statistics of the American Association on Mental Deficiency in cooperation with the National Committee for Mental Hygiene.) p. 19.
9. "Report of the Committee on Statistics." *Proceedings of the American Association on Mental Deficiency, 85th Annual Session,* 1934. (*Journal of Psycho-Asthenics,* 1934. v. 37, p. 412.)
10. Hogben, Lancelot. *Genetic Principles in Medicine and Social Science.* London, 1931. 230 pp., p. 205.
11. Quoted by Hogben, *op. cit.* p. 205.
12. For a detailed and penetrating critique of *The Kallikak Family,* see Abraham Myerson's *Inheritance of Mental Diseases.* Baltimore, 1925. pp. 77–82.
13. Fernald, Walter E. "Thirty Years' Progress in the Care of the Feebleminded." *Proceedings of The American Association for the Study of the Feebleminded,* 1924. p. 212.
14. For a complete and interesting account of this subject, see J. H. Landman's *Human Sterilization.* New York, 1932, 341 pp.
15. *Social Work Year Book,* 1935. Article on "Mental Deficiency," p. 272.
16. Hogben, Lancelot. *Nature and Nurture.* London, 1933. 144 pp., p. 33.

BIBLIOGRAPHY 533

17. *Missouri State Legislature. House Bill No. 290, 1929.*
18. Turner, F. Douglas. "Mental Deficiency." (Presidential Address before Royal Medico-Psychological Association, 1933.) *Journal of Mental Science,* 1933. v. 79, p. 572.
19. Coxe, Warren E. "New York State's Program for the Education of Subnormals in the Public Schools." *Mental Hygiene,* 1934. v. 18, p. 373.
20. Davies, *op. cit.* p. 313.
21. Further advantages of the colony plan are noted in William P. Letchworth's *Care and Treatment of Epileptics.* (New York, 1900. 246 pp., Chapter I.)
22. U. S. Bureau of the Census. *Patients in Mental Institutions, 1944.* Washington, 1947. 247 pp., pp. 36, 160.
23. Shanahan, William T. "Epilepsy." *Social Work Year Book,* 1933. p. 158.
24. Jennings, H. S. *The Biological Basis of Human Nature.* New York, 1930. 384 pp., pp. 250–51.

CHAPTER XVIII

1. Quoted in William G. H. Cook's *Insanity and Mental Deficiency in Relation to Legal Responsibility.* London, 1921. 192 pp., p. 1.
2. In his *Mental Disorder and the Criminal Law,* considered the classic American work on this subject, Sheldon Glueck has drawn up a detailed schema of terminology to prevent confusion in legal and psychiatric terms and concepts regarding mental disorder. (Boston, 1925. 693 pp., pp. 14–15.)
3. Kinberg, Olof. *Basic Problems of Criminology.* Copenhagen, 1935. 436 pp., p. 29.
4. Quoted by Sheldon Glueck, *op. cit.* pp. 129, 131.
5. Hale, Sir Matthew. *History of the Pleas of the Crown.* London, 1678. (1st American ed., Phila., 1847. v. 1, p. 30.)
6. Quoted by Sheldon Glueck, *op. cit.* p. 146.
7. Stephen, James FitzJames. *A History of the Criminal Law in England.* London, 1883. v. 2, p. 158.
8. Weihofen, Henry. *Insanity as a Defense in Criminal Law.* New York, 1933. 524 pp., p. 16.
9. Quoted in Charles Mercier's *Criminal Responsibility.* Oxford, 1905. pp. 170–171.
10. Oppenheimer, Heinrich. *Criminal Responsibility of Lunatics.* London, 1909. 275 pp., p. 251.
11. Ray, Isaac. *Medical Jurisprudence of Insanity.* Boston, 1860 (4th edition). 595 pp., p. 60.
12. *Report of the Sub-Committee on the Medical Aspects of Crime of the National Crime Commission,* 1930. p. 10. (Mimeo.)
13. For a more detailed summary of the advantages of this law, see Winfred Overholser's "The Briggs Law of Massachusetts: A Review and an Appraisal." *American Journal of Psychiatry,* 1934. v. 91, p. 591.
14. Quoted in Sheldon Glueck's *Mental Disorder and the Criminal Law.* p. 499.
15. Rush, Benjamin. *Sixteen Introductory Lectures, . . . upon the Institutes and Practice of Medicine.* Phila., 1811. 455 pp., pp. 369–70.
16. *Chapter 3, Laws of New York, 1800.* "An Act to Pardon John Pastano."
17. See "Institutional Care of the Criminal Insane in the United States," by Mary Harms. *Mental Hygiene,* 1931. v. 19, pp. 135–54.
18. White, William A. *Insanity and the Criminal Law.* New York, 1923. 281 pp., pp. 149–50.

19. The subject of reform in the criminal law is discussed in detail in Sheldon Glueck's *Crime and Justice*. (Boston, 1936. 349 pp.) See especially Chapter VII on "The Prospect of Justice."

CHAPTER XIX

1. *Chapter 31, Laws of 1788, New York.*
2. *Chapter 294, Laws of 1827, New York.*
3. *Collection of all such Acts of the General Assembly of Virginia, of a Public and Permanent Nature.* Richmond, Va., 1803–1808. v. 2, p. 119.
4. Quoted by John Ordronaux, *Lunacy Laws of New York.* Albany, 1878. 517 pp., p. 52.
5. Ray, Isaac. *Medical Jurisprudence of Insanity.* Boston, 1860 (4th edition). p. 369.
6. First published in the United States as *Very Hard Cash.* (New York, 1864 258 pp.)
7. Among her publications were *Mrs. Packard's Prison Life* (Chicago, 1867, 450 pp.); and *The Prisoner's Hidden Life*, or *Insane Asylums Unveiled* (Chicago, 1868, 2 v. in 1).
8. Packard, E. P. W. *Modern Persecution.* Hartford, Conn., 1887. v. 2, pp. 98–100.
9. *Chapter 268, Laws of Massachusetts, 1865.*
10. Dewey, Richard. "The Jury Law for Commitment of the Insane in Illinois." *American Journal of Insanity*, 1913. v. 69, pp. 571–84.
11. *Report of the Commissioners of Lunacy to the Commonwealth of Massachusetts, January, 1875.* Cited by Frankwood E. Williams, *Legislation for the Insane in Massachusetts.* p. 20.
12. Millspaugh, A. C. *Public Welfare Organization.* Washington, D.C., 1935. 700 pp., pp. 263–64.
13. Williams, Frankwood E. *Legislation for the Insane in Massachusetts.* Boston, 1915. 39 pp., pp. 37–38.
14. Russell, William L. "Report of the Committee on the Care of the Insane Pending Commitment." *State Hospitals Bulletin*, 1909. v. 2, pp. 27–34.
15. Davies, Stanley P. "Facilities for Care of Mental Patients Pending Commitment in New York State." *State Hospital Quarterly*, 1925. v. 10, pp. 636–50.
16. Myers, Glenn. "Commitment Laws in California and Elsewhere." *California and Western Medicine*, 1933. v. 39, pp. 313–19.
17. Singer, H. Douglas, and William O. Krohn. *Insanity and the Law.* Phila., 1924. 437 pp., p. 357.
18. Haines, Thomas H. "Parole Procedure in Hospitals for the Insane." *Proceedings of the National Conference of Social Work*, 1920. pp. 159–66.
19. U. S. Bureau of the Census. *Patients in Mental Institutions, 1944.* Washington, 1947, p. 5.
20. Overholser, Winfred, and Henry Weihofen, "Commitment of the Mentally Ill." *American Journal of Psychiatry*, 1946. v. 102, p. 762.
21. *Proceedings of the First International Congress on Mental Hygiene*, 1930. v. 1, pp. 61–62.

BIBLIOGRAPHY 535

CHAPTER XX

1. Kirby, George H. "Modern Psychiatry and Mental Healing." *American Journal of Psychiatry,* 1934, v. 91, pp. 10-11.
2. Discussions by Dr. Hermann Simon. *Proceedings of the First International Congress on Mental Hygiene,* 1930, v. 1, pp. 629-30.
3. *State Hospitals in the Depression.* A survey conducted by the National Committee for Mental Hygiene. New York, 1935. 126 pp., p. 25.
4. Pollock, Horatio M. *Family Care of Mental Patients.* Utica, N.Y., 1936. 247 pp., p. 20.
5. Hamilton, Samuel W., Grover A. Kempf, Grace C. Scholz, and Eve G. Caswell, *A Study of the Public Mental Hospitals of the United States, 1937-39.* U. S. Public Health Service, Supplement No. 164 to the Public Health Reports, Washington, D.C., 1941. 126 pp.
6. The results of my survey were published in a series of about fifty articles, documented with on-the-scene photographs, in the newspaper *PM* of New York City, between January, 1946, and August, 1947. A short account appeared in *Reader's Scope* magazine for August, 1946.
7. *The Care of the Mentally Ill in the State of New York. A Report by a Commission Appointed by Hon. Thomas E. Dewey to Investigate the Management . . . of the Department of Mental Hygiene.* Albany, N.Y., 1944. 124 pp.
8. *Ibid.,* pp. 16, 17, 19, 23-24.
9. The major publication of this material is represented by the booklet, *Out of Sight, Out of Mind,* by Frank I. Wright, Jr. (National Mental Health Foundation, Philadelphia, 1947, 164 pp.)
10. *Report of the Committee on Psychiatric Standards and Policies of the American Psychiatric Assn., May 26, 1946.* (Mimeographed.)
11. "Standards for Psychiatric Hospitals and Out-Patient Clinics Approved by the American Psychiatric Association, 1945-1946." *American Journal of Psychiatry,* 1945, v. 102, pp. 264-69.
12. *U. S. Bureau of the Census, Patients in Mental Institutions, 1945,* U. S. Government Printing Office, Washington, D.C., 1948, *passim.*
13. Hamilton, Samuel W. "American Mental Hospitals." In: *One Hundred Years of American Psychiatry.* New York, 1944. 649 pp., pp. 164-66.

CHAPTER XXI

1. For an excellent discussion of wartime mental health in the civilian population, see Dr. Therese Benedek's *Insight and Personality Adjustment—A Study of the Psychological Effects of War.* New York, 1946, 307 pp.
2. "Psychiatry and the National Defense: Report of a Committee of the Southern Psychiatric Association." *Psychiatry,* 1940, v. 3, pp. 619-24.
3. "National Security" (an editorial) *Psychiatry,* 1941, v. 4, p. 442; "Minimum Psychiatric Inspection—Medical Circular No. 1 (Revised)," *Journal of the American Medical Association,* May 3, 1941, v. 116, pp. 2059-60.
4. U. S. House of Representatives, Subcommittee of the Committee on Interstate and Foreign Commerce, 79th Congress, 1st session. *Hearing on H. R. 2550, A Bill to Provide for, Foster, and Aid in Coordinating Research Relating to Neuropsychiatric Disorders. . . . September 18, 19 and 21, 1945.* Washington, D.C., Government Printing Office, 1945, p. 36.

5. Halloran, Roy D., and Malcolm J. Farrell. "The Function of Neuropsychiatry in the Army." *American Journal of Psychiatry*, 1943, v. 100, pp. 14–20.
6. Deutsch, Albert. "Military Psychiatry in World War II, 1941–1943." In *One Hundred Years of American Psychiatry* (Published for the American Psychiatric Association), New York, 1944.
7. Menninger, William C. "Psychiatric Experience in the War, 1941–1946." *American Journal of Psychiatry*, 1947, v. 103, p. 578.
8. Braceland, Francis J. "Psychiatric Lessons from World War II." *American Journal of Psychiatry*, 1947, v. 103, pp. 587–88.
9. Menninger, *op. cit.* p. 579.
10. U. S. War Dept. Technical Medical Bulletin 203, October 19, 1945. Reprinted in *Mental Hygiene*, 1946.
11. Most noteworthy of those that were published, perhaps, are two articles published in *Psychiatry*, the organ of the William Alanson White Psychiatric Foundation—Dr. Meyer Maskin's "Know Not What They Do" (1946, v. 9, pp. 133–44) and Dr. William Needles' "The Regression of Psychiatry in the Army" (1946, v. 9, pp. 167 ff.)
12. Menninger, *op. cit.* pp. 582–83.
13. Murray, John M. "Accomplishments of Psychiatry in the Army Air Forces." *American Journal of Psychiatry*, v. 103, p. 599.
14. "Discussion." *American Journal of Psychiatry*, 1947, v. 103, p. 605.
15. *Traumatic War Neuroses*. Proceedings of the Conference on Traumatic War Neuroses in Merchant Seamen, January 28, 1943. (*Medical Studies on Merchant Seamen*, No. 1), 163 pp.
16. Administrator of Veterans Affairs. *Annual Report for Fiscal Year ending June 30, 1947* (U. S. Government Printing Office, Washington, 1948), pp. 10, 11, 94, 95, 106, 131.
17. Blain, Daniel. "Highlights of Accomplishments of Neuropsychiatry Program During Past Two Years." Mimeographed, Veterans Administration, Washington, D.C., 6 pp.
18. Menninger, William C. "Lessons from Military Psychiatry for Civilian Psychiatry." *Mental Hygiene*, 1946, v. 30, p. 576.
19. *Ibid.* p. 581.
20. Gregg, Alan. "Lessons to Learn—Psychiatry in World War II." *American Journal of Psychiatry*, 1947, v. 104, p. 220.

CHAPTER XXII

1. Meyer, Adolf. "A Few Trends in Modern Psychiatry." *Psychological Bulletin*, 1904, v. 1, p. 219.
2. *The Problem of Mental Disorder*. A study undertaken by the Committee on Psychiatric Investigations, National Research Council. New York, 1934. 388 pp., p. 9.
3. Wise, P. M. "Presidential Address." *American Journal of Insanity*. 1901, v. 58, p. 84.
4. Freud, Sigmund. "The Origin and Development of Psychoanalysis." *Lectures delivered before the Department of Psychology in Celebration of the Twentieth Anniversary of the Opening of Clark University, September, 1909*. Worcester, 1910. pp. 1–38. The papers of Freud, Jung, Meyer, Jennings, Stern, Boas and Tichener delivered at this memorable session were reprinted in the *American Journal of Psychology*, 1910.

BIBLIOGRAPHY 537

5. Kellogg, Theodore H. "Treatment of Mental Disorders." *A Reference Handbook of the Medical Sciences* (3rd ed., 1916) v. 6, p. 441. It is interesting to note that the same doleful prediction remains unchanged in the 4th edition, published in 1923.
6. *Transactions of the American Medico-Psychological Association,* 1914, pp. 303-24.
7. Rosen, John N. "The Treatment of Schizophrenic Psychosis by Direct Analytic Therapy." *Psychiatric Quarterly,* 1947, v. 21, pp. 3-25.
8. Hutchings, Charles W. "The Results of Ten Years of Malarial Therapy." *Psychiatric Quarterly,* 1936, v. 10, pp. 99-109.
9. Gantt, W. Horsley. "An Experimental Approach to Psychiatry." *American Journal of Psychiatry,* 1936, v. 92, pp. 1907-21.
10. Cotton, Henry A. "The Physical Cause of Mental Disorders," *American Mercury,* 1933, v. 29, pp. 221-25.
11. New York State Temporary Commission on Mental Hospital Problems. *Report on Insulin Shock Therapy.* Albany, 1944. 100 pp.
12. For an excellent account of the shock therapies from a cautiously favorable standpoint, see *Shock Treatments* by Lothar Kalinowsky and Paul H. Hoch. New York, 1946, 294 pp.
13. Ruggles, Arthur H. *Mental Health: Past, Present and Future.* Baltimore, 1934, 104 pp., p. 53.
14. *The Problem of Mental Disorder,* p. 236.
15. Hoskins, Roy G. *The Biology of Schizophrenia.* New York, 1946. 191 pp., p. 167.
16. Meyer, Adolf. "The Psychobiological Point of View." *The Problem of Mental Disorder,* p. 53.
17. Elkind, Henry B., and Maurice Taylor. "The Alleged Increase in the Major Psychoses." *American Journal of Psychiatry,* 1935.
18. Campbell, C. Macfie. *Destiny and Disease in Mental Disorders.* New York, 1935. 207 pp., pp. 197-98.
19. National Committee for Mental Hygiene. *State Hospitals in the Depression.* New York, 1935. p. 1.
20. Quoted by Albert Deutsch, *PM Newspaper,* September 11, 1945.
21. *Report of the Committee for the Investigation of Sterilization.* American Neurological Association, 1935.
22. White, William A. "Psychiatry and the Social Sciences." *American Journal of Psychiatry,* 1928, v. 84, p. 737.
23. Salmon, Thomas W. "Mental Hygiene." In Milton J. Rosenau's *Preventive Medicine and Hygiene* (2nd ed., 1917), pp. 352-53.
24. Chisholm, G. Brock. "The Psychiatry of Enduring Peace and Social Progress." *Psychiatry,* 1946. v. 9, pp. 1-44. Also reprinted, in pamphlet form, by the William Alanson White Psychiatric Foundation, Inc., Washington, D.C.

INDEX

Adair, Governor of Kentucky, message of, in *1821*, 106-7
Admission, voluntary, development of, 429 ff.
After-care movement, 289-91
Agnew (California) Asylum for the Chronic Insane, 241
Alabama, insanity as a defense in, 395
Albany (N.Y.) Hospital, Pavilion F, 293
Alcoholics, in mental hospitals, 454 f.
Alexander of Tralles, 11-12
Allen, J. R., 147
Allen, Nathan, 227, 312, 425
Allgemeine Zeitschrift f. Psychiatrie, founding of, 198
Almshouses as custodial institutions, *see* Poorhouses
American Association for the Study of the Feebleminded, 347, 355, 368, 373
American Association on Mental Deficiency, founding of, 347, 362 ff.
American Bar Association on psychiatry and law, 416
American Epilepsy League, 384*n*
American Foundation for Mental Hygiene, 328, 329
American Journal of Insanity, founding of, 198-200; name changed, 200
American Journal of Psychiatry, *see* American Journal of Insanity
American Medical Association on psychiatry and criminology, 416
American Medico-Psychological Association, *see* American Psychiatric Association
American Neurological Association, 277-78, 289, 512
American Orthopsychiatric Association, 327
American Psychiatric Association, founding and early development of, 191 ff.; "propositions" on asylum construction and standards, 208-12, 237-40; stand on mechanical restraint, 215; on state care, 257, 267; early opposition to state lunacy commissions, 258*n*, 278; resolution on psychiatric education, 283, 313; on reforms in criminal procedure, 416; on standards for modern mental hospitals, 451 ff.; Group for the Advancement of Psychiatry, 514 f.
American Psychoanalytic Society, 490
American Psychological Journal, founding of, 313
Analytical psychology, 491 f.
Annales Medico-Psychologiques, established, 198
Aretaeus of Cappadocia, 9, 188
Army Medical Corps, psychiatric service, 464 ff.; psychiatric nomenclature, 469 f.
Asclepiades of Prusa, 9, 188
Asklepiads, 6-8
Association of Medical Officers of American Institutions for Idiots and Feebleminded Persons, 347; *see also* American Association on Mental Deficiency
Association of Medical Officers of Asylums and Hospitals for the Insane, Great Britain, 191
Association of Medical Superintendents of American Institutions for the Insane, 191 ff.; *see also* American Psychiatric Association
Astrological cures, 13
Astrology and medical prescriptions, 30
Asylums, in medieval Europe, 16; in the 18th century, 55
Asylum Journal at Brattleboro, 200-1

INDEX

Aubanel, Dr., inventor of the crib-bed, 222
Augusta (Maine) State Hospital, 204
Aurelianus, Caelius, 10
Aveyron, wild boy of, 337 f.
Avicenna, 15
Awl, William M., 153, 192, 201-2

Backus, F. F., 342
Bailey, Pearce, 317
Banay, Ralph S., 326
Bancroft, Wilder D., 497
Barker, Lewellys F., 310
Barr, M. W., 361, 369
Barrett, Albert M., 294
Bates, James, 154, 156
Bath (England) Private School for Idiots, 340
Beard, George M., 312
Beers, Clifford W., founder of the mental hygiene movement, 302 ff.; early life of, experiences as a mental patient, 303-5; writes *A Mind That Found Itself*, 306; founds National Committee for Mental Hygiene, 310; founds pioneer Connecticut Society for Mental Hygiene, American Foundation for Mental Hygiene and International Committee for Mental Hygiene, 328, 329; tributes to, 330; death, 331
Bell, Luther V., 151, 155, 168, 192, 197 ff., 204, 273
Bellevue Hospital, 131, 144, 282, 292 ff., 297
Benjamin of Tudela, 16
Bennett, Alice, and non-restraint, 227, 281
Bernstein, Charles, 381, 385
Bethel Colony for Epileptics, Germany, 383
Bethlehem Hospital (Bedlam), 15, 65, 78, 92, 100, 111
Bible, examples of mental disease in, 3
Bicêtre, 88-92, 337 f.
Bill of Rights, 416
Billings, John S., 231-32n, 275
Binet, Albert, 354, 365
Binet-Simon test, 354, 363
Binghamton (N.Y.) State Asylum, 256, 260

Bini, L., 500
Birthright, Inc., 372
Blain, Daniel, 452; *re* psychiatry in the Merchant Marine, 473; report on V.A. neuropsychiatric program, 477 f.
Blanton, Wyndham B., 71
Bleuler, Eugen, 486, 492
Bloomingdale Hospital, 97-102, 113, 136, 152, 155, 192, 202, 274, 298, 421
Blumer, G. Alder, 200, 257, 330
Bly, Nellie, 307
Boarding out system, origin of, 47; in Kentucky, 120; in Mass., 244; for mental defectives, 385 f.; *see also* Family care
Bodine, Joseph L., 227
Boerhaave, Herman, 76, 78, 485
Bonaterre, Professor, 336 f.
Bond, Thomas, 58
Boston, early efforts to establish an asylum at, 66 ff.
Boston Almshouse, insane in, 66-68
Boston City Hospital, 201
Boston House of Industry, in *1833*, 129-30
Boston Lunatic Hospital, 143-45, 192, 201, 223
Boston Nerve Clinic, 296
Boston Psychopathic Hospital, 295, 297, 321, 324
Boston State Hospital, 295
Braceland, Francis J., 467
Bradley, Omar, 475
Brain toxicity, and mental disease, 497
Brattle, Thomas, quoted on witchcraft cases, 37
Breuer, Joseph, 487 f.
Brigham, Amariah, 139, 151, 192, 198 ff., 222, 239, 273, 284, 342
Brigham Hall Asylum, 237
Briggs, Vernon L., 227, 294-95, 405
Briggs Law of Massachusetts, 405 f.
Brill, A. A., 490
Brinkerhoff, Roeliff, 250
British Board of Control, 367n, 445
British Committee of Mental Deficiency, 331
British parliamentary investigation into the condition of the insane, *1815*, 214

INDEX 541

British Royal Medico-Psychological Association, 377
Brooklyn State Hospital, 500
Brosin, Henry W., 514
Brown, George, 347
Browne, Thomas, and witchcraft, 20
Bucknill, John C., 223-24, 227
Buffalo (N.Y.) State Hospital, 211, 256, 281
Bulbocapnine, 497
Burrows, George Man, 134, 136, 138
Burton, Robert, 20
Butler, Cyrus, 170
Butler, John S., 192, 201, 267
Butler Hospital, Rhode Island, 170, 197, 204, 240, 330
Byington, Horatio, 342

Cabot, Richard C., 290
California, mental examination of defendants in, 403, 404
California, early attempts to establish psychopathic hospital in, 291-92; rejection of 1933 commitment bill in, 440
California sterilization law, 372
Campbell, Charles Macfie, quoted, 509
Canada, provision for chronic insane in, 244
Canadian National Committee for Mental Hygiene, 328
Celsus, 11, 27-28
Censuses, Federal, of the mentally ill, *1840-1890*, 231-32; of mental hospitals, 455 f., 507
Central Islip (N.Y.) State Hospital, 457
Central Ohio Lunatic Asylum, 244
Cerletti, U., 500
Chalmers, George, 319
Channing, Walter, 188, 281
Channing, William Ellery, 161-62
Chapin, John B., 296
"Chemical restraint," 443
Chevaillier, A. A., 312
Chiarugi, Vincenzo, 95
Child guidance clinics, census of, 326
Child guidance movement, origin and development of, 323-26
Children's units in mental hospitals, 454

Chipley, Dr., of Kentucky, 239
Chisholm, G. Brock, address, 516
Chittenden, Russell H., 310
Chûhas, or Rat-children, 335
Church bodies, institutions operated by, 456
Civilian lessons from military psychiatry, 479 ff.
Civilian morale in World War II, 460 f.
Clark, James, 218
Clark, L. Pierce, 321
Classification of mental disease, 8, 9, 23, 76-77, 505 f.
Classification, early, of mental patients, 97
Cleaves, Margaret A., 281
Clevenger, Shobal V., 274
Clinics, mental hygiene, *see* Mental hygiene clinics
Clinics, psychiatric, *see* Psychiatric clinics
Cockayne, Oswald, 12
Cogswell, Mason F., 110
Colchester (England) School for Idiots, 340
Colonial legislation, repressive principle in, 43
Colonial settlement law, in Massachusetts, 44
Colonial times, medical practice in, 27 ff.; astrology and medical prescriptions in, 30; provision for the insane in, 39 ff.; care of mental defectives in, 48; medical treatment of the insane in, 48; criminal insane in, 50 ff., 409; houses of correction and workhouses in, 51 ff.; lack of commitment laws in, 419 f.
Colony system, evolution of, 243-45; for mental defectives, 380 ff.; for epileptics, 383 f.
Colorado, mental examination of defendants in, 404
Colorado Psychopathic Hospital, 298
Columbia-Presbyterian Hospital Medical Center, 297
Commissions in Lunacy, 258
Commitment, in Pennsylvania Hospital, 62 ff.; development of laws of, 418 ff.; procedures of, 428 ff.; voluntary and temporary, 431-33;

542 INDEX

Commitment (*Continued*)
in Delaware, 433 f.; detention pending, 434 f.; *habeas corpus* and, 436; suggested reforms, 439; methods of, in New York, 440
Commonwealth Fund, 325
Concord (New Hampshire) State Hospital, 140, 141, 197
Conditioned reflex, 495
Confectio antiepileptica, 27
Confinement, repressive, of the insane, 55-56
Congress on Mental Hygiene, First International, 329; Committee on Legal Measures and Laws, 439
Connecticut, mental defect in, *1856*, 345
Connecticut Lunacy Commissioner, 255
Connecticut Medical Society on the need for an asylum, *1821*, 110-11
Connecticut School for Imbeciles, 345
Connecticut Society for the Relief of the Insane, 111
Connecticut Society for Mental Hygiene, pioneer work of, 310, 315, 328
Conolly, John, 10, 55, 82, 213-15, 221, 225, 340
Conscientious objectors, service in mental hospitals, 451
Constitution, physical, in mental disease, 502
Convulsive therapy in schizophrenia, 498 f.
Cook, George, 237-38
Cook County (Illinois) Asylum, 274
Copp, Owen, 294
Cornell University Medical School, 298
Cottage system, advantages of, 212, 243; evolution of, 241 ff.; in Kankakee (Illinois) State Hospital, 242-43
Cotton, Henry A., 496
County care system, 256, 262-69; in Wisconsin, 234, 262 ff.; in Iowa, 263; census of, 271
Cowles, Edward, 274, 281, 444
Coxe, James, 156
Craig, Oscar, 269, 383
Craig Colony, 383

Cranston (Rhode Island) Asylum for the Incurable Insane, 249
Crime and mental defect, 367
Criminal insane, in colonial times, 50-51; definition of, 409; disposition of, 409 ff.; statutory provisions for, 410 ff.; confinement of, 411; institutions for, 412; release of, 413; suggested reforms, 414 ff.
Criminal law and insanity, 387 ff.
Criminologist and psychiatrist, 415
Crowther, Bryan, 78
Cullen, William, 76, 80-81, 91, 485
Curability of insanity, 132 ff., 510 f.
Curability cult, origin and development of, 132-57
Curtis, George W., 312
Curwen, John, 296
Cutler, Manasseh, 62
Cutler, Nehemiah, 192, 196

Damiens, Robert François, case of, 390
Dana, Charles L., 283, 289
Danielson, Florence H., 359
Dannemora (N.Y.) State Hospital, 410 ff.
Danvers (Mass.) State Hospital, 211
Daquin, Joseph, 95
Dar-al-Maristan in Bagdad, 16
Darwin, Charles, 349 f.
Davenport, Charles B., 359, 365, 373
Davies, Stanley P., quoted, 435
Defectives, pedigrees of, 358 f., 366 f.
Defendants, mental examination of, 403 ff.
Delaware, commitment procedure in, 429, 433 f.
Delinquency, research in, 327
Delinquent mental defectives, provision for, 352
Dementia praecox, 499 f.
Demoniacal possession, as cause of mental disease, 2 ff.; in 17th century America, 31 ff.; and mental defect, 334
Denton, Robert, 15
Dependent insane, colonial relief for, 43, 45, 46, 49; in the early 19th century, 112-13; *see also* State care, Pauper insane, Poorhouses

INDEX 543

Depression, economic effects of, 503 f., 509 f.
Dercum, F. X., 289
Detention wards, 291-93
Dewey, Richard S., 278, 281, 289, 426 ff.
Dickens, Charles, comments of, on American asylums, 144-45, 201
Diderot, Denis, 56
Discharge, methods of, 435
Dix, Dorothea Lynde, 131, 158 ff.; achievements of, 159, 184-85, 186; early life of, 159-62; New England influences on, 163, character of, 164; survey of Massachusetts almshouses and jails, 165; memorial to the Massachusetts Legislature, 165-68; memorial to the Illinois Legislature, 167n; activities in Rhode Island, 169-70; in New Jersey, 171; role in penal reform, 173; efforts in Canada, 174 ff.; appeals for federal provision for insane, 176-79; efforts in Scotland, 179-80; tour of mental hospitals in Europe, 181; work in Civil War, 182; last years of, 185, 190, 197, 233, 235, 236, 239
Dixmont Hospital, Pa., 175
Dongan, Thomas, governor of New York, 44
Doren, G. A., 347
Drake, Daniel, 109
Drugs, therapeutic use of, 497 ff.
Dugdale, Richard L., 350, 359, 366
Duke of York's Law, 46
Dunbar, Flanders, 493
Dwight, Nathaniel, 110

Earle, Pliny, 145-46, 151, 155-57, 192, 202-3, 205, 226, 274, 291, 311
Earlswood (England) School for Idiots, 340
East, E. M., 373
East Cambridge, (Mass.) jail, 158-59
Eastern Lunatic Asylum (State Hospital), Lexington, Kentucky, 71, 106-8, 120, 147, 230
Eastern Lunatic Asylum (State Hospital), Williamsburg, Virginia, founding of, 66, 69-71, 112, 152-53, 192, 196, 230

Eastern New York Custodial Asylum, see Letchworth Village
Eastern State Hospital, Pontiac, Michigan, 261
Eberbach Asylum, Nassau, Germany, 289
Eddy, Thomas, 98-102
Education for the feebleminded, 378 f.
Edward II, king of England, statute re property of the insane, 389
Egypt, ancient, treatment of mental disease in, 3; exorcism in, 4
Ehrlich, Paul, 494
Electric shock therapy, 500 f.
Elizabethan Poor Law, 44
Elkind, Henry B., 508
Elmira Reformatory, 327
Elmore, Andrew E., 265
Endocrine therapy in mental disease, 502 f.
England, early legal provision for insanity in, 389; legal tests for responsibility of the insane in, 391 ff.
English, O. Spurgeon, 493
Epilepsy, Hippocratic theory of, 8
Epileptics, colonies for, 383 ff.
Erskine, Lord, 393, 398
Esquirol, J. E. D., 78, 145, 341, 485
Estabrook, Arthur H., 359, 360, 373
Eugenics, rise of, 300; definition of, 357, practical aims of, 358
Eugenics movement, 356 ff.
Eugenic sterilization, see Sterilization, eugenic
Europe, early asylums in, 16; witchcraft in, 18 ff.
Exhibiting insane for fees, 63 ff.
Exorcism, in Egypt, 4; in medieval times, 17

Falret, Henri L., 237, 289, 339
Family care, in colonial times, 47-48; in Kentucky, 106-7
Family care system, 447 f.
Farrell, Malcolm J., 465
Federal Public Works Administration, building program of, 447
Feeblemindedness, see Mental defect
Felix, Robert H., 513
Fenton, Reuben E., governor of New York, 248

544 INDEX

Fernald, Walter E., 321, 347, 352, 361, 364, 367, 368, 385
Fernald School, *see* Walter E. Fernald School
Ferrus, G. M. A., 338
Fever therapy in general paresis, 494 f.
First International Congress on Mental Hygiene, 329, 439, 445
Fitz James Colony, Clermont, France, 242
Fletcher, Horace, 310
Florida, commitment in, 413, 428
Focal infections, theory of, 496
Fouquier, Francis, governor of Virginia, 69-70
Franklin, Benjamin, 58, 60
Free association, theory of, 488
Freedman, Harry, 465
Freeman, Walter, 501
Freud, Sigmund, 445, 492 f.
Friends Asylum (Hospital), Frankford, Pennsylvania, 95, 97, 108, 136, 202, 206, 241
Fromm-Reichmann, Frieda, 492
Fuller, Margaret, 164
Functional psychoses, prolonged sleep treatment in, 511 f.

Galen, 25
Gallipolis (Ohio) Asylum for Epileptics and Epileptic Insane, 383
Galt, John M., 71, 152 ff., 192, 196 ff.
Galton, Francis, 350, 357 f.
Gantt, W. Horsley, 496
Garrison, Fielding H., 301
General paresis, recent advances in treatment of, 493 f.
George III, king of England, insanity of, 81, 133-34, 393
Georgia, criminal insane in, 410, 414
Georgia Lunatic Asylum, Milledgeville, 140, 457
Gerard's Herball, 28
Germany, eugenic sterilization in, 376 f.
Gheel Colony, 14
Glueck, Bernard, 326
Glueck, Sheldon, 395 f., 416*n*
Goddard, Henry H., 353-54, 359 ff.
Godding, W. W., 184, 194
Gosney, E. S., 372, 373

Government Hospital for the Insane, 184, 240; *see also* St. Elizabeths Hospital
Grant, Madison, 373
Gray, George, 181
Gray, John P., 216, 238 ff., 274, 283, 284, 285
Greece, ancient, mental disease in, 5-9, 11; temple sleep in, 6-7
Greek medicine, contributions of, to mental medicine, 7
Greenhill, James, 30
Gregg, Alan, 482
Griesinger, William, 193
Grimes, John M., 383, 384
Grinker, Roy R., 472
Grinker, Roy R., and John P. Spiegel, *Men under Stress*, 479
Grotius, 272
Guggenbühl, J., 340
Guild of Friends of the Infirm in Mind, England, 289
Gyrator, Dr. Rush's, 79

Habeas corpus, 414, 436
Hack, Arch O., 378*n*
Haines, Thomas H., 437
Hale, John, 31
Hale, Matthew, 19, 388*n*, 391
Halifax (Nova Scotia) Hospital for the Insane, 175
Hall, Basil, 135-36
Hall, G. Stanley, 489
Halloran, Roy D., 465
Hamilton, Samuel W., quoted, 448, 456
Hammond, William A., 227, 276, 282, 283
Hancock, Thomas, will of, 67 ff.
Hard Cash, "reform" novel, 423 f.
Harlem Valley State Hospital, 499
Harrisburg (Pa.) State Hospital, 281
Harsnett, Samuel, Archbishop of York, 22
Hartford Retreat, 110-12, 115, 135-36, 138, 148-49, 152, 192, 195, 198, 200, 201, 255, 267
Harvey, William, 25
Haslam, John, 82
Haviland, C. Floyd, 297
Hawkins, *good and evil* test of, 392
Hawley, Paul R., 475
Hazard, Thomas G., 169

INDEX 545

Healing wells, 13-14
Healy, William, 324, 415n
Heidelberg Psychiatric Clinic, 486
Heinroth, Johann Christian, 193, 203
Helmont, Jean Baptiste van, 25
Hercules, insanity of, 6
Herdman, William J., 293-94
Heredity and mental defect, 349 ff.; rise of study of, 357 ff.; and mental disease, 512; *see also* Eugenics, Sterilization, etc.
Hershey, Lewis B., 464
Hill, Gardiner, 214
Hills, Richard, 244
Hincks, Clarence M., 328, 330
Hines, Frank T., 475
Hippocrates, 8 ff., 25, 229, 485
Hoch, August, 310
Hogben, Lancelot, 358, 366, 374 f.
Holmes, Justice, decision of in *Buck v. Bell* sterilization case, 370
Holt, L. Emmett, 503
Hopkins, Matthew, 18
Horton, E. H., 290
Hoskins, R. G., 503
Hospital, psychopathic, *see* Psychopathic hospital
Hospitals, mental, *see* Mental hospitals; *see also* Institutional care, Institutionalization
Howard, John, 58
Howe, Samuel Gridley, 168, 250, 341-42, 344, 345 f., 355
Hudson (N.Y.) Lunatic Asylum, 192, 196
Hudson River (N.Y.) State Hospital, 256
Human Betterment Foundation, 372
Humanitarianism, rational, rise of, 57; sentimental, philosophy of, 186
Hun, Edward S., 283
Huntington, Ellsworth, 373
Hutchings, Charles W., 495
Huxley, Julian, 358
Hydrotherapy, evolution of, in mental hospitals, 446 ff.
Hypoglycemic therapy, *see* Insulin therapy
Hysteria, 487, 488

Idiocy, definitions, 333, 341n, 355; heredity in amaurotic, 365

Idiots as court jesters, 334
Idiots Act, England, *1886,* 341
Illinois, Conference on the Insane, *1870,* 242, cottage system in, 242-43; personal liberty bill in, 307; compulsory jury trials for the insane in, 426 f.
Illinois Board of State Commissioners of Public Charities, 242, 249, 251
India, feebleminded in, 335
Indiana, statute on compulsory sterilization in, 370; mental examination of defendants in, 403
Indiana State Reformatory, sterilization in, 370n
Individual psychology, 491
Industry, mental hygiene in, 327-28
Infantile sexuality, 488 f.
Insane, provision for in colonial times, 39 ff.; correctional institutions, 51 ff.; almshouses as custodial institutions for, 53, 114 ff.; medical treatment of, in Pennsylvania Hospital, 60 ff.; exhibiting of, 63 ff.; mechanism of terrorization for, 81 ff.; beginnings of humane treatment of, 84 ff.; moral treatment of, 89 ff.; boarding out of, in Kentucky, 106-7, 120; condition of, in New York poorhouses, 130; Dorothea Dix investigates condition of, in jails and almshouses, 166 ff.; regarded as wards of the nation, 177; condition of, in Scotland, 179; non-restraint in care of, 213 ff.; evolution of state care for, 229 ff.; increase of, over general population, 231 ff.; county care of, 234, 256, 262 ff.; evolution of cottage system for, 241 ff.; evolution of colony system for, 243 ff.; state care of, 259 ff.; criminal responsibility of, 389 ff.; tests for, 397 ff.; criminal trials of, 394; criticism of laws relating to criminal responsibility of, 399 ff.; limited responsibility of, in Nebraska, 402 ff.; commitment of, 418 ff.; justifications and limitations of the common law concerning restraint of, 422 ff.; compulsory jury trials for, in Illinois, 426 ff.; detention of,

546 INDEX

Insane (*Continued*)
  pending commitment, 434 f.; discharge and parole of, 435 ff.
Insane, chronic, proposals for provision of, 239 ff.; establishment of state institutions for, 240-41; provisions for, in Canada, 244; county care systems for, 262 ff.
Insane, criminal, *see* Criminal insane
Insane, dangerous, definition of, 410
Insane, dependent, *see* Dependent insane
Insanity, medieval remedies for, 12 ff.; attitude of Moslems towards, 15-16; moral treatment of, 91 ff.; causes of, listed in early hospital statistics, 146; fallacies in reporting cures of, in early statistics, 148; curability of, 148 ff.; and the criminal law, 389 ff.; definitions of, 387 f.; legal concept of, 388; legal provisions for, in Roman law, 389; legal provisions for, in medieval England, 389; criminal responsibility and, 390 ff.; determination of, by jury trial, 438 ff.
Institute of Juvenile Research, 324
Institutional care and treatment, modern trends in, 379 ff., 442 ff.
Institutionalization of the insane, rise of, 186 ff.; aims of, 187 ff.
Insulin therapy for mental disease, 498 ff.
Intelligence quotient (I.Q.), 355, 363
Intelligence tests, American revisions of, 355; limitations of, 363
International Committee for Mental Hygiene, 329
International Congress on Mental Health (1948), 517
Iowa, county care system in, 263; personal liberty bill in, 426
Iowa State Psychopathic Hospital, 298
Isle of Jersey, Dorothea Dix in, 181
Itard, Jean M. G., 335-37

Jackson, James, 103-4
Jacksonville (Illinois) Experimental School for the Feebleminded, 345
Jacksonville (Illinois) State Hospital, 242, 306, 424 f.
Jacoby, George W., 383
James, William, 308, 309, 310, 316
Jarrett, Mary C., 321, 322
Jarvis, Edward, 205, 227, 233
Jefferson Medical College, 282
Jelliffe, Smith Ely, 490
Jennings, H. S., 358, 374, 386
Jewell, J. S., 277
Johnson, Alexander, 315-16, 368
Journal of Nervous and Mental Disease, founding of, 277
Journal of Psycho-Asthenics, founding of, 347
Judge Baker Foundation, 324
"Jukes," the, 350 f.
Jung, C. G., 489 f.
Jury trials, for the insane, in Illinois, 426 ff.; criticism of, 438
Juvenile delinquency, prevention of, 325
Juvenile Psychopathic Institute, 324

Kalamazoo (Michigan) State Hospital, introduction of colony system at, 243-44, 274
Kallikak Family, The, 359, 366
Kankakee (Illinois) State Hospital, cottage system introduced at, 243, 285, 426
Kansas State Board of Charities, 249
Kellogg, Theodore H., 490
Kempf, Grover A., 448
Kentucky, early care and treatment of mentally ill in, 106-8, 120
Kentucky Institution for the Education of Feebleminded Children and Idiots, Frankford, 345
Kentucky Pauper Idiot Act, *1793,* 340
Kenworthy, Marion E., 325
Kerlin, Isaac N., 347
Kirby, George H., 297, 444 f.
Kirkbride, Thomas S., 140, 151, 154, 192, 194, 206-10, 217-18, 281
Kirkbride plan, 210-12
Kite, Elizabeth S., 359
Kittredge, Thomas, 31
Klaesi, 478
Knight, H. M., 346
Kostir, Mary S., 359
Kraepelin, Emil, 485 ff.
Kretschmer, Ernst, 502
Kuhlmann, Fred, 355

INDEX 547

Lathrop, Julia, 310
Laughlin, H. H., 373
Law and insanity, *see* Commitment, Criminal insane, Insane, Insanity
Leopold-Loeb, case of, 403
Letchworth, William P., 250, 383
Letchworth Village, 382
Levy, David, 325, 513
Limited responsibility and mitigation of punishment in criminal trials, 402 f.
Lincoln Asylum, England, 214
Lincoln (Illinois) School for the Feebleminded, 345
Lindpainter, Dr., 289
Linnaeus, 336, 467
Locke, John, 336
Lossing, B. J., quoted, 182
Louis XV, king of France, 390
Louisiana, mental examination of defendants in, 403
Lowell, Josephine Shaw, 351
Lowrey, Lawson, 325
Lucid intervals, theory of, 391
Lunacy, see Insanity, Mental disease
Lunacy, State Commissioner in, in New York, 255-56
Lunacy Commissions, creation of, 258-59
Lunacy Law Reform Society of London, 312
Luther, Martin, 19, 233-34
Lycurgus, laws of, 334

Mackenzie, Colin, 105-6
McFarland, Andrew, 154, 242
McLean Asylum, 102-5, 136, 151, 192, 197, 198, 273, 274, 281, 422, 444
"Mad shirt," 61
Madison (Wis.) State Hospital, 264
Magic and mental disease, 1-2
Magnuson, Paul B., 478
Maine State Hospital, Augusta, 140, 153 ff., 192, 216
Maintenance cost, average, of mental patients, 452
Maisel, Albert, 475
Malnutrition, and mental disease, 503
Manhattan (New York) State Hospital, 286, 287
Manic-depressive psychosis, incidence of, 506

Mann, Horace, 137, 168, 173, 177, 229
Marcy, W. L., governor of New York, 139
Marcy (New York) State Hospital, 495
Marks, Marcus M., 310
Marriage laws for mental defectives, 377
Marsh, Anna, bequest of, 140-1
Maryland, mental examination of defendants in, 404
Maryland Hospital, 105-6
Maryland State Commission of Lunacy, 259
Massachusetts, first statute on insanity, *1676*, 43; colonial settlement law in, 44; poorhouses in, 128; nonrestraint law in, 227; boarding out system in, 244; establishment of a central public welfare body in, 248 ff.; early provision for mental defectives in, 342 f.; provision for defective delinquents in, 352; mental examination of defendants in, 405; law affecting the dangerous insane, *1797*, 420; voluntary admission law in, 432; family care system in, 447
Massachusetts Board of Lunacy and Charity, 259
Massachusetts Board of State Charities, 249, 267, 312
Massachusetts Department of Mental Diseases, 405, 406, 414; traveling clinics of, 379
Massachusetts General Hospital, 104
Massachusetts lunacy commission, *1854*, 233
Massachusetts School for Idiotic and Feebleminded Youth, 343
Massachusetts State Almshouse, *see* Tewksbury Infirmary
Massachusetts State Board of Insanity, 259, 294-96
Massachusetts State Farm, Bridgewater, 352
Mather, Cotton, 32-34, 36*n*
Matteawan (New York) State Hospital, 412
Mechanical restraint, 79, 213 ff., 443
Medical practice in the colonies, 27 ff.

548 INDEX

Medical superintendent, problems of, in mental hospitals, 273, 274
Medicine, preventive, beginnings of, 300-1
Medieval ages, remedies for insanity, 12 ff.; exorcism in, 17
Meduna, L., 500
Mendel, Gregor, and laws of heredity, 354, 357, 365
Menninger, Karl, 452; as director of Winter Veterans Hospital, 476
Menninger, William C., 513, 514; as chief army psychiatrist, 466 f.; re civilian lessons from military psychiatry, 480, 481
Menninger Sanitarium, 456
Mental defect, definition of, 331-32; classification of, 332; and demoniacal possession, 334; hereditary factors in, 349 ff., 374; and social ills, 350; changing concepts in, 354 ff.; psychological criteria for grading of, 363; fields of inquiry in, 364; changing criteria of, 364 ff.; and Mendelianism, 365; and crime, 366; general attitudes towards, 367; segregation in, 368 f.; sterilization in, 369 ff.; environmental influences in, 376, 385; special classes for, 377 f.
Mental defectives, care of, in colonial times, 48; among ancient and primitive peoples, 334; during the Middle Ages, 334-35; early attempts at training, 337 ff.; early provision for, in America, 340 ff.; first state institutions for, 342 ff.; delinquent, provision for, 352; alarmist attitude toward, 352 ff.; classification of, 355, as menace to society, 360 ff.; new classification system for, 362; census of, 369; marriage laws for, 377; registration of, 377; social control of, 377 ff.; mental hygiene clinics for, 378 ff.; census of institutions for, 379 ff.; colony system for, 380 ff.; parole of, 384; boarding out of, 385 f.
Mental disease, and magic, 2; and demoniacal possession, 2 ff.; therapy in, in ancient times, 3 ff.; progress of research in, 283-86; social aspects of, 288 ff.; in the United States Army, 317; chemical approach in, 497 ff.; physique and, 502; endocrine therapy in, 502 ff.; recovery rate in, 505; census of, 505; economic cost of, 505; apparent increase of, 506 f.; effect of depression on, 509 f.; prevention of, 510 ff.; *see also* Insane, Insanity
Mental examination, of defendants, 403 ff.
Mental hospitals, early statistical records in, 145 ff.; early aims and treatment in, 188 ff.; early plans for construction of, 208 ff.; advantages of cottage system in, 212; mechanical restraint in, 221; problems of medical superintendents in, 273, 274; lack of research in, 274 ff.; nurses and women physicians in, 281 ff.; pathological research in, 284; evolution of social service in, 287; evolution of nursing service in, 443 ff.; psychotherapy in, 444; development of occupational therapy in, 445; hydrotherapy in, 446; minimum standards for, 446 ff.; overcrowding in, 447 ff.; during the depression, 447; statistics, 455 f.
Mental hospital administration, criticisms of, 226 ff.
Mental hygiene, origin of term, *1843*, 309 ff.; and social work, 318 ff.; and child guidance movement, 323-26; in prison clinics, 326-27; in industry, 327; organizational growth of, 328-30; internationalization of, 328 ff.; goals, 518 f.
Mental hygiene clinics, 379 ff.; work with the public schools, 379; army, 462 f.
Mental hygiene movement, origin and development of, 300 ff.; influence of World War on, 317 ff.; influence of, on other fields, 318 ff.; influence of, on social work, 322 ff.; state societies, 328 f.; internalization of, 329 f.; child guidance clinics, 326; prison clinics, 326 f.; in industry, 327 f.; organizational growth, 328 ff.
Mental hygiene societies, 328 f.

INDEX

549

Mental patients, census of, 506 ff.
Mental tests, in mental deficiency, 356; critique of, 362 ff.
Merchant Marine, psychiatric service in, 472 ff.
Mesmer, Anton, 488
Meyer, Adolf, 284-87, 289, 297, 309, 310, 445, 483, 486, 503 f.
Michigan, introduction of colony plan in, 244-45; central public welfare authority in, 249n; state care in, 261
Michigan State Psychopathic Hospital, 293-94, 298
Middlesex Asylum, Hanwell, England, 214-15
Middletown (New York) Homeopathic Asylum, 256
Miller, William, and "Millerism," 146-47
Milwaukee (Wisconsin) County Insane Asylum, 265, 266
Minnesota School for the Feebleminded, Faribault, 347
Missouri, sterilization bill in, 375 f.
Mitchell, S. Weir, 276, 279-82, 283
Moniz, Egas, 501
Montessori system in education, 340
Moon, influence of, in mental disease, 30, 82-83, 388n, 391
Moore, J. W., 494
Moral treatment of insanity, rise of, 89 ff.
More, Thomas, 13
Morgan, T. H., 366
Mosher, J. Montgomery, 293
Moslems, attitude of, toward the mentally ill, 15-16
Muller, H. J., 358
Municipal mental hospitals, origin of, 143-45
Murray, John Milne, 472
Murray, Lindley, 93, 100-1
Music therapy in mental hospitals, 445
Myerson, Abraham, 512

Narcosis therapy in mental disease, 498
National Advisory Mental Health Council, 513
National Association for the Protection of the Insane and the Prevention of Insanity, 257, 311-14
National Association for the Study of Epilepsy, 382
National Committee for Mental Hygiene, 301; founding of, 310; objectives of, 314 ff.; surveys of existing mental hygiene facilities by, 316; and development of psychiatric social work, 321; surveys among school children by, 325; psychiatric study of prisoners by, 326; growth of, 328, 379
National Conference of Charities and Correction, see National Conference of Social Work
National Conference of Social Work, 267 ff., 269, 288, 289, 311, 312, 321 ff., 361
National Crime Commission, 404
National Mental Health Act (1946), xvii, 512 f.
National Mental Health Foundation, 451
Navy, U.S., psychiatric service, 467 f.
Nazis, euthanasia program, 376 f.
Nebraska, limited responsibility of insane in, 402 f.
Nebuchadnezzar, insanity of, 3
Nerancy, John T., 442
Nerve clinic, in Philadelphia, 296; in Boston, 296
Neurology, American, rise of, 276 ff.; influence of, in psychiatry, 278 ff.
Neuroses, increase of, 509
Neurosurgery, 501
Newark (New York) Asylum for Feebleminded Women, 352
New England Renaissance, ideals of, 163-64
"New England System" for paupers, 117 ff.
New Hampshire, criminal responsibility in, 397
New Hampshire Asylum, Concord, 140, 141, 154
New Hampshire Commission in Lunacy, 259
New Jersey, county care plan in, 271
New Jersey State Hospital, 496, 502
New Orleans Charity Hospital, 131
New York, pauper insane in, in the early 19th century, 123 ff.; poor-

New York (*Continued*)
houses in, 127 ff.; survey of insane and feebleminded in, *1856*, 233; state care in, 234 ff.; central public welfare body in, 249; provision for chronic insane in, 252 ff.; for mental defectives, 342 ff.; for defective delinquents, 352; care of epileptics, 383; statute of *1788*, 420; commitment methods, 440; investigation of state hospitals, 450 f.
New York City Idiot Asylum, Randall's Island, 345; Insane Asylum, Ward's Island, 203, 314; Lunatic Asylum, Blackwell's Island, 144, 307
New York Hospital, origin and development of, 97-102, 298
New York Mental Hygiene Law, definition of mental defect in, 332 ff.; on temporary commitment, 434; on commitment methods, 440
New York Neurological Society, 257, 277, 278
New York Prison Association, 351
New York Psychoanalytic Society, 490
New York School of Social Work, 321
New York State Asylum for Idiots, Syracuse, 312, 348, 351 ff.; Institution for Defective Delinquents, Napanoch, 352; Lunatic Asylum for Insane Convicts, Auburn, 412
New York State Board of Charities, 252-53, 255 ff., 258, 267, 269, 351, 383
New York State Care Act, *1890*, 229, 259 ff., 262
New York State Commission in Lunacy, 255 ff., 260, 290, 297, 427, 428
New York State Department of Mental Hygiene, 218-19, 297, 428, 447
New York State Lunatic Asylum, *see* Utica State Hospital
New York State Medical Society, 284
New York State mental hospitals, 450 f.
New York State Parole Board, 327
New York State Pathological Institute, *see* New York State Psychiatric Institute
New York State Penal Law, on criminal responsibility, 399

New York State Psychiatric Institute, 285-87, 294, 297-98
Nichols, Charles H., 184, 185, 240
Nielson, W. A., 321
Nightingale, Florence, 281
Noguchi, Hideyo, 494
Nomenclature, psychiatric, 469 f.
Non-restraint, origin and development of, 213 ff.; theory of, 213-14, 224-26; American opposition to, 215 ff., 226 ff.; arguments for, 217 ff.; advocates of, in America, 227-28
Non-restraint law in Massachusetts, *1911*, 227
Norristown (Pennsylvania) State Hospital, 282
North Carolina, state care in Constitution of, 261
North Carolina Board of Public Charities, 249 ff.
Northampton (Massachusetts) State Hospital, 155, 203, 248, 274
Northern State Hospital, Winnebago, Wisconsin, 264
Nurses, first training schools for, 281
Nursing, psychiatric, 444

Occupational therapy, 63, 101, 445 f.
Ohio Board of State Charities, 249, 251, 382
Ohio Hospital for Epileptics, Gallipolis, 383
Ohio State Asylum for the Education of Idiotic and Imbecile Youth, Columbus, 345
Ohio State Hospital, Columbus, 140, 153, 154, 192, 202
Ohio State Lunatic Asylum, Cincinnati, 109-10
Ordronaux, John, 256, 383
Organic psychoses, 506
Oshkosh (Wisconsin) State Hospital, 252
Otis, James, 68
Out-patient department, development of, in mental hospitals, 296-97
Overcrowding in institutions, 447 ff.
Overholser, Winfred, 406, 439

Packard, Mrs. E. P. W., 306-7, 424 f.
Page, Charles W., 227

INDEX

Paine, Thomas, 56, 57
Paracelsus, 21, 22, 27, 488
Paresis, 493 f.
Parole, in institutions for mental defectives, 385; in mental hospitals, 435 f.
Parran, Thomas, 473, 513
Parrish, Joseph, 347
Pathological research, *see* Research
Paulus Aeginata, 11-12
Paupers, insane, care of, in the early 19th century, 116 ff.; "bid off," 117 ff.; contract system for, 120, 126; "dumping" of, 123 ff.; *see also* Dependent insane
Pavlov, and neuroses in dogs, 495 f.
Payne Whitney Psychiatric Clinic, 298
Pedigrees of defective, *see* Defectives
Pennsylvania, first known provision for the insane in, 42; county care plan in, 271; state provision for mental defectives in, 344
Pennsylvania Board of Public Charities, 249, 251
Pennsylvania Hospital, origin and development of, 58-66; Benjamin Rush at the, 77 ff.; 91, 98, 140, 151, 154, 192, 206, 212, 230, 281, 296, 422
Pennsylvania State Committee on Lunacy, 282
Pennsylvania Training School for Feebleminded Children, Elwyn, 344, 346, 361
Pepperell (Massachusetts) Private Asylum, 192, 196
Pereire, Jacob Rodrigues, 338
Performance tests, limitations of, 364
Periodicals, intramural, 200-1
Perkins Institution for the Blind, 342
Personal liberty bill, 4, 25-26
Peterson, Frederick, 289, 297, 310, 383, 494
Pharmacology, contributions of, to psychiatry, 497 ff.
Philadelphia, center of Quaker reforms in the 18th century, 58
Philadelphia Dispensary for the Poor, 74
Philadelphia General Hospital (Old Blockley), 131, 293, 314
Philadelphia Nerve Clinic, 296

Philadelphia Society for Alleviating the Miseries of Public Prisons, 74
Phillips, Wendell, 427
Phillips, William, legacy of, 102-3
Phips, governor of Massachusetts, 38
Phipps, Henry, 316
Phipps Psychiatric Clinic, Baltimore, 297, 324
Physicians, and witchcraft, 20
Physiological concept in mental disease, rise of, 284 ff.
Physique and character, 502
Pierce, Franklin, President, 178-79
Pilgrim (New York) State Hospital, 457
Pinel, Philippe, 5, 9; sketch of, 89 ff.; introduces humanitarian reforms at the Bicêtre, 90; at the Salpêtrière, 90 ff.; influence of, on psychiatric practice, 95, 337, 485
Plater, Felix, 23, 485
Political interference, in state institutions, 453 ff.
Pollock, Horatio M., 447 f.
Poorhouses as custodial institutions for the insane, 53 ff., 114-31; removal of insane from, 246-71; condition of insane in, 130 ff.
Poorhouses, in Massachusetts, 128; in New York, 128
Poor law reform in England, 122
Popenoe, Paul, 372, 373
Powell, T. O., 107-8
Preventive principle, rise of, 300-1
Prison clinics, 326-27
Prisons, mental tests in, 356
Provincial Lunatic Asylum, Toronto, 244
Psychiatric clinics, child guidance clinics, 326; *see also* Mental hygiene
Psychiatric instruction, lack of, in early American medical schools, 282
Psychiatric nursing, *see* Nursing
Psychiatric testimony, 400 ff.
Psychiatry, German, in the early 19th century, 193; American, in the early 19th century, 193 ff.; slow development of, 272 ff.; factors influencing development of, in the late 19th century, 275 ff.; and neu-

Psychiatry (*Continued*)
rology, 277 ff., 464-65; institutional, 279 ff.; social work in, 286 ff.; in World War II, 458 ff.; home front morale, 460 f.; Selective Service, 461; development of 20th century schools of, 483 ff.
Psychoanalysis, evolution of, 487 ff.; opposition to, in America, 489; influence of, 491 ff.
Psychoanalytic Institute (Chicago), 493
Psychoanalytic Review, 490
Psychobiology, 504
Psychology, analytical, 491; individual, 491
Psychoses, *see* Mental disease
Psychosis, manic-depressive, census of, 506 f.
Psychopathic hospitals, evolution of, 291 ff.; types of, 291; functions of, 295 ff.; state, 298
Psychosomatic medicine, 493 ff.
Psychotherapy, evolution of, 444 ff.
Public welfare administration, development of, 246 ff.; central boards for, 248 ff.
Public Works Administration, state hospital projects, 447
Puritanism and witchcraft, 32 ff.
Putnam, James J., 470

Quakers, 57 ff., 92-93, 189
Quincy, Josiah, 122

Raleigh (North Carolina) State Hospital, 175, 261
Rational humanitarianism, philosophy of, 57 ff.
Ray, Isaac, 82, 142-43, 153-54, 192, 197, 203-6, 215-16, 219-20, 258, 274, 282, 310, 398 f., 423
Reade, Charles, 423 f.
Recovery rate, in mental disease, 505
Reed, Andrew, 340
Reed, Walter, 301
Rees, John R., 330, 517
Rehabilitation of veterans, 474 ff.
Reil, Johann C., 199
Renaissance, witch mania in, 19
Repressive principle, in early colonial legislation, 43

Research, in mental disease, 282 ff.
Responsibility, criminal, of the insane, 389 ff.; legal tests for the determination of, 391 ff.
Responsibility, limited, in criminal trials, 402 f.
Restraint, mechanical, 219 ff.; forms used in early mental hospitals, 221; effects of, on patients, 222
Retreat Gazette, Hartford, 200
Rhode Island, commitment methods, 440
Rhode Island Asylum for the Incurable Insane, Cranston, 240
Rhode Island Board of State Charities and Corrections, 249
Richards, J. B., 344, 345
Richards, Mrs. Laura E., 346
Richmond, Mary E., 320, 322
Rockefeller Foundation, 316
Rodman, James, 382
Rogers, A. C., 347
Romano, John, 513
Rome (New York) State Custodial Asylum (State School), 352, 381
Rosen, John Nathaniel, psychiatric technique, 491 f.
Rousseau, J. J., 55
Royal Commission to investigate lunacy system of Scotland, *1855,* 180-81
Ruggles, Arthur H., 331, 502
Rush, Benjamin, achievements of, 72 ff.; early life of, 73; medical system of, 75 ff.; on phobias, 76 ff.; therapeutic remedies of, 77 ff.; invents new mechanical devices, 79 ff.; innovations of, at Pennsylvania Hospital, 83 ff.; reforms instituted by, 84 ff.; influence of, on American psychiatry, 86-87, 91, 94, 189, 190, 408, 422, 517
Russell, William L., 298, 321, 435

Saegert, C. M., 339
Sakel, Manfred, 498 f.
Salem witchcraft, 32-38
Salmon, Thomas W., 272, 297, 316, 317, 325, 328, 442, 515
Salpêtrière, 78, 88, 90 ff., 339
Sanborn, Franklin B., 183, 193, 250, 267

INDEX

Sanctorius, Sanctorius, 26
San Quentin State Prison, classification center, 327
Saul, king of Israel, melancholia of, 3
Scattergood, Thomas, 96
Schizophrenia, *see* Dementia praecox
School children, mental health surveys of, 325; mental tests among, 356
Schrieber, Julius, 466
Schumacher, Henry C., 490
Schurman, Jacob Gould, 310
Schuyler, Louisa Lee, 256-57, 290
Schwarz, Rudolph, 410n
Scot, Reginald, 22
Scotland, conditions of insane in, 179; Royal Commission investigation, *1855*, 180-81
Scottish Rite Masons, Northern Jurisdiction, 485
Scourging, as a remedy for insanity, 13
Screening, psychiatric, 462 f.
Seguin, Edward C., 227, 282, 283, 338-39, 345 ff.
Selective Service, psychiatry and, 461 ff.; statistics, 464, 467
Seneca, 333
Sennert, Daniel, 23
Sentimental humanitarianism, philosophy of, 186
Sequeyra, John de, 71
Seton Institute, Baltimore, 456
Settlement laws and the dependent insane, in colonial times, 45 ff.
Shanahan, William T., 384
Sharp, H. C., 370
Shaw, Chief Justice of Massachusetts, on restraint of the insane, 422 f., 436
Shock therapies, 498 ff.
Simon, Hermann, 445
Simon, Thomas, 354
Sing Sing Psychiatric Clinic, 326
Smith College School of Social Work, 321
Smith, S. Hanbury, 154
Smith, Stephen, 256 ff.
Smythe, James, 105-6
Social environment and mental disease, 514
Social ills, and mental defect, 350, 353

Social psychiatry, 514 ff.
Social reform, founding of national organizations for, 311
Social service, in mental hospitals, 287, 437
Social work, psychiatric, 286 ff.; and mental hygiene, 318 ff.
Société de Patronage, 289
Society for Improving the Condition of the Insane, London, 311
Society of Friends, *see* Quakers
Socio-economic factors in mental disease, 514
Sodium amytal, 498
Soranus of Ephesus, 9
South Carolina State Asylum, Columbia, 108
Southard, E. E., 295, 321-22, 328
Southern Psychiatric Association, 462
Spitzka, Edward C., 279, 282, 283
Spurzheim, 241
St. Boniface Hospital, Florence, 95
St. Dymphna's shrine, 14
St. Elizabeths Hospital, Washington, D.C., 184, 437; *see also* Government Hospital for the Insane
St. John's Provincial Hospital, 175
St. John's wort (hypericon), 29
Stafford, Edward, 29-30
Stanford-Binet test, 363
Stanton, Secretary of War, 182-83
State administration and supervision, systems of, 250 ff.; *see also* State hospitals
State care of the insane, evolution of, 229 ff.; main objectives of, 257; advantages of, 269 ff.; present status of, 271
State Charities Aid Association, New York, 256-57, 290, 297, 311, 434
State hospitals, recent survey of, 448 ff.; official investigations, 450 f.; APA standards for, 452 ff.; statistics, 455 f.
State institutions, rise of, 137 ff.
Statistical methods in early mental hospital reports, 145 ff., 154-55, 202, 205
Stedman, Charles Harrison, 192, 201
Stedman, Henry R., 289
Stephen, James Fitz James, 392

554 INDEX

Sterilization, eugenic, 371 ff., 512; legislation, 375 ff.
Stern, William, 355
Stevenson, George S., 326
Stockton State Asylum, California, 241
Stoddard, T. L., 373
Stokes, Anson Phelps, 310
Stout, A. B., 292
Strecker, Edward A., 472, 513
Stribling, Francis T., 191, 192, 196
Sullivan, Harry Stack, 462
Surgeon General's Office, Division of Neurology and Psychiatry, 317 ff.; in World War II, 465 ff.
Sutton, Dallas G., 461
Sweetser, William, and mental hygiene, 309-10
Sydenham, Thomas, 26, 76
Syracuse (New York) State Institution for the Feebleminded (State School), 344

Taft, Jessie, 322
Tallman, Frank F., 513
Tarumianz, Mesrop A., 451
Taunton (Massachusetts) State Hospital, 248
Taylor, Maurice, 508
Temple sleep, in Greece, 6-7
Tennessee Lunatic Asylum, Nashville, 139-40
Terman, Lewis M., 355
Terrorization in mental therapeutics, 79 ff.
Testimony, psychiatric, 400 f.
Tests, legal, for the responsibility of the insane, 391 ff.
Tewksbury (Massachusetts) Infirmary, 240
Thom, Douglas A., 326
Throop, Enos T., governor of New York, 138
Thurnam, John, 154-55
Todd, Eli, 111-12, 135, 149
Training School for the Feebleminded, Vineland, N.J., 354 f.
Tranquilizer, 79
Treasury of Exorcisms, 17
Trenton (New Jersey) State Hospital, 171, 185, 496
Trials, criminal, psychiatric testimony in, 400 f.; limited responsibility and mitigation of punishment in, 402 f.
Truitt, Ralph P., 325
Tuke, Batty, 218
Tuke, D. Hack, 2, 82, 181, 227, 311, 334, 485
Tuke, Samuel, 96, 99, 101, 111
Tuke, William, 92-95
Turner, Douglas Frank, 377

Unconscious, 488
United Nations World Health Organization, 330; goals, 518 f.
United States Army, mental disease in World War I, 317; in World War II, 458 ff.
"Utica crib," 222-23
Utica (New York) State Hospital, 139, 147, 151, 192, 196, 198, 200, 201, 222, 230, 233, 236, 238, 252-53, 257, 273, 274, 283, 284, 285, 342, 412; *see also* New York State Asylum, Utica

Van Gieson, Ira, 285-87
Vermont Asylum for the Insane (now Brattleboro Retreat), 140-41, 200, 255
Vermont Commissioner of the Insane, 255
Vermont State Care Act, *1886*, 261-62
Vesalius, 26
Veteran rehabilitation, 474 ff.
Veterans Administration, psychiatric and rehabilitation work of, 474 ff.; statistics, 476
Virginia, first state hospital established in, 69-71; law of *1806* on the insane in jails, 421 f.
Vogel, Victor H., 448
Voisin, 339

Waggoner, Raymond, 463
Wagner-Jauregg, Julius, 494
Walker, Clement, 223
Walter S. Fernald State School, Waverley, Massachusetts, 343
Warning out of vagabonds, paupers and insane, in Colonial times, 45
Warren, John Collins, 103-4
Warren (Pennsylvania) State Hospital for the Insane, 296

INDEX

Waterston, R. C., 168
Watts, J. W., 501
Weihofen, Henry, 397, 407, 439
Weiss, Edward, 493
Welch, William H., 330
Western Kentucky Lunatic Asylum, Hopkinsville, 382
Western Lunatic Asylum, Staunton, Virginia, 112, 192, 196
Wet sheet pack, 446
Weyer, Johann, 22
White, Samuel, 192, 194, 196
White, William A., 184, 281, 329, 401, 415, 490, 514; Psychiatric Foundation, 461 ff.
White House Conference on Child Health and Protection, *1930*, 333, 373, 380, 385
Wiggam, A. E., 373
Wigglesworth, Michael, 29
Wilbur, C. T., 347
Wilbur, Hervey B., 312, 343 ff., 351
Wilkinson, John Gardner, 5
Willard, Frances E., 163
Willard, Sylvester D., 236, 238
Willard Act, New York, *1865*, 236 ff., 252 ff., 260
Willard (New York) State Hospital, 236 ff., 238, 240, 252 ff., 260, 264
Williams, Frankwood E., 317, 328, 432, 515
Williams, Roger, 47
Williamsburg, Virginia, first state hospital erected at, 66, 69-71, 233
Willis, Francis, 81, 133-34, 136, 138
Wines, Frederick H., 242-43, 250, 251
Winter Veterans Hospital, 476

Winthrop, John, governor of Connecticut, 29-30
Wisconsin, development of county care of the insane in, 234, 262-69, 271
Wisconsin County Care Act, *1881*, 265-66
Wisconsin, public welfare authority in, 249, 252, 263-68
Wise, Peter M., 289
Witchcraft, in Europe, 18 ff.; and physicians, 20; and puritanism, 32; in Salem, 32 ff.
Witches, insanity of, 20 ff.
Woodward, Samuel B., 111, 138, 149, 151, 191, 192, 194, 195-96, 201, 241-42, 341 f.
Worcester, W. L., 274
Worcester (Massachusetts) State Hospital, 137-38, 155, 169, 191, 192, 195, 201, 230, 241-42, 248, 286, 340, 412, 425, 486
Workhouses and houses of correction, insane in, in Colonial times, 51-53
Workman, Benjamin, 244
Workman, Joseph, 274
World Federation for Mental Health, 329 f.
World War I, influence of, on mental hygiene movement, 317 ff.
World War II, psychiatry in, 458 ff.
Wyman, Rufus, 104

Yates, J. V. N., 123 ff., 127
Yerkes, R. M., 354
York Retreat, 92, 93-95, 96, 99, 100, 102, 110, 111, 154, 181, 196, 311